# EXPLORING DEVIANCE IN CANADA

# OXFORD
## UNIVERSITY PRESS

8 Sampson Mews, Suite 204, Don Mills, Ontario  M3C 0H5
www.oupcanada.com

Oxford University Press is a department of the University of Oxford.
It furthers the University's objective of excellence in research, scholarship,
and education by publishing worldwide in

Oxford   New York
Auckland   Cape Town   Dar es Salaam   Hong Kong   Karachi
Kuala Lumpur   Madrid   Melbourne
Mexico City   Nairobi
New Delhi   Shanghai   Taipei   Toronto

With offices in
Argentina   Austria   Brazil   Chile   Czech Republic   France   Greece
Guatemala   Hungary   Italy   Japan   Poland   Portugal   Singapore
South Korea   Switzerland   Thailand   Turkey   Ukraine   Vietnam

Oxford is a trade mark of Oxford University Press
in the UK and in certain other countries

Published in Canada by Oxford University Press

**Library and Archives Canada Cataloguing in Publication**
Exploring deviance in Canada : a reader / editor, Ed Ksenych.
Includes index.
ISBN 978-0-19-543990-8
1. Deviant behavior—Textbooks.  2. Social control—Textbooks.
3. Canada—Social conditions—Textbooks.  I. Ksenych, Edward,
1950–
HM811.E96 2011          302.5'420971          C2010-906644-8

Oxford University Press is committed to our environment. This book is printed on Forest
Stewardship Council certified paper, harvested from a responsibly managed forest.

**Mixed Sources**
Product group from well-managed
forests and other controlled sources
www.fsc.org   Cert no. SW-COC-000952
© 1996 Forest Stewardship Council

FSC

Printed and bound in Canada.

1  2  3  4 — 14  13  12  11

# EXPLORING DEVIANCE IN CANADA

## A READER

Edited by
**ED KSENYCH**

OXFORD
UNIVERSITY PRESS

# Contents

# Acknowledgements

This book would not have been possible without the help and support of many people. First, I want to acknowledge the significant contribution that my colleague, Jim Cosgrave, has made to this reader. Besides penning an article for it, he gave a good deal of time to discussing ideas as well as reviewing some of the material. I also want to thank several other colleagues who offered thoughtful suggestions: John Baker, Mandy Bergman, David Liu, Tom Malcomson, Rod Michalko, and Tanya Titchkosky.

A special thank you to Tamara O'Doherty for allowing me to use a portion of her MA Thesis as an article, and to Canadian Scholars Press for freely granting us permission to reproduce material from their publications. The book also reflects the influence of three guest speakers who regularly appear in my sociology of deviance course: Adrian Goulborn, Rick Sauvé, and Valerie Scott. As I was selecting articles, I found myself constantly mindful of the rich experiences and insights they have shared in my classes.

I am also very grateful for the support and valuable assistance that Oxford University Press has provided me throughout the publication process. In particular, I want to thank Nancy Reilly, Allison McDonald, and Karri Yano for their valuable suggestions and professional help in making this book possible. As well, I'd like to acknowledge the following Oxford personnel: Eric Sinkins, assistant managing editor, and Steven Hall, senior production coordinator. Finally, I wish to thank the several anonymous reviewers who took the time to read over and comment on the book at various stages of its development.

Dedication
To my sister, Sandra, and my niece and nephew, Jessica and Chris.

# Introduction

This book aims to provide a range of engaging, accessible articles and helpful, interesting commentary to assist students in inquiring sociologically into the topic of deviance and social control. The articles cover some of the more popular themes and topics in these areas, and encourage students to understand and use the sociological perspective to explore questions pertaining to them. The idea for the book emerged from the challenge of developing a one-semester liberal studies elective on deviance for diploma and degree level students in a Canadian college in which the reader would serve as the principal text. Since such electives usually don't have prerequisites, part of the challenge involved finding quality articles that would introduce students to basic concepts and principles while also applying them to the topic area.

There is an unconventional aspect to the collection of 'articles' that comprise this reader. Normally, such a book of readings consists of examples of classical and contemporary sociological theory and research. And these do make up a significant portion of the selections here as well. However, the book also includes a variety of readings not usually found in such books. For instance, you will encounter magazine and newspaper articles as well as monographs, research reports, government fact sheets, interviews, and chapters from books, all of which have been edited and formatted into articles. The point of including such a diverse range of writings is to expose students, not only to examples of sociological theory and research, but also to other forms of discourse about deviance and social control which they can critically reflect upon and analyze sociologically.

The selection of articles and commentary are also based on an approach to teaching the subject that I would like to elaborate on briefly. It is one that

- organizes the content in terms of a framework that emphasizes deviance as a sociological process
- highlights to the role of mass media in the social construction of deviance and the legitimization of social control
- focuses on the Canadian context while recognizing the contributions of sociological research and theory from other countries, notably the United States
- attends to contemporary issues in studying deviance and social control
- reflects current developments in the discipline in a way that remains accessible to students who are new to the field.

## Deviance as a Social Process

The framework that underlies the readings was developed in the context of the course I teach, and it builds on two basic ideas that most sociologists teaching the subject would probably agree with

1. reality is, to an important extent, socially constructed, sustained, and altered

2. behaviours regarded as deviant are part of a more extensive social process related to the nature of group life itself.

The framework also draws on two other ideas that are useful to designing and teaching deviance courses. The first is that teaching college students is best done by teaching inductively (that is, from experience to concepts) rather than deductively (that is, presenting concepts and then applying them), where possible. The second is that conceptualizing deviance as a social process not only presents students with an important sociological insight first noted by Emile Durkheim, but also can be used to structure the rich diversity of material students will be encountering throughout the course.

Let me clarify what is meant by considering 'deviance as a social process'. The question of 'what is deviance?' is usually heard as a question about what kind of behaviour is regarded as deviant and requires social control in a group. But in sociology the question also refers to something more. Deviance is not only a troubling or wrongful behaviour within some particular social context, but also a social process by which a community organizes itself and sustains social order, that is, a particular social arrangement to which its members are generally committed.

To illustrate, consider the following example. Frank is a cantankerous old man who's been in a nursing home for 10 years, half paralyzed from a stroke, but with a clear mind. One evening after dinner he refused to take his evening medication because he said it made him feel too drowsy.

The pattern of behaviours that transpired in this case was as follows. First, the attending nurse reminded him that his doctor had ordered the medication. After further refusal she went to the head nurse and remarked that Frank was being difficult again. The head nurse admonished Frank, but to no avail. The next day, the medication was mashed up in Frank's dinner. Frank noticed the pieces of medication, threw the tray on the floor, and began yelling that they were trying to poison him. After that, he refused to eat any more. Frank's family and doctor were eventually called in to settle him down. The doctor made some adjustments to the medication level, and the family convinced him to be more co-operative. However, for the next couple of months Frank complained about painful bed sores and being left on unemptied bedpans for long periods of time.

The example is not a horrifying violent act, bizarre psychotic behaviour, or scandalous commercial wrong-doing. Yet it is an example of deviance, a rather minor, mundane one. Individuals regularly do behave in ways that vary from or violate norms, values, or beliefs that a group cherishes or feels is necessary to its ongoing organization and way of life, often intentionally. Here, Frank refused to take his evening medication, an act that varied from a routine in the nursing home. Frank's refusal troubled the nursing staff and, when asked afterwards, he said he was aware that it might. Such a 'disturbing act' constitutes the first move in the social process of deviance.

But the nurses' perception of the act, how it became defined and processed, the categories they used to depict him, as well as the collective reactions based on these definitions are also important parts of the above drama. These are the other moves in the social process of deviance. For instance, the nurses could have interpreted Frank's refusal as expressing his legal right to refuse medication (which, when asked afterwards, they were quite aware of), explained the consequences to him, and called in the doctor and the family to discuss the matter. But they didn't. They interpreted it as an expression of a troublesome individual violating established, routine practices within the health care facility. After labelling him as a 'difficult patient' having a relapse into trouble-making, the staff organized their reactions around controlling him for the purpose of maintaining the orderliness of the nursing home.

In situations where individuals behave in ways that disturb prevailing expectations, we usually focus mainly on the disturbing behaviour and the individual who did it. Sociologists don't ignore the 'deviant' individual or the 'deviant behaviour', but they also take into account the process of defining the behaviour and reacting to it. Depicted graphically it looks something like Figure I.1.

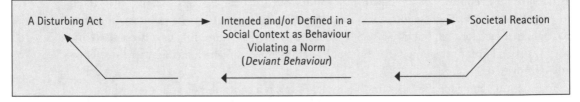

Figure I.1 The Social Process of Deviance

By considering deviance as a social process we give more attention than we ordinarily might to the social context in which the act occurs and how it is being interpreted and reacted to. This includes the means of social control that are brought to bear on the individual seen to be committing the deviant behaviour. Sociologically, the context is perhaps even more important than the act itself. In this case, the immediate context was a government regulated, understaffed, for-profit nursing home. But sociologically, the 'social context' can also extend beyond the immediate environment. For instance, what commonly shared system for dealing with perceived violations of norms was the staff working with?

The nurses were employing a general approach to deviance and social control that has been institutionalized on a national level in Canada as well as in many institutions like hospitals and schools: a crime control model of deviance and social control. Historically Canada's judicial system has been based on the belief that civil liberties can only have meaning in orderly societies. That is, only by ensuring order can society guarantee freedoms. So criminal conduct, as well as actions that could possibly escalate into criminal conduct, are controlled and repressed. This approach is anchored on the national level in Canada's constitutional principle of 'peace, order, and good government'.

By contrast, the American judicial system has historically been based on the belief that the law can be used to defend natural and inalienable individual rights and to protect accused persons from unjust government applications of criminal penalties. In such environments there is a strong pressure to observe the presumption of innocence and intolerance towards mistreatment of the accused. On a national level this is anchored in America's constitutional principle of the right to life, liberty, and the pursuit of happiness.

But to return to deviance as a social process, studying deviance this way does illuminate an unfolding pattern of events that frequently occurs around acts defined as deviant. And its recurrence isn't found just in everyday life. It is also present in how deviance is often portrayed in the mass media. For instance, the basic format for TV crime dramas like *Law and Order* and *CSI* is basically a movement from a graphically depicted disturbing act occurring in the first few minutes, to its definition as a murder in the next few, to a lengthy societal reaction that unifies the audience around key values of American society practised by the police and investigators in successfully detecting and capturing the wrongdoer.

## Current Issues in Deviance and Social Control

I'd also like to comment on how the book addresses various issues in deviance and social control, both public issues and academic ones. As C. Wright Mills noted years ago, public issues are different from personal troubles, not only because they are usually more widespread, but because the source of the problem differs. Strictly speaking, the root of a problem that is a 'personal trouble' primarily concerns an individual's character and his or her immediate environment. By contrast, contending with a 'public issue' reflects an individual's involvement in how people and local environments are organized into historical societies. Generally, a value cherished by publics is being threatend, and there is debate about what the value is and what is threatening it. Often the threat cannot be easily defined in everyday terms because it reflects crises in institutional arrangements, contradictions in social structures, or conflicts arising from historical changes that we are in the grip of. The articles chosen for this book have tried to address some current issues concerning deviance and social control. And these will involve examining some of our basic social institutions as well as the contradictions and ambiguities inherent to them.

Assembling a book of readings also involves contending with issues that concern the sociology of deviance itself. One issue is how to address the double level nature of inquiry. Most areas of inquiry can be fairly easily described in terms of their concrete subject matter. But more analytically, areas of inquiry are animated by fundamental questions and problems. So, the concrete subject matter of deviance and social control usually includes phenomena like provocative social diversions, ways of handling problematic people, mental illness, cults, delinquency, youth gangs, crime, social control agents, prisons, etc. But what are the fundamental problems and questions that underlie these, and are the deeper subject matter of the field? This set of readings recommends using deviance and social control as opportunities to inquire into

- the basic sociological problem of social order, and what deviance and social control tell us about how we organize ourselves and maintain order
- the nature of human sociality, notably how we socially construct reality
- the problem of conscious wrongdoing, or why we choose to do things we usually know will be regarded as disturbing and wrong by a group
- the puzzle of conformity and normalcy, or, why most of us conform and normalize all the particularity and differences that are part of life most of the time
- the question of justice, both theoretically and in practice.

Another issue concerning the sociology of deviance is the current debate over how the topic should be investigated. While the sociology of deviance has a long, rich history, there have been challenges to it as a field of study. First, those advocating a 'critical' approach in sociology centred on themes of equity and social justice have argued that the sociology of deviance often begins by accepting dominant societal definitions of deviant conduct, instead of radically critiquing them from the start. They've noted that the sociology of deviance often reflects an approach to the problem of inequality, difference, and power that emerged in mid-twentieth-century Western societies that were preoccupied with conformity. Instead, much of 'deviance' could be better handled as part of the project of challenging unjust dominant-subordinate relationships and achieving more equitable treatment of those regarded as being different.

Second, criminology has been expanding, and some criminologists argue that deviance, unlike the specific area of crime, is too ambiguous and plagued by relativism. Criminologists have also voiced concern about the heavy use of subjectively-oriented, qualitative research and question its rigour. Finally, some sociologists who have embraced post-structuralist/postmodern theorists, notably Foucault, propose the real topic that has always been behind the sociology of deviance, but bypassed by it, is moral regulation and the imposition of normalcy in an environment of increasingly economically powerful and politically extensive social formations rooted in systems of knowledge that define what is legitimate and what is not.

To some extent, such challenges are part of building academic research areas in the competitive world of contemporary scholarship. At the same time, there is some validity to them. Consequently, in selecting articles, I have tried to incorporate the contributions these criticisms make to understanding deviance and social control. For example, equity and social justice issues are a key concern of several articles, particularly as they relate to youth, women, and minority groups. There is also significant attention given to crime and examples of criminology. This is partly because of the widespread and often misinformed public concern over the forms of deviance it encompasses, and partly because public discourse over crime influences ideas, attitudes, and practices regarding deviance and social control generally. Finally, there are articles that take up Foucault's important work and the themes of moral regulation and the social construction of normalcy.

But it is also important to recognize that each of the approaches has limitations of its own. For the most part, conventional criminology has been a pragmatic, empiricist practice that objectivizes its subject, and bears the well-known strengths and limitations of doing this. While it has important practical concerns such as counting, predicting, and reducing crime, it doesn't seem to be driven by any enduring sociological question or problem beyond the positivist project of scientifically explaining and controlling the world being studied. The position that deviance is another instance of the problem of difference best handled as an equity and social justice issue overlooks the sense in which 'deviants' do not just present a difference, or even a stigmatized difference in need of remedy. Deviance usually involves notions of wrongdoing and harmfulness, or potential harmfulness, to the group and its members, however minor the rule-breaking or possible harm is. And the focus on moral regulation and enforcement of normalcy tends to frame the inquiry in highly institutionalized, political terms of governmentality, the state, power, control, regulation, systems of knowledge, and the politics of discourse. As such it tends to omit or downplay human agency; that is, discussing deviance from the standpoint of the participants who, as social actors, usually consciously and volitionally engage in acts they are aware will be regarded as upsetting, wrong, and so on.

Students new to the sociology of deviance might wonder why I'm mentioning these criticisms of the field before they've even figured out what the field is about. But it's important to be aware that the sociology of deviance and social control can be as contentious as deviance itself.

## The Importance of Theory in Studying Deviance and Social Control

One of the most remarkable aspects of the sociology of deviance is the wide range of concepts and theories that have either been generated out of it or applied to it. Summarizing and covering them all is not only a daunting task in itself (especially in a one semester course), but it can easily overwhelm students, especially if they're not predisposed to inquiring theoretically. In order to cope, they (and often teachers as well) often concretize them as a list of 'viewpoints' rather than treat them as examples of understanding sociologically. The book does contain examples of theoretic writing by Durkheim, Foucault, Goffman, Freud, and Sacks. But the book makes no claim to systematically cover all the theoretical approaches that have been developed to understand deviance and social control. At the same time, taken together, the articles do discuss or exemplify a wide range of theories.

In my experience, the best way to introduce theory is by theorizing in class. As for effectively presenting the diverse approaches pertaining to the field, it's helpful to organize them in very broad groupings, provide a brief overview of any particular theory at the time it's being worked with, and then have students encounter a concrete example of it which can be used to further elaborate on it.

There are two selections in the book that offer such broad groupings. Specifically, Silverman et al. introduce the general categories of 'consensus theories' and 'conflict theories'. Consensus theories would include approaches such as structural-functionalism, strain theories, social bond and social control theories, and theories that emphasize subcultures. Conflict theories would include Marxist approaches, feminist theories, critical post-structuralism, and critical criminological theories. However the contributions of interpretive theories like symbolic interactionism are downplayed in this schema and that needs to be noted.

O'Grady offers a different set of broad categories—'the objectivist-legalistic approach' and 'the social reaction approach'—which highlight the difference between positivist theories that focus on clearly established norms and widespread values, and social constructionist theories. The latter would include symbolic interactionism, Foucault's theory of moral regulation, and critical theory. He also examines the theory implied in the media's general portrayal of deviance and its role in creating moral panic, and uses it as an opportunity to both better understand and critique sociology's current preoccupation with moral panic in the media.

Both of these articles contain frameworks that can be helpful in organizing the diverse approaches that will be encountered in the other readings in the book. Regarding specific theories, I have tried to highlight which particular one is relevant to an article as part of introducing it.

## Sociology as an Exemplary Form of Deviance

There is an ironical quality to the sociology of deviance. While most of the articles exemplify the practice of sociology, together they are also an example of how sociological inquiry itself is inherently a form of deviance. As Peter Berger pointed out in *An Invitation to Sociology,* the sociological perspective debunks, or challenges, both commonsense and official definitions of reality, and transforms the world in which we have lived all our lives in terms of its very meaning and significance. This is not simply an enthusiastic academic sentiment intended to market a discipline. If practised properly, social inquiry really does debunk definitions and transform the world, regardless of the variations in the theoretic or methodological approach with which it is practised.

Sociology disturbs through its very participation in the activity of inquiry, and it generates skepticism and distrust regarding the everyday meaning and understanding of social events. But then this is all part of the particular pleasure, excitement, and danger of sociological inquiry, and of inquiry generally.

April 2010
George Brown College, Toronto, Canada

# Part I  The Question of Deviance

What is deviance, anyway? One of the first challenges that students encounter in taking up the question is what acts count as deviant in a group. What is it about certain behaviours or events that make them deviant rather than usual or generally acceptable? And students quickly point out that deviance involves breaking a norm. That is, it's not just being an exception to some statistical average, but implies violating some socially accepted rule, whether a law or a custom. As such, there's a sense of trouble or wrongfulness associated with deviance.

But the focus of the inquiry shifts when we recognize that the property of deviance resides not so much in a particular kind of behaviour or event, but in how an act is defined and treated by members of a group when it occurs in specific social contexts. It involves decisions that take into consideration which rules are pertinent, who the actors are, what the situation is, and how significant the violation is. This even applies to such seemingly obvious wrongful acts as killing a person.

The situation is complicated further by the fact that there are also varying degrees of seriousness regarding rule-breaking behaviours. John Hagan has offered a useful typology for classifying deviant acts on the basis of their perceived harmfulness, the degree of public agreement regarding the norm, as well as the severity of the social response to such acts.[1] At the top are 'consensus crimes' like homicide and sexual assault. There is widespread agreement among Canadians that these are inherently wrong, harmful, and should be responded to severely. Following this are 'conflict crimes'. These concern acts that may currently be illegal, but over which there is public disagreement regarding their seriousness and how we should respond. For example, Canadians are currently conflicted over the harmfulness of marijuana use and prostitution as well as the appropriateness of existing laws and the consequences of how they've been enforced.

A third type of deviance is 'social deviations' such as addictions or acts stemming from mental disorders. These acts are not violations of laws in themselves, but are regarded as being worthy of attention and intervention on behalf of the individuals themselves and the community at large. Generally, a large proportion of people agree the acts are deviant, somewhat or potentially harmful, and should be subject to some sort of institutional intervention. In some cases sanctions such as shame or public humiliation may be felt to be appropriate. The fourth type of deviance Hagan identified was 'social diversions'. There is an element of provocativeness that accompanies participating in some fads and fashions or varying from what is taken to be conventional and customary. Examples would be sporting spiked hair or vivid hair dyes, at least when they first appeared. But such acts are usually regarded as harmless and receive mild reactions ranging from disdain or mild disgust to indifference to amusement.

The varying character of what counts as deviance highlights the socially negotiated and 'constructed' aspect of it. Part of that variation has to do with the different types of norms that operate in a society. Some norms have been formalized and encoded as laws. However, there are other kinds as well: mores, or moral injunctions about how things ought to be done, and folkways, or everyday customs regarding practical matters like greetings, eating, etc. Part of the variation is also a result of norms at all levels undergoing change with regard to the perceived seriousness and harmfulness of violating them. For instance, consider the shift in the public perception of the harmfulness of tobacco use to oneself and others over the past few decades.

There is a relative quality to what counts as deviant behaviour which can be unsettling. However, while drawing attention to this relativism, sociologists have also found something more. As Erich Goode has pointed out, while there are no actions that are literally condemned everywhere, the condemning of some actions is universal.[2] And this observation becomes the basis of an important sociological insight into deviance and social control. It comes into view when we observe patterns related to the enacting, defining, and reacting to acts that become regarded as deviant. At this level we find deviance referring less to a concrete behaviour that's disturbing or a matter of defining behaviours to be in need of correction and control, than to a sociological process that seems to be inherent in the very nature of group life.

As Durkheim noted a century ago,[3] there is a kind of unfolding drama to this process that's guided by an underlying logic. The initial disturbing act, the activity of defining those acts as deviant, and the nature of the societal reaction are all constituent parts of the unfolding drama. And the underlying logic concerns how we have collectively structured a group and manage its very organization. Through this process the initial disorganizing energy of a disturbing act becomes captured by defining and portraying the act as a deviant behaviour, and then this is used as a basis for clarifying norms and values as well as unifying the group in the process of reacting to it.

These are some of the levels and angles of inquiry that comprise the sociology of deviance. The articles in the first section of the reader use the ambiguity and public debate over what counts as deviance to open up the kinds of questions sociologists ask about it and introduce some basic concepts and ideas that have been developed in sociology to address those questions. This includes crime, which would seem to be the most clear-cut part of the broader concept of deviance. But in sociology it is no settled matter either.

## Notes

1.   Hagan, John. 1994. *Crime and Disrepute*. Thousand Oaks, CA: Pine Forge Press.
2.   Goode, Erich. 1978. *Deviant Behavior*. Englewood Cliffs, NJ: Prentice Hall: 18.
3.   Durkheim, Emile. 1897/1951. *Suicide*. New York: Free Press.
4.   ———1938/1965. *The Rules of Sociological Method*. New York: Free Press.
5.   ———1984. *The Division of Labor in Society*. New York: The Free Press.

# 1

## Introduction

'Furries' aren't doing anything that would be considered illegal, at least in terms of current Canadian or American law. But they generally elicit a reaction from bystanders when they get together. So who are they? Would you consider them an example of deviance ? If so, why? If not, what are they an example of?

## Pleasures of the Fur

*George Gurley*

A moose is loitering outside a hotel in the Chicago suburb of Arlington Heights. The moose—actually a man in a full-body moose costume—is here for a convention . . . and so is the porcupine a few feet away, as well as the many foxes and wolves. Even the people in regular clothes have a little something (ferret hand puppet, rabbit ears) to set them apart from the ordinary hotel guests. One man in jeans and a button-down shirt gets up from a couch in the lobby and walks over to the elevator, revealing a fluffy tail dragging behind him. The elevator doors open. Inside, a fellow is kissing a man with antlers on his head. The other hotel guests look stunned.

'We're a group of people who like things having to do with animals and cartoons', a man in a tiger suit tells a woman. 'We're furries'.

'So cute', the woman says.

Welcome to the Midwest FurFest.

Here, a number of 'furries'—people whose interest in animal characters goes further than an appreciation of *The Lion King*—are gathering together.

At 7:30 p.m., near the front desk, three men known as Pack Rat, Rob Fox, and Zen Wolph are scratching one another's backs—grooming one another, like macaques in a zoo. 'Skritch-ing', they call it. I am tempted to turn around and run. Instead I find myself talking with Keith Dickinson, a self-described 'computer geek'. Not long ago, this man, a 37-year-old from Kansas City, Kansas, was so depressed he could barely bring himself to go to the grocery store. And then it hit him. He started to believe that, somewhere deep down, he was actually . . . a polar bear.

'In normal society', Dickinson says, 'two people who hardly know each other do not walk up and scratch each other's backs. But when you're one of the furs, it's one big extended family'.

Next to him is his skinny, long-haired, fedora-wearing sidekick, a 23-year-old art student named Ian Johnson (nametag: R.C. RABBITSFOOT). Last year, Johnson, who has brought the ashes of his dead cat to the FurFest, persuaded Dickinson to attend another furry convention in Memphis, and that's what did it.

'It's a new way of looking at the world', Dickinson says. 'It's like looking at it with baby eyes, or cub eyes'.

'You regress into a child when you come to a convention', Johnson says, 'because it's that kind of camaraderie, or childishness'.

## Riding with Ostrich

It's night. Ostrich has to run an errand. We get into his Chevrolet Metro and speed away from the Sheraton, toward the nearest mall. The headlights illuminate the road ahead.
Ostrich, whose real name is Marshall Woods, is a compact guy in a denim jacket and blue jeans. He's 39 years old and works as a network administrator at a rubber company in Akron.

'When I was very, very young, I knew I wanted to be some type of animal', he says. 'I didn't necessarily want to be the animal, but I wanted to have the animal shape, as far back as I can remember. It's that way for a lot of people'.

He did normal things, like playing in the highschool marching band . . . but he couldn't stop thinking about cartoon animals. Throughout his teenage and college years, he hid his furriness, thinking it was a 'babyish thing'.

'What the hell', he says. 'Now I'm old and I'm warped, everybody knows it, so I don't bother hiding anything anymore!'

It wasn't until 1994 that he came upon others who shared his interest. He was a chemist at the time, collecting dinosaur stuff on the side. One day he went to a comic-book shop and discovered Genus, a furry comic-book series with sexy characters. 'And I looked at it and I was like, Whoa! This looks pretty much exactly what I'd like to read—I gotta have one of these', he recalls.

Now he writes a newsletter for Ohio Furs, an organization of furries with 87 members.

He got his name after taking some ballet classes and not being very good at it. 'I was sincere but not impressive', he says. 'I guess I was technically competent, but not very much fun to watch. And I was compared to the ostrich ballerinas in Fantasia. They are trying very hard, but they are not quite there'.

In 1998, Ostrich put up a Web site where you can see his animal drawings, his animal-themed poems, and short stories (one of which was published in Pawprints, a magazine for furries), his instructions on how to build a fur suit, and pictures of himself engaged in animal-centred activities. Like the time he made a solo trip to Sea World. 'There's something just inherently cheerful about ducks', reads the text next to one picture on his Web site. 'They seem almost ridiculously optimistic about the world and their place in it'. Next to a photo of sea lions, the caption reads: 'Do they have any idea how cute they look when they beg? Who could refuse them?'

For a while, he concedes, he was a 'plushie', which is the word for a person who has a strong—usually erotic—attachment to stuffed animals. He even wrote a plushie newspaper for a while, but gave it up. 'It doesn't really interest me now', he says. 'I just like to have the stuffed animals around. I would still say I'm a plushophile—I'm just not that interested in it that much sexually. In a casual way, but not really seriously'.

He goes into a store and purchases materials for a puppet-making workshop he is scheduled to lead the next day. Back behind the wheel, Ostrich says, 'I don't like the human form. I never really have. It does not please me. The body, just the flesh, the general design, I just don't like'.

He says he'd prefer to be a lemur or a rabbit and still be intelligent and keep the opposable thumbs. He thinks the technology will be available relatively soon to help him achieve this dream. Talking about all this almost causes Ostrich to miss his exit.

'I. Need. To. Drive. More. Talk. Less'.

Eventually, we pull back into a parking space back at the Sheraton.

'A lot of people here are the very same way. We don't have a lot of deep real-life contact. It's superficial. I kind of skate through society. I mean, you see a lot of people—I see them at work—who have no idea what they're doing, or why, and they sit there and bang along from one hour to the next. As fucked up as I am, I at least know how I feel and what I want to do, and I have the good fortune to have a number of friends who feel the same way'.

Ostrich leads me up to his suite.

It's filled with stuffed animals.

He sits on the chair and says there is a low percentage of women in the fandom, and a preponderance of gay men—or seemingly gay . . . We find as the number of women increases, the number of people who thought they were gay but decided otherwise increases, too. I know a couple of people who thought they were gay until they met a furry girl'.

He gets up.

'In some ways we're very closed off—sort of a subculture. I have trouble looking at it objectively, because it seems so natural. It's how I was my whole life, and all of a sudden, I'm like, Wow, here's a whole bunch of other people like this! Having not come to it from the outside, I have difficulty saying what it actually is, I'm too deeply into it'.

## Some Furry Theory

There are many kinds of furries, but they all seem to have a few things in common. Something happened to them after a youthful encounter with Bugs Bunny or Scooby Doo or the mascot at the pep rally. They took refuge in cartoons or science fiction. After being bombarded by tigers telling them what cereal to eat, camels smoking cigarettes, cars named after animals, airplanes with eyes and smiles, shirts with alligators, they decided their fellow human beings were not nearly so interesting as those animal characters.

But it wasn't so liberating, having these intense feelings, when you thought you were the only person on earth who had them. The second big relevation for most furries came when they got on the Internet. Not only were there others like them, they learned, but they were organized! They started having conventions in the early 90s. Now, such gatherings as the Further Confusion convention in San Jose, California, and Anthrocon in Philadelphia, attract more than 1,000 furry hobbyists apiece. (The Midwest FurFest is a smaller 'con', with about 400 attending.) There are other conventions, too—even summer camps.

The furry group has its own customs and language. 'Yiff' means sex, 'yiffy' means horny or sexual, and 'yiffing' means mating. 'Fur pile' denotes a bunch of furries lying on top of one another, affectionately, while skritching. 'Spooge' is semen—a possible outcome of a fur pile. A 'furvert' is anyone who is sexually attracted to mascots and such.

Many furries have jobs related to science and computers. They role-play on a Web site called 'FurryMUCK', a chatroom kingdom where users pretend they're red-tailed hawks, foxes, and polar bears.

A high number of furries are bearded and wear glasses. Many resemble the animal they identify with (especially wolves and foxes, the most popular 'totems'). Some have googly, glazed, innocent eyes. A few are crazy-eyed.

## A Moment with Mike the Coyote

Down in the lobby, a coyote is sitting on a couch. His nametag reads SHAGGY, but his real name is Mike. Not all the conventioneers want people to know their full names, lest their bosses or parents find out what they're up to on the weekends. Mike the Coyote says he is a security guard in Indiana and has been going to furry conventions since 1992. The Midwest FurFest, he says, is 'very mellow so far, rather surprisingly so, in fact. I hope it stays this way. We don't need the weirdies to fall out of the woodwork. For me, walking around a con with a tail hanging out my butt just seems weird. Just not my particular bag'.

But Mike the Coyote has something for anyone who finds furriness strange: 'Just go look at the Packers and Vikings fans at the game. You think we're weird? Look at the 350-pound guy that's got his body split in colours half and half, he's wearing shorts and paint and nothing else, and he's screaming, 'Vikings!' Oh my God! Anybody involved in beauty pageants? Children's beauty pageants, where they dress the little girls like they're 25-year-old prostitutes—which is just sick'.

## 'There's Something about Raccoons'

One man who didn't make it to the Midwest FurFest is Ostrich's friend Fox Wolfie Galen, the King of the Plushies.

'He's OK', says Jack Below, a 28-year-old on-line worker at Southwestern Bell, who doubles as Spiked Punch, a wolf with a mallet. But, Below adds, Fox Wolfie Galen is 'one of the people I really worry about. I really don't have anything against him: I just think if people really knew the full story on him, it would kind of set a bad image'.

Two months prior to the FurFest, I visited Fox Wolfie Galen, whose real name is Kenneth, at his house in a small Pennsylvania city, where he lives with a roommate and more than a thousand stuffed animals. He was staring at his computer screen, monitoring an on-line auction. He put in a bid of $40.01 for a 40-inch skunk stuffed animal, then lay down on his mattress on the floor.

'I pretty much can't afford to pay more than a dollar an inch for plush', he said, in a voice like that of Bill Murray's gopher-chasing groundskeeper character in *Caddyshack*. 'I like skunks. I mostly collect bunnies, foxes, bears, ferrets, otters, sometimes dinosaurs'.

Fox Wolfie Galen, aged 39, was wearing a Mickey Mouse sweatshirt, green jeans, and thick, red-tinted glasses. (He said his eyesight is so bad that he receives $500 a month from the government; he has no job, rent is $200 a month.) Stuffed animals surrounded him and were stacked up to the ceiling against the wall by his bed. A big Meeko, the raccoon character from Pocahontas, in a Cub Scout uniform was looking at me with a crazed expression.

'That's what I wouldn't mind being in real life'. Fox Wolfie Galen said of the Meeko, which may be the most popular stuffed animal among the plushophiles. Between this one's legs was a little opening, a tear in the seam.

Fox Wolfie Galen had never travelled much beyond his hometown until four years ago, when he went to a furry convention in California with another plushophile he had met on-line. Since then he had made it to conventions in Toronto, Chicago, and Albany, New York.

Plushophilia began for him when he was around seven years old, even though he didn't own any stuffed animals. 'From the time I was born until through high school, I probably touched three or four "plushes",' he said, using the plushophile's term for stuffed animal. 'It wasn't like I couldn't get them. I was interested: I just didn't make the connection. I knew I liked them, because I'd seen them on TV, or if I visited somebody else's house and they had plush. Or if somebody came along in a furry-animal costume, like a high-school mascot, I'd always sit close to where I'd think they'd be coming out'.

After pep rallies he would find himself so aroused that he would have to walk through the school's hallways with a book bag held in front of him. Growing up, he never fantasized about women. 'If a mascot walked into a room surrounded by naked women, I'd be thinking about the mascot', he said.

'I'm not like a person who hasn't had a human mate before', he said. 'I actually have been with four different women in my life, and I can honestly say that none of them have come close to the tactile physical pleasure. Women don't feel like that. Human skin might feel good, it's smooth and everything, but it just doesn't feel the same way'.

For a long time he thought he was the only plushophile on the planet. ' "Plushie" didn't exist in my vocabulary', he said. Then, in 1994, he discovered a Web site that captured his interest. There were some frequently asked questions such as 'Why do you have sex with stuffed animals?' 'Do you actually go on your stuffed animals?' and 'How do you clean your stuffed animals?'

'I'm reading this and I was like, Oh my gosh, somebody else does this? I almost fell over'.

He started his own Web site. There, you can see sexually explicit photos from furry conventions, doctored cartoon stills, and his short stories.

Fox Wolfie Galen said he does have intercourse with his stuffed animals but more often rubs himself externally on the fur. He doesn't believe the stuffed raccoon is alive . . . but he can dream, can't he?

'I'll look at his eyes, and I'm thinking, Oh, it's alive', he said. 'There are people who do kinkier things than me with their plush. Some people put openings in all their plush. Some people even pray to their plushies. There's mutilators. That disturbs me, because they're turned on by destruction of something and I see no reason for it'.

It was getting late. He was still lying on his mattress, now discussing 'crush' videos—a recently outlawed form of pornography made for men who like to watch animals being crushed by women.

'I consider that immoral', he said. 'You heard of Jeffrey Dahmer? He started out doing that stuff. If you could do it to an animal, you could do it to a human'.

He said he wished it were possible to be part man and part beast. But if such a thing were to come about—the advent of hybrid species—he wouldn't want to be alone.

'If I was the only one, they'd find out. They'd put me in a lab and dissect me. You know, it wouldn't be fun. What I'd want is a whole new world where you had, say, Canada was all raccoons, and the United States was all foxes, and Mexico's all badgers, and every country is a different race of animals, and they're all friendly with each other and there's no war'.

In an ideal world, Fox Wolfie Galen would be a ferret, a rat, a skunk, a fox, or a raccoon. 'There's something about raccoons. They actually have fingers, opposable thumbs, and everything. I could imagine a raccoon being half a human and walking on two feet. It would kind of be like a living Disney cartoon'.

But the government would screw it up, he figured.

'They'd probably make some hybrid human resistant to attack, something reptilian, scaly, and hard to kill. So you're probably going to have a whole bunch of alligator men or turtle-shelled men running around. They'll be intelligent, but they'll be slaves to whatever the government wants them to do, like go and kill people. I would only volunteer if we were to be considered at least remotely equal. I'd be a raccoon, most likely'.

I called a taxi and went to the bathroom. When I came back to his lair, Fox Wolfie Galen was in a full-body tiger suit. He was gesturing to a rip in the costume, between his legs.

The taxi arrived.

Outside his house, Fox Wolfie Galen was waving good-bye to me—with a fox hand puppet.

## Calling Dr Pervert

Sex researcher Katherine Gates has written about Fox Wolfie Galen, among others, in her book Deviant Desires: Incredibly Strange Sex (Juno Books, 2000). Now she was sitting down in the living room of her Brooklyn Heights apartment, where she lives with her husband. In the book, Fox Wolfie Galen called sex with stuffed animals a 'sacramental act'.

'How can you not laugh?' Gates said. 'I mean, because it's absurd. Even ordinary sex is pretty damn absurd when you think about it. It's pretty silly, it's pretty awkward, and so I don't think it would be fair to point the finger entirely at these people—but, no, it's funny. And the people who do it for the most part have a great sense of humour about it. Galen is a good example'.

Gates, who is 36 years old, said some plushophiles may not be 'relationship-suitable': 'In some cases—and this might be cruel to say—but we may be wired for the zeta male, the lowest male, to turn to other pursuits besides the pursuit of another human being. These people need a way of having intimacy and pleasure, too'.

Gates's book features chapters on fat admiration, pony play, balloon fetishists, and, on the dark side, the crush freaks. Her Web site, deviantdesires.com, has a forum in which different fetishists can talk to one another—the women who masturbate with bathtub toy boats can talk to the plushies, and so on . . .

Gates admitted she was a pervert, but only in the fantasy realm. 'Little Red Riding Hood', for example: 'I think that's incredibly sexy, and when I was a kid I used to masturbate to the fantasy of being eaten by a pack of wolves. And I still find that sort of thing an exciting image. I can call that into my head when necessary'.

She likes furry stuff, too. 'Take my word for it, I've got a really dirty mind, and my dirty mind has gone to places that are beyond the pale. I think amputee stuff is hot, I think furry stuff is hot. I think slash fiction's hot, but as far as acting stuff out . . . I mean, I've ridden pony boys and pony girls'—people dressed up with bridles and saddles, etc.—'and I found that very exciting, but I'm uninclined to ask my husband to put on a saddle. And we find the ordinary, old vanilla stuff completely satisfying and very, very perfect'.

She considers the plushophiles to have a lot in common with practitioners of vanilla sex. 'They may think about sex as often as we do, which is often, and they may think of stuffed animals instead of Pamela Anderson, but they're very ordinary people', she said. 'Sex is not just what happens to the genitals. Everything is fetish fodder. I can't think of anything in this world that couldn't be sexualized by somebody'.

Back at the convention.

## The Furry Show

Now it's showtime. The Chicago Room is full of furries.

'Y'all ready for a good three, four hours of entertainment?' says Tyger Cowboy, the master of ceremonies.

Babs Bunny is the first act. Basically, it is someone in a bunny outfit hopping around while singing Cyndi Lauper's 'Girls Just Want to Have Fun' in a high-pitched voice.

A group of furries in cat regalia do a few songs from *Grease*. A little boy in the front—a son of the convention chairman, Robert King—has his fingers in his ears.

The Squirrelles sing 'You Can't Hurry Love'. An Elmo muppet does 'Tiptoe Through the Tulips'. Ten seconds into the number, a wolf creeps up and rips Elmo apart. The place goes nuts.

## The Furries Versus the US Army

The next morning, at 11:50, the lobby is full of furries and . . . soldiers in camouflage gear. The 85th Army Reserve Division, headquartered in Arlington Heights, happens to be having a convention here, too—a commanders' conference, during which they're to go over what took place in 2000, and set goals for 2001. The furries in the lobby look baffled. A few military men are smirking. One square-jawed hard-ass stares at the rabbit-eared furry for a moment and, finally, says, 'Yeah!' It's sarcastic. He sounds like a high-school jerk sizing up the class freak. 'Unusual', says a Sergeant Major Jennings.

'I think it's comical, myself', says one of his subordinates. 'God bless America', says the other.

Ostrich comes tearing past them, saying, 'The fur suit parade's about to start!' Soon, about 40 people in mascotwear—the fur suiters—are marching quietly through the lobby. Flash-bulbs pop. Furries in civilian clothes reach out to touch the fur suiters as they go by.

A big puppy.

A wolf with a huge mallet.

A bear eating a raccoon.

'Show us some tail, baby!' says a furry bystander.

'I didn't know rabbits were in season', says an army guy.

A Lieutenant Colonel Flowers is taking it all in good-naturedly. 'A little unusual', he says. 'Of course, they'd probably say the same thing about us'.

A half-kangaroo walks by.

'Pretty good, pretty good, pretty imaginative', the lieutenant colonel says. 'What are they, an advocacy group?'

Another lieutenant colonel, named Farrar, is unfazed. 'Well, when you see people wearing dog collars and chains . . . you know, I went to college', he says. 'It doesn't take much imagination to figure out what these people might be doing behind closed doors. The clean aspect, OK, these guys are cartoon figures, I can see that. But if you go a little left of that, then suddenly you're adding a new dimension to it. It doesn't make me very comfortable. Certainly nothing I agree with. Tantric sex comes to mind. People that have problems'. He thinks some more. 'But we're all getting along!' Without hesitation, he poses for a picture with a brown bear.

Another man in uniform, Lieutenant Patrick George, is chatting with a young raccoon. 'This is something nice to bring kids to', Lieutenant George says.

The raccoon suggests there might be no more war if everyone adopted the furry attitude toward life. Lieutenant George smiles. 'There will always be wars as long as there's people on this earth', he says. 'Not if they all pretend to be animals', the raccoon says, then rejoins the parade.

Lieutenant George has been watching some of the furries. 'Touchy-feely, with each other', he says. 'I noticed that last night. They're scratching each other and laying in the lap. You don't have to be too smart to figure it out. It's easy'. He stops his friendly chuckling, however, when he learns he has been chatting with a guy who might really want to be a raccoon.

'That's different', he says. 'But different people have different beliefs in this world. We can't be the same, we're all individuals. So to each his own'.

## Fox Talk

It's Saturday evening, and a discussion group, 'Foxes in the Fandom', is in progress. It is moderated by a pudgy, bearded man who goes by the name Craig Fox. About two dozen males are present: half look like foxes. Like Randy Foxx and Phallon. And Rowdy Fox, smiling naughtily as his fox hand puppet nibbles on his free hand.

'Do you think movies and books portray foxes evil more, or good more?' Mr. Fox the moderator asks.

'If the main character was a mouse or a rabbit, then the fox would be the evil villain', says Denver, a long-haired guy in an ELTONJOHN.COM T-shirt. 'It also depends if the main character is, for example, a lion. I've run into a couple where the fox is a bumbling sidekick. It depends on basically the line of the food chain with who's the star'.

'Right', says Mr. Fox. 'Um, another thing about foxes, in general, is that—how can I say this?—the fandom looks upon them as extremely yiffy. Why do you think that is?'

There is some giggling.

'If you want to go yiffy', Mr. Fox continues, 'let's look at the rabbits! Whereas foxes actually mate for life, as a general rule'.

Now it's time for tales of real-life fox encounters.

'Has anyone been around an actual fox?' the moderator asks, before telling of how he once went to a petting zoo, where red foxes sat on his head and licked his face.

Denver says he has had 12 encounters with foxes, all in the wild. 'There is one fox that lives in Gloucester, Massachusetts, that apparently likes me, because he has been staring in my window all night'.

Everyone laughs hard.

After everyone agrees that it would be wrong to have a fox as a pet, there is a pause.

'What would people like to see the image of the fox be in the new millennium?' Mr. Fox asks. 'What would you like to see, foxwise?'

'I got a question', says a woman in the back. She is half bat, half cat. 'What's everyone's passion for foxes? Because I don't know anything about it'.

## The Griffin in the Bar

Matt Davis, a slender 30-year-old dude with black close-cropped hair, is in the hotel bar. His T-shirt reads MY SEXUAL PREFERENCE IS NOT YOU. Davis drove up to the Midwest FurFest with a few other furs from Arkansas. He's a security guard and furry artist who fantasizes about being a griffin, which would make him half eagle, half lion.

'I'd be a security-guard griffin', he says, 'I could fly and patrol the area'. He would have a griffin mate who would look like him but 'a little bit thinner-boned' and 'adorable'.

'I've had fantasies that I've spent a long hunt through the forest catching my prey and bringing home to my nest moose and deer, something like that. Something large. Carrying it home to my nest, where my mate is waiting for me, and after eating, we engage in ferocious sex and fall asleep cuddling together in the nest'.

With him is a rotund fellow with long blond hair. He says he is the March Hare (real name: O. Holcomb). 'Being human, first of all, we're not all that cute', he says, 'In fact, we're bare-ass ugly. Second of all, intelligence, while it is a wonderful thing, is not that wonderful. Having what we think is understanding and then realizing it's not is more painful than being hunted down and killed by your predator'. Being furry, on the other hand, is a solution to life. 'It gives me thunder'. Says the March Hare, 'I can walk into any situation and go, 'I am the dude!' It's like having a switch, a psychological switch you can tap into and turn something on'. It helps even when he's flipping burgers, 'You have 30 orders up there', he says, 'If I wasn't the hare, I wouldn't be fast enough to get those 30 orders out—and in under three minutes—and be the dude'.

## The Furry Haters

Later on at the bar, at 2 a.m., a dozen 30-ish patrons, part of a wedding party, are making noise. . . .

'They're freaks', says a blonde who gives her name as Sylvia.

'No', says Johnny, 'Star Trek people that have lost Star Trek. Now they run around with mouse costumes on. Very disturbing'.

'A bunch of freaks running around!' Sylvia insists, 'What is the purpose of the fur costume?'

'Pretty much guys that can't deal with society', Johnny says.

'Bestiality!' Sylvia says.

'It's a shame, because there's a lot of people here who are getting the wrong impression of Chicago', says Johnny . . . It, uh, it just makes me sick. Whitey!'

Whitey comes over. He is wearing a Phish shirt and a red University of Wisconsin cap. 'Oh, these fucking clowns running around?' says Whitey, who is drinking whiskey, smoking a Dunhill, and swaying a bit. 'I'd love to take my 10/22 and take a couple of plink shots at them!'

Today is the opening day of deer season, and Whitey missed it because of his 'dumb-ass' friend's wedding.

'Freaks', Sylvia says, cracking up.

Still, Whitey says he is not one to 'fucking cast judgment on anybody. And if that's their bag of tricks, that's cool, but it's just kind of like, I just think I could come up with a better hobby'. For example? 'Killing real animals', he says. 'Snowmobiling'.

## Toward a Furry Future

A month after the Midwest FurFest, I call Ostrich at his apartment in Ohio. He has been sitting around drawing a picture of a fox and playing with his cat. The FurFest was a success, he says. 'I've heard nothing but good about it'. Ostrich says, 'I've heard two complaints about it, and they're both from known malcontents'. He confirms there was a fair amount of wild sex at the convention: 'Oh yeah, I know there was for a fact. I probably would have been involved in it if I hadn't been so busy'.

Was he still hopeful about the possibility of genetic engineering?

'Oh yeah. That's pretty much the future of the world—there's no way around it. If I can live another 30 or 40 years, I might live several hundred more. Obviously, I'd like to rework my body to make my physical body conform more to my body image. I'd want a tail, I'd want some fur, and, basically, some cute cartoon eyes and stuff. The technology for that's coming. I don't think it's as far off as most people think'.

# 2

## Introduction

In this excerpt from a larger work, Deutschmann introduces us to prescientific approaches to deviance. Among them is demonizing those whose behaviour varies from, or breaks, conventional norms, and is felt to be threatening to the prevailing social order. What are the main characteristics of demonizing? What are the main differences between non-scientific and scientifically inspired approaches to deviance? Explain how the institution of patriarchy can help us understand the witch craze in the Medieval world.

While the author uses the example of the witch craze to illustrate demonizing, this prescientific practice should not simply be relegated to an earlier era. Demonizing continues to be a prevalent way that we, the media, or those in authority, construct deviance in contemporary society as well. What might be some current examples of demonizing being used to discuss deviants?

# Prescientific Approaches to Deviance

*Linda Deutschmann*

In this chapter, we will look at the ways in which deviance was understood before the great transition to rationalism and science ('the Enlightenment') in the late 1600s. Early treatment of deviance was non-causal. The earliest sacred stories (myths) illustrated the character of deviance, and warned people about the consequences of excessive control as well as excessive deviance. The spread and penetration of monotheistic religions—especially Christianity—led to a more causal, but still supernatural, explanation according to which the 'devil' caused deviance and all other ills. Deviance no longer evoked feelings of ambivalence; it was evil, as were those who failed to oppose it. This chapter devotes considerable space to explaining the nature, origins, and consequences of the witchcraft craze that shook Europe from roughly CE 1400 to CE 1700.

Witchcraft is important for the study of deviance because it provides a paradigmatic example (an especially useful model) of the process whereby authorities, sometimes even against resistance from their less powerful subjects, can create deviants. It is relatively easy, looking back through contemporary eyes, to see that 'witches', as seen by the medieval authorities, did not really exist, even if there were then (as now) some people who claimed to have supernatural powers. Once we make clear the way in which the deviantization of witches came about, we can look at other kinds of deviance closer to our own time and raise the same questions. For example, how much of both the glamour and the horror of the 'drug trafficker' is real, and how much is a construct made up of some truths and many inaccuracies? What is the underlying reality, and why is distortion of that reality so common?

# Past and Present Representations of Deviance

## Myths, Parables, and Stories

Before the Enlightenment brought us science, rationality, and an empirically bound reality, people understood life in terms of myths, parables, and stories. These tales described their experiences and, in a non-scientific way, explained them. This tradition is carried on in modern art, drama, and literature that present us with examples of deviance and its consequences. Although they may or may not also provide moral instruction, these stories give us an understanding of how deviance fits into the scheme of things.

The ethical message of each major religion is supported by collections of historical or mythical tales in which various kinds of offences against the powers of creation, or against social regulation, happen. The offence is not always intended by—or even known to—the offender. The response of heaven and earth, however, is usually punitive unless mitigated by ritual reconciliation. The prodigal son, for example, may be welcomed home. For the most part, deviants are expelled from the garden, turned into pillars of salt, or condemned to perform eternal tasks. Temptation and its consequences are the theme of many stories of this kind. Eve was tempted into tasting the forbidden fruit of knowledge. Pandora's curiosity led her to open the box containing all the evils of the world. Buddha, Christ, Mohammed, and other important religious figures all had experience, at least in figurative terms, of demons or temptations.

Secular or magical stories also reinforce cultural images of deviance and control. In Heinrich Hoffman's *Der Struwwelpeter* (1861) (translated by Mark Twain as *Slovenly Peter: Or Cheerful Stories and Funny Pictures for Good Little Folks*), a little girl plays with matches; her dress catches fire, and soon all that remains of her is a pile of ashes, two shoes, and two cats whose tears flow like a stream across the page. In another story, a boy insists on sucking his thumbs and a tailor (with scissor-like legs) leaps across the page to cut them off. Slovenly Peter's long fingernails inspired the film *Edward Scissorhands*, which is itself a moral parable.

Many other children's stories have similar cautionary intentions. The boy who cried wolf when there was no wolf is denied help when he needs it. Little Red Riding Hood talks to a stranger in the woods and gets herself and her grandmother eaten. Cinderella's ugly stepsisters have their eyes plucked out and eaten by doves (Tatar, 1987, p. 182). The vain emperor is revealed as naked. These stories conform to the common cultural practice of warning and admonishing in order to induce polite language, table manners, caution, co-operation, and responsibility.

## Trickster Legends

Despite the above examples, most of our secular tales are ambivalent about deviance in that they do not regard it as unconditionally bad. Indeed, the deviant character is frequently more likable and sympathetic than the characters who teach and correct. This ambivalence about deviance and control is reflected in the culturally universal trickster (Radin, 1972 p. iii) In trickster stories, the smart little guy outwits the stupid, greedy (boring) authorities. The trickster circumvents the usual rules in disrespectful ways.

Unburdened by scruples, tricksters dupe friends, acquaintances, and adversaries alike in the pursuit of their selfish ends and blithely reward their benefactor's generosity with sometimes deadly betrayals. In addition, they have a pronounced weakness for food but are plagued by an inveterate aversion for work, a trait that forces them to rely on trickery to obtain food both in times of want and of plenty (Owomoyela, 1990: 626).

Everything the trickster does is permeated with laughter, irony, wit—and deviance. The trickster is also a god, a god that is not above us all but rather immanent in life itself and in the community. The audience reaction is laughter tempered with awe (Radin, 1972: xxiv).

The trickster takes many forms. He is usually masculine but also gender-bending (Hyde, 1998; Ball, 2001). Even if he sometimes appears as a female he may have a penis that wanders into unacceptable places. He does not take the realities of the human world seriously. In many tales, he shockingly violates many of the customary norms of honesty, mannerliness, and loyalty. When the trickster is present, complacency and comfort are at risk.

Brer Rabbit, Roger Rabbit, and Bugs Bunny have their origins in African trickster figures Anansi and Legba. Their Disneyfication or 'literary sanitation' (Rosenberg, 1998, p. 155) has almost eliminated the demigod features of the original, but they do convey the amusing, iconoclastic, and likeable side of the trickster. One could say the same for Kokopelli, a sanitized and commercialized version of a more complex trickster figure. The trickster also encompasses darker, uncontrolled, less human forces. Batman's archenemy, the Joker, is funny in a campy way. He can take on animal forms or the shape of inanimate objects; and he is violent, unpredictable, homicidal, and sadistic. The mean and mischievous imp Mr Mxyzptlk in Superman comic books combines both comedic and demonic features. Star Wars' Darth Vader is another 'dark' trickster (Iaccino, 1998, p.3) Thus, the trickster embodies the paradox of deviance—its attractiveness and dangers, and its many faces. Joseph Campbell has called him 'The Hero with a Thousand Faces' (Campbell, 1956).

We also find elements of the trickster in rock music (Michael Jackson); the bad heroes of film (Darth Vader), sports (Dennis Rodman), and the arts (Jack Nicholson); and political protests (the antics of masked protesters at demonstrations, for example) (Santinio, 1990). Some of the stories of the Black folk hero Stagolee (Staggerlee) also seem to fit the genre (Leeming & Page, 1999, pp. 172–181). Cross-dressers (people who wear clothes designed for the opposite sex) sometimes fall into the trickster category. They make fun of the established order and question one of its most fundamental dichotomies, the great gender divide. Thus, the essential role of the fool as trickster is a contrary one that upsets the taken-for-granted order of things.

## Contemporary Legends

Contemporary legends differ from legends of the past in that they claim to be factual rather than fantastic. These legends, although highly believable, are based on hearsay rather than fact (Goode, 1992: 306; Pearson, 1984). Some of them are horror stories reflecting urban fears (stolen kidneys, hypodermic needles in phone booths or theatre seats), while some, like the trickster tales, are stories with a humorous, slightly ambiguous moral twist. An example of the first is the perennial legend of the Halloween candy poisoned (by strangers) that stirs up parental anxieties every October (Bennett, 2005; Best, 1985; Brunvand, 1989).

Most students have heard many legends spawned by essay anxieties, such as the one about the student who handed in a recycled essay and received a good mark on it, but with a note from the professor saying 'I only got a C on this, but I always thought it was a lot better than that'. Jan Harold Brunvand, University of Utah English professor and folklorist, has collected hundreds of these tales, which always betray their spuriousness by being told too many times and with far too many embellishments and revisions, and always as told by a reliable source or friend of a friend (Brunvand, 2001, 1981, 1986). Urban legends deal with understandings of deviance and control. They tell us that certain ways of living (deviance, or lack of control) are likely to lead to grief and humiliation, and in the process they express our fears or desire for more order (and sometimes our sense of humour).

## Early Explanations of Deviance: The Demonic Perspective

The earliest recorded attempts to explain rather than describe the nature of deviance did not, as modern science does, seek causes in the empirical world. Deviance, like everything else, was deemed to be caused by forces in the supernatural realm. In theoretical terms, the independent variables were supernatural forces, often demons or devils of some kind, who acted through particular human beings to cause harm in the world. Thus, when floods came, crops failed, farm animals sickened, or women miscarried, people did not look for the causes in nature, physiology, or medicine. Ordinary folks did not understand that mould on the crops could produce hallucinations, miscarriages, and other problems. They looked instead to the supernatural—witches, sorcerers, demons, and the like—as an explanation for these events. In this world, there were no coincidences: if a man walked along a path and something fell on him, someone else must have willed that event to happen by invoking the powers of the supernatural.

Over time, there have been many versions of the demonic perspective, each corresponding with the different ideas about the supernatural that were typical of the particular age and culture.

Monotheistic religions like Judaism, Christianity, and Islam have tended to see the goodness of an all-powerful creator as offset by a single, purely evil power (sometimes personified as a type of devil) bent on wresting power from the Almighty. In the Judaeo-Christian view (which is partially also the view of Islam and which has precursors in Manichaeism and Neoplatonism), the supernatural primarily reflects a cosmic struggle between good and evil, personified by God and the devil (Satan). In the battle for human souls, the devil turns people into deviants. Some people are bad, not just because of what they do to others but also because of their treasonous role in the battle between good and evil. The demonic

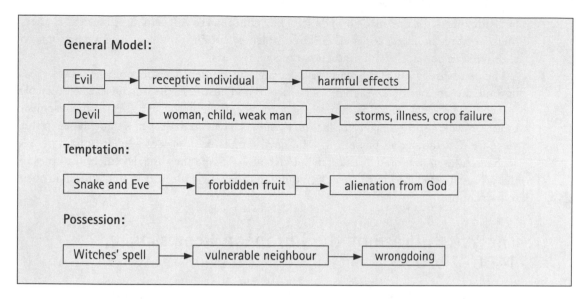

Figure 2.1 The Causal Model of Demonic Deviance

deviant commits physically harmful acts that weaken the system while at the same time challenging the order of things. This view of the world as dualistic, a matter of pure good and stark evil, had a profound impact on conceptions of deviance from the Middle Ages up to the 1970s. Only with the rise of postmodern alternatives has this duality been seriously challenged.

## The Pagan as Deviant

In their efforts to discredit and displace other religions, monotheistic religions have demonized the other religions' gods, made wizards and sorcerers of their sages, and treated their times of ritual ceremony as occasions of demonic celebration (Simpson, 1973). The idea of a Witches' Sabbath, a time when witches supposedly gathered to engage in sex with the devil and his demons, was largely a Christian propaganda distortion of the rites of older religions seen as dangerous pagan cults. Similarly, Baal-Zeebub, the Lord of the Flies, was a fertility god worshipped by the Philistines and other Semitic groups. The Old Testament Israelites transformed him into Beelzebub, a powerful devil. Both the horned Celtic god Cerunnos and the Greco-Roman Pan were remade into Judeo-Christian images of devils with horns and cloven hooves (Russell, 1984, p. 63). Other demonized residuals of pagan times include the immoral or amoral humanlike creatures depicted as elves, fauns, trolls, satyrs, fairies, leprechauns, werewolves, dragons, ghosts, and jinn. Although now the stuff of children's storybooks, these creatures were once an accepted part of everyday life, both feared and respected. Anticipating retaliation if they failed to do so, people spoke kindly about fairies (Briggs, 1978) but also used them to explain such events as a husband gone missing for a year. (The fairies had kidnapped him and made him dance.) Bad children are still sometimes seen as change-lings—evil replacements for good children stolen by goblins or trolls; the deviance of such children is in no way the fault of their parents.

The pantheistic view of the world saw deviance and suffering as phenomena more or less beyond human control. The actions of both gods and hostile spirits were neither predictable nor always preventable. In the monotheistic cosmos, however, humans bear some responsibility for evoking, or giving in to, the forces of evil. The two main paths to deviance in this view are temptation and possession. The devil tempts or possesses weaker human beings such as children or morally weak (irreligious) adults. Sometimes the deviant contributes to the process by dabbling in the occult, indulging in heretical ideas, or living a lifestyle open to corruption.

# The Witch Craze of the European Renaissance, 1400–1700

## Historical Background

Virtually all societies have maintained some beliefs about witchcraft or sorcery. Before the witch craze, European beliefs were similar to those found on other continents. Witches and sorcerers were sometimes feared, sometimes persecuted, but they were often respected and recognized as people who served a useful role in the social order (e.g., by providing charms and amulets to protect people from harm or sickness, or by acting as oracles to decide the innocence or guilt of accused people). Magic directed against political leaders, however, was regarded as treason.

Belief in witches was 'a continuing preoccupation of villagers, but not an obsession' (Garrett, 1977, p. 462). The penalties for unauthorized or malicious practice of witchcraft were commensurate with those enforced for other kinds of assault on individuals or their property.

Before CE 1000, Church canon law (as reflected in the Canon Episcopi of about CE 906, a compendium of popular lore on demons) tended to hold that it was both un-Christian and illegal to believe in the reality of witches (Trevor-Roper, 1969, p. 13; Webster, 1996, p. 77). Witchcraft was not treated as part of the conspiracy theory of the demonic versus God, except for the canon's claim that women who believed themselves able to use love incantations or to fly at night with the pagan goddess Diana were suffering from delusions planted by the devil (Groh, 1987, p. 17). The canon asserted that the folkloric practice associated with such beliefs would disappear as all people became Christian (Ben-Yahuda, 1985, p. 34; Richards, 1990, p. 77). Catastrophes were sent by God to test humankind, and witches were deluded in believing that they could affect such things. In this period, attacks on presumed witches were regarded as superstitious pagan behaviour and some-times resulted in protests to Rome.

Between CE 1000 and 1480, witches and sorcerers (along with other manifestations of supernatural beings) were redefined. Rather than harmless and misunderstood relics of pagan life, they became agents of the devil—a vast subversive conspiracy against everything that was right, orderly, and holy. In fact, many of the accusations made against heretics and witches in this period (incest, infanticide, sex orgies, cannibalism) were the same as those that had been levelled against the early Christians by classical pagan writers (Cohen, 1976; Richards, 1990, p. 78). The process whereby folklore, witchcraft beliefs, ritual magic, and devil worship became one overall and world-shattering conspiracy was neither smooth nor gradual: it was contested in some areas and embraced in others.

The witch craze has been described as a collective psychosis or mania (Trevor-Roper, 1969). Although it has connections with modern fears of Satanism, its scale was much broader and its impact far more devastating. Episodes broke out repeatedly in towns, villages, and cities throughout Europe, the British Isles, and the American colonies, sometimes receding in one area only to break out in others. The exact number of victims is difficult to ascertain, given the widespread (but nonetheless local and episodic) nature of the witch hunt and the fact that records were often not kept at all in the early period. Later records were often destroyed, deliberately or not.

Events such as plagues, wars, and famines were likely to be followed by outbreaks of witch-hunting. In all, somewhere between 100,000 and 200,000 executions probably took place (Barstow, 1995; Ben-Yahuda, 1985, p. 23), although figures as low as 60,000 (Levack, 1987, p. 21) and as high as 500,000 (Harris, 1978, p. 237), and even 9,000,000 (Murray, 1921; Pelka, 1992), have been cited.

## Contributing Factors: The Inquisition and the Malleus Maleficarum

Although the witch craze can be seen as a symptom of the new, dualistic (monotheistic) way of looking at the world, its immediate sources were found within the dominant churches at the time, first among the Roman Catholic authorities, and then the Protestant ones. The witch craze, as a craze, began with the work of the Roman Catholic Inquisition.

The Inquisition caught in its net not only heretics who challenged what the authorities felt were the appropriate forms of belief and behaviour, but also people who, like Galileo, put forward alternative interpretations of the empirical world (Christie-Murray, 1989; Redondi, 1987).

Witch-hunting received a considerable boost from the work of the Franciscan and Dominican brotherhoods. Two Dominicans in particular—Heinrich Kramer (also called Institor) and Jakob Sprenger—played a major role in systematizing and giving shape to the definition of witchcraft as a conspiracy. Together they wrote a treatise on witchcraft called the *Malleus Maleficarium* (*The Hammer of the Witches*) (1971). Originally published in 1486, this was not the first book to codify all that was known or believed of witchcraft—or even the first to set standards for the prosecution of witches—but it was the most systematic, complete, and compelling.

The *Malleus* compiled all the existing sources of belief about witches and witchcraft, most of which were taken from common superstitions, biblical references, Greek and Roman writings, and the confessions of 'witches'. From this material the authors fashioned an impressive work that constructed the image of witch as a terrible danger.

## Explanations for the Craze

The demonic explanation for the witch craze was built on faith, and no amount of empirical evidence could refute it. More worldly interpretations of the causes of witch-hunting can be demonstrated by considering the kinds of people who were accused of witchcraft, the kinds of people who profited from their persecution, and when or under what conditions the accusations were made. All of these aspects are considered in the following list, which summarizes the 16 characteristics of those selected for prosecution as witches in the initial stages of the witch hunt. Once a hunt was under way, of course, no one was completely safe from accusation and conviction, and the only commonality among the victims was the fact that they had been accused.

## Characteristics of the Accused

1.  Women. By most accounts, at least 80 per cent of those executed were women (Kieckhefer, 1976; Levack, 1992a). Thus, to understand the witch hunts, it is necessary first to 'confront the deeply imbedded feelings about women—and the intricate patterns of interest underlying those feelings—among our witch-ridden ancestors' (Karlsen, 1989, p. xiii). The selection of women as targets was hardly surprising given a patriarchal Church that excluded women from all leadership roles and feared them as potential subversives (Worobec, 1995, p. 175). Women who stepped out of their assigned roles as bearers of children and servants to men were especially vulnerable. Thus, women who were 'old maids', widows without family support, sexually promiscuous, or who were lesbians were likely to be targeted (Worobec, 1995, p. 176).

2.  Women in conflict with other women. According to Willis, 'village-level witch-hunting was women's work' (Willis, 1995). Briggs, for example, writes, 'It appears that women were active in building up reputations by gossip, deploying countermagic and accusing suspects; crystallization into formal prosecution, however, needed the intervention of men, preferably of high status in the community' (Briggs, 1996, p. 282). Before the craze, such conflicts would have been settled at the local level and would only very rarely have involved the courts.

3.  Women who gave birth to deformed babies. These infants were regarded as 'Satan's spawn', the product of sexual orgies involving the mother and the devil or his demons.

4.  People seen in the dreams of others (especially if in the form of a sexual partner).

5.  Men or women who claimed to have occult powers. In every society, there have been people with 'second sight', who have forecast the future, dispensed spells or charms, or threatened others with supernatural vengeance. In the 1692 Salem witch trials, the first accused was Tituba, a West Indian servant who entertained the local girls with voodoo and with fortune telling by palmistry. When the girls began falling into unexplained fits, Tituba's employer, the Reverend Parris, beat a confession of witchcraft out of her. People such as Tituba are tolerated in normal times, when there is no anxiety about demonic conspiracies, but are often among the first condemned when such fears are raised (Breslaw, 1996).

6. People believed to be involved in treasonous conspiracies. When the inheritance of a throne could depend on the birth of a living male baby and when poisoning was a major factor in royal succession, the practice of witchcraft for political purposes was often suspected. This form of accusation was particularly common in the early witch-craft trials (around CE 1400). For example, under James III of Scotland, several witches were executed on the grounds that they had been conspiring with the king's brother against the king (Larner, 1980, p. 53).

7. People who got in the way. The most famous witch trial in European history was that of a priest, Urbain Grandier. Grandier was handsome, charming, a brilliant speaker, and popular with parishioners. His support for local power against the central govern-ment made him powerful enemies (a cardinal and the king). The accusation against him involved the 'possession' of a group of Ursiline nuns. These women barked, screamed, blasphemed (swore), and contorted their bodies in erotic ways. Grandier was accused of sorcery. Despite torture, during which all of the bones in his legs and feet were mangled, he refused to confess. He was executed by fire, before a crowed of more than 6,000 who had come for the spectacle (Huxley, 1996, pp. 211–218; Rapley, 1998).

8. People who did not fully accept Church dogma and practice. Besides freethinkers and early scientists, this group consisted of people who continued to follow the customs of the earlier pagan religions. Evidence presented at the heresy trial of Joan of Arc included the fact that she had participated in ancient Celtic practices that were traditional in rural areas but forbidden by the Church.

9. Healers, herbalists, and naturopaths. People involved in issues such as fertility, mid-wifery, and abortion were particularly vulnerable. Known as 'cunning men' and 'wise women' in England, and by equivalent names in Europe, they had 'powers' that were not under the regulation of the authorities (Cassar, 1993, p. 319). Abortion, for exam-ple, was associated with beliefs that newborn babies were being used in obscene rituals with the devil. Curing people by 'magical' means was also condemned. Midwives and herbalists were in competition with the rising all-male, university-based medical estab-lishment, which relied more on logic and dogma than on practical experience (Eastlea, 1980; Watts, 1984, p. 28). People knowledgeable about drugs were also suspect because the effects of drugs such as atropine, henbane, and thornapple, which have narcotic and poisonous properties, seemed to reveal supernatural powers (Worobec, 1995, p. 171). Such, whether they were given to people by women healers, or whether they simply came to them as mould on bread (some fungi that attack grain have LSD-like proper-ties), may lie at the root of beliefs about witches flying at night and being able to change shape (Harris, 1978, p. 190).

10. People blamed for the misfortune of others. Many accusations of witchcraft had their root in quarrels in which one party apparently threatened another, who later became sick or experienced some misfortune. Illnesses attributed to witchcraft or sorcery included 'impotence, stomach pains, barrenness, hernias, abscesses, epileptic sei-zures, and convulsions' (Worobec, 1995, pp. 166–167). Many cases involved beggars who seemed to be retaliating against those who had denied them assistance (Groh, 1987, p. 19; Thomas, 1997, pp. 506, 564), or people who ought to have been seeking

revenge for some previous insult or harm (Worobec, 1995, p. 181). The most frequent cases were those in which someone repudiated a neighbour—usually an old woman seeking a favour—and then attributed personal misfortunes to her (Garrett, 1977, pp. 462–463; Macfarlane, 1970, p. 196). Situations of this kind became increasingly common as the mutual-help systems typical of rural communities were disrupted by population growth and the arrival of early capitalist forms of economy; people who had some wealth began to feel threatened by the rising numbers of beggars and indigents.

11. Exceptional people. Sometimes personal characteristics like an unusual appearance, or perhaps extraordinary success or talent, were seen as the result of a Faustian bargain with Satan. The story of Faust, who sells his soul to the devil in exchange for knowledge and power, goes back to at least to the ninth century. Niccolo Paganini, a composer and violin virtuoso of the 1800s, was treated as a Faustian figure, primarily because his playing was so extraordinary. Canadian fiddler Ashley MacIsaac has similarly been accused of having made a demonic pact (MacIsaac, 2003). Unlike Paganini, MacIsaac will not have to worry about being harmed or refused burial rites.

12. People named by accused witches under torture or persuasion. Almost anyone could be named, but most confessing witches did not try to implicate court officials or other powerful people; such accusations, when they occurred, were often suppressed by the court.

13. People named by those suffering from illness or hardship. In Salem in 1692, the young girls who showed signs of 'possession' (screaming unaccountably, falling into grotesque convulsions, mimicking the behaviour of dogs) named everyone they had a grudge against (Erikson, 1966, p. 142). In total, 142 persons were named, ultimately resulting in the death by hanging of 21 men and women (and one dog). A man who refused to plead either guilty or not guilty was crushed to death under heavy stones; his refusal to enter a plea was interpreted as a denial of the legitimacy of the proceedings. Only when the accusations began to include prominent people (e.g., Lady Phipps, wife of the Massachusetts colony's governor) was the process seriously questioned and, ultimately, rejected (Rosenthal, 1993).

14. People with mental illnesses. Allowed to wander freely—if neglected—in normal times, those suffering from mental illness were particularly vulnerable to being caught up in the witch-hunt. Also singled out were people with psychoneurotic symptoms (manifested, for example, in a failure to react when pricked with a pin) and 'hysterics', who acted out because of physical or emotional stress. As Ben-Yahuda (1985) notes,

> While Freud himself virtually ignored the European witch craze, it contains elements to warm any analyst's heart: cruel and destructive persecutions, women, sex, and violence. These could easily by integrated into psychoanalytic interpretations, emphasizing the projection of hostility, reaction-formation, incestuous wishes, and impulses of the id. (43)

15. People with physical disabilities or neurological disorders. Such individuals might be seem as victims of the witchcraft of others or as suitable partners for Satan. They were

likely to be accused of giving others 'the evil eye'. Also included in this group were the elderly and the physically unattractive.

16. Scapegoats for the system. As long as people believed that plagues, wars, famines, and personal troubles were caused by demons, they needed religious protection. The control of witchcraft became a very significant reason to pay tithes to Church authorities and to obey their rules; only the Church authorities knew how to diagnose and treat supernatural ills, and only they were powerful enough to oppose the devastating powers of Satan. Anyone could be named for the purpose. The witch craze divided people against each other in suspicion and fear and forced them to depend on the Church (Erikson, 1966).

The above list tells us a great deal about the conditions that informed the craze. Whether in Europe, England, or the American colonies, witch-victims represented resistance to the sacred canopy erected over society by their respective churches. Some of these victims were actually deviant in some way. Others served as scapegoats for the threat posed to churches by the fundamental changes that were taking place around the world.

## Disruptive Social Change

Plagues and famines were especially acute in the period between 1400 and 1700, as was social change (Behringer, 1998; Watts, 1984: 7). Events such as Columbus's voyage to Americas in 1492, the opening up of trade routes to the East, and the invention of the printing press all contributed to a growth in knowledge that had the potential to undermine Church rule.

Throughout the witch-craze period, most of the trials were held in the cultural 'borderlands', where social diversity and religious conflict were the greatest, or in places where war and plague had created disorder (Briggs, 1996; Thomas, 1971). Even in later outbreaks, such as in pre-revolutionary Russia (late 1800s), the background of the craze was anxiety-provoking social change and economic upheaval.

Places that were sheltered from change did not develop the craze. For example, while the French were burning Huguenot heretics and witches, the stable French settlement in Canada was not affected; the belief in witches existed, but there was no panic associated with it (Morison, 1955, p. 248). The same was true of Ireland, whose Catholic people were unshaken in their ways and unwilling to make use of the oppressive courts imposed upon them by the English. In Ireland, between 1534 and 1711, only nine proceedings against witches were recorded. Similarly in confidently Catholic Italy and Spain, few witches were burned.

During the eighteenth century the craze finally burned out. Courts gradually ceased to treat witchcraft as a reality other than in its associations with criminal acts, fraud, extortion, or abuse (such as ritual child abuse). The *Criminal Code of Canada*, for example, makes it an offence to pretend to exercise or use any kind of witchcraft sorcery, enchantment or conjuration (Section 365). However, when an Ontario Supreme Court judge said to murderer Peter Demeter (sentenced to five life terms in 1988) 'You certainly appear to ooze evil from every pore of your body', few people in the courtroom thought that Demeter was being told he was 'possessed' or in the service of Satan—nor did they think the judge was joking (Claridge, 1988).

# Modern Beliefs about Demonic Deviance

Despite the predominance of secular definitions of deviance, the demonic remains a theme recognized and sometimes used in our society. The Antichrist has been seen in everything from political opponents and enemy countries to supermarket bar codes (Fuller, 1995). A recent Internet search (2005) on 'Antichrist' turned up George W. Bush, David Hasselhoff (star of Baywatch), Marilyn Manson, the Pope, Harry Potter, Bill Gates, and some quite variable descriptions that reveal ethnic and racial prejudices.

The belief that there is evil in the world does not necessarily result in accusations of demonism and panic over hidden conspiracies. When it does emerge in this form, however, the modern identifying label for those suspected of conspiring is likely to be Satanist, and the suspects are male as often as they are female. Indeed, the emphasis on female witches has receded, and the term 'witchcraft' is rarely used in this sense. A huge divide has emerged between those who use the concepts of Satanism and those who speak of witchcraft. Contemporary witches consider themselves to be practitioners of faiths such as the Mother-Goddess religion. They neither believe in nor worship Satan, and they are usually (but not always) ignored rather than feared by people with different religious convictions (Guiley, 1991; Marron, 1989).

Belief in satanic deviance is, not surprisingly, found mainly (but not exclusively) in areas with a high degree of religious consciousness, such as the Bible Belt areas of Canada and the United States.

## Evil as Metaphor

In modern times, the demonic has become more of a metaphor than an explanation when applied to deviance. Alcoholics speak of the 'devil in a bottle', and many drug addicts see their addiction as a consequence of demonic-like trickery—the drug promises euphoria but delivers death. Some people even see evil behind the apparently secular surface of everyday life:

> The iniquitous roster of evil all around us is an unending list of dark powers that are proliferating: racism, genocide, monstrous crimes, drug gang wars, merciless and random slaughter of innocent civilians, gas bombing of cities, pestilence, famine and war, governmental policies of racial cruelty, death squads, violent or insidious suppression of human rights, forms of slavery, abuse of children, bestial military action against civilians, callousness to the homeless, the AIDS victims and the poor, abuse of the elderly, sexism, rape, wanton murder, cults, terrorism, torture, the unremitting aftermath of past holy and unholy wars, the Holocaust, heinous cruelty and hatred, and the seven deadly sins: wrath, pride, envy, sloth, gluttony, lust, and avarice.
>
> We go on polluting the air, the soil and the water. We think the unthinkable: atomic destruction of civilization and the earth itself. We trash outer and inner space. We literally are in danger of running amok. All the while we feed an unbridled and insatiable appetite for horror; demonic projections are made on enemies

as 'Evil Empire' and 'The Great Satan', governments conspire with organized crime, assassinate, and massacre, destroy the souls of people for power and money, arm nations and individuals, and, as a consequence human beings are now exploding in every corner of the globe. Such things as these are often nourished and cunningly abetted by the media: television, film, newspapers, and even art, literature, and music. (Wilmer, 1988: 2–3)

The witch hunt provides a paradigm that can be applied to events such as the Nazi persecution of the Jews, the McCarthyite 'red scare' in North America, and the overzealous search for child molesters and Satanists. In modern times, demonology is used to explain deviance—generally in its most serious manifestations—only after all natural (as opposed to supernatural) explanations have failed. However, the paradigm can also be applied to more mundane forms of deviance such as drug trafficking when political authorities demonize those forms of deviance.

# References

Ball, M.C. 2001. 'Old Magic and New Fury: The Theophany of Afrekete' in Audre Lorde's *Tar Beach*. *NWSA Journal*, 13(1), 61–83.

Barstow, A.L. 1995. *Witchcraze: A New History of the European Witch-hunts*. San Francisco, CA: HarperCollins.

Behringer, W. 1998. *Witchcraft Persecutions in Bavaria: Popular Magic, Religious Zealotry and Reasons of State in Early Modern Europe* (J. C. Grayson & D. Lederer, Trans.). Cambridge, UK: Cambridge University Press.

Ben-Yahuda, N. 1985. *Deviance and Moral Boundaries: Witchcraft, the Occult, Science Fiction, Deviant Sciences and Scientists*. Chicago: University of Chicago Press.

Bennett, G. 2005. *Bodies: Sex, Violence, Disease and Death in Contemporary Legend*. Jackson MI: University Press of Mississippi.

Best, J. 1985. 'The Razor Blade in the Apple: The Social Construction of Urban Legends'. *Social Problems* 32 (5), 488–499.

Breslaw, E.G. 1996. *Tituba: Reluctant Witch of Salem: Devilish Indians and Puritan Fantasies*. New York: New York University Press.

Briggs, K.M. 1978. *The Vanishing People*. London: B.T. Batsford.

Briggs, R. 1996. *Witches and Neighbors: The Social and Cultural Context of European Witchcraft*. London, UK: HarperCollins.

Brunvand, J.H. 1981. *The Vanishing Hitchhiker*. New York: W.W. Norton.

_____. 1986. *The Choking Doberman and Other 'New' Urban Legends*. New York: Norton.

_____. 2001. *Encyclopedia of Urban Legends*. Santa Barbara, CA: ABC-Clio.

Burman. E. 1984. *The Inquisition: Hammer of Heresy*. New York: Dorset Press.

Campbell, J. 1956. *The Hero with a Thousand Faces*. New York: Meridian Books.

Cassar, C. 1993. Witchcraft Beliefs and Social Control in Seventeeth-Century Malta. *Mediterranean Studies* 3 (2), 316–334.

Christie-Murray, D. 1989. *A History of Heresy*. New York: Oxford University Press.

Claridge, T. 1988. 'You Ooze Evil, Demeter Told, as Judge Adds Two Life Terms'. *Globe and Mail* (July 29), A1.

Cohen, S. 1987. *Folk Devils and Moral Panics: The Creation of Mods and Rockers*. Cambridge, MA: Blackwell.

Eastlea, B. 1980. *Witch-hunting, Magic and the New Philosophy*. Brighton: Harvester.

Erikson, K.T. 1966. *Wayward Puritans: A Study in the Sociology of Deviance*. New York: John Wiley.

Fuller, R.C. 1995. *Naming the Antichrist: The History of an American Obsession*. New York: Oxford University Press.

Garrett, C. 1977. 'Women and Witches: Patterns of Analysis'. *Signs: Journal of Women in Culture and Society* 3 (2), 461–470.

Goode, E. 1992. *Collective Behavior*. Fort Worth: Harcourt Brace Jovanovich.

Groh, D. 1987. 'The Temptation of Conspiracy Theory, Part II'. In C.F. Grauman and S. Moscovici (eds.), *Changing Conceptions of Conspiracy*. Berlin: Springer-Verlag.

Guiley, R.E. 1991. *Harper's Encyclopedia of Mystical and Paranormal Experience*. San Francisco: HarperCollins.

Harris, M. 1978. *Cows, Pigs, Wars, and Witches: The Riddles of Culture*. New York: Random House.

Hoffman, H. 1861. *Slovenly Peter: Or Cheerful Stories and Funny Pictures for Good Little Folks* (M. Twain, Trans.). Philadelphia: John C. Winston.

Huxley, A. 1996. *The Devils of Loudon.* New York: Barnes and Noble.

Hyde, L. 1988. *Trickster Makes This World: Mischief, Myth and Art.* New York: North Point Press (Farrar Straus and Giroux).

Iaccino, J.F. 1998. *Jungian Reflections Within the Cinema: A Psychological Analysis of Sci-Fi and Fantasy Archetypes.* Westport, CT: Praeger.

Karlsen, C.F. 1989. *The Devil in the Shape of a Woman: Witchcraft in Colonial New England.* New York: Random House.

Kiekhefer, R. 1976. *European Witch Trials, Their Foundation in Popular and Learned Culture 1300-1500.* Berkeley, CA: University of California Press.

Kramer, H., and J. Sprenger. 1971. *The Malleus Maleficarum of Heinrich Kramer and James Sprenger.* New York: Dover.

Larner, C. 1980. 'Criminum Exceptum? The Crime of Witchcraft in Europe'. In V.A.C. Gatrell, B. Lenman, and G. Parker (eds.), *Crime and the Law: The Social History of Crime in Western Europe Since 1500.* London: Europa, 49–75.

Leeming, D. & J. Page. 1999. *Myths, Legends and Folktales of America.* New York: Oxford University Press.

Levack, B.P. 1987. *The Witch-Hunt in Early Modern Europe.* New York: Longman.

Macfarlane, A. 1970. *Witchcraft in Tudor and Stuart England.* London: Routledge and Kegan Paul.

MacIsaac, A. 2003. *Fiddling with Disaster.* Lynchberg, VA: Warwick House Publishing.

Marron, K. 1989. *Witches, Pagans, and Magic in the New Age.* Toronto: McClelland-Bantam Seal Books.

Morison, S.E. 1955. *The Parkman Reader: From the Works of Francis Parkman.* Boston: Little, Brown.

Murray, M. 1921. *The Witch Cult in Western Europe.* London: Oxford.

Owomoyela, O. 1990. 'No Problem Can Fail to Crash on His Head: The Trickster in Contemporary African Folklore'. *The World and I* (April), 625–632.

Pearson, I. 1984. 'The Cat in the Bag and Other Absolutely Untrue Tales from Our Urban Mythology'. *Quest Magazine* (November).

Pelka, F. 1992. 'The Women's Holocaust'. *The Humanist* 52 (5), 5–9.

Radin, P. 1972. *The Trickster: A Study in American Indian Mythology.* New York: Schocken.

Rapley, R. 1998. *A Case of Witchcraft: The Trial of Urbain Grandier.* Montreal: McGill-Queen's University Press.

Redondi, P. 1987. *Galileo: Heretic.* Princeton: Princeton University Press.

Richards, J. 1990. *Sex, Dissidence and Damnation: Minority Groups in the Middle Ages.* New York: Barnes and Noble.

Rosenberg, E. 1998. 'Native American Coyote Trickster Tales and Cylcles'. In V. K. Janik & E. S. Nelson (eds,), *Fools and Jesters in Literature, Art and History: A Bio-Bibliographical Sourcebook* (pp. 155–168). Westport, CT: Greenwood Press.

Rosenthal, B. 1993. *Salem Story: Reading the Witch Trials of 1692.* Cambridge, UK, and New York: Cambridge University Press.

Russell, J.B 1984. *Lucifer: The Devil in the Middle Ages.* Ithaca: Cornell University Press.

Santino, J. 1990. 'Fitting the Bill: The Trickster in American Popular Culture'. *The World and I*, April, 661–668.

Simpson, J. 1973. 'Olaf Tryggvason versus the Powers of Darkness'. In Venetia Newall (ed.), *The Witch in History.* New York: Barnes and Noble.

Tatar, M. 1987. *The Hard Facts of the Grimms' Fairy Tales.* Princeton, NJ: Princeton University Press.

Thomas, K. 1971. *Religion and the Decline of Magic.* New York: Charles Scribner's Sons.

Trevor-Roper, H.R. 1969. *The European Witchcraze of the Sixteenth and Seventeenth Centuries.* Harmondsworth: Penguin.

Watts, S. 1984. *A Social History of Western Europe, 1450–1720.* London: Hutchinson University Library and Hutchinson University Library for Africa.

Webster, C. 1996. *From Paracelsus to Newton: Magic and the Making of Modern Science.* New York: Barnes and Noble.

Willis, D. 1995. *Malevolent Nurture: Witchhunting and Maternal Power in Early Modern England.* Ithica, NY: Cornell University Press.

Wilmer, H.A. 1988. 'Introduction'. In Paul Woodruff and Harry A. Wilmer (eds.), *Facing Evil: Light at the Core of Darkness.* LaSalle: Open Court.

Worobec, C. 1995. 'Witchcraft Beliefs and Practices in Pre-Revolutionary Russian and Ukrainian Villages'. *Russian Review* 54, 165–187.

# 3

## Introduction

For most of us, deviance is most vividly represented by crime, although crime is only one aspect of deviance. In this article the authors introduce us to some basic sociological terms used in studying deviance, and examine everyday, sociological and legal definitions of crime. In addition, the authors identify two general kinds of theories that are used to study and analyze deviance—'consensus theories' and 'conflict theories'. How might each of these general approaches help us understand the witch craze discussed in the previous article? Or a more contemporary occurrence such as youth gangs or stripping?

# Lay Definitions of Crime

*Robert A. Silverman, James J. Teevan, and Vincent F. Sacco*

Generally, the legal bureaucracy and the average citizen agree on the acts that should be called crimes. Murder is a crime, as is shoplifting, arson, robbery, fraud, and break and enter. In some instances, however, citizens define acts as criminal when legally they are not. This is apparent in casual conversation when individuals refer to general social ills as crimes. The closing of hospitals, the decreased value of the dollar, the disrespect of youth, none of which is a *legally* defined crime, may thus be defined as crimes by some people. Even more serious examples, such as emotional neglect of children or elderly parents, are generally not criminal matters. For most people, this process of making crime roughly equal to what they consider bad in their society is not an important error (indeed, many are aware that it is wrong), and is certainly quite acceptable in an informal context. For a scientific study of crime, however, the inclusion of the bad or immoral, but not illegal, would make the boundaries of criminology vague and its content almost limitless. For these and other reasons, most criminologists reject such popular definitions of crime.

On the other hand, there are many instances in which crimes legally have occurred but the individuals involved—victim, offender, or both—do not define the act as criminal. Sometimes this is due to ignorance of the law; for instance, the general public is often unaware of the broad extent of the criminal law and how a narrower definition of crime than is legally the case. It is a *Criminal Code* offence, for example, to give trading stamps to purchasers of goods in Canada (section 427), or even to *offer* to transport someone to a common bawdy house (section 211), but few Canadians would be aware of these crimes.

In other instances, it is more disagreement than ignorance, as when people say that what occurred is 'no big deal', that no real crime occurred. Until the modern feminist movement, much spousal abuse fell into this category (cf. Backhouse, 1991). In practice, the definition of acts as crimes or not often depends on the perceptions of the actors involved, how they define the behaviours that have occurred. For example, when one individual strikes another without consent, a criminal assault may have occurred. But suppose it was in fun, as a result of a playful struggle? Most people experience an assault in fun at some time in their lives. The pushing and shoving of children, considered to be a normal part of growing up, is just one example. Among adults as well, and not only when playing hockey and other sports, one finds the equivalents of pushing and shoving matches, little of which is defined as criminal. Even if the force used is excessive and injures one of the participants, the injury is often defined as accidental. The context is thus crucial.

Similarly, some assaults may be considered a part of daily life, and not a crime, by some segments of our society. Hitting an individual, for example, may be viewed as a legitimate way of settling a dispute in some subcultures in Canada today. If both parties agree to this solution, then neither will define the act involved as criminal and neither will call the police.

Suppose, however, that only one of the participants thinks this way or someone is hit, not by a friend or acquaintance, but by a stranger. In such cases, the 'victim' may indeed define the event as a crime and call the police. In this instance, an assault as defined by the *Criminal Code of Canada* (section 265) may have been committed, not because it was *defined* differently. The attacker may even be arrested and prosecuted. Thus, the same use of force may or may not be a crime depending upon the context and upon the actors', especially the victims', perceptions of the situation.

## A Sociological Definition

For sociologists, crimes are a part of a more general category called *deviance* (see Sacco, 1992) and involve the violation of *norms*—social rules that tell people what to do and what not to do in various situations. These rules are passed on to children in any society in a process called socialization and may vary both over time and across different societies. For example, in traditional Inuit culture, infanticide and abandoning the elderly to starve to death were not condemned, but were accepted as means to protect a limited food supply (cf. Edgerton, 1985). In the rest of Canada, strict norms would have prohibited such behaviour. While some societies do not permit the eating of pork, for others beef is not allowed; while most groups prohibit cannibalism, some societies have allowed the practice. The point of these examples is that definitions of deviance are specific to time, place, and circumstances.

Deviance also generally involves, besides the violation of a norm, the possibility of punishment. One measure of how strongly a society feels about its various norms is the punishment or sanction it applies to those who violate them. Since norms range from the important and binding (thou shalt not kill) to the less important and optional (a person should not remain seated when being introduced to another), one would expect different types of reaction to those who violate them. But breaking even the most minor norm usually results in some type of reaction, insignificant though it be in terms of punishment. For example, walking down a street has many behavioural requirements that most of us rarely think of as norms. As you approach a stranger coming toward you, you are expected to avert your eyes at a certain point. If you do not, you have violated a norm, and the reaction to the violation may be anything—from no reaction, to the other individual looking at you, to the verbal challenge, 'What are you staring at?' These less severely sanctioned norms are called *folkways*. *Mores* are those norms whose infractions carry more serious punishments. Violations of mores are seen as more threatening to society—most crimes are violations of mores. But while most criminal laws (for example, those prohibiting sexual assault and theft) are mores, not all mores are laws. For a large part of our society, mores include the permanence of marriage, heterosexuality, and eventually having children. Divorce, homosexuality, and childlessness are not, however, crimes in Canada.

While there have been many attempts to summarize the sociological notion of crime, one of the best is still Gillin's (1945, p. 9) classic statement that crime is

> . . . an act that has been shown to be actually harmful to society, or that is *believed* to be socially harmful by a group that has the power to enforce its belief and that places such an act under the ban of positive penalties.

Gillin's definition includes the ideas that the harm involved can be a constructed (believed) harm and that power determines what will be defined as criminal. That last point is the subject of the next section.

## Conflict Versus Consensus Definitions

Durkheim, one of the founders of sociology, argued that a crime is a violation of a widely held norm or value, an act that attacks what he called the *collective conscience* of a society (1964, p. 79). In this view the criminal law arises out of consensus, out of commonly agreed upon norms and values. Thus, since all or most people would agree that murder, arson, and theft are serious threats to individuals, these acts are defined as crimes. Further, everyone is outraged by such crimes because they weaken and attack the very basis of society.

For conflict theorists, on the other hand, the law is a tool, part of the superstructure of institutions created by the ruling class to serve itself. The law, instead of arising from consensus and providing justice for all, is in reality a weapon of oppression. Conflict theorists disagree among themselves on the role played by the capitalist class in this process, whether it shares its power with other power groups (sometimes called *moral entrepreneurs*) or by and large controls by itself the enactment of laws (cf. Turk, 1993), but they do agree that conflict and power determine the law, not consensus (cf. Young and Matthews, 1992).

Very few sociologists take either of these two extreme positions. Underneath consensus there is always some disagreement or conflict. For example, does euthanasia, abortion, or killing in wartime constitute murder? Inside conflict there is always some consensus and negotiation, for without some co-operation there would be anarchy and lawlessness (cf. Kent, 1990). In addition, there are other more moderate positions on the sources of laws. Some sociologists, for example, have pointed to the role, not just of capitalists, but of the media, especially the publicity given to shocking crimes, and the politics of election years as having important effects on criminal legislation (McGarrell and Castellano, 1991).

**Table 3.1**  Liberal and Radical Perspectives in Defining Care

| Liberal Criminology | Radical Criminology |
| --- | --- |
| DEFINITION OF CRIME: | |
| *Legalistic approach: Crime as behaviour* <br> • leads to an examination of the characteristics and life experiences of the criminal actor; general acceptance of the State <br> • emphasis on cultural variables as they relate to explanations of crime, e.g., how failure in school can lead to crime | *Legalistic approach: Crime as a definition of behaviour made by officials of the State* <br> • leads to an examination of political authority and questioning of the State <br> • emphasis on structural variables as they relate to explanations of crime, e.g., how the whole economic system causes crime |
| ROLE OF CRIMINOLOGISTS: | |
| • criminologists as "expert advisers" to "enlightened leaders" <br> • social research used to provide information for the smooth and efficient running of the State system | • commitment to Praxis, to the application by scientists of their results to improve society <br> • social research used to determine the means by which desired changes can be implemented and inequalities between individuals and group diminished |
| IMAGE OF CRIME AND CRIMINALS: | |
| • crime as a universal phenomenon caused by the inadequacies of human beings; deterministic (controlled by heredity and environment) image of people | • crime as a universal phenomenon due to the conflictual nature of society; human behaviour seen as intentional and goal-oriented (more free will) |
| PRESCRIPTION FOR CHANGE: | |
| • adherence to the rehabilitative ideal: emphasis on changing the nature of individual offenders <br> • adjustment of individuals to the needs of the system | • stresses political nature of crime; emphasis on changing the structural components of society <br> • adjustment of the system to the needs of individuals |

**Source:** Adapted from Cormack-Anthony, A.E. 1980. 'Radical Criminology,' in Robert A. Silverman & James Teevan (eds.), *Crime in Canadian Society*, 2nd ed. Toronto: Butterworths, 246–7.

This discussion is relevant to the definition of crime, since more conservative consensus and more radical conflict theorists might come to quite different definitions. Whereas conservatives would define acts that violate the *Criminal Code of Canada* as crimes, for conflict theorists, some of the building blocks of capitalism should be defined as crimes: for example, the relentless pursuit of profit, the practice of speculation, and the encouragement of over-consumption. Hence, from a conflict perspective, some of the 'real' crimes have not been defined as such; they are not illegal because their victims do not control the law and thus the definition of what constitutes a crime. Thus the concept of ruling-class crimes, legal acts that 'should' be illegal, provides us with another potential definition of crime.

In a less dramatic argument, conflict criminologists criticize criminology's traditional focus on the crimes of the powerless and its relative inattention to the crimes of the powerful (e.g., white-collar crime) and ask whether the media deliberately underplay their reporting of corporate crime, directing public fear to muggers rather than polluters. Comack-Antony (1980) presented a chart that compares and contrasts the ways that radical (conflict) criminology and liberal (consensus) criminology define crime (cf. Burtch, 1992). The chart, slightly modified and reproduced in Table 3.1, illustrates well how one's perspective affects definitions of crime. Before examining it, think about one final example of the point we are making, sometimes called the *social construction* of crime. Is terrorism a crime only if it is unsuccessful? In framing your answer, think about the difference between the storming of the Bastille and the Reign of Terror or of the Boston Tea Party and Louis Riel.

## Legal Definition

Most classic criminology texts agree that criminal law and thus the legal definition of crime is marked by four ideals: politicality, specificity, uniformity, and penal sanction. Politicality means that only government, and in Canada this means the federal government, can make criminal laws; specificity, that the laws are quite precise in their wording, telling exactly what is forbidden (*proscribed*) or demanded (*prescribed*); uniformity, that the laws apply equally to all; and penal sanction, that violators are threatened with a penalty and punishment. A crime is, then, any act or omission in violation of that criminal law. Omission offences include section 129b: 'Everyone who (b) omits, without reasonable excuse, to assist a public officer or peace officer in the execution of duty in arresting a person or in preserving the peace, after having reasonable notice of a requirement to do so . . . is guilty of . . . '.

Legally, then, a crime is a specific act or omission forbidden to all Canadians by Parliament and punishable for all who break that law. The Law Reform Commission of Canada (1974, pp. 1–4) added the following points. (1) Not all acts against the law are crimes. Civil wrongs, called *torts* (for example, wrongful dismissal from a job), are not crimes. Criminal acts are proceeded against by *prosecution* and may result in *punishment*, while civil actions proceed by suit and may result in *compensation*. (2) Although under the *British North America Act* (now the *Constitution Act*, 1982) only the federal government can make a criminal law, the provinces can create provincial *offences* that, while technically not crimes, are treated like crimes. Examples of such legislation include traffic offences and enforced closing of stores on legal holidays. Crimes are thought of as more serious than such provincial offences because (a) they are seen to involve greater harm to individuals, (b) they are more often a violation of fundamental rules, like mores, and (c) 'they are wrongs that any person *as a person* could commit. Offences are more specialized [wrongs] that people commit when playing certain special roles'. For example, individuals disobey speed limits as drivers; they generally commit murders or thefts as individuals (1974, p. 3).

Despite the distinctions between crimes and offences, the consequences to individuals prosecuted for committing any of the many acts prohibited by provincial and municipal legislation and named 'offences' may be similar (or even worse) than the consequence for committing a crime. For violators, then, there may be only a technical difference between a federal *crime* and a provincial *offence*. Thus, for some purposes, the important components of a legal definition of crime are that it is a violation of a law made by any political body, is deemed to be a state rather than a personal matter, and involves threats of punishment rather than compensation.

In a still more technical and legal sense, for an act or omission to be considered a crime, several other conditions are necessary. First, the act must have been legally forbidden before the act was undertaken; that is, the act or omission must be in violation of an already existing law that forbids or commands the act. This means that an act or omission, no matter how ugly, mean, or distasteful, is not a crime if no law exists against it. The main rationale behind this principle is that it would be unfair to punish persons who, when they acted, did so in good faith thinking they were obeying the law. An *ex post facto* (after the fact) law thus cannot designate as criminal an act legal at the time it was committed, and the general ideal of *nullum crimen sine lege, nulla poena sine lege*, that is, no crime without law, no punishment without law, is still an important principle of Canadian jurisprudence. For example, in 1991 the Canadian Supreme Court refused to allow the extradition of two FLQ members to the United States to stand trial for the 1968 hijacking of a plane to Cuba because in 1968 hijacking was not an offence in Canada's *Criminal Code*. That offence was created in 1972. An implication of this principle is that laws must be quite specific and not vague, again applying the logic that the public should know exactly what it legally can and cannot do. Vaguely worded laws would make attempts to obey the law problematic, as people would not be sure if their behaviour would or would not result in penal sanction.

Second, there must be an *actus reus* or act. Merely thinking about or planning to violate the law is generally not a crime, with the exception of the crime of conspiracy (conspiracy to commit offences, *Criminal Code*, section 465). Actually there have never been many conspiracy charges laid in Canada; thus it is fairly safe to say that an *actus reus* is a requirement for a legal definition of crime.

*Mens rea* or criminal intent is a third requirement for a crime. Intentions are not the same as motives (which are the reasons why individuals commit crimes), but instead involve determination and purpose—that individuals intend the consequences of their acts. This means that they know what they are doing, for example, they are not insane, and mean to do what they are doing, for example, the acts were not accidental.

Finally, two additional requirements for the legal definition of a crime are that there should be a causal connection between the *actus reus* and any harm or outcome, and that the *mens rea* and *actus reus* must relate to the same act. These are general rules, ignored in certain circumstances, and sometimes a matter of dispute. For discussion of some of these and similar issues, see the article by Boyd in this section of the book.

## Definitions Made by Police, Prosecutors, and Judges

After Parliament makes the criminal law, the agents of the Canadian criminal justice system, from the police, to Crown prosecutors, to judges, must enforce it, and all may exercise considerable discretion in deciding whether an act or omission is a crime and, if so, which specific crime it is (cf. Kennedy, 1990). For example, suppose one man attacks another and hurts him, and the victim calls the police. Under a strict and static notion of law enforcement and crime, section 267 (assault with a weapon causing bodily harm) of the *Criminal Code* would be enforced by the police: 'Every one who, in committing an assault, . . . causes bodily harm to the complainant, is guilty of an indictable offence and is liable to imprisonment for a term not exceeding 10 years . . . '. The Crown would then prosecute the defendant using the available evidence, the accused would be found guilty, and the convicted criminal would be given a sentence of up to 10 years.

However, there are alternatives to this scenario: (1) the police arrive and the victim indicates that while he did call them, he is not willing to testify against the offender in court. His motives are private, but could include an unwillingness to see the assaulter, often a friend or a relative, sent to trial or even an unwillingness to take time off from work to appear in court as a complainant. The police in most cases will not pursue the incident because they know that they will have insufficient evidence without the testimony of the victim. According to all public records, then, no crime of assault has taken place. The legal code does not indicate that the police have such discretion, but under these conditions it is in fact normal practice. (2) The victim is abusive to the police, and in anger they decide not to record the crime. In fact, the police take many variables into consideration in deciding to write up less serious cases: how busy they are, the type of complainant, and so on. (3) The police do arrest the alleged attacker and charge him with unlawfully causing bodily harm. The Crown is ready to proceed when the defence attorney suggests a deal. If the charge is reduced to assault, punishable by a summary (less serious) conviction (*Criminal Code*, section 266b), the accused will plead guilty. Otherwise, he will plead not guilty to the original charge and insist on a trial. To speed things through the overburdened criminal justice process, the Crown agrees. (4) The police arrest the individual and the Crown proceeds with the case. The defendant pleads not guilty and is able to convince a judge that he in fact did not intend to injure the victim (recall the discussion of *mens rea*). The judge finds the defendant not guilty. Officially, then, no crime of assault causing bodily harm took place.

The combinations of events in the criminal justice system that can occur to redefine an act, compared to the behaviours that actually happened, are thus numerous. In Part 2 of this book, we discuss how these decisions affect official crime statistics. The subject is introduced here to point out that agents of social control must interpret and enforce the law, and the way in which they do so is a part of the process of defining crime (Evans and Himmelfarb, 1996).

## Changing Laws Change Definitions

Many people think of the law as being relatively static. Lawyers know this is not so. The *Criminal Code* is frequently amended by Parliament. Minor changes are routinely made and are based on a 'fine-tuning' of legislation or on recent court interpretations. More important changes take more time and reflect broader social movements. For example, while the public and the mass media both refer to the crime of rape, or forcible sexual intercourse, 'rape' is not a crime in Canada. The sections of the *Criminal Code* dealing with rape were repealed and replaced in a process begun in 1980, partly as a result of the modern feminist movement. These activities are now found under the general heading of assault and are specified as sexual assault (section 271); sexual assault with a weapon, threats to a third party, or causing bodily harm (section 272); or aggravated sexual assault (section 273). The sexual aspect has been downplayed—even penetration is no longer a requirement in the definition of the crime—and the physical harm emphasized. Changing the crime to assault shifted the focus away from the end sought (sexual activity) to the force used, and thus sexual assault joined a slap to the face, a punch to the stomach, or a kick to the groin as assaults to the body. So dramatic was the change in definition that in fact the term 'rape' does not even appear in the index to Carswell's latest *Pocket Criminal Code*. Thus, while many Canadians (including some journalists) call the event previously described a rape, legally, in Canada, no crime of 'rape' exists.

On the other hand, in 1994 in the *R. v. Bernard* case the Supreme Court of Canada made a change with regard to intoxication as a mitigating factor in crimes such as sexual assault. Previously, drunkenness, no matter how severe, could not be used as a defence in such cases. The Supreme Court decided that 'offenders' can be acquitted of sexual assault 'because they were so drunk they did not know what they were doing'. But the Court also said this defence would only be used in the 'rarest' of cases—where the perpetrator was so drunk he was acting like an 'automaton'. Thus the law reflects the priorities of different power groups, sometimes the victims and sometimes the accused.

Changes with larger implications occur even less often. The passage of the *Charter of Rights and Freedoms* (1982) led to many procedural changes (making our criminal justice system more like its US counterpart) and to some substantive changes in the criminal law as well. The charter's protection of free speech led to nullification of parts of the promotion of racial hatred sections of the *Criminal Code* and to modifications to the obscenity law. The most recent major change, however, was the introduction in 1985 of the *Young Offenders Act* (YOA), which replaced the 1970 revision of the *Juvenile Delinquents Act* (originally 1908). The philosophy and effects of the YOA are well documented (cf. Carrington and Moyer, 1994; Corrado, Bala, Linden, and LeBlanc, 1992). It combined a justice model (those accused of delinquency should have the same rights as adults accused of crime, although should be treated somewhat differently) with a crime control model (society must be protected) and largely replaced the welfare model of the JDA (in which the court acted as a wise and judicious parent but often ignored legal safeguards).

Right from the beginning the changes were controversial (cf. Bala, 1997). Some felt that the welfare model philosophy of the old system was superior to the new act. With the introduction of the YOA, youths basically gained the protection of due process (legal safeguards such as right to counsel), but lost some of the informal treatment previously routinely provided under the old act. Some civil libertarians were especially concerned that the new system led to more frequent and longer custody for youths than had occurred under the old act (cf. Clark and Fleming, 1993; Doob and Meen, 1993). At the other end of the spectrum, many, especially among the public, felt that the new age limits provided by the act (12 to 17 instead of the previous lower limit of age 7) allowed younger children (up to age 11) to 'get away with murder' (not to mention sexual assault, robbery, and arson). Children 11 years of age or younger were defined as incapable of having the *mens rea* necessary for crime—a view challenged when people heard of the 11-year-old who sexually assaulted a girl and then taunted the police with his underage status. Perhaps the greatest public concern surrounded the maximum sentences for those age 12 to 17 who commit serious violent crimes, such as the 1994 drive-by shooting of a British man in Ottawa. Many felt that the maximum sentences are too short for some violent crimes and that society deserves greater protection from some young offenders, including trying them in adult court.

Public pressure was successful. In February 1995 the House of Commons passed Bill C-37 (An Act to amend the *Young Offenders Act* and the *Criminal Code*), which dealt with some of the concerns of the public. While the Bill did not change the age range of young offenders, it did increase penalties, especially for the most serious crimes. When the *Young Offenders Act* was initially introduced, the maximum penalty for any crime was three years. This was later raised to five years for some crimes, and a juvenile convicted (in youth court) of first-degree murder could be sentenced to a penalty of ten years. It also visited the issue of transfer to adult court. In the case of murder, attempted murder, manslaughter, or aggravated assault by 16- or 17-year-olds, they would henceforth be dealt with by ordinary (i.e., adult) court unless they could make a successful application to have the case heard in youth court. Hence, the onus was on the teenagers to prove that they should have the privilege of being heard in youth court.

The changes did not go far enough for many, so as this is being written Parliament is considering further changes. To convince a fearful public that they are not just tinkering, a new name has been suggested, the *Youth Criminal Justice Act*. Again, those under age 12 are spared, despite strong pressure to lower the minimum age to 10, but 14- and 15-year-olds convicted of the most serious crimes like murder, aggravated sexual assault, and so on will join 16- and 17-year-olds in being vulnerable to longer sentences. In fact all repeat violent offenders aged 14 to 17 will also be punishable by longer sentences and having their names published upon conviction. These changes reflect that protecting society is the main goal of the criminal law but also that prevention and rehabilitation, including community-based sentences, are important aspects too.

## Conclusions

In summary, there are several definitions of crime from which to choose: (1) acts that violate norms; (2) acts that violate *legal* norms; (3) acts that the participants define as violations of *legal* norms; (4) acts that agents of the Canadian criminal justice system interpret as violations of legal norms; (5) acts for which *mens rea* and *actus reus* have been demonstrated; and (6) acts that, from a conflict perspective, are the 'real' crimes. Each definition may be appropriate under different circumstances. Also remember that whichever definition is chosen, the actual acts defined as criminal are not universal. They are specific to a given time and society.

## References

Backhouse, C. 1991. *Petticoats and Prejudice: Women and Law in Nineteenth-Century Canada.* Toronto: Butterworths.

Bala, N. 1997. *Young Offenders Law.* Concord: Irwin.

Burtch, B. 1992. *The Sociology of Law: Critical Approaches to Social Control.* Toronto: Harcourt Brace Jovanovich.

Carrington, P., and S. Moyer. 1994. 'Trends in Youth Crime and Police Response, Pre- and Post-YOA'.

*Canadian Journal of Criminology* 36, 1–28.

Clark, B., and T. Fleming. 1993. 'Implementing the *Young Offenders Act* in Ontario: Issues of Principles, Programmes and Power'. *Howard Journal of Criminal Justice* 32, 114–126.

Comack-Antony, A.E. 1980. 'Radical Criminology'. In R.A. Silverman and J. Teevan (eds.), *Crime in Canadian society*, 2nd ed. Toronto: Butterworths.

Corrado, R., N. Bala, R. Linden, and M. LeBlanc,

eds. 1992. *Juvenile Justice in Canada*. Toronto: Butterworths.

Doob, A., and J. Meen. 1993. 'An Exploration of Changes in Dispositions for Young Offenders in Toronto'. *Canadian Journal of Criminology* 35, 19–29.

Durkheim, E. 1964. *The Rules of Sociological Method*. New York: Free Press.

Edgerton, R.B. 1985. *Rules, Expectations, and Social Order*. Berkeley: University of California Press.

Evans, J., and A. Himmelfarb. 1996. 'Counting Crimes'. In R. Linden (ed.), *Criminology: A Canadian perspective*, 3rd ed. Toronto: Harcourt Brace Jovanovich.

Gillin, J. 1945. *Criminology and Penology*, 3rd ed. New York: Appleton-Century-Crofts.

Hagan, J. 1992. 'Class Fortification against Crime in Canada'. *Canadian Review of Sociology and Anthropology* 29, 126–139.

Kennedy, L.W. 1990. *On the Borders of Crime*. New York: Longman.

Kent, S. 1990. 'Deviance, Labelling, and Normative Strategies in "The Canadian New Religion/Counter-Cult" Debate'. *Canadian Journal of Sociology* 15, 393–416.

Law Reform Commission of Canada. 1974. *The Meaning of Guilt: Strict Liability*. Ottawa: Information Canada.

McGarrell, E., and T. Castellano. 1991. 'An Integrative Conflict Model of the Criminal Law Formation Process'. *Journal of Research in Crime and Delinquency* 28, 174–196.

Rodrigues, G.P. 1998. *Pocket Criminal Code 1999*. Toronto: Carswell.

Sacco, V. 1992. *Deviance: Conformity and Control in Canadian Society*. Scarborough: Prentice-Hall.

Sacco, V.F., and H. Johnson. 1990. *Patterns of Criminal Victimization in Canada*. Ottawa: Minister of Supply and Services Canada.

Turk, A.T. 1993. 'A Proposed Resolution of Key Issues in the Political Sociology of Law'. In F. Adler and W. Laufer (eds.), *New Directions in Criminological Theory*, vol. 4. New Brunswick: Transaction.

Young, J., and R. Matthews. 1992. *Rethinking Criminology: The Realist Debate*. London: Sage.

## Introduction

The previous article took up the question of what counts as a crime in Canada. Strictly speaking, what does? And from a legal standpoint, what conditions must be met for an act to become a crime? But why do some activities become prohibited by law and become criminalized while others do not in the first place? What criteria or other factors are relevant to deciding what is worthy of being established as law, especially as those particular laws that, when violated, are 'crimes' rather than other kinds of violations?

# What is a Crime?

*Law Commission of Canada*

Criminal law is a punitive response to a perceived problem. It is generally characterized as a necessary evil in a society to stave off the threat of violence, disorder, and danger. However, criminal law deals with more than violence, robbery, and murder. How do we decide whether it is appropriate to use criminal law beyond such offences, and how should we frame our criminal law to deal with such behaviour?[1]

Criminal law rests on the notion of attributing personal responsibility for the crime—there are one or more clearly identifiable individuals to hold accountable for their actions. Consequently, the social, political and cultural context in which the problem occurred disappears into the background. Criminal law both universalizes the problem and individualizes its causes. It universalizes the problem in the sense that it recognizes the claim of the victim as valid and sufficient enough to demand a guarantee of protection by the state. It individualizes the problem by making individuals (mainly individual offenders) responsible for the problem.[2] For example, while we may recognize that child abuse is the result of complex social and psychological factors, we nonetheless place responsibility for such conduct at the individual level.

## Expectations of Criminal Law

Criminal law rests upon several objectives, such as deterring the individual wrongdoer and the general public, as well as reinforcing certain social values and signalling that certain behaviour has been deemed to be undesirable.

We use criminal law because we believe it will deter people from engaging in unwanted conduct. However, deterrence through criminal law varies according to the context, and critics suggest criminal law has failed to prevent people from committing certain crimes. For example, studies on cannabis use in Canada have demonstrated that 25 years of criminalization have had no significant deterrent effect, while the costs of criminalizing cannabis continue to rise.[3]

For many observers, the criminal law carries a powerful symbolic message—it signals that society disapproves of an act and that a formal response by the state is necessary. The struggle to define the symbolic message of criminal law has meant that, over time, laws have been reshaped and reformed to convey certain messages. Different groups play an active role in defining the symbolic message of the criminal law by campaigning on issues of concern and lobbying government to change laws.

The struggle over the symbolic meaning of the law has resulted in a complex system whereby offences are defined differently depending on the context within which the unwanted conduct occurs. For example, the *Criminal Code* differentiates between theft of property that is worth more or less than $5,000, with more serious punishment typically accompanying theft over this amount. The *Code* further differentiates theft from theft accompanied by violence, which is referred to as robbery and is considered serious, often resulting in stiff penalties. Similarly, murder that is premeditated is treated differently and more seriously than an accidental homicide or a death that results from negligent behaviour. In each instance, the criminal law is used to convey different symbolic messages about the seriousness of the offence and how it will be dealt with by the state.

There is certainly no single, timeless and unchanging notion of crime. Alcohol consumption and certain forms of gambling are two examples of conduct that were historically treated as crimes but are no longer regarded as criminal. Conversely, it was not until the 1980s that the rape of a wife by her husband became a *Criminal Code* offence. Marijuana use is an activity that is currently being decriminalized in many countries, while various forms of undesirable conduct resulting from computer use are being subject to increased criminalization. These examples highlight how our ideas about crime change over time as well as shift with our values and beliefs.[4]

Our notions of crime are developed through our experiences, as well as through our interactions with our family, friends, and other people whom we encounter in our daily lives. We also derive our notions of crime from sources such newspapers, television, radio, books, and films. We receive messages about crime and unwanted conduct through these various sources, which in turn help shape our perceptions about what should and should not be criminalized.

A prominent source of information about crime in our society is the media. From television sets to movies, newspapers, and the Internet, we are regularly bombarded with a variety of messages about the nature of crime and its control. The media, and particular television, tend to focus on violent crime, which many observers say creates an inaccurate perception about the level of violent crime in Canada. In this way, the mass media play an important role in cultivating support for punitive solutions by enhancing fears of criminality through the representation of violent crimes.[5]

Fuelled by the fear of crime, a greater sense of insecurity, and the need to take control of one's own safety, individuals are often lured by the commercialization of crime-control products such as house alarms, video surveillance, gated communities, and around-the-clock guard services. Many observers suggest that we are so preoccupied by questions of crime and security that we have become a 'risk society', fixated on how to reduce the 'imminent' potential of criminal behaviour. As a result, the latter part of the twentieth century has witnessed an increasing emphasis on governments adopting a 'law and order' agenda.[6]

During this time there have been increased demands for harsher punishment for offenders.[7] Rates of imprisonment across many western industrialized countries, particularly in the United States, have risen dramatically. In Canada, rates of imprisonment also reached high levels during the 1990s, only to decrease slightly over the last few years. For example, the incarceration rate in Canada peaked in 1994–95 at 153 per 100,000 adults, dropping to 133 per 100,000 in 2000–2001 (D. Hendrick and L. Farmer, 'Adult Correctional Services in Canada, 2000–01' (2002) Juristat: Canadian Centre for Justice Statistics, Statistics Canada, Vol. 22, No. 10, p. 4).

Interestingly, an increased reliance on criminal law and punishment has come at a time when the official crime rate has actually decreased. Contrary to calls to 'get tough' on criminals by implementing a law and order agenda—and reports that crime is expanding and out of control—official crime data actually suggest there has been a decrease in crime over this period. Figure 4.1, developed using data produced by Statistics Canada's Canadian Centre for Justice Statistics, shows the crime rate fell dramatically beginning in the early 1990s, rising only slightly in the past year. As they depend on official crime reporting, crime statistics certainly do not present a complete picture. However, the data suggest that claims

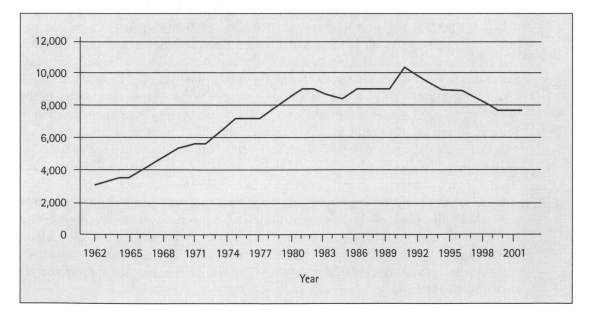

**Figure 4.1 Crime Rate per 100,000 Total Population Canada 1962–2001**

Source: Adapted from Savoie, J. 'Crime Statistics in Canada, 2001.' *Juristat: Canadian Centre for Justice Statistics*, Statistics Canada, 22: 6.

of rising and 'out of control' crime levels—and reports that more punishment and control is necessary—may be erroneous and misplaced.

## Criminal Law and Harm

It is often said that criminal law ought to be reserved for the most serious harms in society. For example, the Ouimet Report (*Report of the Canadian Committee on Corrections: Towards Unity: Criminal Justice and Corrections,* 1969) stated that: 'No conduct should be defined as criminal unless it represents a serious threat to society, and unless the act cannot be dealt with through other social or legal means'. In *Our Criminal Law,* the Law Reform Commission of Canada relied on the harm principle when it argued the criminal law ought to be 'pruned' to better differentiate between 'real crimes' and public welfare or administrative wrongs: 'To count as a real crime an act must be morally wrong. But this . . . is but a necessary condition and not a sufficient one. Not all harmful acts should qualify as real crimes. The real criminal law should be confined to wrongful acts seriously threatening and infringing fundamental social values'.

In 1982, the Department of Justice reaffirmed the relationship between harm and the criminal law in *The Criminal Law in Canadian Society* 'Since many acts may be "harmful", and since society has many other means for controlling or responding to conduct, criminal law should be used only when the harm caused or threatened is serious, and when the other, less coercive or less intrusive means do not work or are inappropriate'. While there may be a consensus that the criminal law ought to be reserved for the most serious harms, the question of what constitutes a 'serious harm' proves more difficult to answer.

Death is perhaps the most serious harm that can be inflicted upon a person. Murder and manslaughter carry the harshest penalties contained in criminal law. But what does this mean in terms of other types of death? As Figure 4.2 indicates, each year the number of deaths that occur in the workplace far outnumber homicides in Canada. Many observers have argued that even when it might be possible to show negligence, deaths in the workplace are rarely treated as criminal events. Rather, we use insurance and regulation to respond to and prevent deaths in the workplace. Gambling is another example of behaviour that is often deemed to be potentially harmful to both the individual and society. For example, gambling is considered harmful to the individual who develops a gambling addiction. At the same time, society is considered harmed by the actions of gambling addicts (for example, the negative impact for family members of gambling addicts and the costs associated with treatment). However, over the last several years there has been an increase in the number of government-run casinos, while private forms of gambling continue to be criminalized. Why is gambling considered harmful when it is organized by individuals but not when done so by governments? Why is gambling a crime in one context and yet decriminalized in another?

The notion of harm tells us that something ought to be taken seriously, but reveals little about how we ought to respond. The examples of murder compared with deaths in the workplace and the decriminalization of some forms of gambling highlight some of the ambiguities and contradictions inherent in our choice of responses.

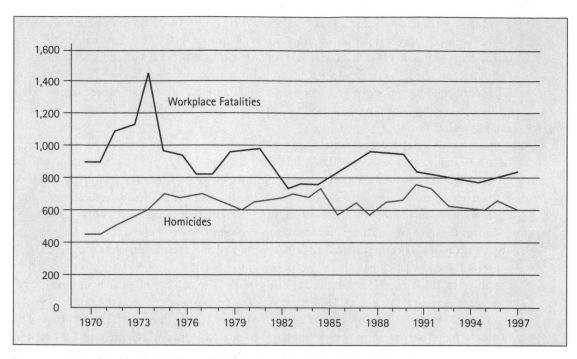

**Figure 4.2 Workplace Fatalities and Homicides Canada: 1970–1997**

Homicide data source: Adapted from Dauvergne, M. 2001. 'Homicide in Canada, 2001' *Juristat: Canadian Centre for Justice Statistics*, Statistics Canada, 22: 7.
Workplace fatalities data source: Adapted from Human Resources and Development Canada, 1999. *Occupational Injuries and their Cost in Canada, 1993–1997*, Ottawa: Human Resources and Development Canada.

We often think that criminal law ought to be reserved for the most harmful behaviours. At the same time, however, when a problem arises, we are tempted to turn to the criminal law as a response. Is clear-cut logging a business practice or environmental degradation?

Is spanking child discipline or abuse? Do circuses entertain or do they abuse animals? Is euthanasia palliative care or murder? The definition of harm is at the heart of many law-reform struggles. Often, the value of criminal law is symbolic—calling something a crime symbolizes our condemnation of the action. But, at the same time, the symbolic power of the criminal law creates an incentive to use criminal law, even when other less coercive responses may be more efficient. In this way, the process of defining something as harmful and calling it a crime creates its own set of contradictions.

Certainly, human conduct can be harmful in several ways. Smoking is bad for one's health but also causes damage to other people through second-hand smoke. Driving too fast may similarly endanger one's life or the lives of others. Jaywalking slows traffic while creating risks for the person who does it. Failing to have a medical checkup is risky for the individual and potentially costly for our health care system. Building a hydro-electric dam detrimentally affects wildlife and those who live off the land. Some of these actions are criminalized, others are regulated, and some are simply frowned upon. Why?

We have a tendency to think that conduct which is harmful to others justifies a greater level of societal intervention than conduct that is harmful only to the individual. But is this a satisfactory distinction? First, what is and is not harmful is often debated. Experts disagree. Politicians disagree. In our day-to-day life, we also question whether harm is 'caused' by certain conduct. However, we often do not know whether certain conduct causes harm and, if so, to what degree. For example, it took many years for science to determine that second-hand smoke was harmful.

Second, even if we agree that certain conduct is harmful, we may disagree on whether it ought to be tolerated, prohibited, or regulated. It is often claimed that if conduct is harmful to others, it warrants a more serious response. However, in a society that recognizes the interdependency of its citizens, such as universally contributing to health care or educational needs, harm to oneself is often borne collectively. There are pressures to regulate and control conduct that primarily harms the individual. The requirements to wear a seatbelt or a helmet for certain activities are examples of a collective decision to protect people against their own risk taking.

Overall, then, what constitutes harmful behaviour is not a question that can be raised in the abstract. It is a question that needs to be asked in the context of a range of possible responses to undesirable conduct. For example, many people may question the imposition of a jail sentence for the failure to wear a seatbelt, but accept that a fine may be appropriate. The distinction between harm to others and harm to oneself is just one element of the decision whether society should intervene in behaviour deemed to be inappropriate.

## Notes

1.  'Our present Criminal Code has its roots in nineteenth-century England. Enacted in 1892, it has undergone a number of ad hoc revisions, with the result that we now have a Criminal Code which does not deal comprehensively with the general principles of criminal law, which suffers from a lack of internal logic and which contains a hodgepodge of anachronistic, redundant, contradictory, and obsolete provisions. The end result is that Canadians, living in one of the most technologically advanced societies in human history, are being governed by a Criminal Code rooted in the horse-and-buggy era of Victorian England'. Law Reform Commission of Canada, (1985–86) 15th Annual Report (Ottawa: Government of Canada) p. 15.
2.  'Criminal responsibility as we know it today, in other words, as a crime against the social order and not an individual victim, appears to be a concept that goes back to the Middle Ages and owes its origins to the increase in royal and religious power that marked this era'. [Translation] L. Viau "Victimes des ambitions royals", Thémis, vol. 30, no. 1, 1995, p. 121.
3.  'We have estimated that approximately 2.5 million people in Canada used cannabis in the last year. In 1999, 21,381 people were charged with the possession of cannabis. This means that only 0.85% of cannabis users were actually charged with possession. It is also important to remember that of the number of people who used cannabis in the last year, many would have used it more than once. As a result, the actual chance of being charged for possession of cannabis in relation to the actual number of offences is in all likelihood much lower than 1 per cent. This certainty raises concerns regarding fairness. In addition, both the effectiveness of the legislation any deterrent effect it may have are seriously in doubt'. Report of the Senate Committee on Illegal Drugs. Cannabis: Our Position For a Canadian Public Policy. (Ottawa: Senate of Canada, 2002) p. 359.
4.  'Restraint in the recourse to criminal law is only one facet of the Commission's mandate to remove anachronisms and anomalies in the law, and to develop new approaches to and concepts of the law in keeping with, and responsive to, the changing needs of Canadian society. It has always been understood by the Commission that the changing needs and perceptions of Canadian society may also urge additions to the Criminal Code of offences not presently prohibited by it, at least not directly and explicitly enough. The same tests which should lead to some Code offences being removed from the Code because (for example) they are no longer perceived as serious threats to our fundamental values, also lead us to conclude that some offences not presently found in the Code should be added to it'. Law Reform Commission of Canada, Crimes Against the Environment Working Paper 44 (Ottawa: Government of Canada, 1985) p. 3.

5.  *'Media representations tend to exaggerate the threat of crime and to promote policing and punishment as the antidote. This is likely to accentuate fear, and thus support for law and order policies'.*  R. Reiner, 'Media Made Criminality: The Representation of Crime in the Mass Media' in M. Maguire, R. Morgan and R. Reiner, eds., *The Oxford Handbook of Criminology*, 3rd ed. (Oxford: Oxford University Press, 2002) p. 407.

6.  *'Such "law and order" talk has become a dominant and daily feature of public culture as we embark on this new millennium. In our latter-day "risk society", security is purportedly in short supply and menacing outsiders imperil us from all sides ... And by all appearances, our pan-Canadian obsession with "the crime problem" has been surging to ever more elevated levels since 1990'.*  R. Menzies, D.E. Chunn and S.C. Boyd, 'Introduction' in R. Menzies, D.E. Chunn and S.C. Boyd, eds., *[Ab]using Power: The Canadian Experience* (Halifax, Nova Scotia: Fernwood Publishing, 2001) p.11.

7.  *'Statistics indicate an increase in the use of incarceration in recent years. From 1986 to 1996, the prison population grew by 26 per cent, the largest increase having occurred between 1988 and 1993, when the number of incarcerated persons grew by 39 per cent. From 1989 to 1995, the federal prison population increased by 22 per cent and the provincial population by 12 per cent. Particularly distressing is the fact that the number of young offenders in custody increased by 26 per cent from 1986 to 1995. The rate of incarceration was over 130 persons per 100,000 inhabitants in 1995, up from 116 in 1985 ...With the exception of the U.S., Canada has the highest rate of incarceration among Western-style democracies'.*  J.P. Brodeur, 'Sentencing Reform: Ten Years After the Canadian Sentencing Commission' in J.V. Roberts and D.P. Cole, eds., *Making Sense of Sentencing* (Toronto: University of Toronto Press, 1999) p. 341.

# 5

## Introduction

'Crime is an integral part of all healthy societies'. With this unusual claim, Durkheim launched a tradition of sociological inquiry into deviance, and provided insights into the subject that continue to be relevant today. His original analysis of crime provided the groundwork for the sociological idea of viewing deviance as a social process with a logic inherent to it. He also developed the concept of *anomie* (or normlessness) to account for pathological levels of deviant behaviour (notably suicide and homicide) that occur when societies are undergoing rapid change. And he theorized we participate in the process of deviance or experience the condition of anomie as part of our involvement in a group's collective consciousness. In these two brief excerpts Durkheim outlines what he means by the concept of the 'collective consciousness' and discusses the nature of the pathological. He also examines the contribution crime makes to a society

such that it becomes integral to the well-being of a healthy group.

Durkheim's concept of a collective consciousness is difficult, in part because the individual and individual consciousness, is valorized in modern societies. But what is Durkheim trying to bring to our attention? And what examples can you think of that illustrate that the idea of a collective consciousness has validity to it?

A key point Durkheim makes in the second selection is that crime, however deplorable to our ordinary understanding of life, does perform important functions in the group as a whole. What are the functions that crime performs? Durkheim's work has influenced the development of more contemporary theories of deviance you will encounter such as functionalism, strain theory, social bond, and social control theory. Do you find his analysis persuasive? Why or why not?

# Crime and the Collective Consciousness *and* The Normal and the Pathological

*Emile Durkheim*

## Crime and the Collective Consciousness

The bond of social solidarity to which repressive law corresponds is one the breaking of which constitutes the crime. We use the term 'crime' to designate any act which, regardless of degree, provokes against the perpetrator the characteristic reaction known as punishment. To investigate the nature of this bond is therefore to ask what is the cause of the punishment or, more precisely, what in essence the crime consists of.

Assuredly crimes of different species exist. But it is no less certain that all these species of crime have something in common. This is proved by the reaction that they provoke from society: the fact that punishment, except for differences in degree, always and everywhere exists. The oneness of the effect reveals the oneness of the cause. Undoubtedly essential resemblances exist not only among all crimes provided for in the legislation of a single society, but among all crimes recognized as such and punished in different types of society. No matter how different these acts termed crimes may appear to be at first sight, they cannot fail to have some common basis. Universally they strike the moral consciousness of nations in the same way and universally produce the same consequence. All are crimes, that is, acts repressed by prescribed punishments. Now the essential properties of a thing lie in those observed wherever it exists and which are peculiar to it. Thus if we wish to learn in what crime essentially consists, we must distinguish those traits identical in all the varieties of crime in different types of society.

An act is criminal when it offends the strong, well-defined states of the collective consciousness.

This proposition, taken literally, is scarcely disputed, although usually we give it a meaning very different from the one it should have. It is taken as if it expressed, not the essential characteristics of the crime, but one of its repercussions. We well know that crime offends very general sentiments, but ones that are strongly held. But it is believed that their generality and strength spring from the criminal nature of the act, which consequently still remains wholly to be defined. It is not disputed that any criminal act excites universal disapproval, but it is taken for granted that this results from its criminal nature. Yet one is then hard put to it to state what is the nature of this criminality. Is it in a particularly serious form of immorality? I would concur, but this is to answer a question by posing another, by substituting one term for another. For what *is* immorality is precisely what we want to know —and particularly that special form of immorality which society represses by an organized system of punishments, and which constitutes criminality. Clearly it can only derive from one or several characteristics common to all varieties of crime. Now the only characteristic to satisfy that condition refers to the opposition that exists between crime of any kind and certain collective sentiments. It is thus this opposition which, far from deriving from the crime, constitutes the crime. In other words, we should not say that an act offends the common consciousness because it is criminal, but that it is criminal because it offends that consciousness. We do not condemn it because it is a crime, but it is a crime because we condemn it. As regards the intrinsic nature of these feelings, we cannot specify what that is. They have very diverse objects, so that they cannot be encompassed within a single formula. They cannot be said to relate to the vital interests of society or to a minimum of justice. All such definitions are inadequate. But by the mere fact that a sentiment, whatever may be its origin and purpose, is found in every consciousness and endowed with a certain degree of strength and precision, every act that disturbs it is a crime.

## The Normal and the Pathological

If there is any fact whose pathological character appears incontestable, that fact is crime. All criminologists are agreed on this point. Although they explain this pathology differently, they are unanimous in recognizing it. But let us see if this problem does not demand a more extended consideration.

Crime is present not only in the majority of societies of one particular species but in all societies of all types. There is no society that is not confronted with the problem of criminality. Its form changes; the acts thus characterized are not the same everywhere; but, everywhere and always, there have been men who have behaved in such a way as to draw upon themselves penal repression. If, in proportion as societies pass from the lower to the higher types, the rate of criminality, i.e., the relation between the yearly number of crimes and the population, tended to decline, it might be believed that crime, while still normal, is tending to lose this character of normality. But we have no reason to believe that such a regression is substantiated. Many facts would seem rather to indicate a movement in the opposite direction. From the beginning of the [nineteenth] century, statistics enable us to follow the course of criminality. It has everywhere increased. In France the increase is nearly 300 per cent. There is, then, no phenomenon that presents more indisputably all the symptoms of normality, since it appears closely connected with the conditions of all collective life. To make of crime a form of social morbidity would be to admit that morbidity is not something accidental, but, on the contrary, that in certain cases it grows out of the fundamental constitution of the living organism; it would result in wiping out all distinction between the physiological and the pathological. No doubt it is possible that crime itself will have abnormal forms, as, for example, when its rate is unusually high. This excess is, indeed, undoubtedly morbid in nature. What is normal, simply, is the existence of criminality, provided that it attains and does not exceed, for each social type, a certain level, which it is perhaps not impossible to fix in conformity with the preceding rules.[1]

Here we are, then, in the presence of a conclusion in appearance quite paradoxical. Let us make no mistake. To classify crime among the phenomena of normal sociology is not to say merely that it is an inevitable, although regrettable phenomenon, due to the incorrigible wickedness of men; it is to affirm that it is a factor in public health, an integral part of all healthy societies. This result is, at first glance, surprising enough to have puzzled even ourselves for a long time. Once this first surprise has been overcome, however, it is not difficult to find reasons explaining this normality and at the same time confirming it.

In the first place crime is normal because a society exempt from it is utterly impossible. Crime, we have shown elsewhere, consists of an act that offends certain very strong collective sentiments. In a society in which criminal acts are no longer committed, the sentiments they offend would have to be found without exception in all individual consciousnesses, and they must be found to exist with the same degree as sentiments contrary to them. Assuming that this condition could actually be realized, crime would not thereby disappear; it would only change its form, for the very cause which would thus dry up the sources of criminality would immediately open up new ones.

Indeed, for the collective sentiments which are protected by the penal law of a people at a specified moment of its history to take possession of the public conscience or for them to acquire a stronger hold where they have an insufficient grip, they must acquire an intensity greater than that which they had hitherto had. The community as a whole must experience them more vividly, for it can acquire from no other source the greater force necessary to control these individuals who formerly were the most refractory. For murderers to disappear, the horror of bloodshed must become greater in those social strata from which murderers are recruited; but, first it must become greater throughout the entire society. Moreover, the very absence of crime would directly contribute to produce this horror; because any sentiment seems much more respectable when it is always and uniformly respected.

One easily overlooks the consideration that these strong states of the common consciousness cannot be thus reinforced without reinforcing at the same time the more feeble states, whose violation previously gave birth to mere infraction of convention—since the weaker ones are only the prolongation, the attenuated form, of the stronger. Thus robbery and simple bad taste injure the same single altruistic sentiment, the respect for that which is another's. However, this same sentiment is less grievously offended by bad taste than by robbery; and since, in addition, the average consciousness has not sufficient intensity to react keenly to the bad taste, it is treated with greater tolerance. That is why the person guilty of bad taste is merely blamed, whereas the thief is punished. But, if this sentiment grows stronger, to the point of silencing in all consciousnesses the inclination which disposes man to steal, he will become more sensitive to the offences which, until then, touched him but lightly. He will react against them, then, with more energy; they will be the object of greater opprobrium, which will transform certain of them from the simple moral faults that they were and give them the quality of crimes. For example, improper contracts, or contracts improperly executed, which only incur public blame or civil damages, will become offences in law.

Imagine a society of saints, a perfect cloister of exemplary individuals. Crimes, properly so called, will there be unknown; but faults which appear venial to the layman will create there the same scandal that the ordinary offence does in ordinary consciousnesses. If, then, this society has the power to judge and punish, it will define these acts as criminal and will treat them as such. For the same reason, the perfect and upright man judges his smallest failings with a severity that the majority reserve for acts more truly in the nature of an offence. Formerly, acts of violence against persons were more frequent than they are today, because respect for individual dignity was less strong. As this has increased, these crimes have become more rare; and also, many acts violating this sentiment have been introduced into the penal law which were not included there in primitive times.[2]

In order to exhaust all the hypotheses logically possible, it will perhaps be asked why this unanimity does not extend to all collective sentiments without exception. Why should not even the most feeble sentiment gather enough energy to prevent all dissent? The moral consciousness of the society would be present in its entirety in all the individuals, with a vitality sufficient to prevent all acts offending it—the purely conventional faults as well as the crimes. But a uniformity so universal and absolute is utterly impossible; for the immediate physical milieu in which each one of us is placed, the hereditary antecedents, and the social influences vary from one individual to the next, and consequently diversify consciousnesses. It is impossible for all to be alike, if only because each one has his own organism and that these organisms occupy different areas in space. That is why, even among the lower peoples, where individual originality is very little developed, it nevertheless does exist.

Thus, since there cannot be a society in which the individuals do not differ more or less from the collective type, it is also inevitable that, among these divergences, there are some with a criminal character. What confers this character upon them is not the intrinsic quality of a given act but that definition which the collective conscience lends them. If the collective conscience is stronger, if it has enough authority practically to suppress these divergences, it will also be more sensitive, more exacting; and, reacting against the slightest deviations with the energy it otherwise displays only against more considerable infractions, it will attribute to them the same gravity as formerly to crimes. In other words, it will designate them as criminal.

Crime is, then, necessary; it is bound up with the fundamental conditions of all social life, and by that very fact it is useful, because these conditions of which it is a part are themselves indispensable to the normal evolution of morality and law.

Indeed, it is no longer possible today to dispute the fact that law and morality vary from one social type to the next, nor that they change within the same type if the conditions of life are modified. But, in order that these transformations may be possible, the collective sentiments at the basis of morality must not be hostile to change, and consequently must have but moderate energy. If they were too strong, they would no longer be plastic. Every pattern is an obstacle to new patterns, to the extent that the first pattern is inflexible. The better a structure is articulated, the more it offers a healthy resistance to all modification; and this is equally true of functional, as of anatomical, organization. If there were no crimes, this condition could not have been fulfilled; for such a hypothesis presupposes that collective sentiments have arrived at a degree of intensity unexampled in history. Nothing is good indefinitely and to an unlimited extent. The authority which the moral conscience enjoys must not be excessive; otherwise no one would dare criticize it, and it would too easily congeal into an immutable form. To make progress, individual originality must be able to express itself. In order that the originality of the idealist whose dreams transcend his century may find expression, it is necessary that the originality of the criminal, who is below the level of his time, shall also be possible. One does not occur without the other.

Nor is this all. Aside from this indirect utility, it happens that crime itself plays a useful role in this evolution. Crime implies not only that the way remains open to necessary changes but that in certain cases it directly prepares these changes. Where crime exists, collective sentiments are sufficiently flexible to take on a new form, and crime sometimes helps to determine the form they will take. How many times, indeed, it is only an anticipation of future morality—a step toward what will be! According to Athenian law, Socrates was a criminal, and his condemnation was no more than just. However, his crime, namely, the independence of his thought, rendered a service not only to humanity but to his country. It served to prepare a new morality and faith which the Athenians needed, since the traditions by which they had lived until then were no longer in harmony with the current conditions of life. Nor is the case of Socrates unique; it is reproduced periodically in history. It would never have been possible to establish the freedom of thought we now enjoy if the regulations prohibiting it had not been violated before being solemnly abrogated. At that time, however, the violation was a crime, since it was an offence against sentiments still very keen in the average conscience. And yet this crime was useful as a prelude to reforms which daily became more necessary. Liberal philosophy had as its precursors the heretics of all kinds who were justly punished by secular authorities during the entire course of the Middle Ages and until the eve of modern times.

From this point of view the fundamental facts of criminality present themselves to us in an entirely new light. Contrary to current ideas, the criminal no longer seems a totally unsociable being, a sort of parasitic element, a strange and unassimilable body, introduced into the midst of society.[3] On the contrary, he plays a definite role in social life. Crime, for its part, must no longer be conceived as an evil that cannot be too much suppressed. There is no occasion for self-congratulation when the crime rate drops noticeably below the average level, for we may be certain that this apparent progress is associated with some social disorder. Thus, the number of assault cases never falls so low as in times of want.[4] With the drop in the crime rate, and as a reaction to it, comes a revision, or the need of a revision in the theory of punishment. If, indeed, crime is a disease, its punishment is its remedy and cannot be otherwise conceived; thus, all the discussions it arouses bear on the point of determining what the punishment must be in order to fulfill this role of remedy. If crime is not pathological at all, the object of punishment cannot be to cure it, and its true function must be sought elsewhere.

## Notes

1. From the fact that crime is a phenomenon of normal sociology, it does not follow that the criminal is an individual normally constituted from the biological and psychological points of view. The two questions are independent of each other. This independence will be better understood when we have shown, later on, the difference between psychological and sociological facts.
2. Calumny, insults, slander, fraud, etc.
3. We have ourselves committed the error of speaking thus of the criminal, because of a failure to apply our rule (Division drt travail social, pp. 395–96).
4. Although crime is a fact of normal sociology, it does not follow that we must not abhor it. Pain itself has nothing desirable about it; the individual dislikes it as society does crime, and yet it is a function of normal physiology. Not only is it necessarily derived from the very constitution of every living organism, but it plays a useful role in life, for which reason it cannot be replaced. It would, then, be a singular distortion of our thought to present it as an apology for crime. We would not even think of protesting against such an interpretation, did we not know to what strange accusations and misunderstandings one exposes oneself when one undertakes to study moral facts objectively and to speak of them in a different language from that of the layman.

# Part II  Constructing Deviance and Normalcy

The sociology of deviance emerged in the mid-twentieth century as an alternative approach to studying phenomena that had been regarded as social pathologies, or harmful to the 'social organism' overall. The social pathological perspective worked with a framework dominated by medical and legal concepts, and it generally accepted the premise that deviance and criminality were immanent properties of deviant and criminal behaviour. By contrast, the sociology of deviance regarded deviance and crime to be problematic in their definition and consequences rather than settled matters, and began attending to how the reality of deviance and crime are 'socially constructed'. That is, they are the result of interpreting and defining situations, justifying these interpretations, and institutionalizing them as part of a common stock of knowledge members of the group can draw upon, as well as politically entrenching them into law. This approach went hand in hand with investigating how normalcy is also socially constructed and maintained on a daily basis by members of a group as part of creating social order.

The rise of criminology in the latter part of the twentieth century represented, in part, an effort to return theory and research to the empirical study of crime focusing on pragmatic questions such as causes, prevention, and effective correction. But since critical approaches in criminology have emerged that focus more on the social and economic environments in which crime occurs, the two areas have become more interrelated. Each approach often draws on concepts, methods, research, and theory from the other, as can be seen in O'Grady's discussion of crime, fear, and risk.

The readings in this section reflect sociology's interest in the socially constructed nature of deviance and normalcy. The articles are attentive to the dynamics involved in defining situations, and providing accounts and justifications as part of engaging in, defining, managing, and/or condemning conduct that is deviant, as well as to how all this occurs in social contexts that involve imbalances in power and authority.

An important aspect of the social construction of deviance is the role that the mass media plays in defining deviance and normalcy as well as in legitimizing social control. And it's important to have some familiarity with media studies as well as to develop media literacy skills given the significant role the mass media plays in portraying deviance and social control and in influencing public perception and discussion. So this section also includes articles that introduce basic concepts, discuss the function of the media in defining and processing deviance, and provide examples of analyzing the content of the mass media.

A key concern in analyzing the ideas, beliefs, and values conveyed in the mass media is just whose system of values, beliefs, and ideas they are. Consensus and conflict theorists generally reflect differing positions on this issue. Consensus theorists argue that the media functions to disseminate a system of norms, values, beliefs, and ideas in order to achieve a widely shared sense of solidarity necessary to work cohesively and coherently together as a group. By contrast, conflict theorists have argued that the media is one of several societal institutions (along with schools, government, and corporations) controlled by the powerful and is used to disseminate an ideology or world view that fundamentally serves their needs and interests at the expense of subordinate groups. The ideology is presented or relied upon as if it were commonsense and becomes, in Gramsci's terms, 'hegemonic', or the dominant way of understanding and seeing the world. People generally come to accept it even though it may not serve their needs and interests.

# 6

## Introduction

The question of what counts as crime was addressed in an earlier reading. Here O'Grady develops the topic further by pointing out that it depends on which theoretical approach to deviance and crime one is working with. First, he considers the 'objectivist-legalist' approach which regards crime in a factual way as violations of the law. Then he compares it with the 'social-reaction' perspective which is attentive to the various ways that crime is socially constructed. Finally, he looks at how crime is portrayed in the mass media, and examines the moral panic that is often part of media accounts of crime.

O'Grady's discussion of the social reaction perspective includes an examination of the role of labelling in defining deviance, conflict theory's focus on the relation between deviant behaviour and how a society is structured, as well as the state's use of moral regulation to control behaviour. Provide an example of each of these other than those given in the article.

While he argues the media does influence public knowledge and views about crime, he cautions us against an overly 'deterministic' view that operates as if there is a direct cause-effect relation between media portrayals and public opinion. Given his cautionary note, what exactly is the influence that the mass media has regarding public knowledge and perceptions of crime?

# Crime, Fear, and Risk

*William O'Grady*

It is common for criminologists to disagree with one another. Many opposing viewpoints exist within the discipline, but defining crime is a topic that, arguably, splits the discipline down the middle. While several different definitions of crime can be identified in the research literature (e.g., Henry and Lanier 2001) it would be fair to say that the majority of these conceptualizations can be captured under one of two broadly based approaches: the objectivist-legalistic position or the social-reaction perspective.

## The Objectivist–Legalistic Approach

Often referred to as a 'value consensus' or 'normative' position, the objectivist-legalistic standpoint understands the definition of crime to be factual and precise.

This point of view typically defines crime as 'something that is against the law'. Such a conceptualization essentially views crime as a violation of legal statutes, where criminality is limited to its legal construction. In Canada, this viewpoint would hold that the study of crime should be restricted to what is contained in *The Criminal Code of Canada*. Tappan, an oft-cited and early adherent of this approach, argues that crime is an intentional act in violation of the criminal law that is subject to penalization by the state (1947: 100). Laws are simply widely shared customs and beliefs that, over time, become codified into legal statutes.

From this perspective, the proper focus of criminology or, for that matter, the goal of criminologists is the analysis of the 'rule-breakers' in society. For this reason, the primary question that stems from the objectivist-legalistic viewpoint becomes, 'What are the causes of criminal behaviour?' Since the definition of what is considered criminal is, for the most part, defined by legal statute, the goal of criminology is a quest to understand why people break the law. To obtain a good sense of how much crime actually exists in any society at any particular point in time, one would simply turn to the facts: official crime statistics.

Those who endorse the objectivist-legalistic approach to the study of crime are no doubt aware that a considerable amount of behaviour takes place in society that may not be against the law but, nevertheless, may cause people harm. Examples of extra-legal behaviour include lawyers who do not adequately represent their client's best interests, some forms of insider trading, and physicians' malpractices that permanently damage or cause the death of their patients. While adherents of the traditional legalistic approach would not deny that people become victims in these types of circumstances, the perpetrators are not violating the criminal law. Until such time when society deems these offences to be criminal, such behaviour is not the proper realm for the study of criminologists.

Several theories of criminal behaviour are informed by the objectivist-legalistic approach. These theories range from biological to psychological to sociological explanations of offending. And Canada's criminal justice system is very much modelled on this objectivist-legalistic approach.

## Crime and Social Reaction

Taken at face value, the objectivist-legalistic approach appears to be straightforward enough: Crime is what is defined by legal statutes, and the purpose of criminology is to find out what causes crime so that policy-makers can implement the initiatives required to combat this social problem.

Until a few decades ago, there really was not a great deal of debate about the way crime was defined by the criminological community. This acquiescence quickly changed with the development of labelling theory in the 1960s (Becker 1963), and later by the various 'critical criminologies' (Taylor et al. 1973) of the 1970s that questioned the objectivist-legalistic approach. Concern was awakened because people had come to see that such a narrow definition of crime assumes that legal definitions reflect widespread social consensus about what is deviant in society (Hagan 1991: 7), and anyone could see that society was anything but consistent in its definitions of deviancy.

Labelling theory theorist Howard Becker argues that social groups *create* deviance by making the rules whose infraction constitutes deviance and then by applying those rules to particular people to label them as outsiders (1973: 9). For Becker 'deviance is not a quality of the act the person commits, but rather a consequence of the application by others of rules and sanctions to the offender. The deviant is one to whom that label has successfully been applied;

deviant behaviour is behaviour that people so label' (1973: 9). In other words, the label is the social reaction to deviancy. However, in a complex society one cannot assume that what is regarded as deviant by the law has been arrived at by universal agreement or social consensus.

At the time, Becker's way of thinking was considered controversial, and no wonder that it was. According to what is sometimes referred to as 'hard' labelling theory, no act—even murder or rape—is inherently criminal. If society does not create the criminal label, then there is no criminal act; crime and deviance are considered to be social constructs. The theory refers to the manner in which individuals and groups create their perceived reality. As a methodological approach, its application involves looking at how social phenomena are produced, institutionalized, and put into practice by humans (Berger and Luckmann 1966). The idea that crime is socially constructed typically produces a more holistic understanding of crime and deviance as elastic in society. If crime is primarily socially constructed, we must at least be alert to the fact that while criminal behaviour is generally regarded to be deviant behaviour, it certainly is not the case that all deviant behaviour has been defined as criminal.

Consider the example of sexual assault. In Canada, sexual assault constitutes both a crime—punishable according to the *Criminal Code*—and an act of social deviance—as the widespread consensus in Canada appears to be that sexual assault is harmful and that such behaviour should not be tolerated. However, other behaviours that are generally considered to be socially deviant—for example, not flushing a public toilet after defecating—are reacted to with repugnance and deemed socially deviant, but by no means does such a behaviour represent a criminal act nor is it punishable on the basis of a legal statute. Consider also behaviours that may be in violation of administrative laws, and subject to a penalty like a fine, but that until recently were not considered by many Canadians to represent a serious social harm. Municipal bylaws prohibiting smoking in bars or restaurants, now in place in many jurisdictions across Canada, are examples of administrative laws and do not fall under the auspices of criminal law. Even though a business may be subject to a fine for a smoking violation, the behaviour would not result in the merchant's having a criminal record.

In essence, social deviance is a continuous variable, that is, deviance is best understood as being an elastic concept or as a 'continuous scale that ranges from the most to the least serious of acts in any given society' (Hagan 1991: 30). The interesting question that arises, then, is why are some behaviours regarded simply as social deviance, other behaviours as breaches of administrative statutes, while a select number of behaviours reach into the criminal realm?

A logical response to this question would be to point out that behaviours deemed by society to be 'criminal' are based on concepts of harm or of socially injurious behaviours, like murder or sexual assault, where it is clear that an individual or social harm has been inflicted. This appears to be a reasonable claim. However, as those who endorse the social-reaction position point out, not all dangerous behaviours that hurt people are against the criminal law. Take the earlier examples of professional malpractice that take place in the legal, medical, and financial services professions. Moreover, certain behaviours that do not appear to be particularly harmful to society are, in fact, against the criminal law and can lead to serious punishment. The possession of illegal drugs provides an example of this latter point. There is neither at present widespread consensus in the research literature on the behavioural and long-term health effects of cannabis use nor are there any known records to indicate that marijuana use can lead to death from overdose; yet the possession of marijuana for non-medicinal purposes is against the law in Canada. Furthermore, anyone found guilty of possessing cannabis faces the possibility of spending a considerable amount of time in prison. Even though the Canadian courts rarely punish marijuana offenders to the full extent of the law, especially for possession of small amounts of the drug, the fact remains that the maximum penalty for marijuana possession (more than 30 grams) in Canada is five years less a day in custody (Controlled Drugs and Substances Act 2005).

This example not only suggests that the level of social and individual harm may not be directly linked to the severity of punishment imposed by society for other criminalized behaviour, but it also alerts us to the idea proposed by the social-reaction perspective that many rules and laws are not endorsed by all segments of Canadian society. The way in which so-called deviant behaviour is understood and reacted to is more largely a reflection of how a society is structured than it is an indication of any pathological traits inherent in those who are labelled as criminals. To argue that crime is socially defined points us in a direction where the meaning of crime can vary across social and cultural contexts. Several examples could be used to illustrate how this is the case. Among the more interesting are laws meant to regulate the distribution and use of drugs. While the violation of drug laws in Singapore can lead to the death penalty or to caning, in other countries drug laws are much less strict. Marijuana is legal to purchase in the Netherlands and one may smoke cannabis openly in certain licensed establishments such as the 'coffee shops' of Amsterdam.

The social-reaction perspective has remained influential since its origins in labelling theory. Not long after labelling theory was introduced, attention shifted away from the study of why people violate social norms to why certain behaviours are labelled as criminal or deviant. This was achieved by investigating the processes by which laws are created or reformed. For example, 'conflict criminologists' or 'critical criminologists', who operate under the assumption that society is in a constant state of divergence, argue that laws come into being within the context of social conflict. So, like the labelling theory perspective, their focus is not on the traits of individual lawbreakers, but on the entire law-making process. The context of social conflict leads the researcher beyond the labelling perspective's narrow critique to examine the dynamics and power imbalances that exist between different groups in society. More specifically, critical definitions of crime generally pay heed to such concepts as social class, race, and gender. For example, the critical position would point out that much of the crime reported on the front page of newspapers or in other news sections usually involves street crime, often being committed by working-class individuals. However, the crimes of the powerful, such as corporate crime, are much more likely to appear in the business section of newspapers. This discrimination based on class suggests, of course, that the crimes committed by the economically powerful are to be taken less seriously than street crime. However, as the critical position points out, there is good reason to believe that crimes committed by the powerful are far more costly to society than crimes committed by the powerless. The point, then, is that the two types of crime are subject to different values in different classes of society and, hence, are subject to different definitions.

A recent perspective in criminology that fits well with the social-reaction position is found in a body of literature that has been influenced by the work of Michel Foucault and his writing on moral regulation. According to this viewpoint, and in keeping with the social-reaction definition of crime, the social regulation of behaviour is not based on widespread social consensus but on moral regulation: a social process that defines what is right and what is wrong in society, encouraging certain forms of behaviour while discouraging others. The process by which behaviour is encouraged or discouraged is mediated by a complex system of social institutions that reward and punish people. While conflict theory views law-creation essentially as a process whereby the powerful—usually economic and political elites—impose their will on others (in the form of norms, values, and ultimately laws), the way that power is understood by moral regulationalists is not so straightforward. While moral regulationists see law-making in terms of judicial power, they do not think populations follow rules simply because of the fear of consequences that would come to bear by getting caught and punished. Rather, other processes, or 'discourses', are at play in society that serve the function of what could be described as social discipline.

For the Foucauldian school, these forms of discipline are of paramount interest (Corrigan 1990). Modes of regulation often included in the study of moral regulation usually imply social controls exercised on low-consensus crime and non-criminal deviance. These social controls affect such social groupings as drug users, prostitutes, exotic dancers, homosexuals, and the poor. One of the more interesting aspects of the moral regulation perspective is that it introduces the idea of self-regulation. That is, it carries the social-reaction perspective of crime and deviance one step beyond laws, lawmakers, and the implementation of direct force and authority to the individual's appropriation of his or her choice of moral behaviour. The moral regulationist maintains that people are self-regulated; that people's identities are socially shaped through 'self-appropriation of morals and beliefs about what is right and what is wrong, possible and impossible, normal and pathological' (Rousmaniere et al. 1997: 3). In keeping with the social-reaction perspective, the moral regulationists are careful to point out that the researcher must ask, 'Whose morals are being regulated, and by whom?'

Even though self-regulation is occurring in society, the criminologist must recognize that groups who are officially morally regulated by the society often resist the efforts by the law to control their behaviour. In this context, one needs to understand the role of the state and how regulation operates in almost every form of state activity from who gets into the country (immigration and citizenship) to how families are defined (taxation) to how the justice system functions. While moral regulation is not confined to the role played by the state, much research in this area does centre on examining the state and how socially appropriate behaviour is defined by the state and is subject to the state's regulatory efforts. The viewpoint of moral regulationists is very much in keeping with the social-reaction perspective; they are not interested in why people are poor, homosexual, or drug users, but simply in how and why groups are controlled, as well as in the ways groups resist that control.

An example of Canadian research that has been informed by the social-reaction approach concerns actions that took place early in the twentieth century in British Columbia. Prior to 1908, the use of heroin and other opiates was not subject to criminal sanction in Canada. In fact, in the late nineteenth and early twentieth centuries, heroin and cocaine were common ingredients in many tonics and elixirs (Carstairs 2005). However, after a series of events pertaining to drug use among the Asian community that occurred in British Columbia at the turn of the century, the Canadian Opium Act was enacted and opiate use across the country was legally censured. What is interesting from a social-reaction standpoint about the creation of such an Act is that there really was not any solid evidence at that time to support the assumption that society in general was concerned about this type of drug use, or that great numbers of people were being adversely affected by the use of opium (Boyd 1991). (This is not to say that contemporary medical research would support the social consensus of that period.) Without social consensus, how did such a law come to be passed by the Canadian Parliament? Becker's notion of moral entrepreneur has been used to attribute the passage of the Opium Act to enterprising individuals or groups, rather than to a societal consensus on the perils of opiate use.

In response to a riot that arose from a labour demonstration that spread to the streets of Vancouver's Chinatown, Deputy Minister of Labour Mackenzie King travelled to British Columbia to investigate. While in Vancouver, King met with Asian merchants—including some who were the proprietors of opium dens—whose properties had been damaged by the rioters and who were seeking financial compensation from the government. During his investigation, King also met with a small number of business people and clergy who were upset by the existence of the opium trade in British Columbia. According to Solomon and Green (1988), King had four main concerns as the result of his visit: (1) opium-smoking was becoming more popular among white people, (2) the Chinese were making vast profits in the opium trade, (3) opium trade was in violation of provincial pharmacy legislation, and finally (4) as a Christian nation, Canada had to set an example for an international campaign against opium (Solomon and Green 1988: 91). The elimination of the 'opium menace' became the primary focus of King's early political career. Under his leadership, Parliament enacted its first prohibitionist drug policy. The 1908 Opium Act 'made it an indictable offence to import, manufacture, offer to sell, sell, or possess to sell opium for non-medical purposes, but prohibited neither simple possession nor use' (ibid.: 92). Ostensibly, the passage of the Act had more to do with political opportunism than with a crystallization of custom or a call from the 'voice of the people'. Today, a century later, simple possession of an opiate in Canada can result in a 25-year prison sentence and the social burden of a serious criminal record.

This example of law-making clearly points out how political imperatives can underlie how social deviance is produced. Equally, the reason why the Opium Act was made into law also illustrates how the classification and regulation of deviant behaviour is by no means based on social consensus or accurate information. There was scant evidence to support the contention that society was in dire need of protection from the activities of opium addicts.

What, then, is crime? Well, it depends on which definition of crime one chooses to endorse. For the criminologist, important implications reside in the definition accepted in terms of the types of questions that will be posed and in the method that will be used in the effort to answer them. If one endorses an objectivist-legalistic definition, then it is quite likely that questions about the causes of crime will be at the forefront of analysis. On the other hand, if one endorses a social-reaction perspective, questions will be addressed that include law-making processes and how crime and deviance become socially constructed.

# Media Portrayals of Crime in Canada

While it is impossible to provide one, straightforward, and agreed-on sociological definition of crime, it is feasible to turn to a locus that does tend to portray crime in a much more uncomplicated and definitive manner: the mass media. Since the 1960s, studies of mass media, particularly of television and of the press, have shown how they play an integral role in how the general public understands the social reality of crime, and why it is crucial to consider these media in understanding how crime is defined in society.

Generally speaking, crime is defined by the media on a basis that is very similar to the objectivist-legalistic viewpoint. In most media accounts of crime (both 'news' and programmed entertainment) crime tends to be defined primarily as events associated with personal fear and risk in which violence is not only commonplace, but its victims are sympathetically portrayed and are often let down by a judicial justice system perceived as being too soft on criminals. While important differences do exist among the various forms of mass media—for example, between newspapers and television—crime reports have in the past played and continue to play a prominent role in news content; estimates of the proportion of total news items devoted to crime coverage have been noted as high as 25 per cent (Surette 1998: 62). Whether through politicians talking about how, if elected, they will 'get tough on criminals' or in dramas depicting crime scene investigations, crime is depicted in the mass media as an ever present part of our culture.

A well-established body of literature has examined the treatment and presentation of crime in the mass media. The two well-accepted findings that have come from this research are, first, that public knowledge about crime and justice is derived largely from the mass media (Surrette 1998), and second that the way crime is portrayed in the media differs considerably from how crime is measured and defined officially, in the official statistics, for example. For some time, scholars have pointed out the generally weak relationship between societal concerns and media presentations about crime and official crime rates (Erickson 1966; Fishman 1978; Hall et al. 1978; Best 1989). Within a Canadian context, a study of youth crime by Sprott (1996) showed that while 94 per cent of youth crime reported in the press focused on youth violence, according to court statistics less than 25 per cent of youth crime is violent—much of which entails relatively minor assaults.

The above research raises questions about the power and ability wielded by the mass media in shaping public understanding about crime and in manipulating viewers' ideas about the appropriate responses for addressing the problem. Without a doubt, the exposure of Canadians to these images of crime is pervasive, as Internet use rises from year to year and just about every Canadian household has at least one television set and watches it, on average, 20-plus hours per week (Statistics Canada 2005).

There is good reason to believe a change has been made in the way crime is depicted in film, television, and the press. A study in England by Reiner and Livingstone (1998) found a decrease in the number of portrayals of property crime, but a steady rise from the 1950s to the mid-1990s in treatments of violent, sexual, and drug-related crime. This analysis concluded that, on the basis of how crime is depicted in the media, society has come to feel more threatened by interpersonal violence and mayhem.

The media are primary sources of information about crime that the public relies on. More-over, the way in which crime is presented in the media does not often correspond to the picture of crime that is painted by official police statistics. According to research, both of these realities are well-accepted. However, there is much less agreement in the research literature about the *effect* that media have in terms of instilling fear of crime in the public. The relationship between the ways the media depict crime and how the public fears crime is neither simple nor direct. For example, one might think that viewers who are exposed to crime in the media on a regular basis would be more fearful of crime than people who watch little television, yet according to the research literature the relationship between a person's levels of exposure to the mass media and their fear of crime is multifaceted.

First, it would be unreasonable to assume that audience members are passive recipients of television, which arguably is the most dominant form of mass media. Sacco (2000) cites the work of Williams and Dickinson (1993), who suggest that television news consumers are actively involved in giving meaning to what appears on their screens. This meaning doubtless is informed by individuals' past experiences and by their own predispositions to interpret what crime means for them. For years, the notion persisted that the media acts like a hypodermic needle, whereby a dose of information is injected to an unsuspecting public who then become directly affected by such a dose. For some decades this notion has been criticized by mass media researchers (e.g., Lazarsfeld et al. 1968) as an overly simplistic model. The mass media are not the public's only sources of information about crime, and other experiences may come to bear on fears and anxieties. Research has shown that the news about crime that travels through interpersonal networks is more likely to induce fear than news that travels over the airwaves of the mass media (Berger 1995). To learn, for instance, about crime through the experiences of a neighbour whose home has been broken into is more persuasive and elevates fear more than hearing about a home invasion in a city that could be 2,000 miles away. Research by Dowler (2003) has shown that survey respondents who were regular viewers of crime dramas were only slightly more likely to fear crime than non-regular viewers. Factors such as gender, age, income, and perceived neighbourhood problems and police effectiveness were much better predictors of fear of crime than was media consumption.

One of the prime data sources for crime and media research has been the newspaper. Examining hard copies or microfiche transparencies of newspapers is not only laborious work, but it also assumes that there exists a one-way vertical communication from the news outlet to the reader. The only opportunity for readers to share their views with other readers was to write letters to the editor or submit short opinion pieces. However, as Jacklin (2009) points out, since most major newspapers today are on-line, the idea of one-way communication is becoming an outdated way of looking at the press. Figure 6.1 provides a useful illustration about how the Internet has changed the relationship between newspapers and their readers.

Even though the idea that the media have a direct influence on public fears about crime is a dubious one, there is reason to believe that the media are capable of distorting public understandings about crime and its control. For instance, in the news media the police can appear to be more effective in apprehending offenders than they actually are. Take the example of illegal drug 'busts'. In recent years, the media have often presented images of police raiding indoor marijuana-growing operations. The scene is familiar: police clad in white, disposable lab coats are captured by television camera crews as they remove large amounts of marijuana and growing equipment from suburban homes, apartments, or other buildings. Often the news clip concludes with a presentation of a cost estimate of the street value of the drugs seized in the operation. While police may have been effective in destroying the particular grow-op in question, any reference to how effective in general the police are in controlling levels of illegal drug production, distribution, and consumption is seldom made. In other words, the public is left with the impression that the police are doing their jobs wonderfully well and that the entire problem of illicit drug production is under control.

Research by Sprott (1996) suggests that the promotion of misconceptions like these have a real impact on what the public believes should be done to confront crime. For example, from population surveys we know that the public thinks that most youth crime is violent. According to Sprott, this false belief leads to the public's opinion that, in the case of youth crime, youth court dispositions are too lenient. When asked to indicate what kinds of cases the respondents were thinking of when youth crime comes to mind, most of those who thought that youth court dispositions were too lenient were thinking of a very small minority of cases: those involving seriously violent repeat offenders. Respondents also had very little accurate knowledge of the operation of the youth court in Canada; they underestimated the severity of dispositions available to the court under the law. The public also believed that the courts were much more constrained than they are in their ability to transfer youth cases to adult court. The view that youth courts are too lenient can best be thought of as a general 'belief', more linked to general views about crime and the criminal justice system than to genuine knowledge or to facts about youth crime and the youth justice system. Thus, not only does this study show that the youth crime coverage in the press does not correspond to the 'statistical

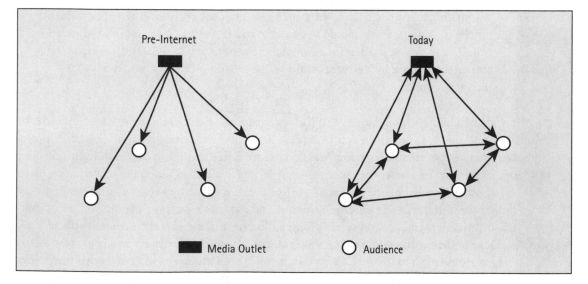

**Figure 6.1 Media and Audience Communication: Pre-Internet and Today**
Source: Jacklin, 2009, p. 13.

reality' of youth crime, it also shows that media coverage can promote public pressure for more punitive measures to deal with youth who come into contact with the criminal justice system.

## Crime and Moral Panics

There is no doubt that media play an important role in constructing crime. Sociologists have developed concepts, therefore, that are intended to better describe the role that communication plays in producing social knowledge about crime. One idea that has been commonly used by criminologists since the 1970s and that is increasingly making its way into public/journalistic discourses about crime is the notion of a 'moral panic'. Influential to this day is a relatively early study by Stanley Cohen (1973), who examined the impact the media play in shaping how crime was defined in England during late 1960s. Not only did the media exaggerate and distort a series of events that began with a stone-throwing incident between the youths of two subcultures (the mods and the rockers) at a seaside village, but the local merchants and the police played an important role in creating what was to become, in Cohen's terms, a moral panic:

> Societies appear to be subject, every now and then, to periods of moral panic. A condition, episode, person, or group of persons emerges to become defined as threat to the societal values and interests; its nature is presented in a stylized and stereotypical fashion by the mass media; the moral barricades are manned by editors, bishops, politicians, and other right-thinking people; socially accredited experts pronounce their diagnoses and solutions; ways of coping are evolved or (more often) resorted to; the condition then disappears, submerges, or deteriorates and becomes more visible. Sometimes the object of the panic is quite novel and at other times it is something that has been in existence long enough, but suddenly appears in the limelight. Sometimes the panic passes over and is forgotten, except in folklore and collective memory; at other times it has more serious and long-lasting repercussions and might produce such changes as those in legal and social policy or even in the way the society conceives itself. (1973, p. 9)

Local merchants who equated youthful wrongdoing with commercial losses lobbied for action so that the fears these youths represented could be controlled or alleviated. All sorts of subsequent youth misbehaviour was taken as evidence that post-war youth in Britain were out of control and were, therefore, in need of increased discipline and surveillance. Each event was portrayed by the media as part of the mods and rockers phenomenon, and the police were arbitrarily stopping, questioning, and sometimes arresting youth who were identified through their appearance as belonging to one of these so-called deviant subcultures. Because of the media exposure, the social reaction posed by the threat was evidenced in the British House of Commons where certain members of Parliament recommended that stiffer penalties be levied to control this outbreak of youth crime.

A number of subsequent studies emerged incorporating this sort of moral panic logic. Interestingly, as in Cohen's original study, much of the targeted activities involved threats posed by youth. For example, there have been studies on moral panics associated with drug use among Israeli youth (Ben-Yehuda 1986); satanic cults (Jenkins and Maier-Katkin 1992); serial killers (Jenkins 1994 ); muggers (Hall et al. 1978); gangs (McCorkle and Miethe 2002); and date-rape drugs (Moore and Valverde 2003).

## Moral Panics in Canada

The moral panic perspective also has informed research on the subject of how crime is defined and reacted to in Canada. One such example stems from a study that was undertaken in Newfoundland. During the mid-1980s, worry was mounting in that province about an apparent rise in crime, particularly violent crime, especially murder and armed robbery. According to Statistics Canada, levels of violent crime in Newfoundland had increased by nearly 40 per cent over a 10-year period. This increase was said to be among one of the greatest for any Canadian province over this same time period (O'Grady 1992: 2). Groups such as the St John's Board Of Trade, some clergy, union leaders, academics, women's groups, and the police all were offering their views about why Newfoundland was suddenly becoming a more violent society, in addition to suggesting what could be done to stem this tide of mayhem. Typical to other studies of moral panics, a 'folk devil' emerged within this discourse and was deemed responsible for the rise in crime: unemployed male youth.

Even though official levels of unemployment historically have been higher in Newfoundland than in other Canadian provinces, during the early to mid-1980s the unemployment rate was extremely high, around 20 per cent. Rates for youth were even higher, and some communities reported levels of youth unemployment that exceeded 30 per cent (Felt and Sinclair 1995). A good example of how the frustrations and blocked opportunities of these youth were seen as being tied to crime is expressed by a witness to the Newfoundland Royal Commission of Unemployment:

> I see the young people in our community getting very upset and possibly there could very well be a sudden rage of the people towards the Government, and maybe in our community, towards whatever groups of people they see as being in authority, which are seemingly not doing anything to help. It's like a time bomb which is very soon, I should think, ready to explode. . . . The correlation between crime and unemployment is a reality. Many individuals find themselves in a rut. As long as the present unemployment situation continues, the crime rate will continue to rise due to the poverty cycle and the social and psychological effects that this cycle has upon the individual (Clarke 1986: 1, 2).

However, after testing the assumptions of these claims, O'Grady (1992) found that there was a discrepancy between actual changes in official crime rates and the concern directed toward the level and character of crime in the province. Levels of violent crime had not increased in the province in any meaningful way, even though sentences for some violent crimes, such as armed robberies, imposed by the judiciary had become more severe. In fact, a major explanation for the 39 per cent rise in the violent crime rate was largely the result of changes in record-keeping and initiatives placed on police by the government to lay assault charges in 'domestic disputes'.

Not only was the moral panic caused by the uncritical examination of crime statistics and increased media attention, but Leyton, who also examined violence in Newfoundland during this same time period, found that the fear of crime was in part generated by the role of interest groups in the province such as politicians, government agencies, professional associations, and social action groups, who had 'discovered' violence and used it to further their own interests (Leyton 1992, p. 191). To quote Stanley Cohen, 'The worse the crime problem becomes, the more professional growth can be justified' (Cohen 1985: 177).

More recent studies of moral panics in Canada have incorporated the concept of 'risk society'. The concept of risk can be traced to the writings of Ulrich Beck, a European social analyst who argues that deep changes to economies, cultures, and social life are a conspicuous feature of global societies. Because of these changes, traditional institutions and social constructs have been transformed and the effect has been an increase in feelings of insecurity (Beck 1992). Certainties of life have been replaced by a state of risk, fear, self-consciousness, and vulnerability (Pile 1999).

In an attempt to integrate the moral panic perspective with notions of risk, a study was undertaken by Doyle and Lacombe about the anxiety over pedophilia in British Columbia. The authors document the frenzy that occurred in that province during the late 1990s over a Supreme Court of British Columbia ruling that struck down the possession provision of the child pornography law. Censuring the possession of child pornography was deemed an invasion of freedom of expression and privacy, according to a judicial ruling. Even though it remained illegal to produce, make, or distribute child pornography, the judgment ruled that it is not illegal to possess such material for private use. Following this ruling, the press, the public, politicians, teachers' unions, and other groups voiced their outrage and concern over this ruling (Doyle and Lacombe 2003: 286). The common concern expressed was the connection between child pornography, pedophilia, and child sexual abuse. According to Doyle and Lacombe, at the centre of the controversy was 'folk devil' Robin Sharpe. Sharpe, a 65-year-old gay male who lived in Vancouver, was targeted not only for being a child pornographer, but also as a pedophile. While not confessing to have been involved in sexual activity with children, Sharpe did point out to the media that sex between adults and children was a long-standing practice in society. Not only were these views widely publicized in the mass media, but a poster campaign was waged in his Kitsilano neighbourhood depicting Sharpe as a menace to society. While the media and others overlooked many aspects of his life that would have 'normalized' the man to some extent, Sharpe not only was depicted as a freak, but was made a scapegoat (ibid.: 287).

For Doyle and Lacombe, Sharpe's unsympathetic treatment needs to be understood as part of a larger moral panic around child abuse, pedophilia, and child pornography. In fact, the authors state that Canada is currently 'engulfed in a moral panic around pedophiles' (ibid.: 304). The authors point out that there has been a sharp increase in the number of alleged cases of child abuse that have been reported to the authorities since the 1970s, even though such reports are not to be taken as indicative of a 'real' increase in the incidence of such behaviour in society. Such an increase in reported cases, in addition to the proliferation of media cases about abused children, has served to heighten social anxieties over such abuse. The authors contend that this attention is associated with rising levels of public awareness and concern over this behaviour. Coupled with the notion presented by 'experts' that the consumption of child pornography leads to pedophilia and with the development of the child as an 'icon' in present-day society, it should not have been a surprise that the case of Robin Sharpe as folk devil evolved as it did.

Moreover, Doyle and Lacombe argue that the proliferation of news media and other new technologies provides more sources in society to alert the public about crime, danger, and risk. In effect, with more channels available from new satellite television technology and the rise of the Internet, fear of crime in society is enhanced and promoted. These sources depend on advertisers for their revenue and are motivated to attract viewers and listeners to purchase the advertisers' products. Such sources are not regulated or limited in their production of attention-catching 'news'. The overall effect of this wave of advertising about criminal behaviour is that criminals have become objects of generalized abhorrence and anxiety and for whom stricter controls and punishments are exacted.

A review of the literature indicates that most attention to crime that has been analyzed according to the moral panic perspective has focused on males. Until recently, public anxieties about crime have not involved 'folk devils' who happen to be female. This situation, however, changed in Canada during the mid-1990s. Research by Barron and Lacombe (2005) explains—in what they call the nasty girl phenomenon—that a new breed of female criminal has emerged and is being portrayed as on the rise in the mass media. Citing the examples of Karla Homolka, who was imprisoned for 12 years in connection to the sexual murders of two Ontario teenage girls (in collaboration with Paul Bernardo) and the events surrounding the beating death of Victoria, British Columbia, teen Reena Virk by seven female teens in 1997, Barron and Lacombe argue that public anxiety around girl violence is beginning to mount. Not only were teen girls thought to be increasingly violent, but the numbers of teen girls who were getting involved in violent crime was thought to be on the rise.

*Nasty Girls* was the title of a CBC television documentary that first aired in 1997. The program investigated teenaged girls' experiences of violence and imprisonment. Barron and Lacombe make the case that this program was a reflection of Canadian society's concern that it had entered into the era of the nasty girl. The documentary juxtaposed the modern teenaged girl, who is shown to be fighting at school, with a young girl from the 1950s, who was dutifully helping her mother with domestic chores. The idea that girls of the past were obedient and respectful to adult authority, whereas girls today are becoming just the opposite, is a theme that is commonly featured in the construction of moral panics. While not focusing on female crime per se, in a book entitled *Hooligan: A History of Respectable Fears* that focused on newspaper accounts of crime and youth in England dating back to the nineteenth century, Pearson (1983) argues that present-day concerns about deviant youth are not unique: Evidence of such concern is longstanding, as is the idea that in the past society was a more caring and civilized place.

The documentary moves on to show the metamorphosis of the good, 'sweet' girl of the past to the violent criminal of the present. The harmful effects of modern popular culture—gangsta rap, sexualized music videos, and teen fashion magazines—are depicted in the documentary as the culprits for the rise of the nasty girl, the new female folk devil of the 1990s. Barron and Lacombe point out that, like other analyses of moral panics, the fears about nasty girls do not correspond to the official statistics that measure the nature and level of young female crime in Canada. For example, the authors point out that the sharp rise in violent crime by young female offenders has more to do with a rise in minor assaults, such as pushing and slapping, than a rise in the number of seriously damaging crimes, such as murder. In fact, this point has been supported in recent research by Sprott and Doob (2004), who have argued that the main reason why the proportion of female younger offenders who have been found guilty in Canadian youth courts in relation to males has increased in recent years is largely the result of the smaller number of males who have appeared in court, not because there has been a landslide of females appearing in court.

Barron and Lacombe then go on to claim that the social construction of the violent girl is linked to a societal backlash against feminism. Quoting Schissel (1997), they write: '[t]he "sugar and spice" understanding of femaleness is often the standard upon which young female offenders are judged, and, in effect, the images of "bad girls" are presented as . . . sinister products of the feminist movement' (Barron and Lacombe 2005, citing Schissel: 107). Similarly, they argue that what troubles society most about the violent girl is that she has come to represent the excesses of the changed social, political, and economic status women have gained through their struggles for equality since the 1960s. The media, they contend, have 'sensationalized the spirit of girl power by positing it as the cause of girl violence' (Barron and Lacombe 2005: 58). Girl power, the source of social anxieties, is the real nasty here; the moral panic over the nasty girl is an outcrop of a desire to return to a patriarchal social order characterized by gender traditionalism and conformity.

## Criticisms of the Moral Panic Perspective

While the concept of 'moral panic' is useful for understanding how crime can be exaggerated and distorted and to concerns about the broader social order, the concept has not been without some criticism. The moral panic framework has been criticized on the basis that it often does not pay enough attention to the fact that all social reaction is not the same, and that audiences today are more sophisticated and less likely to be manipulated by the media than perhaps was the case in the past. For example, McRobbie and Thorton believe that while certain segments of the media exaggerate and distort crime, this is not to suggest that the mass media should be treated as a homogenous entity. They argue that opposing viewpoints are often expressed when it comes to issues related to crime, law, and order. The police, the press, and governing parties do not necessarily operate in a concerted campaign; there is often some organized and articulated opposition (McRobbie and Thorton 1995: 154).

An example of this point can be found in a study by Ericson and Voumvakis, who looked at the coverage given by Toronto newspapers to attacks on women in the 1980s. They found that considerable variation in how these assaults were reported and commented on existed among the *Globe and Mail*, the *Toronto Star*, and the *Toronto Sun*. A more recent example can be found in the wake of a Boxing Day shooting that took place in downtown Toronto in 2005. A 15-year-old girl was killed and six other people were injured by gunfire on normally busy but safe Yonge Street and on the threshold of one of the city's venerable department stores.

An opinion column in the *Toronto Star* was headlined, 'There's no going back to what we once were'. Columnist Rosie DiManno (2005: A6) muses that her 'hometown has become unrecognizable, angry, and malevolent'. The popular columnist further laments that a 'culture of nihilism and reckless wrongdoing has caught up with us' where Toronto could be headed for an 'irreversible ruin, a place of besiegement by crime and wicked malaise'. Words such as these are certainly in keeping with the moral panic perspective in terms of the role that media can assume in playing to the public's anxiety about the threat posed by the perceived growth in ruthless handgun violence.

However, on the very same day, in the same edition of the same newspaper, and only a few pages after the DiManno column, the main editorial of the *Toronto Star* took a completely different slant on this tragic event, opposing the view held by DiManno. While the editorial denounces the crime as a 'senseless' and 'intolerable' act, it also notes that despite the high-profile murders in 2005, the number still was short of the 'record of 88 killings in 1991'. The editorial continued by maintaining that 'Toronto is far from being "just like any big American city" or another "Dodge City" as some critics would have us believe. The streets are not out of control' (*Toronto Star* 2005).

Moore and Valverde (2003: 307) have also challenged the moral panic framework on the basis that understanding social change is not advanced by simply pointing out that 'X or Y fear is not justified by crime statistics'. By emphasizing only that fears about crime are irrational—that is, that crime statistics may be declining while fear and anxiety is increasing—one is suggesting that the only remedy to the problem would be a more informed public. However, Moore and Valverde point out that '[r]ational information and aggregate data don't necessarily counteract moral panics' (ibid.). Rather, they propose that

> [c]ampaigns to stamp out this or that moral evil, we argue, aren't reducible to or completely explained by popular ignorance and unconscious fears, and will not disappear with the application of solid information. No doubt ignorance and unconscious motives are present in popular discourses; but we believe it is high time to get away from the notion that the populace is in the grip of irrational myths and that only the enlightened philosophers (or critical sociologists) can save the world through reason and accurate facts, (ibid.: 308).

In their analysis of the panic surrounding the 'date-rape' drug Rohypnol, Moore and Valverde argue that it is more important to study the 'format than the content of the claims made by various information providers' (ibid.). Informed by a Foucauldian approach to risk management, Moore and Valverde argue that youth are exposed to a mix of messages and formats about date-rape drugs—scientific, statistical data from experts; personal anecdotes as well as moralistic sensational accounts—and perhaps borrowing from the early work of the famous Canadian mass communications expert Marshall McLuhan, Moore and Valverde argue that significance needs to be given to the 'medium' in which these mixed messages are presented as a tool for better understanding moral panics and moral regulation.

Despite these criticisms, the moral panic perspective is a useful way to think about how and why public anxiety about crime surfaces in the way that it does. We are living in a period where information technology is expanding rapidly and many people believe that society is increasingly in need of protection from the risks posed by crime. Criminology can provide insight into the various media in which crime messages are produced for public consumption; as the public embraces that technology, the messages and public response to them will pose substantial, but interesting, challenges for future criminological research.

# References

Barron, Christie, and Dany Lacombe. 2005. 'Moral panic and the nasty girl', *Canadian Review of Sociology and Anthropology* 41, 1: 51–70.

Beck, Ulrich. 1992. *Risk Society: Towards a New Modernity*. London: Sage

Becker, Howard. 1963. *Outsiders: Studies in the Sociology of Deviance*. New York: Free Press.

Ben Yehuda, Nathan. 1986. 'The sociology of moral panics: Toward a new synthesis', *Sociological Quarterly* 4: 495–513.

Berger, Arthur. 1995. *Essentials of Mass Communications Theory*. Thousand Oaks, Calif.: Sage.

Berger, Peter, and Thomas Luckmann. 1971. *The Social Construction of Reality*. London: Allen Lane.

Best, Joel. 1989. *Images of Issues: Typifying Social Problems*. Hawthorne, NY: Aldine de Gruyter.

Boyd, Neil. 1991. *High Society: Legal and Illegal Drugs in Canada*. Toronto: Key Porter Books.

Carstairs, Catherine. 2005. *Jailed for Possession: Illegal Drug Use, Regulation and Power in Canada, 1920 to 1961*. Toronto: University of Toronto Press.

Clarke, Annette. 1986. *Summary—Public Hearing Proceeding: Background Report*. Royal Commission on Employment and Unemployment. St John's: Queen's Printer.

Cohen, Stanley. 1973. *Folk Devils and Moral Panics*. London: Paladin.

———. 1985. *Visions of Social Control*. Cambridge: Polity Press.

*Controlled Drugs and Substances Act*, S.C. 1996, c. 19. 2005 (22 March). *Regulations Amending the Controlled Drugs and Substances Act (Police Enforcement) Regulations*, SOR/2005–72.

Corrigan, Philip. 1990. 'On moral regulation: Some preliminary remarks', in Philip Corrigan, ed., *Social Form, Human Capacities*. London: Routledge.

DiManno, Rosie. 2005. 'There's no going back to what we once were', *Toronto Star*, 28 Dec.

Dowler, Ken. 2003. 'Media consumption and public attitudes toward crime and justice: The relationship between fear of crime, punitive attitudes and perceived police effectiveness', *Journal of Criminal Justice and Popular Culture* 10, 2: 109–26.

Doyle, Kegan, and Dany Lacombe. 2003. 'Moral panic and child pornography: The case of Robin Sharp', in Debra Brock, ed., *Making Normal: Social Regulation in Canada*. Toronto: Thompson.

Ericson, Richard and Sophia Voumvakis. 1984. *New Accounts of Attacks on Women: Comparison of Three Toronto Newspapers*. Toronto: Centre of Criminology.

Erikson, Kai. 1966. *Wayward Puritans: A Study in the Sociology of Deviance*. New York: Wiley.

Felt, Larry, and Peter Sinclair. 1995. *Living on the Edge: The Great Northern Peninsula of Newfoundland*. St John's: ISER.

Fishman, Mark. 1978. 'Crime waves as ideology', *Social Problems* 25: 531–43.

Hagan, John. 1991. *The Disreputable Pleasures: Crime and Deviance in Canada*, 3rd ed. Toronto: McGraw-Hill.

Hall, Stuart, Charles Critcher, Tony Jefferson, John Clarke, and Brian Roberts. 1978. *Policing the Crisis: Mugging, the State, and Law and Order*. London: Macmillan.

Henry, Stuart, and Mark Lanier. 2001. *What Is Crime? Controversies over the Nature of Crime and What Is To Be Done about It*. Lanham, Md: Rowman & Littlefield.

Jacklin, A. 2009. 'Theorizing the effects of new and changing media routines on explanations crime in news'. Unpublished paper. Department of Sociology and Anthropology. University of Guelph.

Jenkins, Philip. 1994. *Using Murder: The Social Construction of Serial Homicide*. New York: Aldine de Gruyter.

Jenkins, J.P., and D. Maier-Katkin. 1992. 'Satanism: Myth and reality in a contemporary moral panic. *Crime, Law and Social Change: An International Journal* 17, 1.

Lazarsfeld, Paul, Bernard Berelson, and Hazel Gaudet. 1968. *The People's Choice: How the Voter Makes Up His Mind in a Presidential Campaign*. New York: Columbia University Press.

Leyton, Elliott. 1992. 'The theatre of public crisis', in Elliott Leyton, William O'Grady, and James Overton, *Violence and Public Anxiety: A Canadian Case*. St John's: ISER.

McCorkle, Richard, and Terrance Miethe. 2002. *Panic: The Social Construction of the Street Gang Problem*. Upper Saddle River, NJ: Prentice-Hall.

McRobbie, Angela, and Sarah Thorton. 1995. 'Rethinking "moral panic" for multi-mediated social worlds', *British Journal of Sociology* 66, 4: 559–75

Moore, Dawn, and Mariana Valverde. 2003. 'Party girls and predators: "Date rape drugs" and chronotopes of gendered risk', in Debra Brock, ed., *Making Normal: Social Regulation in Canada*. Toronto: Thompson.

O'Grady, William. 1992. 'Criminal statistics and stereotypes: The social construction of violence in Newfoundland', in Elliott Leyton, William O'Grady, and James Overton, *Violence and Public Anxiety: A Canadian Case*. St John's: ISER Books.

Pearson, Geoffrey. 1983. *Hooligan*. London: Macmillan.

Pile, Steve. 1999. 'What is a city?', in Doreen Massey, John Allen, and Steve Pile, *City Worlds*. New York: Routledge.

Reiner, Robert, and Sonia Livingstone. 1997. *Discipline or Desubordination: Changing Media Images of Crime*. Final Report ERSC Grant L210252029.

Rousmaniere, Kate, Kari Dehli, and Ning de Coninck-Smith, eds. 1997. *Discipline, Moral Regulation and Schooling: A Social History*. London: Garland Press.

Sacco, Vince. 2000. 'Media constructions of crime', in Robert Silverman, James Teevan, and Vince Sacco, *Crime in Canadian Society*, 6th ed. Toronto: Harcourt Brace.

Schissel, Bernard. 1997. *Blaming Children: Youth Crime, Moral Panics and the Politics of Hate*. Halifax: Fernwood.

Solomon, Robert, and Mel Green. 1988. 'The first century: The history of non-medical opiate use and control policies in Canada, 1870–1970', in J. Blackwell and P. Erickson, eds, *Illicit Drugs in Canada: A Risky Business*. Scarborough, Ont.: Nelson Canada, 88–104.

Sprott, Jane. 1996. 'Understanding public views of youth crime and the youth criminal justice system', *Canadian Journal of Criminology* 38, 3: 271–91.

Sprott, J.B. and A.N. Doob. 2004. 'Changing Models of Youth Justice in Canada', in M. Tonry and A. Doob, eds, *Crime and Justice: A Review of the Research*, Volume 31 Chicago: University of Chicago Press.

Statistics Canada. 2005. *The Daily*, 31 March.

Surrette, Ray. 1998. *Media, Crime and Criminal Justice: Images Are Realities*. Belmont,

Tappan, Paul. 1947. 'Who is the criminal?', *American Sociological Review* 12: 96–102.

Taylor, Ian, Paul Walton, and Jock Young. 1973. *The New Criminology: For a Social Theory of Deviance*. London: Routledge & Kegan Paul.

Williams, Paul and Julie Dickinson. 1993. 'Fear of crime: Read all about it? The relationship between newspaper crime reporting and fear of crime'. *British Journal of Criminology* 33, 1: 33–56.

# 7

## Introduction

Most Canadians, including Torontonians, believe Toronto has one of the highest crime rates in the country and that crime in the city has been on the rise. However, police reports from metropolitan areas across the country indicate that Toronto consistently has one of the lowest crime rates in Canada, both in overall crime and in many specific categories of crime, including violent ones. Moreover, the overall rate in Toronto has been falling since the early 1990s, as it has in most urban areas across the country. How can we account for such misperceptions?

In this selection the author analyzes a newspaper article on crime in Toronto in order to draw attention to both the treatment of crime in the mass media and the importance of being media literate when we consume news. What are the main points about newspaper reporting the author makes? Are they valid in assessing media reports? Has the author omitted any important points we should also take into consideration?

Finally, an important question with any case study such as this is the degree to which the findings can be extended to media reports about crime generally. What position does the author take? Do you accept or reject it, in whole or in part?

## On Rising Crime in Toronto

*Ed Ksenych*

The purpose of this article is pedagogical. Rather than presenting new research or innovative theorizing about either crime or the mass media, it aims to apply some fairly well-established sociological insights concerning the portrayal of crime in the mass media to a particular report from a Toronto area newspaper. Specifically, I want to use the report to examine how the mass media often participates in

- commercializing crime with the result of misleading the public about the realities of crime and social control
- providing a framework for interpreting the information that establishes an inaccurate connection between personal troubles involving crime and crime as a public issue, and
- creating a moral panic that has negative consequences for the police and the public in apprehending those who are endangering the lives of citizens.

Before beginning the discussion, take a moment and read the following newspaper article.[1]

# VIOLENT CRIME RISES IN TORONTO

New statistics on violent crime show an alarming upswing in the numbers of murders, assaults and complaints against the Toronto police force across the GTA.

The numbers, released Thursday, suggest that violence in Toronto is spreading whereas it's declining in other Canadian cities. In Toronto, the murder rate has skyrocketed by more than 25 per cent. There were 47 murders in 1999 which rose to 59 in 2000.

Police point to a rise in rival street gangs as the explanation for the increased street violence.

However, Norm Gardner, chair of the Police Services Board, said the numbers shouldn't spark panic. Gardner says comparing statistics between the two years does not paint an accurate picture. In 1999, he says, the homicide rate was lower than usual.

However, he noted fewer cases are being solved than in previous years. Police say witnesses are afraid to come forward.

The police department has also fuelled more complaints than ever, up by 30 per cent. There were 819 complaints against officers last year. (Metro)

## Mass Media

Discussing the article involves introducing some provisional definitions and ideas pertaining to our topic. This includes the mass media itself. The mass media are embodied in various communication industries that provide newspapers, books, radio, TV, telephone, and internet services, etc. But in sociology mass media doesn't just refer to media industries. It also refers to the type of culture generated by these industries: a culture *generally shared* in *standardized* form by *large numbers of people.*

This is a rather banal description that can easily be passed over. But let's attend to it more carefully. None of the italicized terms are insignificant. Each has implications for what will be regarded as culture (that is, the prevailing way of life and web of meanings shared by a people) by members of a group, and for how culture will be experienced and communicated. Most notably, culture undergoes standardization. But according to what standard? Mass media involves processing culture for mass consumption in a competitive market place. And this involves orienting to the standard of what's common and normal—common ideas, normal prejudices, common tastes, and so on. Otherwise, it won't appeal to, or be readily understood by, the largest number of people possible.

So how does this influence news about crime?

## The Commercialized Mass Media

'The television business is not structured to deliver quality programming to viewers but rather to deliver viewers to advertisers'.[2]

Although commenting on television, Joshua Meyrowitz provocatively presents a basic point about most mass media: they're a business. But what happens to programming when the mass media is subject to commercial interests? More specifically, what effect does communicating through a commercialized mass media have on the content of news? Czerny and Swift[3] point out there is an emphasis on:

1. the intense (there's a selective focus on action and the dramatic)
2. the unambiguous (news is presented in terms of clear and simple moral constructs and simplifies complex issues and events )
3. the familiar (news is presented to fit in with common notions and prejudices)
4. the marketable (the content is geared to consumer taste usually through the use of graphic, sensate content and imagery which often incorporates sex and violence).

Commercialization commodifies news. In doing so it distorts what's being reported upon in the above ways. But *all* communication involves distortion, and commercialization is not the only distorting factor we need to attend to. All media also work with socio-cultural codes that humans create to represent and think about reality. This is especially relevant in the mass media given the emphasis on standardization and the effort to appeal to large numbers of people.

Codes, with their systems of signs, symbols, relations among signs, and rules for interpreting signs, are an important part of how we collectively constitute meaning, or create a meaningful world, together. As Arthur Berger points out, socio-cultural *'codes are highly complex patterns of association we all learn in a given society and culture. These codes . . . affect the way we interpret signs and symbols found in the media and the way we live.'*[4]

Analyzing socio-cultural codes is complex and draws us into the field of semiotics.[5] But for our purposes I want to simply highlight the broadly shared images, ideas, qualities, or attributes that become commonly associated with some thing by members of a group, and as a result, for all practical purposes become aspects of the social reality of that thing. That thing might be a way of life (e.g., organized crime, prostitution, using drugs, etc.), or an activity (e.g., pickpocketing, policing, robbing, etc.), or some other phenomenon (e.g., juvenile delinquency, mental illness, prisons, rehabilitation, etc.).

As an example, consider the concept of 'crime' itself.[6] What comes to mind when one hears the word 'crime'? Strictly speaking, a crime in Canada is an act that violates the *Criminal Code of Canada*. But the word 'crime' doesn't usually evoke images of people cheating on their income tax, stealing materials from their workplace, or storing marijuana in their fridges—all of which are crimes. Nor are these usually reported in our newspapers. As my students repeatedly have told me, the first thing they usually associate with crime is violence in some form or another; all else is secondary. Part of this seems quite understandable. Physically harming human life is serious, and incidents of it disturb both those immediately affected and the community as a whole. Such acts stand out. But there's also a different level of symbolism to this association. All crimes entail 'violating' laws, and the seriousness of such violating is conveyed vividly and readily through an association with 'violence' even though violent crime constitutes only about 12 per cent of all reported crimes in any given year in Canada.[7] In a similar manner, what is usually associated with 'violent crime' is murder even though murder and attempted murder together constitute less than 1 per cent of all violent crime.

But the main function of socio-cultural codes is not to develop associations that provide accurate empirical representations of what actually is the case, although on occasion they might. Their main function is social and symbolic. And a code fulfills this function if it assists us in communicating effectively at a general level. Nevertheless, members of the group using the code may begin to assume or associate the qualities being portrayed in the code as being part of the actual thing being represented or signified.

## Personal Troubles and Public Issues Regarding Crime

We can expect to find the pressures of commercialization as well as the very nature of socio-cultural codes in communication having a distorting effect on all content in the mass media, including news reports about crime. But Vincent Sacco[8] alerts us to another important dimension of news reports about crime. News reports provide a framework for connecting personal troubles and public issues, and often suggest an explanation of the issue.

> *'While the distinction between private troubles and public issues is an important one, these dimensions are not independent. Citizens' personal troubles with crime provide the building blocks out of which public issues are constructed. On the other hand, the warnings of danger implicit in public pronouncements about the seriousness and pervasiveness of crime problems may be a source of private trouble if they increase the fear of crime among those who have routine exposure to such pronouncements.*
>
> *Central to the interplay between individuals' private troubles with crime and the social issue of crime are the mass media. . . . News about crime is most frequently news about the occurrence or processing of private trouble in the form of specific criminal events. . . . Public issues grow up around private troubles when the experiences of individuals are understood as exemplifying a larger social problem, and the news media play a vital role in the construction of such problems (Best, 1989; Gusfield, 1989; Schneider, 1985). . . . Any particular social problem can be framed in many ways, and these various frames imply different causal attributions and prospective solutions (Gusfield, 1989; Schneider, 1985). Because they are able to legitimate some views and to marginalize others, the news media are an important part of this framing process'.*

Most news reports are not just about an incident. The incident is presented as an example of, or tied in with, a broader public issue or social problem, and there is usually an implied or explicit theory, framed in causal terms, about the issue or problem. Later on in his discussion Sacco also notes that these frameworks are usually presented under the authority of a police perspective. All of this can be accomplished quite simply and unobtrusively by reporting, for example, that *'the city's 18th homicide of the year occurred this morning at George Street and Reynolds Avenue. Police suspect it was another instance of an ongoing turf war between rival gangs over supplying drugs in the south end of the city'.* Here the killing is portrayed through the count as an instance of a broader public issue of homicides in the city, and the police reference intimates that this issue primarily concerns street violence involving gangs and drugs. Because of the nature of this particular incident, there is no need to note that Canada's 2004 General Social Survey found that three quarters of violent incidents do not occur on a street or other public place, but in homes and commercial or public institutions (and that figure excludes reported incidents of spousal sexual or physical assault).

Anthony Westell makes a similar point about information and frameworks in news reports, but highlights its significance for political debate and discussion:

> 'If it is true that the quality of public debate is a measure of democracy, then the mass media constitute a vital political institution. The news media provide not only most of the information upon which political discussion must be based, but also the interpretive frameworks that shape the debate. . . . The media . . . define what is normal and respectable in a society, what is debatable and what is beyond discussion by decent, responsible citizens'.[9]

The news and other programming can convey such interpretive frameworks quite explicitly. But often, they are conveyed implicitly in how reports are organized and present information, as we shall see. And media research and theory has been telling us for some time that *how* something is communicated is even more consequential than *what* is communicated with regard to the overall message.[10]

## Generating Moral Panic

A final idea we need to attend to before examining the article is that socio-cultural codes are often developed and used within the mass media as part of creating moral panic with regard to social problems and public issues.[11]

Moral panic refers to the magnification of problems for political effect and arousing moral sentiment. Practically, this often involves persuading the audience to the act of agreement using strategies other than reasonable argumentation or providing strong evidence, such as

- misusing statistics (that is, playing with numbers and definitions of what's being counted)
- repeating words or ideas (that is, making something believable, no matter now far fetched, simply by repeating it over and over again)
- a manipulative and irresponsible use of rhetoric (that is, employing a lot of emotional, moralistic, or dramatic language to convey a point or message)
- demonizing (framing the description and the discussion of something in terms of a bipolar mythic narrative based on a contest between good and evil; fear and courage; order and chaos).[12]

## Rising Crime in Toronto

With these main ideas in mind, let's return to the article. I encountered this news report in a Toronto area newspaper on an early morning commute to work. The Metro is a tabloid newspaper published by Torstar distributed for free throughout the city's transit system, in part, as a public service. And many of the articles are selected, shortened versions of longer articles that appear in the *Toronto Star*.

'*Violent crime rises in Toronto*'. The newspaper headline startled me. Having studied deviance and social control, I was aware that crime rates have generally been declining in Canada and Toronto since 1991. Furthermore, I was aware that violent crime rates have also been generally declining except for occasional rises in some categories, and that Toronto was, and continues to be, one of the safest cities in Canada. That includes comparing Toronto with smaller Census Metropolitan Areas (CMAs) as well as larger ones.[13] So I took a second look. Let's do the same together.

Newspaper reporters and editors are aware that generally readers scan headlines to find ones of interest. Then, they may examine the subheading, and if they're interested, they'll begin reading the article. Most readers usually stop after the first couple of paragraphs. And only the most interested will usually read the article in its entirety. Given this, consider how this article has been organized.

Does the headline actually present an accurate summary of the news being reported by the anonymous author of the article? And what of the subheading? It highlights '**new statistics** on *violent crime show an* **alarming upswing** *in the number of* **murders, assaults and complaints** *against the Toronto police force across the GTA*'.

Then there's the first half of the article itself. '*The* **numbers**, *released Thursday, suggests that* **violence in Toronto is spreading**, *whereas it's* **declining in other Canadian cities**. *In Toronto, the* **murder rate** *has* **skyrocketed** *by more than* **25 per cent**. *There were* **47 murders** *in 1999 which rose to* **59** *in 2000.* **Police** *point to a rise in* **rival street gangs** *as the* **explanation** *for the* **increased street violence**'.

At this point, most readers will usually stop reading. So let's look at what they've encountered and may believe they've accurately understood about the topic being reported upon. There are many things that can be said about the article so far. But notice

- the highlighting and repetition of 'violence' as well as words associated with violence (e.g., murders, assaults, street gangs, street violence) from the beginning to the end of this short portion
- the use of raw numbers rather than rates as well as the omission of any kind of broader historical context for interpreting the numbers beyond one year to the next
- the use of dramatic and emotional language (e.g., new statistics, alarming upswing, spreading (like a disease), skyrocketed, rival gangs)
- the focus on the number of murders as the sole indicator of an article purportedly about 'violent crime in Toronto'
- the explanation of the number of murders by locating the cause of the social problem in rival street gangs, and couching this explanation in a bipolar opposition between 'police' and 'gangs' (good versus evil).

The article is an example of creating moral panic. In it we are presented with an overly simplistic, dramatic explanation of the complex public issue of violent crime that's framed in terms of a familiar, unambiguous demonic framework.

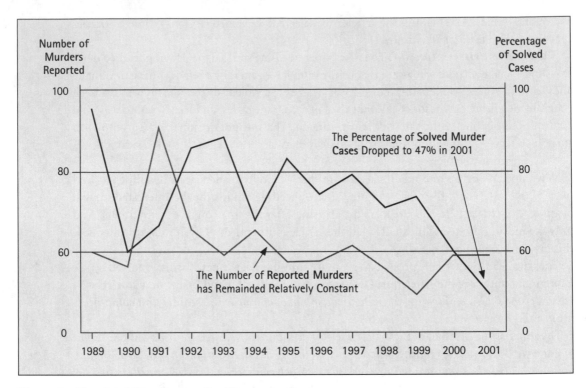

Figure 7.1 Unsolved Murders on the Rise
Homicides Compared with Solved Cases, Annually, in the City of Toronto

Source: Adapted from Metropolitan Toronto Police and *The Globe and Mail*

But what happens when we move on to the second half of the article, the half most newspaper readers typically don't even get to. The second half opens with *'However, Norm Gardiner, chair of the Police Services Board, said* the numbers shouldn't spark panic'. What?!? An anonymous reporter has just informed us in very dramatic terms that we have an 'alarming upswing' in the 'spread of violence' caused by 'rival street gangs'. And now we're being told not to panic. Let's examine the data Mr. Gardiner has in mind but that isn't presented in this article. I've drawn them from another newspaper article published at about the same time in another Toronto newspaper[14] (see Figure 7.1).

These statistics, which track murders over a longer period, indicate that at the time of the article the *number* of murders in Toronto had generally been holding constant for several years (even though the overall population had been increasing). But from 1997 to 1999 the raw number declined significantly. And in 2000, the year this article is reporting on, the raw numbers returned to their usual level. That return to their more usual number was the 'alarming 25 per cent upswing'.

But let's continue with this short article, even though most readers would have probably stopped reading by now. We encounter another 'however'. Only this time it concerns what *really* is the news. '*[Gardiner] noted* fewer cases are being solved *than previous years. Witnesses are afraid to come forward.* The police department has also fueled more complaints than ever, *up by 30 per cent*.

The really significant news was not that violent crime was rising at an alarming rate in Toronto, but that fewer cases were being solved by the police. In the case of murders it dropped from over 70 per cent to under 50 per cent in just two years. And the police located the cause in the failure of witnesses to speak up. At the same time, complaints against the police department trying to solve these cases rose by 30 per cent. So a more accurate headline for the article would have been 'Number of Murders Return to Normal but Police Solving Fewer Cases and Encountering More Complaints'.

## Conclusion

Of course, there are many kinds of reports about crime in newspapers and the mass media overall. And an important question is how representative this report actually is. In my experience, over the years Toronto area newspapers have often presented many reasonably accurate articles about crime. But my contention is that what is going on in this article is more representative of the kind of reporting readers usually encounter than articles which challenge, or offer an alternative to, such reporting.

Nevertheless, the article does finally identify an important problem that needs to be publicly discussed and which continues to be pertinent today: why are fewer citizens assisting police in solving murders?

It is difficult to make valid claims about the effects of media messages on an audience without carefully studying how the audience interprets and processes the messages.[15] But research has indicated for some time that when people believe, even erroneously, that their environment is dangerous, they become fearful, withdraw from community participation, and endorse the state using more punitive measures to respond to crime.[16] I would contend that one reason why citizens in Toronto were not assisting police was that the public is being oriented to as consumers, rather than as citizens, by a commercialized mass media producing crime reports like the one we've examined here.

## Notes

1. 'Violent Crime Rises in Toronto', *Metro*, May 25–27, 2001.
2. Joshua Meyrowitz, 'Television: The Shared Arena', *The World and I*, 1990. As reprinted in Ed Ksenych and David Liu (eds.), *The Pleasure of Inquiry: Readings in Sociology*, Thomson Nelson, 2008: 263.
3. Michael Czerny and Jamie Swift, *Getting Started on Social Analysis in Canada*, 2nd ed. Toronto: Between the Lines Press, 1988.
4. Arthur Asa Berger, *Media Analysis Techniques*, revised edition, Sage, 1991: 23.
5. Ibid. Berger; Roland Barthes, *Mythologies*, Noonday Press/Farrar, Straus and Giroux, 1957; M. Danesi and D. Santeramo (eds.), *Introducing Semiotics: An Anthology of Readings*, Toronto: Canadian Scholars Press, 1992; Wolfgang Iser, *How to Do Theory*, Blackwell, 2006.
6. Law Commission of Canada, *What is a Crime? Challenges and Alternatives: Discussion paper*, Her Majesty the Queen in Right of Canada, 2003.
7. 'Crime Statistics: 2006', *The Daily*, Statistics Canada, Wednesday, July 18, 2007.
8. Vincent Sacco, 'Media Constructions of Crime' in R. Silverman, J. Teevan, and Vincent F. Sacco (eds.). *Crime in Canadian Society*, 6th ed. Toronto: Harcourt Brace, 2000: 11. The references in the quote are to: J. Best, (ed.),

'The Impact of a Crime Wave: Perceptions, Fear, and Confidence in the Police', *Law and Society Review,* 17 (1989): 317–334; J.R. Gusfield, 'Constructing the Ownership of Social Problems: Fun and Profit in the Welfare State', *Social Problems,* 36 (1989), 431–441; J.W. Schenider, 'Social Problems Theory: The Constructionist View', *Annual Review of Sociology,* 11 (1985): 209–229.

9.  Anthony Westell, *The New Society,* McClelland and Stewart, 1977: 73.

10. MacLean, Eleanor, *Between the Lines,* Montreal: Black Rose Press, 1981.

11. Stanley Cohen, *Folk Devils and Moral Panics,* London: MacGibbons and Kee, 1977.

12. See Linda Deutschmann, 'Prescientific Approaches to Deviance' in *Deviance and Social Control,* 4th edition, Thomson Nelson, 2007.

13. 'Crime Statistics: 2006', *The Daily,* Statistics Canada, Wednesday, July 18, 2007.

14. 'Unsolved Murders on the Rise', *Globe and Mail,* December 21, 2001.

15. Sacco, op.cit..; John F. Manzo and Monetta M. Bailey, 'On the Assimilation of Racial Stereotypes Among Black Canadian Young Offenders', *Canadian Review of Sociology and Anthropology,* Vol. 42, No. 3 (2005): 283–300.

16. Craig Haney and John Manzolati, 'Television Criminology' in Elliot Aronson (ed.), readings *About the Social Animal,* 3rd edition, W. H. Freeman, 1981: 125–126; Kenneth Dowler, 'Media Consumption and Public Attitudes Toward Crime and Justice: The Relationship Between Fear of Crime, Punitive Attitudes, and Perceived Police Effectiveness', *Journal of Criminal Justice and Popular Culture,* 10 (2) [2003]: 109–126.

# 8

## Introduction

The concept of function has been important in sociology from Durkheim's early work on. Durkheim theorized that persistent features of a society, including those often regarded as undesirable, are present because, on a social-structural level, they perform functions that contribute to the well-being of the group as a whole. Later, American sociologists elaborated on Durkheim's insight in developing a theoretical approach called structural-functionalism. They noted that the contributions can be 'manifest' (immediately visible and identifiable) as well as 'latent' (hidden and visible only upon careful study and reflection). And they proposed that the contributions related primarily to promoting cohesion, solidarity, group stability, and/or adjustment to changing environmental conditions, both physical and historical.

This approach can also be used to analyze subparts of a group such as social institutions, recurrent practices, ritual activities, narrative patterns, and so on. In these cases, the analysis also examines how the 'structure' contributes to the practical and social tasks the subpart performs in the wider system. And the analysis can become complicated even further by studying how the same phenomenon can be both functional and dysfunctional in a group at the same time.

In this study, Grabe uses the functionalist approach to explore how news about crime contributes to maintaining a moral order, promoting social cohesion, legitimizing social control, and sustaining unequal power relations among groups in American society. Are her arguments equally applicable to Canadian society? Are there any functions that you think she has omitted?

# Television News Magazines and Functionalism

*Maria Elizabeth Grabe*

The injustice and human suffering which result from crime have been well-documented and lamented. Yet, the widespread occurrence of crime persists. Emile Durkheim (1933, 1938, 1951), Kai Erikson (1966), Michel Foucault (1979), and George Herbert Mead (1918) provide a controversial explanation of the persistence and prevalence of crime over the centuries. Unlike the popular belief that crime is a menace that must be obliterated, these scholars argue that crime is an inherent part of a healthy society. Rituals whereby crime is processed and punished function on a number of levels to sustain social structure. Whether there is consensus as to the desirability of the system that is maintained, of course, does not affect the functionality of these rituals in aiding that system's stability.

The existence of crime provides society's members with the opportunity to publicly draw and recognize the line between good and evil. Furthermore, crime rituals promote social cohesion. When the criminal is presented as violating the collective sentiments of a society, its members unify in their condemnation of the criminal. Crime, and the punishment thereof, can also be viewed as a form of social control, where potential criminals are scared into submission to society's rules and regulations.

Beyond the mass media's ritualization of the three Durkheimian functions of crime—to construct morality, promote cohesion, and impose social control—this study is concerned with the mass media's functional presentations of demographic relationships between criminals and victims. According to Gerbner et al. (1979), demographic profiles of violent criminals and the portrayed repercussions of their actions often demonstrate power relations to society's members by communicating 'who gets away with what against whom' (181). Although Gerbner takes a functionalist view on this construction of a social order, he fundamentally opposes the notion that crime, and the mass mediation thereof, is a 'healthy' part of social systems. Instead he views the narratives of crime stories (fictional or non-fictional) as cultivating an oppressing 'scary view' of the world which musters support for police power and ultimately aids in maintaining the status quo.

## The Study of Narrative Content

The above functional views of crime assume the mass dissemination of rituals and myths surrounding the occurrence of criminal acts by which the immorality of deviant behaviour is made known. In other words, crime becomes functional when it is constructed into a narrative and made public. Before the existence of mass media, societies relied on public rituals like torture and executions to demonstrate the notion of justice (Cromer 1978; Erikson 1966; Foucault 1979; Garfinkel 1956; Rusche and Kirchheimer 1939; Schattenburg 1981). In fact, Erikson (1966) links the disappearance of public execution with the development of the newspaper. It is therefore not unreasonable to suspect that contemporary mass media provide the platform for public rituals and communication of myths about crime.

## Crime News as Myth and Ritual

Ericson (1991) observes that the mass media and the justice system constitute two institutions jointly responsible for much of what we learn about the social order. Together they turn events in the physical world into narratives '. . . of what ought to be, fusing facts with normative commitments, values, and myths' (Ericson 1991: 223). Many scholars have described journalism as a process of mythmaking. Following Carey's (1975) ritual view of communication, news is not information but drama—it does not describe the world, but portrays an arena of dramatic forces and action. Along the same lines, Condit (1987), Glasser and Ettema (1989), Ettema and Glasser (1988), Gans (1979), and Knight and Dean (1982) argue that through ritualistic mythmaking, journalism re-inscribes and updates society's consensual views on morality by publicly defining what is right and wrong, innocence and guilt. Gans (1979: 293) goes so far as to claim that the news media helps to 'punish those who deviate from these values'.

In order to investigate the pragmatic potential of news to perpetuate the moral order, promote social cohesion, impose social control, and define power relations, it is necessary to uncover the specific functional myths that underlie crime stories. Durkheim (1933: 65–110; 1951: 335–392) argues that the ritualization of crime is a powerful means to draw publicly the line between good and evil, thereby constructing morality. Thus, if crime news stories play a part in constructing morality, we could expect them to clearly assign the roles of good and evil to police and criminals and to prominently frame crime in terms of the struggle between good and evil. This leads to the first hypothesis:

H1: News stories will frame crime in terms of a struggle between good and evil and primarily assign police and criminals to these roles.

Durkheim (1933: 73–74) and Ericson and Haggerty (1997: 448) theorize that criminal violations of public sentiments provoke a shared outrage aimed at the criminal (and not the societal causes of crime) among society's members which indirectly promotes social cohesion and integration. Fictional television crimes are commonly portrayed as resulting from individual causes such as material greed and psychological instability (Barrile 1980, 1986; Haney and Manzolati 1981). By ignoring possible structural causes for crime, such as poverty or racism, the criminal is portrayed as society's enemy who deserves shared hate and banishment. If crime news stories play a part in promoting social cohesion we could expect them to promote outrage against criminals by presenting them as irrational villains who are responsible for violating society's moral values. This leads to the second hypothesis:

H2: News stories will present criminals as villains who are personally responsible for violating society's moral values.

Durkheim (1933: 65–110; 1951: 335–392) and Ericson and Haggerty (1997: 53, 54 and 360, 361) argue that the processing and punishment of crime provides an opportunity to discourage those who contemplate criminal behaviour and intimidate them into submission to society's rules and laws. Dominick (1973) and Estep and Macdonald (1985) reveal that in television fiction, almost without exception, crime doesn't pay. If crime news stories play a part in promoting social control, they will prominently present the idea that crime is not profitable. This leads to the third hypothesis:

H3: News stories will prominently feature the 'crime does not pay' myth.

According to Gerbner et al. (1979) demographic profiles of criminals and their victims have the narrative potential of communicating society's power structure to its members. Research on fictional narratives reveals the marginalization of women and African Americans. Emphasis on African Americans as society's criminals promotes suspicion and distrust of this race group and when women are routinely featured in fictional crime stories as victims of crime this gender group's vulnerable social position is reaffirmed. If crime news stories contribute to the perpetuation of hierarchical power relationships, we can expect these stories to present women as the victims of crime and African Americans as the criminal villains. This leads to the fourth hypothesis:

H4: News stories will present women as the victims of crime and African Americans as criminals.

# Method

This study focuses on news magazine programs because they feature self-contained narrative segments and allow for relatively lengthy and elaborate storytelling compared to the short and fragmented format of stories on local and national newscasts. In recent times scholars have argued that the distinction between the so-called tabloid and traditional approaches to news reporting is disappearing (Bird 1992; Knight 1989; Knight and Dean 1982). For the purpose of this study, both tabloid and traditional news magazine programs were included in the investigation. The specific tabloid programs are 'Inside Edition', 'A Current Affair', 'American Journal',' and 'Hard Copy'. The specific traditional programs are: 'Dateline NBC', 'Prime Time Live', 'Turning Point', '48 Hours', 'Eye to Eye with Connie Chung', '60 Minutes', 'Day One', and '20/20'.

Instead of a composite month of television programming, the news magazine programs examined in this study were exhaustively sampled over a six month period (October 1, 1994 to March 31, 1995). An additional week of these television broadcasts (April 1–7, 1995) was used in coder training sessions. Half a year of television news magazine programs provided 713 programs and 2,783 individual story segments which amounted to 272 hours of material for the analysis. It is important to use an uninterrupted time period for this study because major crime stories tend to evolve over several weeks and a randomly sampled composite month of television content would only provide fragments of this evolving storytelling process.

# Coding Instrument

Coding was based on what was portrayed, reported, suggested, or implied in the content of the news programs. A crime story is defined as a program segment which features one or more acts of breaking the law as central to the narrative. Only a subset of all segments, based on this criterion, was coded. Segments identified as 'crime stories' by virtue of their focus on crime were analyzed using the portrayed , mentioned, or inferred criminal, victim, and criminal act as three separate recording units. A crime story may have multiple crimes, criminals, and victims, and in such instances, coders coded each criminal, victim, and crime separately. The criminal was identified as the person, group, or organization suggested, suspected, accused, charged, or found guilty of a crime. Three important aspects were considered when coding a criminal. First; the criminal had to be central to the crime narrative. In other words, the criminal had to make a considerable and critical contribution to the construction of the crime narrative. Second, 'suspect', 'accused', 'perpetrator', or 'sentenced criminal' were all coded. Once someone was identified as a criminal suspect (lawfully guilty or not) and presented as such in the story, he or she was included in this investigation. Third, this study also included group and corporate criminality. In such instances, each of the identified members of the corporation or group responsible for the crime were [sic] separately coded as criminals.

The victim was identified as the person or group which suffered due to criminal actions. Four important aspects were considered when coding a victim. First, as with the criminal, the victim had to be central to the crime narrative. Stories may provide criminals without victims. In such instances, only the presented criminal was coded. Second, in cases of group victimization, each central victim appearing, inferred, or described was coded separately. Third, when animals were presented as the victims of a crime, the 'other' option was coded on all items except those related to the severity of the victimization. Finally, in order for someone to be coded as a victim, he or she had to be a direct or primary victim of the criminal act. When acquaintances or family members of the primary victim were portrayed as secondary victims (e.g., they lost the murdered family member) they were not coded as victims.

The crime is the act committed by the criminal, which establishes a relationship with a victim (except of course in the case of a victimless crime). As with the criminal and victim, each criminal act central to the crime narrative was coded. Presentation of the criminal act was scrutinized for its nature, motivation, and the aftermath. The outcome of the crime was examined on a number of different levels. The prevalence of the 'crime doesn't pay' myth, the struggle between good and evil, and the portrayed roles of the criminal, victim, and law enforcement system in the struggle between good and evil were recorded. The coding instrument also assessed the physical and psychological harm done to the victim as a result of the crime.

Criminals and victims were coded for demographic information including gender, race, age, class, occupational status, criminal history of the suspect, and the alleged criminal's guilt or innocence.

## Establishing a Moral Order

The majority of society's members believe in the efficiency, accuracy, and fairness of the criminal justice system. With few exceptions, law enforcement officers are viewed as the protectors of society's members, and the mass media generally reaffirm this notion by portraying the officers of the system as effective and fair in their efforts to guard common morality. In the programs under investigation, law enforcement officers were cast as the good force (78 per cent of cases) fighting against evil criminals in the classic battle between these two forces, confirming Hypothesis 1. The victim was in most cases (91.3 per cent) the helpless good person whom the criminal preyed upon. The criminal took the prominent role as the evil force in 93.5 per cent of cases. By unambiguously assigning police officers to the role of the good force fighting evil, criminals to the role of the evil force, and victims to the role of the helpless prey of evil, clear lines between acceptable and unacceptable behaviour are drawn—thereby contributing to constructing society's moral values.

## Promoting Social Cohesion

Support for Hypothesis 2 was found on two levels. First, the patterned presentation of criminals as guilty, before the criminal justice system has taken its course, prematurely vilifies suspects. Most crime reports preceded the criminal's day in court. Most often (in 86.5 per cent of cases) the suspect was arrested, yet in most cases (69.7 per cent) the outcome of the criminal justice process after the arrest remained unknown. In only 17.9 per cent of cases the arrested criminal was shown to have been found guilty and in only 14.4 per cent of cases was the criminal sentenced. This did not discourage presentations of the criminal as guilty. More than 95 per cent of the portrayed criminals were presented as guilty (see Table 8.1). Similar character assassinations of alleged criminals are common in television fiction (Cromer 1978). Garfinkel (1956) refers to these portrayals as mass mediated degradation ceremonies which

| Table 8.1 Promoting Social Cohesion | | |
|---|---|---|
| Variable | Frequency | % |
| **Criminal Arrested** | | |
| Yes | 1,119 | 86.5 |
| No | 166 | 12.8 |
| Unknown / Other | 8 | 0.7 |
| **Criminal Found Guilty?** | | |
| Yes | 231 | 17.9 |
| No | 162 | 12.5 |
| Unknown / Other | 900 | 69.7 |
| **Implied that the criminal is guilty?** | | |
| Yes | 1,238 | 95.7 |
| No | 37 | 2.9 |
| Unknown / Other | 18 | 1.4 |
| **Implied that the criminal is innocent?** | | |
| Yes | 92 | 7.1 |
| No | 1,196 | 92.5 |
| Unknown / Other | 5 | 0.4 |
| **Motivation** | | |
| Greed | 223 | 17.2 |
| Material Desperation | 13 | 1.0 |
| Protection of Social Status | 336 | 26.0 |
| Psychological Instability | 1,177 | 91.0 |
| Romantic / Domestic Revenge | 714 | 55.2 |
| Alcoholic / Drug Abuse | 168 | 13.0 |
| Avenging Justice | 17 | 1.3 |
| Other Motivation | 30 | 2.3 |

**Note:** The "unknown" option includes cases in which no suggestion or information related to the categorical issue at hand was provided. The "other" item is an attempt to exhaust options within categories. It comprises cases which could not be fitted into either of the options within categories. The motivations of crime were not coded as mutually exclusive categories. This allowed coders to indicate if more than one of the above motivations were presented as the reason for a criminal act.

publicly deliver a curse upon the criminal and call for all of society to witness the ritual destruction of the deviant character. Ultimately these degradation ceremonies serve to promote social solidarity because the members of a society unify in their outrage against the criminal's violation of their common values. The criminal fulfills the important function of representing the evil force in society's never-ending battle against evil. Therefore, it is noteworthy that news magazine programs were quick to turn suspects into guilty and evil criminals.

Second, the criminal was presented as having sole responsibility for violating society's moral values. From Table 8.1 it is clear that, of all the motivations for crime, psychological instability was featured most often. Most important though is that portrayals of individual causes for crime (such as psychological instability, 91 per cent; revenge, 55.2 per cent; protection of social status, 26 per cent; greed, 17 per cent; drug abuse, 13 per cent; and avenging justice, 3 per cent) overshadowed structural causes of crime such as poverty (1 per cent). Barrile (1986) reports similar emphases on individual causes for crime in television fiction and labels it the 'personalized' crime perspective. By virtually ignoring possible structural causes for crime (such as poverty or racism) criminals are portrayed as society's irrational enemies who deserve little sympathy because they presumably act as a result of their own will. In the Durkheimian (1933: 73–74) view, these supposedly self-interested acts that violate the common morality of society's members provoke a shared outrage against the criminal (and not societal institutions), promote social cohesion and integration, and ultimately camouflage the need to change the status quo.

It is noteworthy that 97.7 per cent of all crimes were fully explained in terms of the above motivations (i.e., as a result of greed, material desperation, protection of social status, psychological instability, revenge, alcohol or drug abuse, and avenging justice). The FBI's uniform crime reports provide limited insights into the causes of crime. Yet, there are indications that individual causes of crime play a remarkably small role in motivating criminal behaviour. Only 6.91 per cent of murders are motivated by greed and 4.93 per cent of murders are committed because of revenge (Federal Bureau of Investigation 1994). Nevertheless, the television news magazine world functionally emphasizes individual causes for crime, thereby promoting a view of criminals as self-interested violators of social values.

## Imposing Social Control

As Table 8.2 shows, the vast majority of news magazine reported crimes (88.6 per cent) were violent. Yet, the FBI's uniform crime reports (Federal Bureau of Investigation 1994) indicate a vastly different ratio between violent and non-violent crime: Only 13.4 per cent of crimes are violent. Yet murder was the most prevalent (71.1 per cent) outcome of the criminal act in the news magazine programs. By contrast, FBI (1994) crime statistics indicate that murder constitutes just 0.16 per cent of all crimes and 1.23 per cent of all violent crimes committed in the United States. Only 10.7 per cent of victims in news magazine programs escaped without any physical injuries (see Table 8.2). Psychological injury as a result of the crime appeared prominently (93 per cent) in the news stories under investigation.

This disproportionate emphasis on violence and injury reflects what Gerbner (1988) describes as the process of cultivating fear in television viewers. As we become socialized and

**Table 8.2** Promoting Social Control

| Variable | Frequency | % |
|---|---|---|
| **Crime Type** | | |
| Violent | 1,145 | 88.6 |
| Weapon Used | 871 | 67.4 |
| Sex | 142 | 11.0 |
| Property | 129 | 10.0 |
| Financial | 53 | 4.1 |
| **Physical Harm** | | |
| Killed | 1,102 | 71.1 |
| Serious Injury | 119 | 7.7 |
| Light Injury | 96 | 6.2 |
| Unharmed | 167 | 10.7 |
| Unknown Other | 66 | 4.3 |
| **Psychological Injury** | | |
| Yes | 386 | 93.0 |
| No | 29 | 7.0 |
| Unknown/Other | 0 | 0.0 |
| **Suggested That Crime Doesn't Pay** | | |
| Yes | 952 | 73.6 |
| No | 86 | 6.7 |
| Unknown/Other | 255 | 19.7 |
| **Suggested That Crime Pays** | | |
| Yes | 224 | 17.3 |
| No | 678 | 52.4 |
| Unknown Other | 391 | 30.3 |
| **Punishment Other Than the Criminal Justice System** | | |
| Yes | 419 | 32.4 |
| No | 828 | 64.0 |
| Unknown/Other | 46 | 3.6 |

observe patterned portrayals of violence in the symbolic world of prime time, we make our own calculations about the risk of becoming a victim of crime (Gerbner 1988). If the members of a society are repeatedly instructed that violence and psychological injury are common outcomes of crime, their understanding of the seriousness of this act is greatly inflated.

The drama and narrative potential of crime stories as powerful lessons about social control, morality, social cohesion, and power relations are therefore enhanced.

Social control was further promoted in the content of the programs under investigation by making it clear that crime doesn't pay. This study assessed the prevalence of this crime lesson in two ways. First, the inevitability of a criminal's arrest (86.5 per cent of cases, see Table 8.1) implies that virtually all criminals are brought into the cold light of justice. The tendency to portray law enforcement efforts as swift, effective, and fair is common in television fiction. Knutson (1974: 29) argues that, in television detective series, police officers are presented as dedicated protectors of morality. Haney and Manzolati (1981) did not find a single instance where the 'wrong man' was in custody at the end of television fiction shows. This tendency to portray the police as infallible creates an illusion of certainty and trust in law enforcement (Haney and Manzolati 1981).

Second, the outcome of 73.6 per cent of all crime stories was coded as presenting the 'crime doesn't pay' myth. Even when criminals escaped the long arm of the criminal justice system (32.4 per cent of cases), they faced alternative forms of punishment (i.e., personal tragedy or victimization by another criminal), thereby reaffirming that crime doesn't pay (see Table 8.2).

Narratives about police efficiency and the unprofitability of crime were prominently featured in news magazine crime stories, supporting Hypothesis 3. Public displays of arrests can be interpreted as fear-provoking warnings against criminal pursuits of self-interest. As Durkheim (1933: 86), Mead (1918: 587), and Foucault (1979: 32–69) argued, they are a way of instilling the paralyzing fear of retribution in the minds of those who contemplate evil.

## Reaffirming Power Relations

Hypothesis 4 was also supported. Criminals in news magazine programs are mostly male (85 per cent), African American (53.3 per cent), adult (68.1 per cent), upper-class (50 per cent), and legitimately employed (66.7 per cent). Considering the race and age of criminals, the FBI's demographic profile for criminals differs noticeably from what was found in the content of the programs under investigation. In fact, according to uniform crime reports (Federal Bureau of Investigation 1994) state prison inmates are most often Caucasian (49.1 per cent) and young adults (45.7 per cent). However, similar to the content of news magazine programs, FBI reports indicate that most criminals are employed (67.3 per cent) and male (94.5 per cent).

The focus on African Americans as the group most likely to commit criminal behaviour may contribute to the marginalization of this race group. It is important to note that African American criminals were also portrayed as the most prominent victimizers of both Caucasians (58 per cent) and people from their own race (67.7 per cent, see Table 8.3). These portrayals have the potential to reaffirm Caucasian distrust of African Americans. Indeed, it hardly promotes the social integration of this race.

**Table 8.3** Crosstabulation of Criminal's and Victim's Race and Gender

| Victim | | Criminal | |
| --- | --- | --- | --- |
| Race | Caucasian | African American | Latino |
| Caucasian | 39.2 | 58.0 | 2.8 |
| African American | 29.7 | 67.6 | 2.7 |
| Latino | 40.0 | 10.0 | 50.0 |
| Gender | Male | Female | |
| Male | 75.2 | 24.8 | |
| Female | 94.9 | 5.1 | |

The demographic profile of the victim differs from that of the criminal in all variables but social class. Unlike what is reported in the news magazines programs under investigation, the FBI crime reports indicate that young black males are most likely to become crime victims (Federal Bureau of Investigation 1994).

Caucasian, young adult, upper-class females who are legitimately employed could be viewed as the group most frequently competing with males in the workplace. It is therefore noteworthy that women were presented as most likely to be victims of crime. One can certainly argue that this portrayal serves the existing social order by communicating to aspiring females that they are the group in society most likely to become victims of crime.

Cross-tabulations of gender and labour status reveal that working women (58.7 per cent) were more likely than working men (29.4 per cent) to be victimized in the workplace. Furthermore, the group of working women that was portrayed as victims was also more likely to be victimized in the workplace (58.7 per cent) than at home (31.4 per cent). There is reason to argue that these portrayals send the discouraging message to women that the workplace is a dangerous environment.

As Table 8.3 shows, male criminals were more likely to victimize females (94.9 per cent of female victimizations) than people of their own sex (75.2 per cent of male victimizations). Weapons like knives and guns, as well as the male body itself, were used in the process of victimization. These prominent portrayals of men using weapons and sex against their female victims are an intimidating reaffirmation of male dominance.

The race variable also produced noteworthy results pertaining to sex crimes, the use of weapons other than the body, and ultimately the communication of power relations. Portrayals of the African American as armed and dangerous deepen this group's marginalization and perhaps even perpetuate justification for police brutality against African American offenders.

The relationship between the criminal's gender and the portrayed motivations for the crime offer insight into how society publicly distinguishes between demographic groups. Cross-tabulations of the criminal's gender and motivation for crime reveal that female criminals were presented as more irrational than male criminals. In fact, female criminals were more likely than male criminals to be portrayed as committing crimes because of greed (29.4 per cent vs. 15.6 per cent) and drug or alcohol abuse (86.7 per cent vs. 13.3 per cent). By contrast, the male criminal was motivated by more 'rational' needs (i.e., protection of his social status, 27.9 per cent, versus 1.8 per cent of females). These portrayals emphasize the view of women as unstable, substance abusing, and pathologically greedy beings. This image of women as greedy is further encouraged by the fact that more female (19 per cent) than male (8.8 per cent) criminals were portrayed as committing property crimes. When a society succeeds in constructing demographic distinctions like these, the inclusion and exclusion of distinct groups in different aspects of social life become inevitable.

## Conclusion

This study found support for the notion that the rituals whereby crime is made public serve social functions. In the Durkheimian tradition, the results of this study suggest that crime stories provide a potential means for negotiating society's morality by drawing clear lines between good and evil. Moreover, by frequently and prominently offering the criminal for public scrutiny and by promoting outrage against the criminal's violation of the public's common morality, social solidarity and integration may be promoted.

This study also suggests that the construction of crime narratives involves the casting of demographic groups at different levels of the social order, thereby re-inscribing hierarchical power relations and re-establishing stereotypes. African Americans were presented as criminals who cannot be trusted while women were marginalized as helpless victims, particularly those who dare to leave their homes to pursue careers. These messages are strikingly conservative in times when institutionalized support of women and minorities is supposedly correcting inequalities between race and gender groups. In fact, this study's results support the notion that television mass disseminates messages to nurture the survival of the existing social order.

## References

Barrile, L.G. 1986. 'Television's "bogeyclass"?: Status, motives, and violence in crime drama characters'. *Sociological Viewpoints* 2: 39–56.

Bird, S.E. 1992. *For inquiring minds: A cultural study of supermarket tabloids*. Knoxville, TN: The University of Tennessee Press.

Carey, J.W. 1975. 'A cultural approach to communication'. *Communication* 2:1–22.

Condit, C.M. 1987. 'Crafting virtue: The rhetorical construction of public morality'. *Quarterly Journal of Speech* 73: 23–38.

Cromer, G. 1978. 'Character assassination in the press'. In C. Winick (ed.), *Deviance and mass media* (225–241). Beverly Hills, CA: Sage.

Dominick, J.R. 1973. 'Crime and law enforcement on prime time television'. *Public Opinion Quarterly* 37, 241–250.

Durkheim, E. 1933. *The division of labor in society*. New York: The Free Press.

——— 1938. *The rules of sociological method*. New York: The Free Press.

——— 1951. *Suicide*. New York: The Free Press.

Ericson, R. V. 1991. 'Mass media, crime, law and justice'. *The British Journal of Criminology* 31: 219–249.

Ericson. R.V. and Haggerty. K.D. 1997. *Policing the risk society*. Toronto: University of Toronto Press.

Erikson, K.T. 1966. *Wayward puritans*. New York: Macmillan.

Estep, R., and Macdonald, P.T. 1985. 'Crime in the afternoon; murder and robbery on soap operas'. *Journal of Broadcasting and Electronic Media* 29: 323–331.

Ettema, J.S., and Glasser, T.L 1988. 'Narrative form and moral force: The realization of innocence and guilt through investigative journalism'. *Journal of Communication* 38: 8–26.

Federal Bureau of Investigation. 1994. *Uniform Crime Reports.* US Government Printing Office.

Foucault, M. 1979. *Discipline and punish.* New York: Vintage Books.

Gans, H.J. 1979. *Deciding what's news.* New York: Pantheon.

Garfinkel, H. 1956. 'Conditions of successful degradation ceremonies'. *American Journal of Sociology* 61: 420–424.

Gerbner, G. J 1988. *Violence and terror in the mass media.* Paris, France: Unesco.

Gerbner, G., Gross, L., Signorielli, N., Morgan, M., and Jackson-Beeck, M. 1979. 'The demonstration of power: Violence profile no. 10'. *Journal of Communication* 29: 177–196.

Glasser, T.L., and Ettema, J.S. 1989. 'Investigative Journalism and the Moral Order' *Critical Studies in Mass Communication* 6: 1–20.

Haney, C., and Manzolati, J. 1981. 'Television criminology: Network illusions of criminal justice realities'. *Human Behavior* 12: 278–298.

Knight, G. 1989. 'Reality effects: Tabloid television news'. *Queen's Quarterly* 96: 94–108.

Knight, G., and Dean, T. 1982. 'Myth and the structure of news'. *Journal of Communication* 32: 144–161.

Knutson, P. 1974. 'Dragnet—The perfect crime?' *Liberation* 18: 28–30.

Mead, G.H. 1918. 'The psychology of punitive justice'. *The American Journal of Sociology* 23: 577–602.

Rusche, G., and Kirchheimer, O. 1939. *Punishment and social structure.* New York: Russell and Russell.

Schattenberg, G. 1981. 'Social control functions of mass media depictions of crime'. *Sociological Inquiry* 51: 71–77.

# 9

## Introduction

Sociologists draw attention to the 'socially constructed' nature of deviance. But what is sidestepped in such discussions is the socially constructed nature of normalcy and the ordinary. Sacks argues that, while we all do different kinds of occupational work, every day we also put a lot of work into being 'ordinary', even when we experience troubling events.

Social order depends on our ability to generally predict what will happen next, and to contend with more or less familiar situations. And it requires a good deal of trust in others. So exactly how do people go about being ordinary persons and normalize the vast array of experiences in their everyday lives? For Sacks, the key is language and the way we go about conversing with others in everyday life. This leads him into an examination of the 'technology of conversation', part of a sociological approach called conversational analysis. In this excerpt from a course lecture, he provides us with a few examples of how we do 'being ordinary' and tries to show us why this might be of interest to students. Why might knowing something about how we go about being ordinary and normalizing things be important in studying deviance and social control?

## On Doing 'Being Ordinary'

*Harvey Sacks*

Now, in this course I will be taking stories offered in conversation and subjecting them to a type of analysis that is concerned, roughly, to see whether it is possible to subject the details of actual events to formal investigation, informatively.

The idea is to take singular sequences of conversation and tear them apart in such a way as to find rules, techniques, procedures, methods, maxims (a collection of terms that more or less relate to each other and that I use somewhat interchangeably) that can be used to generate the orderly features we find in the conversations we examine. The point is, then, to come back to the singular things we observe in a singular sequence, with some rules that handle those singular features, and also, necessarily, handle lots of other events.

So, what we are dealing with is the technology of conversation. We are trying to *find* this technology out of actual fragments of conversation, so that we can impose as a constraint that the technology actually deals with singular events and singular sequences of events—a reasonably strong constraint on some set of rules.

The way I will proceed today is, in many ways, nothing like the way I will proceed throughout the rest of the course. In this lecture I will not be attempting to prove anything, and I will not be studying the technology of telling stories in conversation. I will be saying some things about why the study of storytelling should be of interest to anybody. And the loosest message is that the world you live in is much more finely organized than you would imagine.

A good deal of what I will say has its obscure intellectual source in a novel called *Between Life and Death* (trans. Maria Jolas 1970) by Nathalie Sarraute. (I say obscure because if you were to read the book it is not likely that you will find that it says what I say, but with some consideration you might see how it is that I owe what I am saying to this source.)

A kind of remarkable thing is how, in ordinary conversation, people, in reporting on some event, report what we might see to be, not what happened, but the ordinariness of what happened. The reports do not so much give attributes of the scene, activity, participants, but announce the event's ordinariness, its usualness. And if you think of literature or poetry you can perfectly well know that out of any such event as is passed off as, for example, 'It was a nice evening; we sat around and talked', really elaborated characterizations are often presented.

This brings me to the central sorts of assertions I want to make. Whatever you may think about what it is to be an ordinary person in the world, an initial shift is not to think of 'an ordinary person' as some person, but as somebody having as one's job, as one's constant preoccupation, doing 'being ordinary'. It is not that somebody is ordinary; it is perhaps that that is what one's business is, and it takes work, as any other business does. If you just extend the analogy of what you obviously think of as work—as whatever it is that takes analytic, intellectual, emotional energy—then you will be able to see that all sorts of nominalized things, for example, personal characteristics and the like, are jobs that are done, that took some kind of effort, training, and so on.

So I am not going to be talking about an ordinary person as this or that person, or as some average; that is, as a non-exceptional person on some statistical basis, but as something that is the way somebody constitutes oneself, and, in effect, a job that persons and the people around them may be coordinatively engaged in, to achieve that each of them, together, are ordinary persons.

A core question is, how do people go about doing 'being an ordinary person'? In the first instance, the answer is easy. Among the ways you go about doing 'being an ordinary person' is to spend your time in usual ways, having usual thoughts, usual interests, so that all you have to do to be an ordinary person in the evening is to turn on the TV set. Now, the trick is to see that it is not that it *happens* that you are doing what lots of ordinary people are doing, but that you know that the way to do 'having a usual evening', for anybody, is to do that. It is not that you happen to decide, 'Gee, I'll watch TV tonight', but that you are making a job of, and finding an answer to, how to do 'being ordinary' tonight.

So one part of the job is that you have to know what anybody/everybody is doing; doing ordinarily. Further, you have to have that available to do. There are people who do not have that available to do, and who specifically cannot be ordinary.

If, for example, you are in prison, in a room with no facilities at all; say, it has a bench and a hole in the floor and a spigot; then you find yourself doing things like systematically exploring the cracks in the wall from floor to ceiling, over the years, and you come to have information about the wall in that room which ordinary people do not have about their bedroom wall. But it is not a usual thing to say, 'Well, this evening I am going to examine that corner of the ceiling'.

Of course it is perfectly available to anybody to spend an afternoon looking at a wall. You could choose to do that. If you take drugs, you are permitted to do that. But unless you take drugs you would not find yourself allowed to do it, though nobody is around. That is to say, being an ordinary person, that is not a thing you could allow yourself to spend the day doing. And there is an infinite collection of possibilities, of things to do, that you could not bring yourself to do. In the midst of the most utterly boring afternoon or evening, you would rather live through the boredom in the usual way—whatever that is—than see whether it would be less or more boring to examine the wall or to look, in some detail, at the tree outside the window.

There are, of course, people whose job it is to make such observations. If you were to pick up the notebooks of writers, poets, novelists, you would be likely to find elaborated studies of small, real objects. And some novelists' notebooks have extended and detailed observations of character and appearance.

Now, there is a place in Freud's writings where he says, 'With regard to matters of chemistry or physics or things like that, laymen would not venture an opinion. With regard to psychology, it is quite different. Anybody feels free to make psychological remarks'. Part of the business he thought he was engaged in was changing that around; that is, co-jointly to develop psychology and educate laymen, so that laymen would know that they do not know anything about it and that there are people who do, so that they would leave such matters to the experts.

My notion is that, as it is for chemistry and physics, so it is for making distinctive observations about the world and its persons. It is just a thing that, in being ordinary, you do not do. For whole ranges of things that you might figure to be kind of exciting, something like the following talk will be offered (this is not made up, but is actual). Somebody talking about a man she met the night before says:

> He's just a real, dear, nice guy. Just a real, real nice guy. So we were really talking up a storm, and having a real good time, had a few drinks and so forth, and he's real easygoing. He's intelligent, and he's uh, not handsome, but he's nice looking, and uh, just real real nice, personable, very personable, very sweet.

You do not get, from somebody doing 'being ordinary', a report of the play of light on the liquor glasses, or the set of his eyebrows, or timbre of his voice.

I think it is not that you might make such observations but not include them in the story, but it is that the cast of mind of doing 'being ordinary' is essentially that your business in life is only to see and report the usual aspects of any possibly usual scene. That is to say, what you *look* for is to see how any scene you are in can be made an ordinary scene, a usual scene, and that is what that scene is.

Now you can plainly see that that could be a job; that it could be work. The scene does not in the first instance simply present itself, define itself, as insufferably usual, nothing to be said about it. It is a matter of how you are going to attack it. What are you going to see in it? People are regularly monitoring scenes for their storyable possibilities. I give you a grue-some instance of it, from a book called *An Ordinary Camp* (1958) by Micheline Maurel. She reports the first day in a concentration camp. The first hours are horrifying. Then there is a lull. 'Little by little conversation sprang up from bunk to bunk. The rumours were already beginning to circulate. Luckily, the news is good. We'll be home soon. We'll have an unusual experience to talk about'. A way in which his event was dealt with while it was taking place was that in the end it will turn out to have been a good story.

So it seems plain enough that people monitor the scenes they are in for their storyable char-acteristics. And yet the awesome, overwhelming fact is that they come away with *no* storyable characteristics. Presumably, any of us with any wit could make of this half-hour, or of the next, a rather large array of things to say. But there is the job of being an ordinary person, and that job includes attending the world, yourself, others, objects, so as to see how it is that it is a usual scene. And when offering what transpired, you present it in its usual fashion: 'Noth-ing much', and whatever variants of banal characterizations you might happen to use; that is, there is no particular difference between saying 'Nothing much' and 'It was outta sight'.

Whether you were to have illegitimate experiences or not, the characteristic of being an or-dinary person is that, having the illegitimate experiences that you should not have, they come off in just the usual way that they come off for anybody doing such an illegitimate experience.

When you have an affair, take drugs, commit a crime, and so on, you find that it has been the usual experience that others who have done it have had. The ordinary cast of mind would nonetheless be there to preserve the way we go about doing 'being ordinary'. Reports of the most seemingly outrageous experiences, for which you would figure one would be at a loss for words, or would have available extraordinary details of what happened, turn out to be presented in a fashion that has them come off as utterly unexceptional.

My guess is that you could now take that point with you, and, watching yourself live in the world—or watching somebody else, if that is more pleasant—you could see them working at finding how to make it ordinary. Presumably, it would be from such a sort of perceived awareness of, for example, the ease with which, after practice, you see only the most usual characterizations of the people passing (that is a married couple and that is a black guy and that is an old lady) or what a sunset looks like, or what an afternoon with your girlfriend or boyfriend consists of, that you can begin to appreciate that there is some immensely power-ful kind of mechanism operating in handling your perceptions and thoughts, other than the known and immensely powerful things like the chemistry of vision, and so on.

Those sorts of things would not explain how it is that you end up seeing that, for example, nothing much happened; that you can come home day after day and, asked what happened, report, without concealing, that nothing happened. And, if you are concealing, what you are concealing, if it were reported, would turn out to be nothing much. And, as it happens with you, so it happens with those you know. And, further, that ventures outside of being ordinary have unknown virtues and unknown costs. That is, if you come home and report what the grass looked like along the freeway; that there were four noticeable shades of green, some of which just appeared yesterday because of the rain, then there may well be some tightening up on the part of your recipient. And if you were to do it routinely, then people might figure that there is something odd about you; that you are pretentious. You might find them jealous of you. You might lose friends. That is to say, you might want to check out the costs of venturing into making your life an epic.

Now, it is also the case that there are people who are entitled to have their lives be an epic. We have assigned a series of storyable people, places, and objects, and they stand as something different from us. It may be that in pretty much every circle there is a somebody who is the subject of all neat observations, as there are, for society in general, a collection of people about whom detailed reports are made that not merely would never be ventured about others, but would never be thought of about others. The way in which Elizabeth Taylor turned around is something noticeable and reportable. The way in which your mother turned around is something unseeable, much less tellable.

The point is that it is almost everybody's business to be occupationally ordinary; that people take on the job of keeping everything utterly mundane; that no matter what happens, pretty much everybody is engaged in finding only how it is that what is going on is usual, with every effort possible. And it is really remarkable to see people's efforts to achieve the 'nothing happened' sense of really catastrophic events. I have been collecting fragments out of newspapers, of hijackings, and what the airplane passengers think when a hijacking takes place. The latest one I happened to find goes something like this.

> I was walking up towards the front of the airplane and I saw the stewardess standing facing the cabin and a fellow standing with a gun in her back. And my first thought was he's showing her the gun, and then I realized that couldn't be, and then it turned out he was hijacking the plane.

Another, about the hijacking of a Polish plane, goes like this. The plane is now in the midst of being hijacked, and the guy reports, 'I thought to myself, we just had a Polish hijacking a month ago and they're already making a movie of it'. A classically dramatic instance is, almost universally, that the initial report of the assassination of President Kennedy was of having heard backfires.

Let us turn, now, to some fragments of conversation, from tape-recorded telephone calls, in which events that are dramatic, in their way, are being reported. Looking at these reports, we can begin to pick out some of the work involved in doing 'being ordinary'.

Jean: Hello.

Ellen: Jean.

Jean: Yeah.

Ellen: Well I just thought I'd re—better report to you what's happened at Cromwell's today.

Jean: What in the world's happened?

Ellen: Did you have the day off?

Jean: Yah.

Ellen: Well I got out to my car at five thirty. I drove around and of course I had to go by the front of the store.

Jean: Yeah?

Ellen: And there were two police cars across the street and the coloured lady wanted to go in the main entrance there where the silver is and all the (Yeah.) things.

Jean: Yeah.

Ellen: And, they wouldn't let her go in, and he, had a gun. He was holding a gun in his hand, a great big long gun?

Jean: Yeah?

Ellen: And then over on the other side, I mean to the right of there, where the employees come out, there was a whole, oh, must have been ten, uh, eight or ten employees standing there, because there must have been a, it seemed like they had every entrance barred. I don't know what was going on.

Jean: Oh my God.

Let's look at the materials, keeping the events in mind, thinking out what was happening, and playing around with the talk by reference to some way of considering what was happening. I have in mind something like this. When this lady interprets the events, she interprets them so as to find how the police being there involves that they were legitimately there.

We can notice, at least nowadays, that the legitimate presence of the police has become a kind of distributional phenomenon; that is, whereas this lady is able to use the presence of the police to find what was going on, taking it that the police belonged there, others might see the same scene with the same parties taking it that the police were doing something that they had no business doing. That is, if this action took place in a black neighbourhood, watched by black people, then 'the very same scene' would perhaps turn into, for the perception of the parties, an altogether different phenomenon.

There are places where the police can count on the presence of two of their cars to provide for their visible, legitimate presence, such that others will then search the scene to find what the police might be doing that they should be doing, and, for example, pick up on that someone is trying to get into the entrance where the silver is. Whereas there are others who will not at all see the events in that way but, seeing two police cars on the scene, may now look to see what kind of bother the police, by being on the scene, are producing, as compared to what kind of bother they are properly responding to.

That sort of differential organization of the sheer perceiving of an event is of considerable importance for the way in which the fact of the police on the scene tells people that, although there is a trouble, things are okay. For example, that this lady can drive right by the scene knowing that things are more or less well in hand, that something is happening but that the police will take care of it, rather than that something is happening and the police are making it happen.

That sort of phenomenon has become a markedly distributional one, and you ought to learn to appreciate the difficulty involved in groups talking to each other where each of them figures that all they did was to see what was happening. That is, the notion of distributional issues involved is unavailable to either group by virtue of the fact that all they are doing is scanning a scene to see what is happening. They are not arguing anything, they are not imagining anything. They are seeing the scene in some organization. And to tell them that they are imagining it, or that they are making a case, since you perfectly well know what was there to be seen by virtue of what *you* saw, is to put them in a position where they could not really come to understand what you are talking about.

That turns on the fact that each group is specifically committed to a trust of vision, without any conception of what they understand by 'vision'. We can move from here to a discussion of the sorts of utter puzzlement that people have about the kinds of claims that others make about, for example, the police and what they are doing, when each group figures that all they are doing is reporting what they saw and not making a case for anything, being perfectly willing to be fair. This lady is not designing a right-wing report. All she is doing is reporting what she saw. To tell her that it is not what happened is to attack a kind of trust that she has, and should have, in what she simply sees; to propose a situation that would be quite uncomfortable for her to live with; to undermine something that an enormous mass of, in some ways Western, ideology has led her to believe she should, in fact, trust.

The point is, roughly, that it is a culturally and temporally distributional thing that people do or do not trust their eyes. Even such people as those academics who figure that they are attuned to 'the ideological foundations of perception' may not use that sort of attuning to come to appreciate the distrust of vision that some cultures have. The academics see it as a kind of anti-empiricism, where it may not at all be anti-empiricism, but that, in the light of the kinds of troubles that people get into when they take a culturally ordered orientation to vision seriously, a focus on other senses might seem to pay off better.

Another thing—again getting into these kinds of tender problematic areas—this lady is perfectly comfortable as a witness to the scene. And yet you can perfectly well imagine how she would not see herself as a witness at all. In her report there is, for example, no hint of any interest in stopping and helping out, or of getting worried about what is going to happen.

More importantly, there is no hint that she had any fear that somehow, for example, that policeman was about to turn to her and ask her what she was doing there. The massive comfort in her innocence, and in the legitimate audience status that she has, is something that we should give real attention to, in at least this way. It is the kind of thing that we know can be readily shaken. There are times and places where someone would not feel all that comfortable passing such a scene, and—you can readily imagine it—would figure, 'Oh my God, here I am, the first thing that happens is they're going to figure I'm involved'.

That never dawns on our lady. And until it dawns on her, she can have no sense of an empathy with, for example, a kid in the ghetto. And nonetheless I suppose you could bring her to see that; that is, you could show her how her whole sense of innocence affects the whole way she sees the scene. There is no fear on her part at all that anybody is going to mistake her for a party to the scene, though she is perfectly willing to assign others a non-witness, party-to-the-scene status.[1]

Again, there is no feeling on her part that she ought to do anything, and nobody would pretty much figure that she ought to feel that she should do anything. That sort of trust in the ability of the police who are there to handle whatever needs to be handled, and that they will handle it well, is another aspect of the way in which, being a witness, she can sheerly be a witness. One might consider, when one is doing 'being a witness to a scene', the conditions under which your witness status could be transformed in a series of different ways, one of them being into someone who could be seen by others, for example, the lady in the car next to yours, or the man across the street, not as a witness, but possibly as 'a car moving away from the scene'; as 'the escaped robber'. Or, not that you are a witness to a scene that is being ably handled, but that you are somebody who is callously passing it by.

I raise these possibilities because if you read the story you can feel utterly sure that no such issues crossed her mind, and you can then think of scenes in which you have been involved, or others have been involved, in which you see whether or not such issues do emerge, and then focus on what the conditions are that would lead somebody like this lady here to at least have it cross her mind that when the policeman turns around with his gun he is going to shoot her, or tell her to halt; or that somebody else might see her and wonder what in the world she is doing there.

Let us turn, now, to the second fragment. This one occurs at some distance into a telephone call.

Madge: Say, did you see anything in the paper last night or hear anything on the local radio, (unclear) Ruth Henderson and I drove down, to, Ventura yesterday.

Bea: Mm hm.

Madge: And on the way home we saw the – most gosh awful wreck—

Bea: Oh.

Madge: we have ev—I've ever seen. I've never seen a car smashed into sm—such a small space.

Bea: Oh.

Madge: It was smashed,—(unclear) from the front and the back both. It must have been in—caught in, between two cars.

Bea: Mm hm, mm huh.

Madge: Must have run into a car and then another car smashed into it and there were people laid out and covered over on the pavement.

Bea: Mm.

Madge: We were s—parked there for quite a while. But I was going to, listen to the local r—news and haven't done it.

Bea: No I haven't had my radio on either.

Madge: Well I had my television on, but I was listening to uh the blast off, you know.

Bea: Mm hm.

Madge: The uh ah (Yeah.) astronauts.

Bea: Yeah.

Madge: And I, I didn't ever get any local news.

Bea: Uh huh.

Madge: And I wondered.

Bea: Uh huh, no, I haven't had it on . . .

Earlier, I was talking about the constraints set on experiences by 'the ordinary cast of mind'. I want now to focus on entitlement to have experiences. I want to suggest that, in having witnessed this event, and having suffered it as well, in some way (for instance, having had to stop on the freeway in a traffic jam by virtue of it), she has become entitled to an experience. That she is entitled to an experience is something different from what her recipient is entitled to, or what someone who otherwise comes across this story is entitled to.

In part, I am saying that it is a fact that entitlement to experiences are differentially available. If I say it as 'entitlement', you may think of it as not having rights to it, but that is only part of it. It is also not coming to feel it at all, as compared to feeling it and feeling that you do not have rights to it. The idea is that in encountering an event, and encountering it as a witness or someone who in part suffered by it, one is entitled to an experience, whereas the sheer fact of having access to things in the world, for example, getting the story from another, is quite a different thing.

A way to see the matter is to ask the question, what happens to stories like this once they are told? Do stories like this become the property of the recipient as they are the property of the teller? That is, the teller owns rights to tell this story, and they give their credentials for their rights to tell the story by offering such things as that they saw it, and that they suffered by it. Now the question is, does a recipient of a story come to own it in the way that the teller has owned it; that is, can the recipient tell it to another, or feel for it as the teller can feel for those events?

For example, you might, on seeing an automobile accident and people lying there, feel awful, cry, have the rest of your day ruined. The question is, is the recipient of this story entitled to feel as you do? I think the facts are, plainly, no. That is to say, if you call up a friend of yours, unaffiliated with the event you are reporting, that is, someone who does not turn out to be the cousin or the aunt of, the person who was killed in the accident, but just a somebody you call up and tell about an awful experience, then, if the recipient becomes as disturbed as you, or more, something peculiar is going on, and you might even feel wronged—although that might seem to be an odd thing to feel.

Now one reason I raise this whole business, and a way that it is important, is that we could at least imagine a society in which those having experienced something, having seen and felt for it, could preserve not merely the knowledge of it, but the feeling for it, by telling others. That is, if they could feel for it, then anybody they could tell it to could feel for it. Then, plainly, that stock of experiences that others happened to have would not turn on the events that they happened to have encountered, but could turn on the events that anybody who ever talked to them happened to encounter—as we think of a stock of knowledge that we have.

That is to say, if I tell you something that you come to think is so, you are entitled to have it. And you take it that the stock of knowledge that you have is something that you can get wherever you get it, and it is yours to keep. But the stock of experiences is an altogether differently constructed thing. As I say, in order to see that that is so, we can just, for example, differentiate how we deal with a piece of knowledge and how we deal with someone else's experience, and then come to see that experiences then get isolated, rather than that they are themselves as productive as are pieces of knowledge.

Now that fact obviously matters a good deal, in all sorts of ways. Among the ways it comes to matter is that if having an experience is a basis for being aroused to do something about the sorts of things it is an instance of (for example, the state of the freeways, the state of automobiles, the state of whatever else), then plainly the basis for getting things done is radically weakened where those who receive your story cannot feel as you are entitled to feel.

Of course, there is no reason to restrict the matter to misery. Plainly, it holds for joy, as well. Plainly it is specifically an attendable problem that joy is not productive, but that those having such an experience as entitled them to be joyful, telling it to others, they can feel 'good for you' but there are rather sharp limits on how good they can feel for themselves for it, and also, even sharper limits on the good feeling that they can give to a third party with the story.

Again, if we think about it, we can perhaps just see that limited entitlement is not intrinsic to the organization of the world, but is a way we somehow come to perceive and feel about experience, or the way we were taught to do that, which is altogether different from the ways we think about knowledge. It is extremely difficult to spread joy. It is extremely easy to spread information.

Now that is one order of thing—the distributional character of experience and the import of its distributional character for, say, troubles and joys in the world, in, say, sharp contrast to knowledge and its distributional character. You might figure it would be a severe enough kind of fact with regard to people's rights or abilities to have experiences, if they were restricted to those events that they took part in or witnessed, but that is not yet the full story of the kinds of constraints that are set on the possibility of having an experience.

The second sort of constraint is that, if you are going to have an entitled experience, then you will have to have the experience that you are entitled to. You could figure that, having severe restrictions on your chances to have experiences, which turn on, for example, something, in some fashion important, happening to cross your path, or your happening to cross its path, that having happened, well, then you are home free. Once you got it you could do with it as you pleased. No. You have to form it up as the thing that it ordinarily is, and then mesh your experience with that.

That is to say, the rights to have an experience by virtue of, say, encountering something like an accident, are only the rights to have seen 'another accident', and to perhaps have felt for it, but not, for example, to have seen God in it. You cannot have a nervous breakdown because you happened to see an automobile accident. You cannot make much more of it than what anybody would make of it. So we can think of the way that you are entitled to an experience as: you borrow for a while that experience which is available, as compared to you now invent the experience that you might be entitled to.

But since you are so sharply restricted with regard to the occasions of having an experience, then presumably people are happy enough to take them as they come. That is, you are not going to get many surprising new feelings, or whatever, out of this experience, but it is the only experience that you have any chance legitimately to have, so you might as well have it. You might as well form up this automobile-wreck story as an ordinary wreck story rather than attempt to make it into something that would occasion that you are really reaching for experiences. Of course, people are readily seen to be reaching for experience with something that anybody knows is 'just a wreck', 'just a something', and that they make into a life's work.

In that regard, there are a whole bunch of ways that the teller of this story relays to us how she went about bounding this experience. That is to say, what she made of it is told not just the story, but in other ways.

Among the ways that she goes about locating the kind of experience this event was, is that she does not tell it right off in the conversation (and that is not available to you in the excerpt) but she tells it somewhere into the conversation. You will find that stories are specifically differentiated in terms of their importance to the teller by reference to where the teller places them in a conversation.

So, for example, among the ways a teller can make out a story as really important, is to tell it right off. And a way to make it even more important than that is to call to tell it when you figure the other is not available to hear it, for example, to call them up in the middle of the night. Stories are ranked in terms of, and express their status by, your calling somebody up and saying, 'I know you were sleeping, but . . . ', where it is not that they happen to be sleeping, but you call them when they are sleeping, in that if you do not call them then, if you call them when they get up, you have already told them something about the story; that is, it is not so important as you might otherwise want to make it out. So the placing of the story in the conversation and the placing of the conversation in the recipient's life are ways that you go about locating the importance of the story.

Then, of course, she also tells aspects of the story's importance in the telling itself. For example, while it was an important enough experience for her to say to herself, I am going to listen to the radio, other things got in the way of that. She is not embarrassed to say that, instead of that, she watched the astronauts, an action that obviously for some other story would be altogether perverse. For this story it is perfectly okay, and is a way to locate how the events matter, that is, to produce it while indicating that if it came down to trying to find out more, or watching the astronauts, she watched the astronauts.

Aside from that, she could go home and go about her business, as compared to, for example, going home to bed, or, having nightmares all night, or that it in other ways interfered with the life that she was engaged in when this happened. She was coming home, there was the accident, she was stopped for a while, and then she went home and watched the astronauts. That is plainly a way to locate how the story matters, and is plainly an appropriate way for this story. Had she said, 'It ruined the rest of my day', 'I was shaking all over', 'I went to the doctor', 'I had nightmares', then her friend could say, 'Well, you're just oversensitive'. So this business of the character of the experience fitting the conventional status of the event is something that is dealt with in the telling of the story.

At least initially, the blandest kind of formulation we might make is that, although lots of people figure that experience is a great thing, and apparently at least some people are eager to have experiences, they are extraordinarily carefully regulated sorts of things. The occasions of entitlement to have them are carefully regulated, and then the experience you are entitled to have on an occasion that you are entitled to have one is further carefully regulated. Insofar as part of the experience involves telling about it, then the telling of it constitutes one way in which what you might privately make of it is subject to the control of an open presentation, even to someone you thought was a friend.

That is to say, your friends are not going to help you out, by and large, when you tell them some story, unless you tell them a story in the way anybody should tell it to anybody. Then they will be appropriately amused or sorrowed. Otherwise you will find that they are watching you to see that, for example, you are making something big out of something that you are not entitled to make big, or something small that should have been bigger, or missed seeing something that you should have seen, all of which could be deduced by virtue of the way you were required to form the thing up.

Now, I am not by any means saying, 'Let us do away with the ways in which we go about being ordinary', but rather, that we want to know what importance it has. At least one tack we can take is to treat the overwhelming banality of the stories we encounter—in my data, in your own experiences—as not so much something that allows, for example, for statistical analysis of variation, or that makes them therefore uninteresting to study, but as a specific feature that turns on a kind of attitude; say, an attitude of working at being usual which is perhaps central to the way our world is organized.

Jean: Well she said that there was some woman that the—that they were: buhh had held up in the front there that they were pointing the gun at and everything, a k—Negro woman.

Penny: (unclear) No, no.

Jean: What.

Penny: That was one of the employees.

Jean: Oh.

Penny: He ran up to her and she just ran up to him and says what's happened what's aa— well the kids were all laughing about it.

## Note

1.  That the 'coloured lady' who 'wanted to go in . . . where the silver is' was herself a bystander, comes out in a subsequent conversation, between the recipient of the report and someone who was there [GJ].

# 10

## Introduction

Goffman is often mentioned in discussions of symbolic interactionism and its contributions to understanding the social construction of deviance, even though he never considered himself to be one. Nevertheless, much of his 'dramaturgic' (or theatrical) approach to studying everyday social life investigated the importance of presenting a social self, interaction rituals, and role performances in creating social order and a shared sense of the group we belong to at an interactional level. In this excerpt he explores how stigma can affect each of these activities with consequences for both the stigmatized individual and the group.

A stigma is a discrediting attribute, quality, or trait that has the potential of reducing people's evaluation of an individual who possesses it. Goffman points out that the attribute or trait is not in and of itself discreditable. Stigmatizing involves 'normals' defining the trait or attribute as discreditable, then having those that are stigmatized contend with such definitions. And there are a wide range of strategic possibilities in such encounters. Given his discussion, what conditions seem to be necessary for a trait to become regarded as a stigma?

Finally, there are very few of us who do not possess some attribute or trait, or who haven't engaged in some act, that could be regarded as discreditable by others if they knew about it. Perhaps none. So who are the 'normals' Goffman is referring to?

# Stigma and Social Identity

*Erving Goffman*

The Greeks, who were apparently strong on visual aids, originated the term stigma to refer to bodily signs designed to expose something unusual and bad about the moral status of the signifier. The signs were cut or burnt into the body and advertised that the bearer was a slave, a criminal, or a traitor—a blemished person, ritually polluted, to be avoided, especially in public places. Later, in Christian times, two layers of metaphor were added to the term: the first referred to bodily signs of holy grace that took the form of eruptive blossoms on the skin; the second, a medical allusion to this religious allusion, referred to bodily signs of physical disorder. Today the term is widely used in something like the original literal sense, but is applied more to the disgrace itself than to the bodily evidence of it. Furthermore, shifts have occurred in the kinds of disgrace that arouse concern.

## Preliminary Conceptions

Society establishes the means of categorizing persons and the complement of attributes felt to be ordinary and natural for members of each of these categories. Social settings establish the categories of persons likely to be encountered there. The routines of social intercourse in established settings allow us to deal with anticipated others without special attention or thought. When a stranger comes into our presence, then, first appearances are likely to enable us to anticipate his category and attributes, his 'social identity'—to use a term that is better than 'social status' which involves personal attributes such as 'honesty', as well as structural ones, like 'occupation'.

We lean on these anticipations that we have, transforming them into normative expectations into righteously presented demands.

Typically, we do not become aware that we have made these demands or aware of what they are until an active question arises as to whether or not they will be fulfilled. It is then that we are likely to realize that all along we had been making certain assumptions as to what the individual before us ought to be. Thus, the demands we make might better be called demands made 'in effect', and the character we impute to the individual might better be seen as an imputation made in potential retrospect—a characterization 'in effect', a *virtual social identity*. The category and attributes he could in fact be proved to possess will be called his *actual social identity*.

While the stranger is present before us, evidence can arise of his possessing an attribute that makes him different from others in the category of persons available for him to be, and of a less desirable kind—in the extreme, a person who is quite thoroughly bad, or dangerous, or weak. He is thus reduced in our minds from a whole and usual person to a tainted, discounted one. Such an attribute is a stigma, especially when its discrediting effect is very extensive; sometimes it is also called a failing, a shortcoming, a handicap. It constitutes a special discrepancy between virtual and actual social identity. Note that there are other types of discrepancy between virtual and actual social identity, for example the kind that causes us to reclassify an individual from one socially anticipated category to a different but equally well-anticipated one, and the kind that causes us to alter our estimation of the individual upward. Note, too, that not all undesirable attributes are at issue, but only those which are incongruous with our stereotype of what a given type of individual should be.

The term stigma, then, will be used to refer to an attribute that is deeply discrediting, but it should be seen that a language of relationships, not attributes, is really needed. An attribute that stigmatizes one type of possessor can confirm the usualness of another, and therefore is neither creditable nor discreditable as a thing in itself. For example, an individual who desires to fight for his country may conceal a physical defect, lest his claimed physical status be discredited; later, the same individual, embittered and trying to get out of the army, may succeed in gaining admission to the army hospital, where he would be discredited if discovered in not really having an acute sickness.[1] A stigma, then, is really a special kind of relationship between attribute and stereotype, although I don't propose to continue to say so, in part because there are important attributes that almost everywhere in our society are discrediting.

The term stigma and its synonyms conceal a double perspective: Does the stigmatized individual assume his differentness is known about already or is evident on the spot, or does he assume it is neither known about by those present nor immediately perceivable by them? In the first case, one deals with the plight of the *discredited;* in the second with that of the *discreditable.* This is an important difference even though a particular stigmatized individual is likely to have experience with both situations. I will begin with the situation of the discredited and move on to the discreditable but not always separate the two.

Three grossly different types of stigma may be mentioned. First there are abominations of the body—the various physical deformities. Next there are blemishes of individual character perceived as weak will, domineering or unnatural passions, treacherous and rigid beliefs, and dishonesty, these being inferred from a known record of, for example, mental disorder, imprisonment, addiction, alcoholism, homosexuality, unemployment, suicide attempts, and radical political behaviour. Finally there are the tribal stigmas of race, nation, and religion, these being stigmas that can be transmitted through lineages of equally contaminate all members of a family.[2] In all of these various instances of stigma, however, including those the Greeks had in mind, the same sociological features are found: An individual who might have been received easily in ordinary social intercourse possesses a trait that can obtrude itself upon attention and turn those of us whom he meets away from him, breaking the claim that his other attributes have on us. He possesses a stigma, an undesired differentness from what we had anticipated. We and those who do not depart negatively from the particular expectations at issue I shall call the *normals*.

The attitudes we normals have toward a person with a stigma, and the actions we take in regard to him, are well known since these responses are what benevolent social action is designed to soften and ameliorate. By definition, of course, we believe the person with a stigma is not quite human. On this assumption we exercise varieties of discrimination, through which we effectively, if often unthinkingly, reduce his life chances. We construct a stigma-theory, an ideology to explain his inferiority and account for the danger he represents, sometimes rationalizing an animosity based on other differences, such as those of social class.[3] We use specific stigma terms such as cripple, bastard, moron in our daily discourse as a source of metaphor and imagery, typically without giving thought to the original meaning.[4] We tend to impute a wide range of imperfections on the basis of the original one,[5] and at the same time to impute some desirable but undesired attributes, often of a supernatural cast, such as 'sixth sense', or 'understanding'[6]:

> For some, there may be a hesitancy about touching or steering the blind while for others the perceived failure to see may be generalized into a gestalt of disability, so that the individual shouts at the blind as if they were deaf or attempts to lift them as if they were crippled. Those confronting the blind may have a whole range of belief that is anchored in the stereotype. For instance, they may think they are subject to unique judgment, assuming the blinded individual draws on special channels of information unavailable to others.[7]

Further, we may perceive his defensive response to his situation as a direct expression of his defect, and then see both defect and response as just retribution for something he or his parents or his tribe did, and hence a justification of the way we treat him.[8]

Now turn from the normal to the person he is normal against. It seems generally true that members of a social category may strongly support a standard of judgment that they and others agree does not directly apply to them. Thus it is that a businessman may demand womanly behaviour from females or ascetic behaviour from monks, and not construe himself as someone who ought to realize either of these styles of conduct. The distinction is between realizing a norm and merely supporting it. The issue of stigma does not arise here, but only where there is some expectation on all sides that those in a given category should not only support a particular norm but also realize it.

Also, it seems possible for an individual to fail to live up to what we effectively demand of him, and yet be relatively untouched by this failure; insulated by his alienation, protected by identity beliefs of his own, *he feels that he is a full-fledged normal human being, and that we are the ones who are not quite human.* He bears a stigma but does not seem to be impressed or repentant about doing so. This possibility is celebrated in exemplary tales about Mennonites, Gypsies, shameless scoundrels, and very orthodox Jews.

In America at present, however, separate systems of honour seem to be on the decline. The stigmatized individual tends to hold the same beliefs about identity that we do; this is a pivotal fact. His deepest feelings about what he is may be his sense of being a 'normal person', a human being like anyone else, a person, therefore, who deserves a fair chance and a fair break.[9] (Actually, however phrased, he bases his claims not on what he thinks is due *everyone*, but only everyone of a selected social category into which he unquestionably fits, for example, anyone of his age, sex, profession, and so forth.) Yet he may perceive, usually quite correctly, that whatever others profess, they do not really 'accept' him and are not ready to make contact with him on 'equal grounds'.[10] Further, the standards he has incorporated from the wider society equip him to be intimately alive to what others see as his failing, inevitably causing him, if only for moments, to agree that he does indeed fall short of what he really ought to be. Shame becomes a central possibility, arising from the individual's perception of one of his own attributes as being a defiling thing to possess, and one he can readily see himself as not possessing.

The immediate presence of normals is likely to reinforce this split between self-demands and self, but in fact self-hate and self-derogation can also occur when only he and a mirror are about.

The central feature of the stigmatized individual's situation in life can now be stated. It is a question of what is often, if vaguely, called 'acceptance'. Those who have dealings with him fail to accord him the respect and regard which the uncontaminated aspects of his social identity have led them to anticipate extending, and have led him to anticipate receiving; he echoes this denial by finding that some of his own attributes warrant it.

How does the stigmatized person respond to his situation? In some cases it will be possible for him to make a direct attempt to correct what he sees as the objective basis of his failing, as when a physically deformed person undergoes plastic surgery, a blind person eye treatment, an illiterate remedial education, a homosexual psychotherapy. (Where such repair is possible, what often results is not the acquisition of fully normal status, but a transformation of self from someone with a particular blemish into someone with a record of having corrected a particular blemish.) Here proneness to 'victimization' is to be cited, a result of the stigmatized person's exposure to fraudulent servers selling speech correction, skin lighteners, body stretchers, youth restorers (as in rejuvenation through fertilized egg yolk treatment), cures, through faith, and poise in conversation. Whether a practical technique or fraud is involved, the quest, often secret, that results provides a special indication of the extremes to which the stigmatized can be willing to go, and hence the painfulness of the situation that leads them to these extremes. One illustration may be cited:

> Miss Peck [a pioneer New York social worker for the hard of hearing] said that in the early days the quacks and get-rich-quick medicine men who abounded saw the League [for the hard of hearing] as their happy hunting ground, ideal for the promotion of magnetic head caps, miraculous vibrating machines, artificial eardrums, blowers, inhalers, massagers, magic oils, balsams, and other guaranteed, sure-fire, positive, and permanent cure-alls for incurable deafness. Advertisements for such hokum (until the 1920s when the American Medical Association moved in with an investigation campaign) beset the hard of hearing in the pages of the daily press, even in reputable magazines.[11]

The stigmatized individual can also attempt to correct his condition indirectly by devoting much private effort to the mastery of areas of activity ordinarily felt to be closed, on incidental and physical grounds, to one with his shortcoming. This is illustrated by the lame person who learns or relearns to swim, ride, play tennis, or fly an airplane, or the blind person who becomes expert at skiing and mountain climbing.[12] Tortured learning may be associated, of course, with the tortured performance of what is learned, as when an individual, confined to a wheelchair, manages to take to the dance floor with a girl in some kind of mimicry of dancing.[13] Finally, the person with a shameful differentness can break with what is called reality, and obstinately attempt to employ an unconventional interpretation of the character of his social identity.

The stigmatized individual is likely to use his stigma for 'secondary gains', as an excuse for ill success that has come his way for other reasons:

> For years the scar, harelip, or misshapen nose has been looked on as a handicap, and its importance in the social and emotional adjustment is unconsciously all embracing. It is the 'hook' on which the patient has hung all inadequacies, all dissatisfactions, all procrastinations and all unpleasant duties of social life, and he has come to depend on it not only as a reasonable escape from competition but as a protection from social responsibility.
>
> When one removes this factor by surgical repair, the patient is cast adrift from the more or less acceptable emotional protection it has offered and soon he finds, to his surprise and discomfort, that life is not all smooth sailing even for those with unblemished, 'ordinary' faces. He is unprepared to cope with this situation without the support of a 'handicap', and he may turn to the less simple, but similar, protection of the behaviour patterns of neurasthenia, hysterical conversation, hypochondriasis, or the acute anxiety states.[14]

He may also see the trials he has suffered as a blessing in disguise, especially because of what it is felt that suffering can teach one about life and people:

But now, far away from the hospital experience, I can evaluate what I have learned. [A mother permanently disabled by polio writes.] For it wasn't only suffering: it was also learning through suffering. I know my awareness of people has deepened and increased, that those who are close to me can count on me to turn all my mind and heart and attention to their problems. I could not have learned *that* dashing all over a tennis court.[15]

Correspondingly, he can come to reassess the limitations of normals, as a multiple sclerotic suggests:

Both healthy minds and healthy bodies may be crippled. The fact that 'normal' people can get around, can see, can hear, doesn't mean that they are seeing or hearing. They can be very blind to the things that spoil their happiness, very deaf to the pleas of others for kindness; when I think of them I do not feel any more crippled or disabled than they. Perhaps in some small way I can be the means of opening their eyes to the beauties around us: things like a warm handclasp, a voice that is anxious to cheer, a spring breeze, music to listen to, a friendly nod. These people are important to me, and I like to feel that I can help them.[16]

The responses of the normal and of the stigmatized that have been considered so far are ones which can occur over protracted periods of time and in isolation from current contact between normals and stigmatized.[17] This book, however, is specifically concerned with the issue of 'mixed contacts'—the moments when stigmatized and normals are in the same 'social situation', that is, in one another's immediate physical presence, whether in a conversation-like encounter or in the mere co-presence of an unfocused gathering.

    The very anticipation of such contacts can of course lead normals and the stigmatized to arrange life so as to avoid them. Presumably this will have larger consequences for the stigmatized, since more arranging will usually be necessary on their part. Lacking the salutary feedback of daily social intercourse with others, the self-isolate can become suspicious, depressed, hostile, anxious, and bewildered. Sullivan's version may be cited:

The awareness of inferiority means that one is unable to keep out of consciousness the formulation of some chronic feeling of the worst sort of insecurity, and this means that one suffers anxiety and perhaps even something worse, if jealousy is really worse than anxiety. The fear that others can disrespect a person because of something he shows means that he is always insecure in his contact with other people; and this insecurity arises, not from mysterious and somewhat disguised sources, as a great deal of our anxiety does, but from something which he knows he cannot fix. Now that represents an almost fatal deficiency of the self-system, since the self is unable to disguise or exclude a definite formulation that reads, 'I am inferior. Therefore people will dislike me and I cannot be secure with them'.[18]

When normals and stigmatized do in fact enter one another's immediate presence, especially when they there attempt to sustain a joint conversational encounter, there occurs one of the primal scenes of sociology; for, in many cases, these moments will be the ones when the causes and effects of stigma must be directly confronted by both sides.

The stigmatized individual may find that he feels unsure of how we normals will identify him and receive him.[19] An illustration may be cited from a student of physical disability:

> Uncertainty of status for the disabled person obtains over a wide range of social interactions in addition to that of employment. The blind, the ill, the deaf, the crippled can never be sure what the attitude of a new acquaintance will be, whether it will be rejective or accepting, until the contact has been made. This is exactly the position of the adolescent, the light-skinned Negro, the second generation immigrant, the socially mobile person and the woman who has entered a predominantly masculine occupation.[20]

This uncertainty arises not merely from the stigmatized individual's not knowing which of several categories he will be placed in, but also, where the placement is favourable, from his knowing that in their hearts the others may be defining him in terms of his stigma:

> And I always feel this with straight people—that whenever they're being nice to me, pleasant to me, all the time really, underneath they're only assessing me as a criminal and nothing else. It's too late for me to be any different now to what I am, but I still feel this keenly, that that's their only approach, and they're quite incapable of accepting me as anything else.[21]

Thus in the stigmatized arises the sense of not knowing what the others present are 'really' thinking about him.

Further, during mixed contacts, the stigmatized individual is likely to feel that he is 'on',[22] having to be self-conscious and calculating about the impression he is making, to a degree and in areas of conduct which he assumes others are not.

Also, he is likely to feel that the usual scheme of interpretation for everyday events has been undermined. His minor accomplishments, he feels, may be assessed as signs of remarkable and noteworthy capacities in the circumstances. A professional criminal provides an illustration:

> 'You know, it's really amazing you should read books like this; I'm staggered I am. I should've thought you'd read paper-backed thrillers, things with lurid covers, books like that. And here you are with Claud Cockburn, Hugh Klare, Simone de Beauvoir, and Lawrence Durrell!'
>
> You know, he didn't see this as an insulting remark at all: In fact, I think he thought he was being honest in telling me how mistaken he was. And that's exactly the sort of patronizing you get from straight people if you're a criminal. 'Fancy that!' they say. 'In some ways you're just like a human being!' I'm not kidding; it makes me want to choke the bleeding life out of them.[23]

A blind person provides another illustration:

> His once most ordinary deeds—walking nonchalantly up the street, locating the peas on his plate, lighting a cigarette—are no longer ordinary. He becomes an unusual person. If he performs them with finesse and assurance they excite the same kind of wonderment inspired by a magician who pulls rabbits out of hats.[24]

At the same time, minor failings or incidental impropriety may, he feels, be interpreted as a direct expression of his stigmatized differentness. Ex-mental patients, for example, are sometimes afraid to engage in sharp interchanges with spouse or employer because of what a show of emotion might be taken as a sign of. Mental defectives face a similar contingency:

> It also happens that if a person of low intellectual ability gets into some sort of trouble the difficulty is more or less automatically attributed to 'mental defect' whereas if a person of 'normal intelligence' gets into a similar difficulty, it is not regarded as symptomatic of anything in particular.[25]

When the stigmatized person's failing can be perceived by our merely directing attention (typically, visual) to him—when, in short, he is a discredited, not discreditable, person—he is likely to feel that to be present among normals nakedly exposes him to invasions of privacy,[26] experienced most pointedly perhaps when children simply stare at him.[27] This displeasure in being exposed can be increased by the conversations strangers may feel free to strike up with him, conversations in which they express what he takes to be morbid curiosity about his condition, or in which they proffer help that he does not need or want.[28] One might add that there are certain classic formulae for these kinds of conversations: 'My dear girl, how did you get your quiggle'; 'My great uncle had a quiggle, so I feel I know all about your problem'; 'You know I've always said that Quiggles are good family men and look after their own poor'; 'Tell me, how do you manage to bathe with a quiggle?' The implication of these overtures is that the stigmatized individual is a person who can be approached by strangers at will, providing only that they are sympathetic to the plight of persons of his kind.

Given what the stigmatized individual may well face upon entering a mixed social situation, he may, in anticipation, respond by defensive cowering. This may be illustrated from an early study of some German unemployed during the Depression, the words being those of a 43-year-old mason:

> How hard and humiliating it is to bear the name of an unemployed man. When I go out, I cast down my eyes because I feel myself wholly inferior. When I go along the street, it seems to me that I can't be compared with an average citizen, that everybody is pointing at me with his finger. I instinctively avoid meeting anyone. Former acquaintances and friends of better times are no longer so cordial. They greet me indifferently when we meet. They no longer offer me a cigarette and their eyes seem to say, 'You are not worth it, you don't work'.[29]

Instead of cowering, the stigmatized individual may attempt to approach mixed contacts with hostile bravado, but this can induce from others its own set of troublesome reciprocations. It may be added that the stigmatized person sometimes vacillates between cowering and bravado, racing from one to the other, thus demonstrating one central way in which ordinary face-to-face interaction can run wild.

I am suggesting, then, that the stigmatized individual—at least the 'visibly' stigmatized one—will have special reasons for feeling that mixed social situations make for anxious, un-anchored interaction. But if this is so, then it is to be suspected that we normals will find these situations shaky too. We will feel that the stigmatized individual is either too aggressive or too shame-faced, and in either case too ready to read unintended meanings into our actions. We ourselves may feel that if we show direct sympathetic concern for his condition, we may be overstepping ourselves; and yet if we actually forget that he has a failing we are likely to make impossible demands of him or unthinkingly slight his fellow-sufferers. Each potential source of discomfort for him when we are with him can become something we sense he is aware of, aware that we are aware of, and even aware of our state of awareness about his awareness; the stage is then set for the infinite regress of mutual consideration that Meadian social psychology tells us how to begin but not how to terminate.

Given what both the stigmatized and we normals introduce into mixed social situations, it is understandable that all will not go smoothly. We are likely to attempt to carry on as though in fact he wholly fitted one of the types of person naturally available to us in the situation, whether this means treating him as someone better than we feel he might be or someone worse than we feel he probably is. If neither of these tacks is possible, then we may try to act as if he were a 'non-person', and not present at all as someone of whom ritual notice is to be taken. He, in turn, is likely to go along with these strategies, at least initially.

In consequence, attention is furtively withdrawn from its obligatory targets, and self-consciousness and 'other-consciousness' occur, expressed in the pathology of interaction—uneasiness.[30] As described in the case of the physically handicapped:

> Whether the handicap is overtly and tactlessly responded to as such or, as is more commonly the case, no explicit reference is made to it, the underlying condition of heightened, narrowed awareness causes the interaction to be articulated too exclusively in terms of it. This, as my informants described it, is usually accompanied by one or more of the familiar signs of discomfort and stickiness: the guarded references, the common everyday words suddenly made taboo, the fixed stare elsewhere, the artificial levity, the compulsive loquaciousness, the awkward solemnity.[31]

In social situations with an individual known or perceived to have a stigma, we are likely, then, to employ categorizations that do not fit, and we and he are likely to experience uneasiness. Of course, there is often significant movement from this starting point. And since the stigmatized person is likely to be more often faced with these situations than are we, he is likely to become the more adept at managing them.

# Moral Career

Persons who have a particular stigma tend to have similar learning experiences regarding their plight, and similar changes in conception of self—a similar 'moral career' that is both cause and effect of commitment to a similar sequence of personal adjustments. (The natural history of a category of persons with a stigma must be clearly distinguished from the natural history of the stigma itself—the history of the origins, spread, and decline of the capacity of an attribute to serve as a stigma in a particular society, for example, divorce in American upper-middle-class society.) One phase of this socialization process is that through which the stigmatized person learns and incorporates the standpoint of the normal, acquiring thereby the identity beliefs of the wider society and a general idea of what it would be like to possess a particular stigma. Another phase is that through which he learns that he possesses a particular stigma and, this time in detail, the consequence of possessing it. The timing and interplay of these two initial phases of the moral career form important patterns, establishing the foundation for later development, and providing a means of distinguishing among the moral careers available to the stigmatized. Four such patterns may be mentioned.

One pattern involves those with an inborn stigma who become socialized into their disadvantageous situation even while they are learning and incorporating the standards against which they fall short.[32] For example, an orphan learns that children naturally and normally have parents, even while he is learning what it means not to have any. After spending the first 16 years of his life in the institution, he can later still feel that he naturally knows how to be a father to his son.

A second pattern derives from the capacity of a family, and to a much lesser extent a local neighbourhood, to constitute itself a protective capsule for its young. Within such a capsule a congenitally stigmatized child can be carefully sustained by means of information control. Self-belittling definitions of him are prevented from entering the charmed circle, while broad access is given to other conceptions held in the wider society, ones that lead the encapsulated child to see himself as a fully qualified ordinary human being, of normal identity in terms of such basic matters as age and sex.

The point in the protected individual's life when the domestic circle can no longer protect him will vary by social class, place of residence, and type of stigma, but in each case will give rise to a moral experience when it occurs. Thus, public school entrance is often reported as the occasion of stigma learning, the experience sometimes coming very precipitously on the first day of school with taunts, teasing, ostracism, and fights.[33] Interestingly, the more the child is 'handicapped' the more likely he is to be sent to a special school for persons of his kind, and the more abruptly he will have to face the view which the public at large takes of him. He will be told that he will have an easier time of it among 'his own', and thus learn that the own he thought he possessed was the wrong one, and that this lesser own is really his. It should be added that where the infantilely stigmatized manages to get through his early school years with some illusions left, the onset of dating or job-getting will often introduce the moment of truth. In some cases, merely an increased likelihood of incidental disclosure is involved:

I think the first realization of my situation, and the first intense grief resulting from this realization, came one day, very casually, when a group of us in our early teens had gone to the beach for the day. I was lying on the sand, and I guess the fellows and girls thought I was asleep. One of the fellows said, 'I like Domenica very much, but I would never go out with a blind girl'. I cannot think of any prejudice which so completely rejects you.[34]

A third pattern of socialization is illustrated by one who becomes stigmatized late in life, or learns late in life that he has always been discreditable—the first involving no radical re-organization of his view of his past, the second involving this factor. Such an individual has thoroughly learned about the normal and the stigmatized long before he must see himself as deficient. Presumably he will have a special problem in re-identifying himself, and a special likelihood of developing disapproval of self:

When I smelled an odour on the bus or subway before the colostomy, I used to feel very annoyed. I'd think that the people were awful, that they didn't take a bath or that they should have gone to the bathroom before travelling. I used to think that they might have odours from what they ate. I used to be terribly annoyed; to me it seemed that they were filthy, dirty. Of course, at the least opportunity I used to change my seat and if I couldn't, it used to go against my grain. So naturally, I believe that the young people feel the same way about me if I smell.[35]

While there are certainly cases of individuals discovering only in adult life that they belong to a stigmatized tribal group or that their parents have a contagious moral blemish, the usual case here is that of physical handicaps that 'strike' late in life:

But suddenly I woke up one morning, and found that I could not stand. I had had polio, and polio was as simple as that. I was like a very young child who had been dropped into a big, black hole, and the only thing I was certain of was that I could not get out unless someone helped me. The education, the lectures, and the parental training which I had received for 24 years didn't seem to make me the person who could do anything for me now. I was like everyone else—normal, quarrelsome, gay, full of plans, and all of a sudden something happened! Something happened and I became a stranger. I was a greater stranger to myself than to anyone. Even my dreams did not know me. They did not know what they ought to let me do—-and when I went to dances or to parties in them, there was always an odd provision or limitation—not spoken of or mentioned, but there just the same. I suddenly had the very confusing mental and emotional conflict of a lady leading a double life. It was unreal and it puzzled me, and I could not help dwelling on it.[36]

Here the medical profession is likely to have the special job of informing the infirm who he is going to have to be.

A fourth pattern is illustrated by those who are initially socialized in an alien community, whether inside or outside the geographical boundaries of the normal society, and who then must learn a second way of being that is felt by those around them to be the real and valid one.

It should be added that when an individual acquires a new stigmatized self late in life, the uneasiness he feels about new associates may slowly give way to uneasiness felt concerning old ones. Post-stigma acquaintances may see him simply as a faulted person; pre-stigma acquaintances, being attached to a conception of what he once was, may be unable to treat him either with formal tact or with familiar full acceptance:

> My task [as a blind writer interviewing prospective clients for his literary product] was to put the men I'd come to see at their ease—the reverse of the usual situation. Curiously, I found it much easier to do with men I'd never met before. Perhaps this was because with strangers there was no body of reminiscences to cover before business could be gotten down to and so there was no unpleasant contrast with the present.[37]

Regardless of which general pattern the moral career of the stigmatized individual illustrates, the phase of experience during which he learns that he possesses a stigma will be especially interesting, for at this time he is likely to be thrown into a new relationship to others who possess the stigma too. In the many cases where the individual's stigmatization is associated with his admission to a custodial institution such as a jail, sanatorium, or orphanage, much of what he learns about his stigma will be transmitted to him during prolonged intimate contact with those in the process of being transformed into his fellow-sufferers.

As already suggested, when the individual first learns who it is that he must now accept as his own, he is likely, at the very least, to feel some ambivalence; for these others will not only be patently stigmatized, and thus not like the normal person he knows himself to be, but may also have other attributes with which he finds it difficult to associate himself. What may end up as a freemasonry may begin with a shudder. A newly blind girl on a visit to 'The Lighthouse' directly from leaving the hospital provides an illustration:

> My questions about a guide dog were politely turned aside. Another sighted worker took me in tow to show me around. We visited the Braille library; the classrooms; the clubrooms where the blind members of the music and dramatic groups meet; the recreation hall where on festive occasions the blind dance with the blind; the bowling alleys where the blind play together; the cafeteria, where all the blind gather to eat together; the huge workshops where the blind earn a subsistence income by making mops and brooms, weaving rugs, caning chairs. As we moved from room to room, I could hear the shuffling of feet, the muted voices, the tap-tap-tapping of canes. Here was the safe, segregated world of the sightless—a completely different world, I was assured by the social worker, from the one I had just left . . .
>
> I was expected to join this world. To give up my profession and to earn my living making mops. The Lighthouse would be happy to teach me how to make mops. I was

to spend the rest of my life making mops with other blind people, eating with other blind people, dancing with other blind people. I became nauseated with fear, as the picture grew in my mind. Never had I come upon such destructive segregation.[38]

Given the ambivalence built into the individual's attachment to his stigmatized category, it is understandable that oscillations may occur in his support of, identification with, and participation among his own. There will be 'affiliation cycles' through which he comes to accept the special opportunities for in-group participation or comes to reject them after having accepted them before.[39] There will be corresponding oscillations in belief about the nature of own group and the nature of normals. For example, adolescence (and the high school peer group) can bring a marked decline in own-group identification and marked increase in identification with normals.[40] The later phases of the individual's moral career are to be found in these shifts of participation and belief.

The relationship of the stigmatized individual to the informal community and formal organizations of his own kind is, then, crucial. This relationship will, for example, mark a great difference between those whose differentness provides them very little of a new 'we', and those, such as minority group members, who find themselves a part of a well-organized community with longstanding traditions—a community that makes appreciable claims on loyalty and income, defining the member as someone who should take pride in his illness and not seek to get well. In any case, whether the stigmatized group is an established one or not, it is largely in relation to this own group that it is possible to discuss the natural history and the moral career of the stigmatized individual.

In reviewing his own moral career, the stigmatized individual may single out and retrospectively elaborate experiences which serve for him to account for his coming to the beliefs and practices that he now has regarding his own kind and normals. A life event can thus have a double bearing on moral career, first as immediate objective grounds for an actual turning point, and later (and easier to demonstrate) as a means of accounting for a position currently taken. One experience often selected for this latter purpose is that through which the newly stigmatized individual learns that full-fledged members of the group are quite like ordinary human beings:

When I [a young girl turning to a life of vice and first meeting her madam] turned into Fourth Street my courage again failed me, and I was about to beat a retreat when Mamie came out of a restaurant across the street and warmly greeted me. The porter, who came to the door in response to our ring, said that Miss Laura was in her room, and we were shown in. I saw a woman comely and middle-aged, who bore no resemblance to the horrible creature of my imagination. She greeted me in a soft, well-bred voice, and everything about her so eloquently spoke of her potentialities for motherhood that instinctively I looked around for the children who should have been clinging to her skirts.[41]

Another illustration is provided by a homosexual in regard to his becoming one:

> I met a man with whom I had been at school . . . He was, of course, gay himself, and took it for granted that I was, too. I was surprised and rather impressed. He did not look in the least like the popular idea of a homosexual, being well-built, masculine, and neatly dressed. This was something new to me. Although I was perfectly prepared to admit that love could exist between men, I had always been slightly repelled by the obvious homosexuals whom I had met because of their vanity, their affected manner, and their ceaseless chatter. These, it now appeared, formed only a small part of the homosexual world, although the most noticeable one . . .[42]

It may be added that in looking back to the occasion of discovering that persons with his stigma are human beings like everyone else, the individual may bring to bear a later occasion when his pre-stigma friends imputed unhumanness to those he had by then learned to see as full-fledged persons like himself. Thus, in reviewing her experience as a circus worker, a young girl sees first that she had learned her fellow-workers are not freaks, and second that her pre-circus friends fear for her having to travel in a bus along with other members of the troupe.[43]

Another turning point—retrospectively if not originally—is the isolating, incapacitating experience, often a period of hospitalization, which comes later to be seen as the time when the individual was able to think through his problem, learn about himself, sort out his situation, and arrive at a new understanding of what is important and worth seeking in life.

It should be added that not only are personal experiences retrospectively identified as turning points, but experiences once removed may be employed in this way. For example, a reading of the literature of the group may itself provide an experience felt and claimed as reorganizing:

> I do not think it is claiming too much to say that Uncle Tom's Cabin was a fair and truthful panorama of slavery; however that may be, it opened my eyes as to who and what I was and what my country considered me; in fact, it gave me my bearing.[44]

## Notes

1. In this connection, see the review by M. Meltzer, 'Countermanipulation through Malingering', in A. Biderman and H. Zimmer, eds., The Manipulation of Human Behaviour (New York: John Wiley and Sons, 1961), pp. 277–304.
2. In recent history, especially in Britain, low class status functioned as an important tribal stigma, the sins of the parents, or at least of their milieu, being visited on the child, should the child rise improperly far above the initial station. The management of class stigma is of course a central theme in the English novel.
3. D. Riseman, 'Some Observations Concerning Marginality', Phylon, Second Quarter, 1951, 22.
4. The case regarding mental patients is presented by T.J. Scheff in a forthcoming paper.
5. In regard to the blind, see E. Henrich and L. Kriegel, eds., Experiments in Survival (New York: Association for the Aid of Crippled Children, 1961), pp. 152 and 186; and H. Chevigny, My Eyes Have a Cold Nose (New Haven, Conn.: Yale University Press, paperbound, 1962), p. 201.
6. In the words of one blind woman, 'I was asked to endorse a perfume, presumably because being sightless my sense of smell was super-discriminating'. See T. Keitlen (with N. Lobsenz), Farewell to Fear (New York: Avon, 1962), p. 10.
7. A. G. Gowman, The War Blind in American Social Structure (New York: American Foundation for the Blind, 1957), p. 198.

8. For examples, see Macgregor *et al., op. cit.,* throughout.
9. The notion of 'normal human being' may have its source in the medical approach to humanity or in the tendency of the large-scale bureaucratic organizations, such as the nation-state, to treat all members in some respects as equal. Whatever its origins, it seems to provide the basic imagery through which laymen currently conceive of themselves. Interestingly, a convention seems to have merged in popular life-story writing where a questionable person proves his claim to normalcy by citing his acquisition of a spouse and children, and, oddly, by attesting to his spending Christmas and Thanksgiving with them.
10. A criminal's view of this non-acceptance is presented in T. Parker and R. Allerton, The Courage of His Convictions (London: Hutchinson and Co., 1962), p. 110–11.
11. F. Warfield, *Keep Listening* (New York: The Viking Press, 1957), p. 76. See also H. von Hentig, *The Criminal and His Victim* (New Haven, Conn.: Yale University Press, 1948), p. 101.
12. Keitien, *op. cit.,* Chap. 12, pp. 117–129 and Chap. 14, pp. 137–149. See also Chevigny, *op. cit.,* pp. 85–86.
13. Henrich and Kriegel, *op. cit.,* p. 49.
14. W.Y. Baker and L. H. Smith, 'Facial Disfigurement and Personality', *Journal of the American Medical Association, CXII* (1939), 303. Macgregor *et al., op, cit.,* p. 57 ff., provide an illustration of a man who used his big red nose for a crutch.
15. Henrich and Kriegel, *op. cit.,* p. 19.
16. Ibid, p. 35.
17. For one review, see G. W. Allport, *The Nature of Prejudice* (New York: Anchor Books, 1958).
18. From *Clinical Studies in Psychiatry,* H. S. Perry, M. L. Gawel, and M. Gibbon, eds. (New York: W. W. Norton and Company, 1956), p. 145.
19. R. Barker, 'The Social Psychology of Physical Disability', *Journal of Social Issues,* IV (1948), 34, suggests that stigmatized persons 'live on a social-psychological frontier', constantly facing new situations. See also Macgregor *et al., op. cit.,* p. 87, where the suggestion is made that the grossly deformed need suffer less doubt about their reception in interaction than the less visibly deformed.
20. Barker, *op, cit.,* p. 33.
21. Parker and Allerton, *op. cit.,* p, 111.
22. This special kind of self-consciousness is analyzed in S. Messinger et al., 'Life as Theater: Some Notes on the Dramaturgic Approach to Social Reality', Sociometry, *XXV* (1962), 98–110.
23. Parker and Allerton, *op. cit.,* p. 111.
24. Chevigny, *op. cit.,* p. 140.
25. L. A. Dexter, 'A Social Theory of Mental Deficiency', *American Journal of Mental Deficiency, LXII* (1958), 923. For another study of the mental defective as a stigmatized person, see S. E, Perry, 'Some Theoretical Problems of Mental Deficiency and Their Action Implications', *Psychiatry, XVII* (1954), 45–73.
26. This theme is well treated in R. K. White, B.A. Wright, and T. Dembo, 'Studies in Adjustment to Visible Injuries: Evaluation of Curiosity by the Injured', Journal of Abnormal and Social Psychology, *XLIII* (1948), 13–28.
27. For example, Henrich and Kriegel, *op. cit.,* p. 184.
28. See Wright, *op. cit.,* 'The Problem of Sympathy', pp. 233–237.
29. S. Zawadski and P. Lazarsfeld, 'The Psychological Consequences of Unemployment', *Journal of Social Psychology, VI* (1935), 239.
30. For a general treatment see E. Goffman, 'Alienation from Interaction', *Human Relations,* X (1957), 47–60.
31. F. Davis, 'Deviance Disavowal: The Management of Strained Interaction by the Visibly Handicapped', *Social Problems,* IX (1961), 123. See also White, Wright, and Dembo, *op. cit.,* pp, 26–27.
32. Discussion of this pattern can be found in A.R. Lindesmith and A.L. Strauss, *Social Psychology,* rec. ed. (New York: Holt, Rinehart & Winston, 1956), pp. 180–183.
33. An example from an experience of a blind person may be found in R. Criddle, *Love is Not Blind* (New York: W.W. Norton and Company, 1953), p. 21; the experience of a dwarfed person is reported in H. Viscardi, Jr., *A Man's Stature* (New York: The John Day Company, 1952), pp. 13–14.
34. Henrich and Kriegel, *op. cit.,* p. 186.
35 Orbach *et al., op. cit.,* p. 165.
36. N. Linduska, *My Polio Past* (Chicago: Pellegrini and Cudahy, 1947), p. 177.
37. Chevigny, op. cit., p. 136.
38. Keitlen, op. cit., pp. 37–38. A description of the early vicissitudes of a hospitalized polio patient's identification with fellow-cripples is provided in Linduska, *op. cit.,* pp. 159–165. A fictional account of racial reidentification is provided by J. W. Johnson, *The Autobiography of an Ex-Coloured Man,* rev. ed. (New York: Hill and Wang, American Century Series, 1960), pp. 22–23.
39. A general statement may be found in two of E.C. Hughes' papers, 'Social Change and Status Protest', *Phylon*

First Quarter, 1949, 58–65, and 'Cycles and Turning Points', in *Men and Their Work* (New York: Free Press of Glencoe, 1958).

40. M. Yarrow, 'Personality Development and Minority Group Membership', in M. Sklare, *The Jews* (New York: Free Press of Glencoe, 1960), pp. 468–470.

41. *Madeleine, An Autobiography* (New York: Pyramid Books, 1961), pp. 36–37.

42. P. Wildeblood, *Against the Law* (New York: Julian Messner, 1959), pp. 23–24.

43. C. Clausen, *I Love You Honey But the Season's Over* (New York: Hoit, Rinehart and Winston, 1961), p. 217.

44. Johnson, *op. cit.*, p. 42. Johnson's novel, like others of its kind, provides a nice instance of mythmaking, being a literary organization of many of the crucial moral experiences and crucial turning points retrospectively available to those in a stigmatized category.

# Part III  Social Control and Justice

Most of us can give examples of the kinds of constraints we've experienced as a result of being in a group or of having our behaviour controlled as part of the socialization experience we underwent at home and school. But the general experience of constraint and control that is part of life in a group covers over a distinction between the sort of socialization and regulation practices needed to achieve social order, and the sort of control, punishment, and correction which are applied to those who get out of line or are deliberately resisting socialization and regulation.

Strictly speaking, 'social control' refers to the institutions and procedures used to ensure that non-compliant members conform with expected, approved behaviours. The various means a group uses to bring members back into line range from informal practices such as avoidance, gossip, ridicule, and blame, to more formal, serious ones such as economic penalties, rehabilitation, incarceration, and ultimately death. Several articles in this section investigate different ways social control is exercised in contemporary Western societies, from the many informal accommodation practices people use to deal with troublesome individuals to the nature of social control in modern societies and what it's like to do time in a Canadian prison.

Imprisonment is an important public issue today. There has been a growing public sentiment in many Western nations that the current penal system is too lenient, particularly on juvenile offenders. Laws and sentences are not severe enough to act as an appropriate punishment and effective deterrent. Over the past couple of decades, some governments, especially in the US, have been implementing tough law and order policies and programs whose main emphasis has been on increasing punishment, disciplinary rehabilitation, and prisons. To some extent Canada has been following suit.

But do such policies and practices accomplish what their advocates claim? Sociological and criminological research has found some system of punishment is necessary to ensure members comply with norms, values, and beliefs that are integral to the social order of a group, and that such a system will generally deter most of us from committing crimes. But it seems it is the certainty of punishment that is more important than severity.[1] Studies on severity have yielded mixed results. In some cases, especially where there was little to no punishment before, it may decrease reoffending, as with the example of impaired driving.  In other cases it may actually correlate with an increase in reoffending. But overall, it has not been found to have a clear effect as a deterrent.

However there is another unintended consequence of instituting stricter law and order programs and policies, as seen in the example of the US. There is only so much money to give to corrections, and a punitive approach directs it into building more and larger prisons. There is little, if any, money for other kinds of rehabilitative programs. In his 2004 State of the Union address, President Bush acknowledged the problem that was emerging.[2] After years of being tough on criminals by imprisoning them, the first wave of those who had served their time were being released, about 600,000 that year alone. All that most of these prisoners would receive on release would be $20 and a bus ticket. In order to fund the growing prison population, many programs for drug-addiction treatment and job skills had been eliminated. And there were few programs to help integrate the newly released prisoners into society. Moreover, Bush acknowledged it would now take millions more dollars to prevent a criminal underclass from emerging in America as a result of the original policy.

Researchers have known for some time what to expect from incarceration without effective rehabilitation, education or training programs. Why would governments pursue such policies in the first place? In part, this requires investigating the question of justice. Law and order policies are based in a 'retributive' approach to justice that emphasizes discipline and punishment. The concluding articles in this section critique this approach. Specifically, our current approach to justice appears to ignore the many kinds of social injustice that are being experienced by those who often violate the law in the first place. And there may be an important role for a 'restorative' justice system, built on different principles and practices, to complement the existing retributive system.

## Notes

1.  Gomme, Ian McDermid. 2007. *The Shadow Line: Deviance and Crime in Canada, 4th edition*. Toronto: Thomson Nelson: 67–73; Larry Siegel and Chris McCormick. 2006. *Criminology in Canada, 3rd edition*. Toronto: Thomson Nelson: 139–142.
2.  Sanders, Doug. 2004. Jan. 23. '600,000 ex-cons add up to a US headache.' *Globe and Mail*.

# 11

## Introduction

How do we manage people we see as persistently difficult or problematic to interact with? In this article Lynch reports on the results of an assignment he gave to his sociology students. Their task was to interview people who had to deal repeatedly with someone who either they or others regarded as a 'troublemaker'. The aim was to identify the practices people used to live with the problematic person on a daily basis.

Lynch collected the results of his students' findings together into three sets of accommodation strategies, each with a distinctive practical purpose. But sociologically there is often more than one thing going on in social interactions, or various levels of significance to what is occurring. And Lynch found this to be the case here as well. What is it that all these accommodation practices were doing beyond being practical strategies for handling troublemakers? And what is the significance of what he found regarding how we build an orderly social world together?*

# Accommodation Practices

*Michael Lynch*

Accommodation practices are interactional techniques that people use to manage persons they view as persistent sources of trouble. Accommodation implies attempts to 'live with' persistent and ineradicable troubles.[1] Previous studies mention a number of accommodation practices. Lemert (1962) describes how people exclude distrusted individuals from their organization's covert activities by employing methods of 'spurious interaction'. Such forms of interaction are:

> . . . distinguished by patronizing, evasion, 'humouring', guiding conversation onto selected topics, underreaction, and silence, all calculated either to prevent intense interaction or to protect individual and group values by restricting access to them. When the interaction is between two or more persons in the individual's presence it is cued by a whole repertoire of subtle expressive signs which are meaningful only to them. (1962: 8)

Other methods for managing perceived 'troublemakers' include: isolation and avoidance (Lemert, 1962; Sampson *et al.*, 1962), relieving an individual of ordinary responsibilities associated with their roles (Sampson *et al.*, 1962); hiding liquor bottles from a heavily drinking spouse (Jackson, 1954); and 'babying' (Jackson, 1954).

# The Study

This study is an analysis of the results of an assignment which I gave to students in classes on the sociology of mental illness in 1981 and 1982. I instructed students to locate someone in a familiar social environment who was identified by others (and perhaps by themselves) as 'crazy'; the subject need not appear 'mentally ill', but need only be a personal and persistent source of trouble for others. The vast majority of the students had little trouble finding such subjects. I instructed them to interview persons who consistently dealt with the troublemaker in a living or work situation. The interviews were to focus on the practices used by others to 'live with' the troublemaker from day to day. Students who were personally acquainted with the troublemaker were encouraged to refer to their own recollections and observations in addition to their interviews. They were instructed not to interview or otherwise disturb the troublemakers. Each student wrote a five to seven page paper on accommodation practices with an appendix of notes from their interviews.

## The Subjects

The persons the students interviewed described subjects who had already developed to an intermediate stage in the 'natural history of trouble' (Emerson and Messinger 1977). Few troublemakers carried formal designations of mental illness, but each was associated with recurrent organizational troubles. The troubles were defined non-relationally (Goffman 1969); they were attributed to the personal agency of a troublemaker, and any possible mitigating factors were no longer considered pertinent. Although the students and their interviewees claimed a consensus on the fact that *something* was wrong with the troublemaker, just what was wrong was often a matter of speculation. Troublemakers' friends and acquaintances sometimes resorted to amateur psychologizing to account for a subject's 'problem', but often they expressed moral exasperation and disgust, without any mention of a possible 'illness'.

Students and those they interviewed used a rich variety of vernacular epithets for personal character types to identify their subjects. These included common insults, 'crazy' terms used as insults, and a few straightforward 'illness' designators. The following expressions illustrate different shadings in the ambiguity of the troublemakers' statuses as moral offenders and/or 'sick' persons:

1. Commonplace vernacular terms for faults and faulted persons, without reference to insanity: 'bullshitter', 'bird' (as in 'turkey'), 'off the wall', 'spiteful, nasty girl', 'rude and argumentative', 'an obnoxious pest', 'catty', 'space cadet', 'chronic complainer', 'frivolous and ridiculous', and nicknames such as 'Ozone' and 'The Deviant'.
2. Vernacular cognates of madness which do not necessarily compel the serious connotation of illness: 'crazy', 'nuts', 'bananas', 'weird', 'strange', 'unpredictable', 'highly emotional', 'attention seeking and manipulative', 'explosive, angry', and 'sick'.
3. Amateur uses of accounts associated with the helping professions: 'paranoid', 'developmentally disabled', 'chemically imbalanced in the brain', 'low self-esteem', 'obsessed with food', and 'alcoholic'.

Except in a few cases when students reported a specific medical diagnosis, their accounts did not provide unique labels corresponding to stable categories of disorder. They did, however, point to a history of incidents supporting the conclusion that *something* was wrong with the person in question.

Some accounts emphasized that it was impossible to describe just what was wrong with the person. There was far more to the trouble than could be described by a few episodes: 'disgusting eating habits', 'he smells terrible', 'he stands too close to people', 'she asks you to repeat things over and over again', 'she is so promiscuous that one of the fraternities has a song about fucking her!' Not all accounts were wholly negative or rejecting. At least some acquaintances whom students interviewed expressed some affection or attachment to troublemakers, or an obligation to maintain a minimal level of civility toward the person.

In the few cases where the troublemaker had a history of mental or neurological disorder, students reported that their informants used the illness to excuse incidents believed to be symptomatic of the disorder. Such special understandings did not entirely replace more hostile reactions, for many of the 'symptoms' were also personal offences:

> *Margaret explained that she always attempts to start off calm when dealing with Joan and thinking of her as being a 'lonely and sick woman', but that Joan 'gets you so angry that it is difficult to stay level-headed and then I start screaming and have to leave'. (Student report of an interview concerning a 'senile' woman.)*

The students investigated a number of different organizational environments. Fraternities and sororities were most popular, followed by families (both nuclear and extended), dormitory residents, work groups, friendship cliques, athletic teams, and residents of apartment suites and local neighbourhoods. One case dealt with a board and care home; another described a group of students on a retreat. Among the work groups observed were employees of a bookstore, a clothing store, a pharmacy, and a fast food restaurant. One noteworthy case involved a rock and roll band and its crew on a national tour. In each of these cases, membership in the group or organization provided the local basis of the troublemaker's existence. Membership furnished the context for day-to-day interactions with the troublemaker, and for accumulating an oral history of the troublemaker's antics. In the following discussion, I will the use term *members* to refer to all those who knew or related to the troublesome person through common membership in some organized group, network of relationship, acquaintance, or friendship.[2]

Because of the highly sensitive nature of the interactional circumstances which the students were investigating, I repeatedly asked them to respect the privacy of their subjects. They proved to be highly skilled at doing so, perhaps because they relied upon their own skills at performing accommodation practices to hide their inquiries from the troublemaker's attention.

I did not initially design the assignment in order to gather data for my own analysis. However, after reading the students' reports on their observations and interviews I found that despite their variability in descriptive and analytic quality and their obvious shortcomings as data, they described a diversity of accommodation practices, and suggested recurrent features of those practices which were not comprehensively treated in the literature. The information seemed worth reporting and students gave me permission to quote from their papers. I analyzed material from 32 of the student reports, each of which discussed a different case. In the remainder of this paper, all quotes not attributed to sources come from the students' papers.

I have organized accommodation practices under three thematic headings: (1) practices which isolate the troublemaker within the group; (2) practices which *manipulate* the troublemaker's behaviour, perception, and understanding; and (3) practices which members use to influence how others react to the troublemaker. The first set of practices defines and limits the troublemaker's chances for interaction, expression, and feedback within the group. The second set directs the details of the troublemaker's actions and establishes the discrepant meanings of those actions for 'self' and 'other'. The third set includes attempts to make the troublemaker's public identity into a covert communal project.

## Minimizing Contact with the Troublemaker

*Avoiding* and *ignoring* were the two accommodation practices mentioned most often by students. Both were methods for minimizing contact with the troublemaker, and had the effect of isolating the troublemaker within the organizational network. While both were negative methods of behaviour control, attenuating the troublemaker's actual and possible occasions of interaction, they worked quite differently. Avoiding limited the gross *possibility* of interaction, while ignoring worked *within* ongoing occasions of interaction to limit the interactional *reality* of the encounter. Where avoiding created an absence of encounter, ignoring created a dim semblance to ordinary interaction.

### Avoiding

In virtually every student's account, one or more of the members they interviewed mentioned that they actively avoided the troublemaker. Avoidance created an interactional vacuum around the troublemaker. Members managed to stay out of the way of the troublemaker without actually requesting or commanding the troublemaker to stay away from them. Methods of avoidance included individual and joint tactics such as 'ducking into restrooms', 'keeping a lookout for her at all times', and 'hiding behind a newspaper or book'.

Some members were better placed than others within the structure of the organization to avoid the troublemaker. In larger organizations like fraternities and sororities, persons could stake out positions which minimized contact with the troublemaker. In more intimate circles avoidance ran more of a risk of calling attention to the *absence* of usual interactional involvement. Avoidance *did* occur in such intimate groups as families (Sampson *et al.*, 1962), but only at the cost of threatening the very integrity of the group.

### Ignoring/Not Taking Seriously

Ignoring differed from avoiding because it entailed at least some interaction, though of an attenuated and inauthentic kind. One account described conversations with the troublemaker as being 'reduced to superficial "hellos", most of which are directed at her feet; there is an obvious lack of eye contact'. Many accounts mentioned the superficiality of interactions with troublemakers. In some cases this was accomplished by what one student called 'rehearsed and phony responses' to limit the openness of their conversations to a few stock sequences.[3]

Although ignoring entailed interaction, it was like avoidance in that it circumscribed the troublemaker's interactional possibilities. Where avoidance operated to limit, in a gross way, the intersection of pathways between troublemaker and other members, ignoring operated intensively to trivialize the troublemaker's apparent involvements in group activities.[4] Bids for positive notice were ignored, and had little effect on the troublemaker's position within the group.

# Directly Managing the Troublemaker's Actions

Members used a number of more direct interventions to control and limit the troublemaker's behaviour, including humouring, screening, taking over, orienting to local prospects of normality, and practical jokes and retaliations. While such methods had little hope of permanently modifying the behaviour, they were used to curtail episodic disruptions by the troublemaker.

## Humouring

Members often used the term 'humouring' to describe attempts to manage the troublemaker by maintaining a veneer of agreement and geniality in the face of actions which would ordinarily evoke protest or disgust. For example, in the case of 'an obnoxiously argumentative person', members offered superficial tokens of agreement in response to even the most outlandish pronouncements for the sake of avoiding more extreme disruptions.

Humouring was often made possible through insight into recurrent features of the troublemaker's behaviour. Members recognized recurrent situations in ordinary interactions which triggered peculiar reactions by the troublemaker. They developed a heightened awareness of ordinary and seemingly innocuous details of interaction which could touch off an explosive reaction. One student described how her parents managed a 'crazy aunt', who she said was prone to sudden and violent verbal assaults:

> My parents avoided discussing specific topics and persons that they knew distressed her. Whenever she began talking about an arousable [sic] event or person, my parents and her husband attempted to change the subject.[5]

Although members rationalized humouring as a way 'to make it easy for everybody', they did not always find it easy to withhold their reactions to interactional offences. A student wrote about her efforts to prepare her fiancé for a first encounter with her grandmother, said to be suffering from senile dementia, Alzheimer type:

*I attempted to explain to him that he should not say anything controversial, agree with whatever she says, and generally stay quiet as much as possible. [He assured her that everything would be okay, but when he was confronted with the actual grandmother, the assurance proved quite fragile.] That encounter proved to be quite an experience for Charles—we left Grandma's house with Charles screaming back at her for his self-worth.*

Other accounts mentioned the strain and difficulty of trying to humour troublemakers. They described an exceedingly fragile interactional situation which was prone to break down at any moment:

*You don't want to set him off, so you're very careful about what you do and say. You become tense trying to keep everything calm, and then something happens to screw it up anyway: The car won't start, or a light bulb blows. It's all my fault because I'm a rotten wife and mother.*

Humouring often entailed obedience or deference to what members claimed (when not within earshot of the troublemaker) were outrageous or absurd demands:

*Everyone did what she asked in order to please her and not cause any bad scenes.*

In some cases, members exerted special efforts or underwent severe inconvenience for the sake of a person they secretly despised. Not surprisingly, such efforts often, though not always, were exerted by persons over whom the troublemaker had formal authority. In one case the members of a crew travelling with a rock and roll band would set up the troublesome member's equipment before that of the others and set up daily meetings with him to discuss his 'technical needs', while at the same time they believed it was foolish of him to demand such special attention. They described the special meetings and favours as a 'bogus accommodation'. In every case, whether correlated with formal divisions of authority or not, humouring contributed to the troublemaker's sense of interactional power over others.

Humouring always included a degree of duplicity in which members 'kept a straight face' when interacting with the troublemaker or acted in complicity with the troublemaker's premises—premises which members otherwise discounted as delusional or absurd:

*We played along with her fantasy of a boyfriend, 'John'. We never said what a complete fool she was for waiting for him.*

Commonly, members practised *serial* duplicity by waiting until the troublemaker was out of earshot to display for one another's appreciation the 'real' understanding they had previously suppressed:

*They pretend to know what she is talking about, they act as if they are interested . . . they make remarks when she is gone.*

At other times they practised *simultaneous* duplicity by showing interest and serious engagement to the troublemaker's face while expressing detachment and sarcasm to one another through furtive glances, gestures, and double entendres (Lemert, 1962: 8).

> *Those employees who she is not facing will make distorted faces and roll their eyes around to reaffirm the fact that she is a little slow. All the time this occurs Susan is totally oblivious to it, or at least she pretends to be.*

In one fraternity, members devised a specific hand gesture (described as 'wing flapping') which they displayed for one another when interacting with a troublemaker they called 'the bird'.

Members occasionally rationalized their duplicity by describing the troublemaker as a self-absorbed and 'dense' person, whose lack of orientation to others provided ample opportunity for their play:

> *People speak sarcastically to him, and Joe, so wrapped up in himself, believes what they are saying and hears only what he wants to hear.*

## Screening

Jackson (1954: 572) reported that alcoholics' wives attempted to manage their husbands' heavy drinking by hiding or emptying liquor bottles in the house and curtailing their husbands' funds. One student described a similar practice used by friends of a person who they feared had suicidal tendencies. They systematically removed from the person's environment any objects that could be used to commit suicide.

Screening and monitoring of troublemakers' surroundings also occurred in the interactional realm. A few accounts mentioned attempts to monitor the moods of a troublemaker, and to screen the person's potential interactions on the basis of attributed mood. When one sorority's troublemaker was perceived to be especially volatile, members acted as her covert receptionists by turning away her visitors, explaining that she was not in or was ill. In this case members were concerned not only to control the potential actions of the individual, but also to conceal those actions from others, and by doing so to protect the collective 'image' of their sorority from contamination.

## Taking Over

A number of accounts mentioned efforts by members to do activities which ordinarily would be done by someone in the troublemaker's social position. Like published accounts of cases in which husbands or mothers take over the household duties of a wife (Sampson et al.1962), the apartment mates of a troublemaker washed dishes and paid bills for her 'as if she wasn't there'. A circle of friends insisted on driving the automobile of a man they considered dangerously impulsive. Fraternity members gradually and unofficially took over the duties of their social chairman in fear of the consequences of his erratic actions and inappropriate attire. Taking over sometimes included such intimate personal functions as grooming and dressing, as when the spouse of a drunk diligently prepared her husband for necessary public appearances.

# Orienting to Local Prospects of Normality

Yarrow et al. (1955) mention that wives of mental patients sustained efforts to live with their husbands by treating interludes between episodes as the beginnings of 'recovery' rather than as periods of calm before the inevitable storms. By keeping tabs on the latest developments in the troublemaker's behaviour, members were often able to determine when it was 'safe' to treat the troublemaker as a 'normal' person. This method was not always as unrealistic as one would be led to believe from Yarrow et al. (1955). Since most troublemakers were viewed as persons whose difficulties, though inherent, were intermittent, living with them required knowing what to expect in the immediate interactional future:

> I have observed the occasion when a friend at the fraternity house entered the television room; and remained in the rear of the room, totally quiet, watching Danny, waiting for a signal telling him how to act. When Danny turned and spoke to him in a friendly, jovial manner, the young man enthusiastically pulled his chair up to sit next to Danny and began speaking freely.

Members described many troublemakers as persons with likeable and even admirable qualities, whose friendship was valued during their 'good times'. When a member anticipated an encounter with a troublemaker, he or she wanted most of all to avoid touching off a 'bad scene'. The local culture of gossip surrounding a troublemaker tended to facilitate such an aim by providing a running file on the current state of his or her moods. By using the latest news, members could decide when to avoid encounters and when they could approach the troublemaker without undue wariness.

## Practical Jokes and Retaliations

Although direct expressions of hostility toward troublemakers were rarely mentioned, it is possible that they occurred more frequently than was admitted. Practical jokes and other forms of retaliation were designed not to reveal their authors. The troublemaker would be 'clued in' that *somebody* despised him or was otherwise 'out to get' him, but he would be left to imagine just who it was. Some jokes were particularly cruel, and were aimed at the troublemaker's particular vulnerabilities. A member of a touring rock and roll band was known to have difficulty forming relationships with women:

> They would get girls to call his mom and make dates they would never keep. Apparently, the spotlight operator was the author of a series of hot love letters of a mythical girl who was following Moog [a pseudonym for the troublemaker] from town to town and would soon appear in his bedroom. The crew must have been laughing their heads off for days. Moog was reading the letters out loud in the dressing room.

# Influencing the Reaction to the Troublemaker

A group of practices, instead of focusing solely on the troublemaker's interactional behaviour, attempted to control others' *reactions to* and *interpretations of* that behaviour. These accommodations recognized that there could be serious consequences in the reactions of outsiders—non-members—to the troublemaker. Such practices included efforts by members to control the reactions of persons outside the group; and to control assessments not only of the individual troublemaker, but of the group as well. The responsibilities for, and social consequences of, the individual's behaviour were thus adopted by members as a collective project.

## Turning the Troublemaker into a Notorious Character

In stories to outsiders as well as others in the group, members were sometimes able to turn the troublemaker into a fascinating and almost admirable character. A classic case was the fraternity 'animal'. Although litanies of crude, offensive, and assaultive actions were recounted, the character's antics were also portrayed with evident delight. Such descriptions incorporated elements of heroism, the prowess of the brawler, or the fearlessness and outrageousness of a prankster. In one case a student reported that the fraternity troublemaker, nicknamed 'the deviant', was supported and encouraged by a minority faction who claimed to an outsider that he was merely 'a little wild', and that nothing was wrong with him. This faction seemed unembarrassed by, and perhaps a bit proud of, the troublemaker's 'animal' qualities that others might ascribe to the fraternity as well. The quasi-heroic or comical repute of the troublemaker did not overshadow many members' distaste for the disruptions, but it did constitute a supportive moral counterpoint.

## Shadowing

In one instance a group of students living in a dorm arranged covertly to escort their troublemaker on his frequent trips to local bars. He had a reputation for drinking more than his capacity and then challenging all comers to fights. To inhibit such adventures, members of the group volunteered to accompany him under various pretexts, and to quell any disputes he precipitated during the drinking sessions. In the case of the member of the rock and roll band, other members chaperoned him during interviews with media critics. When he said something potentially offensive, his chaperon attempted to turn his statement into a joke. Another account described efforts by a group to spy on a member who they believed was likely to do something rash or violent.

## Advance Notices

As Lemert (1962) points out, members often build a legacy of apocryphal stories about their troublemaker. Stories told by one member to another about the troublemaker's latest antics provided a common source of entertainment, and perhaps solidarity. Some members admitted that they could not imagine what they would talk about with one another if not the troublemaker's behaviour:

> *The highlight of the day is hearing the latest story about Joanie.*

Such gleeful renditions helped to prepare non-members for first encounters with the troublemaker.

A few students mentioned that the troublemakers they studied appeared normal or even charming during initial encounters, but that members soon warned them to be careful about getting involved with the person. Subsequent experience confirmed the warnings, although it was difficult to discern whether this was a result of their accuracy or of the wariness they engendered.

Members of a group that included a persistently troublesome character 'apologized for him beforehand' to persons who shortly would be doing business with him. They also warned women he approached that he was 'a jerk'. In addition to preparing such persons for upcoming encounters, the apologies and warnings carried the tacit claim that 'we're not like him'. This mitigated any potential contamination of the group's moral reputation.

## Hiding and Diluting the Troublemaker

Some fraternities and sororities institutionalized a 'station' for hiding troublemakers during parties and teas where new members were recruited. Troublemakers were assigned out-of-the-way positions in social gatherings and, in some cases, were accompanied at all times by other members whose job it was to cut off the troublemaker's interaction with prospective members.

The methods used for hiding and diluting were especially artful when they included pretexts to conceal from the troublemakers that their role had been diminished. The troublemaker in the rock and roll band was said to embarrass other members with 'distasteful ego tripping' on stage during public concerts. Such 'ego trips' were characterized by loud and 'awful' playing on his instrument and extravagant posturing in attempts to draw the audience's attention to himself. These displays were countered by the sound and light men in the crew.

> *On those nights the sound man would turn up the monitors on stage so Moog sounded loud to himself and would turn down Moog in the [concert] hall and on the radio.*

Simultaneously, the lighting director would 'bathe him in darkness' by dimming the spotlights on him. These practices, in effect, technically created a delusional experience for the troublemaker. They produced a systematic distortion of his perception of the world and simultaneously diminished his public place in that world.

## Covering For/Covering Up

Friends and intimates sometimes went to great lengths to smooth over the damages and insults done to others by the troublemaker. The husband of a 'crazy woman' monitored his wife's offences during her 'episodes' and followed in the wake of the destruction with apologies and sometimes monetary reparations to offended neighbours. Similar efforts at restoring normality also occurred in immediate interactional contexts:

> *Before she will even tell you her name, she is telling you how one day she was hitchhiking and was gang raped by the five men who picked her up. This caused so many problems for her that she ended up in a mental hospital and is now a lesbian. The look on people's faces is complete shock. . . . Those hearing this story for the first time will sit in shock as if in a catatonic stupor, with wide eyes and their mouths dropped open, absolutely speechless. Someone who has already heard this story will break the silence by continuing the previous conversation, . . . putting it on extinction by ignoring it as if she never said anything.*

Members sometimes conspired, ostensibly on behalf of the troublemaker, to prevent the relevant authorities from detecting the existence and extent of the troubles. One group of girls in a freshman dorm deliberately lied to hide the fact that one of their members was having great difficulty and, in their estimation, was potentially suicidal. When her parents asked how she was doing the students responded that she was doing 'fine'. Members tried to contain her problems and to create a 'blockade' around any appearances of her problems that might attract the attentions of university authorities. Once underway, such cover-ups gained momentum, since the prospect of exposure increasingly threatened to make members culpable for not bringing the matter to the attention of remedial agents.

## Discussion

A prevailing theme in the students' accounts of accommodation practices was the avoidance of confrontation. They described confrontation as potentially 'unpleasant', to be avoided even when considerable damage and hardship had been suffered:

> *When students' money began disappearing from their rooms, we had a group meeting to discuss our mode of intervention. Although we all believed Chris was responsible, we did not confront her. Instead, we simply decided to make sure we locked our bedroom doors when not in our rooms.*

In general, a number of reasons for avoiding confrontation were given, including the anticipation of denial by the troublemaker, fear that the troublemaker would create a 'bad scene', and the belief that confrontation would make no difference in the long run.

Less direct methods were used to communicate the group's opinions to the troublemaker. Instead of telling the troublemaker in so many words, members employed a peculiar sort of gamesmanship. Systematic 'leaks' were used to *barely* and *ambiguously* expose the duplicity and conspiracy, so that the troublemaker would realize something was going on, but would be unable or unwilling to accuse specific offenders. Duplicitous gestures or comments which operated just on the fringes of the troublemaker's awareness produced maximum impact.

The successful operation of these practices relied, in part, on the troublemaker's complicity in the conspiracy of silence.

> *Once I was in the room next door to her and the girls were imitating her. Two minutes later she walked in asking [us] to be quiet because she was trying to sleep. I thought I was going to die. Obviously Tammy realized what was going on as the walls are extremely thin; however, Tammy seems to be conspiring on the side of her 'friends' to prevent any confrontation of the actual situation.*

Hostilities were therefore expressed, and retaliations achieved, often with rather specific reference to the particular offences and their presumed source. At the same time, they remained 'submerged' in a peculiar way. They were not submerged in a psychological 'unconscious', since both members and troublemakers were aware of what was going on. Instead, both members and troublemakers made every effort to assure that the trouble did not disturb the overtly normal interaction. 'Business as usual' was preserved at the cost of keeping secret deep hostilities within the organization.

A few accounts did mention instances of explicit confrontation. However, members claimed that such confrontations did not alter troublemakers' subsequent behaviours; instead they resulted in misunderstandings or were received by troublemakers in a defensive or unresponsive way.

Efforts to remove troublemakers from organizations were rarely described, though members of the rock band eventually expelled their troublemaker after he hired a lawyer to redress his grievances against the group. In another case a fraternity 'de-pledged' a new recruit who had not yet been fully initiated. In no other case was an established member removed, although numerous dramatic offences were recounted and widespread dislike for troublemakers was commonly reported.

Taken as a whole, accommodation practices reveal *the organizational construction of the normal individual*. The individual is relied upon both in commonsense reasoning and social theory as a source of compliance with the standards of the larger society. The normal individual successfully adapts to the constraints imposed by social structure. Troublemakers were viewed as persons who, for various reasons, could not be given full *responsibility* for maintaining normality. Instead, the burden of maintaining the individual's normal behaviour and appearance was taken up by others. Troublemakers were not overtly sanctioned; instead, they were shaped and guided through the superficial performances of ordinary action. Their integration into society was not a cumulative mastery learned 'from inside'; it was a constant project executed by others from the 'outside'.

Accommodation practices allow us to glimpse the project of the self as a practical struggle. A semblance of normal individuality for troublemakers was a carefully constructed artifact produced by members. When the responsibility for normality is assumed as an individual birthright, it appears inevitable that conformity or defiance proceeds 'from inside' the individual, just as it appears in commonsense that gender is a natural inheritance. In the latter instance, a transsexual's unusual experience indicates the extent to which the ordinary behaviour and appearance of being female is detachable from the individual's birthright, and can be explicated as a practical accomplishment (Garfinkel 1967). Similarly, for the organizational colleagues of a troublemaker, the elements of normal individuality cannot be relied upon, but must be achieved through deliberate practice. Members together performed the work of minding the troublemaker's business, of guiding the troublemaker through normal interactional pathways, and of filling the responsibilities and appearances associated with the troublemaker's presence for others.[6]

Of course, such projects were less than successful; members complained of the undue burden, disruptions occurred despite their efforts, and the troublemaker was provided with a diminished self and a distorted reality. Perhaps all would have been better off had they 'left the self inside where it belongs'. Nevertheless, accommodation practices enable us to see the extent to which the division between self and other is permeable, and subject to negotiation and manipulation. We can see that individual responsibility for the conduct of affairs is separable from the actual performance of those affairs. Troublemakers were manipulated into a tenuous conformity by members who relied upon the fact that such conformity would be attributed to the individual's responsibility. The individual was thus reduced to the subject of an informal code of responsibility, separable from any substantive source of action (Goffman, 1969: 357).

*The author thanks Renee Anspach, David Davis, Robert Emerson, Harold Garfinkel, Richard Hilbert, James Holstein, Melvin Pollner, and Steven Vandewater for their comments. The exercise on accommodation practices which I used in this research was adapted from a similar exercise used by Robert Emerson and Melvin Pollner in their courses on the Sociology of Mental Illness at the University of California, Los Angeles. During part of this research I was supported by a fellowship from the National Institute of Mental Health's Post-doctoral Training Program in Mental Health Evaluation Research, (# MH 14583). Correspondence to: School of Social Sciences, University of California, Irvine, CA.

## Notes

1. The equally interesting topic of how patients accommodate to their own disorders (Critchley, 1971: 290; O. Sacks, 1974: 227) is not included in this discussion of interactional practices.
2. Here the term *member* does not bear the more radical implication of 'a mastery of natural language', defined in Garfinkel and Sacks (1970: 350).
3. A topic needing further study is how members use greetings and other conversational 'adjacency pairs' (Sacks et al, 1974) to foreclose conversation with troublemakers at the earliest convenient point, but in such a way as not to call attention to their action as a snub.
4. See Wulbert (n.d.) for a poignant discussion of trivializing practices.
5. Jefferson and Lee (1980) characterize some of the detailed ways in which participants in ordinary conversations head off 'troubles talk' and transform it to 'business as usual'. Such procedures are much more varied and intricate than can adequately be described by such phrases as 'changing the subject'.
6. My discussion of the social production of the individual is heavily indebted to Pollner and Wikler's (1981) treatment of that theme. Pollner and Wikler (1981) discuss a family's efforts to construct the appearance of normality for their (officially diagnosed) profoundly retarded daughter. Not only does *normality* become a communal project in these cases, *abnormality* becomes shared as well. One student in my research described an alcoholic's family as 'three characters revolving around a central theme—alcoholism'. The preoccupation with alcohol was shared along with the *denial* that the man's drinking was an official problem.

# References

Bittner, Egan. 1967. 'Police Discretion in Emergency Apprehension of Mentally Ill Persons'. *Social Problems*, 14(3):278-292.

Critchley, MacDonald. 1971. *The Parietal Lobes*. New York: Hafner Publishing Co.

Cumming, Elaine and John Cumming. 1957. *Closed Ranks*. Cambridge, MA: Harvard University Press.

Emerson, Robert and Sheldon Messinger. 1977. 'The Micro-politics of Trouble'. *Social Problems*, 25(2):121–134.

Freeman, Howard and Ozzie Simmons. 1958. 'Mental Patients in the Community: Family Settings and Performance Levels'. *American Sociological Review*, 23(2):147–154.

Garfinkel, Harold. 1967. *Studies in Ethnomethodology*. Englewood Cliffs, NJ: Prentice-Hall.

Garfinkel, Harold and Harvey Sacks. 1910. 'Formal Structures of Practical Actions'. In John McKinney and Edward Tiryakian (eds.), *Theoretical Sociology: Perspectives and Development*. New York: Appleton-Century-Crofts, pp. 337–366.

Goffman, Erving. 1961. *Asylums*. Garden City, NY: Doubleday.

———. 1969. 'The Insanity of Place'. *Psychiatry*, 32(4):352–388.

Henry, Jules. 1972. *Pathways to Madness*. New York: Random House.

Hollingshead, August and Frederick Redlich. 1958. *Social Class and Mental Illness*. New York: Wiley.

Jackson, Joan. 1954. 'The Adjustment of the Family to the Crisis of Alcoholism'. *Quarterly Journal of Studies on Alcohol*, 15(4):562–586.

Jefferson, Gail and John Lee. 1980. 'The Analysis of Conversations in Which Anxieties and Troubles Are Expressed'. Unpublished report for the Social Science Research Counsel, University of Manchester, England.

Lemert, Edwin. 1962. 'Paranoia and the Dynamics of Exclusion' *Sociometry*, 25(1):2–20. Mayo, Clara, Ronald Havelock, and Diane Lear Simpson. 1971. 'Attitudes Towards Mental Illness among Psychiatric Patients and Their Wives'. *Journal of Clinical Psychology*, 27(1):128–132.

Myers, Jerome and Bertram Roberts. 1959. *Family and Class Dynamics*. New York: Wiley.

Pollner, Melvin and Lynn Wikler. 1981. 'The Social Construction of Unreality: A Case Study of the Practices of Family Sham and Delusion'. Unpublished paper, Department of Sociology, University of California, Los Angeles.

Sacks, Harvey, Emanuel Schegloff, and Gail Jefferson. 1974. 'A Simplest Systematics for the Organization of Turn Taking in Conversation:' Language. 50(4): 696–735.

Sacks, Oliver. 1974. *Awakenings*. New York: Doubleday.

Sampson, Harold, Sheldon Messinger, and Robert Towne. 1962. 'Family Processes and Becoming a Mental Patient'. *American Journal of Sociology*, 68(1):88–98.

Spitzer, Stephan, Patricia Morgan, and Robert Swanson. 1971. 'Determinants of the Psychiatric Patient Career: Family Reaction Patterns and Social Work Intervention'. *Social Service Review*, 45(1):74–85.

Srole, Leo, Thomas Langer, Stanley Michael, Marvin Opler, and Thomas Rennie. 1962. *Mental Health in the Metropolis: The Midtown Manhattan Study*. New York: McGraw-Hill.

Wulbert, Roland, n.d. 'Second Thoughts about Commonplaces'. Unpublished paper, Department of Sociology, Columbia University (circa 1974).

Yarrow, Marian, Charlotte Schwartz, Harriet Murphy, and Leila Deasy. 1955. 'The Psychological Meaning of Mental Illness in the Family'. *Journal of Social Issues*, 11(4):12–24.

## Introduction

Foucault's work has been influential in understanding various aspects of social control, including the role of dominant 'discourses' (or institutionalized systems of what counts as knowledge and is perceived as truth in a society) in the state's regulation of moral behaviour, and how groups resist that control. His analysis of the modern penal system is itself part of a larger study that examines how modern society is basically a 'disciplinary society' regardless of its affirmation of humanitarian ideals, rights, and freedoms. In this excerpt from Discipline and Punish he focuses on the shift in penal style that occurred in France and elsewhere over the past two centuries, namely, a shift from the spectacle of punishing the body of the condemned to the apparently more humane exercise of discipline and punishment in the prison. What are the main changes that accompany this shift in penal style? Foucault uses the terms 'political technology' and 'soul' in his discussion. What does he mean by them?

# The Body of the Condemned

*Michel Foucault*

On 2 March 1757, Damiens the regicide was condemned 'to make the *amende honorable* before the main door of the Church of Paris' where he was to be 'taken and conveyed in a cart, wearing nothing but a shirt, holding a torch of burning wax weighing two pounds'; then, 'in the said cart, to the Place de Grève, where, on a scaffold that will be erected there, the flesh will be torn from his breasts, arms, thighs, and calves with red-hot pincers, his right hand, holding the knife with which he committed the said parricide, burnt with sulphur, and, on those places where the flesh will be torn away, poured molten lead, boiling oil, burning resin, wax, and sulphur melted together and then his body drawn and quartered by four horses and his limbs and body consumed by fire, reduced to ashes, and his ashes thrown to the winds' (*Pièces originales . . .* , 1757: 372–374).

Bouton, an officer of the watch, left us his account: 'The sulphur was lit, but the flame was so poor that only the top skin of the hand was burnt, and that only slightly. Then the executioner, his sleeves rolled up, took the steel pincers, which had been especially made for the occasion, and which were about a foot and a half long, and pulled first at the calf of the right leg, then at the thigh, and from there at the two fleshy parts of the right arm; then at the breasts. Though a strong, sturdy fellow, this executioner found it so difficult to tear away the pieces of flesh that he sets about the same spot two or three times, twisting the pincers as he did so, and what he took away formed at each part a wound about the size of a six-pound crown piece.

'After these tearings with the pincers, Damiens, who cried out profusely, though without swearing, raised his head and looked at himself; the same executioner dipped an iron spoon in the pot containing the boiling potion, which he poured liberally over each wound. Then the ropes that were to be harnessed to the horses were attached with cords to the patient's body; the horses were then harnessed and placed alongside the arms and legs, one at each limb'.

Eighty years later, Léon Faucher drew up his rules 'for the House of young prisoners in Paris':

Art. 17. The prisoners' day will begin at six in the morning in winter and at five in summer. They will work for nine hours a day throughout the year. Two hours a day will be devoted to instruction. Work and the day will end at nine o'clock in winter and at eight in summer.

Art. 18. *Rising.* At the first drum-roll, the prisoners must rise and dress in silence, as the supervisor opens the cell doors. At the second drum-roll, they must be dressed and make their beds. At the third, they must line up and proceed to the chapel for morning prayer. There is a five-minute interval between each drum-roll.

Art. 19. The prayers are conducted by the chaplain and followed by a moral or religious reading. This exercise must not last more than half an hour.

Art. 20. *Work.* At a quarter to six in the summer, a quarter to seven in winter, the prisoners go down into the courtyard where they must wash their hands and faces, and receive their first ration of bread. Immediately afterwards, they form into work-teams and go off to work, which must begin at six in summer and seven in winter.

Art. 21. *Meal.* At 10 o'clock the prisoners leave their work and go to the refectory; they wash their hands in their courtyards and assemble in divisions. After the dinner, there is recreation until 20 minutes to 11.

Art. 22. *School.* At 20 minutes to eleven, at the drum-roll, the prisoners form into ranks, and proceed in divisions to the school. The class lasts two hours and consists alternately of reading, writing, drawing and arithmetic.

Art. 23. At 20 minutes to one, the prisoners leave the school, in divisions, and return to their courtyards for recreation. At five minutes to one, at the drum-roll, they form into work-teams.

Art. 24. At one o'clock they must be back in the workshops; they work until four o'clock.

Art. 25. At four o'clock the prisoners leave their workshops and go into the courtyards where they wash their hands and form into divisions for the refectory.

Art. 26. Supper and recreation that follows it last until five o'clock; the prisoners then return to the workshops.

Art. 27. At seven o'clock in the summer, at eight in winter, workshops; bread is distributed for the last time in the workshops. For a quarter of an hour one of the prisoners or supervisors reads a passage from some instructive or uplifting work. This is followed by evening prayer.

Art. 28. At half-past seven in summer, half-past eight in winter, the prisoners must be back in their cells after the washing of hands and the inspection of clothes in the courtyard; at the first drum-roll, they must undress, and at the second get into bed.

The cell doors are closed and the supervisors go the rounds in the corridors, to ensure order and silence. (Faucher, 1838: 274–282)

We have, then, a public execution and a time-table. They do not punish the same crimes or the same type of delinquent. But they each define a certain penal style. Less than a century separates them. It was a time when, in Europe and in the United States, the entire economy of punishment was redistributed. It was a time of great 'scandals' for traditional justice, a time of innumerable projects for reform. It saw a new theory of law and crime, a new moral or political justification of the right to punish; old laws were abolished, old customs died out.

Among so many changes, I shall consider one: the disappearance of torture as a public spectacle. Today we are rather inclined to ignore it; perhaps, in its time, it gave rise to too much inflated rhetoric; perhaps it has been attributed too readily and too emphatically to a process of 'humanization', thus dispensing with the need for further analysis.

Punishment, then, will tend to become the most hidden part of the penal process. This has several consequences: it leaves the domain of more or less everyday perception and enters that of abstract consciousness; its effectiveness is seen as resulting from its inevitability, not from its visible intensity; it is the certainty of being punished and not the horrifying spectacle of public punishment that must discourage crime; the exemplary mechanics of punishment changes its mechanisms. As a result, justice no longer takes public responsibility for the violence that is bound up with its practice.

The disappearance of public executions marks therefore the decline of the spectacle; but it also marks a slackening of the hold on the body.

Generally speaking, punitive practices had become more reticent. One no longer touched the body, or at least as little as possible, and then only to reach something other than the body itself. It might be objected that imprisonment, confinement, forced labour, penal servitude, prohibition from entering certain areas, deportation—which have occupied so important a place in modern penal systems—are 'physical' penalties; unlike fines, for example, they directly affect the body. But the punishment-body relation is not the same as it was in the torture during public executions. The body now serves as an instrument or intermediary: if one intervenes upon it to imprison it, or to make it work, it is in order to deprive the individual of a liberty that is regarded both as a right and as property. The body, according to this penalty, is caught up in a system of constraints and privations, obligations and prohibitions. Physical pain, the pain of the body itself, is no longer the constituent element of the penalty. From being an art of unbearable sensations, punishment has become an economy of suspended rights. If it is still necessary for the law to reach and manipulate the body of the convict, it will be at a distance, in the proper way, according to strict rules, and with a much 'higher' aim. As a result of this new restraint, a whole army of technicians took over from the executioner, the immediate anatomist of pain: warders, doctors, chaplains, psychiatrists, psychologists, educationalists. By their very presence near the prisoner, they sing the praises that the law needs: they reassure it that the body and pain are not the ultimate objects of its punitive action. Today a doctor must watch over those condemned to death, right up to the last moment—thus juxtaposing himself as the agent of welfare, as the alleviator of pain, with the official whose task it is to end life.

The modern rituals of execution to this double process: the disappearance of the spectacle and the elimination of pain. The same movement has affected the various European legal systems, each at its own rate. The same death for all—the execution no longer bears the specific mark of the crime or the social status of the criminal; a death that lasts only a moment—no torture must be added to it in advance, no further actions performed upon the corpse; an execution that affects life rather than the body.

Punishment had no doubt ceased to be centred on torture as a technique of pain; it assumed, as its principal object, loss of wealth or rights. But a punishment like forced labour or even imprisonment—mere loss of liberty—has never functioned without a certain additional element of punishment that certainly concerns the body itself: rationing of food, sexual deprivation, corporal punishment, solitary confinement. Are these the unintentional, but inevitable, consequence of imprisonment? In fact, in its most explicit practices, imprisonment has always involved a certain degree of physical pain. The criticism that was often levelled at the penitentiary system in the early nineteenth century (imprisonment is not a sufficient punishment: prisoners are less hungry, less cold, less deprived in general) that was never explicitly denied: it is just that a condemned man should suffer physically more than other men. It is difficult to dissociate punishment from additional physical pain. What would a non-corporal punishment be?

There remains, therefore, a trace of 'torture' in the modern mechanisms of criminal justice—a trace that has not been entirely overcome, but which is enveloped, increasingly, by the non-corporal nature of the penal system.

If the penality in its most severe forms no longer addresses itself to the body, on what does it lay hold? The answer of the theoreticians—those who, about 1760, opened up a new period that is not yet at an end—is simple, almost obvious. It seems to be contained in the question itself: Since it is no longer the body, it must be the soul. The expiation that once rained down upon the body must be replaced by a punishment that acts in depth on the heart, the thoughts, the will, the inclinations. Mably formulated the principle once and for all: 'Punishment, if I may so put it, should strike the soul rather than the body' (Mably 1789: 326).

During the 150 or 200 years that Europe has been setting up its new penal systems, the judges have gradually, by means of a process that goes back very far indeed, taken to judging something other than crimes, namely, the 'soul' of the criminal.

It would be wrong to say that the soul is an illusion, or an ideological effect. On the contrary, it exists, it has a reality, it is produced permanently around, on, within the body by the functioning of a power that is exercised on those punished—and, in a more general way, on those one supervises, trains, and corrects, over madmen, children at home and at school, the colonized, over those who are stuck at a machine and supervised for the rest of their lives. This is the historical reality of this soul, which, unlike the soul represented by Christian theology, is not born in sin and subject to punishment, but is born rather out of methods of punishment, supervision, and constraint. This real, non-corporal soul is not a substance; it is the element in which are articulated the effects of a certain type of power and the reference of a certain type of knowledge, the machinery by which the power relations give rise to a possible corpus of knowledge, and knowledge extends and reinforces the effects of this power. On this reality reference, various concepts have been constructed and domains of analysis carved out: psyche, subjectivity, personality, consciousness, etc. On it have been built scientific techniques and discourses, and the moral claims of humanism. But let there be no misunderstanding: It is not that a real man, the object of knowledge, philosophical reflection, or technical intervention, has been substituted for the soul, the illusion of the theologians. The man described for us, whom we are invited to free, is already in himself the effect of a subjection much more profound than himself. A 'soul' inhabits him and brings him to existence, which is itself a factor in the mastery that power exercises over the body. The soul is the effect and instrument of a political anatomy; the soul is the prison of the body.

That punishment in general and the prison in particular belong to a political technology of the body is a lesson that I have learnt not so much from history as from the present. In recent years, prison revolts have occurred throughout the world. There was certainly something paradoxical about their aims, their slogans, and the way they took place. They were revolts against an entire state of physical misery that is over a century old: against cold, suffocation, and overcrowding, against decrepit walls, hunger, physical maltreatment. But they were also revolts against model prison, tranquilizers, isolation, and the medical or educational services. Were they revolts whose aims were merely material? Or contradictory revolts: against the obsolete, but also against comfort; against the warders, but also against the psychiatrists? In fact, all these movements—and the innumerable discourses that the prison has given rise to since the early nineteenth century—have been about the body and material things. What has sustained these discourses, these memories, and invectives are indeed those minute material details. One may, if one is so disposed, see them as no more than blind demands or suspect the existence behind them of alien strategies. In fact, they were revolts, at the level of the body, against the very body of the prison. What was at issue was not whether the prison environment was too harsh or too aseptic, too primitive or too efficient, but its very materiality as an instrument and vector of power. It is this whole technology of power over the body that the technology of the 'soul'—that of the educationalists, psychologists, and psychiatrists—fails either to conceal or to compensate, for the simple reason that it is one of its tools.

# References

Faucher, L. 1838. *De la reforme des prisons.*
de Mably, D. 1789. *De la législation, Oeuvres complètes,* IX.
*Pièces originales et procédures du procès fait à Robert-François Damiens, III,* 1757.

# 13

## Introduction

If we don't have any direct experience to rely upon, our perceptions of prison life often become based on news stories and fictional representations. Julian Roberts' interview with a lifer named Al is intended to give us a more accurate idea of what actually goes on in a correctional institution. Most 'lifers' are doing time for murder. Those sentenced to life for first degree murder must spend at least 25 years in prison, while those sentenced for second degree murder spend between 10 and 25 years, depending on the judge's decision. How does Al's description of prison life compare with what you expected? In what ways does Al's discussion support or conflict with the points Foucault made about the modern penal system in the previous article?

## Life in Prison: Interview with a Lifer

*Julian V. Roberts*

*Al was 31 years old when he was sentenced to life-25. He had served five years at the time of the interview.*

It's hard to describe a typical day: you get up, go for breakfast, come to work, go through the motions more than anything else. I'm fortunate, I think, in that I've got a job that actually has some responsibility inside the prison, which is really exceptional. And it also takes some time and occupies time to help it pass. But after the workday is over, if you're not into playing floor hockey in the gym or lifting weights, then it leaves little else. The library is only open for an hour, and it's watch TV or play bridge in the unit.

Can I describe how I expect my sentence to proceed? No, I can describe how it's supposed to work, and the way it's supposed to work is that, through displaying what CSC [Correctional Service of Canada] considers appropriate behaviour, I should earn reduced security. And, based on their programs and their goals and all this type of stuff, I should already be in a medium [security institution], but because I'm political within the institution, I think it will be a long time before I ever see one. I applied for a medium, but I think it'll be a long time before I ever see one. As far as the sentencing and parole [is concerned], anybody serving a life sentence with a parole eligibility date of more than 15 years is allowed to apply to the court that sentenced them—what they call the Court of Competent Jurisdiction—for a judicial review after 15 years (see preceding chapter). And in this review, you can be awarded a reduced parole eligibility date; you can be told you're getting nothing, or you can be told to come back again in *x* number of years. Assuming you win judicial review, you then become parole-eligible. That doesn't mean you're going to get parole; you're just now eligible to apply to the National Parole Board. And they'll set up a pass program, whatever all else, at that time, but as far as looking forward to it, it's 10 years down the road before I can even go through the judicial review, so I don't even think about it; it's a day at a time.

I was 31 years old, didn't quite know what to expect . . . you've seen all the TV movies and the hype and everything else, and prison is nothing like the hype. But one of the attitudes that I had was that, first of all, I was not going to get political. And I did. The prison system works on its own set of rules called the Commissioner's Directives in the Penitentiary Service Regulations, and if you buck the system, if you say that the CD is wrong, or if you even say the administration isn't living up to this policy or that policy, you're considered political. And, if you're going to be political, then you had better be actively political in that you're elected to a position because those that are elected to positions are protected a little bit from the backlash of the administration. And those that are not elected to positions will find themselves on an airplane and waking up in a French-speaking prison in the morning.

I got political first of all in Edmonton over the education system—or lack of education system I guess is a better way to describe it—to a point where it *cost* me a transfer to Kent, which was all to my betterment because I'd been trying to get to Kent anyway, and they'd turned me down on three different occasions. But once I spoke out publicly and it was broadcast on the news, against the education system in Edmonton, I was on an airplane to Kent very quickly. Education is the only really positive thing within prison. Once you've got it, they can't take it away from you. It doesn't matter what else there is. If you buy a TV, they can take it away from you, they can say you can't have that in your cell. If you do hobby work, they can take that away from you. They can take away the right to do hobby work. Once you've educated yourself, at whatever level, whether you've achieved grade 6, grade 8, or a university degree, that's a thing you've got and it's in you—they can't take it away.

I'm active with the lifers group. I'm also the Inmate Committee rep for my living unit. Elected positions. I won't sit back and watch injustices against fellow prisoners. Many of them are under-educated and not capable of speaking out for themselves except in a violent tone because that's what they've known all their lives. And I can handle it reasonably and rationally, so I'll speak out for them, and it causes strife. I'm doing more time in a max than I should because of it, but so be it. Over the last month, there seems to have been some movement on the part of this administration towards actually following the mission statement [of Correctional Services] and adjusting to it. And, I think it's because of pressures that have been brought to bear over the previous nine months, from April of last year, when the mission statement first came out. Inmates are actually starting to use the mission statement when they're filing grievances. Because up until a month ago, and I've said it in writing to the administration of Kent, that I firmly believe that the administration of Kent takes the mission statement as a public relations document that was issued by the Commissioner to appease the politicians and the public, and they have no intention of putting it into policy. It will, I think, in a few years, have an impact, but it's going to take years.

Life imprisonment is a tough sentence. I mean, how do you describe it? It's the rest of your life. You're sentenced to prison not for 10 years or 25 years as people tend to believe; you're sentenced to prison for life. The sentence is life imprisonment with no eligibility for parole for at least 25 years. That doesn't mean you're getting out in 25. That means you can apply. And nobody can fathom it. Nobody has served it yet because it's only been in place since 1976. As I said, nobody can fathom it, nobody can really imagine what it's like to do it, and everybody has to do it differently because each person is an individual and has his own personality. I tend to say 'one day at a time'. One day at a time . . . get up in the morning and see what the day brings. And, when the day is over, well that's past; there's no sense dwelling on it. Let's get up tomorrow and do one day again.

If you want to get into simple mathematics, shortly after you come into the system, you get a letter from the parole board and—this is really nice of them—you're sentenced to life-25, and you get a letter from the parole board that says your parole-eligibility date is, in my case, April 13, 2010; however, you may apply for day parole on April 13, 2007! Really magnanimous of them. And they tell you, you must serve 9,131 days. Yes, they tell you exactly—you must serve 9,131 days . . . they've got it all counted out for you, including leap years, and it's just appalling. You can't afford to sit here and dwell on the fact that you've got 20 years to go, or 21, or 19, or however close you happen to be getting. You can't dwell on that because it's unmanageable. I think if lifers started to dwell on the fact that they've got 20 years to go, or 19 years to go, the suicide rate would be so high that they might as well bring back the death penalty. The difference between this death penalty and the death penalty they had before was they got it over with quick; now they make you suffer. They even have a neat little deal in the Commissioner's Directives where, if you're unhealthy to the point where it is life-threatening, you can't refuse medical attention! They can stick you in a hospital and keep you alive, so you have to continue to serve your sentence, You're sentenced to life, but they won't *let* you die.

How can you describe the different types of guys? There's guys like myself that have never had a conflict with the law in their life, there are career criminals who've gone out and robbed banks, and in some cases, that's all they've done is rob banks. There are others that shot somebody in the course of a robbery and therefore are serving life for that. There are drug dealers that have killed people in drug deals and are serving life for that It's as varied as anywhere else. The best way to describe a prison population, I guess, is a microcosm of the general population of this country. Except that it's single sex. I don't worry about [whom] I'm living with. They all realize that I'm in here doing life-25 because I killed somebody, not because I walked into a drug store and grabbed a bag of whatever, or grabbed a bank teller's cash drawer or something like that. It's because somebody pissed me off and they're dead. And the guys around me know that. And it's the same with every other lifer. The guys around them realize also that they're in here because they killed somebody. There's a degree of respect, you know. This is this man's space.

Within that, there's also the guidelines within the prison, and I'm not talking now about administrative rules; these are prisoners' rules. You've got the rules, you live within them, and you stay within them. And as long as you're within those rules, really nobody's going to bother you.

The reports that are written by institutional staff are unimportant. They're written by semi-professional people who are taught how to write reports, not necessarily how to evaluate people, that sit there, thinking that because they've taken a case management course, they're now psychologists and have the answers to all your problems. And I have a great deal of trouble with them. CSC thrives on paperwork, like any other bureaucracy, and what's written determines whether you go down in security, whether you get a proper parole board, all that kind of stuff. But to me, it's unimportant. I know who I am, I can respect the person I see in the mirror in the morning, and I really don't care what they write. Everybody gets the opportunity to read and sign them; a lot of guys will just stuff them back in front of their case management officer. I haven't had a case management report done on me since August of '88. They're supposed to be done every four months, but the staffs afraid to write about me because they know I'll challenge any lies they put in there.

Most of the jobs in here are meaningless. There are some jobs that aren't: The guys working the grill in the kitchen are learning a good skill. Working in the cabinet shop, they can learn a good skill if they put themselves to it, but most of the other jobs are delivering the toilet paper to the living-units—pretty important task, well it is; everyone's got to have toilet paper, right—but, you know, it's not exactly what you would call a job. A kitchen job is pulling the meal wagons down to the closed units—that's a job; all you do is pull this wagon through the courtyard three times a day. That's your total workday. Pretty tough job, pretty meaningful stuff; I can see a person getting a lot out of that, knowing how to pull a wagon across the city of Vancouver, or whatever. You know, maybe they'll be able to deliver papers or something significant when they can get out because that's all that job is going to lead to.

The Commissioner's Directives suggest that 'there be a meaningful work placement', This is the term they use for every prisoner in the institution. And I've already described what's meaningful—delivering toilet paper. That's all meaningful employment as far as the institution is concerned, There is supposed to be work placement available, full-time placement for every prisoner in the institution, There's not. I don't know what can be done about it, if anything. It's just the structure of the prison that says it is or isn't going to work, and there just isn't that much work. I don't know what can be done. By the time you've been in long enough to be going through your appeals and everything else, and that's when you finally realize that, yes, I'm going to serve this sentence, you've found a full-time job. And usually one that you're comfortable with. A lot of the guys aren't interested in meaningful work; they're interested in picking up enough inmate pay to keep themselves in tobacco and cans of Coke or coffee, whatever it is they're interested in, never mind the rest.

I'm fully aware of the fact that I don't require maximum-security handling—my work supervisor will tell you I don't require maximum-security handling, and you know yourself from dealing with me that I don't. On the other hand, I can go through this prison and show you many that do. So, I can't say 'eliminate maximum-security prisons'. They certainly need a better method of assessment, a fairer method of determining who does and doesn't get transfers so the decisions aren't personal. I've taken some political action, filed a grievance against this staff member or that staff member, or whatever, and won that grievance, and now that staff member is making a decision on whether or not I move down in security. It's now become a persona 1 decision instead of one that should be made rationally and objectively.

For me, the question is, in the end, only academic. I believe I'm going to die in prison. Maybe in 1990, maybe in the year 2000, maybe in the year 2010. The environment is such that I am living with, and considered one of Canada's most dangerous or most unmanageable prisoners. That's why I'm in a max. That is what a max is supposed to be for: Canada's most dangerous or most unmanageable prisoners. Based on that fact—and I live in a population of 140 or 150 of Canada's most undesirable people—there's a good chance that somebody, for some foolish reason, could decide they're taking me out. They're drunk on brew, they're pilled up, I've done something they didn't like. And the same holds true for me. I'm not likely to, but I could. I honestly believe I'll die in prison. Because I'm a fatalist. When my time is here, it's here, and there's nothing I can do about it. You can't speed it up, you can't slow it down.

I think I have definitely matured, if that's the right word, and I'm not even sure that that is. I think things through a lot more, a lot deeper, than I ever did on the street. On the street, it was just, sort of, oh well, if you screw it up, you can fix it tomorrow. Well, in here, you screw it up, and you may not see tomorrow, you know! So, yeah, you think things through a lot more closely. People in here, most of them, manage to function at the mental age that they should have been at and weren't at when they came in here. They should have been developing functionally as 18, 19, and 20-year-olds, and weren't. Now they are. They won't go beyond that, they'll serve 25 years and come out as a 20-year-old. Because they've missed the things that I did from 20 to 30 years of age and the things that you did from 20 to 30 years of age; they've never had the opportunity to do it, and without doing it, you can't mature past it. The things that you did from 30 to 40 years of age I've never had the opportunity to do because I came to jail at 31. When I get out, I'll behave like a 31-year-old. Lifers don't reoffend when they're paroled. I think it's like point nine per cent have reoffended, or something like that, less than one per cent. That doesn't mean they don't have the problems and other struggles if you try to reintegrate with the friends you had before you came in. They've lived those 25 years, they've got 25 years of life experience that you don't have, and you can't conceive of what they're talking about because of it, so you have to go back to associating with younger people that haven't had that life experience because it's the only way you can survive. And they do the same thing with prisoners when they get out of jail . . . we go out at, at 56, when I'm parole-eligible, and I start running around with 29 and 31-old people; they're going to say, like, there's something psychologically wrong with this man.

If I come out at 56, as a 31-year-old, after 25 years in prison, I'll be the same mental age as my children. How do you deal with that? Assuming that I make it through this sentence, if I'm fortunate enough to, and I pray that I am, I don't want to die any more than any other person; I like living just as much as anybody else and if I make it through, I still wouldn't see my children. I would make a point of not seeing them. It's far better for them to have me not interfere with their life in any way, shape, or form.

What will I do then? Oh, I'm going fishing. If I get out, I'm going back to Northern Manitoba where I grew up; I'm going to build a little cabin on the side of the lake, and I'm going fishing. I'll go into town and get supplies, and say 'hi' to people, and report to the parole officer and whatever, and go fishing. To hell with the world. I'm dropping out of society; I have absolutely no respect left for the Canadian government whatsoever. One of the things I did was three years in the army—I loved my country, believe it or not, very much. I loved my country. Definitely didn't agree with the politics, but when I was out there, I had the right to vote, the right to change things within the framework of the law. After having gone through what they call the 'justice' system, which is inappropriately named—it's something like 'military intelligence', the words don't fit together—and what I've seen within this prison, I have absolutely no respect left for this country whatsoever. I don't want anything to do with it. I'll do whatever time they tell me I have to do until I'm eligible for parole. Once I'm out, goodbye. I don't want to see them again, I don't want anything to do with them.

There's nothing to be gained except retribution for the life I took. There's no rehabilitation whatsoever. If there is any rehabilitation, it's in spite of the system, not because of it. It's because the person decides that he's going to do something for himself during that time period. Even the nonsense of maybe losing the university program—the fight and the struggle to keep it—just so that we can educate ourselves. Taxpayers cry because we're getting university education. Some of them claim, well look, this prisoner's getting a university education, and I can't afford to send my daughter. Well, let me tell you that it costs more—I don't know the exact figures, but something like seven dollars per man, per hour—to put them in a shop than it does to put them in a classroom. If they think that the prison industry system is there to make money and help them pay for the cost of their incarceration, they're wrong, because prison industries lose money. And, as I say, it costs more for security to keep them locked in their cells than it does to put them in a classroom. You can put 20 or 30 prisoners, students, in a classroom under the supervision of one person. You put them in any other area, and you're dealing with a much lower ratio—you don't have 20 or 30 to one.

I want nothing to do with society at all any more. Once you've been convicted by the courts and turned over to the penitentiary system, you now come under different legislation and they take away many of the rights that ordinary citizens have, besides the right of freedom, which naturally has to be taken away. I'm not suggesting that I shouldn't be in prison—I killed somebody. Yes, I should be doing time for it.

# 14

## Introduction

What is justice? Do young people receive it? In this polemical article, Hogeveen challenges Canada's 'vengeance as justice' approach to youth crime and argues that it draws our attention away from the various forms of injustice experienced by many young people as well as the general silencing of youth in modern Western societies. He specifically focuses on the injustices of child poverty, the racism that Aboriginal youth confront, and the neglect of girls as both victims and offenders in the current youth justice system. His concluding judgment is a severe one. But given his supporting arguments, is it a 'just' one?

# Is There Justice for Young People?

*Bryan Hogeveen*

A recent article in the *Peterborough Examiner* proclaimed, 'Youth "Justice" a joke'. A mother had been compelled to write to the paper after a group of 'teenagers' verbally accosted her 12-year-old daughter. While the mother assured readers that she had taught her daughter 'to be polite, mannerly, and to respect other people', she contended that the Youth Criminal Justice Act (YCJA)—Canada's legislation governing offenders between the ages of 12 and 17— was making her job exceedingly difficult (O'Brien 2004). Parents, it seemed, were afforded no assistance from the Act. While this mother was certain that she could call upon the law to deliver *justice* for her daughter, the police informed her otherwise. If the YCJA provided no recourse for injured parties, where were parents (and their daughters) to turn for redress? An article with a similar refrain entitled 'Youth Justice?' appeared in the *Halifax Daily News*. The reporter suggested that youth typically 'mock the system' and scoffed at a sentence of nine months' probation and 30 hours of community service for a young person convicted of tying a cord around a cat's neck and dragging it into the woods with the intention of killing it (Aikenhead 2004).

Embedded in these newspaper stories is a discursive construction of today's generation of youth as somehow more criminal, disrespectful, and precocious than youth in times past. For example, the second author stated, 'kids from previous generations didn't think they could get away with murder, so they didn't try.' Intrinsic to this statement is the ubiquitous assumption that somewhere in time (often when the writer was young) lies a golden era when juvenile deviance was hardly a problem. Our past, then, was a simpler time when youth respected elders, were silent, and obeyed their parents. Such an understanding of contemporary young people belies the absolute condition whereby youth have *always* discontented and troubled adults. In 469 BCE Socrates lamented, 'the children now love luxury. They have bad manners, contempt for authority, they show disrespect for adults and love to talk rather than work or exercise. They contradict their parents, chatter in front of company, gobble down their food at the table and intimidate their teachers.' This statement could just as easily have been typed on a computer as scribbled on parchment.

Troublingly, this conception of young people as predatory criminals and of the law as offering little recourse remains pervasive in an era of steadily *declining* youth crime rates. Focusing attention exclusively on adolescent patterns of offending masks such *in*justices confronting youth as inequality, silencing, and oppression. Admittedly, youth do commit crimes. However, they are at the same time highly overrepresented in rates of victimization and poverty, a fact often concealed in the preoccupation with patterns of criminality and efforts to strengthen juvenile justice legislation. Moreover, a particularly disturbing consequence of Canada's 'vengeance as justice' paradigm is the gross overrepresentation of Aboriginal youth in centers of detention. As a group, Native adolescents are among the most disadvantaged in Canadian society; they are also the most punished. While Native youth are the most disparaged, homeless, poor, and drug addicted youth, as well as 'squeegee kids', are other targets deemed suitable for public vengeance. Justice, it seems, is something done to young people, not something to which they are entitled. A different rendering of *justice* for youth would view them as requiring protection in the form of systems and a populace that respects their heritage, age, condition of life, and situation. To date, however, Canada falls well short of this ideal.

## What Is Justice?

We live in an era in which war, prison overcrowding, genocide, ethnic cleansing, and vigilantism are often justified in the name of justice. But what, exactly, *is* justice? Canadians employ the term as if its meaning were self-evident. Scholars trying to explore the meaning of justice find arriving at an adequate definition fraught with difficulty. While academics have done well in exploring how the question 'what is justice' is debated, they have yet to arrive at a definitive answer (Hudson 2003). Contemporary *theoretical* conceptions proceed from principles of *distribution* derived from philosophical and legal perspectives. Classical justice theorists such as John Stuart Mill, David Hume, and Immanuel Kant, and more contemporary philosophers such as John Rawls offer normative principles intended to guide the allocation of society's limited resources (wealth, opportunity, income, etc.). These distributive theories of justice embrace everything from how situations facing the poor and downtrodden are handled to how society regulates violations of its criminal code. David Miller (1999, 1) offers the following succinct and powerful definition of this theoretical tradition: it involves 'how the good and bad things in life should be distributed among the members of a human society'. However rational this definition may seem, it is abstract, divorced from real life problems, structural disparities, and institutional discrimination (Young 1990). As such, resources are distributed such that the most affluent benefit while the poor and visibly different spiral into desolation and misery.

A significant part of the difficulty in answering the question 'what is justice?' centres on the fundamental ambiguity in the word itself. For example, it can refer to the bureaucratic structure for administering the legal process. Canada boasts a federal Department of *Justice*, which embodies and reflects this convention. It can be used in law and legislation to imply the impartiality of the system (e.g., the Youth Criminal *Justice* Act). Moreover, *justice* suggests a connection with law and order campaigns in which victims declare that they are owed retribution for pain suffered. In this context, *justice* being done means an ethic of punishment that delivers obvious signs of unpleasantness to offenders. This kind of justice can also reflect the public's desire to amend law, often in relation to existing but flawed legislation that seemingly promotes *in*justice. Until 2003 when the YCJA became law, Canadian youth were governed under the Young Offenders Act (YOA). Throughout the period leading up to legislative change, the YOA was consistently hailed as inequitable because it was seen as debasing the victims of juvenile deviance. Newspaper headlines suggested that federal young offender legislation was to blame for victimization and that tougher legislation would prevent the harm done to the injured (Hogeveen 2005).

For many, justice has been intimately connected with inalienable and omnipresent rights enshrined under legislation. For example, the Charter of Rights and Freedoms (Canada 1982) guarantees Canadian citizens and permanent residents: a) freedom of conscience and religion; b) freedom of thought, belief, and expression; c) freedom of association; d) the right to vote; and e) the right to life, liberty, and security of the person. Nevertheless, until very recently youth did not enjoy access to these guarantees in the same way that adults did. Under law and in society, children were traditionally not afforded dignity or respect, but were instead treated as chattel belonging to their father. The movement toward assigning rights to children, according to Katherine Covell and Brian Howe (2001), went through three fundamental stages. It passed from a laissez-faire philosophy in which children were considered parental property, to a humanitarian and sentimental rationale of children as a separate class of partially formed individuals, to the current discourse of children as people entitled to individual rights.

A turning point in rights allocation for youth occurred on 20 November 1989 when the United Nations Convention on the Rights of the Child was unanimously adopted. A convention is an expression not only of a moral stand but 'also of a legal agreement and international obligation' (Covell and Howe 2001: 20). In 1991 Canada ratified the convention, which comprises 41 articles divided into two broad categories:

1. civil and political rights, which include the right to self-determination and protection from arbitrary arrest
2. economic, social, and cultural rights, which include the right to health care and education and freedom of religion.

According to Hammarberg (1990), human rights and protections set out by the convention can usefully be divided into three broad groups, often referred to as the three Ps: provision, protection, and participation. Rights of *provision* imply that youth must be afforded basic welfare, which includes the right to survival and development, education, and to be cared for by parents. Articles under the *protection* rubric ensure that children are sheltered from abuse, economic exploitation, discrimination, and neglect. Youth are also accorded the right to *par-*

*ticipation*, which involves freedom of speech, freedom of religion, and the right of expression (Denov 2004).

Despite Canada's agreement to abide by the convention's conditions, substantial gaps remain between the state's promise and the real world. One of the greatest concerns for youth advocates is the general lack of awareness about the convention and the rights youth are guaranteed therein. According to Doob and Cesaroni (2004), youth have little understanding of what exactly rights are. Barry Feld (2000) suggests that young people typically see rights as something they are allowed to do and conditional on other conduct. Thus they do not understand the consequences of waiving their right to silence, for example, when a police officer warns them against self-incrimination. A study of high school students by Peterson-Badali and Abramovich (1992) found that very few youth could identify the most basic legal principles, such as the youth court's age jurisdiction (12–17). Moreover, when asked with whom their lawyer could share privileged information, many young people were certain that their legal representative was obliged to inform their parents and the judge what they revealed in confidence. To what extent are rights meaningful if young people are unaware of their implications and how they are exercised?

Equating rights with justice is spurious—at best. Rights conventions are of little utility when their intricacies are not widely known, understood, or distributed. They tend to float above relationships among individuals and provide little guidance on the ethical responsibility of one person to another. Rights discourses provide very little direction to those addressing inequality and subjugation in an *un*just society. Recall that rights and social goods are not equally distributed throughout the Canadian population. People on the margins are grossly overrepresented in poverty and incarceration rates. Is this a just state of affairs? If working-class and minority youth have become the foremost clients of state services that deliver pain and experience higher rates of poverty, it is *not* as a result of some innate propensity toward crime and unemployment. Rather, it is because they are trapped at the intersection of three transformations distinct to the neo-liberal organization of society that have targeted the visibly different and the socially marginal: economic globalization, dismantling the social welfare net, and intensifying penal strategies have all contributed to greater inequality and unequal distribution of scarce societal resources in favour of the affluent (Wacquant 2001). During the late 1990s, to paraphrase the title of Jeffrey Reiman's (1979) seminal work, the rich were getting richer while the poor were receiving prison. If justice is to ensure equal distribution of resources and goods to societal members, it would appear that Canada is moving in a most peculiar direction, especially as the situation pertains to young people.

## Justice and the Poor?

Child poverty continues to rise despite a booming economy and federal and provincial coffers bursting at the seams. In the current neo-liberal ethos, the gulf between the rich and the poor continues to widen. Statistics gathered by the federal government's Canadian Council on Social Development illustrate this growing divide most clearly. Between 1984 and 1999, the average net worth of the country's poorest families dropped by 51 per cent while for the wealthiest it increased by 42.7 per cent. Moreover, the number of familial units that paid more than 50 per cent of their gross income on rent rose by 43 per cent between 1990 and 1995 (Lee and Engler 2000). Burgeoning poverty rates are not the product of economic backwardness, recession, or decline. They are, however, conditioned by mushrooming inequality experienced in a context of widespread economic evolution and opulence. Perhaps the most puzzling element of the new marginality is that it is growing in an era characterized by a robust economy and sturdy growth that has benefited privileged members of Western society (Wacquant 1999). Although on the surface these two phenomena seem contradictory, they are in fact linked. Indeed, the shift to a new knowledge-based and global economy translates into a polarized workforce in which increased employment opportunities for the highly educated and technically trained abound while millions of unskilled labour jobs are lost to overseas production sites and automation (Ley 1996; Lévesque 2002; Enloe 1990). Although the country's economy continues to hum along, fewer are profiting from it. The further the neo-liberal economy proceeds, the more invasive and widespread poverty will become. The result is greater numbers of families looking to the state for assistance, which puzzlingly seems unwilling to offer *real* help.

The social welfare net that caught and propped up the downtrodden throughout most of the twentieth century has been seriously eroded as the neo-liberal economy continues to gain pace. Indeed, between 1986 and 1996, as measured in constant dollars, Alberta welfare benefits for a single individual deemed employable were slashed by 42.5 per cent while single parents with a child saw their benefits eroded by 23.6 per cent (Canadian Council on Social Development 2004). While poverty rates continue to climb, the net traditionally in place to soften the impact has been stripped away. Even the benefits available to ameliorate the conditions of the most vulnerable—Canada's children—are currently being clawed back by the state. For example, the National Child Benefit provides families with annual incomes of less than $22,615 with $126 per month for the first child and decreasing amounts for subsequent children. However, under a scheme initiated by the federal government, only working families are now allowed to keep the money while those most in need—individuals on social assistance and disability pensions—are denied support payments altogether (Della-Mattia 2004). Compare this with the $45 million per year that the Alberta government doles out to subsidize the local horse-racing industry. A growing group of destitute individuals, who require the greatest assistance, are having to scrounge for the crumbs that remain after services that the government deems more important (such as horse-racing) get their cut.

Tragically, youth are the hardest hit. According to the Canadian Council on Social Development, children between the ages of 15 and 24 had the highest poverty rate in Alberta. The council's 2003 report, *Campaign 2000: Report card on child poverty in Canada* (Canadian Council on Social Development 2003a), provided convincing evidence that despite seven years of economic prosperity, over a million children in this country continue to live in poverty. These figures establish that more children are poor than in 1989 when Parliament unanimously pledged to eradicate child poverty by the year 2000. Poverty, however, is not an equal opportunity oppressor. *Campaign 2000* presented evidence that 42 per cent of immigrant children lived in destitution compared with 17.4 per cent of non-immigrants of the same age. Moreover, 41 per cent of Aboriginal youth living off reserves were counted among the most impoverished (Canadian Council on Social Development 2003b).

Despite growing numbers and increasing need, provincial funding has not kept pace. To manage the excesses of and fallout from the current economic climate, state officials have not extended social welfare assistance to needy parents but resorted to pruning child welfare budgets and cutting jobs. The Children's Aid Society (CAS) of Halifax, for example, was forced in 2002 to cut a million dollars from its budget over a mere six months (Mills 2002). Funding cuts of this magnitude have serious and often severe implications because child welfare workers become overextended and managers feel pressure to reduce spending. In this desperate environment, youth in need have routinely been denied essential helping services such as treatment sessions and educational programs. Older youth have also seen essential and relatively inexpensive programs relegated to the dustbin of the neo-liberal state. While seemingly innocuous, bus passes allow the poor to cross the urban landscape to attend school or hold jobs. Without this resource, youth often lose their jobs and/or are expelled from school for non-attendance. Moreover, throughout the late 1990s many youth were incarcerated for breaching conditions attached to probation orders. For the most part, they were considered in contempt of court for failing to comply with a court order, typically their failure to fulfill community service hours. A typical scenario might involve a young person sentenced to 20 hours of community work as restitution for a minor infraction. All too often, young people who appear before Canada's courts are impoverished, which curtails the mere act of travelling across town to fulfill their community service obligation. Taking the young person's non-compliance as a sign of disrespect and contempt for authority, the youth court judge counterintuitively sentences the recalcitrant youth to additional hours of community service. The cycle continues until the frustrated judge surrenders and orders the offender incarcerated. This all too common and tragic occurrence could easily be prevented *if* resources were used intelligently.

While Canadians favoured tax breaks for corporations and the richest segments of society, they campaigned at the same time for increased rates of incarceration for young people—the most costly (both economically and socially) mode of penalty. This situation is particularly troubling when we consider that a great number of young people are incarcerated for relatively *minor* forms of deviance. Indeed, a great number of inmates were sentenced to prison for such 'heinous' breaches of public order as failure to comply with court orders and property-related crimes. Perhaps as a result of the public's appetite for punishment, Canada's rate of incarceration for young people exceeds that of the all Western nations—including the United States (Hogeveen 2005). While Canadians could in the past point to greater tolerance toward the recalcitrant on their part than their American counterparts, these statistics suggest that 'we' are more like 'them' than many would like to believe.

More troubling still is that individuals warehoused in Canada's centres of detention are almost exclusively from the most marginal classes. Instead of distributing welfare benefits to the poor and suppressed, Canadians have placed this class under the authority of the criminal justice system. While social welfare schemes were shrinking, programs that coercively targeted the poor were expanding. Consider, if you will, the amount of relief that could be administered for the resources devoted to incarcerating excessive numbers of young people. Reflect on how much tuition could be paid with the $50,000 to $100,000 required to detain one young person for a year. Indeed, set against the backdrop of the type of crimes for which these youth are being detained, this expenditure seems extreme. Throughout the 1990s, when the tendency to lock up juvenile offenders was at its peak, so too was the erosion of welfare. One could interpret this as an indication that the only institutions and social programs Canadians were willing to support were those that delivered the most obvious signs of pain to the destitute and marginal. In effect, centres of detention have become the social service to which the poor and oppressed have the readiest access. More than any other group, Aboriginal youth have felt the sting of the state's penal governance of poverty and marginality.

## Justice and Indigenous Youth?

Throughout history, Aboriginal peoples have been subjected to intrusive and invasive modes of state-level control aimed at reform, assimilation, and subjugation (Anderson 1999; Hogeveen 1999). Wherever the Euro-Canadian state encountered indigenous people, the Native land was quickly vacated to make way for white settlement and capitalist expansion. Among the tools of colonialism employed to regulate and shore up the Anglo vision of the country's founders were the North-West Mounted Police (forerunner of the RCMP), law, reserves, a pass system, children's forced adoption by white families, and residential schooling. With the closure of residential schools and with many indigenous peoples now living off reserves, institutions of detention are now on the front lines when it comes to controlling the indigenous 'other'. Penal practices are applied to Aboriginal people with special diligence and severity. Ceaselessly denied entry into Euro-Canadian institutional life, increasing numbers of Native youth have been pushed through the state's justice process to the point that it is now, I think, possible to talk about the criminalization of indigenousness.

Government reports and investigations have consistently pointed to a gross overrepresentation of Native adolescents at the most punitive end of the system (Royal Commission on Aboriginal Peoples 1993; 1996). Peter Carrington and Jennifer Schulenberg (2004) suggest that indigenous adolescents are 20 per cent more likely to be charged when apprehended than non-Aboriginal youth. Moreover, Aboriginal youth are more likely to be denied bail, to spend more time in pre-trial detention, and to be charged with multiple offences (often for administrative violations) and are less likely to have legal representation in court proceedings (Roberts and Melchers 2003; Statistics Canada 2000). While Aboriginal youth accounted for 5 per cent of the total youth population in 1999, they occupied 24 per cent of the beds in Canadian detention centres. More tragic is the situation confronting indigenous youth in Canada's prairie provinces. In Saskatchewan and Manitoba, three-quarters (75 per cent for Manitoba and 74 per cent for Saskatchewan) of youth sentenced to custody were identified as Aboriginal while less than 10 per cent of Manitoba's youth population is Native (Statistics Canada 2000). No group has been more touched by Canada's appetite for youth incarceration than the First Nations.

Buttressing this systematic subjugation of those considered alien to the national body is the coincident dismantling of welfare programs during a period of intensified poverty among indigenous peoples—especially children. Not only are Aboriginal people highly overrepresented among the street population, they are more likely to be living in urban poverty and inhabiting living quarters deemed overcrowded than the general Canadian population (Canadian

Council on Social Development 2003b). According to Aboriginal activist Cindy Blackstock (2003), Canada's indigenous peoples would rank 78th on the United Nations' Human Development Index (HDI)—which measures poverty, literacy, education, and life expectancy. Canada itself consistently ranks first. The HDI, developed by Pakistani economist Mahbub ul Haq, has become the standard means of measuring overall well-being, and especially child welfare, through three basic categories:

- *long and healthy life* as indicated by life expectancy at birth
- *knowledge* as measured by adult literacy rate
- *standard of living* as derived from gross domestic product per capita

When compared to people in the rest of the world, Canadians are well situated. But hidden among facts and figures is a long-silent, oppressed, and subjugated population. Colonialism, it seems, is not an embarrassing period in the long-forgotten Canadian past. Instead it continues to rear its ugly head.

Given that the Aboriginal population is much younger than the Canadian average, the predicament facing the nation-state promises to shape the future of this country in very dramatic ways. A 2003 report by the Canadian Council on Social Development stated that the median age for Aboriginals was 24.7 compared to 37.7 for non-Aboriginals. Moreover, children 14 and under made up 33 per cent of the Aboriginal population compared to just 19 per cent for non-indigenous peoples. However, this growing group of young Aboriginals is more likely to live in poverty. More than half of all Aboriginal children were considered poor while only 23.4 per cent of all Canadian children suffered under this unfortunate condition (Canadian Council on Social Development 2003b).

## Justice for Girls?

Youth, especially the poorest and most marginalized, face pervasive discrimination, silencing, and victimization. While young people are often presented in media and popular discourse as particularly troubling, they are at the same time troubled (Tanner 1996). The latter part of this equation receives far less scrutiny than the former but is no less problematic. According to data gathered by Statistics Canada, those most likely to receive the sharp end of 'justice' are at the same time the most vulnerable to crime as well as social and economic subordination and are thus most in need of protection. Highlights of the *General social survey* suggest that youth are highly overrepresented as victims of crime. In 1999 youth aged 12 to 17 constituted 8 per cent of the population but were victims in 16 per cent of violent offences. The same study revealed that girls were overrepresented as victims of violent crime, especially sexual deviance (Statistics Canada 2001a).

Throughout history, the youth justice system has tended to neglect girls both as victims and as offenders. This is not surprising given that young girls have been highly underrepresented in crime statistics. Early criminologists and youth justice officials used this underrepresentation to bolster the view that wayward girls must somehow be defective. Discourses around female deviance embedded in traditional and positivist criminology illustrate this tendency. The founding *fathers* of criminology, such as Cesare Beccaria in 1778, Charles Hooton in 1939, and Otto Pollak in 1950, portrayed female offenders as a defective lot, the product of inferior breeding as well as biological and anatomical inferiority (Snider 2004). By the turn of the nineteenth century, offenders were considered mentally weak, but following the logic set out above, female 'deviants' were 'more terrible than any man' in that they were 'less intelligent, more passive, more deficient in moral sense, but stronger in sexual instincts' (Snider 2004: 232). Flowing out of this discourse were 'capricious and arbitrary status' offences—a category of offences that applies solely to youth, which if committed by an adult would not result in arrest (i.e., drinking, incorrigibility, truancy, and curfew violations)—that aimed to control female sexuality by incarcerating those who flouted norms of 'emphasized femininity', which stressed the importance of piety, domesticity, and above all monogamous heterosexual marriage.

Juvenile court officials cast a wide net over what they deemed 'sexuality'. Girls did not have to be caught in the act to be admonished by state actors. Franca Iacovetta (1999) charged that parents often brought their girls to the attention of police on the basis of neighbourhood gossip. Indeed, the mere suggestion of sexual activity could initiate state proceedings against young girls. Throughout the late nineteenth and early twentieth century, girls were routinely incarcerated for such aberrant conduct as holding hands or being out after dark in the wrong part of town in the company of a boy. Although girls drew the attention of juvenile court officials for their wayward sexuality, boys were detained for reasons not directly linked to violations of the normative sexual order. Instead, they were arrested for defying elite standards of appropriate conduct for working-class males by refusing to work, rejecting school, disobeying the law, and disrespecting their parents' requests for appropriate conduct.

Court records reveal the sexual double standard. Lauren P., who arrived in Canada from Ireland during the 1910s, was sent to live in an industrial school for the 'heinous crime' of flirting with boys at gasoline stations, staying out late, and going to movies—'often with rouge and lipstick' (Hogeveen 2002). Boys suffered no such intrusion into their lives or invasion of their bodies. Indeed, on a very revealing occasion a young boy, fearful he had impregnated his girlfriend, timidly asked his probation officer for advice. The officer promptly ordered the impudent youth to be tested for venereal disease and do his *manly* duty toward his girlfriend. A similar confession would have landed a female youth in an industrial school for an indefinite period.

Not only was girls' sexuality policed through juvenile court and industrial school intervention, race relations were also governed through state-sponsored intrusion. A familiar refrain from white Anglo-Celtic elites who dominated social, economic, and political life during the early twentieth century was that 'the nation' was in danger of decline (Valverde 1991). In the eyes of many, 'nation' was a generic term that referred to those of Anglo descent while racialized 'others' were viewed with increasing suspicion. By the 1910s a widely accepted racial hierarchy was firmly established in Canada. This ordering was not solely structured by skin colour but also by degrees of whiteness. The mostly British upper middle-class professionals who spearheaded eugenics campaigns—promoting forms of social control aimed at improving the racial qualities of future generations (Garland 1985: 142)—constituted themselves and 'the nation' in opposition to immigrants from other cultures. Anglo-Celtic elites, bolstered by eugenics discourse, created a purportedly common-sense racial logic that associated whiteness with the 'clean and the good, the pure and the pleasing'(Jackson 2000; Roediger 1991; Morrison 1992). It followed then that 'white' girls found associating with boys considered 'other' required training and reformation for the good of 'the nation'.

*In*justices experienced by girls continue under contemporary youth justice regimes, in part because they remain 'too few to count' within the youth justice system (Adelberg and Currie 1987). Despite some modest increase in numbers, female young offenders constitute one fifth of all cases appearing in youth court. Their infrequent appearance before magistrates and in centres of detention helps to explain why relatively few youth justice resources are set aside for female offenders—it does not, however, excuse it. This condition is felt throughout the youth justice process as more and more female youth are subjected to institutional arrangements, risk assessment, and programming designed by men on the basis of boys' experience. Given that theoretical foundations have been developed out of male experience, females are excluded as subjects of knowledge and authorized knowers. The implications are profound. Existing theories of crime and deviance predict the greatest deviance by the most marginalized, alienated, and devalued by society. However, this condition applies to women much more than it does to men. Yet despite being devalued and alienated, girls do not commit crime at anywhere near the rate of boys (Reitsma-Street 1999). Thus it would be very useful if theoretical interpretations of juvenile criminality and the programming that flows from it reflected girls' experience. However, that has not been the case.

The dearth of resources devoted to female programming and lack of attention to girls' experience have further implications. For instance, while Alberta operates and maintains support for numerous open-custody beds (institutions that are not locked) for male youth, only four are set aside for females. This situation is particularly egregious: incarcerated girls sentenced to open custody are not cascaded down to house arrest but relegated to locked units when open-custody beds are unavailable.

Clearly, girls' encounters with the young offender system, both historically and today, serve to further their marginalization and foster additional injustices.

## Voices of Youth?

The foregoing conditions have been produced by adult-conceived and implemented policy and practice. But if they are to be ameliorated, who should undertake the task? Who, we may ask, knows better what it is like to be young than those who occupy that generational position? The problem, however, is that youth are silenced. They are the subjects of adult-inspired intrusions, not their authors. In Western society, in fact throughout the global social field, adult views structure action and shape societal infrastructure while youthful voices remain silenced and frequently nullified. When the input of youth is solicited—which is hardly customary—it is often as an afterthought or as an aside. While the 'otherness' of young people renders them unique, it is often used to justify their exclusion as decision-makers in institutional arrangements that fundamentally affect their lives. Western discourse constitutes children as partially formed, in need of training and maturity—but most significant, inferior to adults.

Institutional arrangements that dot the Canadian landscape function to censor youth and fix them in a subordinate position. No one has to state overtly that youthful voices are less intelligent, barely cogent, and inferior to adults; it is simply understood. Indeed, pervasive discourses such as 'children should be seen and not heard' function to entrench the view that youth are somehow less than and 'other' to adults. However, this discourse is anchored in much more tacit albeit powerful ways. The fact that youth are not given the right to vote until they reach their eighteenth birthday speaks volumes about their silence (Mathews 2001). Moreover, when we consider the terms 'teacher', 'politician', and 'judge', we automatically assume that it is adults about whom we are speaking. But do youth have nothing of value to contribute to these important domains? Hardly. They find themselves on the outside, invited to participate only when something is being imposed on them—without, of course, any choice on their part. This order of things does not need to be taught in schools: it just is. Nevertheless, it is patently obvious through a cursory glance at the institutional hierarchy. Put simply, adults occupy all positions of influence.

This condition exists because of the way that fundamental resources are distributed throughout the social order. Those with the influence to speak and be heard derive their legitimacy from the field in which they exert their dominance. They are the spokespersons of the dominant order and work to ensure the continued existence of the status quo. In Western society, age is currency, and those who have accumulated the most experience as measured by years—only to a certain point, of course—inherit the symbolic power that accrues with it.

According to social theorist Pierre Bourdieu, every established social order necessarily makes its own arbitrariness seem a natural condition (Bourdieu 1977: 164). In Canadian society, where traditional hierarchies based on age remain relatively stable, our order of things appears self-evident, innate, and ordinary. Or to put it succinctly, in Canadian society the great majority are fully aware of their social positions and conduct themselves accordingly. In this order there remains little room for youth to manoeuvre into a more agreeable position. It would seem that the normative social order is fated to be replicated generation after generation. Those who benefit from the established order prefer not to unsettle the status quo. It is only the subordinated who have an interest in pushing back societal limits in order to expose the capriciousness of the presupposed order. Therefore, youth are left the task of unsettling the traditional norms that silence them.

In Edmonton, Alberta, a group of enterprising youth, despondent over their silence, has challenged contemporary orthodoxy by establishing and administering the world's only 'youth for youth' restorative justice program. A well-established definition of restorative justice suggests that it is an alternative criminal justice process whereby 'parties with a stake in a particular offence come together to resolve collectively how to deal with the aftermath of the offence and its implications for the future' (Marshall 1996, 37). In opposition to traditional youth justice processes in which adults predominate, the Youth Restorative Action Project (YRAP) was created, designed, and implemented and is currently administered by youth. It is made up entirely of young people—between 14 and 21, ranging from honours students to ex-offenders and recovering drug addicts—who consult with offenders to decide on appropriate sanctions within the frame of restorative justice. Adults are accorded no decision-making power and are almost entirely excluded from proceedings except in rare instances when they are called upon to provide clarification on technical points of law. YRAP paves the way for new discursive potentials and novel understandings that recognize the injustices and exclusions contained within established youth justice practice.

Unfortunately, YRAP is the exception rather than the rule. Youth continue to be silenced and nullified in matters that affect them directly. Only when the norms that reinforce adult privilege are exposed and the resulting social order is no longer considered inevitable can amendments be suggested.

## Conclusion

Given the silencing of young people, their experiences of poverty, the racism that confronts certain segments, and the dislocation of girls in juvenile justice, we can safely conclude that there is no justice for youth. But what would *justice* look like? Given that those for whom justice remains elusive are subjugated, marginalized, and racialized populations, *justice*, broadly conceived, would imply an ethic of how to be *just* with an to the 'other'. The problem, however, is that universal pronouncements such as the Canadian Charter of Rights and Freedoms and the UN Convention on the Rights of the Child provide little guidance toward this end. We should, therefore, not be fully satisfied with such endeavours. Satisfaction with the application of conventions and charters reduces the language of justice to questions of rights and conceals the tyranny over the poor, the indigenous, the female, and the silent.

## References

Adelberg and C. Currie. 1987. *Too few to count: Canadian women in conflict with the law.* Vancouver: Press Gang Publishers.

Blackstock, C. 2003. 'Same country, same land, 78 countries apart'. Unpublished paper.

Bourdieu, P. 1977. *Outline of a theory of practice.* Cambridge, UK: Cambridge University Press.

Canada. 1982. *Canadian Charter of Rights and Freedoms.* Ottawa: Government Printer.

———. 2004. 'Canada Child Tax Benefit for July 2004–July 2005'. www.nationalchildbenefit.ca/ncb/govtofcan4.html.

Canadian Council on Social Development. 2003a. *Campaign 2000: Report card on child poverty in Canada.* Ottawa: Canadian Council on Social Development.

———. 2003b. *Aboriginal children in poverty in urban communities.* www.ccsd.ca/pr/2003/aboriginal.htm.

———. 2004. *Percentage change in welfare benefits in Canada.* www.ccsd.ca/factsheet/fs_96wel.htm (retrieved 7 December 2004).

Carrington, P., and J. Schulenberg. 2004. 'Introduction: The Youth Criminal Justice Act: A new era in Canadian juvenile justice?' *Canadian Journal of Criminology an Criminal Justice* 46 (2):219–23.

Covell, K., and B. Howe. 2001. *The challenge of children's rights for Canada.* Waterloo, ON: Wilfrid Laurier University Press.

Della-Mattia, E. 2004. 'Martin fingers Liberals for child benefit clawback'. *Sault Star* 22 November: A4.

Denov, M. 2004.'Children's rights, juvenile justice, and the UN Convention on the Child: Implications for Canada'. In K. Campbell (Ed.), *Understanding youth justice in Canada.* Toronto: Pearson.

Doob, A., and C. Cesaroni. 2004. *Responding to youth crime in Canada.* Toronto: University of Toronto Press.

Enloe, C. 1990. *Bananas, beaches and bases: Making feminist sense out of international politics.* Berkeley: University of California Press.

Feld, B. 2000. '"Juveniles" waiver of legal rights: Confessions, Miranda, and the right to counsel'. In T. Grisso and R.G. Schwartz (Eds), *Youth on trial: A developmental perspective on juvenile justice.* Chicago: University of Chicago Press.

Garland, D. 1985. *Punishment and welfare.* London: Gower. *Bibliography 333*

Hammarberg, T. 1990. 'The UN Convention on the Rights of the Child and how to make it work'. *Human Rights Quarterly* 12 (1):97–105.

Hogeveen, B. 1999. 'An intrusive and corrective government: Political rationalities and the governance of Plains Aboriginals 1870–1890'. In R. Smandych (Ed.), *Governable places: Readings on governmentality and crime control*. Aldershot, UK: Dartmouth.

———.2002.'Mentally defective and feeble-minded juvenile offenders: Psychiatric discourse and the Toronto juvenile court 1910–1930'. *Canadian Bulletin of Medical History* 20 (1):43–74.

———. 2005. '"If we are tough on crime, if we punish crime, then people get the message": Constructing and governing the punishable young offender in Canada during the late 1990's. *Punishment and Society* 7 (1):73–89.

Hudson, B. 2003. *Understanding justice: An introduction to ideas, perspectives, and controversies in modern penal theory*. Philadelphia: Open University Press.

Iacovetta, F. 1999. 'Gossip, contest and power in the making of suburban bad girls: Toronto, 1945–60'. *Canadian Historical Review* 80 (4):585–623. *338 Bibliography*

Jackson, C. 2000. 'Waste and whiteness: Zora Neale Hurston and the politics of eugenics'. *African American Review* 34 (Winter):639–60.

Lee, K., and C. Engler. 2000. *A profile of poverty*. Ottawa: Canadian Council on Social Development.

Lévesque, A. 2002. 'Le travail des femmes à l'heure de la mondialization néo-libérale'. *Canadian Woman Studies/Les cahiers de la femme* 21/22 (4/1):151–5.

Ley, C. 1996. *The rise and fall of development theory*. London: James Currey.

Marshall, T. 1996. 'The evolution of restorative justice in Britain'. *European Journal on Criminal Policy and Research* 4 (4):21–43.

Mathews, H. 2001. 'Citizenship, youth councils and young people's participation'. *Journal of Youth Studies* 4 (3):299–318.

Miller, David. 1999. *Principles of social justice*. Cambridge, MA: Harvard University Press.

Mills, D. 2002. 'Children will be protected despite cutbacks'. *National Post* 3 October.

Morrison, T. 1992. *Playing in the dark: Whiteness and the literary imagination*. New York: Vintage.

O'Brien, N. 2004. 'Youth "justice" a joke'. *Peterborough Examiner* 4 October: A4.

*Olympia*. 1938. Leni Riefenstahl, producer and director. Germany.

Peterson-Badali, M., and R. Abramovich. 1992. 'Children's knowledge of the legal system: Are they competent to instruct legal counsel?' *Canadian Journal of Criminology* 34 (2):139–60.

Reiman, J. 1979. *The rich get richer and the poor get prison: Ideology, class and criminal justice*. New York: Wiley.

Reitsma-Street, M. 1999. 'Justice for Canadian girls: A 1990s update'. *Canadian Journal of Criminology* 41 (3):335–58.

Roberts, J., and R. Melchers. 2003. 'The incarceration of Aboriginal offenders'. *Canadian Journal of Criminology* 45 (2):170–89.

Roediger, D. 1991. *Wages of whiteness: Race and the making of the American working class*. New York: Verso.

Royal Commission on Aboriginal Peoples. 1993. *Aboriginal peoples and the justice system*. Ottawa: Minister of Supply and Services.

Royal Commission on Aboriginal Peoples. 1996. *Bridging the cultural divide: A report on Aboriginal peoples and criminal justice in Canada*. Ottawa: Minister of Supply and Services.

Snider, L. 2004. 'Female punishment: From punishment to backlash'. In C. Sumner (Ed.), *The Blackwell companion to criminology*. Malden, MA: Blackwell.

Statistics Canada. 2000. *Youth in custody and community services in Canada, 1998–9*. Ottawa: Centre for Justice Statistics.

———.2001a. *A profile of criminal victimization: Results of the 1999 General Social Survey*. Ottawa: Statistics Canada.

Tanner, J. 1996. *Teenage troubles: Youth and deviance in Canada*. Scarborough, ON: Nelson.

Valverde, M. 1991. *The age of light, soap, and water: Moral reform in English Canada, 1885–1925*. Toronto: McClelland and Stewart.

Wacquant, L. 1999. 'Urban marginality in the coming millennium'. *Urban Studies* 36 (10):1639–47.

———. 2001. 'Deadly symbiosis: When ghetto and prison mesh'. *Punishment and Society* 3 (1):95–134.

Young, I.M. 1990. *Justice and the politics of difference*. Princeton, NJ: Princeton University Press.

# 15

## Introduction

Recently many groups have argued that Canada's retributive justice system and punitive penal model have been ineffective in dealing with crime and delinquency on various levels. Increasing attention is being given to using 'restorative justice processes' to address crime and delinquency, the concerns of victims, and the effects of crime on the community. This abridged version of *Transforming Relationships Through Participatory Justice* provides an overview of restorative justice and some of the public discussion of it. The full report is available on line at Dsp-psd.pwgsc.gc.ca/Collection/JL2-22-2003E.pdf.

What is restorative justice? How does it differ from retributive justice? What are its advantages, disadvantages as well as some of the main concerns with it? In the final analysis, do you think it can be an effective and appropriate approach to crime and delinquency in Canada?

The difference between retributive and restorative justice is also relevant in informal social contexts. Restorative justice is connected to Carol Gilligan's work on masculine and feminine systems of valuing. In *In a Different Voice* (1982), Gilligan argues that gender formation involves developing a system of valuing or morality based on different experiences boys and girls have of the mother-child relationship.

The 'masculine' system is centred around individual rights and works with a notion of justice as fairness. Its aim is to objectively arrive at resolutions to moral dilemmas that all rational persons would agree upon by developing and objectively applying an abstract system of rules and principles to situations. Aggression, which is what generally leads to violating another's rights, is viewed as an unruly impulse to be controlled by law.

The 'feminine' system is centred around responsibility and is a more narrative, contextually attentive approach to resolving moral issues. It works with a notion of justice as 'caring' which requires taking into consideration the relationships among all the people involved, the general context, and the specific circumstances of an action in arriving at resolutions that are attentive to how everyone involved will be affected. Aggression is treated as an outcome of a fractured human connection or failed relationship in need of repair.

In your experience, do men generally adopt a more retributive approach and women a more restorative approach when dealing with issues involving wrong-doing in settings like the home, school, or workplace?

# Restorative Justice

*Law Commission of Canada*

## Introduction to Participatory Justice Processes

Conflict, and our response to it, is an enduring feature of our lives. We encounter conflict in our families, at work, at school, and in most other aspects of our lives. Conflict causes pain and loss. It damages people and property, sometimes irreparably. Conflict has the potential to destroy relationships between people. But conflict can also have positive effects. Conflict can define boundaries, both in a physical sense and in a social sense. It can establish limits to what is and is not acceptable behaviour. On an individual level, conflict provides an opportunity for growth and moral development. We may learn from our mistakes. We may learn to develop an appreciative understanding of the interests and concerns of others. At the community level, conflict provides an opportunity to discuss the values that underpin rules and regulations, to examine their assumptions, and to test their validity against opposing claims.

There are many strategies for resolving conflicts. Some of these strategies are healthy, others are not. We often ignore neighbours who play their music too loudly. We may tolerate offensive behaviour because the process for making a complaint is too difficult. We may negotiate with clients who will not abide by a contract. We may avoid locations that are perceived as dangerous. As consumers, we often accept the fact that we receive inferior products or service rather than complain. And, occasionally, we use the justice system—both the criminal law, and the civil, and administrative remedies—to resolve some of our conflicts.

Over the past several decades, some Canadians have become dissatisfied with how the formal justice system operates. Tribunals are frequently seen as unresponsive to the needs of people in conflict; conflicts are framed in legal language, rather than in terms of how individuals experience them; remedies often do not provide adequate redress for those who have been harmed; and the process is frequently time-consuming, costly, and confusing. The frustrations with conventional dispute processing—including excessive formalism, processing delays, and limited efficacy in resolving problems—have stimulated the growth of the restorative justice movement.

The dominance of the adversarial framework in Canadian law is an expression of our commitment to principled and just outcomes. While these commitments continue to be central to our understanding of a just society, they are also increasingly seen as insufficiently flexible to respond to diverse social relationships in a changing socio-demographic context. Adjudication can destroy personal and social relationships. Its commitment to formal equality can appear naïve in light of economic and other disparities among Canadians and its focus on the protection of individual rights may neglect the impact of conflict on collective coexistence and on particular communities. Finally, the adjudicative system has a limited range of outcomes: probation, fines, and incarceration in the criminal justice system, and monetary compensation in the civil justice system. Often, these outcomes fail to address the needs and desires of the parties involved in the conflict.

Can we do better? Is it possible to imagine a way to frame and to respond to conflicts that provides more satisfactory outcomes while safeguarding principles of justice? How do we safeguard the justice values of the adjudicative model without limiting our capacity to resolve conflict in a way that is more meaningful to those involved in disputes? There is a case to be made both for change and for caution.

## Restorative Justice

What is restorative justice? Most people would recognize that restorative justice is a different way of thinking about crime and conflict, but just what makes it different?

There are many ways of thinking about restorative justice, and each offers a different insight into how conflict is understood and resolved. Some proponents focus on restorative justice as a program or a specific type of intervention, such as victim–offender mediation or sentencing circles. Other proponents place a greater emphasis on the outcome of restorative justice processes. They focus on restorative justice as a way of healing victims, offenders, and the community.

The starting point for the Commission is that restorative justice is a process that brings victims, wrongdoers, and the community together to collectively repair harm while satisfying each participant's conception of justice. This report adopts this process-centred conception of restorative justice.

The adversarial process is **event based**. The key driver for the adversarial criminal justice system is the event that caused a conflict: how the event is defined and shaped goes a long way in determining how the conflict is resolved. The criminal justice process revolves around establishing that the act occurred and that the accused is or is not guilty. Either an accused can plead guilty to committing the act, or the case can go to court where evidence is presented to prove or disprove that the accused is criminally responsible.

Restorative justice is **relationship based**. Restorative justice processes focus on helping the victim to come to terms with the aftermath of the crime, holding the offender accountable for the crime and its consequences and, where appropriate, re-establishing their relationship in the community.

Restorative justice processes embody a set of values, which point toward a process, or set of processes, for addressing how individuals are affected by conflict. Restorative justice processes attempt to facilitate the personal growth and recovery of both the victim and the offender and, where warranted, to transform their relationship and restore some basis of understanding and common purpose. Restorative justice principles emphasize respectful and inclusive processes that exemplify many of the values of procedural justice (sometimes described as 'justice as process').[1] The orientation of restorative justice favours consensual outcomes over imposed ones. Therefore a set of process values—for example, personal voice, dialogue, respect for other participants and respect for outcomes—flow directly from restorative justice principles. There is also an important relationship between the types of processes implied and promoted by restorative justice principles and the desired or anticipated outcomes of restorative processes.[2]

# The Context

The principles of restorative justice have deep roots in both Western and non-Western traditions. Some argue that a move toward a restorative model of justice is perhaps best understood as a return to the roots of justice. While the roots of restorative justice can be traced back to antiquity, in its modern form restorative justice emerged in the 1970s.[3] This section will review the rise of restorative justice in Canada.

## The Failure of the Punitive System

Over the past two decades, many have argued that the adversarial model has not helped lower the crime rate nor contributed to greater public safety; until recently, crime rates and incarceration rates continued to rise.[4]

The limitations of the justice system are particularly acute for Aboriginal people.[5] Aboriginal people are significantly overrepresented in the prison system. In 2000–01, Aboriginal people accounted for 19 per cent of provincial and territorial sentenced admissions to custody and 17 per cent of federal sentenced admissions to custody, but constituted only 2 per cent of the adult Canadian population, according to 1996 census counts. The overrepresentation of Aboriginal people in the prison system is particularly evident in western and northern Canada. These data suggest that a punitive penal model has had limited, if any, impact on rates of crime and reoffending, particularly among Aboriginal people.

High crime rates and high rates of incarceration lead many to question the functioning of the justice system.[6] During the 1970s and 1980s many countries adopted the 'just deserts' model of punishment.[7] 'Just deserts' is premised on the belief that offenders ought to be punished in direct proportion to the wrong they have committed.[8] Under this model, proportional punishment is seen as a measure of true justice. The relative severity of sentences must be closely linked to the nature of the offence and tempered by the principle of parsimony— the principle that the least restrictive sanction necessary to achieve defined social purposes should be imposed. The concept of 'just deserts' is couched in moral terms; indeed, it is understood as 'an integral part of everyday moral judgment'.[9]

Unlike other countries, Canada did not adopt the 'just deserts' model. A parliamentary committee headed by David Daubney, then a member of Parliament, was convened to address the recommendations of the Sentencing Commission's report. Daubney's committee recommended that Parliament explore alternatives to imprisonment, including the use of restorative justice.

## Victims' Movements

The disillusionment of victims and their families with the criminal justice system has been a highly significant factor in the growth of restorative justice initiatives. The past 20 years have seen a significant growth in the number of lobby organizations representing the interests of the victims of crime. These organizations are variously described as victims' rights, or victim advocacy groups and victim support programs. These groups have highlighted the alienation of victims in a prosecutorial system in which the state stands in the shoes of victims and effectively excludes them from the process. The victim is not a party to the criminal prosecution of the accused, but only a witness to the crime.

Victims are largely left out of the court process, except in their role as witnesses. It is assumed that the interests of the state and those of the victim are the same. Most victims need a public affirmation that what occurred to them was wrong, and the criminal justice system is capable of responding to that need. However, many victims also want answers to questions, questions that the criminal courts are not structured to answer such as 'Why did this happen to me?' and 'Will I be compensated for my damaged property?' Victims' rights organizations have also expressed concerns about procedural issues. They feel that they have been excluded from the process and have lobbied for greater control over, and input into, decisions that are made regarding how cases are processed through the system. Finally, victims lack important information about what happens to offenders as they progress through the correctional system.

In response to victims' rights movements, some efforts have been made in Canada in the past decade to refocus the justice system on the unmet needs of the victims of crime.[10] One example is the introduction of victim impact statements into the sentencing process.[11] Victim impact statements may be read by the victim into the court record. This requires special permission from the judge. When they are read in court, victim impact statements are not subject to cross-examination, nor are they made under oath.

## The Emergence of a Community Justice Movement

Another significant factor in the evolution of restorative justice initiatives has been the development of a social movement that seeks a return to local decision-making and community-building, independent of the formal justice system. Advocates of community justice have argued that no amount of system reform could eliminate the effects of institutionalization and bureaucratization, which treat all individuals as formally equal, thereby failing to recognize the reality of diversity and power differences.[12] Conflict is often seen by the state as a negative force, something to be controlled and eliminated, thereby taking away the opportunity to discuss conflicting values, which are often at the root of conflicts.[13] In contrast, community-based justice initiatives can encourage the peaceful expression of conflict, build respect for diversity, and promote responsibility-taking by the community.[14] Another important theme in community justice projects is an attachment to social justice issues, such as tolerance and inclusiveness, environmental care and stewardship, and fair working environments.[15]

An early Canadian community justice initiative is Community Justice Initiatives of Kitchener/Waterloo, established in 1978. Like many community dispute resolution programs, this type of initiative offers intervention and facilitation for both criminal and civil disputes—also for matters in which no legal steps have been taken.[16] Many of the values of community-based justice are especially significant for faith communities, which have often been at the forefront of initiatives in community justice.[17] In Canada, the Mennonite community has played an enormous role in furthering the development of restorative justice, as has the Church Council on Justice and Corrections.

People who are not members of a faith also have the opportunity to give meaning to their experiences of conflict through participation in community justice. Neighbourhood justice centres have often originated in very large urban environments, which are often characterized as culturally individualist.[18]

Participation in community panels and boards and other informal dispute resolution processes represents an important effort to build community identity in these settings.

One further characteristic of the community justice movement is important to note. This is a focus on the lessons of experience, or 'what works'.[19] Disillusionment with the formal criminal justice system has led to a willingness to innovate and experiment in an effort to do things better. This is reflected in the history of neighbourhood justice centres, the continuing development of new programs and processes (such as healing circles and group conferencing), a strong commitment to seeing results in action, and a growing interest in program evaluation that is faithful to the consensus-based goals of community restorative justice.[20] While individual advocates and community justice activists are undoubtedly influenced by theoretical work on the values and principles of restorative justice, community models are primarily grounded in practical experience.

## Aboriginal Community Justice

The roots of restorative justice are particularly strong in Canadian Aboriginal communities. Aboriginal leaders have developed initiatives in response to an overwhelming need for emotional and spiritual healing in their communities. Moreover, in many Aboriginal communities, restorative justice initiatives are a part of a larger movement to assert control over governance functions.

In many cases, traditional healing and spiritual practices have been taken up as restorative justice measures, so justice practices have come to reinforce and extend the influences of those traditions in the communities.[21] The 'circle' is symbolic and, in some cases, sacred. It is used extensively across many Aboriginal communities as a form of social control and governance. A crime against an individual has an impact on the whole community because everyone is connected through relationships and through belief and value systems based on connections with land, animals, and spirits. In some communities, a crime committed by an individual must be repaired by the extended family or clan, and amends must be made to all other families or clans. Specific rituals exist to fulfill these reconciliatory and compensatory obligations. The unwillingness to break an offender's connections to the community is exemplified in the statement of the Hollow Water researchers: 'The People of Hollow Water do not believe in incarceration . . . The difference in Hollow Water is that offenders face their responsibilities with the love, respect, and support which the Anishnabe people believe are due to all creatures'. [22]

The Tsuu T'ina Provincial Court in Alberta is an Aboriginal court. It has mostly Aboriginal personnel, including an Aboriginal judge, an Aboriginal crown prosecutor, many of the clerks of the court and administrative staff are Tsuu T'ina Band members. The intent of the Tsuu T'ina peacemakers' process is to resolve disputes, avoid the courts, get to the underlying causes of the actions, restore community relationships and bring back a sense of harmony to the community.[23]

We would be ignoring important cultural differences if we were to suggest that restorative justice fits into a worldview that is shared by all Aboriginal communities.[24] The Aboriginal Healing Foundation notes that clear and generic healing principles and processes have not evolved 'because of the necessity for communities to develop their own models and processes which are closely linked with their own cultures, resources, and needs'.[25] It may also be unwise to accept restorative justice processes as distinctly Aboriginal.[26] Finally, the

Aboriginal Women's Action Network (AWAN) notes that the rush to implement restorative justice processes in some Aboriginal communities may place victims in danger of re-victimization, particularly for victims of violent or sexual assaults.[27]

# The Policy Framework

## Restorative Justice and the *Criminal Code*

The sentencing principles set out in the *Criminal Code* provide legislative support for the implementation of restorative justice processes.[28] Although the *Code* says that sentences ought to be proportional to the harm caused by the act, the principle of proportionality is balanced by another provision that states that an offender should not be deprived of liberty if less restrictive sanctions may be appropriate in the circumstances. Moreover, recent amendments[29] introduced, for the first time, a provision that explicitly refers to alternatives to incarceration—which might include sanctions agreed to through restorative processes—to be considered when a court imposes a sentence. This provision also emphasizes the need to give special consideration to alternatives in the case of Aboriginal offenders.

In addition, imposing conditional sentences[30] is also an option in a restorative process. Considerable case law has been generated regarding the appropriate conditions for imposing a conditional sentence. The Supreme Court of Canada makes it clear that a conditional sentence is 'generally . . . more effective than incarceration at achieving the restorative objectives of rehabilitation, reparations and promotion of a sense of responsibility in the offender'[31,32] and that 'restorative sentencing goals do not usually correlate with the use of prison as a sanction'.[33] Moreover, the Supreme Court points out that a conditional sentence, properly imposed, can meet the goals of both denunciation and deterrence.[34]

## UN Declaration of 'Basic Principles on the Use of Restorative Justice Programmes in Criminal Matters'

The United Nations Commission on Crime Prevention and Criminal Justice developed a draft resolution, 'Basic Principles on the Use of Restorative Justice Programmes in Criminal Matters'.[35] Canada has taken a leading role in sponsoring this resolution and hosted a major meeting of international experts in October 2001 to draft a set of basic principles for further consideration by this Commission. The 'Basic Principles on the Use of Restorative Justice Programmes in Criminal Matters' lends strong international support to the concept of restorative processes and outcomes at 'all stages' of the criminal justice process. The principles of the declaration emphasize party self-determination and voluntariness and refer to the need for procedural safeguards, including the availability of legal advice and full provision of information to participants in advance of any restorative process.[36]

Most significantly, perhaps, the Declaration calls for national governments to take steps— through consultation between criminal justice authorities and program administrators— to develop guidelines and standards for the operation of restorative justice processes.

## Department of Justice Canada's Values and Principles of Restorative Justice in Criminal Matters

Following the release of the United Nations declaration, the Department of Justice Canada launched a round of consultations to develop a statement of values and principles of restorative justice in criminal matters and guidelines for restorative justice programs that could be used in Canada. The values and principles document establishes 11 basic principles and procedural safeguards for the use of restorative justice, and a set of program guidelines.

## Basic Principles and Procedural Safeguards for the Use of Restorative Justice

1. Participation of a victim and an offender in a restorative justice process should be based on their free, voluntary and informed consent. Each party should receive a clear explanation of what the process might involve and the possible consequences of their decision to participate. Consent to participate may be withdrawn at any stage.
2. The victim and offender must accept as true the essential facts of the offence, and the offender must accept responsibility for the offence.
3. The facts must provide sufficient evidence to proceed with a charge, and the prosecution of the offence must not be barred at law.
4. The offender has the right to seek legal advice before and at all stages of the process.
5. Referrals to a restorative process can occur at all stages of the criminal justice system, from pre-charge diversion through to post-sentencing and post-release from custody in appropriate cases, and taking into account relevant prosecution policies.
6. Referrals to and conduct of a restorative process must take account of the safety and security of the parties and any power imbalances between victim and offender with respect to either person's age, maturity, gender, intellectual capacity, position in the community or other factors. In particular, implied or explicit threats to the safety of either party, and whether there is a continuing relationship between the parties, must be of paramount concern.
7. All discussions within the restorative process, other than those conducted in public, must remain confidential, unless agreed to the contrary by the victim and offender, and may not be used in any subsequent legal process.
8. The admission of responsibility by the offender for the offence is an essential part of the restorative process, and cannot be used as evidence against the offender in any subsequent legal process.
9. All agreements must be made voluntarily and must contain only reasonable, proportionate, and clear terms.
10. The failure to reach or to complete a restorative agreement must not be used in any subsequent criminal proceedings to justify a more severe sentence than would otherwise have been imposed on the offender.
11. A restorative justice program should be evaluated regularly to ensure that it continues to operate on sound principles and to meet its stated goals.

# Restorative Justice Processes

It is within this context that restorative justice processes emerged in Canada. In this section, we review some of the more common forms of restorative justice in use in Canada.

## Victim–Offender Mediation

Victim–offender mediation (VOM) and victim–offender reconciliation programs (VORPs) are among the earliest models of contemporary restorative justice processes. In VOM and VORPs the offender and the victim are voluntarily brought together—either before sentence or sometimes many years after sentence and incarceration—in the presence of a trained mediator.[37] In Kitchener, Mark Yantzi and Dave Worth asked a judge to permit them to try a different approach in dealing with two young offenders arrested for vandalism. The approach was to allow the victims and the offenders to take a key role in deciding the most appropriate method of responding to the harm done by the conflict. A satisfactory resolution—direct reparations—was reached, and the first Canadian VORP was born. Since then, the scope of mediation practices has grown considerably.

VOM and VORPs usually rely heavily on a volunteer base, and they are now generally located within the criminal court. Many VOM programs are formally sponsored by probation or youth justice departments, which make referrals of individual cases. Some programs work closely with Crown prosecutors to select cases appropriate for referral to mediation.[38] Sometimes a local criminal court judge will recommend that a matter be referred to mediation.[39]

In common with other restorative justice initiatives, referral into mediation can take place at any of four points in the processing of a criminal event: police entry point (that is, pre-charge); Crown entry point (that is, post-charge but pre-trial); court entry point (generally at the sentencing stage); and corrections entry point (following incarceration and before release).[40,41]

Intervention at any of these four points requires a close working relationship with the formal justice system. These schemes can function as a form of diversion from the formal justice system and they are often built into existing alternative-measures programs that are operated by community agencies in cooperation with justice officials.[42] In some programs, when a referral takes place pre-charge, an offender may not receive a criminal record since there is no formal finding of guilt by a criminal court.[43]

In addition, rather than operating as an alternative to punishment, some restorative justice processes operate after sentencing, with the express purpose of providing an opportunity for a victim and offender to meet to exchange information.[44]

## Community and family group conferencing

Originating in family group conferencing, which was developed and applied to youth justice processes in New Zealand,[45] conferencing models are now widely used in restorative justice initiatives. A coordinator will invite the family and friends of both the victim and the offender to participate in a discussion to explore appropriate ways to address the offending behaviour and desired outcomes for the family or the community. Those involved will then develop a plan for monitoring the offender's future behaviour and set out any reparative elements deemed necessary. Conferences are seen as an effective means of ensuring follow-through on agreed outcomes because of the larger number of individuals who are asked to commit to the rehabilitation plan.[46] This is in marked contrast to traditional criminal procedure in which community input into sentencing is rarely, if ever, available.[47]

## Sentencing Circles

Sentencing circles operate in many Aboriginal communities in Canada. Sentencing circles allow victims, offenders, community elders, other community members, and court officials to discuss the consequences of a conflict and explore ways of resolving it. Restitution for damages and reintegration of the wrongdoer into the community are high priorities. Community members play an active role in assisting the victim and the wrongdoer with the healing process. Some of these circles—for instance, the Circle Sentencing model developed in the Yukon by Judge Barry Stuart [48,49]—operate within the formal justice system as an alternative to the conventional sentencing process, and include justice professionals (police, probation officers, defence counsel, Crown counsel, and judges).

Circles are also sometimes used if cases are diverted from the justice system into alternative-measures programs (usually reserved for first-time youth offenders). Other circles are simply a gathering of those most concerned about the offender and the victim, and any other community members with an interest in the process.

## Community Boards or Panels

Community panels are made up of volunteers drawn from the community who meet formally with offenders and victims to facilitate a discussion of appropriate outcomes. Again, panel hearings can be conceived either as a pre-charge diversion from the formal system or as an alternative means to determine an appropriate sentence after a guilty plea has been entered.

Following a discussion (or 'hearing'), the panel and the offender make a contract stipulating what the offender will do during a probationary period. There is an emphasis on reparation and responsibility-taking by the individual offender. The probation contract is generally supervised by members of the panel, but in the event of breaches[50] the offender will be referred back to the court for sentencing.

## Other Participatory Processes

Besides VOM and community circles and panels, a range of other restorative justice practices has evolved, and innovative processes continue to emerge. For example, restorative justice principles have influenced the development of many school-based programs, including peer mediation training and anger management education.[51] In addition, circle processes have been used to address school-based conflicts.[52] Churches in Canada are also exploring restorative justice applications such as circle processes and mediation to deal with disputes in local church congregations.

Restorative justice processes also take place in prisons with incarcerated offenders, preparing them for reintegration into their communities.[53] For example, the Correctional Service of Canada (CSC) has shown a strong commitment to the principles of restorative justice by establishing a Restorative Justice and Dispute Resolution Branch that works with internal and external partners. Successful restorative opportunities have been created through victim-offender mediation of serious crime, surrogate programs, peacemaking circles and other initiatives. At several penitentiaries, inmates, community members, and staff have collaborated to create Restorative Justice Coalitions that have advanced educational initiatives.

# Objectives of Restorative Justice

The diverse origins of restorative justice initiatives, as well as the wide range of practice models, makes developing shared objectives and values for restorative justice processes a challenging task. It is, however, possible to distil from these practices a set of objectives and values that animate most restorative justice processes.

## Denouncing Unacceptable Behaviour

Restorative justice processes do not take a value-free approach to anti-social behaviour. Denunciation of certain behaviours is an objective of restorative justice, just as it is in the formal retributive model.[54] However, the process of arriving at a denunciation is quite different from that used by the adversarial criminal justice system, and the measure of what is unacceptable is examined in a broad context.

Restorative justice attempts to deliver 'deliberative justice' that is not circumscribed by legal definitions.[55] Restorative justice processes aim to identify the locus of responsibility and assess the impact of the harm caused by the behaviour in question, rather than meeting pre-existing criteria of harm. Restorative justice is a flexible response to the circumstances of the behaviour. Nonetheless, the commitment of restorative justice to identifying unacceptable behaviours and to acting to minimize their impact and reduce potential repeat offending means that restorative justice processes go beyond dealing with particular incidents and cases of law-breaking and harm, and offer a general social mechanism for the reinforcement of standards of appropriate behaviours.[56]

Of course, the assessment of behaviours as inappropriate and unacceptable does not take place in a vacuum. Participants in restorative justice processes are undoubtedly affected by their knowledge and experience of the existing criminal law, their degree of proximity to the offender and the behaviour, and the prevailing social climate in relation to crime and recidivism. There are also entrenched assumptions—although these are now being challenged in a few restorative justice processes[57]—about the appropriateness of restorative justice for serious crime. These assumptions reflect wider external values about punishment and imprisonment.

This pluralism gives rise to concerns about delegating the authority to denounce and forgive certain types of conduct to restorative justice processes, which may function inside or outside the formal justice system. The development of standards for acceptable and unacceptable behaviour can be a vehicle for progressive and community development, as well as for the intolerance and even tyranny of homogeneous groups. This is a particular concern if there are already entrenched inequalities of power and privilege within the community.[58]

## Support for Victims

The focus on the offender in the state prosecutorial model means that the expertise of justice professionals is oriented toward offenders, not victims. Restorative justice processes reconceptualize the victim as the focal point in the conflict resolution process. As a consequence, the victim's role is central to restorative justice processes—victims are provided a voice, an opportunity to ask questions and a process in which to confront their fears.[59] Further, by participating in decision-making, victims can exercise some power regarding outcomes.

When they participate, victims are generally satisfied with restorative justice processes. Most evaluation studies report a high rate of victim satisfaction with these processes. A recent study by Justice Canada found that restorative justice programs, when used in appropriate cases, are effective methods of improving satisfaction for both victims and offenders, increasing offender compliance with restitution and decreasing recidivism when compared with more traditional criminal justice measures.[60] Wemmers and Canuto[61] reviewed the literature on victims' experiences with restorative justice. Their review showed that most victims who participated in a restorative justice program were satisfied with their experiences and that they benefited from the process, particularly through meetings with the offender. Victims participate in restorative justice programs to seek reparation, help the offender, confront the offender with the consequences of the crime, and ask questions, such as why the offence was committed.

While generally promising, victim-satisfaction data have some limitations. First, it is important to distinguish between victims of minor crimes and those of serious crimes. Are satisfaction rates as high for victims of serious crimes as they are for those of minor crimes? Second, high satisfaction scores may be a result of self-selection. For example, it is possible that victims who participated in a restorative justice process had a positive attitude toward mediation prior to participating in the process. Third, it is necessary to examine the relationship between victim satisfaction and demographic variables such as age, gender, race and ethnic origin. Finally, evaluations must examine why some victims refuse to participate in restorative justice processes.[62]

Preliminary evaluation data on victim satisfaction are promising, but this is only part of the story. Victims' personal accounts are perhaps more revealing of the ways in which restorative justice processes can meet the needs of victims in the aftermath of crime. Many personal accounts testify to the power of the processes to facilitate healing and closure for victims.[63]

Another practical dimension of victims' needs that appears to be met by restorative justice initiatives is follow-through with agreed reparations and restitution. Like civil mediation, restorative processes claim a higher rate of individual compliance with outcomes that are consensually agreed to than do orders imposed by a court. Further, and perhaps more importantly, victims may receive an apology as a result of a participatory process—apologies are not generally available to them in the adversarial process.[64]

Nonetheless, significant concerns persist about the capacity of restorative justice to place victims at the centre of the process of resolution, especially initiatives operating within the formal criminal justice system and including justice officials. Can restorative justice really be victim oriented? It is not clear that, given the opportunity, victims would jump at the chance to engage in face-to-face dialogue with an offender. A number of programs report low rates of take-up by victims invited to participate in either mediation or group conferencing.[65] A further concern is that some victims may be pressured—by their families, communities or perhaps program advocates—to participate in restorative processes in which they feel uncomfortable or even intimidated.

Aboriginal women in particular have voiced fears that women who have experienced sexual or physical abuse may feel pressured to participate in community circles, despite feeling unsafe. While many Aboriginal women recognize the debilitating effects that the adversarial justice system has on Aboriginal communities and want to support alternative ways of resolving conflict, they question whether their concerns and their interests can be met in their communities as they currently exist.

More broadly, restorative justice processes must include specific protection for vulnerable populations. For example, a significant number of individuals who get caught up in the criminal justice system have mental health problems, which may impair their ability to make an informed decision to enter into a restorative justice program. Special care should be taken to ensure that they have the cognitive capacity to meaningfully participate in the process. Once the restorative justice process commences, a mental health professional should be available to provide services when required.

Seniors are another potentially vulnerable segment of the population. A study conducted for the Commission examined how the justice system responds to the financial exploitation of the elderly.[66] Many individuals who are exploited are reluctant to ask the police to intervene in what is perceived as a family matter. For example, some elderly victims do not want to take legal action against their children, while others who have been abused 52 and financially exploited tend to feel guilt and shame about what has happened to them, particularly if the abuser is a relative.[67]

## The Reform of Individual Offenders Through Active Responsibility-Taking

Retribution as a sentencing philosophy has evolved into a moral choice for its advocates, regardless of its instrumental value in reducing recidivism. The retributive model understands responsibility-taking as essentially passive.[68] The offender receives a punishment for engaging in prohibited conduct. It is an acknowledgment of responsibility for past actions, with no sense of taking responsibility for the consequences of the behaviour.[69] Moreover, it is imposed on the offender by the state, instead of being assumed or actively embraced by the offender.

Restitution succeeds where retributive theories fail in relating the punishment to the circumstances of the actual offender and victim and focusing on forward-looking behaviour—both making amends and dealing with other consequences of the offence. Restorative justice processes have a component of restitution attached to them. In their focus on the individual offender and victim, restitution and restorative justice share many objectives and values. What distinguishes restorative justice from restitution is its enlarged lens, which includes the wider community surrounding the individual offender and victim. Whether using VOM or larger group processes—such as circles, community panels, or group conferencing—restorative justice has the central objective of encouraging offenders to take responsibility for their actions, not so much in relation to the state as in relation to the individual victims and the communities in which they live.[70] Circles and group conferences enable other community members to be included in responsibility-taking indirectly (for example, by encouraging offenders to take authentic responsibility for the impact of their actions) and perhaps also directly (by sharing in the sense of vulnerability that crime creates for a community).

A circle setting also facilitates the development of group norms and group identity, challenging offenders to take responsibility for the impact of their behaviour, rather than allowing them to hide behind the technical language and rules of the courtroom. The circle includes offenders, making them a part of the group rather than outsiders.

The adversarial criminal justice system equates the attribution of responsibility to a conviction, and conviction is a win–lose proposition: the accused is either guilty or not guilty. Most restorative justice processes allow for a much more nuanced approach to responsibility. In many conflicts, including those that result in criminal charges, the accused may be guilty of the criminal charge and may be fully or partially responsible for the conflict. This is a key difference between restorative justice processes and the adversarial system. In many situations, the accused is both legally guilty and fully responsible for the crime—for example, a typical case of robbery, break and enter, or drunk driving resulting in death. In other situations, the accused may be legally guilty of the crime, but the question of responsibility is less clear-cut.

Restorative justice aims to increase the effectiveness of our response to crime in terms of community order and peace. Functionally, this means both reducing levels of individual recidivism and, more widely, preventing crime. But an effective response to crime also has a broader and deeper meaning for restorative justice advocates and for actively engaging the community in the dispute resolution process.[71] Restorative justice advocates argue that peace and order can be achieved by expanding community control and narrowing state control over the justice system. While there are fears that restorative justice may expand the state's social control—'net widening'[72]—many argue that the devolution of dispute resolution processes is a way of building stronger, healthier communities.[73]

Traditionally, the jury has been the primary method of involving the community in the justice system.[74] Restorative justice processes suggest a departure from this traditional way of incorporating the community. Juries and community members in a restorative justice process perform many of the same functions. Both examine the facts of the case, both add a layer of accountability, both act as the conscience of the community, and both are a buffer against oppressive and unjust law. The two differ, however, in at least two significant ways. First, juries are supposed to be impartial. Impartiality is a cornerstone of the Canadian justice system. Unlike juries, community representatives in restorative justice processes are not impartial. Second, whereas juries represent communities in the abstract, community representation in restorative justice processes is concrete. The families of the victim and offender, the people who live in the area, those who know the conflicting parties, and those who have a vested interest in the outcome of the case participate directly in the proceedings.

Restorative justice offers the possibility of harnessing the power of individuals to create the social capital required to build strong communities. **Social capital** refers to the elements of social organization, such as networks, norms, and social trust, that foster coordination and cooperation for mutual benefit.[75] Social capital helps create interconnections between community members and networks of civic engagement. The interconnectedness of community members often encourages trust, discourages political and economic opportunism, and facilitates collaboration for a common goal.

Communities, however, are complex. Communities can be highly stratified by race, gender, class, or age. Communities can be inclusive, but they can also impose membership conditions that are highly exclusionary and unjust. Many women's groups, including Aboriginal women's groups, have cautioned about the danger of accepting 'the community' as an unqualified social good. There are real concerns that restorative justice will reproduce many of the inequalities of the current adversarial process.

AWAN conducted focus groups with women in rural Aboriginal communities in British Columbia.[76] It reported that violence in some rural Aboriginal communities in British Columbia was so pervasive that it had become normalized. Moreover, when women spoke out against violence, their voices were silenced.

There is always a danger that restorative justice processes may produce 'counterfeit communities'. Restorative justice is part of a larger movement, in which governments are entering into partnerships with communities. These new partnerships raise a number of issues regarding the relationship between governments and communities. Partnerships are voluntary arrangements between two or more individuals or organizations that agree to work co-operatively toward a common goal. Partnerships must involve a willingness on the part of government to share power and decision-making with the community. But community members must also be encouraged to assume control of the decision-making process. A restorative justice program in which experts act on victims and offenders or otherwise exert control over the process is not a partnership, regardless of how much information these experts share with their 'clients'.

Restorative justice principles see conflict within communities as an opportunity for dialogue and change—as a means to better understand the dimensions of peaceful order in a truly inclusive way.[77] The community must take responsibility for high levels of both control and support if peace and order are to be established and maintained, resisting the slide to taking a punitive approach (characterized by high control and low support) or to becoming overly permissive (characterized by low control and high support).[78]

## Identifying Restorative, Forward-Looking Outcomes

A broadly shared objective for restorative justice processes is the use of constructive, contextually appropriate, and forward-looking outcomes or restorative resolutions. Instead of basing sentencing on predetermined rules with a strong retributive flavour, restorative justice processes strive for outcomes that satisfy a wide group of stakeholders (of whom the Crown is just one). Fair punishment should also have a forward-looking component, for example, apology and reparation by the offender, community service of some sort and, when warranted, a term of incarceration.

When determining an appropriate outcome, those involved in a restorative justice process reflect on the needs of victims, offenders, and members of the community. Restorative justice processes do not rule out a term of incarceration as one component of a restorative resolution to a conflict, but they generally are resistant to using incarceration as a reflex reaction to a crime. For example, incarceration may not be the most appropriate punishment if it deprives a family of the principal breadwinner or deprives a community of a person who can contribute positively.

There is also a preventive aspect to forward-looking outcomes.[79] 'Prevention' includes the prevention of further interpersonal harm and, if possible, the neutralization of the social harms caused by continuing power imbalances. The objectives of restorative processes are met if the processes are responsive to these types of practical, forward-looking criteria, rather than being overwhelmed by conventional assumptions about the intrinsic moral value of punishment.

# Core Process Values for Restorative Justice

What types of processes and practices best result in achieving the objectives of restorative justice?

## Participation

A key process value of restorative justice is to engage victims and offenders in resolving a conflict. Restorative justice objectives can only be met if victims and offenders are permitted to participate in the conflict resolution process. Participation offers several advantages: having a voice in the conflict resolution process, being listened to, and having control over how a conflict is resolved. Participation in the conflict resolution process increases one's sense of fair treatment. Each of these elements is discussed below.

Experience suggests that the expression of an individual voice in a determinative process has value in itself regardless of the impact on eventual outcomes.[80] Writing about mediation processes, some authors [81] argue that the self-expression that empowers the speaker by giving voice to his or her concerns and goals is itself a legitimate objective for the process of dialogue, regardless of whether an agreed, or a 'good' outcome results.

The Commission's consultations and research have shown that victims and offenders experience a strong need to articulate thoughts and express feelings about the crime in question.[82] A meeting format that enables a face-to-face exchange of information and perspectives is often key to the premise of restorative justice that 'truth' is established through personal experience and interaction. Among other things, discussion can challenge assumptions about the other side's motivations and rationale, fill in gaps or explode theories about the meaning of one another's acts, and challenge stereotyping of motives and behaviours.[83]

A parallel element to having a voice is being listened to.[84] Being listened to is strongly associated with validation and the acknowledgment of one's losses or suffering. Acknowledgment and validation are strongly advocated by a growing number of mediation practitioners and scholars who propose what is sometimes described as a communication frame for negotiation and dialogue (as contrasted with the settlement frame, which focuses on the delineation of the technical and factual issues to resolve the presenting dispute).[85] 'The need to be heard is often as important as the need to resolve the problem'.[86]

The importance of face-to-face dialogue in giving voice to both offender and victim, as well as others affected by the behaviours, highlights the need for a skilful third party, whether acting as a circle moderator, mediator, panel chair, or in some other position. It is important that the third party ensure that these values are maintained throughout the dialogue, for example by requiring respectful listening and shared talking time. However, the third party must not 'take' the opportunity for conciliation, or at least better understanding, from the parties by over-structuring and controlling the dialogue.[87]

## Respect for All Participants

Respectful behaviour toward all participants in a circle, a mediation or other restorative justice forum is a necessary corollary of the principle of face-to-face dialogue. However, it is not an inevitable consequence and, in the often emotionally charged environment of victim–offender interaction, it is worth stating explicitly as a key process value for restorative justice. Respectful treatment is a procedural value and need not be identical to structural equality of the parties, something which might be difficult to achieve in a criminal justice context. The offender will usually have already accepted responsibility for the wrongful conduct, and the victim will already have been seen as the wronged person, thereby establishing a structural inequality from the outset. While circles and other restorative processes cannot provide structural or psychological equality, they must be explicit and proactive in their commitment to respectful treatment of all participants, including offenders. Significant in achieving this goal is the effort of restorative justice practices to place the problem, and not the person, at the centre of the process. The offender often cares deeply what the victim thinks about them.[88] The opportunity for face-to-face dialogue can reduce or alleviate the tendency to demonize the offender and enables the beginnings of mutual respect.

## Community Empowerment

Another key process value for restorative justice is the participation of the community, whether delineated by family ties, membership in a geographically defined group (for example, neighbourhood or residents of an Aboriginal community, etc.), or some other connection to the victim or offender or affected community. The concept of community involvement has provoked some skepticism, especially outside more closely knit communities such as Aboriginal groups or smaller rural communities. Questions that are raised include: Who decides who should participate in a circle or other restorative justice process? Is participation by invitation only—the practice with family group conferencing[89]—or can anyone sit in the circle to discuss fair outcomes when an offender has admitted a charge? The victim may feel that the circle is stacked with friends and supporters of the offender.[90] Who speaks for the wider community in the circle, and with what legitimacy and what mandate?

To better understand the significance of participation as a process value in restorative justice, it is important to link it to the notion of empowerment. This means that the participants in the process see the problem not just as something that affects their lives now, but as something that may continue to affect their community and see that the problem requires the attention of more than just the two formal parties—the Crown and the offender—or even these two parties and the victim.

If this ideal notion of community empowerment is not to descend into community tyranny and vigilantism, it is critical that when community members discuss accountability for anti-social or criminal behaviour, they do more than look for an individual to blame. Instead, participation must be based on a genuine recognition that the wider group—the neighbourhood, the school, or the extended family circle—has a role to play in the restorative process. This includes working with the offender to enable him or her to take personal responsibility by 'harnessing sources of social control within families, schools, and neighbours as well as among public institutions'.[91]

## Commitment to Agreed Outcomes

Restorative justice practices vary widely in the degree to which they rely on formal enforcement and compliance monitoring. In some programs, any breach of the terms of a restorative resolution may result in referral back to a trial judge for formal sentencing. In other situations, including some types of community service and some Aboriginal circles, there is less formal monitoring and greater reliance on the integrity and honour of the offender. However, data collected from restorative justice processes suggest that voluntary compliance rates are high.[92]

## Flexibility and Responsiveness of Process and Outcomes

This fifth and final process represents an important tenet of the restorative justice movement. A tension arises between, on the one hand, the goal of providing respectful and respected processes for a dialogue that reflects individual and community needs and, on the other hand, the need for structure and control. The very nature of restorative justice processes and their emphasis on informality rejects the one-size-fits-all approach of the traditional adjudicative model. Moreover, some of the concerns about the potential for the tyranny of community are only properly addressed if communities are self-conscious about their assumptions of good or fair process and ensure that they can be responsive to both cultural diversity and individual needs. But there is also pressure for protocols and the emergence of claimed orthodoxies in restorative justice, just as in other areas of innovation. To resist this temptation to recreate a rigid and unresponsive process or set of processes, the restorative justice movement must continuously reaffirm the importance of process flexibility and creativity.

The same issues arise in relation to outcomes. The commitment of restorative justice to consensual and context-sensitive outcomes as the end result of facilitated dialogue processes does not mean that there is no recognition of relevant rules and principles, experience in past cases, and so on; it means simply that this is also a part of, and not all of, the context in which an outcome is fashioned by these participants. Again, there is pressure to produce outcomes that can be matched to identifiable standards and do not go soft on offenders, pressure that needs to be resisted if restorative justice is to remain committed to its core goals and values.

## Notes

1. See, for example, J. Thibaut, L. Walker, S. LaTour and S. Houlden, 'Procedural Justice as Fairness' (1974) 26 *Stanford Law Review* 1271; and J. Thibaut and L. Walker, *Procedural Justice: A Psychological Analysis* (New York: Erlbaum, 1975).
2. For example, the United Nations, in articulating and adopting its 'Basic Principles for the Use of Restorative Justice Programs in Criminal Matters', describes 'restorative outcomes', as agreements reached 'as a result of restorative process'; further, 'Restorative outcomes include responses and programs such as reparation, restitution and community service'. See 'Basic Principles for the Use of Restorative Justice Programmes in Criminal Matters', at III (3) and see the further discussion of the United Nations principles of restorative justice available on-line: www.restorativejustice.ca/National Consultation/BasicPrinciplesBody.htm.
3. One of the first references to 'restorative justice' is linked to Albert Eglash who used the term in his 1977 article 'Beyond Restitution: Creative Restitution'. See A. Eglash, 'Beyond Restitution: Creative Restitution' in J. Hudson and B. Galaway, eds., *Restitution in Criminal Justice* (Lexington: Lexington Books, 1975) at 91.
4. For a review of Canadian crime statistics, see Canadian Centre for Justice Statistics, Canadian Crime Statistics (Ottawa: Statistics Canada, 2001); D. Garland, *The Culture of Control: Crime and Social Order in Contemporary Society* (Chicago: University of Chicago Press, 2001).
5. For a review of Aboriginal over-representation in the criminal justice system, see Canadian Welfare Council, *Indians and the Law: A Survey Prepared for The Honourable A. Laing* (Ottawa: Canadian Welfare Council, August 1967) 42; Alberta Task Force, *Justice On Trial: The Report of the Task Force on the Criminal Justice System and Its Impact on the Indian and Métis People of Alberta* (Edmonton: Government of Alberta, 1990); Manitoba, *Report of the Aboriginal Justice Inquiry of Manitoba*, Volume 1: *The Justice System and Aboriginal People* (Winnipeg: Queen's Printer, 1991); Indian Justice Review Committee (Canada), *Report of the Saskatchewan Indian Justice Review Committee* (Regina: The Committee, 1992); C. LaPrairie, *Examining Aboriginal Corrections in Canada* (Ottawa: Ministry of the Solicitor General, 1996); Canada, Royal Commission on Aboriginal Peoples, *Bridging the Cultural Divide: A Report on Aboriginal People and Criminal Justice in Canada* (Ottawa: Supply and Services Canada, 1996); and M. Jackson, 'Locking Up Natives in Canada' (1988–89) 23:1 *University of British Columbia Law Review* 216.
6. D. Garland, *The Culture of Control: Crime and Social Order in Contemporary Society* (Chicago: University of Chicago Press, 2001); D. Cayley, *Expanding Prison, The Crisis in Crime and Punishment and the Search for Alternatives* (Toronto: Pilgrim Press, 1999); and N. Christie, 'Conflicts as Property' (1977) 17:1 *British Journal of Criminology* 1.
7. A. Von Hirsch, *Doing Justice: The Choice of Punishments: Report of The Committee for the Study of Incarceration* (New York: Hill and Wang, 1976); and A. Von Hirsh, *Past or Future Crimes: Deservedness and Dangerousness in the Sentencing of Criminals* (New Brunswick: Rutgers University Press, 1985).
8. Canadian Sentencing Commission, *Sentencing Reform – A Canadian Approach: Report Of The Canadian Sentencing Commission* (Ottawa: Canadian Sentencing Commission, 1987) at 143–144.
9. A. Von Hirsch, 'Penal Theories' in M. Tonry, ed., *The Handbook of Crime and Punishment* (Oxford: Oxford University Press, 1998) at 666. In the 1980s, the Canadian Sentencing Commission studied the criminal sentencing process in Canada. The Sentencing Commission recommended that Parliament adopt 'just deserts' as the paramount consideration governing the determination of a sentence; it proposed a two-pronged reform strategy. First, a legislative statement of sentencing principles was to be made. Then a rigid system of guidelines would be imposed—offences would be ranked according to severity, and each offence would have a presumptive sentence. The proposals represented an attempt to create a system of sentencing based on proportionality, where the most important factor in sentencing would be the gravity of the offence, rather than the offender's past convictions. Past convictions would be only one factor among many to be taken into account in determining the sentence within the presumptive range or in deciding whether to depart from the

presumptive sentence. Canadian Sentencing Commission, *Sentencing Reform – A Canadian Approach: Report Of The Canadian Sentencing Commission* (Ottawa: Canadian Sentencing Commission, 1987).

10. For an exhaustive review of the rise of the victims' movement in Canada and policy responses to this movement, see K. Roach, *Due Process and Victims' Rights: The New Law and Politics of Criminal Justice* (Toronto: University of Toronto Press, 1999).

11. Section 722 of the Canadian *Criminal Code*. Provincial legislation also establishes procedures for the submission of such statements (see below). Parole boards are also empowered to ask for victim impact statements when considering a request for the reduction of a term of ineligibility for parole; see *Criminal Code* s. 645.63(1)(d). See generally, The Honourable Justice C. Hill, 'Expanding Victims' Rights' in A.D. Gold, ed., *Alan D. Gold's Collection of Criminal Law Articles* on-line: www.quicklaw.com (Quicklaw: GOLA [database], 1999).

12. For a classic exposition of the arguments for a rejection of the state system and the development of community-based justice, see R. Shonholtz, 'Neighborhood Justice Systems' (1984) 5 *Mediation Quarterly* 3.

13. L. Nader, 'Controlling Processes in the Practice of Law: Hierarchy and Pacification in the Movement to Reform Dispute Ideology' (1993) 9:1 *Ohio State Journal on Dispute Resolution* 1.

14. For example, N. Christie has written about this tendency of the formal criminal justice system to attempt to 'explain conflicts away' and, in particular, to ignore their relationship to socio-economic and class structures. Christie, *supra* note 8 at 6.

15. K. Pranis recognizes this tension when she writes that '[c]ommunity justice seeks equal consideration for the well-being and wholeness of all community members . . . [W]ell-being requires *being able to meet one's own needs without harm to others and being able to exercise control in one's life*' (italics added). K. Pranis, 'Restorative Justice, Social Justice and the Empowerment of Marginalised Communities' in G. Bazemore and M. Schiff, eds., *Restorative Community Justice: Repairing Harm and Transforming Communities* (Cincinnati: Anderson Publishing Co., 2001) 287 at 288.

16. G. Husk, 'Making Community Mediation Work' in J. Macfarlane, ed., *Rethinking Disputes: The Mediation Alternative* (Toronto: Emond Montgomery, 1997) at 282.

17. M.L. Hadley, ed., *The Spiritual Roots of Restorative Justice*. SUNY Series in Religious Studies (Albany: State University of New York Press, 2001).

18. Robert Redfield devised the folk-urban continuum, which describes the evolution of a rural community to an urban society and the changes that result. These include the loss of both the original homogeneity and the cohesion of established social practices. Redfield's work is described in I. Schulte-Tenckhoff, *The Concept of Community in the Social Sciences and Its Juridical Relevance* (Ottawa: Law Commission of Canada, September 2001) at 14–15.

19. See the discussion in T.F. Marshall, *Restorative Justice: An Overview* (London: Home Office, 1998) at 3.

20. For example, a workshop on program evaluation presented by Dr. Avery Calhoun of the University of Calgary drew a very large crowd at the Canadian Criminal Justice Association's 2002 conference in Gatineau, Quebec.

21. Solicitor General of Canada and the Aboriginal Healing Foundation, *Mapping the Healing Journey: The Final Report of a First Nation Research Project on Healing in Canadian Aboriginal Communities* (Ottawa: Solicitor General of Canada, 2002) at 21.

22. Aboriginal Peoples Collection of Canada, *The Four Circles of Hollow Water* (Ottawa: Public Works and Government Services Canada, 1997) at 10.

23. J. Ryan and B. Calliou, *Aboriginal Restorative Justice Alternatives: Two Case Studies* (Ottawa: Law Commission of Canada, 2002).

24. *Supra* note 22, at 7.

25. Aboriginal Peoples Collection of Canada, *The Four Circles of Hollow Water* (Ottawa: Public Works and Government Services Canada, 1997) at 11.

26. E. LaRocque, 'Re-examining Culturally Appropriate Models in Criminal Justice Applications' in M. Asch, ed., *Aboriginal and Treaty Rights in Canada: Essays on Law, Equity and Respect for Difference* (Vancouver: University of British Columbia Press, 1997) at 75–76, suggests that there is a 'growing complex of reinvented 'traditions' which have become popular even while lacking historical or anthropological contextualization'.

27. W. Stewart, A. Huntley, and F. Blaney, *The Implications of Restorative Justice for Aboriginal Women and Children Survivors of Violence: A Comparative Overview of Five Communities in British Columbia* (Ottawa: Law Commission of Canada, July 2001) at 28.

28. *Criminal Code*, R.S.C. 1985, c. C-46, s. 718.

29. *Ibid.* at 718.2(e).

30. A conditional sentence is a term of imprisonment that is served in the community. A number of criteria have to be met before an offender can be sentenced to serve his or her term of custody in the community under supervision. First, the sentence cannot exceed two years less one day. Second, if the offence carries a minimum penalty, the offender cannot receive a conditional sentence. Third, the judge must be convinced

that the presence of the offender in the community (rather than prison) does not pose a danger to the public. Finally, the judge must be convinced that a conditional sentence is consistent with the purpose and principles of sentencing that are contained in the *Criminal Code*. For more information see: 'What Is a Conditional Sentence?' Conditional Sentencing Series Fact Sheet 1 (Research and Statistics Division, Department of Justice Canada), on-line: www.canada.justice. gc.ca/en/ps/rs/rep/fs_cs_001e.pdf (date accessed: 17 September 2003).

31.  *R. v. Proulx* [2000] S.C.R. 6, 2000 SCC 5, online: QL.

32.  *Ibid.* at para. 22.

33.  *Ibid.* at para. 19.

34.  Chief Justice Lamer stated that 'there may be certain circumstances in which the need for denunciation is so pressing that incarceration will be the only suitable way in which to express society's condemnation of the offender's conduct'. But, he continued, 'Judges should be wary of placing too much weight on deterrence when choosing between a conditional sentence and incarceration. The empirical evidence suggests that the deterrent effect of incarceration is uncertain'. Chief Justice Lamer, in *Proulx* at paras. 106–107.

35.  United Nations Economic and Social Council, 'Basic Principles on the Use of Restorative Justice Programmes in Criminal Matters' (Vienna: Commission on Crime Prevention and Criminal Justice, 2002), on line: www. restorative justice.org/rj3/UNdocuments/UNDecBasicPrinciplesofRJ.html (date accessed: 17 September 2003).

36.  Note that the United Nations Principles were the focus of an on-line discussion facilitated by the Network for Conflict Resolution in 2002–2003.

37.  For a classic description of this VOM process, see M. Umbreit, 'Mediation of Victim–Offender Conflict' (1988) 31 *Journal of Dispute Resolution* 84.

38.  For example, the now defunct Dispute Resolution Centre of Ottawa-Carleton.

39.  For example, the Ottawa Collaborative Justice Project has received the majority of its referrals from pre-trial judges. For more information see on-line: www.ccjc.ca.

40.  B. Archibald, 'A Comprehensive Canadian Approach to Restorative Justice: The Prospects for Structuring Fair Alternative Measures in Response to Crime' (prepared for delivery at the 1998 Conference on Making Criminal Law Clear and Just, Queen's University, Kingston, Ontario, November 1998).

41.  In theory, intervention can also occur before the engagement of the formal justice system, for example, if the community becomes alerted to schoolyard bullying issues at a local school. Intervention at this early stage is an important restorative justice principle, but in VOM and VORP, as in other restorative justice processes, this type of early intervention is relatively less common than the four system entry points described above. Intervention can also occur before the engagement of the justice system, but it is more complex to identify, document and evaluate for the purposes of policy development.

42.  For example, in Nova Scotia, an extensive new program of restorative justice initiatives builds on the work of alternative-measures programs. See A. Thomson, *Formal Restorative Justice in Nova Scotia: A Pre-implementation Overview* (prepared for delivery at the Annual Conference of the Atlantic Association of Sociologists and Anthropologists, Fredericton: October 1999) at 7, online: http://ace.acadiau.ca/soci/agt/justice/restorative justice.htm (date accessed: 17 September 2003).

43.  M. Peterson, 'Developing a Restorative Justice Program: Part One' (2000) 5:3 *Justice as Healing* 1, online: www. usask.ca/nativelaw.

44.  Marshall and Merry, reporting on UK programs, found that 76 per cent of UK VOM programs operate post-sentence. See T. Marshall and S. Merry, *Crime and Accountability: Victim/Offender Mediation in Practice* (London: Home Office HMSO, 1990) at 8.

45.  See, for example, J. Hudson, A. Morris, G. Maxwell and B. Galaway, eds., *Family Group Conferences: Perspectives on Policy and Practice* (Australia: Federation Press, 1996).

46.  See Marshall, *supra* note 19, at 20.

47.  Gerry Ferguson points out that in recent history the best-known example of a criminal jury attempting to have input into sentencing was in the trial of Robert Latimer (*R. v. Latimer*, [2001] 1 S.C.R. 3); the jury's request was brushed off by the trial judge. See G. Ferguson, *Community Participation in Criminal Jury Trials and Restorative Justice Programs* (Ottawa: Law Commission of Canada, 2001) at 140.

48.  For example, the much-recognized efforts of Judge Barry Stuart in the Yukon and the work of a local Justice with the Hollow Water project in Manitoba. See B. Stuart, 'Sentencing Circles: Making Real Differences' in J. Macfarlane, ed., Rethinking Disputes: The Mediation Alternative (Toronto: Emond Montgomery, 1997); T. Lajeunesse, *Evaluation of Community Holistic Circle Healing: Hollow Water First Nation.* Volume 1: *Final Report* (Ottawa: Solicitor General of Canada, 1996)

49.  M. Peterson notes that Judge Fafard of Saskatchewan has participated in 60 to 70 sentencing circles and has never rejected a circle recommendation. See M. Peterson, *supra* note 43 at 81. For a comprehensive description of the philosophy, rationale and practices of circle sentencing, see the judgment of Justice Stuart, in *R. v. Moses*, [1992] Y.J. No. 50, [1992] 3 C.N.L.R. 116 (QL).

50. One study estimates that 17 per cent of offenders fail to complete their agreements. See L. Kurki, 'Restorative and Community Justice in the United States' (2000) 27 *Crime and Justice* 235.

51. A number of individual schools have implemented restorative justice processes for resolving conflict. In British Columbia, the Fraser Region Community Justice Initiatives agreed to work with a school district to explore how restorative justice principles might be applied throughout the local school system. This project is one of the first of its kind to implement restorative justice as a collaborative effort and in a comprehensive manner throughout an entire school district. See C. Bargen, *Safe Schools: Strategies for a Changing Culture* (prepared for delivery at the 6th International Conference on Restorative Justice, Simon Fraser University, Vancouver, B.C., June 2003).

52. The Youth Canada Association works to understand conflict and promote peace-building through restorative processes among Canadian youth. See online: www.youcan.ca/.

53. Many examples in the introduction to the recent book by Bazemore and Schiff fall into this fourth category. G. Bazemore and M. Schiff, eds., *Restorative Community Justice: Repairing Harm and Restoring Communities* (Cincinnati: Anderson Publishing, 2001) at 1-4.

54. Kathleen Daly, for example, argues that proponents of restorative justice often overstate the philosophical divide that exists between restorative justice and retributive justice. K. Daly, 'Revisiting the Relationship Between Retributive and Restorative Justice' in H. Strang, and J. Braithwaite, eds., *Restorative Justice: Philosophy to Practice* (Aldershot: Ashgate, 2000) 33. See also A. Von Hirsch, J.V. Roberts, A. Bottoms, K. Roach and M. Chiff, eds., *Restorative Justice and Criminal Justice: Competing or Reconcilable Paradigms* (Oxford: Hart Publishing, 2003).

55. J. Braithwaite, 'Restorative Justice' in M.H. Tonry, ed., *The Handbook of Crime and Punishment* (Oxford: Oxford University Press, 1998) at 239.

56. T. Wachtel, and G. Gold, 'Restorative Justice in Everyday Life' in H. Strang and J. Braithwaite, eds., *Restorative Justice and Civil Society* (New York: Cambridge University Press, 2001) 114.

57. For example, the work of Dave Gustafson with serious crimes at the Fraser Region Community Justice Initiatives. See D. Gustafson and S. Bergin, *Promising Models in Restorative Justice: A Report for the Ministry of the Attorney-General of British Columbia* (Victoria: Ministry of the Attorney-General, 1998); and the work of the Ottawa Collaborative Justice Project, which targets serious crimes, including cases of robbery, robbery with a weapon, weapons offences, break and enter, theft over $5,000, fraud, assault, assault causing bodily harm, impaired driving causing bodily harm or death, and careless driving or dangerous driving causing bodily harm or death. As well, the John Howard Society of Manitoba is in the early stages of developing a restorative justice program for domestic assault. L. Maloney and G. Reddoch, *Restorative Justice and Family Violence: A Community-based Effort to Move from Theory to Practice* (prepared for delivery at the 6th International Conference on Restorative Justice, Simon Fraser University, Vancouver, B.C., June 2003).

58. For example, the systemic sexism and tolerance of violence against women in some Aboriginal communities is described in W. Stewart, A. Huntley and F. Blaney, *The Implications of Restorative Justice for Aboriginal Women and Children Survivors of Violence: A Comparative Overview of Five Communities in British Columbia*, supra 27, at 26–31.

59. Tony Marshall and Susan Merry have suggested that the process of face-to-face dialogue between victim and offender can enable victims to explore and sometimes dismantle stereotyping views they held of offenders, in general, and the offender who harmed them, in particular. See Marshall, *supra* note 44.

60. J. Latimer, C. Dowden and D. Muise, *The Effectiveness of Restorative Justice Practices: A Meta-analysis* (Ottawa: Department of Justice, 2001).

61. J. Wemmers and M. Canuto, *Victims' Experiences with, Expectations and Perceptions of Restorative Justice: A Critical Review of the Literature.* (Ottawa: Policy Centre for Victims Issues, Department of Justice Canada, 2001).

62. For a review of the literature on restorative justice evaluations, L. Kurki, 'Evaluating Restorative Justice Practices' in A. Von Hirsch, J. Roberts, A. E Bottoms, K. Roach and M. Schiff, eds., *Restorative Justice and Criminal Justice: Competing or Reconcilable Paradigms* (Oxford: Hart Publishing, 2003).

63. See, for example, M. Ruth, Stories of Negotiated Justice (Toronto: Canadian Scholar's Press Inc., 2000); and W. Derksen, *Confronting the Horror: The Aftermath of Violence* (Winnipeg: Amity Publishers, 2002).

64. In *Restoring Dignity*, the Law Commission of Canada provides an overview of the qualities of a meaningful apology and the role of meaningful apologies in the justice process. See Law Commission of Canada, *Restoring Dignity: Responding to Institutional Child Abuse in Canadian Institutions*, (Ottawa: Law Commission of Canada, March 2000). See also S. Alter, *Apologising for Serious Wrongdoing: Social, Psychological and Legal Considerations* (Ottawa: Law Commission of Canada, May 1999) at the sections entitled 'Acknowledgement of the Wrong Done' and 'Accepting Responsibility for the Wrong Done'.

65. For example, victim participation in the long-standing Winnipeg project is reported as just 10 per cent. J. Bonta, S. Wallace-Capretta and J. Rooney, *Restorative Justice: An Evaluation of the Restorative Resolutions*

*Project* (Ottawa: Solicitor General of Canada, 1998). See also the data presented by D.R. Karp and L. Walther on victim participation in the Vermont Community Reparative Boards in G. Bazemore and M. Schiff, eds., *Restorative Community Justice: Repairing Harm and Transforming Communities* (Cincinnati: Anderson Publishing Co., 2001) at 210-211.

66. D. Poirier and N. Poirier, *Why Is It So Difficult to Combat Elder Abuse and, in Particular, Financial Exploitation of the Elderly?* (Ottawa: Law Commission of Canada, July 1999).

67. H.B. Eisenberg, 'Combating Elder Abuse Through the Legal Process' (1991) 3:1 *Journal of Elder Abuse and Neglect* 65; and C. Spencer, *Diminishing Returns: An Examination of Financial Responsibility, Decision Making and Financial Abuse Among Older Adults in British Columbia* (Vancouver: Gerontology Research Centre, Simon Fraser University, 1996).

68. For a description of 'passive' contrasted with 'active' responsibility-taking, see M. Bovens, *The Quest for Responsibility* (New York: Cambridge University Press, 1998) at 26–38.

69. J. Braithwaite and D. Roche, 'Responsibility and Restorative Justice' in G. Bazemore and M. Schiff, eds., *Restorative Community Justice: Repairing Harm and Transforming Communities* (Cincinnati: Anderson Publishing Co., 2001) at 63-65.

70. M. Achilles and H. Zehr, 'Restorative Justice for Crime Victims: The Promise and the Challenge' in G. Bazemore and M. Schiff, eds., *Restorative Community Justice: Repairing Harm and Transforming Communities* (Cincinnati: Anderson Publishing Co., 2001) at 91.

71. See, for example, the discussion in D. Cayley, 'Security and Justice for All' in H. Strang and J. Braithwaite, eds., *Restorative Justice and Civil Society* (New York: Cambridge University Press, 2001) at 211–213.

72. S. Cohen, *Visions of Social Control* (Oxford: Polity, 1986). See also K. Roach, 'Changing Punishment at the Turn of the Century: Restorative Justice on the Rise (2000) 42:3 *Canadian Journal of Criminology* at 255; J. Braithwaite, 'Restorative Justice: Assessing Optimistic and Pessimistic Accounts' (1999) 25 *Crime and Justice* 1 at 89.

73. D. Moore, 'Shame Forgiveness and Juvenile Justice' (1993) 12:1 *Criminal Justice Ethics* 3.

74. Ferguson, *supra* note 47.

75. R. Putnam, *The Decline of Civil Society: How Come? So What?* (prepared for delivery at the John L. Manion Lecture, Canadian Centre for Management Development, Ottawa, 22 February 1996), at 4.

76. Stewart, *supra* note 27.

77. Some sociologists advance the theory that there is a relationship between various communities and the levels of types of crime committed therein. Work under this paradigm explores community influences on individual development. See, for example, P. Wikstrom, 'Communities and Crime' in M. Tonry, ed., *The Handbook of Crime and Punishment* (New York: Oxford University Press, 1998) at 269.

78. Wachtel, *supra* note 56 at 116–117.

79. T.F. Marshall, *Restorative Justice: An Overview* (London: Home Office, 1998) at 3.

80. T. Tyler, K. Rasinki and N. Spodick, 'The Influence of Voice on Satisfaction with Leaders: Exploring the Meaning of Process Control' (1985) 48 *Journal of Personality and Social Psychology* 72.

81. R.A. Bush and J.P. Folger., *The Promise of Mediation: Responding to Conflict Through Empowerment and Recognition* (San Francisco: Jossey-Bass, 1994) especially 84–89.

82. M.S. Umbreit, *Victim Meets Offender: The Impact of Restorative Justice and Mediation* (Monsey: Criminal Justice Press, 1994) at 101.

83. See also the discussion in J. Macfarlane, 'Why Do People Settle?' (2001) 45 *McGill Law Journal* 663 at 709–710.

84. Testing four possible limitations on the satisfaction associated with a high degree of process control, Tyler found that the only factor that significantly reduced or eliminated this satisfaction was when the final decision-maker (where outcomes were imposed) did not appear to give due consideration to the disputants' view. See T. Tyler, 'Conditions Leading to Value Expressive Effects in Judgments of Procedural Justice: A Test of Four Models' (1987) 52 *Journal of Personality and Social Psychology* 333.

85. See D.M. Kolb and Associates, *When Talk Works: Profiles of Mediators* (San Francisco: Jossey-Bass, 1994) at chapter 1. This is also sometimes described as a 'therapeutic' style of mediation. See S. Silbey and S. Merry, 'Mediator Settlement Strategies' (1986) 8 *Law and Society Policy Review* 7; and see also L. Riskin, 'Mediator Orientations, Strategies and Techniques' (1994) 12 *Alternatives* 111.

86. R. Albert and D. Howard, 'Informal Dispute Resolution Through Mediation' (1985) 10 *Mediation Quarterly* 99

87. G. Davis, 'The Theft of Conciliation' (1985) 32 *Probation Journal* 7.

88. This was explicitly stated as important to more than half the sample in Umbreit's study of four American VOM programs. Umbreit, *supra* note 82 at 103.

89. Family group conferencing generally uses a community-of-care model to determine who should be present at the circle.

90. S. Retzinger and T. Scheff, 'Strategy for Community Conferences: Emotions and Social Bonds' in B. Galaway

and J. Hudson, eds., *Restorative Justice: International Perspectives* (New York: Criminal Justice Press, 1996) 315.

91. C. LaPrairie, 'The "New" Justice: Some Implications for Aboriginal Communities' (1998) 40:1 *Canadian Journal of Criminology* 61 at 67.

92. See, for example, data on compliance and completion of agreements in Marshall, *supra* note 14 at 18; and in the context of civil mediation, see C. McEwen, and R. Mainman, 'Small Claims Mediation in Maine: An Empirical Assessment' (1984) 33 *Maine Law Review* 244.

# Part IV    Sexual Deviance

Sexual deviance usually encompasses pornography, phone sex, stripping, prostitution, incest, adultery, and sexual relations with minors. The area often also includes discussions of homosexuality and intersexuality, a term that refers to individuals with various combinations of male and female genitalia. But the articles in this section focus mainly on prostitution because it is an ongoing public issue in Canada. Over the past few years, hundreds of sex workers have gone missing or been murdered, a situation recently brought to public attention by the Pickton murder trial. While two thirds of Canadians may disapprove of prostitution because they find it immoral,[1] the public has also become uneasy over disregarding these occurrences because 'they're just sex workers'. In addition, prostitution activists have recently launched a lawsuit challenging the constitutionality of Canada's prostitution laws.

Prostitution is an example of what Hagan calls a 'conflict crime', that is, an activity involving public disagreement over its injuriousness and wrongfulness, even though it is illegal. The debate has focused on the following main options: 1) to continue to criminalize it and punish prostitutes along with their clients; 2) to legalize it and establish areas that are licensed, regulated, and managed by the government; 3) to decriminalize it and regulate it like any other business; and 4) to focus on rehabilitating or reforming prostitutes as well as their users.

Analyzing public issues sociologically involves investigating their connection to values that the publics feel are being threatened and to strains, contradictions, or transformations in the institutions and systems that structure society. Here, a significant contradiction appears in Canada's prostitution laws. Strictly speaking, the act of buying and selling sexual services has always been legal in Canada. At the same time, several sections in the *Criminal Code* criminalize activities pertaining to the selling of sexual services: 1) procuring, or getting persons to become prostitutes; 2) living on the avails of a prostitute (that is, living with a prostitute or off a prostitute's earnings); 3) being found in, or running, a common bawdy house (that is, keeping or resorting to a place for the purpose of prostitution); and 4) communication, or offering to buy or sell sexual services in public.

A second contradiction concerns the values that are being threatened. It often surfaces in debates, not only over prostitution, but over other practices regarded as sexually deviant. Acts of sexual deviance are generally subjected to a great deal of moral censure. And the societal institutions established to regulate sexual relations—marriage, family, and kinship systems—are usually backed by equally strong moral injunctions. However, these dominant moral discourses often invoke 'nature' as part of justifying why the normative institutions and practices are right and those varying from them are wrong. So, for instance, one might hear that a family ought to be comprised of a married heterosexual couple with children because it is the kind of grouping found in nature. Of course, such a position overlooks the vast variety of sexual behaviours and ways of rearing young actually found in the animal world, as well as the diverse range of practices and arrangements regarding sex, marriage, and family that are regarded as normative in societies around the human world. But it also entails a contradiction which anthropologist Claude Lévi-Strauss noted and explored.[2] If something is 'natural', or based in nature, then why does it need to be enforced so vigorously by moral command, injunction, or regulation? So what exactly is the problem posed by human sexuality for human societies such that its solution requires a great deal of moral regulation that often tries to ground itself in nature?

Investigating such contradictions is not just of academic interest. Canada's current approach to the conflicted nature of public opinion and its prostitution laws effectively leaves prostitution criminalized. But a troubling consequence of this is that it drives prostitution underground leaving prostitutes vulnerable to predators and abuse, especially street prostitutes.

An additional problem that arises in the public discussion of prostitution as well as other forms of sexual deviance in Canada is stereotyping. Much of the sociological research into sexual deviance has been to debunk stereotypes and provide a more accurate portrayal of the practice and the people involved in it, whether prostitutes, strippers, or consumers of pornography. While there is validity to some of the negative views and claims generally associated with prostitution in the case of defamilied juvenile prostitutes engaged in 'survival sex', sociological research into adult prostitution in Canada consistently finds that most prevailing conceptions are surprisingly incorrect.[3]

## Notes

1. A Leger Marketing Survey found prostitution was considered immoral by 68 per cent of adults (76 per cent women; 59 per cent men) as reported in *Metro*, June 12, 2006.
2. Claude Lévi-Strauss, 'The Family', from Harry L. Shapiro, *Man, Culture, and Society, Revised Edition*, Oxford University Press, 1969.
3. Special Committee on Pornography and Prostitution (The Fraser Commission), *Pornography and Prostitution: Report of the Special Committee on Pornography and Prostitution*, Ottawa: Department of Justice, 1985.

# 16

## Introduction

The victimization experienced by street-based sex workers has led many people to conclude that prostitution is inherently dangerous. However, street-based workers are the minority of sex workers in Canada. Can their experiences be generalized to other types of prostitution? This article is an excerpt from an exploratory study of women's experiences working in off-street prostitution venues in Vancouver, BC. O'Doherty's original study contained a victimization survey that examined various forms of victimization of off-street sex workers as well as in-depth interviews with 10 off-street sex workers that explored their working conditions, safety, stereotypes of prostitution, and law reform. This article shares the results of the in-depth interviews.

Do female off-street sex workers face the same degree of violence and other types of victimization as female street-based sex workers? What recommendations do the interviewees make regarding law reform? And what are the reasons for their recommendations? Finally, what theoretic approach would help us account for O'Doherty's findings?

The complete results and recommendations of O'Doherty's study are available on Professor John Lowman's Prostitution Research Page at http://24.85.225.7/lowman_prostitution/HTML/publications.html .

## Off-Street Commercial Sex

*Tamara O'Doherty*

Vancouver's Downtown East-Side (DTES) is notorious for drugs, prostitution, and violence. At least 69 women, most of whom were associated with the street-based sex industry, have gone missing from this area since the late 1970s.[1] Research reveals that up to 98 per cent of women who work on the streets of the DTES experience violence from clients, pimps and other sex workers (Currie, Laliberte, Bird, Rosa, Noelle and Sprung 1995; Lowman and Fraser 1996; Cler-Cunningham and Christensen 2001). The high levels of violence reported by street workers are not unique to Canada: researchers from other countries—including the United States, England, The Netherlands and Sweden—have similarly concluded that street-based sex workers are exposed to inordinately high levels of violence (Brewis and Linstead 2000; Kuo 2002; Sanders 2005; Working Group on the Legal Regulation of the Purchase of Sexual Services 2004).

While the victimization experienced by street-based sex workers around the world has led some researchers to argue that prostitution is inherently dangerous (Dworkin 1993; Farley 2004; Raphael and Shapiro 2004; Raymond 2003), others assert that prostitution is not always violent, and that criminalization produces working conditions that facilitate violence against sex workers (Betteridge 2005; Bindman and Doezema 1997; Canadian HIV/AIDS Legal

Network 2005; Kempadoo and Doezema 1998; Lewis, Maticka-Tyndale, Shaver and Gillies 2005; Lowman 2005; Network of Sex Work Projects n.d.; Pivot Legal Society 2003; Rekart 2005).

> The criminal law and its enforcement encourage violence against sex workers, contribute to the continued low income of sex workers who have few options but to work on the street because of their poverty and other issues such as addictions, and increase those sex workers' risk of being exposed to HIV. (Canadian HIV/AIDS Legal Network 2005, p. 44)

Section 213 of the *Criminal Code of Canada* prohibits public communication for the purpose of prostitution. This section has garnered much criticism since its inception in 1985. The Canadian HIV/AIDS Legal Network concluded that the communicating provision has done little to reduce street prostitution, and argued that the criminal status of prostitution, 'has contributed, both directly and indirectly, to the risk of violence and other health and safety risks faced by sex workers in Canada' (2005, p. 45).

The communication provision aspires to prevent the nuisance attributed to traffic and loitering (Lowman 1998); its purpose is to eliminate the public display of prostitution. Lowman asserts that the nuisance-eradication approach has forced women to work in isolated, poorly lit areas of Vancouver. The communication provision has had the unintended effect of reducing street-based sex workers' negotiating powers: in order to avoid potential criminal charges, street sex workers must enter vehicles quickly and accept clients without first coming to an agreement about the services to be provided and the costs of the transaction (Lewis, Maticka-Tyndale, Shaver, and Gillies 2005; Davis 1994). Lowman (2000) argues that the nuisance philosophy behind the communication provision has contributed to escalating violence rates for street-based sex workers:

It appears that the discourse on prostitution of the early 1980s, dominated by demands to 'get rid' of prostitutes, created a social milieu in which violence against prostitutes could flourish. (p.18)

Many people and organizations around the world have called for the decriminalization of the sex industry to ameliorate working conditions and improve safety for sex workers. Some of the international organizations which support decriminalization include the World Health Organization (WHO), the International Labor Organization (ILO), Amnesty International, Human Rights Watch, Anti-Slavery International and the Global Alliance Against Trafficking in Women (GAATW). Two Canadian legal organizations have recently undertaken in-depth analyses of the effects of prostitution laws on the health and safety of sex workers (Pivot Legal Society 2003; Pivot Legal Society 2006; Canadian HIV/AIDS Legal Network 2005). Both concluded that decriminalization is necessary to reduce the violence experienced by sex workers.

In opposition to this view, radical feminists argue that the act of prostitution is itself an example of violence against women, and should be abolished. To this end they seek to criminalize the sale of sex on the grounds that 'prostituted women' are victims, and they support criminally prohibiting both procuring and sex purchasing (Dworkin 1993; Farley 2004;

Raphael and Shapiro 2004; Raymond 2003). The claim that prostitution is violence against women is partly political—radical feminists deny that women ever 'consent' to prostitute— and partly empirical: they assert that all prostitutes are victims of violence. It is this latter claim that my thesis sets out to investigate.

Given that researchers consistently report high violence rates in street-based prostitution, the act of selling sex via the street is clearly dangerous. But are rates of violence in other parts of the industry the same?

> In order to assess the validity of the feminist argument that prostitution is dangerous, we must establish the extent to which these hazards exist and the extent to which they are linked to the commoditization of sex. Only then can we assess whether or not they can be used to justify the position that prostitution should be eliminated and prostitutes rehabilitated for their own good. (Shaver 1988, p. 84)

Approximately 80 per cent of the sex industry in BC occurs *off-street* (Benoit and Millar 2001; Lowman 2005; Pivot Legal Society 2006). Weitzer (2000) cautions that, 'when it comes to prostitution, the most serious blunder is that of equating all prostitution with street prostitution, ignoring entirely the indoor side of the market' (p. 4). Data from research conducted with street-based sex workers may not be generalizable across the industry. At present, we do not have a comprehensive understanding of the experience of sex workers in different parts of the off-street commercial sex industry. Do women providing in-call and out-call services experience the same degree of victimization as street-based workers? Do in-call and out-call workers experience the same degree of risk of victimization? Is the experience of prostitution always an experience of violence? Can women sell sex without experiencing violence?

To begin exploring women's experiences of violence in off-street prostitution, my thesis focuses on women working in massage parlours, escort agencies, or independently out of their own homes in Vancouver, BC. There were two components to this research: a) a victimization survey examining interpersonal violence and other harmful activities, such as theft and client refusals to wear condoms; and b) in-depth interviews with 10 off-street sex workers exploring themes such as working conditions, safety, stereotypes of prostitution, and law reform.

The project was concerned with the exchange of sexual services for remuneration by *consenting adults*. Because the term 'sex work' could include erotic massage, exotic dancing, telephone sex operations, escorting, domination services, and pornography as well as prostitution, I used the term 'prostitution' to refer to direct-contact sexual services performed for remuneration. I used the term 'sex worker' to refer to the people who sell these sexual services.[2]

## Working in the Off-Street Sex Industry

This section focuses on the results of 10 interviews I conducted as part of my overall study. It examines working conditions in the off-street sex industry, and describes participants' recommendations for law and social policy reforms.

All of the interview participants reported that their main reason for participating in this project was to explain what working in their segment of the sex industry was really like; they wanted to combat stereotypes about women who sell sex. These women stressed their desire for the general public and the government to understand that the experience of sex work is not homogenous: individuals engage in sex work for many different reasons and in many different circumstances. For most of my participants, the decision was primarily financial: sex work can offer a very high wage without the need for specific training or education.

Some women reported working in the industry because they enjoy their work, and they enjoy providing a positive sexual experience for men.

> And then there are the lonely postmen who are shy, don't know how to seduce women or aren't very good in the dating department. And when I see him, I make him feel good himself because he's actually quite sexy. And he's quite skilled and I am able to find what is sexy about every one of my clients.
>
> *Interview 9*

> And what about the guy who's got the coke-bottle bottom glasses, he's the guy who nobody will have sex with . . . what would you do if you couldn't even pay for sex? . . . I've seen guys dumpster diving and then standing at my door with the money in their hands. Their once a year treat—once a year shower for that matter—come in and they are so freaked out it almost makes me scared . . . I've been in bed with men who are blind or quadriplegic. Climbed right into the extended care bed . . . It's totally wonderful to do those kinds of things.
>
> *Interview 2*

> I mean these guys don't want to be seeing me—they want to be home with you—if only . . . like this one old guy with Parkinson's—he just wished his wife would touch him. And I'm like . . . Oh my god. It's so sad on such a deep level . . . So, I love most of my clients. I can honestly say, for the most part, I connect really well with my clients and they are really sweet. Especially with the type of sex I offer—they really do come to me for tenderness. And I like to do that healing, have good intentions.
>
> *Interview 4*

The ability to choose to work in the sex industry featured prominently in the discussion regarding entrance. All of the participants were adamant that their decision to work in the industry was consciously made, and all of them were indignant that people should question their choice.

> I just wish people would stop judging what I do as breaking something they think should be sacred and feeling sorry for girls like me. Why? Respect me. Help those that are really being exploited. I'll let you know if I am, but how can I be if I'm the boss of my business and not at the mercy of the streets and a rough agency? In a perfect world we'd all wish

*for the perfect job and a great income and to not have to do anything hard for it. But whether I'm an escort or not, everyone deals with this dilemma of doing jobs that pay great but aren't perfectly enjoyable. In most cases, as in mine, you have your ups and downs, likes and dislikes about it. There is no perfection. They didn't outlaw the most dangerous job in the world, crabbing in Alaska, just because the chances of being killed were higher than what I do . . . the men make huge money and THEY choose to take that risk based upon informed knowledge and it's legal! Same with ocean welding or mining! Why is what I do any worse when at my elite level there is next to no cases of death or violence caused by occupation!*

*Interview 6*

The interview participants were asked to identify the 'best' parts of the job. The wages were certainly one of the best parts. One woman responded that the friendships she had built with other women in the industry were the best part of her work. The other two most common answers were: a) the freedom of operating as an independent; and b) the confidence or self-esteem that can be gained through sex work.

*The best part is the freedom I have. I work whenever I want, I can charge whatever I'm comfortable with, and I have no boss to exploit me or otherwise make life difficult (which is what I experienced in every other job I've ever had).*

*Interview 10*

Interview participants explained that the negative impact sex work can have on personal relationships was the biggest cost of their work. Some of the women felt isolated because they could not discuss their work with family and friends unless they were willing to be truthful about their occupation. One of the women said that she felt she could not have a family while she worked in the sex industry. Another doubted that she would be able to find a partner who would accept her work. Two of the women had serious concerns about negative long-term effects the work could have on women, and the social stigma attached to being a sex worker. One woman said that she did not see any negatives associated with her work.

There was a great deal of variety in styles of sex work. One woman worked independently as a masseuse who did not offer 'full service' to her clients (no sexual intercourse). Two women worked independently on part-time schedules because they had other occupations. Some of the women worked solely on an out-call basis, while others preferred to work out of their residences. Three of the women explained that their dates were typically full-evening affairs or weekend trips.

Some of the women want everything about the transaction to be open and directly stated. Others prefer not to discuss details and just let the date unfold. These latter women were more likely to describe their work as 'companionship': they were being paid for their time, not for specific services. Almost all of the women said that the flexibility and the ability to structure the work the way they wanted was one of the best parts of independent sex work.

When it comes to their future expectations, one of the interview participants was looking to end her career in the sex industry. Another woman was looking to end 'in the near future': she explained that the double life she was required to live was beginning to wear on her. The other eight women had no plans for leaving the sex industry at the time of the interview.

The women explained that one of the more difficult aspects of sex work relates to leaving the industry. Two participants suggested that transitioning out to more legitimate work would be very difficult because they were unsure what kind of work they could do that would match their current income. One woman who had exited a couple of times explained that she had done so only to satisfy a partner: she always returned to sex work because she preferred it to other work. Experiences of violence prompted one of the women to leave the industry on at least one occasion.

## Combating Stereotypes

One of the main reasons that the interview participants gave for sharing their stories was to try to help the general public and the academic community see what their work is really like. They all felt that there are too many misconceptions and hurtful stereotypes about women who engage in sex work. These stereotypes include the assumed homogeneity of the work, victimization, exploitation, and the lack of choice women are presumed to have. This section examines these women's experience of stereotypes and the stigmatizing of sex workers.

### Homogeneity of Sex Work

> Like everything else in the world, we are all different girls, we all have different circum-
> stances—it is very hard to blanket everybody. You just can't generalize. Everyone's got-
> ten into it for different reasons, even in the high end. I mean we don't even consider each
> other competition, because we all have our own way of doing things and likewise we all
> have our reasons for being here.
>
> Interview 8

Some of the most important lessons to take from this research are that women engage in off-street sex work for many different reasons, they work in many different ways, and they come from many different backgrounds. Two of the women began working in the sex industry at around 30 years of age. One woman came from a 'very wealthy background', four others said they had very 'normal' backgrounds. Two women started sex work when they were teenagers living on the street. One woman had never worked in a 'straight job'—her experience was completely limited to the sex industry. Nine had held other types of jobs, four of whom were working in a 'straight job' at the time of the interview in addition to their sex work.

### Victimization

The interview participants expressed their frustration with the assumption that they had experienced childhood sexual abuse, emotional trauma, or that there was simply something 'wrong with them'. This stereotyping seems to be the only way people who are not involved in the sex industry can make sense of women who choose to prostitute. One interview participant said that she was labelled 'mentally ill' by her mother: this was the only way the mother could understand her daughter's involvement in the sex industry. Another woman expressed her frustration with common assumptions by asking, 'Am I unicorn? Do I not exist?' The interview participants were especially critical of 'feminists'.

> *It's so amazing that there are people who are like, 'I am woman, hear me roar', who come to a complete stop on this.*
>
> Interview 6

> *I think it is really sad when crazy right wing feminists – I mean if you're calling yourself an educated woman, someone who is free-thinking and a feminist who breaks through moulds - then don't shut yourself off to other opinions, because they are just as valid.*
>
> Interview 4

## Exploitation

The participants were asked how they responded to the allegation that the sex industry exploits and harms all women. Their responses ranged from anger at the 'ignorance' underlying the allegation, to deciding to share their experiences in order to disprove the allegation, to questioning its accuracy.

> *Those allegations make me angry. I think it's incredibly arrogant for someone to say that they know the nature of the work of ALL women in this industry. It's a very ignorant and offensive thing to say. When people say things like that, I feel like I'm being treated like a young child who can't make her own decisions about what to do. I think these allegations come from people who refuse to believe that there can be positive things about the sex trade, and don't bother considering all the information that is available.*
>
> Interview 10

One of the women argued that, to address the question about exploitation, we need to take the socio-economic position of women into consideration:

> *I believe that in a world with such significant socio-economic imbalances, it is often financial disparity or other vulnerabilities that lead women into this business. If you took those factors away, if we had a just world and prostitution still existed, I would accept prostitution as being non-exploitative and I don't think I'm going to see that in my day. Furthermore, unlike other service industries, the commoditization or value is mostly based on objectification rather than the quality of the service. Now in regards to whether or not the sex trade harms women outside the trade, I would have to agree with this statement to the extent that, say, the modeling industry (for example) portrays unrealistic expectations of what women should look like, or porn represents an unrealistic*

*perception of female sexuality . . . And even though I do struggle with the contradictions, saying that it is exploitative is a generalization and that means I am forcing my position on to the other women around me.*

*Interview 7*

Six women identified working conditions as being the primary source of exploitation in the sex industry. They described how the need to advertise their services results in sex workers having to pay exorbitant rates simply because of the nature of the work. Further, they suggested that the amount of money some agencies make from sex workers, the systems of fines that are often imposed, and requirements by some agencies that staff offer unsafe sexual services were all forms of exploitation.

## Agency: The State of Exerting Power[3]

All of the women who participated in the interviews insisted that they made conscious choices to work in the sex industry. Two women stated that were it not for their financial need, they would not choose sex work. However, six women commented that they work because they want to: they did have other sources of income and still chose to continue working as sex workers.

*I have options. That's all I can say. I have a degree, I have a job, and it's good extra cash. I meet interesting people and I feel good about myself.*

*Interview 8*

Another common misconception is that sex workers drug themselves in order to cope with the work. Nine of the women interviewed explicitly stated that they make a point of never doing any kind of drug while working. Four women said that they limited their alcohol consumption to one or two glasses of wine during the course of a date. These self-imposed restrictions arise from the woman's desire to remain in control throughout the date.

Questions relating to how much agency these women exercise extend beyond their initial decision to work in the sex industry; they concern sex workers' power to control sex transactions. Women were asked how they felt about the assertion that men buy sex from women because they want to be able to exert power over women. All the respondents were adamant that this was not the case in their experience—if anything, the reverse is true: these women consider sex work to empower them.

*It's a very empowering thing. I don't really know how to describe it. Only someone who's actually done it would understand. Anyone who thinks the man is in power in these transactions has never worked—the women are controlling these transactions.*

*Interview 1*

Many participants described their work as meeting the aspirations of many feminists: they do what they want with their bodies, with partners they choose, and in conditions they choose. Some of the women described themselves as the ultimate feminists.

The participants' sense of power was greatest when they felt they were in control of the circumstances of their work. The women I interviewed all operated independently. They were in a position to structure their work in a way that felt comfortable. The women defined their own boundaries of comfort for physical acts. For them, sex work was not about selling unrestricted sexual access to their bodies. Women often commented that 'it's not all about sex' or 'the work is so much more than sex'. Five of the women provided examples of dates where no sex actually occurred: they were being paid for their companionship.

## Stigmatization

Synonyms for the word 'stigma' include shame, dishonour, and disgrace. Prostitution is often viewed as disgraceful, shameful, and dishonorable. Five women discussed issues relating to the sense of shame attached to their work. It appears that one of the primary effects of this stigma is to prevent women from 'coming out' about their work. They did not want certain people to know about their occupation because of the reaction it would occasion. While sex workers may feel completely comfortable about their work, they may choose to keep it hidden in order to avoid judgment. One woman explained that while all of her friends and family knew about her work, she chooses not to identify herself as a sex worker ' . . . in the company of people who may have the power to make my life difficult' (Interview 7).

Women suggested that there is a more negative stigma towards women who actively seek work in the industry. When prostitution can be explained away as the result of drug addictions, abuse, or coercion, people seem to be much more accepting of the prostitute, whom they can see as a victim. Women who stand firmly behind their decisions to sell sex are treated as anomalies and dismissed. As one participant explained:

> From what I have found, a lot of people are comfortable accepting you if you were a hooker but you left it in your past. Not many people are comfortable if you are a hooker'.
>
> *Interview 7*

# Participants' Recommendations about Law Reform

One of the main goals of this project was to provide a means by which women could voice their recommendations for law reform to the academic and legal communities. Respondents were asked how to make the work 'safer'. The questionnaire concluded with an open-ended question asking for additional comments, thereby giving respondents an opportunity to make whatever recommendations they liked. Twenty-one of the respondents wrote additional comments, the majority of which expressed the need for law reform and increased education about the nature of off-street sex work. In the following section, I outline the main recommendations that emerged over the course of the interviews and in the survey responses.

## Decriminalization

*This job is as legitimate as any other and should be completely legal. What people choose to do with their own time and bodies is nobody's business unless somebody is being harmed.*

*Interview 10*

All of the individuals who participated in this project firmly opposed the criminalization of sex work. The following comments suggest that a double standard underlies the criminalization of prostitution:

*At its most fundamental form, whenever someone doesn't understand—especially people not in this industry—my favourite line is to say, Let's back up a bit. Do you think there should be a law against a woman being a slut? Really—is a woman free to do whatever she wants with her own body? Forget about the money for a second. Can I go out and fuck a different guy every day or should there be a law against that? It may not sit well with you, you may have no respect for a 'loose' woman, but really, if I want to go out, chase different guys, fuck different men, fuck three guys in one night and then go back to the bar for more, should there be a law against that? You'd be hard pressed to find someone to say yes. Then what changes when I decide that I want to ask for money? Are you trying to say that women should be available for free? Is that really what you're trying to say? A woman is free to be a slut, as long as she doesn't want to ask for money. . . . It's really hard to justify criminalization of prostitution when you start from that premise . . . As soon as the compensation enters the equation it turns scary.*

*Interview 1*

Generally, the respondents were not afraid of being charged with a criminal prostitution offence: they reported that the likelihood of police intervention in their work is extremely low or non-existent. For them, the biggest risk of working in the industry is being identified as a sex worker and facing social consequences. However, as argued below, the quasi-legal status of sex work in Canada does affect off-street sex workers in the following ways: it has an important impact on the way agencies are structured; it affects how well informed individuals are upon entering the industry; it limits sex workers' abilities to openly negotiate the terms of transactions; and the legal status can deter individuals from turning to the police when they are criminally victimized.

Escort agencies were identified as a potential source of exploitation. The interview participants asserted that, while escort agencies and massage parlours are necessary for many individuals who are either not able to or are unwilling to run their own business, they should be subject to employment standards and they should be structured as non-exploitatively as possible. However, because of the current legal regime, agencies are able to operate in ways that are not in the best interests of workers. Respondents reported a system of fines for being late or for calling in sick. Some agencies charge workers a 'book on' fee whereby the worker pays the agency for the privilege of getting dates. In some organizations workers are required to pay between 40 per cent and 60 per cent of the hourly rate to the agency as the agency cut. In addition, workers are expected to 'tip' the phone girls, the drivers (if one is provided, otherwise they have to drive themselves or pay for their own transportation), and the management (if applicable). If the workers do not tip the phone girls, they will not get clients referred to them.

Many of the participants understood that one of the reasons agencies require such high rates from their workers is the high cost of operating an 'adult entertainment' establishment. The advertising fees such establishments are charged in comparison to other licence fees are exorbitant. One woman explained that fees upwards of $30,000 annually are charged for an advertisement in the local telephone directory. Licensing fees can be extremely high, and many establishments are charged higher than average rental fees, in part due to their questionable legal status. Agency operators, municipal governments, advertisers, and landlords all reap additional profit out of the sex business because of its marginal legal status; ironically, in the process they all appear to live partly on the avails of prostitution, a criminal offence.[4]

Sex work is an underground occupation. This is largely due to the social stigma attached to the work, and the criminal and municipal prohibitions against it. The law silences sex workers thereby reducing the amount of information available to individuals who are considering entering the industry. One of the most common recommendations is to provide access to information about how to work safely and provide training for women getting into the business. Participants recommended that there be training to provide women with necessary customer service and other skills unique to escort work. However, training cannot legally occur in Canada as it may be considered procuring (s. 212), communication for the purposes of prostitution (s. 213), or aiding or abetting someone to become a prostitute (s. 212(1)(d)). Training is important to the protection of the health and safety of escort agency and massage parlour workers:

*Well, if you're going to run a place where you don't expect someone to risk their health, give them the tools to show someone a good time for an hour. If you're going to charge someone $300, and they go to do the things they want to do— 'Oh no, you can't kiss me, you can't touch me down there, no you can't perform oral sex on me, no, I'm not touching your dick without a condom on it'—the guy's going to be pissed off. You can't justifiably run an establishment where you let girls charge $300 for sex and don't give them some sort of knowledge of how to entertain someone. So, it eclipses mere occupational health and safety, you can't just tell someone, don't do this and don't do this and don't do this because those will all risk your health—what are you going to tell them to do—just lay there? If you're going to charge top dollar, then give someone the tools and the knowledge they need to entertain someone for an hour. Further, this training should be provided by a certified public health nurse but it's impossible to organize that when the service (sex work) is illegal.*

*Interview 1*

The criminal laws have a much more significant impact on the lives of street-based sex workers. All of the women interviewed expressed concern about the safety of women who work the street. They discussed how wrong it felt to know that while they were able to work free from violence, other women who are doing essentially the same work are risking their lives.

> *A lot of us see it as really nasty that we can do what we do, and I haven't heard about any violence . . . we could ask a cop if we get lost where the Four Seasons is, and that's fine. But these girls on the DTES are just getting slaughtered. I mean, how can that be happening? What is going on? It's just disgraceful. A lot of us actually feel guilty about that because we're going to these nice hotels, being taken for dinner, I mean it's something that is essentially the same thing and these girls are being killed, or beat up or raped and maimed.*
>
> *Interview 5*

However, while off-street workers are not subject to enforcement of the criminal laws like street workers, women who work indoors are often misinformed, unaware or confused about the legalities of their work. This confusion can result in sex workers' safety being compromised. While s. 213 of the *Criminal Code* is directed towards street-based sex work, many off-street workers believe that they are not allowed to openly discuss the terms of the exchange either by phone or by email. This does not deter people from engaging in acts of prostitution (which is technically *not* a criminal offence), it only serves to prevent people from discussing their boundaries and services offered prior to the meeting. Similarly, some women reported a reluctance to report incidents to police officers for fear of legal or social repercussions.

One woman revealed how her recent report of being harassed was turned against her when the police became involved.

> *I have reported experiences of harassment, when harassment escalated to my neighbours receiving flyers (mock advertisements). This encounter involved the RCMP's vice unit coming and having a discussion over coffee. Our discussion involved vice officers telling me my work was illegal and my responding by quoting sec. 210 of the* Criminal Code. *The officers instructed me to make efforts to exit the trade within the next three months. I made them aware that I would leave 'when I am good and ready to'. The officers then made threats about arrest and ministry involvement. I told them they could do whatever they felt they needed to and escorted them to the door. I proceeded to get a lawyer the next day in case they followed through on their threats. The officers did not come back as they said they would in three months, nor was I arrested, nor was there any involvement from the Ministry of Children and Families.*
>
> *Interview 7*

## Legalization, Licensing, and Taxes

The majority of the women interviewed balked at the idea of legalizing and licensing the industry. Their main fear was that licensing would result in their losing their independence, and force them into a situation where they would be pimped by the government.

*But that would be something that could harm my business with legalization. Anything coming in would have some restrictions and right now there are none. I mean there are some things I could see would be reasonable, like having a medical test every couple of months, but if they made you join a union, I wouldn't be into that. My business is my business. And there are discretion issues, too. If everyone knew you were an escort, and they see you with a guy, they'll assume he's a client. I think that's problematic. If it is regulation and my real name is going to be somewhere, I don't want to give out my real name for safety.*

*Interview 5*

One of the women was in the process of applying for her escort licence at the time of the interview. None of the other eight independent women had licences—either because they knew that they did not need to have a licence to work independently, or because they did not want to formally associate themselves with the adult entertainment industry for fear that it would lead to some kind of repercussion.

*I wonder if it could not involve licensing. Like just create a safe zone where women could work and it's not heavily regulated. Because I don't see a lot of women who work the street being willing to walk in get a licence and give out their real names. Then you are suddenly in the radar. Like, right now, as far as I'm concerned nobody knows my real name. As far as I know. So, no I wouldn't want to register.*

*Interview 8*

When it came to taxation, four women said that sex workers are often unaware of the tax implications of their work. Some sex workers are reluctant to claim income associated with escorting or massaging for fear that identifying their occupation to the federal government would eventually harm them financially, legally, or in some occupationally-related way. However, failure to declare income may negatively affect a person's ability to purchase real estate or get a credit card. One of the women described the problem this way:

*I realized that for a lot of women in this business, the fact of being (or feeling) unable to declare income is a seriously limiting factor in life. How does one get credit or a mortgage without having proof of income? I guess I've taken those things for granted because I've always had a regular job with a decent income, but it seems that relatively few women in this business are able to lead 'normal' financial lives. I've also noticed that despite the relatively good incomes this business brings, a lot of women are scrambling for rent money at month's end. Why is this? Perhaps the very fact that they cannot put their income down on paper and that everything is cash based prevents women from ever really analyzing their finances (budgeting, etc.).*

*Interview 8*

Another woman explained how it is difficult to deal with Revenue Canada because sex workers cannot get accurate information about how to declare their income because they cannot find out what expenses can legitimately be deducted.

## Employment Standards and Occupational Health and Safety

One common suggestion was that employment standards should apply to adult entertainment establishments. One woman suggested that the agencies should have a set of guidelines imposed, but that these guidelines should be developed by experiential individuals. They should include rules eliminating the system of fines and 'book on' fees, ensuring clean and safe working conditions, and creating specific health and safety guidelines to protect sex workers. The system should include resources for sex workers, such as financial advice, personal and career counselling, training or education opportunities, and access to medical services. Participants suggested that advertisers should apply the same rates to all businesses and stop imposing exorbitant rates on adult entertainment services. This would assist in bringing operating costs down, and reduce the percentage that agencies take from the hourly rate.[5]

> It makes me angry the way that the agencies take so much money. It's a common complaint. And I think that sometimes girls will flip from agency to agency looking for a better deal, but I mean these people are making tons of dough. And who's the person that's giving their body? It's wrong . . . 10 per cent—that's reasonable! That's like what an agent for an athlete would charge. After all, it's a promotional agency. Yeah, there's some booking and whatever, but take a booking fee and then charge a percentage—that's fair.
>
> *Interview 9*

Occupational health and safety was a concern for several women in both the survey and the interview samples. Condom use during intercourse appears to be a non-negotiable part of sex work in this particular segment of the industry. However, this does not extend to condom use during other risky sexual activities like oral sex. Many women reported being asked by a prospective client to have sex without a condom, and reported that some agencies pressure escorts to provide certain sexual services, such as oral sex, without a condom.

> One of the biggest concerns for women who work in the sex industry is GFE (Girl Friend Experience) sessions. There are people who know it's a health risk but it's just like people who smoke. You don't light up a cigarette and think it's healthy for you, just like you don't provide a bareback blowjob and think that it's healthy for you. But given what you're being compensated for, you decide well, the risk is going to be this percentage; well . . . maybe you'll go with that.
>
> *Interview 1*

The practices in GFE sessions vary depending on the worker.[6] Some women offer unprotected oral sex as a part of the experience. Others simply offer a higher level of intimacy and activities such as cuddling and kissing.

*Every woman has to make her own decision about what she is willing to do and take a calculated risk. Ideally, we would all take our health seriously . . . Really, unless you abstain from sexual activities, there is some risk involved. I do take some risk, but much less than some others. E.g. I perform oral sex unprotected in some situations. It is a part of the GFE I offer and expected as a part of GFE in a lot of places. . . . If it wasn't expected by most, I wouldn't offer it, especially since it actually impedes my skills.*

*Interview 7*

While there is a stereotype that clients would all prefer to have unprotected sex, one interview participant mentioned that she had been turned down by a prospective client because she offered unprotected oral sex. She explained that it is important to be open and honest about the type of activities that you are willing to do so that clients can make their own decisions. Five of the interview participants stressed their opinions that 'civilian' women were far more likely to engage in risky sexual behaviour than they were.

*You are probably at a greater risk to get an STD from a civilian pickup at a bar because for us, if we get an STD, we're out of business. We're done. We've got to go back to work wherever, at a shoe store, and we don't want to do that, we're having fun. But if it's a pickup, and you're drunk and she's never going to see you again, why would she tell you? And then, you're going to come to us and give it us and then we're going to give it to other clients? That's not happening. They assume that since you're in the profession, you might be willing to take the risk. They don't think about it from a business sense.*

*Interview 5*

Sex workers report being instructed by managers in agencies to do visual and manual checks to ensure that clients are not infected with STDs prior to engaging in activities. As five interviewees explained, they would refuse to have sex with anyone who exhibited any symptoms of an STD. The women interviewed took their health very seriously and insisted on regular medical testing. Some of the women expressed their frustration at the fact that some clients continue to request unsafe practices:

*It's not the women that have to change their opinion because many of them—again, there are some that just don't know any better—but that's not the majority of it. So, it's not the ignorance—it's the demand side of it. It infuriates me because there's less risk to them. It's not that they're ignorant, it's that they are not fluid receptive. So, there's very little risk to them and all the risk is borne by the provider. So, yes it's the demand side that has the money and that will dictate the services and the prices. . . . Public information campaigns would be great because it's ultimately the demand side of the equation that has to change their opinion.*

*Interview 1*

## Access to Information about the Sex Industry

*I feel there is a lot of misunderstanding and misconception about this industry—an industry that is so broad, a spectrum that is so immensely wide—and people's opinions are largely jaded by centuries of religious confines . . . Of course there are women who are coerced into this industry and not treated well. But the more exposure that is brought to the real underlying situation in the industry, the real circumstances we work in, the reality of the clients we see, the more possibility for enlightenment. The thing is they don't know it could be better—that's the problem. And the public makes you feel that you have to hide and that you are an outcast.*

*Interview 9*

Most of the women who participated in this project recommended that there be greater access to information about the sex industry, about the different types of sex work, and the options available to people who are considering sex work.

*Make it a more open working environment so that there are choices as opposed to it's either A or B, there's nothing in the middle. And we should be encouraging people, educating people on how to enter the industry rather than this whole 'sink or swim' . . . You can imagine all sorts of circumstances that aren't like the choice I made (just because), I want them to know what they're deciding and what the options are . . . if they knew they could run a little ad and work for themselves, or if they knew that there were body rub places . . . I think it's like a pre-emptive strike: if you have the tools to make the decision then you'll make a better decision.*

*Interview 2*

*I had a colleague contact me and we had this wonderful talk and she was like, 'wow—if I had known these things when I first started out, I definitely would have done things differently. But nobody knows; you either figure it out or you get lost. Women get lost because there's no education. That's not fair—because the public doesn't want to know about it? That's just not fair.*

*Interview 9*

Sex workers need access to information about the law, financial advice, tax implications, and increased access to medical information. They strongly recommend that clients be given more information about STDs and sex in general. The interview participants assigned the responsibility for stigmatization of sex workers to society in general. The harmful stereotypes and condemnatory attitudes contribute more to stigma than the act of selling sex.

*I would like to be able to say, 'I'm a professional elite independent escort' and not feel afraid I'm going to be arrested, ridiculed or judged wrongly as 'loose', 'slutty' or 'pathetic'. I feel proud of myself what I've achieved and angry that I have to keep it a secret and feel the shame of others. I'm not ashamed—it's other people's issues because of ignorance.*

*Interview 6*

*I don't think it has much to do with the profession. I think the profession catches the end result of problems that are already there in society and it's a further expression of insecurity.*

*Interview 5*

The legal and academic communities need more information about the heterogeneity of sex work, and they need to base their laws and theories on more inclusive research.

*I agreed to participate in the research as I believe it is important to shed light about the reality of the sex trade, at least from my experience. This is useful and any person who's studying it academically can't get a genuine perception of the business without people who have been genuinely in it.*

*Interview 7*

## Socio-Economic Factors

*I think the biggest problem is that girls get into this out of desperate circumstances. Whether it's because of an addiction or just poor financial management, it's a worry when someone becomes dependent on this.*

*Interview 8*

Most of the women interviewed (8 out of 10) felt quite strongly that one of the key reasons they have positive experiences working in the sex industry is because they are not completely dependent on the income generated. Five of the women said that it is when women are in difficult financial positions that they accept more risky behaviour, and it is in these circumstances that women take chances they otherwise would not take. Two women suggested that the sex industry is ideal for circumstances when women find themselves suddenly in extreme financial need (widows, women who are leaving abusive husbands etc.).

*I would like to say no [I wouldn't encourage women to enter this industry], but I have known women in desperate situations. My best friend had an abusive partner and felt she couldn't leave. I did encourage her because it is a fast source of income.*

*Interview 7*

Another woman suggested that the current stigmatization of prostitution makes work in the sex industry undesirable.

*The hard part about that question is if the environment still exists the way it is, then I don't really think it's a good idea. Look at the ways in the past, the times where courtesans were running the country. In those times, ladies of the palace would ask for their daughters to be taken into servitude because of the wonderful life that was given to the courtesans, their education, the only women allowed in the library . . . Yeah, so it depends on the political environment. I think that things are changing, I like to think that things are changing. I can see a movement towards acceptance on a broader scale of the industry itself.*

*Interview 2*

Four women perceived the political climate surrounding sex work to be changing. They hope that people are gaining more tolerance of different forms of female sexuality and that attitudes toward sex workers are changing.

*Societies where they are more accepting of it, like Europe, the level of safety is different. It's almost as though society creates the risk because of the stigma that's attached. Now that being said, I feel that we are at a point right now, in the development where things are starting to change—both in terms of clients' willingness and acceptance of certain things.*

*Interview 9*

## Conclusions

In this research I sought to find out how much violence and other kinds of victimization occur in various kinds of off-street sex work. The findings indicate that it is possible for women to work safely in the sex industry and that, contrary to radical-feminist assertions, violence is *not* inherent to prostitution. If women are able to sell sex off-street without experiencing violence, then we must look to conditions unique to the street to determine why street-based sex workers face such high levels of violence. Perhaps, as Lowman (2000) suggests in his discussion of the 'discourse of disposal', society's treatment of street level sex workers as disposable nuisances has contributed to the high rates of violence.

The act of selling sex does not necessarily cause sex workers to experience violence, and we need to stop basing policy on the idea that a causal link has been established. It is exploitative working structures and the quasi-legal status of prostitution that severely compromise sex workers' safety. Therefore, much of the responsibility for the current levels of violence and harm experienced by sex workers in Canada must be attributed to Canada's prostitution laws.

## Notes

1. The latest Missing Women Poster maintained by the RCMP Joint task force for Missing Women has 69 names and pictures.
2. See Bindman & Doezema (1997) for a discussion regarding terminology.
3. Source: www.wordreference.com
4. See Pivot (2006) for more information on the various structures of agencies.
5. See Pivot (2006) for more recommendations related to occupation health and safety.
6. See also Pivot (2006): pp.27-28.

# References

Benoit, C. and Millar, A. 2001. *Dispelling Myths and Understanding Realities: Working Conditions, Health Status and Exiting experiences of Sex Workers*. Retrieved June 15, 2004 from web.uvic.ca/~cbenoit/papers/DispMyths.pdf

Betteridge, G. 2005. *Sex, Work, Rights: Reforming Canadian Criminal Laws on Prostitution*. Canadian HIV/AIDS Legal Network. Retrieved August 1, 2006 from www.nswp.org/pdf/AIDSLAW-SWREFORM-2005. PDF

Bindman, J and Doezema, J. 1997. *Redefining Prostitution as Sex Work on the International Agenda*. Network of Sex Work Projects. Retrieved January 20, 2003 from www.walnet.org/csis/papers/redefining. html

Brewis, J. and Linstead, S. 2000. *Sex, Work and Sex Work: Eroticizing Organization*. London: Routledge.

Canadian HIV/AIDS Legal Network. (2005) *Sex, Work, Rights: reforming Canadian criminal laws on prostitution*. Retrieved June 15, 2006 from www.aidslaw.ca

Canadian HIV/AIDS Legal Network. (2007) *Not up to the Challenge of Change: An analysis of the report of the Subcommittee on Solicitation Laws*. Retrieved February 10, 2007 from www.aidslaw.ca

Cler-Cunningham, L. and Christensen, C. 2001. *Violence Against Women in Vancouver's Street level Sex Trade and the Police Response*. Written for PACE Society. Retrieved January 29, 2007 from www.pace-society.ca

Currie, S., Laliberte, N., Bird, S., Rosa, N., and Sprung, S. 1995. *Assessing the Violence Against Street-Involved Women in the Downtown Eastside/Strathcona Community*. Dowtown Eastside Youth Activities Society and Watari Research Society, Ministry of Women's Equality, Vancouver, BC.

Davis, S. 1994. *Prostitution in Canada: Invisible Menace or Menace of Invisibility?* Commercial Sex Information Service. Retrieved January 22, 2003 from www.walnet.org/ csis/papers/index.html

Dworkin, A. 1993. *Prostitution and Male Supremacy*. Speech delivered at, 'Prostitution: From Academia to Activism', sponsored by the Michigan Journal of Gender and Law at the University of Michigan Law School, October 31, 1992. Retrieved September 29, 2006 from www.nostatusquo.com/ACLU/dworkin/MichLawJourI.html.

Farley, M. 2004. 'Bad for the body, bad for the heart: prostitution harms women even if legalized or decriminalized'. *Violence Against Women*, *10* (10), 1087–1125.

Kempadoo, K and Doezeman, J, (eds.). 1998. *Global Sex Workers: Rights, resistance and redefinitions*. (pp.1–28) New York: Routledge.

Kuo, L. 2002. *Prostitution Policy: Revolutionized Practice through a Gendered Perspective*. New York, New York University Press.

Lewis, J., Maticka-Tyndale, E., Shaver, F. and Gillies, K. 2005. *Health, security and sex work policy*. Presentation to the House of Commons Subcommittee on Solicitation Laws (SSLR), Ottawa. Retrieved September 29 from web2.uwindsor.ca/courses/sociology/maticka/star/presentation_list.html

Lowman, J. 1998. 'Prostitution Law Reform in Canada'. *Toward Comparative Law in the 21st Century*. Institute of Comparative Law in Japan (eds.), Tokyo: Chuo University Press, 919–946.

Lowman, J. 2000. 'Violence and the Outlaw Status of (Street) Prostitution'. *Violence Against Women*, 6 (9), 987–1011. Retrieved January 19, 2004 from mypage.uniserve.ca/~lowman/violence2/MurdPro.pdf

Lowman, J. 2005. Submission to the Subcommittee on Solicitation Laws of the Standing Committee on Justice, Human Rights, Public Safety and Emergency Preparedness. Retrieved September 29, 2006 from mypage.uniserve.ca/~lowman/

Lowman, J and Fraser, L. 1996. *Violence Against Persons who Prostitute: The British Columbia Experience*. Technical Report No. TR1996-14e. Ottawa: Department of Justice Canada. Retrieved May 15, 2004 from mypage.uniserve.ca/~lowman/

Network of Sex Work Projects. (n.d.) *Introduction to the issues regarding sex work*. Retrieved January 28, 2003 from www.nswp.org.

Pivot Legal Society. 2003. *Voices for Dignity: A call to end the harms caused by Canada's Sex Trade Laws*. Retrieved May 20, 2004 from www.pivotlegal.org/sextradereport/1long.html

Pivot Legal Society. 2006. *Beyond Decriminalization: Sex Work, Human Rights and a New Framework for Law Reform*. Retrieved September 30, 2006 from www.pivotlegal.org/pdfs/BeyondDecrimLong Report.pdf

Raphael, J and Shapiro, D. 2004. 'Violence in Indoor and Outdoor Prostitution Venues'. *Violence against Women*. 10(2), 126–139.

Raymond, J. 2003. *10 Reasons for Not Legalizing Prostitution*. Coalition Against Trafficking in Women International (CATW). Retrieved June 20, 2006 from www.rapereliefshelter.bc.ca/issues/prostitution_legalizing.html

Rekart, Michael. 2005. *Sex Work Harm Reduction*. Lancet, 366 (9503), 2123-2134.

Sanders, T. 2005. *Sex Work: A Risky Business*. England, Willan Publishing.

Shaver, F. 1988. 'A critique of the feminist charges against prostitution'. *Atlantis*, 4(1), 82–89.

Weitzer, R. 2000. *Sex for Sale: Prostitution, Pornography and the Sex Industry*. New York: Routledge.

Working Group on the legal regulation of the purchase of sexual services. 2004. *Purchasing Sexual Services in Sweden and the Netherlands: Legal Regulation and Experiences*. Ministry of Justice and the Police.

# 17

## Introduction

Things are not as straightforward as they seem. With this, Bruckert begins her study of the world of strip clubs. While she both acknowledges and resists the moral assumptions and everyday perceptions which we usually use to interpret the setting and what occurs within it, Bruckert asks us to listen to the views of those working in the industry. What emerges is that the setting is less about entertainment and sex than how stripping is a lot of work.

At the same time, the stripper is in a disreputable occupation and engaged in labour of which the public generally disapproves. How do these workers handle the stereotypical assumptions, disapproval, and stigma associated with their jobs? Do they utilize any of the 'neutralization techniques' identified by Sykes and Matza to defuse or disarm the moral censure often directed at them? In what ways is stripping 'women's work'? Bruckert's study draws on the sociological approaches of conflict theory, feminism, and symbolic interactionism. But precisely in what ways?

## The World of the Professional Stripper

*Chris Bruckert*

If you wandered into one of the over 200 strip clubs in Ontario, you might notice the dim lighting, the pool tables and video games, the continually running pornographic movies, and the smell of stale beer. You might notice that this is clearly a 'male space' that is, somewhat ironically, defined by the presence of (some) women. Women in scant attire 'hanging out', women sitting and listening with apparently rapt attention to men, women at some phase of undress dancing on stage, women in champagne rooms[1] dancing for, or talking with, (clothed) men who are sitting only inches away from their naked bodies. At first glance the scene appears so imbued with the markers of gendered oppression, objectification, and exploitation that analysis is hardly necessary. Nonetheless, things are not as straightforward as they seem. From the perspective of the women 'deep' in conversation or dancing on the stage, strip clubs are not about entertainment, or immorality, or sex. They are about work.

In this chapter we explore the work of strippers through the lens of feminist labour theory. Using an approach informed by Marxism, symbolic interactionism, and feminism allows us to shift between analytic levels and consider the intersection and tension between market economy, social and gender relations, regulatory frameworks, dominant discourses, labour processes, and work site practices. When we step outside of morally loaded assumptions and attend to *the* understanding of industry workers, it is quickly apparent that strippers' work is both similar to and markedly different from other working-class women's labour.[2]

# From Entertainment to Service

The trajectory of labour of Ontario's strippers over the last three decades speaks to the unique position of strip clubs as both commercial enterprises embedded in the market economy and, at the same time, the product and focus of dynamic social processes including moral and legal regulation. It also illustrates how broader labour market trends and economic shifts not only position clubs to exploit strippers but also condition the nature of that exploitation. In the mid and late 1970s strippers were entertainers who, in exchange for wages,[3] performed five sets of four songs (three fast, one slow floor show) during their six-hour shift. During the 1980s and into the 1990s Canada experienced periods of recession, a general stagnation of fiscal growth, and high rates of unemployment (Phillips 1997: 64). During this period of economic restructuring, manufacturing jobs were displaced, the service sector expanded exponentially, and women's labour market position was destabilized (Luxton and Corman 2001). For working-class women labour market reorganization resulted in a move into labour-intensive consumer service sector employment characterized by low pay, low capital-labour ratio, limited job security, poor working conditions, and non-standard labour arrangements such as part-time, casual, and seasonal work. In principle protected through labour legislation, in practice marginal, non-unionized workers in this sector have limited recourse to legal protection and are susceptible to a range of exploitive practices (Duffy and Pupo 1997). In addition, the vanishing social safety net compounded the vulnerability, economic need, and domestic responsibilities of this social strata. As a result, workers were not only, by default, increasingly employed in the service sector but situated to embrace work in the growing non-standard labour market, including casual and flexible self-account work, as an income-generating strategy that allowed them to fulfill their many social and personal obligations.

It was in this context of economic decline and dwindling options for working-class women that the new industry innovation of table dancing[4] was introduced in the early 1980s and used to justify cutting dancers' pay to $30 or $40 a day. At the same time shifts were increased from six to eight hours, and bar fees[5] were implemented. By the early 1990s as the economy continued to spiral downward threatening even the 'bad jobs' in the service sector, clubs went from exploiting workers to the full appropriation of their labour. Many dancers found their pay eliminated, as they were offered the option of working for 'tips' or not at all. In short, in Ontario between 1980 and 2000 stripping was 'de-professionalized',[6] dancers were redefined as service providers, wages were reduced, and the labour requirements were substantially increased.

Today, while some dancers continue to work 'on-schedule' earning between $35 and $45 for an eight-hour shift, most work as 'freelancers'[7] receiving no financial compensation from the club. Under either arrangement, dancers are expected to pay the established bar fee of between $10 and $20, follow house rules, remain in the bar for a predetermined period of time—hanging out and 'looking like a hooker' (Debbie)[8]—and perform between one and five three-song 'sets' on stage. Similar to other subcontracting relations (i.e., electricians) exotic dancers are responsible for furnishing tools, in this case music, costumes, and transportation. In exchange for labour, fees, and compliance with the expectations of the club, the bar provides the labour site— the physical space (bar, chairs, champagne rooms) and other coordinated and necessary labour by disk jockeys, bartenders, servers, and doormen. This setting is, of course, crucial. Without it, a dancer cannot solicit the private dances that constitute her income.[9]

In spite of receiving no or minimal pay the workers' labour and general deportment remains under the control of management, who establish the house rules governing attire and behaviour, expectations of stage shows, interactions with customers, and services offered in the champagne rooms. Compliance is realized through economic sanctions in the form of fines and by the club's power to deny access to customers. A dancer who is defined as troublesome, who complains 'too much', who doesn't follow the house rules, or who leaves with a customer may be suspended or barred permanently. 'Troublesome' dancers also risk being blacklisted. This can have dire consequences, since the marked dancer will be unable to pursue her trade anywhere in the city. Put this way, today strippers are in a contradictory space—on the one hand they are managed like employees and subject to disciplinary regimes if they fail to comply, while on the other hand they are denied the pay and protection generally associated with employment.

The exploitative nature of managerial attempts to extract maximum labour power notwithstanding, there have also been positive implications for workers in the shift from entertainment to service. With de-professionalization and lower labour costs, a new industry standard of continuous stages and lots of 'girls' emerged. These changes in turn meant new employment opportunities and an opening up of the labour market as the demand increased. They also conditioned the relationship between management and dancers in new ways. Their limited commitment to a particular labour site affords individual dancers greater levels of autonomy and allows them to determine, within particular confines, where, when, and how much they work. Since the club no longer pays workers but exchanges fees and labour site access for free labour, the ability of management to control labour has been somewhat eroded. This is exacerbated by the managerial need for a stable work force and their subsequent hesitancy to alienate the dancers on whom they rely. This is particularly true for women with considerable organizational assets (i.e., a 'sexy' appearance, a client list).

Moreover, the new organization not only conditions labour relations but also interacts with class to shape the labour site itself. In the past, the nature of the entertainment-based industry compelled dancers to work full-time and travel 'the circuit'. These conditions effectively excluded many women workers who embraced other 'respectable' social roles: children, partners, school commitments, other jobs. Today, dancers can opt to work full-time, part-time, or occasionally; and either never, or only periodically go 'on the road' in response to particular financial difficulties. In real terms this, coupled with the impoverishment of women workers in Canada generally, opened up the industry to reputable working-class women and women from middle-class families whose eroding economic position (coupled with ideological changes regarding the meaning of nudity) has rendered morally suspect labour increasingly tenable. Tina, a sole-support mother, started working as a stripper when after years of steady employment she found herself:

> On welfare for seven months. And it was hard and . . . I saw those, ah, those ads [in the newspaper]. And one day I decided to, to go, to try it y'know. But it was scary. I was 29 years old and I didn't know what was going on there.

Like Tina, these new workers need to overcome their own stereotypical assumptions about strip clubs; however, those who effectively deconstruct the dominant discourses sometimes remain in the occupation for considerable periods of time. In turn, as these new workers bring to the labour site their own class culture and investment in respectability, these values have become embedded in the industry structure itself. Today, the markers of rough working-class culture—practices (partying, drugs), appearance (cut-off jean shorts, tattoos), values (being 'solid'), and language (talking tough)—are either absent from strip clubs or are limited to one token 'rough bar'.[10]

In 1973, amendments to the provincial Liquor Control Act expanded the definition of 'theatre' (Ontario 1973) and made it possible in Ontario to combine alcohol and nudity in a legal commercial endeavour. Since then, the trajectory of strip clubs in the province reveals how the complex interplay between market economy and labour structure shapes the labour process in marginal spheres at the same time as the labour process shapes the class origin of the available employee base. Workers are then positioned in a contradictory class location: they are both independent entrepreneurs who manage their own business—thus, are the bourgeois—and employees who sell (or in this case exchange) their labour power and who rely on, and must comply with the expectations of, an individual capitalist—in this case, the proletariat.

## The Job

When we shift our focus and apply the feminist labour lens to the question of labour practices, another set of questions emerges. What does the work entail? What skills and competencies are workers expected to bring to the labour site? What strategies do dancers employ to negotiate the occupational hazards? What are the particular challenges of the job? In addition, by retaining the focus on class, we are also positioned to ask: How does strippers' labour compare to that of working-class women more generally?

## The Stage

A woman working in a strip club as a stripper first and foremost has to *act* like a *stripper;* whether she is on the stage or not, she is always *performing*. This involves both the ceremony common to visible employees of 'playing [her] condition to realize it' (Goffman, 1959: 76) and the fact that the dancer is allowed some creativity, although, like actors generally, she is required to assume a role that is not her own, nor of her making (Henry and Sims, 1970). To entertain, she has to 'do a stage'. This public erotic labour involves the ability to perform for, but also interact with, the audience, whose very presence legitimates the work.[11] In addition, a stripper's act requires a degree of comfort with nudity, a willingness to expose herself physically, and a self-assured and confident presentation-of-self. Many strippers develop a strong stage presence and are often competent dancers, proficient not only in the standard stripper 'moves' but able to incorporate, and execute (in very high heels) their own eclectic mix of ballet, jazz, acrobatics, aerobics, and posing. On stage a dancer must continue to smile or at least assume the appropriate sexually vacant expression—'I think about doing laundry or watch the TV' (Debbie) —in the face of apathy and, sometimes, taunts. These kinds of verbal comments touch not only on her performance but, in light of the gendered appearance-imperative, on her value as a woman. In short, she needs to develop the capacity to distance herself from the negative evaluation of the audience.

Although obscured by the performance component and nudity, stage shows are physically demanding labour. And, like so much physical labour, it can be dangerous.[12] In addition to the risks inherent to dancing in stiletto heels, there is the threat of infectious disease. While many dancers take protective measures,[13] the dressing rooms, washrooms, stage, and pole are, at least in some clubs, not particularly well-maintained. The work is also exhausting and technically difficult: 'Pole work is a lot of hanging upside down, it's a lot of balance, muscle technique. It's hard to look sexy when you're upside down and all the blood's rushing to your head!' (Diane). Put another way, the 'moves' can only be erotic if they appear effortless and natural, a feat that necessitates practice, skill, and considerable muscle development.[14] In short, constructing sexuality is not natural or easy but hard *work*; however, the more effective the illusion, the more sexual the portrayal, the more the *work* is invisible.

The question becomes: How is erotic labour understood and negotiated by participants? Perhaps the most telling finding was how few comments were made by interviewees about sexuality. It appeared to be largely incidental. While dominating public consciousness, nudity, sexual presentations, and interactions are normalized within the cultural environment of the strip club, so that the erotic nature of the labour is essentially a non-issue for participants.

Perhaps more important still are the meanings scripted onto the labour. A dancer engages with the indicators of sexuality, and these links to the erotic appear to define her job as a stripper. However, this explicitly erotic labour operates at the level of the visible body. It is not about sex but nudity and the visual presentations of the erotic: 'You manipulate your body in a certain way and you throw a sexual aspect to it' (Debbie). Put another way, dancers engage in surface acting where 'the body not the soul is the main tool of the trade. The actor's body evokes passion in the *audience,* but the actor is only *acting* as if he has the feeling' [emphasis in original] (Hochschild 1983: 37). The eroticized setting, available props, and their own expectations may ensure that the audience defines the entertainers as sexual.

## The Floor

As previously noted, today's dancers must continually negotiate two discrete, and sometimes conflicting, jobs during their work day. The quasi-contractual obligation is to perform strip-tease shows and 'hanging out'—tasks for which she receives not a paycheque but attains access to customers. As self-account service workers, all or most of the worker's income is directly paid by customers in fee-for-service arrangements. In order to 'make her money' dancers must first solicit and sell their private dances by convincing 'a guy that he really wants a dance' (Debbie). Here labour practices are constrained not only by house rules but also by individual inclination. Some dancers flatly refuse to approach customers: 'Some girls go around and ask, "Hi baby how you doing" and start shaking their things in front of him. No! I don't like that at all. I just wait for them. If they want me bad enough, they'll come and get me, they'll signal me or tell the waitress' (Rachel). Others 'work the floor'—socializing and engaging promising-looking customers in conversation. The most aggressive hustlers greet all customers. At a minimum they 'give them the eye, just like you would in a bar' (Debbie).

Having 'sold' her service, the dancer accompanies the patron to the champagne room where she seeks to maximize her income by employing a variety of special skills. 'Once they come and get me, they're screwed. They're stuck with me, and I'm gonna keep them and siphon out every last dime I can get' (Rachel). While this may entail dirty dancing, more frequently dancers employ 'straight' strategies to maximize income:

> I don't stop [dancing] until they tell me to stop, and then I tell them how much. I don't do one dance and then sit . . . I used to do that, one dance and that's it. Then you don't get another dance. So I just keep dancing. (Sally)

In the champagne room a dancer needs to encourage the customer, retain his attention and good will, and yet remain firmly in control of the situation. The challenges have increased with the media and public discourses throughout the lap-dancing debates. Apparently, customers frequently equate surface presentations of sexuality with actual sexuality, so that dancers are wrongly presumed to be, if not prostitutes, then highly promiscuous. Today '99 per cent by the customers, oh yes, "You must have a price" . . . the way society is, they're allowed to expect it' (Marie). This means that an individual dancer is required to cope with customers' anticipation of sexual fulfillment while she labours in an environment where she is presumed to be, but cannot be, sexually available.

Not surprisingly, given the physical space and discursive parameters, making money also renders dancers vulnerable to physical or sexual aggression. As a result, they must remain vigilantly attentive to clues that identify potentially dangerous patrons (body language, conversation, approach, intoxication). Dancers also routinely rely on each other for protection— 'In the champagne room we're all watching each other's back' (Debbie)—and most of the more experienced dancers have perfected strategies that maximize their control of the interaction.

## Emotional Labour

While erotic labour, either on the public stage or in the relatively private champagne rooms, appears to define strippers' labour, in practice strippers are increasingly required not only to engage in the surface acting essential for the selling and providing of private entertainment services but also to provide an interpersonal social service that necessitates a unique set of skills and strategies. Here Arlie Hochschild's (1983) concept of emotional labour has resonance.[15] Many customers are only marginally interested in nude entertainment whether it is on the public stage or in a private champagne room. Instead these men come to strip clubs because they 'want someone to talk to' (Rachel) and will 'spend a couple of hundred bucks and they sit there and talk to a girl that's nice to them and makes them feel good for a few hours' (Diane).

For the dancer, this parody of social relations necessitates 'playing a game . . . It depends on the guy, the drippier you are, the more money you'll make. The more you laugh at his jokes, the more money you'll make' (Sally), In essence, the dancer presents a cynical performance (Goffman 1959: 18), instrumentally and consciously playing to the expectations of an audience of one.

Essentially, a dancer's livelihood depends on her ability to recreate social relations and 'treat them like they're people. You don't just treat them like they're a ten dollar bill' (Rachel). Interactions are routinized charades where dancers create the illusion of a novel interaction with a 'special' person. In short, strippers' daily labour involves not only continual performance— playing the role of a stripper—but also adopting other personas, in effect playing a number of roles, within a particular spectrum of possibilities, consecutively and sometimes concurrently:

> I used to give every guy a different age depending on what they wanted. I also gave different stories, but that's complicated to keep track of. Sometimes I acted really young and walk[ed] around the club in a skirt being cutesie. You don't even have to look that young, just act young. It's really weird. Different guys want different things. (Sarah)

Like other direct service workers, a stripper has to be able to manage her emotions and anger in the face of ignorant and trying customers. However, there is something more—she participates in a financial interaction that masquerades as a social relationship with its sense of reciprocity: 'I should probably have my PhD in psychology by now for all the problems I've listened to and all the advice I've given' (Rachel). Social relationships are normally defined by mutual concern. In the strip club, however, the appearance of concern becomes a commodity that is purchased, 'I feel guilty when they tell me things. Because personally I don't give a shit. But I have to pretend I do' (Jamie). Notably, unlike the professionals to whom Rachel compares herself, a dancer has neither the language nor the professional training on which to rely to guide her through the interaction; instead, she has to improvise as she continually reinvents herself and adapts her performance.

Although talking to customers appears to be a rather innocuous activity, many dancers express exasperation: 'You have to go sit down with the guy and blah blah blah blah blah blah blah blah. I hate that' (Tina). In fact, the most distress was voiced by research participants about this activity. On reflection, this is not surprising. As capitalism expands and the service industry swells to include the supply of emotional and interpersonal services (for men) in a commercial imitation of authentic social relationships,[16] the boundaries are being blurred and the product is not only the service but the server herself. For strip industry workers, this means they are alienated not just from their bodies—through their physical capacity to work or their labour power—nor from their surface sexual self-presentation in a way that was normal in burlesque theatres. They are alienated from something more—their social selves:

> Temporarily you're someone you're not, just for this guy, just so you can get his money. If he wants to believe something then you just play right along with it. 'Ya I'm from wherever' and make yourself up to be something you're not (Sally).

The result is a disassociated sense of self, so that 'I pretend I'm somebody else and I get all glamorous and I go into work. I'm a completely different person in the club, a completely different person' (Debbie). Workers are very explicit about the need to distance and separate their different selves: 'I have a very distinct difference between my job and my life, and I find if I mix the two of them that I can't keep it straight' (Ann). This assumption of separate identity is in part facilitated by the use of stage names so that 'on stage I'm Kim so that's not me either' (Alex). It would appear that, as new areas of social and interpersonal life are transformed into services to be bought, the alienation inherent to the labour process in societies is also extended into a new arena.

## Stripping is Women's Work

To summarize the discussion so far, when we abandon morally loaded assumptions, explore labour structure and practices, and 'normalize' the labour of strippers by making links to the 'reputable' work of working-class women, similarities start to emerge. Today strippers are contractual own-account workers who experience the same sorts of issues confronting other working-class women in Canada, including a non-supportive work environment; exploitation and oppression by owners and managers, non-standard labour arrangements, lack of security, and minimal protection by the state. As part of the burgeoning consumer service sector they, like many other direct service workers, do a job that requires erotic and emotional labour. The job itself is physically exhausting, emotionally challenging, and definitely stressful.[17] Success is contingent on the development of complex skills and competencies including performance, construction of sexuality, sales, and finely tuned interpersonal skills. The very existence of these skills belie the customary focus on deviance rather than work process in much of the literature. Of course, that these skills are largely dismissed, or rendered invisible, is not unique to the strip trade but characterizes many working-class women's jobs (Gaskell 1986). It does, however, affirm once again the relative and subjective nature of what is defined as skills.

It is women's work in another way as well. Traditionally women were expected to provide men with nurturance, care, and support. Dancers provide this service for men who 'want someone to listen to their problems' (Sarah) on the market on a fee-for-service basis. Suspending, momentarily, what it says about the state of alienation in advanced capitalist society that men are prepared to pay $10 for every four minutes[18] they spend in the company of a woman ($85 per hour if they take the flat rate[19]), we can appreciate that this is fully consistent with the move of capital into the types of services traditionally performed in the home. In the context of intimate relations, this empathetic support is not experienced as particularly challenging; within the labour market, it proves to be difficult, emotionally taxing labour that requires both surface and deep acting and the implementation of complex skills. Like so much of the labour women do, it is obscured, even to participants, by the context in which it occurs and the taken-for-granted nature of the competencies. That is to say, not only is the labour structured so that work is interspersed with social interaction, but emotions do not 'fit' into the language of work, so that while the strippers are fully aware that 'it's hard on your head after a while' (Diane), they are, nonetheless, sometimes not fully cognizant of this as *labour* activity.

# But Not a Job Like Any Other!

Recognizing this work as labour, we must exercise caution. While we can legitimately make links to more reputable labour sites for almost every aspect of the dancer's work, few jobs require this combination of skills and necessitate that the worker operate in such a complex and emotionally taxing labour environment. In this last section, we attend to specificity and consider stripping as a *marginal* labour activity and reflect on the implications for workers.

First, we need to consider that stripping is a stigmatized labour location.[20] While participation in the paid labour force is a taken-for-granted imperative for most Canadians, the nature of an individual's work is something they are presumed to choose. 'Choosing' a labour market location that is on the margins of legality, morality, or propriety can have profound implications, as the stigma of labour location is transformed into a stigma of the worker (Polsky 1969).

These workers must contend with moral righteousness and stereotypical assumptions in interpersonal relations and in a range of social and economic areas from housing—'some places don't rent to strippers' (Diane) —to finance—'it's hard to get credit in a bank' (Marie) —that are generally assumed to operate outside of moral consideration. Put another way, *working* as a stripper becomes *being* a stripper, an identity marker with very real implications in the lives of women in the industry and that shapes the worker's experience of the wider world.[21] While most dancers deconstruct the discourses and challenge the assumptions that underlie the stigma (prostitution, drug abuse, immorality) and effectively manage their personal and social identities, they must, nonetheless, continually engage in social and personal exchanges where their labour location is understood to be definitive.

The implications of participating in 'disreputable' labour extend beyond questions of identity and social interaction. Dancers must also negotiate a web of state regulatory practices unknown to employees in more 'reputable' occupations. Throughout the 1980s and into the early 1990s, in response to claims made by community groups that linked strip clubs to increased crime and vice, municipalities throughout Ontario began to regulate the industry through severe zoning restrictions, banning clubs from residential areas, restricting the clubs to commercial zones, and stipulating no-strip-club parameters around churches and schools. They also introduced licensing that required the newly designated 'exotic entertainment parlour attendants' to purchase annual licences under threat of fines and even imprisonment.[22] The nature of the licensing is revealing and speaks to the moral subtext of these strategies. In principle, these controls are intended to regulate the industry in the interests of broader society; in practice, they not only stigmatize and marginalize workers but also further restrict the employment options of women workers: some clubs are 'zoned' out of existence, while live entertainment ceases to be economically viable for smaller clubs in light of the hefty annual fees.

# Conclusion

If I have done my job well, it should be clear to the reader that the work women perform in strip clubs, is *hard* work. In order to be able to practise her trade, a dancer has to appear periodically on stage, dance, and remove her clothes for a roomful (or worse, *not* a roomful) of men 'for free'. In order to 'make her money', she has to present herself as an attractive 'sexy' woman, sell her service to an individual patron, and retain his attention by engaging in erotic and/or emotional labour while carefully maintaining physical and psychological boundaries. In the champagne room, her naked body may well be inches from her client, but she is continually being monitored by the manager, the doorman, other dancers, and the police. Like a rape victim, if she is inappropriately touched, she is held responsible and sanctioned. All the while she has to cope with the particular stress of working in a leisure site as well as deal with the chaotic environment and interpersonal conflicts that abound. When she leaves the labour site, she continues to engage with the stigmatized nature of her occupation, managing her social and personal identity as well as coping with the stereotypical assumptions of her friends, intimate partners, and the state agencies with whom she interacts. In other words, while we can legitimately make links to more reputable labour sites for almost every aspect of the dancer's work, there are few jobs that require this combination of skills and necessitate that the worker operate in such a complex and emotionally taxing labour environment. Furthermore, the implication of stigma means that the labour has far-reaching costs in the worker's personal life.

At the same time, the implications of having a 'job like no other' are not all bad. Unlike most workers who provide traditional women's work on the open market, a stripper is well compensated for her labour. Furthermore, not only does the job offer her a flexibility and autonomy seldom available to working-class women, it allows her to develop competencies that are useful outside the labour site—assertiveness, boundary maintenance, and interpersonal skills. In addition, although her work may leave her frustrated and angry, it also affords her a broader vision, enhanced self-esteem, good body image, comfort with her sexuality, and confidence—all worthwhile attributes and ones that many women continue to struggle to realize.

## Notes

1.  These cubicles, measuring perhaps three feet by five feet each, are equipped with two (most often vinyl) chairs facing each other, an ashtray and a ledge to hold drinks. While the cubicles are usually hidden from the general view of the club, they are open to be monitored by anyone passing down the aisle between them.
2.  This chapter is based on data gathered during a year of participant observation in a southern Ontario strip club, 15 in-depth, semi-structured interviews with women working as strippers, and a series of interviews with other industry employees including managers, doormen, bartenders, waitresses, and disk jockeys. For a more detailed description of the methodology or for a further development of the arguments see Bruckert (2002).
3.  Wages ranged from $275 to $600 a week in the late 1970s.
4.  Table dances are a one-song strip show performed at the patron's table. Today, in spite of the advertised availability of $5 table dances, these are rare. Most dancers simply refuse to remove their clothes in the middle of the bar. At any rate, most patrons are easily persuaded to enjoy the privacy afforded by the champagne rooms, where for $10, the stripper either dances on a stool or sits in close proximity to the customer and moves—a dance in name only.
5.  Dancers are required to pay bar fees or 'DJ fees' of between $10 and $20 per shift. In practice this means that the dancer must 'pay to work there' (Jamie). Depending on the club, these fees compensate the disk jockey and sometimes the bartender, who also receive no pay in the traditional sense.
6.  This redefining of labour as semi-skilled is consistent with the trend towards de-skilling that Braverman (1974) identified as characteristic of twentieth century capitalism. That de-skilling is ideologically and economically

useful (for capitalists) is revealed when we realize that throughout the 1980s and 1990s, at the same time as skills were being denied, employers in mainstream sectors of the labour market were establishing inordinate educational requirements (Rinehart 1996:78). It would appear that labour-dependent personal service industries capitalize on existing age, gender, and racial stratifications by hiring marginal workers and then justify their low wages through reference to their marginal status (Reiter 1991:148).

7.  DERA (Dancer's Equal Rights Association of Ottawa) estimates that one in four Ottawa dancers are 'on-schedule' (DERA 2001).

8.  On-schedule dancers are booked for eight-hour shifts, while freelancers must remain for a minimum period—usually four or five hours—established by the bar.

9.  To perceive these arrangements as anomalous risks reaffirming marginality by locating it outside of established labour practices. In fact, in the way it is organized, stripping is comparable with the non-stigmatized service occupation of realty. Like strippers, real estate agents are in such a paradoxical relation to their 'employers' that the term is hardly appropriate. Realtors are actively recruited by brokers; they are hired, and they can be fired. But since they receive no direct financial remuneration for their labour from their employer, the relationship is nuanced. In exchange for legal protection and access to the necessary legitimizing context (including the use of the name, licence, and insurance), means of production (phone services, office space, and technical support), the realtor commits her or himself to a particular brokerage firm (including providing 'free' labour staffing the office).

10. There was a particular irony here. While the dominant discourse increasingly defines stripping as immoral, the clubs and workers are becoming progressively more committed to respectability: 'they think of it as a business now, y'know, the newer generation; it's more like a business instead of just the stereotyped thing that people used to do. The girls are keeping their money. A lot less drugs' (Rachel). Furthermore, young women from the rough working-class, who wear the markers with pride, are being marginalized within the industry. It is precisely these women whose employment options are restricted and who are the most exploited population of workers.

11. Her agency is noteworthy. Far from being solely an object of the male gaze, it is the dancer who establishes the interaction with the audience and determines the pace, actions, and movement of the show. The audience's reading of her sexualized form does not erase her authorship. We see this clearly when a dancer enacts a fine parody as she plays with her own and her audience's sexuality, although she is usually quite careful, given the economic power dynamic, not to let the audience in on the joke.

12. While not all working-class jobs are manual, physically challenging jobs are overwhelmingly working-class. Consequently, the labour sold frequently has a socially unacknowledged (though recognized by the wage-labourers themselves) youth imperative and uncompensated costs in terms of health and well-being (Dunk 1991; Houtman and Kompier 1995:221).

13. These include bringing their own towels to sit on and sometimes their own cleaning materials.

14. In addition, creating an erotic persona necessitates countless hours of labour in appearance, clothes, makeup, and sometimes tanning salons or plastic surgeries.

15. Hochschild (1983) argues that, rather than simply selling her mental and physical labour, the modern service worker must now engage in emotional labour. This requires the worker, in exchange for a wage, to 'induce or suppress feeling in order to sustain the outward countenance that produces the proper state of mind in others' (1983:7) and engage in 'deep acting' by re-creating personal experiences in a commercial setting. Such a worker must manage her feelings not just for private social relations (which we all do), but as a commodity to benefit the corporation that pays her wage. The process, which requires her to transform her smile into a sincere smile, cannot avoid creating a sense of alienation from feelings (Hochschild 1983:21).

16. It is possible that capitalism is responding to the market and exploiting men's insecurity in the changing gender relations that characterize the latter half of the twentieth century. With the erosion of male power that 'is based on the compliance of women and the economic and emotional services which women provided' (Giddens 1992:132), men struggle with the new expectations and their own need for intimacy (Giddens 1992:180).

17. For dancers 'role overload', identified as a key contributor to workplace stress (Levi et al., 1986:55) is normal. Dancers have to constantly negotiate two separate, sometimes conflicting, jobs during their work day. The quasi-contractual obligation of the stripper is to perform strip-tease shows and 'hang out'—'looking like a hooker' (Debbie) —tasks for which she receives not a paycheque but the opportunity to 'make her money'; that is, to take the chance to utilize the profitable skills of soliciting and playing the game. Her job not only requires her to fulfill a number of roles at the same time but also to continually manage the emotional and sexual demands of patrons. She must try to maximize her income while simultaneously engaging in boundary maintenance to protect her emotional and physical space. In addition, dancers are subject to the stress shared by other labourers engaged in emotional work (Adelmann 1995:372) as well as the particular stressors shared by entertainers—performance anxiety and a fear of even minor physical injury that can effectively curtail their career (Sternbach 1995): 'I can't work with black eyes, I can't work with big scars across my face' (Jessie).

18. These prices were in effect in 1999.
19. These prices were in effect in 1999.
20. Of course, other occupations are also stigmatized—morticians, custodians, and used car salespeople, to name a few.
21. It is also a 'sticky' stigma infecting those around the dancer as well (Goffman 1963:30), so that her family may be, or may perceive themselves to be, stigmatized. Certainly, those who share her labour site are. It is also sticky in the sense of enduring even after participation in the industry has ceased. The almost inevitable linguistic designation of *ex*-strippers in the media speaks to an understanding that participation in the trades legitimates continued assumptions of immortality.
22. In 2001, there is considerable provincial disparity. Some municipalities, such as London and Kitchener, require clubs, but not attendants, to purchase licences. In municipalities that continue to license dancers, costs can be quite high. In Windsor, dancers must pay $225 plus administration and photo fees annually.

# References

Adelmann, P. 1995. 'Emotional labour as a potential source of job stress'. In S. Sauter and L. Murphy (eds.), *Organizational risk factors for job stress*. Washington: American Psychological Association.

Braverman, H. 1974. *Labour and monopoly capital; The degradation of work in the twentieth century*. New York: Monthly Review Press.

Bruckert, C. 2002. *Taking it off, putting it on: Women in the strip trade*. Toronto: Women's Press.

DERA. 2001. Mission statement. Ottawa: Dancers' Equal Rights Association of Ottawa Carleton. (n.p.)

Duffy, A. and Pupa, N. (1997). *Part-time paradox*. Toronto, McClelland & Stewart.

Dunk, T. 1991. *It's a working man's town: Male working-class culture in northwestern Ontario*. Montreal: McGill-Queen's University Press.

Gaskell, J. 1986. 'Conceptions of skill and work of women: Some historical and political issues'. In R. Hamilton and M. Barreti (eds.), *The politics of diversity, feminism, Marxism and nationalism*. London: Verso.

Giddens, A. 1992. *The transformation of intimacy*. Palo Alto, CA. Stanford University Press.

GoHman, E. 1959. *The presentation of self in everyday life*. New York, Doubleday.

———— 1963. *Stigma*. Upper Saddle River, NJ, Prentice Hall.

Henry, W. and Sims, J. 1970. 'Actors' search for a self'. *Trans-Action* 7, 11.

Hochschild, A. 1983. *The managed hear: Commercialization of human feeling*. Berkeley, CA: University of California Press.

Houtman, I. and Kompier, M. 1995. 'Risk factors and occupational risk groups for work stress in the Netherlands'. In S. Sauter and L. Murphy (eds.), *Organizational risk factors for job stress*. Washington: American Psychological Association.

Levi, L., Frankenhauser, M. and Gardell, B. 1986. 'The characteristics of the workplace and the nature of its social demands'. In S. Wolf and A. Finestone (eds.), *Occupational stress: Health and performance at work*. Littleton, MA. PSG Publishing.

Luxton, M. and Corman, J. 2001. *Getting by in hard times: Gendered labour at home and on the job*. Toronto: University of Toronto Press.

Ontario. 1973. 'An act to amend the liquor licence Act'. (Chapter 68, 69). *Statutes of the Province of Ontario*. Toronto: Thatcher.

Phillips, P. 1997. 'Labour in the new Canadian political economy'. In W. Clement (ed.), *Understanding Canada: Building the new Canadian political economy*. Montreal: McGill-Queen's University Press.

Polsky, N. 1969. *Hustlers, beats and others*. Garden City, NJ. Anchor Press.

Reiter, E. 1991. *Making fast food*. Montreal, McGill-Queen's University Press.

Rinehart, J. 1996. *The tyranny of work: Alienation and the labour process*. 3rd ed. Toronto: Harcourt Brace.

Sternbach, D. 1995. 'Musicians: A neglected working population in crisis'. In S. Sauter and L. Murphy (eds.), *Organizational risk factors for job stress*. Washington: American Psychological Association.

# 18

## Introduction

Prostitutes and prostitute activists generally argue that prostitution is just another job and point out that most individuals in the trade enter it by choice. However, even prostitute advocates make an important distinction between adult prostitution and the sexual exploitation often associated with juvenile prostitutes engaged in 'survival sex'.

In this abridged version of his study, Hodgson investigates juvenile prostitution in Toronto and finds it to be a strategy to cope with the poverty, loneliness, and vulnerability of being a defamilied youth. But unlike adult prostitution, Hodgson finds that males perform a significant and highly manipulative role in getting juveniles to enter the business.

What exactly are the methods used? How can we best assist youth who find themselves in the situation outlined by Hodgson?

Hodgson's study highlights the relevance of socialization, subcultural groups, and making choices in socio-economic conditions that are not of one's choosing in taking on a 'deviant career'. But for those who have been introduced to any of the following theories, a further question. To what extent does his study support or challenge Sutherland's differential association theory, Cloward and Ohlin's theory of differential opportunities, Hirshi's social bond theory, or the liberal or more radical feminist perspectives?

## Juvenile Prostitutes

*James F. Hodgson*

This monograph is presented in the format of a sociological exploratory study that examines the interactions between male street sex trade managers (street pimps) and female street sex trade workers (street prostitutes). The specific aim of this examination is to provide an extended, applied, conceptual analysis of the pimp-prostitute relationship. There have been numerous studies and much research on prostitution, but there has been very limited examination of the role that pimps play in the 'prostitution scene'. Many reports on prostitution vaguely mention the involvement of pimps and often fail to move their examination beyond cursory comments regarding their role. Therefore, pimps are often portrayed as secondary actors in street prostitution subculture.

Some reports describe the pimp-prostitute relationship as one of 'mutual functional interdependence.' This 'mutual functional model' suggests that pimps play a role in assisting and providing necessary services to prostitutes. Prostitutes are often portrayed as entrepreneurs, and pimps are often dismissed as assistants in many studies of street prostitutes. It is asserted in this text that these accounts do not accurately depict or describe how central the pimp's role is manifest within street prostitution subculture. This examination provides a much needed critical analysis of the role that pimps play in the recruitment, the training, and the compelling of women to work as prostitutes.

This inquiry details that pimps are, indeed, significant primary actors who are involved in producing and reproducing the subculture of street prostitution. Therefore, this work focuses directly on the role that pimps play in promoting and regenerating street prostitution.

This analysis develops and facilitates a qualitative methodological inquiry into the pimp-prostitute relationship. Specifically, elements of qualitative analysis are exercised throughout this study to demonstrate the methodological process of qualitative approaches to under-standing social phenomena. A social typology of adolescent prostitutes is generated to assess emerg-ent social research that attempts to identify characteristics of juvenile prostitution. This examination includes the analysis of determining the role of pimps and how central the pimp's role remains in the prostitute's life. The procurement methods that pimps employ and the characteristics of the relationship that develop will disclose the level of vulnerability and dependence, the gender relations, the psychological coercion, the training, the application of the trade, the working relations, the violence and abduction, and the consequences of this exposure.

Preliminary perusal of the available data illustrates that children as young as 10 years of age are exchanging sexual acts for money in many urban centres. The estimated number of children employed as sex trade workers ranges on any given day from 10,000 on the streets of Canada to 100,000 on American streets. Of course, there are problematic features of gathering reliable statistical assessments of the numbers of children and adolescents working as prostitutes. However, most officials working in the child-care services recognize that juvenile prostitution has become a reality on the social landscape in most urban jurisdictions.

Although quantitative analysis of the scope of this social problem provides limited disclosure, social and legal research indicates that each year hundreds of children are experiencing severe social conditions and circumstances. The results of these dysfunctional social conditions are that a significant number of children eventually find themselves working as street prostitutes. The data demonstrate that a significant number of children are 'falling through the cracks' of child welfare systems. Many of the children are victims of abuse at home and are further victimized by inadequate school and child welfare responses.

Juvenile prostitutes are not fallen women, sluts, or whores, but are, in fact, our children. It is obvious that child-care and police agencies are competing for our children on the streets— the competitors are the pimps. The pimps have developed and provide a complete system of outreach, intake, on-the-job training, peer support, protection, and work incentives for young women. Can our child-care agencies compete with the opportunities that are provided by pimps?

The definition of 'pimp' and 'prostitute' employed within the framework of this study is determined from the current legal interpretation of the legislation contained in the *Criminal Code of Canada*. Section 212. (1), (2), (3) of the *Criminal Code* is commonly called the 'pimp legislation' within the legal community and outlines 11 offences that upon conviction would indeed label one as a pimp. Three of the offences are listed here to provide a general definition and understanding of the legal concept of a pimp. Greenspan (1994:207) outlines Section 212. (1) of the *Criminal Code*:

Every one who:
  (d) procures or attempts to procure a person to become,
      whether in or out of Canada, a prostitute,
  (h) for the purpose of gain, exercises control, direction or
      influence over the movements of a person in such a
      manner as to show that he is aiding, abetting or
      compelling that person to engage in or carry
      on prostitution with any person or generally,
  (j) lives wholly or in part on the avails of prostitution of
      another person
is guilty of an indictable offence and liable to imprisonment for a term not exceeding 10 years.

The definition of 'prostitute' utilized within this study is drawn from the current legal interpretation of case law. A prostitute is defined as 'one who completes sex acts in exchange for money or goods'. These definitions are offered to clarify how these terms are understood within a legal context. It is within this legal context that the terms 'pimp' and 'prostitute' are utilized in this examination.

The dynamics of the pimp-prostitute relationship are determined by the methods that pimps select to procure and exercise control of women for the purposes of prostitution. The method that pimps select to procure and exercise control is directly dependent on the age and the level of vulnerability of the women. Subsequently, the nature of the relationship varies. This work asserts that the dynamics of this interaction between pimps and prostitutes are not those of mutual functional interdependence, but ones in which pimps exhort various levels of exploitation, degradation, dominance, and manipulation regardless of what method of procurement and control they choose to invoke.

# Juvenile Prostitutes:  A Social Typology

## Background and Family Composition

Many of the juveniles interviewed for this project disclosed that they were not running to the street to become involved in prostitution, but, in fact, were running from abusive situations at home. Often the street was the only perceived option. This sense of limited options is illustrated in the following comments by Lori and Karen respectively:

> It was really shit at home. It didn't matter what I did, it wasn't right. They drove me fucking crazy. They would search my room and everything. My dad kept accusing me of taking drugs, which was bullshit. Even my grades weren't good enough. I couldn't stay there any more. I had to leave. I didn't know where I was going, but I just had to get out.
>
> *Interview: 13-year-old: April 9, 1991*

I didn't know anything about the street. I didn't have anything. But when you arrive, you learn fast. You have to or you die. But anything was better than living at home. They had screwed up my head so much I just ran. But I learned everything I needed within a few days. You can learn quick.

*Interview: 14-year-old: February 6, 1989*

The idea of prostitution, in most cases, became a factor for consideration by women after they arrived on the street. These women did not have any original intention of working as prostitutes before leaving their places of abode.

It is important to point out here that 90 per cent of the respondents of this study under 18 years of age were living away from their families because of various levels of family breakdown. Most were in the care of child-care agencies and others were living with friends. An unpublished report prepared by the Hospital for Sick Children, entitled 'Sexually Transmitted Infections In Adolescent Prostitutes In Toronto' (1989: 1), highlights findings of dysfunctional characteristics:

Most adolescent prostitutes are runaways, though not all runaways become prostitutes. These young people have often escaped from a variety of adverse circumstances including physical and sexual abuse, incest, parental alcoholism and violence, sexual intercourse at an early age with few or no meaningful relationships, negative sexual labelling among peers. . . . This young, unskilled population turns to 'the street' as their new home with its attraction of a socially accepting peer group, easy access to drugs and a variety of activities which may be perceived as exciting and often illicit. Drug dealing and prostitution then become the means to finance this lifestyle.

## Family Characteristics

Beverley McKeddie, director of a youth intervention services program in Toronto, highlights the many different circumstances that have significance in developing positive and negative family characteristics. Again, keep in mind that the dysfunctional characteristics of the family force children to run to the streets. During an interview with Ms McKeddie on March 17, 1994, she reported that all of the families that come to the attention of her agency are suffering from dysfunctional behaviourial reactions that are generated by many factors including economic crisis. However, the expression of dysfunctional family relations is depicted by the individual trauma being played out by the children. This individual trauma is the result of experiences of sexual, physical, psychological, and verbal abuse and neglect that the child has endured within the family structure.

McKeddie reports that many of these dysfunctional characteristics are expressed as covert abuse in that less than adequate parenting skills are fostered, which results in neglecting the needs of the children within the family unit and, therefore, the family, structure and component do not meet the children's needs. Moreover, for many of these children, running from the family unit becomes a coping skill. McKeddie describes the characteristics of these children who run from their homes. These characteristics include: low to no self-esteem; self-delusions; poor physical hygiene; very little understanding of right and wrong; and no boundaries to behaviour.

The family relationships described by the respondents were indeed less than functional. Dysfunctional aspects of family life reveal that, for most, positive family relationships were not possible because of the deteriorating family conditions. Table 18.1 highlights the family relationships as disclosed by the respondents. The majority of the respondents emphasized the detrimental relationship that was experienced and the feeling of urgency to remove themselves from this oppressive, painful and destructive environment.

## History of Sexual, Physical, and Psychological Abuse

Sexual, physical, and psychological abuse at home is another area that needs to be examined to fully understand the environment. Obviously, this type of abuse would affect the nature of the family relationship, not to mention the victim's self-esteem and feelings of acceptance and rejection. Table 18.2 provides a breakdown of the incidence of sexual, physical, and psychological abuse reported by the respondents. Although much debate continues as to the causality of such abuse and the incidence of adolescent prostitution, the data clearly show a high incidence of abuse among the respondents.

If nothing else, the data disclose that physical, sexual, and psychological abuse force adolescents from their homes and onto the street where prostitution may be one of several methods of street survival.

## Concluding Typology

In concluding this social typology of adolescent prostitutes many characteristics can be categorized. l) These young people are not running to the street but are running from acute

### Table 18.1  Family Relationships

|  | No. | % |
| --- | --- | --- |
| Respondents removed from home by child-care authorites | 63 | 33 |
| Respondents can live at home but do not want to | 25 | 13 |
| Respondents cannot return home | 46 | 24 |
| Return home intermittently | 41 | 21 |
| Difficulties living at home | 11 | 6 |
| Reported good relations at home | 8 | 4 |
| Total | 194 | 100 |

| **Table 18.2** Incidence of Sexual, Physical, or Psychological Abuse | | |
|---|---|---|
| | No. | % |
| Physical abuse | 70 | 36 |
| Sexual abuse | 39 | 20 |
| Psychological abuse | 41 | 21 |
| All three | 32 | 16 |
| Total abuse reported | 182 | 94 |
| Neither type of abuse reported | 12 | 6 |
| Total number of respondents | 194 | 100 |

crisis circumstances and experiences in their home environment. 2) These children and adolescents arrive on the street in an extremely physically and psychologically vulnerable condition. 3) The dysfunctional aspects of their family life varied, but the issue of the inability to cohabitat with family members was prevalent. 4) Significant numbers came from single-parent households. 5) Most reported some level of either sexual, physical, or psychological abuse at home, and some reported all three levels of abuse. 6) The obvious ramifications of these dysfunctional family settings are the diminished scholastic accomplishments of the adolescents; most did not proceed past the ninth grade. 7) Adolescent prostitutes represent all ages with a mean age of fourteen-and-one-half. 8) Exploration of socio-economic status suggests that adolescent prostitutes represent various levels of income groups. However, significant evidence suggests that there is indeed an overrepresentation of adolescents from the impoverished and working-class economic groups. 9) The physical and mental health of these adolescent prostitutes can only be described as extremely desperate, vulnerable, volatile, and self-destructive. 10) Although the majority of the adolescent prostitutes were Caucasian, an overrepresentation of blacks and indigenous people is reported to be involved in this environment. 11) Drugs and other intoxicants play a significant role in this street subculture and are one of the instrumental factors that facilitate the immersion of these vulnerable groups into prostitution.

## Procurement: The Pimp's Game

The data and self-reports reveal that women who had no previous prostitution-related experiences are being procured directly or indirectly into this lifestyle by pimps. The self-reports disclose that pimps play an instrumental role in the recruit's procurement into prostitution. As suggested, there are two distinctly different methods of procurement that pimps utilize. It is asserted within this research that pimps vary their methods of procurement after giving consideration to such contingencies as age and level of vulnerability. It is asserted here that pimps who discover a woman in highly vulnerable circumstances will utilize the seduction method of procurement. Pimps, upon discovering women who appear to be in control of their environment, employ the stratagem method of procurement.

This finding may be somewhat surprising to some observers of social exchange, as these methods of procurement are contrary to the preconceived image of how pimps operate. The societal image represented through media and popular literature conventionally depicts the pimp as using physical, coercive means to compel women into prostitution. These portrayals often suggest that women are abducted from the street and are subsequently administered various addictive drugs to compel their dependency to prostitution and to their pimp. The data reflect that this method of procurement is not utilized, but, instead, pimps employ methods of seduction and/or stratagem and not abduction. Closer analysis of the self-reports is offered here to further understand how pimps orchestrate their complex system of procurement.

## Seduction Method of Procurement

The method of procurement by 'seduction' that the self-reports disclose suggests that an extremely compounded projection of events is applied by pimps to seduce women into prostitution. Pimps seduce women into prostitution strategically displaying various levels of affection, attraction, and concern. These elements of emotional support bond women to pimps, and, subsequently, the women to prostitution.

The self-reports describe pimps as usually making the initial contact by way of general conversation about the need for cigarettes or inquiries as to the woman's presence in town. Early in this conversation, the pimps will ask if she is 'live' or if she has a 'man'. This appears to be the pimps method of determining whether or not women are working as prostitutes or know the prostitution game. Within this subculture, to be 'live' is to be working as a prostitute, and 'square' indicates not working as a prostitute. The connotations given to this terminology, within this subculture, suggest that it is the norm in this lifestyle to be 'live' and certainly not acceptable, if not deviant, to be 'square'. This strategy being played out is represented in the comments made by Cindy:

> He just came up to me and said, 'You live or memorex?' I said, 'What are you talking about?' He never did answer, but he took me out to a couple of clubs that night. He began looking after me; actually, he wouldn't let me out of his sight.
>
> *Interview: 15-year-old: July 9, 1991*

During this initial contact with the pimp, the candidate is asked several questions about her present circumstances. Pimps ask about her current situation such as age, location of residence, closest family, how long in the city, etc. This allows the pimp to make a quick assessment of her vulnerability, then choose the appropriate method of procurement.

Pimps appear to assess the recruit's level of emotional vulnerability and to supply her with affection and attention to fill the void. The self-reports indicate that emotional attachment appears to have the greatest impact on the women and that they would, indeed, do anything for their pimps.

Most of the self-reports indicate that during the candidate's early introduction to the pimp, she did not know nor did the pimp disclose that he was a pimp. If she discovered that her new-found friend and companion was a pimp, often she did not terminate the relationship because the pimp did not mention anything to her about working as a prostitute. Kathy describes her pimp:

> I figured that he cared too much for me to want me to work; I mean he loved me. I begun to learn that he had some girls working for him, but I figured that I was his girlfriend and the others were his business. I guess I was a little naive about that.
>
> *Interview: 16-year-old: October 8, 1990*

The next step applied by pimps appears to be an extremely critical development in the candidate's journey into prostitution. This step immerses the candidate into the world of prostitution by exposing her to numerous prostitutes and pimps. The candidate usually receives this exposure at after-hours night clubs or at various hotels. This exposure allows the new candidate to hear about the excitement of the street and the adventures associated with prostitution as described by prostitutes and pimps. This sense of excitement is further escalated for the candidate when pimps supply various drugs such as cocaine and marijuana. One young prostitute, Rebeca, describes the all night visits and drug use at the night clubs:

> Yea it was crazy, there were pimps and whores coming and going, like drugs everywhere, it was like 'every night was a Saturday night'.
>
> *Interview: 14-year-old: November 7, 1991*

A significant number of the self-reports describe this 'every night was a Saturday night' concept. Exposure to these clubs and their occupants appears to have tremendous impact on the young recruit's life as she begins to bond more strongly with the pimps and to this escalated lifestyle of apparent excitement and adventure. The candidates observe women going out for the evening to work as prostitutes, and returning with the 'trap' (money earned by completing acts of prostitution). These prostitutes speak of their adventures and travels of the past five hours and of the strange requests made by dates (customers).

## Psychological Coercion: 'Choosing Time'

The monetary cost of caring for and 'turning out' young women is substantial. The hotel rooms, food, taxis, drugs, and all the other necessary items are expensive. Pimps suggest that the women can assist their financial standing by 'turning a trick'. If she rejects this suggestion the pimp then suggests that she should leave or go home. Pimps tell them that they can no longer subscribe to the 'family'. This threat of being deprived of their pimp and a lifestyle to which they have developed a strong attraction appears to have extreme impact on what they decide to do. If she leaves, she is without her new-found special person and lifestyle. If she stays, she must work as a prostitute. These events being played out are captured in comments by Elizabeth:

Billy said that we needed money and that he had to leave to go back to Philadelphia if he couldn't get more money, He more or less said that he couldn't afford to keep looking after me. We suddenly didn't even have enough money for food or cabs. Billy became really miserable and unhappy. He asked me to help out by turning a few tricks. I did feel somewhat obligated, I mean I needed to help out, I mean he helped me out so much. I knew he would have to leave if I didn't help. It didn't seem so bad at the time.

*Interview: 14-year-old: May 20, 1991*

A study completed by Enables (1978:209) suggests that some subjects that she interviewed reported that 'they started prostitution because they were in love with the pimp and felt prostitution was necessary to maintain their relationship with him'.

Pimps often subject women to a form of reverse psychology to entice them to stay and start working as prostitutes. The reports reveal that pimps often tell women that they can leave at anytime and encourage them to telephone their families. This seems to increase the desire and will to stay with the pimp. Therefore, she believes that it is her decision in 'choosing' to stay and work as a prostitute for the pimp. The term 'choosing' is used to describe when the women must decide if they are going to work as a prostitute or not and for which pimp. Arlene reported exercising 'her choice' in staying with her new acquaintances:

It was my choice, like he didn't force me or anything. We needed more money and he asked me to help. It was my decision. He didn't force me; I could have gone back to the home, but I didn't want to do that.

*Interview: 14-year-old: February 2, 1991*

Cecil, a pimp, commented on the concept of choosing:

You can't physically force them to do it because they will just 'chunk' you off. You've got to plead to their other side, their emotional side, their common sense side. They have to believe it's them helping out.

*Interview: 18-year-old: March 20, 1989*

## Strategem Method of Procurement

The self-reports from women who are in less vulnerable circumstances, as described earlier, suggest that the pimp's approach is very direct in illustrating that he wants them to work for him as prostitutes. This method of procurement is labelled the 'stratagem method of procurement'. The reports advise that pimps talk about the large amounts of money that can be earned, the glamour of travel, adventure, and other grandiose images resembling the lifestyles of the rich and famous. Pimps suggest that they can develop this new lucrative, romanticized career and will provide all the support and protection that the young recruit needs. The stratagem method of procurement being played out is illustrated in comments from Beth and Karen respectively:

He walked up to us in the club and introduced himself as 'Jade'. He was all decked out. He started talking about his business and we asked more about it. He said it was providing escorts for old men. He told us we could make $400 to $500 a night if we wanted to. He said he takes all his employees to Hawaii once a year as a bonus plan. He was very business about it. He even gave me his card and told me to call him if I was interested.

*Interview: 18-year-old: July 28, 1991*

I was in the shopping mall and he approached me and asked if I was a model. I wasn't and he started telling me about the modelling business. He was telling me how I would make two and three thousand dollars a week with a body like mine. He said that with his brain and my body we could make a lot of money. He said that I could purchase a new Mercedes through his company after the first year of work.

*Interview: 17-year-old: June 10, 1991*

Women acquired by this method of procurement appear to be lured into the 'prostitution game' by pimps who utilize false promises and images of grandeur.

Pimps who practise this stratagem method of procurement appear to portray themselves as managers who will accommodate the candidate's break into the sex trade business. Fitzroy, who was working as a pimp, provides some insight on the notion of sex trade managers:

Hey, I manage their affairs, I make sure they are safe. I look after them. I make sure that they feel safe. I make sure they have a good time . . . I get them ready for the street and groom them so they can be successful . . . You have to approach it like a business.

*Interview: 26-year-old: June 11, 1988*

The reports advise that a pimp gives the recruit detailed instructions of what services a pimp provides and, of course, what she is required to pay a pimp for this service, which usually works out to 60 or 70 per cent of the 'trap'.

Women procured by this method, as those who are procured by seduction, think that it is their own rational decision to get involved in prostitution. A pimp, as with the seduction method, tells the candidate that they do nothing by force. Lori reports this notion of 'free choice' by commenting:

He outlined the game and told me what he would do for me. He told me about all the money I could make and all the wonderful places I could go. He talked about all the clothes I could buy. He then said it was my choice, I could just waste my life and be poor all my life or take control and do something for myself. He said he would be around if I chose to become involved. I ended up seeing him the next night at the club and I decided to give it a try.

*Interview: 18-year-old: January 18, 1991*

# Training: Getting Started

If the woman chooses to stay with the pimp and her new street friends, she 'chooses' to become involved in prostitution, as the seduction method of procurement suggests. If she is convinced by the pimp's exaggerated description of prostitution, she 'chooses' to be involved in prostitution, as the stratagem method of procurement demands. The next stage is a significant one in the further immersion into the prostitution environment. The training process will be examined to expose the job training strategies and orientation procedures that pimps employ in developing young women for prostitution. Moreover, this examination moves beyond analysis of the street rules and regulations, to reveal the 'socialization processes' and the 'subcultural components' that are engendered and imposed while 'learning the game'. The revealing of the socialization process and the subcultural components expose the strategies that pimps utilize to indoctrinate new recruits to conform without question to the rules, expectations, and roles as imposed by pimps and the street environment.

The training and subsequent bonding to prostitutes, pimps, and the street environment ensure adherence to the ideology represented on the street. The ideology embraced within the prostitution environment is produced and reproduced, which contributes to neutralizing the individual identity of the new recruit and weakens any attachment to previously learned values and norms. The recruit's complete immersion into this environment facilitates the internalization of the 'prostitution role'. This adoption and internalization of the prostitution role serves to ensure the recruit's adherence to the pimp and the street subculture.

As the self-reports disclose, if a woman 'chooses', it means that the pimp will need to train her to work as a prostitute. The self-reports suggest that the young women are turned out usually by pimps with assistance from their 'wife-in-law'. The wife-in-law is the pimp's 'main lady' or the prostitute that a pimp trusts with the task of turning out a new candidate. The training consists of being apprised of all the rules of the street sex trade business. The number one rule is 'don't tell the police that you have a pimp', and the number two rule is 'don't hold back trap' (money). The number three rule is 'don't talk to other pimps', and the number four rule is 'don't talk to the police any longer than you have to'. The candidate is also instructed on how to recognize plain-clothes police officers, bad dates, and dangerous situations, how to perform various sex acts, condom use, the exchange of money, how much money to charge for various sex acts, how much money to make each night, and other essential knowledge that they are required to know if they are to survive in this game of sex for money.

Caplan (1984: 140) suggests that pimps have developed a system of 'outreach, intake, orientation, job development, on the job training, housing, peer support, role models, and incentive programs that are all part of what he offers'. Pimps and their wives-in-law provide the necessary information and training to facilitate the recruit's further involvement in the prostitution environment. This immersion moves the candidate closer to the initiating ritual of 'turning the first trick', to get her ready to 'break' for the first time, thus securing her commitment to the sex trade.

## Applying the Trade: The 'First Trick'

The females are told that their pimp or one of the 'players' are close by if they need anything. The females are sent out on the street with the wife-in-law to 'turn her first trick'. The first trick establishes her newly acquired position in the family. The self-reports describe the experience of turning the first trick as exciting, but at the same time frightening. The pimp's wife-in-law usually went with the new recruit on the 'first date', in an attempt to reduce the fear that the candidate may be experiencing. Many women characterize the first date as embarrassing, but submit that it is over quickly and generates money swiftly. Marlene describes her first trick:

> It was embarrassing standing on the street, like everyone going by was looking at us because they know that we are working, but the guy drove up and we went with him. I did what I had to and made my first 60 dollars. It was easy, I guess but I never looked back, everything was happening so fast. I remember how happy and excited Kenny was when I told him that I broke. He made me feel good about all of it.
>
> *Interview: 14-year-old: June 17, 1991*

The self-reports depict the importance of turning that first trick and the subsequent endorsement that is received from the pimp.

The significance of turning the first trick within this subculture is indeed material in its implications and consequences. The turning of the first trick further immerses the recruit deeper into the prostitution environment. This 'socialization process' serves to bond her to other prostitutes and to the street subculture. This ensures adherence to the ideology represented and fostered by the pimp. Female prostitutes are 'socialized' to embrace the street subculture and are therefore required to internalize the values and beliefs of the street in order to belong to the family. The cultural values and norms of the street subculture include many behaviours and beliefs that may be contrary to those expressed by the dominant culture. Heather describes this internalization of the street subculture:

> Ya, I couldn't believe how fast everything was happening and I couldn't believe the things I was doing. I mean, I was a new person, I mean I was doing things that I never would have done before. Especially some of the sex things. I started acting that part and I was proud of it. I sort of loved to see the reaction to straight people when I told them I was a 'Hoe'.
>
> *Interview: 16-year-old: April 10, 1990*

Within the street prostitution subculture, the values and norms express many behaviours that would receive much negative stigma within the dominant culture. Such activities and values as law-violating behaviour, fearlessness, daring, shrewdness, excitement, danger, and freedom from external constraints of the conventional norms and values of the family, state, or school are all expressions that are manifest, endorsed and encouraged within this street subculture. The prostitute is required to internalize these norms and values and therefore internalize the roles and attitudes of street prostitution. This internalizing ensures that the woman begins to see herself within the social role of 'prostitute' and therefore will play out that role. The official labelling of deviant or delinquent behaviour results in the internalization of a delinquent or deviant self-image or conscience, and hence, continued involvement in delinquent or deviance activities or, in this case, continued participation in prostitution.

Turning the first trick has other significance in regards to the role of pimps. Pimps appear to realize the importance of this immersion to new values and norms within this street subculture. The self-reports disclose that it becomes most evident that the prostitute's status with her pimp changes significantly after she turns the first trick. The pimp immediately imposes a 'turning out fee' or 'street charge', she is now financially indebted to the pimp. This significant change in status reduces the woman to property or an investment that can be redeemed or exploited for considerable financial reward. This change in status appears to affect the pimp-prostitute relationship considerably as the working relations descend to violence.

## Working Relationships: The Descent to Violence

### Seduction/Strategem to Abduction

Women in the self-reports, for the most part, describe the relationship with their pimp as very satisfying and pleasant during the outset of their encounter, regardless of which method of procurement their pimp utilized. However, as described earlier, many of the women begin to question the relationship within a short period of time. With the relationship deteriorating, many prostitutes disclose that they would be subjected to physical abduction by pimps. If the woman attempts to leave her pimp or violates one of his rules, she is often subjected to being abducted from the street and physically disciplined by the pimp. Kathy and Sharon, respectively, describe being abducted and assaulted after leaving their pimp:

> I had left Jason and wanted to take a break from working so I just hid out at a couple of hotels. I was able to hide out for four days until he caught me. He actually choked me out. He beat me and I was black and blue all over. He made me work three times as hard to make up for the lost money. He watched me continuously for three weeks after that.
>
> *Interview: 15-year-old: April 18, 1990*

> When I left, Keven caught me at the mall and told me to come with him or he would slit my throat right there on the spot. He took me back to the hotel and beat me. He kept saying that he had invested too much time in me to let me chump him off like that. He told me I would have to pay him $4000 if I wanted to leave.
>
> *Interview: 13-year-old: June, 17 1987*

Pimps claim a 'colour of right' over prostitutes, as they have invested time and energy in turning out. This abduction is usually described as violent and results in the woman being

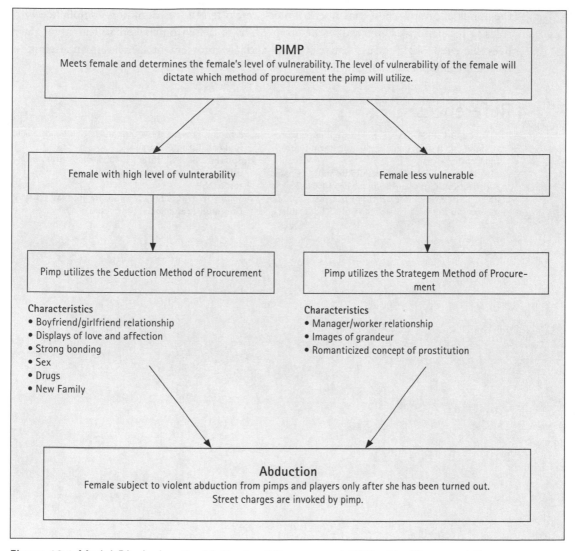

Figure 18.1 **Model Displaying the Methods of Procurement Utilized by Pimps and the Resulting Incidents of Abduction**

physically forced to continue to engage in prostitution. Figure 18.1 illustrates this shift to abduction regardless of the method of procurement that pimps employ.

The Toronto Street Youth Project Report (1986) reveals that pimps are the most frequent physical abusers of young prostitutes under 16 years of age. The Badgley Report (1984: 118) also documents this high incidence of physical abuse inflicted on prostitutes by pimps in noting that 'four in five girls who had worked for pimps had been beaten, and in some instances, seriously injured by these men'. Eighty-five per cent of the subjects interviewed for this effort revealed that they had been endangered by violent abductions and several physical assaults at the hands of pimps. These violent encounters were often the result of non-compliance with rules or regulations as imposed by the pimp. Many of these women were so fearful for their lives that they sought the assistance of social and law enforcement agencies in an attempt to escape the apprehension and terror.

## References

Badgley Report. 1984. *Sexual Offenses Against Children in Canada*. Ottawa: Canadian Government Publishing Centre.

Caplan, Gerald. 1984. 'The Facts of Life about Teenage Prostitution'. *Crime and Delinquency*, 30: 69–74.

Enables, G. 1978. *Juvenile Prostitution in Minnesota: The Report of a Research Project*. St Pauls: The Enablers, Inc.

Greenspan, Edward. 1994. *Annotated Criminal Code of Canada*. Toronto: Carswell.

Hospital for Sick Children. 1989. *Sexually Transmitted Injections in Adolescent Prostitutes in Toronto*. Toronto: N.P.

*Toronto Street Youth Project*. 1986. Toronto: Ministry of Community and Social Services: n.p.

# Part V | Mental Illness and Psychiatry

Mental illness is a distinctive form of deviance. It is an example of 'ascribed deviance'; that is, it involves behaviours, predispositions or physical traits defined as deviant even though the individuals have not chosen their condition. Often these are characteristics or qualities which individuals are born with or which biologically beset them, and over which they have little or no control. Of course, people contending with disabilities or disfiguring diseases vary or differ from what is usually or normally the case and haven't chosen their conditions either. But while mental disorders are not deliberately chosen, they are often treated as a more serious form of ascribed deviance because the disorders can precipitate behaviours that are, or could be, harmful to oneself or others. An example would be serious forms of psychosis such as sociopathy where an individual derives some satisfaction from inflicting harm on another but feels no remorse in doing so. Or anorexia or depression where an individual could take his or her own life.

But how do we determine if someone is experiencing a mental illness, or if a disturbing act is a consequence of a mental disorder rather than an individual idiosyncracy, an unfamiliar cultural practice, or, as we saw in the reading on the medieval witch craze, a manifestation of evil? As such, the topic of mental illness goes hand in hand with psychiatry. The articles in this section consider psychiatry from a sociological perspective by viewing it as a social institution involved in social control within modern societies and as part of the broader phenomenon of the medicalization of social control.

Throughout the twentieth century, the medical profession increasingly became involved in the exercise and legitimizing of social control over a wide range of problems. It was Talcott Parsons who first theorized that modern medicine does not just diagnose and treat illness, but also adjudicates and manages it as a minor form of deviance. The adjudicating and managing works with a language of the 'normal', 'pathological', or 'abnormal', and what is managed is an ill person's exemption from the usual responsibilities of members within the community. The familiar school policy of having to provide doctor's notes for late assignments or an absence from class would be an example. With psychiatry, the involvement in the modern process of social control is even more explicit.

The American Psychiatric Association represents the psychiatric establishment in North America. Its authoritative diagnostic handbook, the *DSM-V (2002): the Diagnostic and Statistical Manual of Mental Disorders*, covers a wide range of disorders including organic mental syndromes and disorders, schizophrenic disorders, mood disorders, delusional disorder, anxiety disorders, and personality disorders.

Although there are various approaches in psychiatry, the one which dominates the profession is based on a 'medical model'. This refers to the professional ideology that mental disorders have a physiological foundation, whether biochemical, neurological, genetic, etc., and hence are 'mental illnesses'. While 'psyche' originally referred to the soul or mind of an individual, the focus of much current psychiatry has been on the brain, the neurological system, and the hormonal system. As a result, a significant form of treatment involves drugs and surgical interventions.

Sociological studies of psychiatry often reflect a conflict-theory approach and have been critical of it for neglecting the influence of social, economic, and political conditions in contributing to psychic distress as well as in defining it as solely an individual's mental disorder. They have also been critical of how diagnosing becomes a form of labelling, and of the significant imbalance in power and authority in the client-psychiatrist relationship.

The point of such studies is not to dismiss the realities of psychological distress, anguish, destructive behaviours, or frightening experiences which afflict many. Nor is it intended to trivialize the work undertaken by those who have tried to help people with such afflictions. Rather they indicate that psychiatry, as a social institution, can be as puzzling and worthy of investigation as the disorders it treats.

Finally, while there are many theorists who have made major contributions to the field of psychiatry, some have also contributed to understanding deviance and social control more generally, such as Sigmund Freud. Freud's work not only offers an inquiry into why people who know what's right might do what's wrong. At the end of his career, he used his psychoanalytic work on the psyche and psychological disorders to explore more sociological topics such as the relationship between human happiness and society as well as the origins of human society.

# 19

## Introduction

The following reading is abridged from Freud's *Civilization and Its Discontents*, his last book. After working on a psychoanalytic theory of personality, psychosexual development, and psychological disorders, Freud turned his attention to the broader topic of the nature and historical development of the human animal. This context can be difficult to relate to. We generally think about our lives as individuals located in a particular society in the present time. But what if we considered our lives and our society in terms of humanity and human history as a whole? For Freud the results are troubling. Humans in general have a difficult time being happy. And those in more advanced 'civilizations' seem to have even more difficulty than those living in more 'primitive' societies.

But Freud's inquiry can be challenging for other reasons too. He assumes some familiarity with his psychoanalytic theory of human nature and the conflicted self. So you may need to introduce yourself to some of his basic ideas. Those that are relevant here are: his concept of the human personality as a psychic structure comprised of three component parts ('id', 'ego', and 'superego'); the conflict that exists in humans between the generative life instinct (*libido*, or *Eros*) and the destructive death instinct (*Thanatos*); the tension that develops between our instinctual forces and the cultural requirements of living together in a group; the ego's effort to find practical, reasonable solutions for satisfying our needs and desires in culturally appropriate ways; and, the emergence of different kinds of psychological strategies for resolving the tension (including 'sublimation' and 'defense mechanisms' like 'repression').

Freud's overall theory offers some explanation of why individuals who know what's culturally expected sometimes do what will be seen as wrong. But it also provides a theory of the origin of human society, and explores how the dynamic, conflicted relation between individual and group is more complex than just an opposition between a free solitary individual and a group requiring obedience and conformity.

Some guiding questions to keep in mind as you read: what are the three main sources of unhappiness that Freud identifies, and which is the most significant? How does he explain the origin of human societies? What problem inevitably arises when individuals are parts of groups? And how do groups bind themselves together in the face of this problem? Finally, after hearing his argument, what do you think of his view that people in more 'primitive' societies might actually be happier than those living in more 'civilized' societies?

# Why Is It So Difficult for People to Be Happy?

*Sigmund Freud*

## I. The Sources of Human Unhappiness

[Let us turn to the] question of what men themselves show by their behaviour to be the purpose and intention of their lives. What do they demand of life and wish to achieve in it?

The answer to this can hardly be in doubt. They strive after happiness; they want to become happy and to remain so. This endeavour has two sides, a positive and a negative aim. It aims, on the one hand, at an absence of pain and unpleasure, and, on the other, at the experiencing of strong feelings of pleasure. In its narrower sense the word 'happiness' only relates to the last. In conformity with this dichotomy in his aims, man's activity develops in two directions, according as it seeks to realize—in the main, or even exclusively—the one or the other of these aims.

As we see, what decides the purpose of life is simply the program of the pleasure principle. This principle dominates the operation of the mental operation from the start. There can be no doubt about its efficacy, and yet its program is at loggerheads with the whole world, with the macrocosm as much as the microcosm. There is no possibility at all of its being carried through; all the regulations of the universe run counter to it.

We are threatened with suffering from three directions: from our own body, which is doomed to decay and dissolution and which cannot even do without pain and anxiety as warning signals; from the external world, which may rage against us with overwhelming and merciless forces of destruction; and finally from our relations to other men. We tend to regard it as a kind of gratuitous addition, although it cannot be any less fatefully inevitable than the suffering which comes from elsewhere.

It is no wonder if, under the pressure of these possibilities, men are accustomed to moderate their claims to happiness—just as the pleasure principle itself, indeed, under the influence of the external world, changed into the more modest reality principle—if a man thinks himself happy merely to have escaped unhappiness or to have survived his suffering, and if in general the task of avoiding suffering pushes that of obtaining pleasure into the background. Reflection shows that the accomplishment of this task can be attempted along very different paths; and all these paths have been recommended by the various schools of worldly wisdom and put into practice by men. An unrestricted satisfaction of every need presents itself as the most enticing method of conducting one's life, but it means putting enjoyment before caution, and soon brings its own punishment. The other methods, in which the avoidance of unpleasure is the main purpose, are differentiated according to the source of the unpleasure to which their attention is chiefly turned. Some of these methods are extreme and some moderate; some are one-sided and some attack the problem simultaneously at several points. . . .

Our enquiry concerning happiness has not so far taught us much that is not already common knowledge. And even if we proceed from it to the problem of why it is so hard for men to be happy, there seems no greater prospect of learning anything new. We have given the answer already by pointing to the three sources from which our suffering comes: the superior power of nature, the feebleness of our own bodies, and the inadequacy of the regulations which adjust the mutual relationships of human beings in the family, the state, and society. In regard to the first two sources, our judgment cannot hesitate long. It forces us to acknowledge those sources of suffering and to submit to the inevitable. We shall never completely master nature; and our bodily organism, itself a part of that nature, will always remain a transient structure with a limited capacity for adaptation and achievement. This recognition does not have a paralyzing effect. On the contrary, it points the direction for our activity. If we cannot remove all suffering, we can remove some, and we can mitigate some: the experience of many thousands of years has convinced us of that. As regards the third source, the social source of suffering, our attitude is a different one. We do not admit it at all; we cannot see why the regulations made by ourselves should not, on the contrary, be a protection and a benefit for every one of us. And yet, when we consider how unsuccessful we have been in precisely this field of prevention of suffering, a suspicion dawns on us that here, too, a piece of unconquerable nature may lie behind—this time a piece of our own psychical constitution.

When we start considering this possibility, we come upon a contention which is so astonishing that we must dwell upon it. This contention holds that what we call our civilization is largely responsible for our misery, and that we should be much happier if we gave it up and returned to primitive conditions. I call this contention astonishing because, in whatever way we may define the concept of civilization, it is a certain fact that all the things with which we seek to protect ourselves against the threats that emanate from the sources of suffering are part of that very civilization.

It is time for us to turn our attention to the nature of this civilization on whose value as a means to happiness doubts have been thrown. We shall not look for a formula in which to express that nature in a few words, until we have learned something by examining it. We shall therefore content ourselves with saying once more that the word 'civilization'[1] describes the whole sum of the achievements and the regulations which distinguish our lives from those of our animal ancestors and which serve two purposes—namely to protect men against nature and to adjust their mutual relations.[2] In order to learn more, we will bring together the various features of civilization individually, as they are exhibited in human communities.

The first stage is easy. We recognize as cultural all activities and resources which are useful to men for making the earth serviceable to them, for protecting them against violence of the forces of nature, and so on. As regards this side of civilization, there can be scarcely any doubt. If we go back far enough, we find that the first acts of civilization were the use of tools, the gaining of control over fire, and the construction of dwellings.

We recognize, then, that countries have attained a high level of civilization if we find that in them everything which can assist in the exploitation of the earth by man and in his protection against the forces of nature—everything, in short, which is of use to him—is attended to and effectively carried out.

But we demand other things from civilization besides these, and it is a noticeable fact that we hope to find them realized in these same countries.

Beauty and cleanliness and order obviously occupy a special position among the requirements of civilization. No one will maintain that they are as important for life as control over the forces of nature or as some other factors with which we shall become acquainted. And yet no one would care to put them in the background as trivialities. That civilization is not exclusively taken up with what is useful is already shown by the example of beauty, which we decline to omit from among the interests of civilization. The usefulness of order is quite evident. With regard to cleanliness, we must bear in mind that it is demanded of us by hygiene as well, and we may suspect that even before the days of scientific prophylaxis the connection between the two was not altogether strange to man. Yet utility does not entirely explain these efforts; something else must be at work besides.

No feature, however, seems better to characterize civilization than its esteem and encour-agement of man's higher mental activities—his intellectual, scientific, and artistic achieve-ments—and the leading role that it assigns to ideas in human life. Foremost among those ideas are the religious systems, on whose complicated structure I have endeavoured to throw light elsewhere.[3] Next come the speculations of philosophy; and finally what might be called man's 'ideals'—his ideas of a possible perfection of individuals, or of peoples, or of the whole of humanity, and the demands he sets up on the basis of such ideas.

The last, but certainly not the least important, of the characteristic features of civilization remains to be assessed: the manner in which the relationships are regulated—relationships which affect a person as a neighbour, as a source of help, as another person's sexual object, as a member of a family and of a State. Here it is especially difficult to keep clear of particular ideal demands and to see what is civilized in general. Perhaps we may begin by explaining that the element of civilization enters on the scene with the first attempt to regulate these social relationships. If the attempt were not made, the relationships would be subject to the arbitrary will of the individual: that is to say, the physically stronger man would decide them in the sense of his own interests and instinctual impulses. Nothing would be changed in this if this stronger man should in his turn meet someone even stronger than he. Human life in common is only made possible when a majority comes together which is stronger than any separate individuals. The power of this community is then set up as 'right' in opposi-tion to the power of the individual, which is condemned as 'brute force'. This replacement of the power of the individual by the power of the community constitutes the decisive step of civilization. The essence of it lies in the fact that the members of the community restrict themselves in their possibilities of satisfaction, whereas the individual knew no such restric-tions. The first requisite of civilization, therefore, is that of justice—that is, the assurance that a law once made will not be broken in favour of an individual. This implies nothing as to the ethical value of such a law. The further course of cultural development seems to tend towards making the law no longer an expression of the will of a small community—a caste or a stra-tum of the population or a racial group—which, in its turn, behaves like a violent individual towards other, and perhaps more numerous, collections of people. The final outcome should be a rule of law to which all—except those who are not capable of entering a community—have contributed by a sacrifice of their instincts, and which leaves no one—again with the same exception—at the mercy of brute force.

The liberty of the individual is no gift to civilization. It was greatest before there was any civilization, though then, it is true, it had for the most part no value, since the individual was scarcely in a position to defend it. The development of civilization imposes restrictions on it, and justice demands that no one shall escape those restrictions. What makes itself in a human community as a desire for freedom may be their revolt against some existing injustice, and so may prove favourable to a further development of civilization; it may remain compatible with civilization. But it may also spring from the remains of their original personality, which is still untamed by civilization and may thus become the basis in them of hostility to civiliza-tion. The urge for freedom, therefore, is directed against particular forms and demands of civilization or against civilization altogether. It does not seem as though any influence could induce a man to change his nature into a termite's. No doubt he will always defend his claim to individual liberty against the will of the group. A good part of the struggles of mankind centre round the single task of finding an expedient accommodation—one, that is, that will bring happiness—between this claim of the individual and the cultural claims of the group; and one of the problems that touches the fate of humanity is whether such an accommodation can be reached by means of some particular form of civilization or whether this conflict is irreconcilable.

At this point we cannot fail to be struck by the similarity between the process of civilization and the libidinal development of the individual.

In most cases this process coincides with that of the *sublimation* (of instinctual aims) with which we are familiar, but in some it can be differentiated from it. Sublimation of instinct is an especially conspicuous feature of cultural development; it is what makes it possible for higher psychical activities, scientific, artistic, or ideological, to play such an important part in civilized life.

Finally, and this seems the most important of all, it is impossible to overlook the extent to which civilization is built up upon a renunciation of instinct, how much it presupposes precisely the non-satisfaction (by suppression, repression, or some other means?) of powerful instincts. This 'cultural frustration' dominates the large field of social relationships between human beings. As we already know, it is the cause of the hostility against which all civilizations have to struggle. It will also make severe demands on our scientific work, and we shall have much to explain here. It is not easy to understand how it can become possible to deprive an instinct of satisfaction. Nor is doing so without danger. If the loss is not compensated for economically, one can be certain that serious disorders will ensue.

But if we want to know what value can be attributed to our view that the development of civilization is a special process, comparable to the normal maturation of the individual, we must clearly attack another problem. We must ask ourselves to what influences the development of civilization owes its origin, how it arose, and by what its course has been determined.[4]

## The Origin of Civilization

The communal life of human beings has a two-fold foundation: the compulsion to work, which was created by external necessity, and the power of love, which made the man unwilling to be deprived of his sexual object—the woman—and made the woman unwilling to be deprived of the part of herself which had been separated off from her—her child. Eros and Ananke [Love and Necessity] have become the parents of human civilization too. The first result of civilization was that even a fairly large number of people were now able to live together in a community. And since these two great powers were co-operating in this, one might expect that the further development of civilization would proceed smoothly towards an even better control over the external world and towards a further extension of the number of people included in the community. Nor is it easy to understand how this civilization could act upon its participants otherwise than to make them happy.

Before we go on to enquire from what quarter an interference might arise, this recognition of love as one of the foundations of civilizations may serve as an excuse for a digression which will enable us to fill in a gap which we left in an earlier discussion.

We said there that man's discovery that sexual (genital) love afforded him the strongest experiences of satisfaction, and in fact provided him with the prototype of all happiness, must have suggested to him that he should continue to seek the satisfaction of happiness in his life along the path of sexual relations and that he should make genital erotism the central point of his life. We went on to say that in doing so he made himself dependent in a most dangerous way on a portion of the external world, namely, his chosen love-object, and exposed himself to extreme suffering if he should be rejected by that object or should lose it through unfaithfulness or death.

A small minority are enabled by their constitution to find happiness, in spite of everything, along the path of love. But far-reaching mental changes in the function of love are necessary before this can happen. These people make themselves independent of their object's acqui-escence by displacing what they mainly value from being loved on to loving; they protect themselves against the loss of the object by directing their love, not to single objects but to all men alike; and they avoid the uncertainties and disappointments of genital love by turning away from its sexual aims and transforming the instinct into an impulse with an inhibited aim. What they bring about in themselves in this way is a state of evenly suspended, steadfast, affectionate feeling, which has little external resemblance any more to the stormy agitations of genital love, from which it is nevertheless derived.

The love which founded the family continues to operate in civilization both in its original form, in which it does not renounce direct sexual satisfaction, and in its modified form as aim-inhibited affection. In each, it continues to carry on its function of binding together considerable numbers of people, and it does so in a more intensive fashion than can be effected through the interest of work in common. The careless way in which language uses the word 'love' has its genetic justification. People give the name 'love' to the relation between a man and a woman whose genital needs have led them to found a family; but they also give the name 'love' to the positive feelings between parents and children, and between the broth-ers and sisters of a family, although we are obliged to describe this as 'aim-inhibited love' or 'affection'. Love with an inhibited aim was in fact originally fully sensual love, and it is so still in man's unconscious. Both—fully sensual love and aim-inhibited love—extend outside the family and create new bonds with people who before were strangers. Genital love leads to the formation of new families, and aim-inhibited love to 'friendships' which become valuable from a cultural standpoint because they escape some of the limitations of genital love, as, for instance, its exclusiveness. But in the course of development the relation of love to civiliza-tion loses it unambiguity. On the one hand love comes into opposition to the interests of civiliza-tion; on the other, civilization threatens love with substantial restrictions.

Psychoanalytic work has shown us that it is precisely these frustrations of sexual life which people known as neurotics cannot tolerate. The neurotic creates substitutive satisfactions for himself in his symptoms, and these either cause him suffering in themselves or become sources of suffering for him by raising difficulties in his relations with his environment and the society he belongs to . . . But civilization demands other sacrifices besides that of sexual satisfaction.

When a love-relationship is at its height there is no room left for any interest in the environ-ment; a pair of lovers are sufficient to themselves, and do not even need the child they have in common to make them happy. In no other case does Eros so clearly betray the core of his being. His purpose of making one out of more than one; but when he has achieved this in the proverbial way through the love of two human beings, he refuses to go further.

So far, we can quite well imagine a cultural community consisting of double individuals like this, who, libidinally satisfied themselves, are connected with one another through the bonds of common work and common interests. If this were so civilization would not have to withdraw any energy from sexuality. But this desirable state of things does not, and never did, exist. Reality shows us that civilization is not content with the ties we have so far allowed it. It aims at binding the members of the community together in a libidinal way as well and employs every means to that end. It favours every path by which strong identifications can be established between the members of the community, and it summons up aim-inhibited libido on the largest scale so as to strengthen the communal bond by relations of friendship. In order for these aims to be fulfilled, a restriction upon sexual life is unavoidable. But we are unable to understand what the necessity is which forces civilization along this path and which causes its antagonism to sexuality. There must be some disturbing factor which we have not yet discovered.

The clue may be supplied by one of the ideal demands, as we have called them,[5] of civilized society. It runs: 'Thou shalt love thy neighbour as thy self'. It is known throughout the world and is undoubtedly older than Christianity, which puts it forward as its proudest claim. Yet it is certainly not very old; even in historical times it was still strange to mankind. Let us adopt a naïve attitude towards it, as though we were hearing it for the first time; we shall be unable then to suppress a feeling of surprise and bewilderment. Why should we do it? What good will it do us? But, above all, how shall we achieve it? How can it be possible? My love is something valuable to me which I ought not to throw away without reflection. It imposes duties on me for whose fulfillment I must be ready to make sacrifices. If I love someone, he must deserve it in some way. (I leave out of account the use he may be to me, and also his possible significance for me as a sexual object, for neither of these two kinds of relationship comes into question where the precept to love my neighbour is concerned.) He deserves it if he is so like me in important ways that I can love myself in him; and he deserves it if he is so much more perfect than myself that I can love my ideal of my own self in him . . .

But if he is a stranger to me and if he cannot attract me by any worth of his own or any significance that he may already have acquired for my emotional life, it will be hard for me to love him. Indeed, I should be wrong to do so, for my love is valued by all my own people as a sign of my preferring them, and it is an injustice to them if I put a stranger on a par with them. . . .

On closer inspection, I find still further difficulties. Not merely is this stranger in general unworthy of my love; I must honestly confess that he has more claims to my hostility and even my hatred. He seems not to have the least trace of love for me and shows me not the slightest consideration. If it will do him any good he has no hesitation in injuring me, nor does he ask himself whether the amount of advantage he gains bears any proportion to the extent of the harm he does to me.

The element of truth behind all this, which people are so ready to disavow, is that men are not gentle creatures who want to be loved, and who at the most can defend themselves if they are attacked; they are, on the contrary, creatures among whose instinctual endowments is to be reckoned a powerful share of aggressiveness. As a result, their neighbour is for them not only a potential helper or sexual object, but also someone who tempts them to satisfy their aggressiveness on him, to exploit his capacity for work without compensation, to use him sexually without his consent, to seize his possessions, to humiliate him, to cause him pain, to torture, and to kill him. *Homo homini lupus.*[6] Who, in the face of all his experience of life and of history, will have the courage to dispute this assertion? As a rule this cruel aggressiveness waits for some provocation or puts itself at the service of some other purpose, whose goal might also have been reached by milder measures. In circumstances that are favourable to it, when the mental counter-forces which ordinarily inhibit it are out of action, it also manifests itself spontaneously and reveals man as a savage beast to whom consideration toward his own kind is something alien.

The existence of this inclination to aggression, which we can detect in ourselves and justly assume to be present in others, is the factor which disturbs our relations with our neighbour and which forces civilization into such a high expenditure [of energy]. In consequence of this primary mutual hostility of human beings, civilized society is perpetually threatened with human beings, civilized society is perpetually threatened with disintegration. The interest of work in common would not hold it together; instinctual passions are stronger than reasonable interests. Civilization has to use its utmost efforts in order to set limits to man's aggressive instincts and to hold the manifestations of them in check by psychical reaction-formations. Hence, therefore, the use of methods intended to incite people into identifications and aim-inhibited relationships of love, hence the restriction upon sexual life, and hence too the ideal's commandment to love one's neighbour as oneself—a commandment which is really justified by the fact that nothing else runs so strongly counter to the original nature of man. In spite of every effort, these endeavours of civilization have not so far achieved very much. It hopes to prevent the crudest excesses of brutal violence by itself assuming the right to use violence against criminals, but the law is not able to lay hold of the more cautious and refined manifestations of human aggressiveness. The time comes when each one of us has to give up as illusions the expectations which, in his youth, he pinned upon his fellow men, and when he may learn how much difficulty and pain has been added to his life by their ill-will. At the same time, it would be unfair to reproach civilization with trying to eliminate strife and competition from human activity. These things are undoubtedly indispensable. But opposition is not necessarily enmity; it is merely misused and made an *occasion* for enmity.

If civilization imposes such great sacrifices not only on man's sexuality but on his aggressivity, we can understand better why it is hard for him to be happy in that civilization. In fact, primitive man was better off in knowing no restrictions of instinct. To counterbalance this, his prospects of enjoying this happiness for any length of time were very slender. Civilized man had exchanged a portion of his possibilities of happiness for a portion of security. We must not forget, however, that in the primal family only the head of it enjoyed this instinctual freedom; the rest lived in slavish suppression. In that primal period of civilization, the contrast between a minority who enjoyed the advantages of civilization and a majority who were robbed of those advantages was, therefore, carried to extremes. As regards the primitive peoples who exist today, careful researches have shown that their instinctual life is by no means to be envied for its freedom. It is subject to restrictions of a different kind but perhaps of greater severity than those attaching to modern civilized man.

## Psychoanalytic Theory, the Aggressive Instinct, and Civilization

In none of my previous writings have I had so strong a feeling as now that what I am describing is common knowledge and that I am using up paper and ink . . . to expound things which are, in fact, self-evident. For that reason I should be glad to seize the point if it were to appear that the recognition of a special, independent aggressive instinct means an alteration of the psychoanalytic theory of the instincts.

We shall see, however, that this is not so and that it is merely a matter of bringing into sharper focus a turn of thought arrived at long ago and of following out its consequences. Of all the slowly developed parts of analytic theory, the theory of the instincts is the one that has felt its way the most painfully forward.[7] And yet that theory was so indispensable to the whole structure that something had to be put in its place. I took as my starting point a saying of the poet-philosopher, Schiller, that 'hunger and love are what move the world'. Hunger could be taken to represent the instincts which aim at preserving the individual; while love strives after objects, and its chief function, favoured in every way by nature, is the preservation of the species. Thus, to begin with, ego-instincts and object-instincts confronted each other. It was to denote the energy of the latter and only the latter instincts that I introduced the term 'libido'. Thus the antithesis was between the ego-instincts and the 'libidinal' instincts of love (in its widest sense) which were directed to an object. One of these object-instincts, the sadistic instinct, stood out from the rest, it is true, in that its aim was so very far from being loving. Moreover it was obviously in some respects attached to the ego-instincts; it could not hide its close affinity with instincts of mastery which have no libidinal purpose. But these discrepancies were got over; after all, sadism was clearly a part of sexual life, in the activities of which affection could be replaced by cruelty. Neurosis was regarded as the outcome of a struggle between the interest of self-preservation and the demands of the libido, a struggle in which the ego had been victorious but at the price of severe sufferings and renunciations.

Every analyst will admit that even today this view has not the sound of a long-discarded error. Nevertherless, alterations in it became essential, as our enquiries advanced from the repressed to the repressing forces, from the object instincts to the ego.

Starting from speculations on the beginning of life and from biological parallels, I drew the conclusion that, besides the instinct to preserve living substance and to join it into ever larger units,[8] there must exist another, contrary instinct seeking to dissolve those units and to bring them back to their primaeval, inorganic state. That is to say, as well as Eros there was an instinct of death. The phenomena of life could be explained from the concurrent or mutually opposing action of these two instincts. It was not easy, however, to demonstrate the activities of this supposed death instinct. The manifestations of Eros were conspicuous and noisy enough. It might be assumed that the death instinct operated silently within the organism towards its dissolution, but that, of course, was no proof. A more fruitful idea was that a portion of the instinct is diverted towards the external world and comes to light as an instinct of aggressiveness and destructiveness. In this way the instinct itself could be pressed into the service of Eros, in that the organism was destroying some other thing, whether animate or inanimate, instead of destroying its own self. Conversely, any restriction of this aggressiveness directed outwards would be bound to increase the self-destruction, which is in any case proceeding.

I know that in sadism and masochism we have always seen before us manifestations of the destructive instinct (directed outwards and inwards), strongly alloyed with eroticism; but I can no longer understand how we can have overlooked the ubiquity of non-erotic aggressivity and destructiveness and can have failed to give it its due course in our interpretations of life . . . I remember my own defensive attitude when the idea of an instinct of destruction first emerged in psychoanalytic literature, and how long it took before I became receptive to it.

The name 'libido' can once more be used to denote the manifestations of the power of Eros in order to distinguish them from the energy of the death instinct.[9] It must be confessed that we have much greater difficulty in grasping that instinct; we can only suspect it, as it were, as something in the background behind Eros, and it escapes detection unless its presence is betrayed by its being allowed with Eros. It is in sadism, where the death instinct twists the erotic aim in its own sense and yet at the same time fully satisfies the erotic urge, that we succeed in obtaining the clearest insight into its nature and its relation to Eros. But even where it emerges without any sexual purpose, in the blindest fury of destructiveness, we cannot fail to recognize that the satisfaction of the instinct is accompanied by an extraordinarily high degree of narcissistic enjoyment, owing to its presenting the ego with a fulfillment of the latter's old wishes for omnipotence. The instinct of destruction, moderated and tamed, and, as it were, inhibited in its aim, must, when it is directed towards objects, provide the ego with the satisfaction of its vital needs and with control over nature.

In all that follows I adopt the standpoint, therefore, that the inclination to aggression is an original, self-subsisting instinctual disposition in man, and I return to my view that it constitutes the greatest impediment to civilization. At one point in the course of this enquiry I was led to the idea that civilization was a special process which mankind undergoes, and I am still under the influence of that idea. I may now add that civilization is a process in the service of Eros, whose purpose is to combine single human individuals, and after that families, then races, peoples, and nations, into one great unity, the unity of mankind. Why this has to happen, we do not know; the work of Eros is precisely this.[10] These collections of men are to be libidinally bound to one another. Necessity alone, the advantages of work in common, will not hold them together. But man's natural aggressive instinct, the hostility of each against all and of all against each, opposes this program of civilization. This aggressive instinct is the derivative and the main representative of the death instinct which we have found alongside of Eros and which shares world-dominion with it. And now, I think, the meaning of the evolution of civilization is no longer obscure to us. It must present the struggle between Eros and Death, between the instinct of life and the instinct of destruction, as it works itself out in the human species. This struggle is what all life essentially consists of, and the evolution of civilization may therefore be simply described as the struggle for life of the human species.[11]

The fateful question for the human species seems to me to be whether and to what extent their cultural development will succeed in mastering the disturbance of their communal life by the human instinct of aggression and self-destruction. It may be that in this respect precisely the present time deserves a special interest. Men have gained control over the forces of nature to such an extent that with their help they would have no difficulty in exterminating one another to the last man. They know this, and hence comes a large part of the current unrest, their unhappiness, and their mood of anxiety. And now it is to be expected that the other of the two 'Heavenly Powers', eternal Eros, will make an effort to assert himself in the struggle with his equally immortal adversary. But who can foresee with what success and with what result?[12]

## Notes

1. In view of Freud's sweeping pronouncement ('I scorn to distinguish between culture and civilization') and of a similar remark towards the end of 'Why War?', it seems unnecessary to embark on the tiresome problem of the proper translation of the German word 'Kultur'. We have usually, but not invariably, chosen 'civilization' for the noun and 'cultural' for the adjective. [From Editor's Note to *The Future of an Illusion* (1927) translated in S. Freud, Standard Edition (24 volumes), London and New York, from 1953.]
2. See *The Future of an Illusion* (1927).
3. Cf. *The Future of an Illusion* (1927).
4. Freud returns to the subject of civilizations as a 'process' . . . in his open letter to Einstein, *Why War?* (1933) in S. Freud, Collected Papers (5 volumes), London, 1924–1950.
5. ' "Civilized" Sexual Morality' (1908), *Standard Ed.*, 9, 199.
6. 'Man is a wolf to man'. Derived from Plautus, *Asinaria* II, iv, 88.
7. Some account of the history of Freud's theory of the instincts will be found in the Editor's Note to his paper 'Instincts and Their Vicissitudes' (1915), *Standard Ed.*, 14, 113 ff.
8. The opposition which thus emerges between the ceaseless trend by Eros towards extension and the general conservative nature of the instincts is striking, and it may become the starting point for the study of further problems.
9. Our present point of view can be roughly expressed in the statement that libido has a share in every instinctual manifestation, but that not everything in that manifestation is libido.
10. See *Beyond the Pleasure Principle* (1920), translated in S. Freud, Standard Edition, 18, 3.
11. And we may probably add more precisely, a struggle for life in the shape it was bound to assume after a certain event which still remains to be discovered.
12. The final sentence was added in 1931—when the menace of Hitler was already beginning to be apparent.

## Introduction

Heitzeg's focus in this article is on disorders usually diagnosed in infancy, childhood, and adolescence. It is the largest category of disorders in the American Psychiatric Association's manual of mental illnesses. What does this mean? And how can we account for it?

However, the article is also about the social institution of psychiatry and its involvement in social control as much as the treatment of mental illness. What are the key characteristics of psychiatry as a social institution? What role does psychiatry perform in the socialization and control of young people? Finally, to what extent can conflict theories, such as those based on the work of Karl Marx, Max Weber (pluralist conflict theory), or Foucault's theory of moral regulation help us understand Heitzeg's discussion of the psychiatric diagnosis and treatment of disorders among young people as well as the social organization of psychiatry itself?

# Medical Deviance and DICA: Disorders Usually First Diagnosed in Infancy, Childhood, or Adolescence

*Nancy Heitzeg*

It is fitting that the Disorders Usually First Diagnosed in Infancy, Childhood, or Adolescence (DICA) is the first and largest diagnostic category in the DSMIV. Its placement and inclusivity clearly illustrate the discretion inherent in the medical model, as well as the pervasive overlap with other models of social control. All the diagnostic categories included in DICA are simultaneously subject to the informal social control of family, school, or media, as well as the formal social control of the juvenile justice system. Further, it is an indicator of the nature and extent to which juveniles are subject to an ever-widening net of norms and sanctions.

The disorders included in this diagnostic category fall into several general subclassifications: mental retardation; learning disorders; motor skills disorders; communications disorders; pervasive developmental disorders; attention-deficit and disruptive behaviour disorders; feeding and eating disorders of infancy or early childhood; tic disorders; elimination disorders; and other disorders of infancy, childhood, or adolescence.[1] In earlier editions of *Diagnostic and Statistical Manual of Mental Disorders*, eating disorders (i.e., anorexia nervosa and bulimia nervosa) and gender identity disorders were also included in DICA. The justification was the earlier age of onset for these disorders. Although these two disorders are now primarily in adult diagnoses, they still are believed to be rooted in childhood or adolescent experiences. Further, many adults receive diagnoses which are listed in DICA; this is especially true for the attention-deficit disorders. Juveniles may additionally be diagnosed with any other disorder listed in DSMIV. Frequently they are diagnosed with substance-use or manic-depressive disorders. This DSMIV classification, then, is not limited to juveniles; its title is based on the assumption that these disorders are usually first diagnosed in infancy, childhood, or adolescence.

The DICA category encompasses an incredible range of problematic conditions. Everything from severe retardation to slight difficulties with math is included here. Discretion and the scope of medical model control is further maximized by the fact that what constitutes many of these disorders might actually be indicative of typical childhood or adolescent behaviours. For example, we might expect most children to exhibit anxiety over separation from their loved one, or many adolescents to undergo distress over identity, popularity, and career goals. It is difficult to imagine how one might clearly distinguish the 'normal' developmental process from mental illness.

This diagnostic category is further complicated by the almost perfect overlap that exists between these disorders and the informal and formal models of social control. Much of what is included here, especially those disorders involving disruptive behaviour or development, is fundamentally related to informal relations with family or at school. Still others have as their primary symptomology evidence of legal violations and disregard for formal rules. Trouble at home, school, or with the law becomes the diagnostic criteria for a mental illness. This is overlap in the most complete sense.

The discretion and overlap that characterize DICA is yet another example of the rule-laden status of juveniles. The young have more rules—informal, medical, formal—than any other social group. They are subject to the informal social control of family and school, the organizational co-optation, stereotyping, and censorship of media, the all-encompassing diagnostic categories of DSMIV, and the complete array of administrative, civil, and criminal law. The multitude of norms governing youth in each model merges and overlaps to create a seamless web of social control. This is evidenced by the juvenile justice system, which draws from all three models to expand the rules that further limit the rights of juveniles. Whether such extensive social control is warranted is beside the point. It will soon be clear that the combined approach of informal, medical, and formal control mechanisms results in the near total subjugation of juveniles to the rules. It is to these youth-oriented rules—first medical, then the overlapping informal and formal—that we now turn.

## Societal Reaction to DICA

The conditions and associated behaviours enumerated in the DICA category may be defined and controlled as deviant medically, informally, or formally. While many were once controlled exclusively by informal mechanisms, and later by law, the medical model presently has simultaneous jurisdiction over all these problems of youth. Each of these models of social control, and the norms and sanctions they apply to juveniles, will be examined in detail.

## Medical Definition and Control of DICA

DSMIV's definition of the Disorders Usually First Diagnosed in Infancy, Childhood, and Adolescence includes a broad range of conditions. These disorders may vary in their severity and longevity. Some represent rather minimal problems; others, pervasive and severely debilitating disorders. Some of these disorders are short-lived, while others are persistent conditions that never result in full recovery.

As already noted, the DICA classification includes several subcategories of disorders, which will be discussed in the following pages.

## Disorders Related to Development: Mental Retardation, Learning Disorders, Motor Skills Disorders, Communication Disorders, Pervasive Developmental Disorders

The developmental disorders involve some disturbance in the 'acquisition of cognitive language, motor, or social skills'. The developmental delay may be general, involving an overall lack of normal progress, or it may be limited to a specific area of skill acquisition. All these disorders have their onset before age 18, although many may appear in very early childhood. The developmental disorders include several specific conditions. Included are mental retardation, learning disorders, communication disorders, motor skills disorders, and the pervasive developmental disorders.

The essential features of mental retardation are 'significantly subaverage general intellectual functioning' with impairments in social skills, communication, and daily living skills. Onset must be before the age of 18, and may be further evidenced by lack of personal independence and social responsibility. Degree of severity is measured by standard IQ levels, and may be mild (IQ 50–55 to 70), moderate (IQ 35–40 to 50–55), severe (IQ 20–25 to 35–40), or profound (IQ below 20 or 25).

Other developmental disorders are less pervasive and severe. This subset of disorders refers to developmental delays in specific areas: learning, motor skills, and communication. The difficulties detailed here are much less pervasive and problematic than with other developmental disorders. The learning disorders involve arithmetic, expressive writing, or reading 'skills, as measured by a standardized, individually administered test, markedly below the expected level'. The communication disorders are similarly diagnosed by standardized measures, and include delays in articulation, as well as expressive and receptive language. And, finally, the motor skills disorder is defined as marked impairment in the development of motor coordination.

These disorders represent very specific intellectual and physical conditions that may affect at least 10 per cent of school-age children. It is important to remember that diagnostic criteria are based on standardized measures that may be flawed. In addition, these developmental delays, however problematic, often seem to run their course without psychiatric intervention. Viewing them as 'mental illnesses' must be questioned. Being behind in one's reading skills, for example, certainly seems very different from hearing strange voices who instruct you to kill. Earlier editions of DSM even acknowledged this point: 'The inclusion of these categories in a classification of 'mental disorders' is controversial, since many children with these disorders have no other signs of psychopathology. Further, the detection and treatment of many of these disorders usually take place within schools rather than the mental health system.

The pervasive development disorders are characterized by significant social and physical underdevelopment. The essential feature of these disorders is the qualitative impairment of reciprocal social interaction, in the development of verbal and non-verbal communication skills, and in imaginative activity. Onset usually occurs before age three, and may also be associated with abnormalities in cognitive skills, posture and motor behaviour, odd responses to sensory input, self-injurious behaviour, and abnormalities in eating, drinking, sleeping, and mood. Included are autism (i.e., markedly abnormal development in social interaction and communication with a restricted repertoire of activity); Rett's disorder (i.e., abnormal physical, motor, and social development); childhood disintegrative disorder (i.e., regression in physical, communicative, and social development after two years of normal progress); Aspergers's disorder (i.e., severe and sustained impairment in social interaction and the development of restricted, repetitive patterns of behaviour, interests, and activities), and unspecified pervasive developmental disorders.

## Attention–Deficit and Disruptive Behaviour Disorders

These disorders are 'characterized by behaviour that is socially disruptive and is often more distressing to others than to the people with the disorders'. Included here are *attention deficit hyperactivity disorder (ADHD), oppositional defiant disorder, and conduct disorder.* The symptoms of these disorders essentially constitute rule-breaking behaviour, i.e., violations of the informal norms of home or school and activities that are status or criminal offences.

Attention deficit hyperactivity disorder is characterized by varying degrees of inattention, impulsiveness, and hyperactivity. The onset of ADHD is usually before age four, although one-third of those affected may continue to exhibit symptoms throughout adulthood. DSMIV indicates that ADHD may be anywhere from three to nine times more common in males than in females. Symptoms may disrupt social interaction at home, school, work, and among peers. Symptoms include fidgeting, distractibility, impatience, short attention span, difficulty in following instructions, and lack of recognition of danger. See Table 20.1.

The symptoms of conduct disorder are violations of formal rules, especially the criminal law. Juvenile status offences are also included. In many respects, it also parallels the adult anti-social personality disorder. DSMIV notes that unchecked conduct disorders may develop into adult anti-social personality disorder. Further, children of adults with anti-social personalities are much more likely to be diagnosed with conduct disorders. Conduct disorder may also be linked with substance-use disorders and ADHD. Again, diagnoses are nearly five times more common for males than for females. Conduct problems include stealing, lying, running away from home, truancy, arson, and cruelty. See Table 20.2.

## Table 20.1 Diagnostic Criteria for Attention-Deficit Hyperactivity Disorder

A.   Either (1) or (2):

(1)  six (or more) of the following symptoms of inattention have persisted for at least 6 months to a degree that is maladaptive and inconsistent with developmental level:

*Inattention:*
(a)  often fails to give close attention to details or makes careless mistakes in schoolwork, work, or other activities
(b)  often has difficulty sustaining attention in tasks or play activities
(c)  often does not seem to listen when spoken to directly
(d)  often does not follow through on instructions and fails to finish schoolwork, chores, or duties in the workplace (not due to oppositional behaviour or failure to understand instructions)
(e)  often has difficulty organizing tasks and activities
(f)  often avoids, dislikes, or is reluctant to engage in tasks that require sustained mental effort (such as schoolwork or homework)
(g)  often loses things necessary for tasks or activities (e.g., toys, school assignments, pencils, books, or tools)
(h)  is often easily distracted by extraneous stimuli
(i)  is often forgetful in daily activities

(2)  six (or more) of the following symptoms of **hyperactivity–impulsivity** have persisted for at least 6 months to a degree that is maladaptive and inconsistent with developmental level:

*Hyperactivity:*
(a)  often fidgets with hands or feet or squirms in seat
(b)  often leaves seat in classroom or in other situations in which remaining seated is expected
(c)  often runs about or climbs excessively in situations in which it is inappropriate (in adolescents or adults, may be limited to subjective feelings of restlessness)
(d)  often has difficulty playing or engaging in leisure activities quietly
(e)  is often "on the go" or often acts if "driven by a motor"
(f)  often talks excessively

*Impulsivity:*
(g)  often blurts out answers before questions have been completed
(h)  often has difficulty awaiting turn
(i)  often interrupts or intrudes on others (e.g., butts into conversations or games)

B.   Some hyperactive-impulsive or inattentive symptoms that caused impairment were present before age 7 years.

C.   Some impairment from the symptoms is present in two or more settings (e.g., at school [or work] and at home).

D.   There must be clear evidence of clinically significant impairment in social, academic, or occupational functioning.

E.   The symptoms do not occur exclusively during the course of a Pervasive Developmental Disorder, Schizophrenia, or other Psychotic Disorder and are not better accounted for by another mental disorder (e.g., Mood Disorder, Anxiety Disorder, Dissociative Disorder, or a Personality Disorder).

*Code* based on type:

**314.01 Attention–Deficit/Hyperactivity Disorder, Combined Type:** if both Criteria A1 and A2 are met for the past 6 months.

**Table 20.1** (Continued)

**314.00 Attention–Deficit/Hyperactivity Disorder, Predominantly Inattentive Type:** if Criterion A1 is met but Criterion A2 is not met for the past 6 months.

**314.01 Attention Deficit/Hyperactivity Disorder, Predominantly Hyperactive-Impulsive Type:** if Criterion A2 is met but Criterion A1 is not met for the past 6 months.

**Coding Note:** For individuals (especially adolescents and adults) who currently have symptoms that no longer meet full criteria. "In Partial Remission" should be specified.

**Source:** American Psychiatric Association, *Diagnostic and Statistical Manual of Mental Disorders*, 4th edition (Washington, DC: APA, 1994), pp. 83–85.

Oppositional defiant disorder is characterized by a pattern of lesser rule-breaking behaviour. The symptoms here involve the violations of informal norms, particularly those related to social interaction with parents, other adults, and peers. Onset is usually in adolescence, with symptoms more evident in interactions with adults the child knows well. Substance-use disorders and ADHD again might be associated. The symptoms are indicative of what many might term 'typical' adolescent behaviour, and, interestingly enough, DSMIV notes that 'children with the disorder are likely to show little or no signs of the disorder when examined critically'. The symptoms include a short temper, argumentativeness, defiance, resentment, and a refusal to accept rules and to accept responsibility for their behaviour—some might say, the typical teenager. See Table 20.3.

# Eating Disorders

The *eating disorders* involve disturbances in eating behaviour. Until DSMIV, DSM included anorexia nervosa and bulimia nervosa in this subclassification. Pica and rumination disorder of infancy are primarily disorders of very young children, and are equally prevalent among both sexes. Pica is usually a disorder of infants or very young children, and involves repeatedly 'eating nonnutritive substances, such as paint, plaster, string'. Similarly, rumination disorder of infancy involves disturbance in the very young, characterized by 'repeated regurgitation, without nausea or associated gastrointestinal illness'.

# Tic Disorders

These disorders are characterized by tics, 'involuntary, sudden, rapid, recurrent, nonrhythmic, stereotyped, motor movements or vocalizations'. Tics feel as if they are irresistible, are made worse under stress, and may be simple or complex. Children who suffer from tics may have had head trauma or central nervous system abnormalities. Tics, whether chronic or transient, are three times more common in males than in females. Onset may be as early as age one or as late as age 21. They may be short-lived or lifelong.

**Table 20.2** Diagnostic Criteria for 312.8 Conduct Disorder

A.  A repetitive and persistent pattern of behaviour in which the basic rights of others or major age-appropriate societal norms or rules are violated, as manifested by the presence of three (or more) of the following criteria in the past 12 months, with at least one criterion present in the past 6 months:

*Aggression to people and animals*
(1)  often bullies, threatens, or intimidates others
(2)  often initiates physical fights
(3)  has used a weapon that can cause serious physical harm to others (e.g., a bat, brick, broken bottle, knife, gun)
(4)  has been physically cruel to people
(5)  has been physically cruel to animals
(6)  has stolen while confronting a victim (e.g., mugging, purse snatching, extortion, armed robbery)
(7)  has forced someone into sexual activity

*Destruction of property*
(8)  has deliberately engaged in fire setting with the intention of causing serious damage
(9)  has deliberately destroyed others' property (other than by fire setting)

*Deceitfulness or theft*
(10)  has broken into someone else's house, building, or car
(11)  often lies to obtain goods or favours or to avoid obligations (i.e., "cons" others)
(12)  has stolen items of nontrivial values without confronting a victim (e.g., shoplifting, but without breaking and entering; forgery)

*Serious violations of rules*
(13)  often stays out at night despite parental prohibitions, beginning before age 13 years
(14)  has run away from home overnight at least twice while living in parental or parental surrogate home (or once without returning for a lengthy period)
(15)  is often truant from school, beginning before age 13 years

B.  The disturbance in behaviour causes clinically significant impairment in social, academic, or occupational functioning.

C.  If the individual is age 18 years or older, criteria are not met for Antisocial Personality Disorder.

*Specify type based on age at onset:*
**Childhood–Onset Type:** onset of at least one criterion characteristic of Conduct Disorder prior to age 10 years
**Adolescent–Onset Type:** absence of any criteria characteristic of Conduct Disorder prior to age 10 years

*Specify severity:*
**Mild:** few if any conduct problems in excess of those required to make the diagnosis and conduct problems cause only minor harm to others
**Moderate:** number of conduct problems and effect on others intermediate between "mild" and "severe"
**Severe:** many conduct problems in excess of those required to make the diagnosis or conduct problems cause considerable harm to other

**Source:** American Psychiatric Association, *Diagnostic and Statistical Manual of Mental Disorders*, 4th edition (Washington, DC: APA, 1994), pp. 90–91.

**Table 20.3** Diagnostic Criteria for Oppositional Defiant Disorder

A. A pattern of negativistic, hostile, and defiant behaviour lasting at least 6 months, during which four (or more) of the following are present:

(1) often loses temper
(2) often argues with adults
(3) often actively defies or refuses to comply with adults' requests or rules
(4) often deliberately annoys people
(5) often blames others for his or her mistakes or misbehaviour
(6) is often touchy or easily annoyed by others
(7) is often angry or resentful
(8) is often spiteful or vindictive
(9) has deliberately destroyed others' property (other than by fire setting)

B. The disturbance in behaviour causes clinically significant impairments in social, academic, or occupational functioning.

C. The behaviours do not occur exclusively during the course of a Psychotic or Mood Disorder.

D. Criteria are not met for Conduct Disorder, and, if the individual is age 18 years or older, criteria are not met for Antisocial Personality Disorder.

Note: Consider a criterion met only if the behaviour occurs more frequently than is typically observed in individuals of comparable age and development level.

Source: American Psychiatric Association, *Diagnostic and Statistical Manual of Mental Disorders*, 4th edition (Washington, DC: APA, 1994), pp. 93–94.

## Elimination Disorders

The two disorders cited here—functional encopresis and functional enuresis—are essentially toilet training issues. The elimination disorders are defined as involuntary and repeated defecation and urination into 'places not appropriate for that purpose (e.g., clothing or floor)'.

## Other Disorders of Infancy, Childhood, or Adolescence

As usual, DSMIV has a residual category for disorders not classified elsewhere. Identity disorder is one of the minor and typical childhood responses as mental illness. Reactive attachment disorder describes a condition that results from child abuse or neglect.

Identity disorder is characterized by 'severe subjective distress regarding uncertainty about a variety of issues relating to identity, including three or more of the following: Long-term goals, career choice, friendship patterns, sexual orientation and behaviour, religious identification, moral value systems, or group 'loyalties'. Impairment in social or occupational (including academic) functioning is a result of the symptoms.

Reactive attachment disorder of infancy or early childhood describes a condition that results from abuse or neglect. Such a child would have a markedly disturbed ability to relate to others and would have received harsh or negligent child care. As usual, DSMIV has a residual category for disorders not classified elsewhere. Included are separation anxiety disorder (i.e., excessive anxiety concerning separation from home); selective mutism (i.e., consistent failure to speak in specific social situations); stereotypic movement disorder (i.e., repetitive, non-functional motor behaviour); and reactive attachment disorder (i.e., disturbed and inappropriate social interaction as a result of abuse or neglect).

Almost any conceivable behaviour or condition of infancy, childhood, or adolescence might potentially result in a psychiatric diagnosis. DSMIV's definition of these disorders is broad enough to encompass everything from severe retardation to a mild stutter, from autism to occasional bedwetting, from anxiety to adolescent rebellion. If, indeed, DSMIV's definitional scope is warranted, are there any youth who are *not* mentally ill? And, if all youth are ill, doesn't the medical distinction between ill and well lose all meaning? Are all these conditions really comparable, i.e., do we need to distinguish between issues related to physical development and those of a cognitive or social nature? Are all these conditions really 'illnesses', i.e., do they really have an objective cause and a potential medical cure? And, are all these conditions really problems, i.e., might at least some be a reasonable response to an endless array of rules and adult-inflicted pressures to conform and comply?

Even the APA acknowledges that it may be 'controversial' to refer to some of these conditions as 'mental disorders'. Being below one's reading level or refusing to clean one's room may be problematic, but it is difficult to imagine that psychiatric intervention is warranted. And, given labelling theories' concern over the impact of societal reaction on self-concept, one might wonder if psychiatric diagnoses for such commonplace and minimal difficulties might actually do more harm than good. Perhaps there are alternatives to the medicalization of childhood deviance that might be effective for dealing with conditions outlined by DICA.

The inherent difficulties with this diagnostic category is complicated by the medical model's lack of context. Under some conditions, the conditions and behaviour entailed in DICA might not be deviant at all. Consider, for example, the case of oppositional defiant disorder. If the youth in question lives in a situation where he or she is subject to abuse and/or neglect, might we not expect—even encourage—anger, annoyance, arguments, and defiance of adult requests or rules? A comparable illustration might be made with reference to the attention deficit hyperactivity disorder. Is this really a mental illness or a response to situational contingencies? Fidgeting, distractibility, talking or blurting out answers to questions, and interrupting might just as well be responses to a boring, overstructured, understimulating classroom setting. Implicit in DICA, and throughout much of the social control of youth, is the assumption that adults and their rules are always right, and that children or adolescents who question them are always wrong. This may not be the case.

The medical model's control and treatment of DICA also raises questions. First and foremost is the highly controlled age status of the clients. Unlike adults who often voluntarily seek psychiatric treatment, juveniles are almost universally referred by adults: parents, teachers, or juvenile justice personnel. Their entrance into the medical model is involuntary. The juvenile in American society has severely curtailed rights. Juveniles do not have the right to refuse psychiatric treatment. Here, as in the juvenile justice system, it is assumed that any adult's estimation of the problems and required course of social control is valid. To quote Supreme Court Justice William Rehnquist, '[Juveniles] unlike adults are always in a state of custody'.[2] It matters little whether that custody is centred at home, at a psychiatric facility, or in a court-ordered juvenile detention centre. Part of the social meaning of juvenile is that one is never fully free, but is always subject to the overarching adult control: informal, medical, or formal. Juveniles who are diagnosed and treated for DICA have no choice of or input into their treatment.

Those who receive a DICA diagnosis are primarily treated with somatic therapy, institutionalization (both public and private), and individual behaviour modification techniques. Often, these treatment options are used in combination.

The primary somatic treatment of DICA is the administration of psychotropic medications. Its most widespread use is the treatment of attention deficit hyperactivity disorder (ADHD). The use of drugs to treat this disorder actually predates the diagnostic category itself. (Prior to 1957, ADHD was more generally referred to as a 'childhood behaviour disorder'. Initially, it applied to impulsive, overactive children, but it has been broadened to include those who do not pay attention. Female teenagers and even adults are now more likely to receive this diagnosis. A support group for children and adults with attention deficit disorder—CHADD—claims 28,000 members nationwide.[3]) The disruptive behaviour and learning difficulties associated with ADHD were first treated with amphetamines in 1937.[4] Charles Bradley noted the 'paradoxical' effect stimulants had on hyperactive children; rather than becoming more active, they were subdued. The development of Ritalin (a stimulant with amphetamine-like qualities, but few side effects) in the mid-1950s paved the way for the widespread treatment of ADHD with drugs. Since its FDA approval in 1961 for use with children, Ritalin has become the treatment of choice for ADHD diagnoses. ADHD is now the most common childhood psychiatric problem; anywhere from three per cent to 20 per cent of all elementary and secondary students have been labelled ADHD. The rate of treatment for this disorder has been doubling every four to seven years, and as many as 750,000 children are being treated with Ritalin; in the past four years, prescriptions for Ritalin have increased 390 per cent.[5] Its use continues, despite psychiatry's inability to pinpoint any biological basis for ADHD, or even to fully understand exactly why Ritalin produces calming effects in hyperactive children.

The use of Ritalin is not without controversy. Many have argued that it is overused and serves as a mere social control mechanism, rather than an effective treatment. Indeed, school personnel have been shown to have a much looser definition of ADHD than have medical professionals.[6] It is possible that these recommendations for ADHD diagnosis and treatment are based on the self-serving motive of behaviour control. Others have expressed concern over Ritalin's sometimes negative side effects. Lawsuits totalling millions of dollars have been filed nationwide on behalf of parents who claim their children have been adversely affected. It has been charged that Ritalin numbed children's senses and produced insomnia, loss of appetite, and psychotic episodes. Still others suggest that ADHD is a set of symptoms, not a disease per se. Consequently, it is argued, ADHD should be treated holistically (i.e., through chiropractic and diet) to get to the root of the problem.[7]

Despite these objections, the APA still advocates the use of Ritalin as the treatment of choice for ADHD. Psychotropic medications also are used in the treatment of other DICA diagnoses. Antidepressants, antipsychotics, and sedatives are frequently prescribed for juveniles. These medications are used for the treatment of several DICA conditions, as well as for other

DSMIV diagnoses that juveniles may additionally receive: schizophrenia, mood disorders, obsessive-compulsive disorders, anxiety disorders, and substance-use disorders. The question of whether psychotropic medications are an effective treatment for mental illness or just a mechanism for behavioural control is always open; it is particularly relevant in regard to the treatment of adolescents. Evidence shows that prescriptions are used too readily, as a first rather than last resort, and inordinately used for such conditions as conduct disorders.[8] Further, these medications are most frequently used for juveniles in conjunction with institutionalization, a fact that lends credence to the argument that psychotropic drugs may be used to control rather than treat.

Institutionalization is another increasingly popular approach to the treatment of DICA. Throughout the 1970s and 1980s, juvenile admissions to psychiatric facilities doubled. Juvenile admissions to both public and private institutions totalled over 270,000. Much of this increase is accounted for by admissions to private hospitals. In 1971, 7,668 juveniles were admitted to such facilities; by 1988, that number had increased to over 99,000.[9] In 1992, an additional 135,000 youths were admitted to in-patient treatment facilities for alcohol and drug use.

While adults are usually institutionalized for serious psychotic episodes, substance use, or other obsessive-compulsive disorders, juveniles are often hospitalized for much lesser disorders. Conduct and oppositional defiant disorders are a common reason for institutionalization. Presently, symptoms may be as minimal as the 'out-of-control behaviour' cited on an actual patient chart: '1) Refusing to contribute to the family, 2) Dirty clothes left out, 3) Dirty room, 4) Consistent antagonism'.[10] While such quintessential adolescent behaviour may warrant societal reaction, it is unlikely that institutionalization in a psychiatric facility is necessary.

The minor disorders for which juveniles are committed are only part of the problem. Failure of informal social control mechanisms at home or at school, in conjunction with the high-pressure, profit-motive approach of many private hospitals, may be the two largest contributors to the dramatic rise in juvenile admissions to psychiatric hospitals. Juveniles are most likely to be committed by their parents.[11] Because they are minors, this is viewed as voluntary commitment, regardless of the juvenile's wishes. It is subsequently exceedingly easy for parents to commit a 'problem child'; the child has no legal standing to review their admission, nor the freedom to leave.

Parents are often encouraged to commit children to private facilities via fear-inducing advertising and pressures to commit rather than seek outpatient options. Considering that such institutional treatment may cost as much as $27,000 per month, it is not surprising that referral often means automatic admittance. The number of clients admitted increases the amount of money paid to the institutions. The argument that all of this is really done only for the best interests of the child is further weakened by an analysis of insurance coverage on length of stay. Children and adolescents with private insurance remained in private hospitals an average of 32 to 38 days; those covered by HMOs stayed an average of approximately 16 days; those covered by Medicaid/Medicare stayed an average of 13 days; while juveniles with no coverage remained only about 10 days on average.[12] In other words, a patient's length of stay seems determined *not* by need but by their insurance benefits. This would seem to indicate that profit, combined with parental inability to exert effective social control, lies at the root of increased juvenile psychiatric admissions. Psychiatric institutionalization may not be appropriate for dealing with the juvenile's problem; it is, however, a simple and lucrative solution for the attendant adults.

Juveniles are also treated with behaviour modification therapies. These may often be used in concert with psychotropic medications or institutionalization. This approach has been applied to the treatment of disruptive behaviours and elimination disorders, as well as juvenile cases of obsessive-compulsive behaviour and substance use.[13] Positive and negative reinforcement involving token economic tier systems and punishments have all been tried. Behaviour modification of juvenile psychiatric problems may be individually oriented; more often, however, a group approach involving family or peers is preferred. While behaviour modification may result in the reduction of original symptoms, it does not address the underlying causes for the juvenile's behaviour.

Finally, DSMIV's developmental disorders, especially learning disorders and communication disorders, are not technically treated by psychiatrists. These disorders are most often dealt with within the context of the school system. Special-education sections and speech therapy are the major methods of addressing these developmental delays.

The Disorders Usually First Diagnosed in Infancy, Childhood, and Adolescence, then, encompass a monumental range of behaviours and conditions that are treated with a variety of therapies. Discretion is maximized here; almost any child potentially could be labelled with this diagnostic category. Juveniles are vulnerable to unchallenged medical model control.

## Notes

1. American Psychiatric Association, *Diagnostic and Statistical Manual of Mental Disorder*, 4th edition (Washington, DC: APA, 1994). All subsequent quotations or references to APA or DSMIV are to this edition.
2. Michael S. Serrell, 'Reining in Juveniles and Aliens: The High Court Rules in Preventive Detention and Deportation', *Time*, 18 June 1984, p. 76; *Schall v. Martin*, 104 S. CT. 2403 (1984).
3. Peter Conrad and Joseph W. Schneider, *Deviance and Medicalization: From Badness to Sickness*, reprint of the 1980 edition (Philadelphia: Temple University Press, 1992), pp. 156–161; Claudia Wallis, 'Life in Overdrive', *Time*, 8 July 1994, pp. 43–50.
4. Conrad and Schneider, *Deviance and Medicalization*, p. 156; C.A. Bradley, 'The Behaviour of Children Receiving Benzedrine', *American Journal of Psychiatry*, 30 (November 1937): 577–588.
5. Conrad and Schneider, *Deviance and Medicalization*, pp. 156–157, 285; Doctors of Chiropractic International, 'What Have They Done to Our Children?' *The Spinal Column*, January/February 1989, p. 2; D.J. Safer and Joe Krager, 'A Survey of Medication Treatments for Hyperactive/Inattentive Students', *Journal of the American Medical Association*, 260 (1988): 2256–2259; Wallis, 'Life in Overdrive'.
6. Conrad and Schneider, *Deviance and Medicalization*, p. 285.
7. DCI, 'What Have They Done?' p. 2.
8. Conrad and Schneider, *Deviance and Medicalization*, p. 158; Katherine Barrett and Richard Green, 'Mom, Get Me Out of Here!' *Ladies Home Journal*, May 1990, pp. 98–106.
9. Lisa A. Merkel-Holguin, *The Child Welfare Stat Book 1993* (Washington, DC: The Child Welfare League of America Inc., 1993); Barrett and Green, 'Mom, Get Me Out of Here', p. 103.
10. Ibid., p. 104.
11. Ibid.
12. Ibid., p. 103.
13. Ibid., p. 104; Conrad and Schneider, *Deviance and Medicalization*, pp. 231–235.

## 21

### Introduction

Rosenhan's classic study of schizophrenia and psychiatric hospitals challenges the commonsense belief that we can easily distinguish the normal from the abnormal, the sane from the insane. Or that if 'we' can't, the 'professionals' can. But as he tells us, *the evidence is simply not compelling*.

The article illustrates the importance of Howard Becker's work on labelling and its place in the process of defining and controlling deviance. Labelling is not just calling someone a name. It is an evaluative practice that both describes and explains a behaviour by attributing a quality to the individual, especially to the individual's character. Once the category is applied, it becomes the basis for social expectations about the individual, provides a framework for interpreting their behaviours, and justifies our treatment of them. For example, as a label 'vagrant' is not just a description of an individual who is homeless and living off handouts; it also carries with it an implicit explanation of why the individual lives this way. There's something about the individual's moral nature or character that leads them not to live as people normally do.

So how did the diagnosis of 'schizophrenia' operate as a label in the psychiatric hospitals that Rosenhan studied? Who was aware of its use as a label and who wasn't? Given Rosenhan's findings, what strategies can be implemented in psychiatric facilities to lessen the negative impact of labelling upon individuals?

## Being Sane in Insane Places

*D.L. Rosenhan*

If sanity and insanity exist, how shall we know them?

The question is neither capricious nor itself insane. However much we may be personally convinced that we can tell the normal from the abnormal, the evidence is simply not compelling. It is commonplace, for example, to read about murder trials wherein eminent psychiatrists for the defence are contradicted by equally eminent psychiatrists for the prosecution on the matter of the defendant's sanity. More generally, there are a great deal of conflicting data on the reliability, utility, and meaning of such terms as 'sanity', 'insanity', 'mental illness', and 'schizophrenia'.[1] Finally, as early as 1934, Benedict suggested that normality and abnormality are not universal.[2] What is viewed as normal in one culture may be seen as quite aberrant in another. Thus, notions of normality and abnormality may not be quite as accurate as people believe they are.

To raise questions regarding normality and abnormality is in no way to question the fact that some behaviours are deviant or odd. Murder is deviant. So, too, are hallucinations. Nor does raising such questions deny the existence of the personal anguish that is often associated with 'mental illness'. Anxiety and depression exist. Psychological suffering exists. But normality and abnormality, sanity and insanity, and the diagnoses that flow from them may be less substantive than many believe them to be.

At its heart, the question of whether the sane can be distinguished from the insane (and whether degrees of insanity can be distinguished from each other) is a simple matter: do the salient characteristics that lead to diagnoses reside in the patients themselves or in the environments and contexts in which observers find them? . . . [T]he belief has been strong that patients present symptoms, that those symptoms can be categorized, and, implicitly, that the sane are distinguishable from the insane. More recently, however, this belief has been questioned. . . . [T]he view has grown that psychological categorization of mental illness is useless at best and downright harmful, misleading, and pejorative at worst. Psychiatric diagnoses, in this view, are in the minds of the observers and are not valid summaries of characteristics displayed by the observed.[3–5]

Gains can be made in deciding which of these is more nearly accurate by getting normal people (that is, people who do not have, and have never suffered, symptoms of serious psychiatric disorders) admitted to psychiatric hospitals and then determining whether they were discovered to be sane and, if so, how. If the sanity of such pseudo-patients were always detected, there would be prima facie evidence that a sane individual can be distinguished from the insane context in which he is found. . . . If, on the other hand, the sanity of the pseudo-patients were never discovered, serious difficulties would arise for those who support traditional modes of psychiatric diagnosis. Given that the hospital staff was not incompetent, that the pseudo-patient had been behaving as sanely as he had been outside of the hospital, and that it had never been previously suggested that he belonged in a psychiatric hospital, such an unlikely outcome would support the view that psychiatric diagnosis betrays little about the patient but much about the environment in which an observer finds him.

This chapter describes such an experiment. Eight sane people gained secret admission to 12 different hospitals.[6] Their diagnostic experiences constitute the data of the first part of this chapter; the remainder is devoted to a description of their experiences in psychiatric institutions. . . .

## Pseudo-patients and Their Settings

The eight pseudo-patients were a varied group. One was a psychology graduate student in his 20s. The remaining seven were older and 'established'. Among them were three psychologists, a pediatrician, a psychiatrist, a painter, and a housewife. Three pseudo-patients were women, five were men. All of them employed pseudonyms, lest their alleged diagnoses embarrass them later. Those who were in mental health professions alleged another occupation in order to avoid the special attentions that might be accorded by staff, as a matter of courtesy or caution, to ailing colleagues.[7] With the exception of myself (I was the first pseudo-patient and my presence was known to the hospital administrator and chief psychologist and, so far as I can tell, them alone), the presence of pseudo-patients and the nature of the research program was not known to the hospital staffs.[8]

The settings were similarly varied. In order to generalize the findings, admission into a variety of hospitals were sought. The 12 hospitals in the sample were located in five different states on the East and West coasts. Some were old and shabby, some were quite new. Some were research-oriented, others not. Some had good staff-patient ratios, others were quite understaffed. Only one was a strictly private hospital. All of the others were supported by state or federal funds or, in one instance, by university funds.

After calling the hospital for an appointment, the pseudo-patient arrived at the admissions office complaining that he had been hearing voices. Asked what the voices said, he replied that they were often unclear, but as far as he could tell they said 'empty', 'hollow', and 'thud'. The voices were unfamiliar and were of the same sex as the pseudo-patient. . . .

Beyond alleging the symptoms and falsifying name, vocation, and employment, no further alterations of person, history, or circumstances were made. The significant events of the pseudo-patient's life history were presented as they had actually occurred. Relationships with parents and siblings, with spouse and children, with people at work and at school, consistent with the aforementioned exceptions, were described as they were or had been. Frustrations and upsets were described along with joys and satisfactions. These facts are important to remember. If anything, they strongly biased the subsequent results in favour of detecting sanity, since none of their histories or current behaviours were seriously pathological in any way.

Immediately upon admission to the psychiatric ward, the pseudo-patient ceased simulating *any* symptoms of abnormality. In some cases, there was a brief period of mild nervousness and anxiety, since none of the pseudo-patients really believed that they would be admitted so easily. Indeed, their shared fear was that they would be immediately exposed as frauds and greatly embarrassed. Moreover, many of them had never visited a psychiatric ward; even those who had, nevertheless, had some genuine fears about what might happen to them. Their nervousness, then, was quite appropriate to the novelty of the hospital setting, and it abated rapidly.

Apart from that short-lived nervousness, the pseudo-patient behaved on the ward as he 'normally' behaved. The pseudo-patient spoke to patients and staff as he might ordinarily. Because there is uncommonly little to do on a psychiatric ward, he attempted to engage others in conversation. When asked by staff how he was feeling, he indicated that he was fine, that he no longer experienced symptoms. He responded to instructions from attendants, to calls for medication (which was not swallowed), and to dining-hall instructions. Beyond such activities as were available to him on the admissions ward, he spent his time writing down his observations about the ward, its patients, and the staff. Initially these notes were written 'secretly', but as it soon became clear that no one much cared, they were subsequently written on standard tablets of paper in such public places as the dayroom. No secret was made of these activities.

The pseudo-patient, very much as a true psychiatric patient, entered a hospital with no foreknowledge of when he would be discharged. Each was told that he would have to get out by his own devices, essentially by convincing the staff that he was sane. The psychological stresses associated with hospitalization were considerable, and all but one of the pseudo-patients desired to be discharged almost immediately after being admitted. They were, therefore, motivated not only to behave sanely, but to be paragons of co-operation. That their behaviour was in no way disruptive is confirmed by nursing reports, which have been obtained on most of the patients. These reports uniformly indicate that the patients were 'friendly', 'co-operative', and 'exhibited no abnormal indications'.

## The Normal Are Not Detectably Sane

Despite their public 'show' of sanity, the pseudo-patients were never detected. Admitted, except in one case, with a diagnosis of schizophrenia[9], each was discharged with a diagnosis of schizophrenia 'in remission'. The label 'in remission' should in no way be dismissed as a formality, for at no time during any hospitalization had any question been raised about any pseudo-patient's simulation. Nor are there any indications in the hospital records that the pseudo-patient's status was suspect. Rather, the evidence is strong that, once labelled schizophrenic, the pseudo-patient was stuck with that label. If the pseudo-patient was to be discharged, he must naturally be 'in remission'; but he was not sane, nor, in the institution's view, had he ever been sane.

The uniform failure to recognize sanity cannot be attributed to the quality of the hospitals. . . . Nor can it be alleged that there was simply not enough time to observe the pseudo-patients. Length of hospitalization ranged from 7 to 52 days, with an average of 19 days. The pseudo-patients were not, in fact, carefully observed, but this failure clearly speaks more to traditions within psychiatric hospitals than to lack of opportunity.

Finally, it cannot be said that the failure to recognize the pseudo-patients' sanity was due to the fact that they were not behaving sanely. While there was clearly some tension present in all of them, their daily visitors could detect no serious behavioural consequences—nor, indeed, could other patients. It was quite common for the patients to 'detect' the pseudo-patients' sanity. . . . 'You're not crazy. You're a journalist, or a professor [referring to the continual note-taking]. You're checking up on the hospital'. While most of the patients were reassured by the pseudo-patient's insistence that he had been sick before he came in but was fine now, some continued to believe that the pseudo-patient was sane throughout his hospitalization.[10] The fact that the patients often recognized normality when staff did not raises important questions.

Failure to detect sanity during the course of hospitalization may be due to the fact that . . . physicians are more inclined to call a healthy person sick . . . than a sick person healthy. . . . The reasons for this are not hard to find: it is clearly more dangerous to misdiagnose illness than health. Better to err on the side of caution, to suspect illness even among the healthy.

But what holds for medicine does not hold equally well for psychiatry. Medical illnesses, while unfortunate, are not commonly pejorative. Psychiatric diagnoses, on the contrary, carry with them personal, legal, and social stigmas.[11] It was therefore important to see whether the tendency toward diagnosing the sane insane could be reversed. The following experiment was arranged at a research and teaching hospital whose staff had heard these findings but doubted that such an error could occur in their hospital. The staff was informed that at some time during the following 3 months, one or more pseudo-patients would attempt to be admitted into the psychiatric hospital. Each staff member was asked to rate each patient who presented himself at admissions or on the ward according to the likelihood that the patient was a pseudo-patient. . . .

Judgments were obtained on 193 patients who were admitted for psychiatric treatment. All staff who had had sustained contact with or primary responsibility for the patient—attendants, nurses, psychiatrists, physicians, and psychologists—were asked to make judgments. Forty-one patients were alleged, with high confidence, to be pseudo-patients by at least one member of the staff. Twenty-three were considered suspect by at least one psychiatrist. Nineteen were suspected by one psychiatrist *and* one other staff member. Actually, no genuine pseudo-patient (at least from my group) presented himself during this period.

The experiment is instructive. It indicates that the tendency to designate sane people as insane can be reversed when the stakes (in this case, prestige and diagnostic acumen) are high. But what can be said of the 19 people who were suspected of being 'sane' by one psychiatrist and another staff member? Were these people truly 'sane?' . . . There is no way of knowing. But one thing is certain: any diagnostic process that lends itself so readily to massive errors of this sort cannot be a very reliable one.

## The Stickiness of Psychodiagnostic Labels

Beyond the tendency to call the healthy sick—a tendency that accounts better for diagnostic behaviour on admission than it does for such behaviour after a lengthy period of exposure—the data speak to the massive role of labelling in psychiatric assessment. Having once been labelled schizophrenic, there is nothing the pseudo-patient can do to overcome the tag. The tag profoundly colours others' perceptions of him and his behaviour.

From one viewpoint, these data are hardly surprising, for it has long been known that elements are given meaning by the context in which they occur. . . . Once a person is designated abnormal, all of his other behaviours and characteristics are coloured by that label. Indeed, that label is so powerful that many of the pseudo-patients' normal behaviours were overlooked entirely or profoundly misinterpreted. Some examples may clarify this issue.

Earlier I indicated that there were no changes in the pseudo-patient's personal history and current status beyond those of name, employment, and, where necessary, vocation. Otherwise, a veridical description of personal history and circumstances was offered. Those circumstances were not psychotic. How were they made consonant with the diagnosis of psychosis? Or were those diagnoses modified in such a way as to bring them into accord with the circumstances of the pseudo-patient's life, as described by him?

As far as I can determine, diagnoses were in no way affected by the relative health of the circumstances of a pseudo-patient's life. Rather, the reverse occurred: the perception of his circumstances was shaped entirely by the diagnosis. A clear example of such translation is found in the case of a pseudo-patient who had had a close relationship with his mother but was rather remote from his father during his early childhood. During adolescence and beyond, however, his father became a close friend, while his relationship with his mother cooled. His present relationship with his wife was characteristically close and warm. Apart from the occasional angry exchanges, friction was minimal. The children had rarely been spanked. Surely there is nothing especially pathological about such history. . . . Observe, however, how such a history was translated in the psychopathological context, this from the case summary prepared after the patient was discharged.

This white 39-year-old male . . . manifests a long history of considerable ambivalence in close relationships, which began in early childhood. A warm relationship with his mother cools during his adolescence. A distant relationship to his father is described as becoming very intense. Affective stability is absent. His attempts to control emotionality with his wife and children are punctuated by angry outbursts and, in the case of the children, spankings. And while he says that he has several good friends, one senses considerable ambivalence embedded in those relationships also. . . .

The facts of the case were unintentionally distorted by the staff to achieve consistency with a popular theory of the dynamics of a schizophrenic reaction.[12] Nothing of an ambivalent nature had been described in relations with parents, spouse, or friends. . . . Clearly, the meaning ascribed to his verbalizations (that is, ambivalence, affective instability) was determined by the diagnosis: schizophrenia. An entirely different meaning would have been ascribed if it were known that the man was 'normal'.

All pseudo-patients took extensive notes publicly. Under ordinary circumstances, such behaviour would have raised questions in the minds of observers, as, in fact, it did among patients. Indeed, it seemed so certain that the notes would elicit suspicion that elaborate precautions were taken to remove them from the ward each day. But the precautions proved needless. The closest any staff member came to questioning these notes occurred when one pseudo-patient asked his physician what kind of medication he was receiving and began to write down the response. 'You needn't write it', he was told gently. 'If you have trouble remembering, just ask me again'.

If no questions were asked of the pseudo-patients, how was their writing interpreted? Nursing records for three patients indicate that the writing was seen as an aspect of their pathological behaviour. . . . Given that the patient is in the hospital, he must be psychologically disturbed. And given that he is disturbed, continuous writing must be a behavioural manifestation of that disturbance, perhaps a subset of the compulsive behaviours that are sometimes correlated with schizophrenia.

One tacit characteristic of psychiatric diagnosis is that it locates the sources of aberration within the individual and only rarely within the complex of stimuli that surrounds him. Consequently, behaviours that are stimulated by the environment are commonly misattributed to the patient's disorder. For example, one kindly nurse found a pseudo-patient pacing the long hospital corridors. 'Nervous, Mr. X?' she asked. 'No, bored', he said.

The notes kept by pseudo-patients are full of patient behaviours that were misinterpreted by well-intentioned staff. Often enough, a patient would go 'berserk' because he had, wittingly or unwittingly been mistreated by, say, an attendant. A nurse coming upon the scene would rarely inquire even cursorily into the environmental stimuli of the patient's behaviour. Rather, she assumed that his upset derived from his pathology, not from his present interactions with other staff members. . . . [N]ever were the staff found to assume that one of themselves or the structure of the hospital had anything to do with a patient's behaviour. One psychiatrist pointed to a group of patients who were sitting outside the cafeteria entrance half an hour before lunchtime. To a group of young residents he indicated that such behaviour was characteristic of the oral-acquisitive nature of the syndrome. It seemed not to occur to him that there were very few things to anticipate in a psychiatric hospital besides eating.

A psychiatric label has a life and an influence of its own. Once the impression has been formed that the patient is schizophrenic, the expectation is that he will continue to be schizophrenic. When a sufficient amount of time has passed, during which the patient has done nothing bizarre, he is considered to be in remission and available for discharge. But the label endures beyond discharge, with the unconfirmed expectation that he will behave as a schizophrenic again. Such labels, conferred by mental health professionals, are as influential on the patient as they are on his relatives and friends, and it should not surprise anyone that the diagnosis acts on all of them as a self-fulfilling prophecy. Eventually, the patient himself accepts the diagnosis, with all of its surplus meanings and expectations, and behaves accordingly. . . . (see note 5).

## Powerlessness and Depersonalization

Eye contact and verbal contact reflect concern and individualization; their absence, avoidance and depersonalization. The data I have presented do not do justice to the rich daily encounters that grew up around matters of depersonalization and avoidance. I have records of patients who were beaten by staff for the sin of having initiated verbal contact. During my own experience, for example, one patient was beaten in the presence of other patients for having approached an attendant and told him, 'I like you'. Occasionally, punishment meted out to patients for misdemeanours seemed so excessive that it could not be justified by the most radical interpretations of psychiatric canon. Nevertheless, they appeared to go unquestioned. Tempers were often short. A patient who had not heard a call for medication would be roundly excoriated, and the morning attendants would often wake patients with, 'Come on, you m—f—s, out of bed!'

Neither anecdotal nor 'hard' data can convey the overwhelming sense of powerlessness which invades the individual as he is continually exposed to the depersonalization of the psychiatric hospital. . . .

Powerlessness was evident everywhere. The patient is deprived of many of his legal rights by dint of his psychiatric commitment.[13] He is shorn of credibility by virtue of his psychiatric label. His freedom of movement is restricted. He cannot initiate contact with the staff, but may only respond to such overtures as they make. Personal privacy is minimal. Patient quarters and possessions can be entered and examined by any staff member, for whatever reason. His personal history and anguish is available to any staff member (often including the 'gray lady' and 'candy striper' volunteer) who chooses to read his folder, regardless of their therapeutic relationship to him. His personal hygiene and waste evacuation are often monitored. The [toilets] may have no doors.

At times, depersonalization reached such proportions that pseudo-patients had the sense that they were invisible, or at least unworthy of account. Upon being admitted, I and other pseudo-patients took the initial physical examinations in a semi-public room, where staff members went about their own business as if we were not there.

On the ward, attendants delivered verbal and occasionally serious physical abuse to patients in the presence of other observing patients, some of whom (the pseudo-patients) were writing it all down. Abusive behaviour, on the other hand, terminated quite abruptly when other staff members were known to be coming. Staff are credible witnesses. Patients are not.

A nurse unbuttoned her uniform to adjust her brassiere in the presence of an entire ward of viewing men. One did not have the sense that she was being seductive. Rather, she didn't notice us. A group of staff persons might point to a patient in the dayroom and discuss him animatedly, as if he were not there.

One illuminating instance of depersonalization and invisibility occurred with regard to medications. All told, the pseudo-patients were administered nearly 2100 pills. . . . Only two were swallowed. The rest were either pocketed or deposited in the toilet. The pseudo-patients were not alone in this. Although I have no precise records on how many patients rejected their medications, the pseudo-patients frequently found the medications of other patients in the toilet before they deposited their own. As long as they were co-operative, their behaviour and the pseudo-patients' own in this matter, as in other important matters, went unnoticed throughout.

Reactions to such depersonalization among pseudo-patients were intense. Although they had come to the hospital as participant observers and were fully aware that they did not 'belong', they nevertheless found themselves caught up in and fighting the process of depersonalization. . . .

## The Consequences of Labelling and Depersonalization

Whenever the ratio of what is known to what needs to be known approaches zero, we tend to invent 'knowledge' and assume that we understand more than we actually do. We seem unable to acknowledge that we simply don't know. The needs for diagnosis and remediation of behavioural and emotional problems are enormous. But rather than acknowledge that we are just embarking on understanding, we continue to label patients 'schizophrenic', 'manic-depressive', and 'insane', as if in those words we had captured the essence of understanding. The facts of the matter are that we have known for a long time that diagnoses are often not useful or reliable, but we have nevertheless continued to use them. We now know that we cannot distinguish insanity from sanity. It is depressing to consider how that information will be used.

Not merely depressing, but frightening. How many people, one wonders, are sane but not recognized as such in our psychiatric institutions? How many have been needlessly stripped of their privileges of citizenship, from the right to vote and drive to that of handling their own accounts? How many have feigned insanity in order to avoid the criminal consequences of their behaviour, and, conversely, how many would rather stand trial than live interminably in a psychiatric hospital—but are wrongly thought to be mentally ill? How many have been stigmatized by well-intentioned, but nevertheless erroneous, diagnoses? . . . [P]sychiatric diagnoses are rarely found to be in error. The label sticks, a mark of inadequacy forever.

Finally, how many patients might be 'sane' outside the psychiatric hospital but seem insane in it—not because craziness resides in them, as it were, but because they are responding to a bizarre setting, one that may be unique to institutions which harbour neither people? Goffman (see note 4) calls the process of socialization to such institutions 'mortification'—an apt metaphor that includes the processes of depersonalization that have been described here. And while it is impossible to know whether the pseudo-patients' responses to these processes are characteristic of all inmates—they were, after all, not real patients—it is difficult to believe that these processes of socialization to a psychiatric hospital provide useful attitudes or habits of response for living in the 'real world'.

## Notes and References

1. P. Ash, *J. Abnorm. Soc. Psychol.* 44, 272 (1949); A.T. Beck, *Amer. J. Psychiat.* 119, 210 (1962); A.T. Boisen, *Psychiatry* 2, 233 (1938); N. Kreitman, *J. Ment. Sci.* 107, 876 (1961); N. Kreitman, P. Sainsbury, J. Morrisey, J. Towers, J. Scrivener, *ibid.*, p. 887; H.O. Schmitt and C.P. Fonda, *J. Abnorm. Soc. Psychol.* 52, 262 (1956); W. Seeman, *J. Nerv. Ment. Dis.* 118, 541 (1953). For an analysis of these artifacts and summaries of the disputes, see J. Zubin, *Annu. Rev. Psychol.* 18, 373 (1967); L. Phillips and J.G. Draguns, *ibid.*, 22, 447 (1971).
2. R. Benedict, *J. Gen. Psychol.* 10, 59 (1934).
3. See in this regard H. Becker, *Outsiders: Studies in the Sociology of Deviance* (Free Press, New York, 1963); B.M. Braginsky, D.D. Braginsky, K. Ring, *Methods of Madness: The Mental Hospital as a Last Resort* (Holt, Rinehart and Winston, New York, 1969); G.M. Crocetti and P.V. Lemkau, *Amer. Sociol. Rev.* 30, 577 (1965); E. Goffman, *Behaviour in Public Places* (Free Press, New York, 1964); R.D. Laing, *The Divided Self: A Study of Sanity and Madness* (Quadrangle, Chicago, 1960); D.L. Phillips, *Amer. Sociol. Rev.* 28, 963 (1963); T.R. Sarbin, *Psychol. Today* 6, 18 (1972); E. Schur, *Amer. J. Sociol.* 75, 309 (1969); T. Szasz, *Law, Liberty and Psychiatry* (Macmillan, New York, 1963); *The Myth of Mental Illness: Foundations of a Theory of Mental Illness* (Hoeber Harper, New York, 1963). For a critique of some of these views, see W.R. Gove, *Amer. Sociol. Rev.* 35, 873 (1970).
4. E. Goffman, *Asylums* (Doubleday, Garden City, N.Y., 1961).
5. T.J. Scheff, *Being Mentally Ill: A Sociological Theory* (Aldine, Chicago, 1966).
6. Data from a ninth pseudo-patient are not incorporated in this report because, although his sanity went undetected, he falsified aspects of his personal history, including his marital status and parental relationships. His experimental behaviours therefore were not identical to those of the other pseudo-patients.
7. Beyond the personal difficulties that the pseudo-patient is likely to experience in the hospital, there are legal and social ones that, combined, require considerable attention before entry. For example, once admitted to a psychiatric institution, it is difficult, if not impossible, to be discharged on short notice, state law to the contrary notwithstanding. I was not sensitive to these difficulties at the outset of the project, nor to the personal and situational emergencies that can arise, but later a writ of habeas corpus was prepared for each of the entering pseudo-patients and an attorney was kept 'on call' during every hospitalization. I am grateful to John Kaplan and Robert Bartels for legal advice and assistance in these matters.
8. However distasteful such concealment is, it was a necessary first step to examining these questions. Without concealment, there would have been no way to know how valid these experiences were; nor was there any way of knowing whether whatever detections occurred were a tribute to the diagnostic acumen of the staff or to the hospital's rumour network. Obviously, since my concerns are general ones that cut across individual hospitals and staffs, I have respected their anonymity and have eliminated clues that might lead to their identification.
9. Interestingly, of the 12 admissions, 11 were diagnosed as schizophrenic and one, with the identical symptomatology, as manic-depressive psychosis. This diagnosis has a more favourable prognosis, and it was given by the only private hospital in our sample. On the relations between social class and psychiatric diagnosis, see A.B. Hollingstead and F.C. Redlich, *Social Class and Mental Illness: A Community Study* (Wiley, New York, 1958).
10. It is possible, of course, that patients have quite broad latitudes in diagnosis and therefore are inclined to call many people sane, even those whose behaviour is patently aberrant. However, although we have no hard data on this matter, it was our distinct impression that this was not the case. In many instances, patients not only singled us out for attention, but came to imitate our behaviours and styles.
11. J. Cumming and E. Cumming, *Community Ment. Health* 1, 135 (1965); A. Farina and K. Ring, *J. Abnorm. Psychol.* 70, 47 (1965); H.E. Freeman and O.G. Simmons, *The Mental Patient Comes Home* (Wiley, New York, 1963): W.J. Johannsen, *Ment. Hygiene* 53, 218 (1969); A.S. Linsky, *Soc. Psychiat.* 5, 166 (1970).
12. For an example of a similar self-fulfilling prophecy, in this instance dealing with the 'central' trait of intelligence, see R. Rosenthal and L. Jacobson, *Pygmalion in the Classroom* (Holt, Rinehart, and Winston, New York: 1968).
13. D.B. Wexler and S.E. Scoville, *Ariz. Law Rev.* 13, 1 (1971).

# Part VI  Youth and Deviance

The articles in this section address various topics concerning youth and deviance: delinquency, gangs, irreverent youth cultures, and the worrisome influence of violence in the mass media on youth. But a key part of the sociological investigation of youth and deviance concerns, not deviance, but the social construction of youth itself as a life stage or age category in modern societies.

Generally, youth are viewed in a contradictory way: as vulnerable and in need of help and protection; and also as potentially unruly, oppositional, and in need of discipline and control. As an age category they are often associated with delinquency and crime, non-conformity, and challenging authority, and are treated as a 'social problem' despite the generally conventional and non-offensive morality held and practised by most young people. For example, a survey of youth in several countries, including Canada and the US, found that youth internalize many of society's key cultural values.[1] They attach importance to trustworthiness, courtesy, helping those worse off, eating healthily, having a life partner, and working hard. But they often express less enthusiasm for society's major social institutions such as marriage and church, or for conventional indicators of success like accumulating material possessions and fame.

So where does the view of youth as a social problem come from? Much of it is rooted in how the social category of youth has been constructed and instituted in modern societies. Social historians have found that the age category of youth is not so much a natural developmental stage found among humans everywhere as a relatively recent socio-cultural invention that emerged during the process of industrialization in the West. From then on, youth have been regarded as either a minor form of deviance in itself or predisposed to deviant behaviour if left unmonitored and unsupervised. By contrast, the experience of childhood and youth in many other parts of the world varies considerably from that of Western societies. In many countries, children are regularly employed in factories, are involved in sex work, or are pressed into fighting wars.

This modern conception of youth is not just of historical interest. It is important for understanding the relationship between youth and deviance. The social status of youth is ambiguous and is accompanied by conflicting expectations because young people are regarded as 'adult-essing'. As a result of laws that embody this conception of youth, young people are marginalized from society economically and politically, and placed in an elongated state of dependency on adults and adult institutions. The only way to legitimately overcome this ambiguous social status and marginalization is to age and go through a lengthy period of enforced education.

Having large numbers of young people go through such conditions of social strain and ambiguity at the same time has had consequences. It establishes a social environment for the emergence of distinct patterns of behaviours and understandings such as adolescent identity problems; youth cultures and countercultural movements; youthful involvement in delinquent ('status offences') and criminal activities; and sadly, rates of suicide which are several times higher than the homicide rates that most adults and the media are concerned about (Statistics Canada data.[2])

## Notes

1.  Campbell, Murray. 'Wealth and fame? Not for these kids'. *Globe and Mail*. Friday, November 19, 1999.
2.  Over the past half decade the homicide rate for youths 12–17 in Canada has been around 1.7 per 100,000; but the official suicide rate for males 15–19 has been about 15 per 100,000, and for females about 5 per 100,000. See Statistics Canada, CANSIM, table 102-0551, Catalogue no. 84F0209X. Last modified: 2008-02-26.

## Introduction

In this excerpt from a larger work on youth and deviance, Tanner examines the current public concern over youth misbehaviour, youth cultures, and gangs. He argues that behind these public issues is a significant social historical fact: the prevailing view of youth in modern societies is based not so much on a natural developmental stage as on a relatively recent socio-cultural construction that emerged during the process of industrialization in the West. Moreover, this modern idea of youth regards the age category to be inherently a minor form of deviance, or at least prone to deviance.

What events were crucial to the development of our modern ideas of childhood and youth? What are the consequences of the institutionalization of these age categories for growing up in our society, especially with regard to participating socially, economically, and politically within it? To what degree might the very marginalization of youth from full participation in society and the ambiguous nature of this socially-constructed age category be a factor in why and how some young people engage in the deviant activities that they do? Finally, to what extent can Merton's strain theory help us understand youthful misbehaviour, youth cultures, and involvement in gangs?

# Deviant Youth: The Social Construction of Youth Problems

*Julian Tanner*

Nearly 10 years ago, on 20 April 1999, I was a vicarious witness to the shootings at Columbine High School in Littleton, Colorado. Sitting in front of my *TV* set, I learnt about the two masked and heavily armed male students who had fatally wounded 12 of their fellow students and a teacher before shooting themselves.

Very quickly, media coverage of the event moved from reporting the basic facts to putative explanation. A wide range of possible causes were identified and discussed at length: media violence, particularly the violent nature of much popular culture; an emergent 'Goth' sub-culture (specifically the 'trench coat Mafia'); parental neglect; the overlooking of 'obvious' warning signs of trouble ahead by parents, teachers, and local law enforcement agents; and the easy availability of lethal firearms.

While Columbine was neither the first, nor the last, example of a school shooting, it remains the most pivotal one. It has set the standard by which all shootings are now judged and interpreted—in particular, what school shootings are said to represent. More broadly, the Columbine incident had the immediate effect of concentrating the public mind on the dispositions and behaviour of young people. For many people, but especially adults, the name 'Columbine' has become a one-word summation for a wide range of deeply held fears about the collective condition of contemporary youth. In particular, Columbine is taken as evidence that today's young people are more violent and aggressive than their predecessors.

This was not the first time that young people have been viewed in this way. In fact, as far as crime and deviance is concerned, this is how they are routinely viewed . . . In this regard, it is instructive to turn to a newspaper heading from the *Globe and Mail*: 'Another outbreak of street-gang fighting has reawakened citizens to the extent of the problems these young people present'.

What incident do you imagine is being described here? An outbreak of swarming at a suburban shopping mall? Gang violence between Bloods and Crips in Toronto or rival gang factions in Vancouver? Both are reasonable guesses, but both are wrong. The headline is, in fact, from an editorial in the *Globe and Mail* from January 1949—over 60 years ago. The street fighters in question were, in fact, boys—the 'Junction Boys', a then-prominent gang based in Toronto's West End. Their delinquent activities included car theft, breaking and entering, liquor offences, street brawls, and inciting riots (with baseball bats) in communities other than their own. Politicians and newspapers explained and deplored their behaviour in terms of broken homes, declining moral standards, and—this was in the days before television, don't forget!—violent gangster movies.

The 1949 *Globe and Mail* editorial was resurrected by journalist Colin Vaughan to introduce his own, more recent, commentary on youth gangs in Toronto (*Globe and Mail*, 8 June 1992). The title of his article, 'Everything old seems new again, to teens' sums up his thesis: for all its apparent novelty, contemporary teenage behaviour is not really very different from that of the past. Vaughan points out that the idea that Canada's largest city has, until recently, been immune to crime ('Toronto the Good') is a myth; from the beginning Toronto has had its fair share of gang conflicts. In support of his argument he describes the 'Jubilee Riots' of 1875, when Protestant Orangemen attacked Irish Catholic immigrants on city streets, and recalls the notorious Christie Pit riots of 1933 when, toward the end of a long, hot summer, young Jews were set upon by juvenile Fascists (members of the 'Swastika Club'). Fighting fanned out along Bloor Street as both sides called in reinforcements. A sequel of sorts took place in 1965, when a neo-Nazi rally at a downtown park was protested. . . .

Colin Vaughan . . . is not alone in seeing basic similarities between contemporary teenagers and their predecessors. The British criminologist Geoffrey Pearson reached a similar conclusion and made it the starting point for his own investigation of the nature of the 'youth problem' in the United Kingdom. His book, entitled *Hooligan* (1983), begins with an examination of mid-1970s press coverage of youth (mis)behaviour and finds a now-familiar concern with a juvenile crime problem that seemingly has no precedent, the prescribed solution for which is sought in stiffer punishments for young offenders. Furthermore, Pearson found that the troubled present was compared with an apparently more tranquil past. Contemporary media commentators and politicians were able to recall a time—roughly 20 years earlier—when young people were not out of control, schools were still able to exert authority over the young, family values were intact, parents were more willing and able to supervise their children, police were not handcuffed by petty bureaucratic rules, and the courts were able to administer appropriately severe punishments.

Intrigued by this rosy view of the 1950s, Pearson then examined newspaper coverage of youth behaviour from that time. And what did he find? Virtually the same concerns and arguments expressed in roughly the same language! In the 1950s, juvenile crime was seen as a new and disturbing problem; the youth of the nation was being corrupted by post-war affluence, and so forth. Again, there was a harking back to a time, 20 years earlier, when young people had not been a problem. Proceeding in this manner, Pearson delves further and further back into British history, trying to find a time when youthful deviance was not a source of anxiety. Always the crime-free 'golden age' is reckoned to be 20 years prior to the present and, therefore, a perpetually elusive utopia.

What are the sociological implications of Pearson's observations? First, and most obviously, anxieties about the delinquent activity of youth have a long pedigree. There is very little that is new about our current concerns with raves, squeegee kids, swarming, youth gangs, or violence in schools and the media. As we shall see, our Victorian forebears were scarcely less concerned about unsupervised and uncontrolled youth on the streets than we are today. Second, the myth of the 'good old days' influences our thinking about and prescriptions for contemporary juvenile offenders: if delinquency was once less of a problem than it is now, today's problems can be solved by doing what they did yesterday. The usual assumption is that juveniles were punished more harshly in the past and that is the reason why delinquency was less of a problem (Bernard 1992: 13). Third, studying reactions to delinquent behaviour is as important a task for students of crime as studying the behaviour itself. This is partially a matter of acknowledging that how we respond to youth—what we celebrate, tolerate, or condemn—tells us much about society's moral boundaries. But more importantly, studying our reactions to delinquency alerts us to the fact that objective social conditions alone do not give rise to social problems such as crime and deviance.

## Social Constructionism and Youth Deviance

Over the past several decades, sociologists have pondered the nature of social problems and the threat that they pose to society. Using delinquency as our example, the traditional argument is that delinquency is a problem because the anti-social behaviour of adolescents is dangerous and damaging to persons and property within the community. This might be called an objectivist approach to social problems. The focus is on norm-violating behaviours, particularly behaviour that is evaluated negatively because of the harm and injury it causes. Researchers working in this tradition enquire about the causes of delinquency and might ask, for instance, 'What sorts of backgrounds do delinquents come from?', 'What kinds of early childhood experiences have delinquents had?", 'Does exposure to rap music lead to violent behaviour?' From a second, more recent perspective, delinquency is a problem simply because it has been defined or labelled as a problem. This is referred to as a constructionist approach to social problems, and its proponents believe:

> that our sense of what is or is not a social problem is a product, something that has been produced or construed through social activities. When activists hold a demonstration to attract attention to some social condition, when investigative reports

publish stories that expose new aspects of the condition, or when legislators introduce bills to do something about the conditions, they are constructing a social problem. (Best 1989: xviii)

Social constructionists are less interested in the behaviour itself, and more interested in how certain conditions become recognized as social problems. They point out that some objectively harmful or dangerous conditions never achieve social problem status, while others become serious social problems without much evidence that they are very injurious—or that they even exist at all. On the one hand, for example, cheating on income-tax returns is not always regarded as a serious social problem even though the behaviour results in a significant revenue loss for governments, and, in turn, hardship for citizens reliant upon various forms of social welfare. Satanic crime, on the other hand—involving the kidnapping and mutilation of children by devil worshippers—has been deemed a serious social problem, at least in the United States, without much evidence to support the claims of the whistleblowers drawing attention to these practices (Sacco 2005: 8).

Constructionists interested in the problem of youth are more likely to pose questions about media representations of youth gangs than about the causes of gang behaviour. They might also ask 'Why do we care more about youth gangs than youth homelessness?' Or—Vince Sacco's question—'Why do we become excited about the violent content of rap music but seem to have little to say about the violent content of country music?' (2005: 8).

## Media Portrayals of Youth Deviance

As Pearson's study suggests, media reportage of young people in general accentuates the negative, a tendency confirmed by another British study. A content analysis of a sample of national and local newspapers revealed that the vast bulk of youth stories had a negative orientation in that they concentrated disproportionately on deviant activities (Porteous and Colston 1980, cited in Muncie 1984).

Although no equivalent Canadian study has been conducted, two researchers have reported on a brief review of the *Toronto Star* during the first week of December 1990. They found that on each day of the week, at least one story managed to link youth with crime . . . Needless to say, youth gangs are a particularly attractive topic for news organizations. For an example of how they get reported on, we can again turn to the *Toronto Star*, which in the fall of 1998 mounted an extensive three-part investigation of what it saw as a growing problem in Canada's largest city.

The series was prominently displayed—literally, front-page news—and began with the claim that there were 'more than 180' youth gangs operating in Toronto. Where did this seemingly high number come from? Not from official data gathering agencies: neither Statistics Canada nor police departments across the country categorize criminal incidents according to whether or not they are 'gang related'. Nonetheless, it does appear that reporter Michelle Shepherd relied heavily on police information for her story. But one problem with this source is that police officers are only provided with vague legal guidelines regarding the dimensions of gang behaviour. Bill C-95, for instance, advises that a gang entails 'five or more individuals engaged in criminal activity'. However, according to the *Globe and Mail*, police also define a youth gang as 'two or more persons engaged in anti-social behaviour who form an allegiance for a common criminal purpose, and who individually or collectively are creating an atmosphere of fear and intimidation within a community' (*Globe and Mail*, 2 November 1998).

In the absence of more precise and generally agreed upon criteria about what constitutes gang activity, different commentators are free to come up with their own best estimates regarding the nature of teen gangs . . . Indeed, if a gang can be said to exist with as few as two members, the anti-social behaviour in question is not specified, and the criteria for 'fear and intimidation within a community' are a matter of judgment, it is not difficult to see how the 'more than 180' might be arrived at and why citizens might be scared of the teenagers in their neighbourhoods.

Similarly, the essentially loose and discretionary criteria employed in gang spotting can lead to the misidentification (and misinterpretation) of casual and informal small group activity among adolescents as 'gang-related behaviour'. For instance, are we to understand that the numerous small cliques of kids who hang around smoking outside high schools or the bunch of kids who act up on the bus or subway on the way home from school are engaged in gang activity? If the police decide to define such behaviour in gang terms, and subsequently issue warnings and make arrests, then the size and scope of the gang problem is only going to get bigger.

But the *Toronto Star* reporter did not use only police sources for her story; she also collected information from students themselves in the form of questionnaires completed outside school premises. Again, the focus was on, among other things, gangs. Students were asked whether there were gangs in their school and, if so, did they belong to one? Over half of the respondents affirmed a gang presence in their school and 10 per cent reported gang membership.

The problem with these questions is that they are predicated on the assumption that the reporter asking the question and the students answering them are in agreement about how we define gang behaviour. Is gang activity and gang membership limited to robbing and stealing, dealing drugs, and violent and aggressive behaviour or does it also include hanging out with your friends, playing sports, or going to parties and clubs together? Since the content of gang behaviour was not specified in the question, it is hard to know what meaning to attach to the information supplied by respondents.

Overall, the theme of the series was that a crime problem was getting out of control; that official statistics suggesting otherwise were misleading; that school boards were deliberately suppressing information about youth-gang activity; and that although Toronto was not yet like Los Angeles, this was the (downward) direction in which things were heading: 'Bloods and Crips. The chilling gang names have never meant much north of the border. Now they do' (*Toronto Star* 26 October 1998: B1).

The message of escalating gang activity in Toronto was not conveyed just by facts and figures, however. Information was also relayed visually in the form of a computer-enhanced full-colour map entitled 'Toronto youth gang territories', which detailed the geographic location of each of the 180 named gangs. I suggest that this illustrated guide to youth gang operations in Toronto has the effect of making teenage gangs appear more numerous, organized, predatory, and geographically diffuse than they really are. The other likely effect of this visual presentation is an increased fear of youth crime. . . .

The commonsense view about the relationship between the mass media and youth crime is that the journalists who write the stories that attract our attention are simply recording events as they unfold. According to this argument, media accounts about youth crime provide a more or less faithful reflection of an objectively existing social problem (Muncie 1984; Surette 1992). However, media organizations do much more than just report the facts. Whether they realize it or not, journalists shape how their readers, viewers, and listeners feel and think about the behaviour of youth. Research on media institutions indicates that the news that we consume is the result of a selection process. Items for inclusion in news reports compete for time and space; stories about deviant youth have an advantage in this competitive process because they are deemed highly 'newsworthy' (Muncie 1984). . . .

These comments are not meant to suggest that the media invent or fabricate news stories about youth deviance, or that the problems of delinquency and crime would suddenly stop if journalists stopped writing about them (Muncie 1984: 20). Rather, the main point to be made about the reporting and presentation of youth stories is that they exaggerate and sensationalize events and situations, often presenting atypical cases as representative and, in so doing, they construct a problematic image of youth that does not always correspond to actual behaviour.

If media reports had no effect upon how audiences view deviance, these details would be interesting but of no real consequence. But research suggests that media presentations of crime issues affect public perceptions of the criminal justice system. For instance, surveys conducted for the Canadian Sentencing Commission found that members of the public overestimated the amount of crime in Canada; they believed that rates of recidivism are higher and that maximum sentencing penalties are lower than they really are, and they underestimated the severity of penalties routinely administered (Corrado and Markwart 1992).

Tellingly, the majority (95 per cent) of respondents also revealed that they derived their knowledge about crime in Canada predominately from the mass media. The commission also found—as have several American studies—that violent crime is overrepresented in news stories about crime. In fact, stories reporting that by the time a young person graduates from high school, he or she will have been witness to 'x' number of both real and fictional stabbings, shootings, murders, and so forth have become something of a cliché. *Time* magazine, in a cover story on 'Our Violent Kids' (12 June 1989), has put that figure in the United States at 200,000 (Acland 1995: 14, 147).[1] Violent crime is actually more likely to appear in print and broadcast items than in real life! This has a predictable effect. Surveys conducted in Canada, the United States, and the UK reveal that the general public believes crimes of violence form a much higher proportion of the total volume of youth crime than they really do (Roberts 2004). Roberts also reports misconceptions about the direction of youth crime (ever upwards) and overstates the ratio of youth crime to adult crime. . . .

## Youth, Moral Panics, and Deviancy Amplification

By this stage, it will probably not surprise you to discover that the mass media have been held responsible for creating particularly exaggerated fears about youth problems, fears that have been referred to as 'moral panics' (Cohen 1973). Stanley Cohen coined this term after witnessing clashes between rival groups of 'mods' and 'rockers' on the beaches of England in the mid-1960s and analyzing media interpretations of those events. Media coverage was, in fact, intense, driven by a combination of fear, anxiety, and moral outrage about what this episode said about the condition of the British nation.

Cohen concluded—like Pearson after him—that many of the claims made about delinquent youth had been made before and were, in fact, part of a repetitive cycle in which the mass media were heavily implicated:

> Societies appear to be subject, every now and then, to periods of moral panic. A condition, episode, person, or group of persons emerges to become defined as a threat to societal values and interests; its nature is presented in stylized and stereotypical fashion by the mass media; the moral barricades are manned by editors, bishops, politicians, and other right-thinking people; socially accredited experts pronounce their diagnoses and solutions; ways of coping are evolved or (more often) resorted to; the condition then disappears, submerges, or deteriorates and becomes more invisible. Sometimes the object of the panic is quite novel and at other times it is something which has been in existence long enough, but suddenly appears in the limelight. Sometimes the panic passes over and is forgotten, except in folklore and collective memory; at other times it has more serious and long-lasting repercussions and might produce such changes as those in legal and social policy or even in the way the society conceives of itself. (Cohen 1973: 9)

The conditions and incidents that become the object of moral panic are, for the most part, fairly predictable (Cohen 2002: viii). Some have been mentioned already: youth violence and gangs, drugs, and the harmful effects of the mass media. Cohen suggests that moral panics occur at times of profound but scarcely understood social change, when established values and beliefs are believed to be threatened. 'Folk devils'—witches in seventeenth-century New England, or mods and rockers in mid-twentieth-century Britain—are identified as external threats to established values and institutions against whom 'normal society' can unite and rally.

It is no coincidence that most moral panics involve the young. This is because, at least in part, their successful socialization into conformist behaviour is made problematic by their susceptibility to anti-social influences. These influences tend to occur when the major agencies of socialization—the family, the established church, the school system—appear to be breaking down, and when young people seem to be out of control. In Cohen's analysis, for instance, the fights between the mods and the rockers were seen by media commentators as a consequence of too much affluence, too much leisure, and the end of compulsory military training (national service). Post-war changes had weakened the influence of traditional authority (as vested in family, school, and religion), and gang fights at seaside resorts were one highly visible result.

As the case of the mods and rockers shows, in Britain the deviant and delinquent behaviour of working-class youth is most likely to inspire moral panics, particularly if their activities include violence and aggression. Often the frightening and discreditable activities of youth are traced back to the corrupting influences of popular entertainment and culture—an argument that has a long pedigree (Sacco and Kennedy 1994: 215).

In Victorian times, it was believed that the crime melodramas available in cheap theatres would induce imitative behaviour among their young working-class audiences. In the course of the twentieth century, rising rates of youthful crime have been linked at different times to the spread of horror and crime comics, dime-store novels, gangster movies, rock-and-roll music, and, more recently, slasher films (or, as the British call them, 'video nasties'). The contemporary concern with video games is also part of this tradition. However, the most common focus is television. Our concern in the past with *Ninja Turtles* and *Mighty Morphin Power Rangers* or, less obviously, *The Simpsons* or *South Park*, reflects a prevailing belief that the mass media exert a powerful and negative effect upon a young and impressionable audience, resulting in high rates of youthful crime, particularly violent crime (Murdock 1982; Barrat 1986). . . .

While the idea of 'moral panics' is a British one, moral panics about youth have been produced in North America as well.[2] Here, however, race has been the catalyst more often than class. It is often minority youth who have been assigned the folk devil role, setting in motion both heavy-handed policing and suspect media accounts. . . .

## More Panics, Proportionality, and Social Construction

Some students of crime and deviance are uncomfortable with the moral panic concept. They believe that the term implies that individuals panic, in a psychological sense, in the face of conditions and episodes they find unsettling (Sacco 2005: 5). In repost, we should emphasize that the 'panic' in 'moral panic' is not meant literally, as a psychological diagnosis, but as a metaphor referring to the impact of macro social forces upon the well-being of a society. Secondly, critics invoke questions about proportionality. They ask: How do we know, exactly, when we are observing, or experiencing, an overreaction to a criminal event? What is the benchmark by which we judge the level of response to one incident a moral panic, while the response to another one is credited as reasonable anxiety? Thirdly, and relatedly, some people claim that the problem with crime is not our exaggerated response to it but the very opposite, that some serious crimes are not treated seriously enough. For example, there are many people in the black community who feel that not enough attention is paid to the black victims of violent crime, or to their concerns about racial profiling.

Finally, there is the relationship between moral panics and social constructionism to consider. These two concepts have much in common. There are clear overlaps in their subject matter, theoretical assumptions (particularly the emphasis upon claims making), and research methodology (content analysis of the media); many researchers draw no hard and fast distinction between the two concepts. . . .

However, while moral panics may not be a prerequisite for social problem construction, their existence certainly makes that outcome more likely. In some cases—school violence comes to mind—problematic behaviour in the form of truancy, skipping classes, mild forms of bullying or teasing, and classroom disruption by unruly students is sufficiently routine or commonplace that it takes a major catastrophe, a singular dramatic event, to turn normal concerns into a fully fledged panic. Columbine was, of course, that one defining episode. . . .

Some commentators have recently begun to suggest that young people are now growing up in a 'risk' society. Although it has a number of sources and referents, this argument has become associated with the German social theorist, Ulrich Beck. He proposes that a wide range of economic, social, and cultural changes are transforming human societies; that the old institutions and social constructs are unable to affect social norms and cultural expectations; and that many of the certainties of life have been removed and replaced by a state of 'risk' (Beck 1992).

Many parts of this argument apply to, or can be made to apply to, the experiences of the young. For instance, it is claimed that the transition from school to work has become increasingly problematic because of global changes in the nature of economic life (Krahn and Lowe 1997; Marquard 1998). In the Maritime provinces, for example, sons can no longer anticipate following their fathers into the fishing industry; more generally, a good education no longer guarantees a good job.

Although young people today have more choices than earlier generations, they also face more constraints. More importantly, the old markers of class and gender that traditionally guided young people toward, or away from, particular futures have lost their determinative influence. Decision making—which career to pursue, what sort of education to get, if and when to get married and have children—is becoming not only riskier but also more individualized.

This thesis has not gone unchallenged. Growing up has never been easy—indeed, the various difficulties involved with doing so have given rise to over 50 years of 'youth culture', as we will see in a moment. Is the process really harder now than throughout the 1930s or during and just after the Second World War? Is it really the case that class and gender, or race for that matter, have lost their ability to shape life chances or lifestyle choices?

These criticisms notwithstanding, the influence of Beck's ideas has been such that researchers have started to ponder the range of 'risks' that young people encounter in the course of their daily lives (Furlong and Cartmel 1997). Indeed, as far as young people and deviance is concerned, risk has been interpreted quite literally in terms of victimization and the dangers that both it and offending pose to the successful attainment of adult status.

The strategic position that young people occupy in social imagery about crime and deviance—in particular, the idea that they are both 'troubling' and 'troubled'—also means that their behaviour is regularly used as a barometer of, or cipher for, the moral health or sickness of the community (Cohen 1973; Gilbert 1986; Davies 1990). . . . However, the danger of imbuing the behaviour of the young with important symbolic meaning is that it leads to images of adolescent deviance that do not always correspond with reality . . . The facts are that most young people are not in serious conflict with society, do not hold values that clash with those of the parental generation, and do not engage in the types of deviance that adults find most troubling.

This is periodically confirmed by social surveys, one example of which is Bibby's investigation of the social attitudes of Canada's teenagers (Bibby 1985). On a wide range of issues—what they value, what they enjoy, their religious beliefs, occupational ambitions, sexual mores—teenagers are revealed to be utterly conventional in their choices and preferences, expressing views that their parents would not find outrageous. In fact, these findings exemplify a more general point: most children are remarkably like their parents and are 'distinguished from one another, and by the same variables, as are adults' (Campbell 1969: 877).

## The Invention of Adolescence and Delinquency

If, as I am suggesting, there is a gap between the perception and reality of adolescent deviance, what factors have encouraged the view that youth is a particularly difficult and problematic stage in the life-cycle? Why do images of trouble and deviance colour so many people's understanding of adolescence?

The answer to these questions can be found in changes in the economic and social organization of society that have occurred over the past 200 or so years and that have had the cumulative effect of removing the young from adult society. The problematic image of modern youth is a consequence of their emergence as a separate, distinct, age-based social category.

Given the contemporary preoccupation with the transgressions—both real and imagined—of juveniles, it is hard to conceive of a time when the young were not so collectively burdened with the stigma of deviance. Yet the fact is that before the middle of the nineteenth century they were rarely a subject of public concern. For instance, the word 'adolescence'—so much a part of contemporary discourse about the young—was rarely used outside of scientific writings before the turn of the century (Kett 1971: 97). Modern assumptions about youth—particularly the idea that young people are naturally inclined toward rebellion and non-conformity—are of relatively recent vintage; their origins can be traced back to the modern world created by the industrial revolution of the eighteenth and nineteenth centuries. Prior to that time no clearly defined intermediate stage between childhood and adulthood existed . . . Medieval French children, for instance, often worked alongside adults from the age of seven onwards. This egalitarian participation in economic activity extended into non-work time as well. Children were present at, and participated in, all the great ceremonies and rituals of the life cycle—including death—to a degree that would be unheard of today. Children were treated, in effect, as little adults; this was indicated by their dress, games, and legal status. Similarly, when they broke the law and were caught by the authorities, the chronologically young were responded to in the same (or similar) punitive manner as adult offenders. They were neither treated more leniently nor were they placed in separate juvenile prisons. The law recognized no meaningful distinction among violators on the basis of age, and therefore there was no legal designation of delinquency.

What changed all of this? The short answer is that human societies became increasingly age-differentiated as a result of the industrial revolution. The connection between the two events is sometimes made quite explicit, as in Frank Musgrove's observation that 'the adolescent was invented at the same time as the steam engine' (Musgrove 1964: 33).

When Musgrove talks about adolescence being 'invented', or when sociologists discuss the social construction of youth, what they mean is that those intermediate age-based categories that we now take for granted and use more or less interchangeably did not exist on any grand scale prior to the transformations ushered in by the industrial era.

At the risk of oversimplifying what was a very complex process, two key transitions associated with industrialization have relevance for arguments about the social construction of adolescence and delinquency: (1) the transitions from an agriculturally-based economy and society to an industrial one and (2) from home-based work (the cottage system) to the factory system.

Early versions of the factory system depended upon the relatively simple labour power provided by men, women, and children. However, the development of increasingly sophisticated machine technology, which was cheaper and more productive than human muscle power, eventually led to the displacement of large numbers of workers. The subsequent labour surplus resulted in plunging wage rates. In the face of competition for scarce jobs from cheap child labour, male factory workers campaigned through their trade unions to restrict the employment of children in the mines and factories. A similar goal was simultaneously sought by other individuals and groups, albeit for very different reasons. Humanitarian reformers opposed the hiring of children on the grounds that the conditions and terms of employment in the factory system were sufficiently harsh and exploitative that the young should not be subjected to them. This alliance of male industrial workers and humanitarian reformers secured the passage of legislation that checked the use of child labour. As the nineteenth century progressed, the streets of major Canadian, American, and European cities were, therefore, increasingly filled with the unemployed youth now displaced from the production system.

In order to survive, they needed to steal. The urban milieu facilitated this objective by bringing the impoverished young into contact both with their potential victims and with other youth with whom they could forge predatory networks. What subsequently became recognized as juvenile delinquency was originally property crime committed on city streets by young, working-class males directed against upper-class adults. For the first time in history, thanks to industrialization and urbanization, property crime had become the main form of criminal activity in society; and most of it was committed by young people (Bernard 1992). This is not to suggest that all of the activities of nineteenth-century street youth were criminal. Working (selling newspapers and matches and so on) and playing were more important. . . .

Nonetheless, their work and leisure activities disturbed middle-class observers—reformers, clergymen, journalists—who deplored the morally corrupting lifestyle in which they were engaged. The introduction of compulsory education was one means of controlling street urchins and providing the sort of moral training and direction that was lacking in their home lives.

These concerns were particularly acute in Canada because Great Britain had used Canada as a dumping ground for the orphans and destitute of its own cities. Between the 1860s and 1920, Britain exported 90,000 children to Canada (Bean and Melville 1989). Their presence was something of a mixed blessing. On the one hand, they solved a perennial problem facing Canadian farmers—the shortage of cheap labour. Although it is doubtless the case that some children's lives were improved immeasurably by their involuntary migration to the New World, many others were ruthlessly exploited. They often worked 16-hour days on isolated homesteads, were badly abused, and never saw their families or native country again. As one contemporary participant put it, 'Adoption, sir, is when folks gets a girl to work without wages' (Sutherland 1976: 10).

However, the economic advantages of cheap labour were offset by law and order considerations. Their origins as members of an impoverished underclass made them particularly
vulnerable to the lure of the criminal life. Likewise, their early experiences rendered them
a source of contamination, spreading criminal values throughout Canada's major cities. . . .

From roughly 1883 onwards, reformers became more and more convinced that committing young offenders to common lock-ups was counter-productive—such institutions were
little better than schools for crime. Determined to prevent boys and girls from graduating to
the 'burdensome ranks of paupers, drunkards and criminals' when they grew up, they argued
for separate penal institutions for juveniles (Sutherland 1976: 91). . . .

# The Juvenile Delinquents Act of 1908

The official history of juvenile delinquency in Canada begins in 1908. Following similar legislative initiatives in the United States and Great Britain, the first piece of legislation pertaining
specifically to juveniles was passed in that year. The Juvenile Delinquents Act (JDA) had the
deliberate effect of legislating the distinction between adult and young offender, a distinction
which we now take for granted. A separate juvenile court and a probation service were two of
its most enduring features.

The legislative intent of the reformers was two-fold. First, the legislators felt that treating
old and young criminals alike was inhumane: the indiscriminate use of harsh punishment
violated, to use the modern parlance, the civil rights of the young. Second, reacting to juvenile offenders as hardened criminals and placing them in adult prisons extinguished any possibility of reform. Unlike adult criminals—who were largely beyond redemption—there was
still hope that inner-city street youth could be saved. On the one hand, therefore, the young
were seen as being particularly prone to crime and deviance but, on the other hand, they were
viewed as being most conducive to reform.

Applying these ideas resulted in legislation that not only targeted a diverse set of conditions—law-breaking, pauperism, and dependency—but also a wide range of prohibited
acts. The Juvenile Delinquents Act in Canada, and its counterpart in other parts of the
English-speaking world, ensured that young people got in trouble with the law for a much
larger number of offences than did adult offenders. Although some youth crime was the
same as adult crime (robbery, assault, theft), there were other offences for which young
people, and young people alone, were liable to arrest, punishment, and treatment (Frith,
1985). These latter violations are known collectively as status offences. They included the
consumption of alcohol, truancy, running away from home, refusal to obey parents, having delinquent friends, and the use of profanity—activities that were illegal solely because
the individuals who engaged in them were underage.[3] The broad scope of what counted as
delinquency is evident in revisions to the original Act, passed in 1924. According to the law,
a delinquent was:

> any child who violates any provision of the *Criminal Code* or of any Dominion or
> provincial statute, or of any by-law or ordinance of any municipality, or who is guilty
> of sexual immorality or any similar form of vice, or who is liable by reason of any

other act to be committed to an industrial school or juvenile reformatory under the provisions of any Dominion or provincial statute. (quoted in West 1984: 33)

The age of minimal legal responsibility was kept at seven, and the upper age limit (that is, the age at which a young offender became an adult offender) varied according to province: 16 in Ontario, Alberta, New Brunswick, Nova Scotia, PEI, the Yukon, Saskatchewan, and the Northwest Territories; 17 in British Columbia and Newfoundland; and 18 in Manitoba and Quebec. The most severe sentence the juvenile court could impose was institutionalization in a training school where the emphasis was upon discipline and character training. It is also worth noting that, along with a broad definition of delinquency, judges were granted considerable discretion regarding the punishment that wrongdoers should receive, the severity of which was determined not by the seriousness of the offence but by the 'needs' of the offender—as decided by judges and probation officers (West 1984).

## Adolescents, Delinquency, and Youth Culture

Although the history of delinquency begins with nineteenth-century street youth, the concerns aroused by their public behaviour quickly spread to include all adolescent activity. In the view of prominent Victorian opinion-makers, the nature of adolescence made all young people susceptible, or vulnerable, to the lures of delinquency.

From the beginning, adolescence has never been merely a transitional stage between childhood and adulthood. It has invariably been seen as a time of turmoil and conflict. Academics writing at the turn of the century are primarily responsible for this viewpoint. These experts—mainly psychologists and psychiatrists—were of the opinion that every young person skirted with delinquency because rebellion was a natural and universal characteristic of this intermediary stage in the life cycle.

The person most closely identified with this interpretation of adolescence was a prominent pioneer psychologist, G. Stanley Hall, a man much influenced by the work of Charles Darwin and his thesis regarding the biological evolution of the species. Hall argued that just as the human species as a whole passed through a series of stages in its development, so too did each individual human being. The human species and its individual units thus evolved through conditions of early animal primitivism into refined, civilized, mature entities. Paralleling Darwin's designation of an intermediate stage in the evolution of the species, Hall identified a similar phase in individual development: adolescence, a time of *sturm und drang* (storm and stress) that Hall felt corresponded to an equally unstable and tumultuous phase in the development of human civilization. Hall similarly allowed the biological doctrine of recapitulation to mould his views on the origins of juvenile delinquency, which he saw as the outcome of a clash between the 'savage' inclinations of youth and the civilizing influences of society (Kett 1977: 255).

His prognostications unleashed a series of books on the adolescent years and inspired a coterie of experts prepared to counsel on the problem of youth. His assertions about the 'natural' sources of adolescent rebellion were quickly and eagerly embraced by the educators and welfare workers of the day and had a significant effect upon the development of a justice system that caters specifically to the needs of those who are no longer children but not yet adults. Moreover, and not coincidently, Hall's storm and stress model of adolescence influenced subsequent debate about rising juvenile crime, the effects of popular entertainment, and the relationship between the two (Murdock 1982: 64).

Hall, and the psychologists who followed him, operated with a view of adolescence that concentrated on the inborn inclination of young people toward problematic behaviour. Although they focused upon structural and cultural factors rather than individualistic ones— adolescence was both a social and a personal experience—the early sociologists shared the same problem-centred view of their subject matter.

In the 1940s sociologists began to draw attention to the growing importance of a separate, sub-society of adolescence; the premier American sociologist of the day, Talcott Parsons, referred to this 'society within a society' as a 'youth culture' (1942). Parsons was the leading light of the then-dominant sociological paradigm of functionalism. However, it was left to other sociologists working within the same functionalist paradigm to enlarge upon the origins and nature of youth culture. The fullest flowering of the functionalist view was provided by S.M. Eisenstadt (1956). For Eisenstadt, youth culture was an outcome of disruptions in the transition from childhood to adulthood characteristic of industrial society and manifested as generational differences and conflicts. Some elaboration of these complexities is in order.

Functionalists view social institutions as a set of interrelated parts that contribute to the smooth functioning of the whole. Hence, the function of the family is to equip children with an understanding of the basic norms of society, and the function of the educational system is to prepare the young for their future occupational roles. Successful fulfillment of the tasks allocated to society's various component institutions leads to strong social integration; weak integration leads to conflict. Intergenerational conflict is seen as a consequence of a poor fit—weak integration—between age-groups and society. Weak integration, and hence generational conflict, is seen as being particularly pronounced in advanced industrial societies because of the problematic nature of the transition from childhood to adulthood. . . .

Industrialization has ruptured the transitional process because an increasingly complex and constantly evolving division of labour has meant that appropriate job skills cannot be taught informally in the bosom of the immediate family. As a result, the preparation for future adult work roles has been transferred from the nuclear family setting to specialized educational institutions.

The elongated training period required for occupational roles and the absence of a ritual that publicly acknowledges the arrival of adulthood are seen as creating ambiguities and uncertainties for the young regarding their role and status in society. Their exclusion from adult work roles and subsequent confinement in a separate educational institution has cultivated a collective sense of marginality and distinctiveness.

It is the gap between what the family is no longer capable of delivering (occupational skills and training) and what an increasingly complex economy requires (specialized and extended periods of occupational training in educational institutions) that gives rise to autonomous youth groups. . . .

Other factors have only served to make youth groups and youth culture even more important in the years following the Second World War. First, the massive increase in the birth rate

after 1945—the 'baby boom'—meant that the young made up an increasingly large proportion of the total population. In Canada, the 10 years between 1951 and 1961 saw the number
of 15–19-year-olds in the population increase by over a million (Owran 1996: 145). Second,
and as one would expect, the baby boom had a huge impact on the schools, colleges, and
universities of most Western nations. More young people were spending increasing amounts
of time in the education system where they interacted more or less exclusively with their
peers. The common, age-specific character of their experiences engendered a collective self-
consciousness regarding their distinctive location in society.

These feelings were, in turn, reinforced by another increasingly ubiquitous influence: the
machinations of a growing teenage leisure industry that was not slow to realize that the young
constituted a new and largely untapped market. For the first time ever, consumer goods,
services, and entertainment—movies, magazines and, in particular, popular music—were
pitched specifically at the expanding youth population. Appealing to what were felt to be
universal age-specific needs, emotions, and experiences, the youth-oriented leisure industries helped nurture a view of the young as a unique, distinctive, and homogeneous social
category, united in their tastes and interests . . .

For many adults, the preoccupations of youth—new music, new fashions, new dances, fast
cars, fast food—spelled trouble: more and more 'ordinary' adolescents 'looked and behaved
like juvenile delinquents' (Gilbert 1986: 17). High school was where ordinary adolescents
('teenagers') were increasingly forced to rub shoulders with the more obviously delinquent.
As clear-cut distinctions between deviancy and conformity started to break down, the term
'teenager' (invented at about the same time as 'youth culture', in the 1940s) became increasingly interchangeable with, and indistinguishable from, delinquency. This development is
nicely illustrated by an (apparently) popular joke of the time in which one suburban housewife tells another: 'My husband was two hours late getting home the other night. Oh, my
God, I thought, the teenagers have got him' (Murdock and McCron 1976: 18).

As James Gilbert points out, what gave these fears added substance was the fact that, beginning in the 1950s, fewer working-class and minority youth were dropping out of school.
In Canada, 1954 marked the first time that more than 50 per cent of 14–17-year-olds were in
school; by 1960, 66 per cent of this age group were students (Owram 1996: 145). No longer,
therefore, were the traditional folk devils confined to the mean streets and neighbourhoods
of the inner cities where they had first emerged in the nineteenth century: delinquent values
and networks had now found a place in high school, where they exerted a pernicious influence on ordinary teenage culture (Gilbert 1986). . . .

## Notes

1. The inference contained in these headlines, of course, is that witnessing violence on the television or at the
   movies increases the prospects of real-life violence. However, while there is little doubt that adolescents and
   children are constantly exposed to media violence, there is considerably less agreement about what this exposure means for adolescent behaviour. Here are some reasons why I am skeptical about claims that the mass
   media makes any significant direct contribution to real-life violence.
      First, Young Canadians and Americans are exposed to much the same kinds of media programming, and
   yet the United States has significantly higher crime rates—particularly violent crime rates. Similarly, European

youth watch many of the same violent movies (though probably fewer of them) and enjoy much the same kinds of music and yet have much lower rates of violent crime than their North American counterparts. Second, all theories of media influence concentrate on violent crime but crimes of violence are not common among young people. Thus, even if the media effects on teenage violence and aggression are real and substantial, we are left wondering why a steady consumption of violent movies and anti-authority rock songs and videos have produced mainly minor property crimes (Sacco and Kennedy 1998: 272–3).

Third, as I have emphasized throughout this chapter, popular culture has routinely been blamed for the ills of society, particularly adolescent violence. In this regard, it is worth remembering that the most murderous gang of the twentieth century were the Nazis, the leadership of which were highly cultured men who enjoyed the music of Wagner and Beethoven and other classical German masters. Does anybody ever claim that their genocidal behaviour was caused by their preferences for high culture (Morrison 1997)?

2.  Though not as regularly as in the UK. It has been suggested that moral panics are an endemic feature of British life because of the highly competitive nature of the British newspaper industry. A large number of national daily newspapers vie for readers by deliberately provoking controversy over moral issues (Thompson 1998.)

3.  Status offences have been formally eliminated from youth criminal justice legislation. However, it still appears that young offenders, particularly female ones, are subject to judicial intervention for a much broader range of wrongdoings than are adults (Bell 1994; Chesney-Lind 1997).

# References

Acland, C. 1995. *Youth, murder, spectacle.* Boulder: Westview Press.

Barrat, D. 1986. *Media sociology.* London: Tavistock.

Bean, P., and J. Melville. 1989. *Lost children of the empire.* London: Unwin Hyman.

Beck, U. 1992. *Risk society: Towards a new modernity.* London: Sage.

Bell, S. 1994. 'An empirical approach to theoretical perspectives on sentencing in a young offender court', *Canadian Review of Sociology and Anthropology* 31 (1): 35–64.

Bernard, T. 1992.*The cycle of juvenile justice.* New York: Oxford University Press.

Best, J. 1989. *Images of issues: Typifying contemporary social problems.* New York: Aldine de Gruyter.

Bibby, R. 1985. *The emerging generation: An inside look at Canada's teenagers.* Toronto: Irwin.

Campbell, E. 1969. 'Adolescent socialization', in *Handbook of socialization theory*, D. Goslin, ed. Chicago: Rand McNally.

Chesney-Lind, M. 1997. *The female offender: girls, women and crime.* Thousand Oaks, CA: Sage.

Cohen, S. 1973. *Folk devils and moral panics.* London: MacGibbons and Kee.

Cohen, S. 2002. 'Moral panic as cultural politics', in *Folk devils and moral panics*, 3rd ed. New York: Taylor and Francis.

Corrado, R., and A. Markwart. 1992. 'The evolution and implementation of a new era of juvenile justice in Canada', in *Juvenile justice in Canada: A theoretical and analytical assessment,*

Davies, J. 1990. *Youth and the condition of Britain.* London: Athlone Press.

Eisenstadt, S. 1956. *From generation to generation.* Glencoe, IL: Free Press.

Frith, S. 1985. 'The sociology of youth', in *Sociology: New directions*, M. Haralabos, ed. Ormskirk: Causeway Press.

Furlong, A., and F. Cartmel. 1997. *Young people and social change: Individualization and risk in late modernity.* Buckingham: Open University Press.

Gilbert, J. 1986. *A cycle of outrage.* New York: Oxford University Press.

Kett, J. 1971. 'Adolescence and youth in nineteenth century America', in *The family in history*, T. Rabb and R. Rothberg, eds. New York: Harper & Row.

———. 1977. *Rites of passage.* New York: Basic Books.

Krahn, H., and G. Lowe. 1997. 'School–work transitions and post modern values: What's changing in Canada?', in *From education to work: Cross-national perspectives*, W. Heinz, ed. Cambridge: Cambridge University Press.

———. 1998. *Work, industry and Canadian society*, 3rd ed. Scarborough: Nelson Canada.

Marquard R. 1998. *Enter at your own risk: Canadian youth and the labour market.* Toronto: Between the Lines.

Morrison, B. 1997. *As if: A crime, a trial, a question of childhood.* New York: Picador USA.

Muncie, J. 1984. *The trouble with kids today: Youth and crime in postwar Britain.* London: Hutchinson.

Murdock, G. 1982. 'Mass communication and social violence', in *Aggression and violence*, P. Marsh and A. Campbell, eds. Oxford: Blackwell.

Murdock, G., and R. McCron. 1976. 'Youth and class: The career of confusion', in *Working class youth culture*, G. Mungham and G. Pearson, eds. London: Routledge and Kegan Paul.

Musgrove, F. 1964. *Youth and the social order.* London: Routledge and Kegan Paul.

Owram, D. 1996. *Born at the right time: A history of the baby boom generation*. Toronto: University of Toronto Press.

Parsons, T. 1942. 'Age and sex in the social structure of the United States', *American Sociological Review* 7: 604–16.

Pearson, G. 1983. *Hooligan*. London: Macmillan.

Sacco, V., and L. Kennedy. (1994). *The criminal event*. Toronto: Nelson.

Sacco, V. 1998. *The criminal event*, 2nd ed. Toronto: Nelson.

———. 2005. *When crime waves*. Thousand Oaks, CA: Sage.

Shepherd, M. 1998. *Toronto Star*, 26 October, B1.

Surette, R. 1992. *Media, crime and criminal justice: Images and realities*. Pacific Grove, CA: Brooks/Cole.

Sutherland, N. 1976. *Children in English-Canadian society: Framing the twentieth-century consensus*. Toronto: University of Toronto Press.

Thompson, K. 1998. *Moral panics*. London and New York: Routledge.

Vaughan, C. 1990. 'Everything old seems new again, to teens', *Globe and Mail*. (n.d.)

West, W.G. 1984. *Young offenders and the state*. Toronto: Butterworths.

## 23

### Introduction

Youth gangs are a popular issue in Canada. But what do we really know about them? The following selection is the outcome of combining two information sheets that are part of a series published by the NCPC and available on the government's Public Safety website (www.publicsafety.gc.ca). [Date Modified: 2008-01-10]. After reading them, respond to the questions you'll find at the end.

---

# Youth Gangs in Canada: What Do We Know? *and* Youth Gang Involvement: What Are the Risk Factors?

*NCPC of Public Safety Canada*

## Youth Gangs in Canada: What Do We Know?

**The National Crime Prevention Centre (NCPC) of Public Safety Canada** is committed to developing and disseminating practical knowledge to address the problem of youth gangs. This information sheet is part of a series on youth gangs. It includes highlights from the 2002 Canadian Police Survey on Youth Gangs as well as other sources of information on youth gangs.

To implement effective prevention and intervention strategies, we must start by understanding the nature and scope of the youth gang problem. This document presents an overview of current knowledge about youth gangs in Canada, including their connections with guns and drugs.

### What is a Youth Gang?

Youth gangs typically consist of young people who

- self-identify as a group (e.g. have a group name)
- are generally perceived by others as a distinct group
- are involved in a significant number of delinquent incidents that produce consistent negative responses from the community and/or law enforcement agencies.[1]

There are other important characteristics of a youth gang that help us to understand the phenomenon. The Montréal Police Service's definition of 'youth gang' explicitly incorporates the anti-social and delinquent behaviours that are distinctive of youth gangs. It defines a 'youth gang' as

> An organized group of adolescents and/or young adults who rely on group intimidation and violence, and commit criminal acts in order to gain power and recognition and/or control certain areas of unlawful activity.[2]

## Who Joins Youth Gangs?

The 2002 Canadian Police Survey on Youth Gangs and other sources suggest that youth gang members cut across many ethnic, geographic, demographic, and socio-economic contexts.[3] However, youth at risk of joining gangs or already involved in gangs tend to be from groups that suffer from the greatest levels of inequality and social disadvantage.[4]

Aboriginal youth are more vulnerable to gang recruitment and organized crime than non-Aboriginal youth and they are increasing in numbers and influence in Western Canada.[5]

Many youth who join gangs have also been identified as youth who are using drugs and already involved in serious and violent crime. Furthermore, youth who display higher levels of previous delinquency are more likely to remain in the gang.[6]

The reasons for joining a youth gang are various. Some youth seek excitement; others are looking for prestige, protection, a chance to make money, or a sense of belonging.[7]

## Results of the Canadian Police Survey on Youth Gangs

Youth gangs are not just an urban phenomenon. They are active across the country in both large and small communities.[8]

Results of the Canadian Police Survey on Youth Gangs and other sources suggest that youth gangs are a growing concern in many Canadian jurisdictions, although not to the same extent as in the United States. Comparisons between the two countries show that almost twice the percentage of jurisdictions in the United States report active youth gangs as compared with those in Canada (see Table 23.1).

The Survey asked police officers to estimate the number of youth gangs in their jurisdiction. According to these estimates:

- Canada has 434 youth gangs with roughly 7,000 members nationally (see Table 23.2).
- Ontario has the highest number of youth gangs and youth gang members in absolute terms, with 216 youth gangs and 3,320 youth gang members. Saskatchewan is second (28 youth gangs and 1,315 members), followed by British Columbia (102 youth gangs and 1,027 members).[9]
- For the country as a whole, the vast majority of youth gang members are male (94 per cent).[10]

**Table 23.1**  Comparison of Youth Gangs in Canada and the United States

|  | US (2000) | Canada (2001) |
| --- | --- | --- |
| Population | 281,421,906 | 30,007,094 |
| Percentage of jurisdictions reporting youth gang activity | 40% | 23.7% |
| Estimated number of youth gangs | 24,500 | 434 |
| Estimated number of gang members | 772,500 | 7,071 |
| Density per 1000 population | 2.75 | 0.24 |

Source: Astwood Strategy Corporation (2004)

- Almost half (48 per cent) of all youth gang members are under the age of 18. Most (39 per cent) are between 16 and 18 years old.[11]
- The largest proportion of youth gang members are African Canadian (25 per cent), followed by First Nations (21 per cent) and Caucasian (18 per cent).[12]
- Police agencies and Aboriginal organizations indicate that there is a growing percentage of female gang membership in western Canadian provinces, including British Columbia (12 per cent), Manitoba (10 per cent) and Saskatchewan (9 per cent).[13]

## Gangs, Crime and Violence

The movement of gang members from one jurisdiction to another appears to have an impact on the criminal activities and involvement of youth, as does the return of gang-involved youth or adult inmates from correctional facilities.[14]

From a prevention perspective, it is vital to understand that youth involvement in crime and violence is linked with the experience of the gang itself.[15]

In the United States, studies of large urban samples show that youth gang members are responsible for a large proportion of all violent adolescent offences. On average, 20 per cent of gang members were responsible for committing about 80 per cent of all serious violent adolescent offences.[16]

While similar offence data is not available in Canada, a quasi-national study of the criminal careers of a birth cohort[17] found that 16 per cent of alleged young offenders who were classified as chronic offenders were responsible for 58 per cent of all alleged criminal incidents.[18]

## Gangs, Guns, and Drugs in Schools

Gun violence in major cities in Canada has been a growing concern, especially in Toronto, Edmonton, Calgary, Vancouver, and Montreal.[19]

**Table 23.2** Comparison of Youth Gangs and Youth Gang Members, Nationally and by Province, 2002

| Area | Number of Youth Gangs | Number of Youth Gang Members | Youth Gang Members per 1,000 Population |
|---|---|---|---|
| Canada | 434 | 7071 | 0.24 |
| British Columbia | 102 | 1027 | 0.26 |
| Alberta | 42 | 668 | 0.22 |
| Saskatchewan | 28 | 1315 | 1.34 |
| Manitoba | 15 | 171 | 0.15 |
| Ontario | 216 | 3320 | 0.29 |
| Québec* | 25 | 533 | 0.07 |
| Nova Scotia | 6 | 37 | 0.04 |
| New Brunswick | 0 | 0 | 0 |
| Prince Edward Island | 0 | 0 | 0 |
| Newfoundland and Labrador | 0 | 0 | 0 |
| Yukon | 0 | 0 | 0 |
| Northwest Territories | 0 | 0 | 0 |
| Nunavut | 0 | 0 | 0 |

*Data was collected on only four police agenies in the Province of Québec. As a result, the percentage of jurisdictions reporting active youth gangs in Québec (i.e., 100%) must not be considered representative of the entire province.

Source: Astwood Strategy Corporation (2004)

Gun violence is also more prevalent among street gangs that involve primarily young men less than 30 years of age.[20]

The Drugs, Alcohol and Violence International (DAVI) study, a joint Canada-US effort, provides important evidence about the relationships between gangs, guns, and drugs in Toronto and Montreal. A total of 904 male students (grades 9 to 12), school dropouts, and young offenders were interviewed. The results indicate that

- There is a correlation between gang presence in schools and the availability of both guns and drugs in schools.
- 18.7 per cent of boys (ages 14 to 17) in Montréal and 15.1 per cent in Toronto have brought a gun to school.
- School dropouts who get involved in drug selling are at higher risk of being involved in gun-related violence.[21]

## Conclusion

Most youth who join gangs have already been involved in crime, violence, and illegal drug use. The prevalence and scope of youth gang involvement varies across the country, but the 'gang effect' of increased delinquency, drug use, and violence is a common thread.

Integrated, targeted, and evidence-based community solutions are necessary to reduce and prevent the proliferation of gangs, drugs, and gun violence. More information is available on youth gangs in Canada at www.publicsafety.gc.ca/ncpc and www.safecanada.ca.

# Youth Gang Involvement: What Are The Risk Factors?

**The National Crime Prevention Centre (NCPC) of Public  Safety Canada** is committed to developing and disseminating  practical knowledge to address the problem of  youth gangs. This information sheet is one of a series providing information related to youth gang involvement.  It is designed to assist those who are concerned  about youth gangs and who are working to help prevent  youth from becoming involved in gangs or to help them  leave gangs.

The vast majority of young people never get involved in  crime or join gangs. Those who do join gangs tend to have  specific risk factors that influence their involvement and membership in gangs.

To effectively prevent youth from joining gangs it is  essential to understand these risk factors.

## What is A Risk Factor?

Risk factors can be defined as life events or experiences that  are associated with an increase in problem behaviours, such  as drug use or gang activities.[22]  For example, being the child of a single parent who is often  absent from the home and lacks adequate support can be  considered a risk factor. The negative influence of a friend[23] or  sibling can be another.

Risk factors can be divided into five categories:

- individual characteristics
- peer group
- school
- family
- community

## Major Risk Factors

Long-term studies of adolescents in Canadian and American  cities (Montreal, Seattle, Washington, and Rochester) suggest  that the most important risk factors for gang involvement include

- negative influences in the youth's life
- limited attachment to the community

- over-reliance on anti-social peers
- poor parental supervision
- alcohol and drug abuse
- poor educational or employment potential
- a need for recognition and belonging

The Seattle study found that children and youth are two to four times more likely to join gangs if they are affected by these factors.[24]

Youth at risk or already involved in gangs tend to be from groups that suffer from the greatest levels of inequality and social disadvantage.[25]

## Major Risk Factors Associated With Youth Gang Involvement

Individual

- prior delinquency
- illegal gun ownership
- drug trafficking
- desire for group rewards such as status, identity, self-esteem, companionship and protection
- anti-social attitudes
- aggression
- alcohol and drug use
- early or precocious sexual activity
- violent victimization

Peer Group

- high commitment to delinquent peers
- street socialization
- gang members in class
- friends who use drugs or who are gang members
- interaction with delinquent peers
- pre-teen exposure to stress

School

- poor school performance
- low educational aspirations, especially among young females
- negative labelling by teachers
- high levels of anti-social behaviour
- few teacher role models
- educational frustration

- low attachment to school
- learning difficulties

Family

- family disorganization, including broken homes and parental drug and/or alcohol abuse
- family violence, neglect, and drug addiction
- family members in a gang
- lack of adult and parental role models, parental criminality, parents with violent attitudes, siblings with anti-social behaviours
- extreme economic deprivation

Community

- social disorganization, including high poverty and residential mobility
- high crime neighbourhood; neighbourhood youth in trouble
- presence of gangs in the neighbourhood
- availability of or perceived access to drugs in the neighbourhood
- availability of firearms
- cultural norms supporting gang behaviour
- feeling unsafe in neighbourhood

Source: Adapted from Howell (1998, 2005).

## Evolving Risk Factors

Gang involvement is a process that happens over time. This process is influenced by the life trajectory and individual, familial, and social experiences of a young person.

Several studies indicate that risk factors associated with gang involvement are present long before a youth joins a gang.[26] For example, youths who were the most behaviourally and socially maladjusted in childhood were found to be the most likely to join and stay in gangs for several years.[27]

Unless appropriate actions are taken to address the factors that result in more serious crime or gang involvement, early negative life experiences and subsequent involvement in crime will only reinforce the path towards continued delinquency.

Additionally, it appears that not only entry into gangs, but also prolonged membership is associated with a greater risk of delinquency.[28]

## Risk Factors and Prevention

The identification of the specific risk factors associated with youth gang involvement helps us determine where and how to focus prevention efforts.

Briefly, we know that

- The more risk factors that a youth experiences, the more likely he or she is to join a gang. Research also suggests that the presence of risk factors in *multiple categories* increases the probability of gang involvement.[29]
- The increase in gang violence and crime in some Aboriginal communities has been attributed in part to an increasing youth population, inadequate housing, drug and alcohol abuse, a high unemployment rate, lack of education, poverty, poor parenting skills, the loss of culture, language, and identity, and a sense of exclusion.[30]
- Gang cohesion, culture, and lifestyle are also important considerations. A Montreal study of 756 boys showed that gang members display higher rates of delinquent behaviours and drug use than non-gang members.[31]

The above-mentioned Montreal study also provides evidence for a significant 'gang effect' among youth gang members linked to the experience of the gang itself.

This gang effect adds to the social and family risk factors that may be present prior to joining a gang.

## Protective Factors and Prevention

In addition to preventing youth from joining gangs, it is important to reduce membership duration for youth who belong to a gang and to provide appropriate services (drug treatment, employment and educational opportunities) once they leave the gang.

Strengthening protective factors plays an important role in reducing youth gang involvement. Protective factors are positive influences that mitigate the impact of risk factors and decrease the likelihood of problem behaviour.

Drawing on evidence regarding gang prevention, the *Community Solutions to Gang Violence* project in Edmonton helps increase protective factors among youth by

---

**Box 23.1** Community Solutions to Gang Violence (CSGV)

This initiative is most concerned with young people who come together to engage in profit-driven criminal activity and violence.

With a large number of partners in the fields of law enforcement, health, and child and social services, this project put together a community-wide action plan and network of support to find solutions to the gang violence problems in the Greater Edmonton Area. This involved developing a comprehensive listing of risk and protective factors related to gang involvement.

In addition, CSGV has launched a website (www.csgv.ca) that keeps people informed of ongoing activities and provides resources, tools, and information that can be used to prevent young people from being drawn into gangs.

- building positive relationships and patterns of interaction with mentors and pro-social peers
- creating positive social environments through community, family and service organizations
- promoting social and economic policies that support positive youth development.

## Conclusion

Understanding why some young people join gangs while others do not is key to effective prevention efforts.

Current research suggests the need to address specific risk factors that lead youth to violence and gangs. It is also important to enhance protective factors that can play a role in keeping youth out of gangs.

More information on prevention strategies to address the risk and protective factors associated with youth gang involvement is available at www.publicsafety.gc.ca/ncpc and www.safecanada.ca.

# Discussion Questions

Now that you've read the two information sheets, consider the following comments and questions. In their 2005 report 'Youth Gangs in Canada', the Canadian Research Institute for Law and the Family noted that the definition of youth gang is quite problematic for police, policy makers, and the public for various reasons. Perceptions of what constitutes a youth gang vary across regions depending on the gang issues particular to an area, and this is further complicated by the inappropriate labelling of youth social groups by outsiders.

Regarding these fact sheets, much of the data, including the tables, is taken from a 2002 Canadian Police Survey on Youth Gangs published by the Astwood Strategy Corp. But that study did not actually work with a common or generally accepted definition of youth gang. It left it up to the police who were surveyed to decide on how to define it. Although the police perspective on youth gangs is important, what limitations or implications result from this approach to defining gangs? To what extent can we claim to 'know' something about youth gangs based on the 'facts' in the fact sheets?

Finally, Travis Hirshi has developed social bond (or social control) theory to account for juvenile delinquency. Basically, he theorized that weak bonds to conventional activities (like school and sports) as well as to conventional authority figures and role models (like parents, teachers, religious leaders, sports figures) enable, rather than cause, involvement in deviant activity. A strong social bond is evident in the attachment an individual has to authority figures and peers, his/her commitment to conventional activities through actual involvement in them, as well as his/her belief in the norms, values, and ideas that make up the conventional world. Do the risk factors identified in the report basically confirm or challenge Hirshi's theory? What factors are presented that are beyond the original scope of Hirshi's theory? Were any factors unclear in their meaning?

# Notes

1. Canada. Royal Canadian Mounted Police. *Environmental Scan: Features: Focus on Youth Gangs*. Ottawa: Royal Canadian Mounted Police, 2006.
2. Montréal. Montréal Police Service. *Provincial Action Plan on Street Gangs*. Québec: Department of Public Security, National Coordinating Committee, 2004 [Meeting, Toronto, May 25, 2005].
3. Astwood Strategy Corporation. *2002 Canadian Police Survey on Youth Gangs*. Ottawa: Public Safety and Emergency Preparedness Canada, 2004.
4. Wortley, Scot and Julian Tanner. "Social Groups or Criminal Organizations? The Extent and Nature of Youth Gang Activity in Toronto" in *From Enforcement and Prevention to Civic Engagement: Research on Community Safety* / edited by Bruce Kidd and Jim Phillips. Toronto: Centre of Criminology, University of Toronto, 2004: 59–80.
5. Richter-White, Holly. *Direct and Indirect Impacts of Organized Crime on Youth, as Offenders and Victims*. Ottawa: Royal Canadian Mounted Police, Research and Evaluation Branch, Community Contract and Aboriginal Policing Service, 2003; RCMP, 2006.
6. Gatti, Uberto, Richard E. Tremblay, Frank Vitaro and Pierre McDuff. "Youth Gangs, Delinquency and Drug Use: A Test of the Selection, Facilitation, and Enhancement Hypotheses," *Journal of Child Psychology and Psychiatry* 46(11), (2005): 1178–1190.
7. RCMP (2006); Wortley et al., 2004.
8. RCMP (2006); Astwood Strategy Corporation (2004).
9. Astwood Strategy Corporation, 2004.
10. Ibid.
11. Ibid.
12. Ibid.
13. Ibid.; Federation of Saskatchewan Indian Nations (FSIN) (2003). *Alter-Natives to Non-Violence Report: Aboriginal Youth Gangs Exploration: A Community Development Process*. Saskatchewan: FSIN, 2003.
14. Canada. Correctional Service Canada (2002). *An Examination of Youth and Gang Affiliation within the Federally Sentenced Aboriginal Population*. Ottawa: Correctional Service Canada, 2002; Astwood Strategy Corporation (2004).
15. Gatti et al., 2005.
16. Thornberry, Terence P., David Huizinga and Rolf Loeber. "The Causes and Correlates Studies: Findings and Policy Implications," *Juvenile Justice* 10, 1, (2004): 3–19.
17. The study used linked data from Statistics Canada's *Youth Court Survey* and *Adult Criminal Court Survey* to describe the court careers, up to the 22nd birthday, of Canadians born in 1979/80.
18. Carrington, Peter, Anthony Matarazzo and Paul deSouza. "Court Careers of a Canadian Birth Cohort," *Crime and Justice Research Paper Series*, no. 6. Ottawa: Canadian Centre for Justice Statistics, 2005.
19. Dauvergne, Mia and Geoffrey Li. "Homicide in Canada, 2005" *Juristat* 26, 6, (2006). Ottawa: Canadian Centre for Justice Statistics.
20. Canada. Criminal Intelligence Service Canada (CISC). *2006 Annual Report on Organized Crime in Canada*. Ottawa: CISC, 2006.
21. Erickson, Patricia G. and Jennifer E. Butters. *Youth, Weapons and Violence in Toronto and Montréal*. Report prepared for Public Safety and Emergency Preparedness Canada, Ottawa, 2006. Policing Service, Research and Evaluation Branch, Royal Canadian Mounted Police, 2003.
22. Howell, James C. "Moving Risk Factors into Developmental Theories of Gang Membership," *Youth Violence and Juvenile Justice* 3, 4 (2005): 334–354.
23. Ibid.
24. Hawkins, J. David and John A. Pollard, (1999). "Risk and protective factors: Are both necessary to understand diverse behavioral outcomes in adolescence?," *Social Work Research* 23, 3: 145–158.
25. Wortley, Scot and Julian Tanner. "Social Groups or Criminal Organizations? The Extent and Nature of Youth Gang Activity in Toronto" in *From enforcement and prevention to civic engagement: research on community safety*/edited by Bruce Kidd and Jim Phillips. Toronto: Centre of Criminology, University of Toronto, 2004: 59-80; Federation of Saskatchewan Indian Nations (FSIN), 2003.
26. Howell, James C. (2005).
27. Gatti, Uberto, Tremblay, Richard E., Vitaro, Frank and McDuff, Pierre. "Youth gangs, delinquency and drug use: a test of the selection, facilitation, and enhancement hypotheses," *Journal of Child Psychology and Psychiatry* 46, 11 (2005): 1178–1190; Hill, 2001.
28. Ibid.

29. Wyrick, Phelan and James C. Howell. "Strategic Risk-Based Response to Youth Gangs." *Juvenile Justice Journal* 9, 1 (2004).
30. Federation of Saskatchewan Indian Nations (FSIN). *Alter-Natives to Non-Violence Report: Aboriginal Youth Gangs Exploration: A community development process.* Saskatchewan, FSIN, 2003; Lafontaine et al., 2005; Royal Canadian Mounted Police, 2006.
31. Gatti et al., 2005.

# References

Astwood Strategy Corporation. 2004. *2002 Canadian Police Survey on Youth Gangs.* Ottawa: Public Safety and Emergency Preparedness Canada.

Carrington, Peter, Anthony Matarazzo and Paul deSouza. 2005. 'Court Careers of a Canadian Birth Cohort'. Crime and Justice Research Paper Series, no. 6. Ottawa: Canadian Centre for Justice Statistics.

Correctional Service Canada. 2002. An Examination of Youth and Gang Affiliation within the Federally Sentenced Aboriginal Population. Ottawa: Correctional Service Canada.

Criminal Intelligence Service Canada (CISC). 2006. *Annual Report on Organized Crime in Canada.* Ottawa: CISC.

Dauvergne, Mia and Geoffrey Li. 2006. 'Homicide in Canada, 2005' *Juristat* 26 (6). Ottawa: Canadian Centre for Justice Statistics.

Erickson, Patricia G. and Jennifer E. Butters. 2006. *Youth, Weapons and Violence in Toronto and Montréal.* Report prepared for Public Safety and Emergency Preparedness Canada. Ottawa.

Federation of Saskatchewan Indian Nations (FSIN). 2003. Alter-Natives to Non-Violence Report: Aboriginal Youth Gangs Exploration: A Community Development Process. Saskatchewan: FSIN.

Gatti, Uberto, Richard E. Tremblay, Frank Vitaro and Pierre McDuff. 'Youth Gangs, Delinquency and Drug Use: A Test of the Selection, Facilitation, and Enhancement Hypotheses,' *Journal of Child Psychology and Psychiatry* 46, 11 (2005), pp. 1178–1190.

Hawkins, J. David and John A. Pollard. 'Risk and Protective Factors: Are Both Necessary to Understand Diverse Behavioral Outcomes in Adolescence?', *Social Work Research,* 23, 3, (1999) pp. 145–158.

Hill, Karl G., Christina Lui and J. David Hawkins. 2001. *Early Precursors of Gang Membership: A Study of Seattle Youth.* Washington, D.C.: Office of Juvenile Justice and Delinquency Prevention.

Howell, James C. 2005. 'Moving Risk Factors into Developmental Theories of Gang Membership,' *Youth Violence and Juvenile Justice,* 3, 4, pp. 334–354.

Lafontaine, Tanya, Ferguson, Myles and J. Stephen Wormith. 2005. *Street Gangs: A Review of the Empirical Literature on Community and Corrections-Based Prevention, Intervention and Suppression Strategies.* Saskatchewan, University of First Nations, University of Saskatchewan.

Montréal. Montréal Police Service. Provincial Action Plan on Street Gangs. Québec: Department of Public Security, National Coordinating Committee, 2004 [Meeting, Toronto, May 25, 2005].

Richter-White, Holly. 2003. *Direct and Indirect Impacts of Organized Crime on Youth, as Offenders and Victims.* Ottawa: Community Contract and Aboriginal Policing Service, Research and Evaluation Branch, Royal Canadian Mounted Police.

Royal Canadian Mounted Police. 2006. *Environmental Scan: Features: Focus on Youth Gangs.* Ottawa: Royal Canadian Mounted Police.

Shader, Michael. 2003. *Risk Factors for Delinquency: An Overview.* Washington, D.C., U.S. Department of Justice, Office of Juvenile Justice and Delinquency Prevention.

Thornberry, Terence P., David Huizinga and Rolf Loeber. 2004. 'The Causes and Correlates Studies: Findings and Policy Implications', *Juvenile Justice* 10, 1, pp. 3–19.

Wortley, Scot and Julian Tanner. 2004. 'Social Groups or Criminal Organizations? The Extent and Nature of Youth Gang Activity in Toronto' in *From Enforcement and Prevention to Civic Engagement: Research on Community Safety,* edited by Bruce Kidd and Jim Phillips. Toronto: Centre of Criminology, University of Toronto, pp. 59.

Wyrick, Phelan and James C. Howell. 2004. 'Strategic Risk-Based Response to Youth Gangs,' *Juvenile Justice Journal,* 9, 1. Washington, D.C., U.S. Department of Justice, Office of Juvenile Justice and Delinquency Prevention, 2004. PS4-37/1-2007E-PDF 978-0-662-45551-6.

## Introduction

Youth cultures began emerging soon after the appearance of youth as a life stage in the early twentieth century, starting with the 'flappers' and their 'zoot' suits. Despite varying styles, youth cultures usually distinguish themselves from 'adult' culture in terms of language, fashion, music, art, and issues of gender as well as the overall theme of control. As Baron has noted in his study of Vancouver punks, youth cultures generally exhibit an 'opposition-by-inversion' of selected aspects of dominant adult culture, and an appeal to defiance or rebellion.

For instance, in response to growing support for autocratic order in the 30s and 40s, youth said 'swing'. In response to expectations about conforming to middle class, suburban life in the 50s, youth said 'go bohemian'. In response to the discipline and control of mass production, youth said 'rock'n'roll'. In response to liberating the world through war in the 60s and 70s, youth said 'make love'. In response to accumulating material goods as a sign of success in the 80s, youth said 'don't work; wear torn clothes, garbage bags, and safety pins instead.' And in response to the recent silence of governments and the public in North America on issues like racial inequality, oppression, and poverty in the midst of growing affluence, corporate power, and a growing class of elites, youth said, 'let's rap, because we're not gonna stop talkin' about these things'.

But much of the defiance is diffuse and symbolic. And however oppositional their messages, youth cultures often undergo commercialization and assimilation by the very system they are apparently critiquing. In this case, what are the ironical results of the commercialization and mass consumption of hip hop? Is Brym's critique applicable to all hip hop? Finally, has hip hop actually had any impact on changing the existing social order?

# Hip Hop from Caps to Bling

*Robert J. Brym*

## 1.8 Million Black Men Are Missing

Nobody should be surprised that a popular subculture rooted in the lives of African-American men focuses so tightly on violence and death. About a third of African-American households enjoy annual incomes of US$50,000 a year or more, but for the roughly one-quarter of African Americans who live in poverty, violence and death are a big part of everyday life.

One indicator of the disproportionate amount of violence faced by African-American men is the **sex ratio**, the number of men per 100 women in a population. In most of the world, the sex ratio is about 96. There are about 96 white American men for every 100 white American women, for example. More men than women work in dangerous jobs and engage in high-risk behaviour such as smoking and excessive alcohol consumption. Besides, women are the hardier sex, biologically speaking. That's why there are fewer men than women in most populations.[1]

Among African Americans, however, the sex ratio is less than 87, an extraordinarily low figure. Assuming that a sex ratio of 96 is normal, we can conclude that 9 black men are missing for every 100 black women (since 96 minus 87 equals 9). Given 19.3 million black women in the United States in 2004, that works out to about 1.8 million missing black men. In 2004 there were 16.7 million black men in the United States but there should have been 18.5 million (calculated from US Census Bureau 2006).

Many missing black men died violently. The homicide rate is the number of murders per 100,000 people in a population. The black male homicide rate in the United States was nearly 39 in 2003, but reached about 60 in Illinois, Louisiana, and Pennsylvania. In contrast, the homicide rate was 5.7 for the United States as a whole and 1.7 for Canada.

In 2003, nearly 6,000 more black men than black women were murdered in the United States. But homicide is not the only cause of excess deaths among black men. In addition, about 4,000 more black men than black women died accidentally, mainly due to car accidents and drug overdoses. About 2,500 more black men than black women died of AIDS, and about 1,000 more black men than black women committed suicide (calculated from National Center for Injury Prevention and Control 2006; see Kubrin, Wadsworth, and DiPietro 2006). These figures oblige us to conclude that the destruction of the lives of poor African-American men by violence and high-risk behaviour is horrifyingly routine. It is therefore to be expected that violence and death would form central themes in their cultural expression.

## Social Origins of Hip Hop

The situation of the African-American community as a whole has improved since the 1960s. The civil rights movement created new educational, housing, and job opportunities for African Americans and resulted in the creation of a substantial black middle class. The United States became a more tolerant and less discriminatory society. Yet in the midst of overall improvement, the situation of the roughly one-quarter of African Americans who live in poverty became bleaker.

After World War II, and especially in the 1960s, millions of southern Blacks migrated to northern and western cities. Many were unable to find jobs. In some census tracts in Detroit, Chicago, Baltimore, and Los Angeles, black unemployment ranged from 26 to 41 per cent in 1960. Many of the migrants were single women under the age of 25. Many had children but lacked a husband and a high school diploma.

The race riots of the 1960s helped to persuade the government to launch a 'war on poverty' that increased the welfare rolls. In 1973, the American poverty rate fell to 11.1 per cent, its lowest point ever. After 1973, however, everything went downhill. Manufacturing industries left the inner city for suburban or foreign locales, where land values were lower and labour was less expensive. In the three decades following 1973, the proportion of the American labour force employed in industry fell from about one-third to one-fifth. Unemployment among African-American youth rose to more than 40 per cent. Middle-class blacks left the inner city for the suburbs. The migration robbed the remaining young people of successful role models. It also eroded the taxing capacity of municipal governments, leading to a decline in public services. Meanwhile, the American public elected conservative governments at the state and federal levels. They cut school and welfare budgets, thus deepening the destitution of ghetto life (Piven and Cloward 1977: 264–361; 1993; Wilson 1987).

With few legitimate prospects for advancement, poor African Americans turned increasingly to crime and, in particular, the drug trade. In the late 1970s, cocaine was expensive and demand for the drug was flat. So in the early 1980s, Colombia's Medellin drug cartel introduced a less expensive form of cocaine called 'rock' or 'crack'. Crack was not only inexpensive—it also offered a quick and intense high, and it was highly addictive. Crack cocaine offered many people a temporary escape from hopelessness and soon became wildly popular in the inner city. Turf wars spread as gangs tried to outgun each other for control of the local traffic. The sale and use of crack became so widespread it corroded much of what was left of the inner-city African-American community (Davis 1990).

The shocking conditions described above gave rise to a shocking musical form: hip hop. Stridently at odds with the values and tastes of both whites and middle-class African Americans, hip hop described and glorified the mean streets of the inner city while holding the police, the mass media, and other pillars of society in utter contempt. Furthermore, hip hop tried to offend middle-class sensibilities, black and white, by using highly offensive language.

In 1988, more than a decade after its first stirrings, hip hop reached its political high point with the release of the album *It Takes a Nation to Hold Us Back* by Chuck D and Public Enemy. In 'Don't Believe the Hype', Chuck D (Carlton Douglas Ridenhour) accused the mass media of maliciously distributing lies. In 'Black Steel in the Hour of Chaos', he charged the FBI and the CIA with assassinating the two great leaders of the African-American community in the 1960s, Martin Luther King and Malcolm X. In 'Party for Your Right to Fight', he blamed the US government for organizing the fall of the Black Panthers, the radical black nationalist party of the 1960s. Here, it seemed, was an angry expression of subcultural revolt that could not be mollified.

# Hip Hop Transformed

However, there were elements in hip hop that soon transformed it (Bayles 1994: 341–62; Neal 1999: 144–8). For one thing, early, radical hip hop was not written as dance music. It therefore cut itself off from a large audience. Moreover, hip hop entered a self-destructive phase with the emergence of gangster rap, which extolled criminal lifestyles, denigrated women, and replaced politics with drugs, guns, and machismo. The release of 'Cop Killer' by Ice T (Tracy Marrow) in 1992 provoked strong political opposition from Republicans and Democrats, white church groups, and black middle-class associations. 'Cop Killer' was not hip hop, but it fuelled a reaction against all anti-establishment music. Time/Warner was forced to withdraw the song from circulation. The sense that hip hop had reached a dead end, or at least a turning point, grew in 1996, when rapper Tupac Shakur (Parish Crooks) was murdered in the culmination of a feud between two hip hop record labels, Death Row in Los Angeles and Bad Boy in New York (Springhall 1998: 149–51).

If these events made it seem that hip hop was self-destructing, the police and insurance industries helped to speed up its demise. In 1988, a group called Niggas With Attitude released 'Fuck the Police', a critique of police violence against black youth. Law enforcement officials in several cities dared the group to perform the song in public, threatening to detain the performers or shut down their shows. Increasingly thereafter, ticket holders at hip hop concerts were searched for drugs and weapons, and security was tightened. Insurance companies, afraid of violence, substantially raised insurance rates for hip hop concerts, making them a financial risk. Soon, the number of venues willing to sponsor hip hop concerts dwindled.

While the developments noted above did much to mute the political force of hip hop, the seduction of big money did more. As early as 1982, with the release of Grandmaster Flash and the Furious Five's 'The Message', hip hop began to win acclaim from mainstream rock music critics. With the success of Run-DMC and Public Enemy in the late 1980s, it became clear there was a big audience for hip hop. Significantly, much of that audience was composed of white youths. As one music critic wrote, they 'relished . . . the subversive "otherness" that the music and its purveyors represented' (Neal 1999: 144). Sensing the opportunity for profit, major media corporations, such as Time/Warner, Sony, CBS/Columbia, and BMG Entertainment, signed distribution deals with the small independent recording labels that had formerly been the exclusive distributors of hip hop CDs. In 1988, *Yo! MTV Raps* debuted. The program brought hip hop to middle America.

Most hip hop recording artists proved they were eager to forego political relevancy for commerce. For instance, Wu-Tang Clan started a line of clothing called Wu Wear, and, with the help of major hip hop recording artists, companies as diverse as Tommy Hilfiger, Timberland, Starter, and Versace began to market clothing influenced by ghetto styles. Independent labels, such as Phat Farm and FUBU, also prospered. The members of Run-DMC once said that they 'don't want nobody's name on my behind' but those days were long past. By the early 1990s, hip hop was no longer just a musical form but a commodity with spin-offs. Rebellion had been turned into mass consumption.

## Bling

Some hip hop artists come from the inner city, have criminal backgrounds, served time in prison, and glorify the gangster lifestyle. As of this writing, Curtis '50 Cent' Jackson is probably the best known among them. Some hip hop artists remain true to their political birthright. For example, Chuck D's mother was a Black Panther activist, and to this day he is engaged in raising black political consciousness as a writer, publisher, and producer. It seems, however, that a large number of prominent hip hop artists emulate the gangster lifestyle neither because it reflects their origins nor because they regard it as a political statement but simply because it is stylish and profitable to do so. Their backgrounds have nothing in common with drug suppliers, pimps, and gang leaders, and their politics are mainstream or nonexistent. Even in the early years of hip hop, a gap between the biographies of many hip hop artists and their public personae was evident for those who took the time to do a background check. Three examples:

- DMC (Darryl McDaniels) was part of the legendary Run-DMC, the first hip hop group that looked like it ran with a gang and had just come off the street corner. Run-DMC was credited with bringing hip hop into the mainstream in the 1980s. Yet DMC was born into a solidly middle-class, suburban family. His parents were college-educated. He was described by rock critic Bill Adler as a good Catholic school kid, a mama's boy (Samuels 2004: 149).
- Another infamous figure was Ice T. He is often credited with starting the gangster rap movement with his single, '6'n the Morning'. He released 'Cop Killer' in 1992, causing a national scandal. Yet Ice T completed high school and served in the army as a ranger in the 25th Infantry. He now continues serving the forces of good by playing a detective in the TV show *Law and Order: Special Victims Unit*.
- Flavor Flav (William Jonathan Drayton, Jr.) was a member of the notorious Chuck D and Public Enemy. Yet he graduated high school and attended Adelphi, an old, respected college in Long Island, New York. He trained as a classical pianist. After a stint on the reality TV show *The Surreal Life*, he made a living co-starring in another reality TV show, *Strange Love*, with Brigitte Nielsen, a Danish actress once married to Sylvester Stallone. His latest TV venture is *The Flavor of Love*, in which 20 single women who profess to adore him move into a 'phat crib' in Los Angeles and compete for his affections.

## Table 24.1   Brand Names in Top 20 Songs, 2005

| Brand | Number of Mentions |
|---|:---:|
| Mercedes-Benz automobile | 100 |
| Nike sports shoes | 63 |
| Cadillac automobile | 62 |
| Bentley automobile | 51 |
| Rolls-Royce automobile | 46 |
| Hennessy cognac | 44 |
| Chevrolet automobile | 40 |
| Louis Vuitton luggage | 35 |
| Cristal champagne | 35 |
| AK-47 assault rifle | 33 |
| Total | 509 |
| Average mentions/song | 25.5 |

Source: Adapted from *Agenda Inc.* (2005): 4–7. Courtesy of Agenda Inc., http://agendainc.com

| Table 24.2 Top Brand Name–Dropping Artists, 2005 | |
| --- | --- |
| Artist | Number of Brands |
| 50 Cent | 20 brands in 7 songs |
| Ludacris | 13 brands in 6 songs |
| The Game | 13 brands in 2 songs |
| Ciara | 10 brands in 4 songs |
| Jamie Foxx | 6 brands in 1 song |
| Kanye West | 6 brands in 1 song |
| Lil' Jon | 6 brands in 2 songs |
| Tricky Daddy | 6 brands in 2 songs |
| Total | 80 brands in 25 songs |
| Average brands/song | 3.2 |

Source: Adapted from *Agenda Inc.* (2005): 4–7. Courtesy of Agenda Inc., http://agendainc.com

My contention that the 'getting-money game plan' drives many hip hop artists is supported by the near-worship of luxury commodities in much of their music. Consider Tables 24.1 and 24.2, based on the top 20 songs of 2005 on the Billboard charts, almost all of which were in the hip hop genre. Table 24.1 shows how many times the 10 most frequently mentioned brands were referred to in the top 20 songs. Table 24.2 lists the eight recording artists who referred to brands most frequently. The numbers tell a fascinating story. Each of the top 20 songs of 2005 mentioned brands 25.5 times on average. Assuming the average song is two-and-a-half minutes long, that works out to a brand mentioned every six seconds. From this point of view, hip hop is a lot like one of those soap commercials that rely mainly on brand name repetition to ensure that consumers keep the product in mind when they go grocery shopping. Only, in the world of hip hop, the good life is strongly associated not with laundry detergent but with driving a Mercedes, wearing Nikes, drinking Hennessy cognac, and packing an AK-47.

## Street Cred

The runaway financial success of some hip hop artists can rob them of what they call 'street cred'. One's claim to be a pimp or a cop killer can lose credibility when one shops at Salvatore Ferragamo and lives in the suburbs.

Successful hip hop artists have responded to the problem of street cred in three ways. First, some decide to give up any pretense of street cred by using their money to insulate themselves from the inner city. A Diddy or a Will Smith (formerly the Fresh Prince) makes no bones about catering to a largely white, suburban, culturally and politically mainstream, middle-class audience. They never lived in the inner city and apparently have no plans to visit any-time soon.

Successful hip hop artists whose audience appeal derives from their self-characterization as street toughs often take a more dangerous tack. They may live in the wealthy suburbs but they still frequent the inner city, where some of them were born. Many of them are undoubt-edly nostalgic about inner-city life, but they seem also to be motivated to visit the clubs and street corners of their old 'hood to show that they have not sold out. The trouble is that permanent residents often envy their wealth and fame; and this resentment can easily boil over into lethal violence. Famous hip hop artists who were shot and killed visiting their old neighbourhoods after striking it rich include Scott La Rock (Scott Sterling) in 1987 (the first high-profile hip hop slaying), Run-DMC's Jam Master Jay (Jason Mizell) in 2002, and Proof (DeShaun Holton), Eminem's right-hand man and member of D-12, in 2006 (Dawsey 2006). A compromise between rejecting the inner city and visiting it as a rich tourist involves staging gun battles for public consumption. For example, in March 2005, a sidewalk gunfight broke out near hip hop radio station WQHT in New York City between the entourages of hip hop star The Game and his former mentor, 50 Cent. The Game had hinted that he might record with one of 50 Cent's rivals, so 50 Cent expelled The Game from his inner circle. The gunfight followed. Four years earlier, on the same street corner, a similar incident occurred between followers of Lil' Kim, one of the few female hip hop stars, and rival Capone after Capone's group had referred to Lil' Kim as 'lame' in their appropriately titled song 'Bang, Bang'. In both gunfights, the hip hop stars' followers discharged many rounds of ammunition at close range but damage was minor. Total casualties in the 2001 and 2005 gun battles combined: one man shot in the leg in 2005.

It seems plausible that the gunfights were actually for show. They help to reinforce the violent image and street cred of the hip hop stars involved. Hip hop stars are multimillion-aire members of the music elite but the gunfights confer 'the illusion of their authenticity as desperate outlaws' (Haj du 2005). In that light, shootouts are low-risk investments by savvy businesspeople. Lil' Kim's shootout certainly paid off handsomely. She claimed in front of a Grand Jury that two of her associates were not present at the 2001 gunfight. But witnesses contradicted her testimony and WQHT's security tape showed her holding a door open for one of the men. She was subsequently sentenced to a year and a day in prison for perjury. The two weeks preceding her imprisonment on 19 September 2005 were videotaped for a reality show on Black Entertainment Television. The first episode of *Lil' Kim: Countdown to Lockdown* was the most watched series debut in the network's 25-year history. It has not been disclosed how much Lil' Kim earned for her efforts (Associated Press 2005; Strong 2006).

# The Three Promises of Hip Hop

## Identity

[M]an ain't like a dog . . . because . . . he know about death . . . [W]e ain't gonna get no move on in this world, lyin' around in the sun, lickin' our ass all day . . . [S]o with this said, you tell me what it is you wanna do with your life.

DJay (Terrence Howard), a pimp, to Nola (Twyn Manning), one of his prostitutes, in *Hustle and Flow* (2005)

People create, share, and socially transmit languages, beliefs, symbols, values, material objects, routine practices, and art forms to help them survive and prosper. Sociologists call the sum total of these responses to real-life problems **culture**. Medicine, Christianity, the Russian language, and the pulley help people cope, respectively, with ill health, questions about the meaning of life, the desire to communicate, and the need to raise heavy objects. Hip hop is no different. It is also a response to real-life problems.

For example, the 2005 box-office hit *Hustle and Flow* tells the story of how DJay responds culturally to his life problems. Knowing that we will die, we must choose how to live meaningfully or be reduced to an existence little better than that of a dog, says DJay. He finds that he can achieve self-fulfillment by giving up his life as a pimp and giving voice to the joys and frustrations of the life he knows in the largely black, poor, violent, downtown core of Memphis, Tennessee. He becomes a hip hop artist. Artistic self-expression renders his life meaningful and rewarding. It gives him a sense of identity.

To operate in the world, all people must develop a sense of who they are and what they can do (and who they aren't and what they can't do). The construction of identity is a lifelong task; people may alter their occupational, religious, national, ethnic, and even sexual identity as they mature and their circumstances change. But adolescence is the stage of life when most people lay the foundation for future development. It is typically a turbulent period, full of tentative experiments, exuberant strivings, the emulation of heroes, self-doubt, false starts, and confrontation with stubborn authority. By means of these experiments, strivings, and so forth, adolescents form a baseline identity. Particular styles of popular music—unique patterns of rhythm, melody, and lyrics—express adolescent struggles in particular social contexts and give them form. That is why popular music is so meaningful and important to most adolescents (and most nostalgic adults) (Gracyk 2001).

Minor currents in hip hop oppose violence, crime, drugs, and the mistreatment of women, but the dominant identity promoted by the genre is that of proud, arrogant, violent, criminal, misogynistic, black hyper-masculinity. The identity is largely a response to the degrading effects of racism on the self-esteem of black men in the American inner city. Take persistent poverty and bad schools, remove social services and industrial jobs, introduce crack and gang wars, and you soon get hip hop (Dyson 2006). Nelson George, the genre's leading historian, writes that hip hop is 'a system of survival' and 'an invigorating source of self-empowerment' (George 1998: 50). It negates middle-class sensibilities because many black men believe that middle-class sensibilities have tried to negate them.

## Upward Mobility

George is correct to note that 'hip hop didn't start as a career move but as a way of announcing one's existence in the world' (George 1998: 14). Nonetheless, a career move it soon became. If hip hop's first promise was to provide a sense of black male identity in the context of the American inner city in the 1970s and 1980s, its second promise was to serve as a path of upward social mobility out of that context. (Upward mobility refers to movement up a system of inequality.)

Yet hip hop's lure resembles the largely false hope offered by professional sports. In 2004, the National Basketball Association, the National Football League, and Major League Baseball employed 3,911 players of whom 1,650 were Black (see Table 2.3). That's 1,650 out of roughly 5 million black men between the ages of 18 and 40. The odds of an African-American man in the 18–40 age cohort being a top professional athlete are 3,030 to 1. If he lives to the age of 80, he has a better chance (3,000 to 1) of getting struck by lightning in his lifetime (estimated from 'Facts about Lightning', 2006; US Census Bureau 2002b). Although statistics on the subject are not available, it is evident that the odds of an African-American man becoming a hip hop star are considerably worse than his odds of becoming a top professional athlete; the black men who become well-known hip hop artists even at the regional level, let alone nationally or internationally, number in the low hundreds, not the low thousands.

The poor black youth who regard professional athletes and hip hop artists as role and mobility models have little chance of realizing their dreams, all the more so because their unrealistic aspirations often deflect their attention from a much safer bet—staying in school, studying hard, and pursuing an ordinary career (Doberman 1997). The odds of an African-American man in the 18–40 age cohort being a physician are roughly seven times better than the odds of his being a professional athlete or a well-known hip hop artist, and the odds of his being a lawyer are roughly 14 times better (estimated from Holmes 2005; King and Bendel 1995; US Census Bureau 2002a). Yet because so many young African-American men seek to follow the career paths and emulate the lifestyles (including the criminality) of a 50 Cent or an Allen Iverson, too few of them sing the praises of Dr James McCune Smith, the first

**Table 24.3** African-American Men in Professional Sports, 2004

| Sport | Players | Black Players | Black as a Percentage of Total |
|---|---|---|---|
| National Football League | 1,842 | 1,228 | 67 |
| National Basketball Association | 478 | 311 | 65 |
| Major League Baseball | 1,591 | 111 | 7 |
| Total | 3,911 | 1,650 | 42 |

Note: The disproportionately large number of black players in the NBA and the NFL is sometimes used to defend the view that blacks are *genetically* superior athletes (Entine, 2000). However, no genetic evidence of black athletic superiority exists. Besides, non-blacks dominate many sports, including hockey (Canadians and Russians), swimming (Australians), gymnastics (East-Europeans and Chinese), and soccer (West-European and South Americans). Superiority of particular racial, ethnic, and national groups in certain sports is the result of unique combinations of climate, geography, history, culture, and government and private-sector sponsorship, not genes.

Source: Adapted from Lapchick (2004: 15, 26, 35). *2004 Racial and Gender Report Card*, Orlando, FL: University of Central Florida. http://www.bus.ucf.edu/sport/public/downloads/2004-Racial_Gender_Report_Card.pdf (accessed 29 April 2006) pp. 15, 26, 35.

African-American doctor, or seek to emulate the uncool but respectable accomplishments of TV's Dr Heathcliff Huxtable. In 2005, the number of black law students in the United States fell to a 12-year low despite a growing black population (Holmes 2005).

An important lesson about the nature of culture lies embedded in this story. Culture is created to solve human problems, as we have seen. But not all elements of culture solve problems equally well. Some elements of culture even create new problems. After all, the creators of culture are only human. In the case at hand, it seems that by promoting unrealistic hopes for upward mobility and encouraging a lifestyle that draws young African-American men away from school, hard work, and the pursuit of an ordinary career, hip hop culture badly shortchanges them.

## Power

Like hip hop's promise of upward mobility, its assurance of power has proven largely an illusion.

We saw that hip hop emerged among African-American inner-city youth as a counsel of despair with strong political overtones. Many commentators believed that by reflecting the traditions, frustrations, and ambitions of the community that created it, hip hop would help the otherwise isolated voices of poor black youth sing in unison, shape a collective identity, and engage in concerted political action to improve the conditions of all African Americans (cf. Mattern 1998).

There are still radical political currents in hip hop. For the most part, however, it has become an apolitical commodity that increasingly appeals to a heterogeneous but mainly white, middle-class audience. As one of hip hop's leading analysts and academic sympathizers writes, 'the discourse of ghetto reality or 'hood authenticity remains largely devoid of political insight or progressive intent' (Forman 2001: 121).

Hip hop substantially lost its politics for three reasons. First, as one industry insider notes, 'Mainstream media outlets and executive decision-makers . . . fail to encourage or support overt political content and militant ideologies because . . . "it upsets the public"' (KRS-One cited in Forman 2001: 122). The recording industry got excited about hip hop precisely when executives saw the possibility of 'crossover', that is, selling the new black genre in the much larger white community. For them, hip hop was an opportunity little different from that offered by Motown in the 1960s. They apparently understood well, however, that to turn hip hop into an appealing mass-marketed commodity it had to be tamed and declawed of its political content so as not to offend its large potential audience. If they needed to be sensitized to the need to tone down the rhetoric, the political opposition to hip hop that was stimulated by gangster rap and songs like 'Cop Killer' in the early 1990s certainly helped. That opposition was the second reason hip hop lost its politics. Third, hip hop artists themselves contributed to the depoliticization of their music. For the most part untutored in politics, history, and the social sciences, they are unequipped to think clearly about the public policies that are needed to help the black underclass and the specific forms of political action that are needed to get the black underclass to help itself. At most, they offer the flavour of rebelliousness, the illusion of dissent, giving members of their audience the feeling of being daring and notorious rule breakers and revolutionaries but offering nothing in the way of concrete ideas, let alone leadership.

Vladimir Lenin, leader of the Russian Revolution of 1917, once said that capitalists are so eager to earn profits they will sell the rope from which they themselves will hang. But he underestimated his opponents. Savvy executives and willing recording artists have taken the edge off hip hop to make it more appealing to a mass market, thus turning dissent into a commodity (Frank and Weiland 1997). Young consumers are fooled into thinking they are buying rope to hang owners of big business, political authorities, and cultural conservatives. Really, they're just buying rope to constrain themselves.

Part of this chapter first appeared on-line as 'Hip Hop from Dissent to Commodity' at http://www.societyinquestion4e.nelson.com/article1.html.

## Notes

1.  There are important exceptions. In Asia and North Africa, women suffer markedly poorer access to food and health services than men. Moreover, in China, India, Singapore, Taiwan, and South Korea, ultrasound tests are widely used to determine the sex of babies before birth, and abortion of female fetuses is common. In such countries, the ratio of men to women is unusually high—about 106 (Brym and Lie 2007: 588; Sen 1990; 2001).

# References

Agenda Inc. 2005. 'American Brandstand 2005'. On the World Wide Web at www.agendainc.com/brandstand05.pdf (accessed March 2006).

Associated Press. 2005. 'Lil' Kim Sentenced to a Year in Prison'. *MSNBC.com* 6 July. On the World Wide Web at www.msnbc.com/id/8485039/ (accessed 20 April 2006).

Bayles, M. 1994. *Hole in Our Soul: The Loss of Beauty and Meaning in American Popular Music*. Chicago: University of Chicago Press.

Brym, R.J. and Lie, J. 2007. *Sociology: Your Compass for a New World*, 3rd ed. Belmont, CA: Wadsworth.

Davis, M. 1990. *City of Quartz: Excavating the Future in Los Angeles*. New York: Verso.

Doberman, J. 1997. *Darwin's Athletes: How Sport Has Damaged Black America and Preserved the Myth of Race*. Boston: Houghton Mifflin.

Dyson, M. E. 2006. *Come Hell or High Water: Hurricane Katrina and the Color of Disaster*. New York: Basic Civitas Books.

'Facts about Lightning'. 2006. *LEX18.com*. On the World Wide Web at www.lex18.com/Global/story.asp?S=1367554&nav=menu203_3 (accessed 29 April 2006)

Forman, M. 2001. 'It Ain't All about the Benjamins: Summit on Social Responsibility in the Hip-Hop Industry'. *Journal of Popular Music Studies* 13: 117–23.

Frank, T. and Weiland, M., eds. 1997. *Commodify Your Dissent: Salvos from the Baffler*. New York: W.W. Norton.

George, N. 1998. *Hip Hop America*. New York: Penguin.

Gracyk, T. 2001. *I Wanna Be Me: Rock Music and the Politics of Identity*. Philadelphia: Temple University Press.

Holmes, T.E. 2005. 'Blacks Underrepresented in Legal Field: ABA Report Shows Stark Contrasts in the Career Tracks of Lawyers'. *Black Enterprise* August 2005. On the World Wide Web at www.Findarticles.com/p/articles/mi_m1365/is_1_36/ai_n15674277/pg_2 (accessed 30 April 2005).

King, G. and Bendel, R. 1995. 'A Statistical Model Estimating the Number of African-American Physicians in the United States'. *Journal of the National Medical Association* 87, 4: 264–72.

Kubrin, C.E., Wadsworth, T., and DiPietre, S. 2006. 'Deindustrialization, Disadvantage and Suicide among Young Black Males'. *Social Forces* 84: 1,559–79.

Lapchick, R. 2004. *2004 Racial and Gender Report Card*. Orlando FL: University of Central Florida. On the World Wide Web at www.bus.ucf.edu/sport/public/downloads/2004_Racial_Gender_Report_Card.pdf (accessed 29 April 2006).

Mattern, M. 1998. *Acting in Concert: Music, Community and Political Action*. New Brunswick NJ: Rutgers University Press.

National Center for Injury Prevention and Control. 2006. 'WISQARS Leading Causes of Death Reports, 1999–2003'. On the World Wide Web at webapp.cdc.gov/sasweb/ncipc/leadcaus10.html (accessed 15 April 2006).

Neal, M.A. 1999. *What the Music Said: Black Popular Music and Black Public Culture*. New York: Routledge.

Piven, F.F., and Cloward, R.A. 1977. *Poor People's Movements: Why They Succeed, How They Fail*. New York: Vintage.

———. 1993. *Regulating the Poor: The Functions of Public Welfare*, updated ed. New York: Vintage.

Sen, A. 1990. 'More than 100 Million Women Are Missing'. *New York Review of Books* 20 December: 61–6.

———. 2001. 'Many Faces of Gender and Inequality'. Frontline 18: 27 October–9 November. On the World Wide Web at www.hinduonnet.com/fline/fl1822/18220040.htm (accessed 20 April 2005).

Springhall, J. 1998. *Youth, Popular Culture and Moral Panics: Penny Gaffs to Gangsta-Rap, 1830–1996*. New York: Routledge.

Strong, N. 2006. 'Lil' Kim's Reality Show Scores Highest Debut in BET History'. Allhiphop.com 14 March.

On the World Wide Web at www.allhiphop.com/hiphopnews/?ID=5460 (accessed 23 April 2006)

US Census Bureau. 2002a. 'Table 1. United States—Race and Hispanic Origin: 1790 to 1990'. On the World Wide Web at www.census.gov/population/documentation/twps0056/tab01/xls (accessed 29 April 2006).

———. 2002b. 'Table 3. Black or African-American Population, by Age and Sex for the United States: 2000'. On the World Wide Web at www.census.gov/population/cen2000/phc-t08/tab03.xls (accessed 29 April 2006).

Wilson, W.J. 1987. *The Truly Disadvantaged: The Inner City, the Underclass, and Public Policy*. Chicago: University of Chicago Press.

## Introduction

What is the stereotype of the young black Canadian? How does the media contribute to this stereotype? In what ways do black Canadians—and especially black young offenders—identify with and embrace these stereotypes?

This sociological study investigates the influence of racial stereotypes of blacks in the media on their self-concepts and identity. Specifically, it examines to what extent the interviewees' views of themselves incorporate the 'gangsta' stereotype frequently portrayed in the mass media as part of their black identity. The authors address not only if, but also how, stereotypical views may influence an audience. While most interviewees recognized and related to the 'gangsta' stereotype, they also assessed other stereotypical views of blacks in deciding which to relate to. So why did these individuals choose to adopt the 'gangsta' image to the extent that they did?

# On the Assimilation of Racial Stereotypes among Black Canadian Young Offenders

*John F. Manzo and Monetta M. Bailey*

This paper investigates the assimilation and iteration of racial stereotypes among black[1] Canadians by inspecting open-ended interviews with eight black or mixed-race respondents who are adjudicated young offenders. The focus of this investigation is on whether, and to what extent, this assimilation can be observed in interviewees' discourse and, moreover, whether the speakers' self-concepts entail their incorporation of 'criminal' as an aspect of black identity.

An association between race and criminal justice processing in Canada has been documented, particularly with respect to black and native persons. Wortley (1999) notes that, in 1997, native persons represented about four per cent of the population but constituted 14 per cent of federal prison inmates. Black persons accounted for roughly two per cent of the population while representing over six per cent of those in federal correctional institutions. Native persons had an incarceration rate of 184.85 per 100,000 persons, while that of black Canadians was 146.37; non-native, non-black Canadians were incarcerated at a rate of about 100 per 100,000 (Wortley 1999: 261).

This evident association between race and crime (or incarceration), among other factors, has led many in society to develop negative stereotypes of persons based on their racial identities. In Canada, these negative impressions stem not only from actual experiences of prisoners in the criminal justice system, but also from images in North American culture and media. Despite the relatively small black population in Canada, Canadians are almost certainly familiar with the image of the black 'gangsta' from media imagery imported from the US, a nation with more than six times the population of black persons, per capita, and embracing a black population with a history, culture, and level of social segregation different from that in Canada.

Mass-cultural images of black Canadians, it would seem, not only motivate stereotyping on the part of those who are not Black, they should also influence racial identities and related self-concepts among black persons themselves. This paper considers results of a study that investigated the association between crime and the formation of a racial identity among black young offenders. The study entailed open-ended interviews on topics including police-minority relations, the racialization and criminalization of their racial groups, the connection between their lifestyle and cultural influences such as rap music, and the relationship between their racial group and the dominant (white) culture.

The focus of this paper is on the responses given by respondents with regard to the social depiction of their race, the possible impact of this depiction in their racial identity formation, and the relationship between this depiction and their criminal actions. First, we consider how the youth believe their racial group is portrayed in society. We then ascertain if they believe these images comprise 'criminal' elements. Finally, we investigate whether and how this portrayal has been internalized by these youth to inform or influence their criminal actions.

## Theoretical Perspectives

We consider 'race' to be a socially constructed, malleable, interpersonally relevant and, thus, a 'micro'-level phenomenon; we also recognize that 'race' has an historical and otherwise 'macro' social resonance and meaning that exists over and above individuals' perception of and claims to it. For these reasons, the theoretical perspectives of this paper adopt views that partake of both historical and social-interactional construal of race. This paper deploys social construction perspectives as developed by Berger and Luckmann (1966) with notions of the historically embedded construction of race derived from post-colonial theory (Fanon 1967; Said 1978), and, at the level of lived and lively social experience, we rely on the notion of cultural transmission that is based on the contributions of C. Wright Mills (1963) with respect to what he termed 'vocabularies of motive'. The first two of these theories account for 'race' as socially and historically defined and embedded, as aspects of a cultural endowment that is given and, more clearly for post-colonial theory, imposed, on persons; the last theoretical theme considers how, through what concrete discursive means, the content of racial typifications is 'taught' to occupants of those historically and socially constructed racial categories.

Social construction theory (cf. Berger and Luckmann 1966) maintains that individuals define themselves based on social conceptions of the group to which they claim membership. Social construction theory holds that the basis for 'subjective' reality is in fact the social world: The self is created through a dialectical, reflexive relationship between the individuals and their social milieux. Social construction theory thus argues that persons see themselves in the same terms that society views them.

With respect to racial identity and criminal propensities, social constructionists such as

Blakey (1999), Holdaway (1997), Rodkin (1993) and Schiele (1998) argue that most social theories about race and crime tend to reify race and ignore the social process that is involved in the creation of racial categories. Such theories do so by treating race as endogenous to the person and assigned as any other biological feature. We, on the other hand, side with constructionists who view 'race' not as a static, ascribed quality of persons but as a process achieved and learned through social interaction and as a consequence of the receipt of cultural definitions of race. This construction of race is known as racialization, a process through which meanings and definitions become associated with what become socially defined as different racial categories. It is the way in which race is constructed in everyday life and becomes, in effect, 'real' in society and to the individual.

Colonial theory adds to social-construction approaches by accounting for social conceptualizations of race based on historical relations among different racial and ethnic groups. In his seminal *Black Skin, White Masks*, Fanon (1967) proposes that, in a former colonial society, socially accepted modes of thought were based on the views of the dominant, 'colonizing' group. The culture, language, and customs of the colonizers come to be normative and to be considered superior to both local indigenous cultures and to those who were part of subsequent non-white diasporas to post-colonial societies. Thus, in North American society, definitions and stereotypes of races, among other topics, are created and organized by persons of Northern and Western European origin. Colonial theorists see present-day society as evincing the racial relationships and subjugation that characterized colonial times. Negative images associated with minority groups therefore derive from a colonial history, and the self-concepts that minority persons adopt owe to their place vis-à-vis white persons historically. . . .

Our research is . . . finally informed by the notion of 'cultural transmission', which suggests concrete ways through which negative self-concepts and stereotypes are adopted through social praxis. Cultural transmission theories concern how popular culture, among other discursive forms, can influence individual action. Cultural transmission theory also proposes how individuals justify their seemingly deviant actions by referring to socially accepted accounts for doing so, such as 'I am owed this money, so I am not really stealing it', or 'I am defending my family's honour by harming this person; I am not committing a crime'. These statements are known as 'vocabularies of motive' (Mills 1963) and were most famously explicated in 'drift theory', as developed by Sykes and Matza (1957). Vocabularies of motive are cognitive and linguistic concepts that furnish motives (before the fact) and accounts (after the fact; cf. Lyman and Scott 1968) for committing certain classes of behaviours. The concept has seen greatest use as an explanation for the tendency for persons to drift in and out of criminal or otherwise deviant behaviour, as with studies that encompass deviant acts from non-criminal activities like cheating on tests (McCabe 1992), to suicide (Stephens 1984), rape and murder (Scully and Marolla 1984). The concept has also informed understandings relating to the motivations of some victims of domestic violence to remain with their abusers (Ferraro and Johnson 1983); 'vocabulary of motive' thus need not only be a resource to permit the forming of motive to commit deviant or criminal acts. With respect to the topics under investigation here, cultural transmission is important in understanding how Black persons may internalize societal depictions of themselves as resources to "motivate" them to behave in manners consistent with those stereotypes. These cultural messages must, moreover, come from concrete sources of communication, and our research suggests that these can and do emerge from discourses in popular media. As such, we argue that media not only 'teach' racial stereotypes (in positive as well as pejorative senses), but also that these stereotypes themselves can facilitate criminal and otherwise deviant motives and rationalizations. . . ).

# Methodology

## The Sample

This paper examines interviews with respondents from a study entailing interviews of eight black or mulatto young offenders between 14 and 18 years old in Alberta, Canada. Three were in open-custody residential 'group homes', and five were in secure custody at a youth detention facility. The ages and placements for each interviewee are indicated the first time each is cited in this report.

The second author, who is herself a black Canadian originally from Barbados, conducted the interviews. As part of our protocol for the protection of human subjects and following the insistence of our gate-keeping agencies, she was not permitted to inquire about our subjects' crimes (although they were, of course, permitted to discuss or allude to them themselves . . .).

# Findings

## Respondents' Perspectives on Societal Views of Black Persons

Overall, respondents expressed, unsurprisingly, the view that stereotypical ideas of black persons did exist socially, and that these images owed largely to what the youths construed as representations depicted in media and in the larger culture. The respondents seemed, moreover, to identify with these stereotypes, some more than others.

## Stereotypes of Blacks

Respondents suggested that stereotypes of Blacks were of two categories. First, people saw Blacks as being 'dangerous', as possessing at best defiant attitudes and at worst criminal tendencies, in line with what might be called a 'gangsta' image. Although the respondents demonstrated a partial acceptance of this stereotype in that they also stated that style of dress influences how they judge other black persons, they expressed some anger that non-Blacks did this. They were quite vocal in their objection to others placing Blacks into categories, and determining membership in a category according to style of dress. This objection was largely founded on the fact that the respondents believed that when others viewed them, based on their style of dress, as in the 'gangsta' category, they associated criminal behaviour with it.

The second stereotype that respondents noted saw black persons as entertainers, that is, as athletes, actors, musical performers, and so on. This view of Blacks is not mutually exclusive with respect to the 'gangsta' image; indeed, the essence of 'gangsta' is demonstrated by a look adopted by rap stars and other black celebrities, including some athletes. Consequently, respondents stated that they believe that many people in society assumed that they were criminals. Carl (16, secure custody) said,

> . . . because I'm black, everybody looks at you like . . . a gangsta, playa, baller, right. I don't look at myself like that but everyone else calls me that, like 'What's up, thug?', you know, like a gangsta . . . because you are black you gotta be a thug, you gotta be a gangsta, that's how they all think. They look at you and if you're not that then you are not popular, you are not really black. I think that's all wrong though.

Black respondents generally believed that social evaluations of them were more negative than positive. The question of how they believed they were seen by members of society drew responses such as: 'Probably bad things, like you are, I don't know, in gangs . . . like we are going to steal or something', or . . . 'some people think that black people are always bad, they're always in gangs, this and that, right'. One respondent deployed the notion of 'stereotype' that such perceptions comprise. Desmond (17, secure custody) stated, 'People assume that I am in a gang when I'm walking around with all my friends. Like that's a straight-up stereotype right there. And then, like coming in here, they think "Oh he's black, he did this", so it's the same thing that everybody else is thinking. Stereotype'. The issue arises in accordance with our research questions as to where these stereotypes come from. In every interview, the interviewees' overwhelming response was that media played an important part in promoting views of black persons and black culture. The respondents' utterances on these matters follow.

## Portrayals of Blacks in the Media

The respondents saw the overall portrayal of Blacks in the media as mixed, with respect to the relative amount of positive and negative imagery that are portrayed, but saw these images as conforming to stereotypes regardless. For example, respondents reflected on how black persons are shown possessing special talents, as athletes in particular sports or as entertainers in a very delimited range of arts (as rappers or comedians, for example).

The other way they are seen in the media, from our respondents' experiences, was as criminals. The interesting thing about the criminal portrayal was the judgment associated with it depended on the media outlet. Some respondents noted that, usually in the news and mainstream media, the criminal image that Blacks had was seen as negative, while in media intended for black (almost always African-American) audiences, this image, even when the black persons in them were in fact depicted as criminals, had more positive connotations . . .

While Daniel (17, secure custody) seemed to recognize that the portrayal of Blacks in the media was mixed in the ways expressed by the other respondents, he implied that the negative representations were more common than positive ones:

> They look like—like criminals and stuff like that. Only some, only some 'cause some black people are talented and positive people, you know, sometimes. But sometimes

they just, I don't know, sometimes they look bad. Like I know like when you're sitting watching TV and stuff, they make them look like people from the ghetto and stuff like that all the time. Like every black person's from the ghetto and stuff, and do a lot of crime and stuff like that.

Daniel further expressed that he believed that the negative views of Blacks in society could be attributed to the depictions of Blacks in the media.

. . . lots of people think of black people as thugs and robbing people and stuff, you know . . . Like some people think that a black person's not normal. They just think—like how there's a lot of crime and stuff because of movies and stuff, you know, and how black people that are in the movies, they all live in ghettos and stuff and all do crime and stuff like that. I just think that that's how people see us.

Given this reporting of negative media imagery, the question emerges as to how respondents themselves adopted or rejected those images as constituting their views of themselves.

## Respondents' Perspectives on the 'Gangsta' Image

It became clear that the majority of respondents felt some connection to a 'gangsta' image. The respondents defined this image as specific to Blacks, and as opposed to the 'normal' social depiction of Whites as not 'gangsta'. While the youths under study here allowed that some Blacks were 'normal', respondents also saw 'gangstas' or 'thugs' as uniquely black constructs. Moreover, respondents expressed no desire to assume a conventional, socially acceptable image. These respondents all suggested that their refusal to conform to 'normal' social types, to which some outrightly referred to as 'looking and acting white', meant that they were seen as that particular other known as 'gangstas'. They chose to embrace this image . . .

This gangsta image encompasses at once dress, language, and demeanour. The style of dress entailed an African-American 'street' sensibility, comprising labels such as Sean John; however, despite the evident importance that appearance should play in being a 'gangsta', respondents were more likely to address the demeanour or 'attitude' that 'gangsta' encompasses. One aspect of demeanour entails the linguistic performance of gangstas, and indeed the gangsta argot is marked by profanity and a specialized vocabulary, as Ricky articulates:

. . . [others] don't swear as much as we do, they don't use profanity or whatever as much as we do. They don't use slang as much as us, they're like, 'Hey, how are you?'; we are like 'Wha's up man?' or something like that. I don't know, to [others] our language or our slang, our gangsta language to them is hard.

Gangsta demeanour encompassed a self-presentation that would best be described as carefree but threatening, because all acknowledged that when challenged or 'dissed' they could then marshal violence. Kobe interpreted the difference between the black and white attitudes this way:

> White people are more snotty. Black people are I think, are more relaxed, you know. 'Cause I have—some of my friends are black friends and they're just, like, into chillin' and all that . . . Basically, I think white people are more snotty and more rude.

This attitude was one that the respondents thought afforded Blacks more fun than other groups. However, the carefree attitude was juxtaposed by the tough attitude that 'gangstas' had when they were upset. When referring to a friend, Carl said,

> . . . he's like 'hard', like he doesn't care what he does, like me. I can do something, I don't care what you do, but if you cross me you wouldn't expect me to hit you or something like that, but I'll pop you without even caring . . .

Finally, the gangsta image was marked by the prevalence of smoking marijuana, which most respondents admitted to, and associated with their definition of a gangsta. Some respondents commented on the crimes they committed while smoking 'weed'; others noted that they were often approached as a source of it. It was also an aspect of the 'carefree' attitude described earlier . . .

It was clear, then, that the majority of respondents identified to some extent with the 'gangsta' type. This identification is seen not only in the style of dress that the respondents embraced, but also in the attitude that they held towards others. This was apparent in Ricky, who stated that he wished others to think the following of him:

> Like if you mess with me, like I'll kill you . . . like I don't care, that's my attitude, I don't care . . . In my mind what I think of it is, if you do something to me, I think of it as this: A nigga never forgets.

The youths deployed the word 'nigga' recurrently. Several respondents, explicitly or implicitly, made the distinction between a 'nigga' and a 'gangsta'. Ricky suggested that a 'gangsta' just 'goes around and causes trouble, or jacks somebody for no reason', on the other hand, a 'nigga' 'beats up somebody, but there is a reason'. For these youth, there was more pride and, one may conclude, social acceptability in being a 'nigga' than in a being a 'gangsta'. Thus, it is fair to say that some of the youth identified more closely with the image of a 'nigga' rather than that of a 'gangsta'. It should also be noted that most of the youth did not make this distinction, and that it is fair to say that most respondents could be said to identify with both typologies.

## History and Black Identity

Post-colonial theory recommends that black persons' views of themselves will partake of the historical position of black peoples vis-à-vis their oppressors. Questions emerge, however, concerning which black peoples' history, which oppressors, and where, exactly, these images would come from. When respondents reported knowledge of the history of black persons in North America, this knowledge was gleaned from televised imagery and the unavoidable

American influence that it contains. This is important because, like most black persons in Canada, all but one of these respondents' black ancestors emigrated to Canada from the West Indies, mostly Jamaica, rather than from the United States; an additional respondent's family had immigrated from Africa. In addition, all of the respondents were Canadian citizens, yet not one demonstrated any knowledge of the history of blacks in Canada. Moreover, most admitted little knowledge of the history of Jamaica (or any other Caribbean nation) or its race politics . . .

[W]ith some exceptions, respondents were largely unaware of the history that attached to black identity and, in particular, the history relevant to their own ancestries. However, post-colonial theory suggests that the effect of the past provides for an unseen shaping of one's contemporary worldview. We would not have expected that respondents would state the precepts of post-colonial theory explicitly, or that they would have to know about their own ancestors' experiences with colonialism in order to experience its latent effects. They should, however, appear to be aware of those posited effects when they speak of their oppression; however, even this discussion does not completely support the tenets of post-colonial theory, because respondents' views did not clearly suggest that they saw themselves as oppressed. The following excerpts demonstrate this finding.

## Respondents' Views on 'Oppression'

Most respondents suggested that there were disadvantages associated with being Black in Canada, but they expressed pride in being Black. The interviewees suggested, in general, that while there was racism in society, they did not believe themselves to be seriously affected by it, even while admitting to being influenced by and sometimes judged unfairly due to the currency of a 'gangsta' image of Blacks. The reason behind this may be that black respondents seemed to take pride in some of the stereotypes of their race, both positive and negative. These depictions included stereotypes that Blacks are especially talented in certain sports, and as entertainers, but some also took pride in evincing images such as 'gangstas' and 'thugs'. Many also claimed that they simply did not care what others' views of them were in the first place; indeed, we note that respondents even deployed a fatalistic view of societal opinions of them as a variety of vocabulary of motive, one that said, to paraphrase, 'if this is how society sees me, I might as well act in this way'.

With respect to perceptions of 'oppression', respondents were in fact able to identify some areas in which they believed that their race put them at a relative disadvantage. Some indicated that they believed that stereotypical views of Blacks would make it more difficult for them to acquire certain jobs, and that Blacks were often under the surveillance of police and private security. None, however, indicated that these complications made it impossible for them to achieve their goals.

The youth evidenced internalization of negative stereotypes in a process consistent with the claims of 'vocabulary of motive' and related approaches in criminology, which address how persons justify deviant behaviours by marshalling cognitive and linguistic scripts that serve as motives, rationalizations, or excuses for those behaviours. Dale exemplified this tendency when he said, 'A lot of people think I'm bad, so why would I care?'. . .

Youth assented to other stereotypes as well. For example, Desmond, Daniel, and Carl all embraced the stereotype that Blacks are skilled athletically. Desmond, when asked what characteristics distinguished Blacks from other racial groups, stated:

> Some physical characteristics, 'cause when—like we're more built than other people and we're more physical, can do things better, some things. Like we're quicker in running, like athletes. We're more athletic and stuff like that . . .

Carl, however, appeared to be the only respondent who saw this stereotype as misleading, albeit one that always permits him to 'automatically play' despite his very surprising and counter-stereotypical admission that he 'can't play ball, right?'

> People look at you like because you are Black you can do that. Like in here, at this place, they are like, 'Good, you can play ball right?' But I can't play ball. Right? But they just think that all black people can play ball. They always want me on their teams . . . not for hockey though or for volleyball—but for basketball or baseball. 'Cause I'm Black I automatically play . . . just 'cause I'm Black I should be athletic, not for, like, the joy of the game . . .

The interviewees consistently demonstrated beliefs that society saw them in negative terms, but they also showed evidence of internalizing and even coveting those characteristics. It should be noted that none of the youth said anything along the lines of 'all black people are criminal'; it is not in this sense that we mean that the interviewees 'internalized' either negative or positive stereotypes. They allowed that 'Black' comprises diversity. However, the youth interviewed all identified with 'gangsta'. In addition, they saw this image as a generally desirable one for them, and many of them admitted that they have engaged in behaviour that supports such a representation. Their claimed knowledge of society's opinion of them permitted these youth to relinquish responsibility for their criminality; they merely acted in accordance with how, they believed, they were seen by other people.

## Conclusions

The participants in this study articulate a view of themselves and of black persons in general that is consistent with certain stereotypes. This finding supports the claims of social construction and post-colonial theories, both of which anticipate that a member of any racial minority—particularly one whose history entailed overt oppression, discrimination or slavery—would adopt self-images in line with those prescribed and maintained by the larger society. However, it is vital that we emphasize that our findings do not support these theories *tout court*; in particular, the implication of victimization tacit in social construction and, especially, post-colonial theory is not clearly present in our respondents' discourses. Yes, their self-concepts appear riddled, in one sense, with the typifications of 'Black' provided them in their cultures. Paradoxically, in accepting, to varying degrees, the existence of these social stereotypes, our respondents were also distancing themselves from mainstream (especially 'white') society by embracing them. Not only do the interviewees admire and in some cases aspire to 'gangsta', but they also take pride in certain other stereotypes, for example that Blacks are good athletes, actors, rappers, and singers. While these youth sometimes expressed frustration with the stereotypes, they also supported them in their responses.

Of course, any social status comprises behavioural, performative aspects—'roles', in other words—and so we must ask to what extent these youths' acceptance and internalization of certain racial typologies (such as 'gangsta' or 'nigga', which, despite the positive claims about this status, would appear to have certain deviant associations as well) had consequences for their behaviours, especially their criminality. We argue that this association is evident. The respondents here had all been adjudicated as young offenders, and although we did not overtly discuss specific crimes, we note that these youth took pride in their own 'gangsta' aspect, using it as a way to differentiate them from the dominant culture. Such a finding clarifies the importance of considering the content of communication and the ways in which it is received and deployed by its audience. In our study, the cultural imagery of the 'gangsta' furnished not only a stereotype for the youth here to lay claim to, it also furnished a resource for motivating and justifying criminal activity. To reiterate a point made earlier in this paper, the perspectives of social construction/post-colonialism might elucidate that black persons adopt stereotypes of themselves as their own identities; these theories do not, however, elucidate how this is done or how the stereotypes themselves might impel deviant behaviours. In incorporating all of these theoretical views, we have here accounted for both sides of the problem.

We believe that pride in their racial group demonstrated for these youth a form of resilience that had both positive and negative connotations. In a culture where they are aware of negative racial associations, it is helpful and hopeful for these youth to identify aspects of their race as positive and to take pride in them. However, a problem arises when the aspect that they choose to embrace is inherently criminal and, quite possibly, criminogenic, such as the gangsta image that these youth have adopted and that they extol. We believe that a deeper problem is a lack of viable alternatives for these youth, which is demonstrated in limited role models, a lack of knowledge of the history of their culture, and a society that advertises a limited view of an entire, diverse racial group. To innovate on cultural transmission approaches, the 'culture' in this case 'transmits' precious little in terms of an identity that Black youth might adopt. In a world in which the only viable alternatives are sport (for males), entertaining, or crime, it is unsurprising that Black youth, in Canada and elsewhere, ally with the option that requires the least specialized talent.

## Note

1.  Our use of the term 'black', and not 'African-Canadian' or 'West-Indian Canadian' is preferable since it comprises all those of African heritage. We use this term to refer to both black and mixed race or 'mulatto' speakers, since both groups in this study identify as "black."

# References

Berger, P. and Luckmann, T. 1966. *The Social Construction of Reality: A Treatise in the Sociology of Knowledge*. New York: Anchor Books.

Blakey, M. 1999. 'Scientific racism and the biological concept of race.' *Literature and Psychology*, Vol. 13, No. 1, pp. 1–29.

Fanon, F. 1967. *Black Skin, White Masks*. New York: Grove Weidenfeld.

Ferraro, K. and Johnson, J. 1983. 'How women experience battering: The process of victimization.' *Social Problems*, Vol. 39, No. 3, pp. 325–35.

Holdaway, S. 1997. 'Some recent approaches to the study of race in criminological research: Race as a social process.' *British Journal of Criminology*, Vol. 37, No. 3, pp. 383–401.

Lyman, S.M. and Scott, M.B. 1968. 'Accounts.' *American Sociological Review*, Vol. 33, No. 1, pp. 46–62.

McCabe, D. 1992. 'Influence of situational ethics on cheating among college students'. *Sociological Inquiry*, Vol. 82, No. 3, pp. 365–74.

Mills, C.W. 1963. 'Situated actions and vocabularies of motive'. In *Power, Politics and People*. I.L. Horowitz (ed.). New York: Oxford University Press, pp. 439–52.

Rodkin, P. 1993. 'The psychological reality of social constructions'. *Ethnic and Racial Studies*, Vol. 16, No. 4, pp. 633–56.

Said, E. 1978. *Orientalism*. Harmondsworth, UK: Penguin.

Schiele, J. 1998. 'Cultural alignment, African American male youths and violent crime'. *Journal of Behavior in the Social Environment*, Vol. 1, No. 2, pp. 165–81.

Scully, D. and Marolla, J. 1984. 'Convicted rapists' vocabulary of motives: Excuses and justifications'. *Social Problems*, Vol. 31, No. 4, pp. 530–44.

Staples, R. 1975. 'White racism, Black crime, and American justice: An application of the colonial model to explain crime and race'. *Phylon*, Vol. 36, No. 1, pp. 14–22.

Stephens, B. 1984. 'Vocabularies of motive and suicide'. *Suicide and Life-Threatening Behavior*, Vol. 14, No. 2, pp. 243–53.

Sykes, G. and Matza, D. 1957. 'Techniques of neutralization: A theory of delinquency'. *American Sociological Review*, Vol. 22, No. 4, pp. 664–70.

Tatum, B. 2000. *Crime, Violence and Minority Groups*. Aldershot, UK: Ashgate Publishing.

Wortley, S. 1999. 'A northern taboo: Research on race, crime and criminal justice in Canada'. *Canadian Journal of Criminology*, Vol. 41, No. 1, pp. 261–74.

Young, R. 1990. *White Mythologies: Writing History and the West*. London: Routledge.

# Part VII | Street Crime

The articles in this section address various issues regarding violent crime, including how to effectively respond to it. 'Street crime' is the informal term for interpersonal criminal violence, and it's used here deliberately to draw attention to some of the misconceptions we encounter when we investigate violent crime. Street crime suggests violent crimes usually occur on the streets and involve strangers. But as Canada's 2004 General Social Survey found, three-quarters of violent incidents occur in commercial or public institutions and people's homes (and this tabulation excludes incidents of spousal assault). And violent incidents usually involve people who do know each other, notably in the case of homicides, assaults, and sexual assaults. Although violent crime has a high public profile, government statistics based on police reports indicate that it usually constitutes around 12 per cent of all reported crime in any given year, with homicides making up under 1 per cent of reported violent crime.

An important contribution of social scientific studies has been to challenge and debunk misconceptions often spawned by sensationalized portrayals of crime in both the news and entertainment. One approach to doing this involves the difficult work of gathering valid and reliable statistics. Criminology, in particular, has focused on the precise measurement and prediction of crime using quantitative methods that are attentive to matters of definition and methods of gathering statistics. More critical forms of criminology extend this attention to the social, political, and economic environments in which crime occurs.

Sociological studies often employ more qualitative research methods, attend to how crime, like other forms of deviance, is a social process, and address areas that are more theoretically ambiguous in nature. For instance, what counts as violence? Or criminal violence? A violent act may seem self-evident, but it occurs in a social context and undergoes interpretations, judgments, and varying reactions. Conventionally, violence refers to any interaction in which physical force is used to manipulate another. But such a generic definition ends up including some behaviours that are socially approved or at least tolerated, and excluding behaviours that are experienced as 'violent' even though they don't involve physical force itself such as deliberate psychological abuse and social humiliation. Similarly, what counts as criminal violence may exclude incidents where force is applied to those not legally regarded as human beings such as lynching blacks, killing women, and physically assaulting children—all of whom were not legally regarded as persons during certain periods of Western history.

An important concept in studying violence is 'normative suspension', and it underscores the importance of social context in defining and reacting to an act as a deviant behaviour. The term is typically applied to events that occur in a leisure context, like sports. There, the regular rules of society are removed and replaced by more lax, though still restrictive, rules developed and enforced by those participating in the activity. For instance, much of the behaviour that goes on in a hockey or football game would end up in a courtroom if it occurred outside of the sport. But normative suspension can also be useful in examining many public issues beyond the context of sports, as we'll see in the next section.

Another example of sociological research concerns the structure of violent transactions, which highlights how deviance is a social process, often a spiralling one as we saw in the example of Frank at the beginning of the book. Some kinds of interactions are more likely to result in violent outcomes than others. Studies have found assaults and homicides are often bound up with 'fights'[1] or 'arguments'. Fights are frequently character contests in which participants try to save face at each other's expense. They exhibit a common pattern of escalation beginning with an attack by one party on the character of another. The other person then attempts to engage in some mildly aggressive identity-saving retaliation which provokes a sustained or heightened attack by the first party, and so forth until it spirals out of control. The chances of the contest escalating out of control are heightened by the presence of bystanders, especially if they adopt postures of neutrality or encouragement.

Finally, discussions of violent crime often introduce statistics. But it is important to be attentive to how the statistics have been gathered as well as what kinds of events are being counted, or not counted. For while crime statistics may be part of the descriptive activity of counting disreputable violence, they are usually also part of the project of controlling such violence. And concealed behind any display of statistical data are always questions concerning what exactly is in need of being controlled and what isn't, as well as issues of definition and interpretation. As we saw in Chapter 4, workplace fatalities resulting from violations of the Health and Safety Act far outnumber homicides, but usually aren't counted in crime statistics. What may be omitted in how we currently classify and enforce interpersonal criminal violence?

## Notes

1.  Luckenbill, D.F. 1977. 'Criminal homicides as a situated transaction', *Social Problems*. 25: 176–86; and D.F. Luckenbill and D.P. Doyle. 1989. 'Structural position and violence: developing a cultural explanation', *Criminology*. 27 (3): 419–436.

## Introduction

Studies of the social construction of deviance frequently find that the media as well as medical or judicial authorities portray the 'criminal' as committing the crime for psychological reasons like pathological greed or some other disorder. Social, economic, or political factors are downplayed or often completely ignored. This, in turn, contributes to a public image of 'them' as a different from 'us'. But there are cases where some very grizzly violent crimes are committed for seemingly pathological reasons. Here we are introduced to serial killer Michael Wayne McGray. Although McGray's acts are horrifying, sociologically McGray is quite familiar. He fits a prevalent, ideal typical image of the 'criminal' as a calculating, remorseless, violent person—or sociopath—who brings terror to many of those he encounters. And as Anderson points out, she really does find McGray terrifying.

At the same time, in terms of those who are imprisoned for crimes, McGray is not typical. About 9 out of 10 of offenders in Ontario's provincial prisons are sentenced for non-violent offences, and about two thirds of offenders in Canada's federal system are there for non-violent offences. So what is to be done with individuals like McGray? And what do we do with a correctional system designed to treat clients as if they were like McGray when most often they're not?

# One on One with a Killer

*Erin Anderson*

When I first meet the man claiming the slaughter of 16 people and the title as Canada's most horrifying serial killer, he is asking after his mom like any good son.

She has been receiving crank calls, it seems, and her health is frail, and Michael Wayne McGray pleads with a prison official for time tonight to phone her, to make sure she's okay. When he is promised the call, he relaxes back into his chair. We're left alone, with a wall of glass between us.

And Mr McGray begins, ever so nonchalantly, to talk about the killings. How it made him feel good to stab those prostitutes in the dark. How eagerly the gay men took him home, never suspecting. How the death and pain and blood of it all fuelled his fantasies for months.

He never flinches once in the telling. His soft voice sounds the same tallying victims as it did speaking of his mother. To anyone watching, we might be chatting about the Oscars.

The guards at the maximum-security prison where Mr McGray has begun his life sentence, after pleading guilty to first-degree murder in Moncton on Monday, are not taking any chances. They joke about 'his urges', but they know that he has threatened to kill a guard if he has the chance, and he is not allowed around other prisoners.

I put in the request on Tuesday for an interview, and, for two days, prison officials had told me that Mr McGray wasn't feeling up for visitors of any kind—he was fighting his homicidal 'urges', what he calls his 'hunger'.

On Wednesday, he apparently smashed the television in his room. But by Thursday, he was prepared to talk, and I headed to Renous, about 150 kilometres by bumpy highway north of Moncton.

Before my trip, police warned me to be extra careful with him—one officer helpfully described how it would only take a second for such a hulking man to slip his shackled wrists over my head and snap my neck, if he felt so inclined.

There was never a chance of that happening. The glass divider penned him in, and the guards watched us from a window overlooking the room.

But every so often, Mr McGray would casually drag his fingers across the glass surface while making some point, and though I knew I couldn't be in any danger, I had to fight the instinct to jump away.

He is still the man who strangled a Moncton woman named Joan Hicks with his bare hands, beat her head against her bathroom wall, and then slashed her throat just to make certain she was dead.

And I have seen the sickening crime-scene photo of what happened next to her 11-year-old daughter Nena, who so loved the Maple Leafs and was learning French.

Even if Mr McGray's story is true and another man killed the girl, he was still there in her bedroom when she was strung up—just for show—in her polka-dotted underwear, among the clothes in her closet. (A second murder charge against Mr McGray for Nena's death was stayed this week, after his guilty plea.)

We sit across from each other in the prison interview room for about 90 minutes, speaking by phone. I ask my questions and try not to linger too long on the answers, and he recounts the killing of all those people—a string of lonely gay men and prostitutes and homeless drug addicts—with careful civility, but not even a play at remorse.

He doesn't have anything 'against' homosexual men, he informs me; they're just easy to kill.

He is also uncertain of specific dates—he says he criss-crossed the country so often he can't remember when he was where—which will make it harder for police to prove that he is telling the truth.

'I remember places by the victims', he says.

He claims to have killed at least once a year since 1985, in such cities as Ottawa, Calgary, Vancouver, and Toronto—and even two people across the border in Seattle.

On request, he starts matter-of-factly listing them off; the two prostitutes he stabbed in Vancouver, a gay man in Montreal, an acquaintance named 'Fluff' in the south end of Saint John, two women in Nova Scotia.

He says he could lead the way to the body he buried in Toronto's High Park, in, he believes, the summer of 1997—a claim the city's police said yesterday that they consider dubious.

It's possible Mr McGray killed people in Toronto 'and we are looking into it', Det. Sgt Doug Grady said.

But the homicide detective suggested that the man is 'playing games' and is getting his kicks by trying to get the country's police 'running all over hell's half-acre'.

'We just want to get his blood', Det. Sgt Grady said, suggesting that DNA testing will tell more about Mr McGray's activities than his boasts ever will.

When I ask Mr McGray for names, he shrugs. He did not take the time to learn their names, he says.

Police have already charged him, in the wake of his own statements, with the stabbing deaths of two gay men in Montreal in 1991, and the 1987 killing of an acquaintance after a failed taxi robbery in Saint John.

Mr McGray suggests that he wants to bring closure to the families, but he says he won't talk to police until three conditions are met: He doesn't want to be charged with any more killings, as he is already serving the maximum sentence; he wants treatment, and he doesn't want any accessories charged in relation to the killings.

But the RCMP has said it cannot negotiate with him, certainly not before learning details of his claims. 'It's like putting a gun to our head', said Sergeant Wayne Noonan, a Halifax RCMP spokesman. Too many jurisdictions and too many families are involved, and any deal could taint the statement for use in court later.

Mr McGray does not want to spend the rest of his life in segregation, but he accepts there is little chance that he will ever be freed. 'I know that I'm going to spend the rest of my life in prison, and I think I belong here'.

A few times during the interview, he loses his temper—because I suggest to him that he might not be telling the truth.

When this happens, he spits out an obscenity and his voice starts to rise. Then, he switches back to his soft tone, as if reining in his anger.

He is a large man, and has a pot-belly and black beard, both acquired since his arrest for the killings of Joan and Nena Hicks in March, 1998. His hair is puffy, and his eyes brown, and if you didn't know whom you were talking to, you might consider them soulful.

In any event, I look him in the eyes as little as possible—how do you meet the gaze of someone telling you that he stays sober when he kills so that the memories are sharper? Whenever our eyes meet, he is never the first to look away.

Mr McGray was born in Collingwood, Ontario, and grew up in Yarmouth, Nova Scotia, a struggling fishing village a few hours southwest of my hometown. While he was mulling over his biographies of serial killers, and feeding his urges, I would have probably been playing basketball there with my junior high school.

He claims to have found his first victim, not far away, on the road to Digby. Her name was Elizabeth Gail Tucker, and she was 17, hitchhiking to a fish plant job, when Mr McGray says he and a friend picked her up.

He is not sure where his 'urge' comes from, he says, or how it started. He knows only he can't control it.

Maybe it grew out of an unhappy childhood as the second youngest of six siblings, with a father who worked as a welder and was an abusive alcoholic in between.

He says it was there even before he suffered sexual and physical abuse at a group home near Shelbourne, where he was sent for being 'unmanageable' at home.

Whatever the cause, he says he quickly discovered that he liked killing; he 'liked it a lot'.

At 3:40p.m., prison official Rick Matthews knocks on the glass and gives me two minutes to wrap up the interview.

Once more, we go over the list of cities where he says he has left bodies, and his tally remains the same.

He doesn't slip up—but he doesn't get specific either. He tells me that he hopes his story gets out there, so that perhaps the police will make him a deal.

He's not seeking notoriety, he insists, but just wants help so that the killing stops and, maybe, his nightmares will go away.

When the time's up and Mr Matthews returns, Mr McGray says, 'Call me any time'. Then he hangs up his phone and stands at the door waiting for the guards.

I don't see him look back. And that is a good thing.

# 27

## Introduction

Discussions of crime often involve comparisons among countries. Both Canada and the US have highly developed data gathering systems that yield a stream of statistical information readily available to the public. But there are important differences to consider when comparing data from both countries.

As mentioned in the introduction to this book, historically the justice systems are based on two very different judicial approaches to wrongdoing—the crime control and due process approach. The differences also extend to how crimes are legislated and punished. In Canada the federal government has the responsibility for legislating what will be defined as 'crimes', whereas the provinces develop laws and regulations whose violations result in torts and offences. In the US the individual states have a greater influence in defining and processing crimes. There are also important differences in categorizing crimes. For instance, while the US has rape laws, in the early 1980s Canada legislated sexual assault laws to replace rape. The overall category of sexual assault is comprised of three levels that include actions ranging from harassment to forced intercourse. As a result, a simple comparison of US rape statistics with Canadian statistics on the overall category of sexual assault would be invalid.

In this selection, Torrey draws attention to other differences in how national statistics are generally collected in each country. What else should we keep in mind with regard to statistics about crime and other forms of deviance?

## Data Gold Mines and Minefields: Doing Comparative Research on Canada and the United States

*Barbara Boyle Torrey*

Canada and the United States provide a gold mine of opportunities to do comparative, quantitative research. They have two of the best statistical systems in the world, and they have many sources of nationally representative data that can be used for comparative purposes. Comparative research, however, can also be a minefield of misconceptions, misunderstandings, and misinterpretations. Even when there are quantifiable data available to use in comparisons, mistakes can easily be made.

The statistical systems in the two countries are both excellent but quite different, which can lead to considerable confusion. Canada has a centralized statistical system, which is managed by Statistics Canada (www.statcan.ca). The United States has a decentralized statistical system with more than 30 government agencies independently funding national data collections. In addition, many household surveys in the United States are funded by the federal government but conducted and managed by the academic and private profit sectors. To many Canadians, this looks like statistical anarchy, and it makes finding American data challenging.

Countries collect data on the issues that concern them the most. Race relations has been such an important issue in the United States that people have been asked their race on censuses and surveys for over two centuries. A lot of American statistics on health, education, and living arrangements are categorized by race because of its importance in both the historical and current affairs of the country. Therefore, it is surprising to Americans that Canada doesn't collect data on race; instead, it collects data about ancestry and, for some purposes, will aggregate some ancestry categories to define a 'visible minority'. Questions about race and visible minorities reflect how differently the two countries have dealt with some of their most important social issues. These differences also illustrate how comparative, quantitative research can turn researchers into statistical anthropologists.

Privacy of publicly collected data is a critical issue for both countries. Strict privacy provisions in the *Statistics Act* govern Canadian data managed by Statistics Canada. The individual records are made available through 11 Research Data Centres (RDCs) where strict controls are maintained to ensure that no one's privacy can be compromised. Statistics Canada and the Social Sciences and Humanities Research Council (SSHRC) fund the RDCs. Data from 33 surveys are available at these RDCs. The Data Liberation Initiative (DLI) has made some, but not all, of Statistics Canada's more aggregated survey data available to 68 Canadian universities. Moreover, a lot of aggregated data is available on the Statistics Canada website.

The US Census Bureau also has strict privacy laws governing the use of micro data on population and household surveys. It has also established RDCs in nine locations in the United States where a researcher, after being sworn in as a Census Bureau 'employee', can have access to detailed records. A number of other government agencies in the United States fund surveys, which are taken by both public and private organizations. In many cases the data from these surveys are aggregated, documented, and deposited in the Inter-University Consortium for Political and Social Research (ICPSR; www.icpsr.umich.edu) at the University of Michigan or are available through the survey firms that collected them.

There is a hierarchy of data sources that should be considered in doing comparative research. The data at the top of the hierarchy are those collected jointly by the two countries because their comparability is vouched for by the two statistical agencies. The major recent example is the joint *Canada/United States Survey of Health, 2002–03*. Statistics Canada and the US National Center for Health Statistics developed the questionnaire, used the same collection techniques, and analyzed the data jointly.

Another source of comparable data can come from studies by statistical offices, which harmonize existing data. These studies tend to have a lot of footnotes describing comparability issues with the data, but they still provide data comparisons that are reliable and unique. A good example is Statistics Canada's recent study of crime in Canada and the United States.[1] Another is the adjustment made to unemployment statistics in a recent article published by the US Bureau of Labor Statistics.[2]

A third source of comparable data for Canada and the United States are international organizations, which compile, document, and maintain international databases. The best organizations struggle to make data as comparable as possible and document what differences remain. Because these international organizations are dependent on member countries reporting their data, it is a slow process.

The most difficult data to use for comparative research are those that come directly from a statistical office or survey organization and that have not been harmonized with similar data from the other country. These unadjusted data can create minefields for the unsuspecting. Some surveys in the two countries have identical names but different purposes. Others have similar purposes but actually have asked different questions.

Finally, national-level data may mask regional variation in countries that are as heterogeneous as Canada and the United States. In many ways, this should not surprise us. Within the United States itself there are enormous regional and racial variations. Canada is the same. Provincial loyalties remain strong, and to this can be added Aboriginal identities and Quebec's deep sentiments.[3] Therefore, national data need to be handled with care and sub-national data used when possible to show the variation among the states and provinces.

## Notes

1. Maire Gannon, 'Crime Comparisons Between Canada and the United States', *Juristat*, Canadian Centre for Justice Statistics, Statistics Canada Catalogue no. 85-002-XPE Vol. 21,11.
2. Constance Sorrentino and Joyanna May, 'US Labor Market Performance in International Perspective', *Monthly Labor Review* (June 2002): 15–35.
3. See Nelson Wiseman, 'Provincial Political Cultures', in Christopher Dunn, ed., *Provinces: Canadian Provincial Politics* (Peterborough, ON: Broadview Press, 2004). Wiseman explores the ways in which each province is a fragment of its older founding society, with different metaphorical images being attached to them as they evolved.

## Introduction

This abridged Juristat report uses statistical data gathered by the police and the courts as well as victimization surveys to examine the extent and nature of sexual offences in Canada. The focus of this edited version is on sexual assault and excludes other sexual offences such as pornography or prostitution-related offences.

Why does the crime of rape no longer officially exist in Canada? What types of sexual offences are there in Canada, and how are they defined? Why do victims often not report such offences to the police? Are there any patterns regarding the victims and the accused? Finally, compare and contrast the prevailing cultural ideas and treatment of women in North America today with those outlined by Deutschmann in her article on the witch craze in medieval society.

# Sexual Offences in Canada

*Rebecca Kong, Holly Johnson, Sara Beattie, and Andrea Cardillo*

Over the past two decades, understanding and awareness of sexual offences, as well as responses to these behaviours, have undergone many changes. On the legislative front, this transition began with the 1983 amendments to the *Criminal Code* that replaced the crimes of rape and indecent assault with a three-tier structure of sexual assault. The goals of these amendments were to emphasize the violent rather than the sexual nature of such crimes, and to increase victims' confidence in the criminal justice system and willingness to report these crimes to the police (Department of Justice 1985). Amendments also eliminated immunity for those accused of sexually assaulting a spouse, removed reference to the gender of victims and perpetrators, and restricted the admissibility of evidence about the complainant's prior sexual history. Further, in 1988, *Criminal Code* provisions specific to sexual offences against children were implemented.

More recently, with the evolution in technology and globalization, legislators and policymakers have had to react to emerging issues of child pornography, the luring of children over the Internet, and trafficking in persons for the purpose of sexual exploitation. Child prostitution is also an issue of concern. Child prostitutes are generally viewed as victims of exploitation and abuse who are in need of assistance, although they may still be charged with prostitution-related offences (Bittle 2002).

This article presents statistical data on the extent and nature of sexual offences. The data used in the report are from Statistics Canada and include police statistics from the Uniform Crime Reporting (UCR2) Survey[1] and the Homicide Survey, and court data from the Adult

Criminal Court Survey and the Youth Court Survey. This article also presents analysis from the 1999 General Social Survey on Victimization, which collected information from a representative sample of Canadians 15 years of age and older on their experiences as victims of crime.

## Trends in Sexual Offences Reported to the Police

*Sexual offences* in this article includes sexual assault levels 1, 2, and 3, as well as the category of 'other sexual offences' which are a group of offences designed primarily to protect children from sexual abuse (see Box 28.1 *Sexual Offences Defined* on page 332 for *Criminal Code* definitions of these offences).

In 2002, 27,094 incidents involving sexual offences were reported to police in Canada. Sexual assault level 1 (the category of least physical injury to the victim) accounted for 88 per cent of these. Other sexual offences accounted for 10 per cent, and sexual assault levels 2 and 3 accounted for the remaining 2 per cent.

Among the 2.4 million *Criminal Code* incidents reported by police in 2002, sexual offences accounted for just 1 per cent, a proportion that has not changed for the last 10 years. Among the 303,294 *violent* incidents reported by police, total sexual offences accounted for 9 per cent, with sexual assaults (levels 1, 2, and 3) making up 8 per cent and other sexual offences accounting for 1 per cent (Figure 28.1).

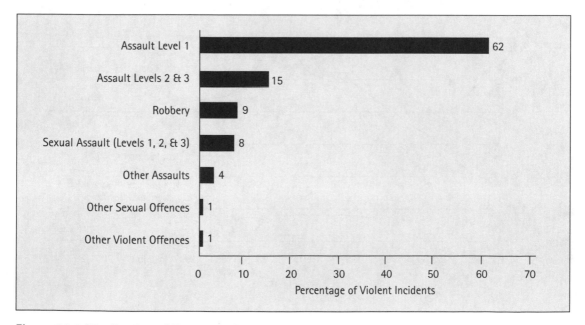

**Figure 28.1 Distribution of Reported Violent Offences, 2002**

Source: Uniform Crime Reporting Survey, Canadian Centre for Justice Statistics, Statistics Canada.

## Recent Decline in Sexual Offences Reported to Police

After the passage of the reform legislation in 1983, the rate of total sexual offences reported to police began to increase (see Figure 28.2). The increase continued until 1993, peaking at 136 incidents per 100,000 population. This trend has been driven by sexual assault level 1. Rates of sexual assault levels 2 and 3 declined between 1983 and 2002, while rates of other sexual offences fluctuated.

This dramatic rise in the overall rate of police-reported sexual offences following the introduction of the new legislation has been the subject of much analysis. In general, researchers have found insufficient evidence to attribute the rise solely to legislative reform, but suggest that other related social changes also encouraged victims to come forward (Roberts and Gebotys 1992; Roberts and Grossman 1994; Department of Justice 1985). Examples of social changes during this period are: improvements to the social, economic, and political status of women; a heightened focus on victims of crime and the growth in services and initiatives to support them, including sexual assault centres; special training

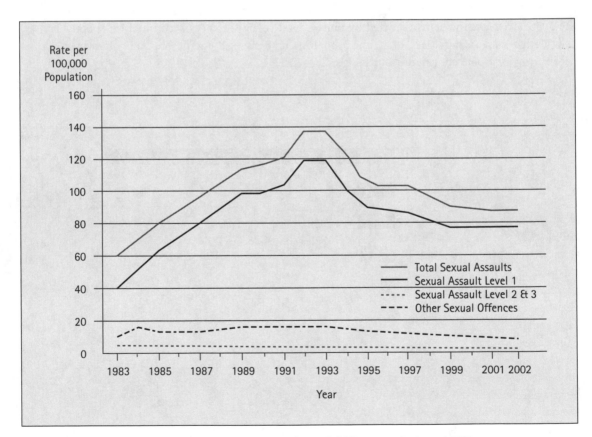

**Figure 28.2 Trends in Rates of Police-Reported Sexual Offences, 1983 to 2002**

Source: Uniform Crime Reporting Survey, Canadian Centre for Justice Statistics, Statistics Canada.

of police officers to deal with victims, and; the growth of treatment teams in hospitals trained to respond to victims of sexual assault and gather evidence that could be used at trial (Clark and Hepworth 1994).

After the peak in 1993, the rate of sexual offences reported to the police then declined, which parallels the overall downward trend for violent offences. Possible explanations for these declines are recent shifts in the age structure of the population and changing social values. Declines in rates of sexual offences coincided with a decrease in the proportion of the population aged 15–34. Since young adults have higher rates of criminal victimization and offending than other age groups, crime rates can be expected to decline as their share of the population declines. Changing social values related to sexual assault have also coincided with an aging population, and the combined effect may be more important than demographic shifts alone.

In 2002, the rate of reported sexual offences remained at 86 incidents per 100,000 population, virtually unchanged from the previous year. While the 2002 rate was 36 per cent below the 1993 peak, it was still 47 per cent higher than in 1983.

The rate for sexual assault level 1 has declined 35 per cent from the peak figure in 1993 and has remained stable since 1999. Rates for sexual assault levels 2 and 3 are relatively low, so small changes in the rates can result in large changes in percentage terms. These offences declined steadily since 1993, by 60 per cent. The rate of other sexual offences declined by 40 per cent over this time period.

## Homicides Involving Sexual Violence and Prostitution

Criminal incidents are classified in the Uniform Crime Reporting Survey according to the most serious in the incident (see Methodology section, at end of article). Sexual assault levels 2 and 3 are classified as more serious than most other crimes, but sexual assault level 1 will be classified lower than the more serious forms of physical assault (levels 2 and 3) if they occurred in the same incident. Sexual assaults that precipitate a homicide will likewise be classified as homicides. However, the more detailed Homicide Survey shows that, between 1991 and 2001, 184 homicides out of a total of 6,714 (less than 3 per cent) were preceded by sexual assault toward the victim. Most of these incidents had an identified accused (89 per cent) and the vast majority of these accused (98 per cent) were male. The majority of sexual assault-related homicides (82 per cent) involved female victims. About half of all victims were under age 25 and 14 per cent were children under 15. In contrast, two-thirds of accused were 25 years of age or older.

Prostitutes are at a heightened risk of violence and homicide. Between 1991 and 2001, a total of 50 homicides in Canada were identified by police as occurring in the context of prostitution and victims were either clients or prostitutes.[2] Two-thirds (33) of these victims were female and one-third (17) were male. Four-in-ten were under the age of 25. In only 33 cases was an accused identified, a rate for solved cases that is lower than for homicides overall (66 per cent compared to 79 per cent).

## Box 28.1  Sexual Offences Defined

The term *sexual offences* encompasses a wide range of criminal acts in the *Criminal Code of Canada*. Such conduct ranges from unwanted sexual touching to sexual violence resulting in serious physical injury or disfigurement to the victim. It also includes special categories of offences designed to protect children from sexual abuse.

In this article, the term *sexual assault* includes the following *Criminal Code* offences:

(a) Sexual assault level 1 (s.271)—an assault committed in circumstances of a sexual nature such that the sexual integrity of the victim is violated. Level 1 involves minor physical injuries or no injuries to the victim. This is a hybrid offence and may be prosecuted as an indictable offence (with a maximum sentence of 10 years imprisonment (or by way of summary conviction (with a maximum sentence of 18 months imprisonment or $2,000 fine).[2]

b) Sexual assault level 2 (s. 272)—sexual assault with a weapon, threats, or causing bodily harm. Level 2 is an indictable offence carrying a maximum sentence of 14 years imprisonment. A mandatory minimum sentence of four years in prison is imposed if a firearm is used.

c) Aggravated sexual assault (level 3)—sexual assault that results in wounding, maiming, disfiguring, or endangering the life of the victim. Level 3 is an indictable offence carrying a maximum sentence of life imprisonment. A mandatory minimum sentence of four years in prison is imposed if a firearm is used.

The term *other sexual offences* includes a group of offences that are meant primarily to address incidents of sexual abuse directed at children. The *Criminal Code* offences included in this category are

a) Sexual interference (s. 151)—the direct or indirect touching (for a sexual purpose) of a person under the age of 14 years using a part of the body or an object. This is a hybrid offence and may be processed as an indictable offence (with a maximum sentence of 10 years imprisonment) or by way of summary conviction.[3]

b) Invitation to sexual touching (s. 152)—inviting, counselling, or inciting a person under the age of 14 years to touch (for a sexual purpose) the body of any person directly or indirectly with a part of the body or with an object. This is a hybrid offence and may be processed as an indictable offence (with a maximum sentence of 10 years imprisonment) or by way of summary conviction.

c) Sexual exploitation (s. 153)—a person in a position of trust or authority towards a young person or a person with whom the young person is in a relationship of dependency, commits sexual interference or invitation to sexual touching. 'Young person' refers to a person between 14 and 18 years of age. This is a hybrid offence and may be processed as an indictable offence (with a maximum sentence of five years imprisonment) or by way of summary conviction.

d) Incest (s. 155)—sexual intercourse with a person to whom one has a known defined blood relationship. This is an indictable offence carrying a maximum sentence of 14 years imprisonment.

e) Anal intercourse (s. 159)—with the exception of married couples and other persons over the age of 18 who consent and who engage in these acts in private. This is a hybrid offence and may be processed as an indictable offence (with a maximum sentence of 10 years imprisonment) or by way of summary conviction.[4]

f) Bestiality (s. 160)—Anyone who commits or compels another person to commit bestiality is guilty of a hybrid offence and may be processed as an indictable offence (with a maximum sentence of 10 years imprisonment) or by way of summary conviction.

# Victimization Survey Reports of Sexual Assault

Victimization surveys provide an alternative to police statistics in that they interview victims directly about their experiences of crime and therefore include both incidents that were reported to the police and those that were not reported. This is an important source of information in the case of sexual assault since these crimes are among the least likely to be reported to police. Statistics Canada's 1999 General Social Survey (GSS) on Victimization found that victims 15 years of age and older did not report 78 per cent of sexual assaults to the police that year.[5] This is considerably higher than the unreported rate for robbery (51 per cent), physical assault (61 per cent), and break and enter (35 per cent).

The 1999 GSS measures two aspects of sexual assault victimization: sexual attack and un-wanted sexual touching. These are measured by the following two questions:[6]

1. *Sexual attack: During the past 12 months, has anyone forced you or attempted to force you into any unwanted sexual activity by threatening you, holding you down, or hurting you in some way?*
2. *Unwanted sexual touching: During the past 12 months, has anyone ever touched you against your will in any sexual way? By this I mean anything from unwanted touching or grabbing, to kissing or fondling.*

According to the GSS definition, an estimated 502,000 Canadians 15 years and older living in the 10 provinces had experienced a sexual assault in the 12 months prior to the survey. This translates into a rate of 21 incidents per 1,000 population age 15 and older (33 per 1,000 women and 8 per 1,000 men). The change in the rate of sexual assault over the last GSS on Victimization in 1993—16 per 1,000 population—was not statistically significant (See Besserer and Trainor 2000).[7]

These figures do not count sexual assaults perpetrated by spouses. An in-depth module in the 1999 GSS addressed the issue of spousal violence separately and found that, overall, 8 per cent of women and 7 per cent of men reported some type of violence by a common-law or marital partner in the five years preceding the survey. Among those victims, 20 per cent of women and 3 per cent[8] of men reported experiencing at least one incident of sexual assault (defined as sexual attack only in the case of spouses). This amounts to an estimated 138,000 women and 14,000 men who were sexually assaulted by a spousal partner over the five year period.

Because they include a large number of incidents not reported to the police, victimization surveys produce estimates that are higher than rates derived from police statistics. This is the case even though sexual assaults recorded in victimization surveys exclude those committed against children under 15 years old, and the population residing in institutions or in Canada's three territories.

## Most are Unwanted Sexual Touching, Most Victims Women

The majority of sexual assault victimizations reported to the 1999 GSS (involving perpetrators other than spouses) were unwanted sexual touching (77 per cent) as opposed to sexual attack against women (82 per cent), and half of all victims were 15–25 years of age.

**Table 28.1** Reasons for Not Reporting Violent Crimes to the Police, 1999

| | Sexual | | Robbery | | Assault | |
|---|---|---|---|---|---|---|
| | No. (000s) | % | No. (000s) | % | No. (000s) | % |
| Total Incidents Not Reported to Police | 391 | 100 | 116 | 100 | 754 | 100 |
| **Deal With in Another Way** | | | | | | |
| Yes | 237 | 61 | 56 | 49 | 432 | 57 |
| No | 153 | 39 | 60 | 51 | 320 | 42 |
| Don't Know/Not Stated | 0 | 0 | 0 | 0 | 0 | 0 |
| **Not Important Enough** | | | | | | |
| Yes | 195 | 50 | 48 | 41 | 392 | 52 |
| No | 194 | 50 | 69 | 59 | 361 | 48 |
| Don't know/Not stated | 0 | 0 | 0 | 0 | 0 | 0 |
| **Personal Matter and Did Not Concern the Police** | | | | | | |
| Yes | 194 | 50 | 44 | 38 | 226 | 30 |
| No | 195 | 50 | 72 | 62 | 527 | 70 |
| Don't Know/Not Stated | 0 | 0 | 0 | 0 | 0 | 0 |
| **Did Not Want to Get Involved With the Police** | | | | | | |
| Yes | 182 | 47 | 58 | 50 | 268 | 36 |
| No | 207 | 53 | 59 | 50 | 484 | 64 |
| Don't Know/Not Stated | 0 | 0 | 0 | 0 | 0 | 0 |
| **Police Couldn't Do Anything About It** | | | | | | |
| Yes | 130 | 33 | 55 | 48 | 244 | 32 |
| No | 260 | 66 | 61 | 52 | 509 | 68 |
| Don't Know/Not Stated | 0 | 0 | 0 | 0 | 0 | 0 |
| **Fear of Revenge** | | | | | | |
| Yes | 73 | 19 | 32 | 27 | 74 | 10 |
| No | 317 | 73 | 85 | 73 | 678 | 90 |
| Don't Know/Not Stated | 0 | 0 | 0 | 0 | 0 | 0 |
| **Police Wouldn't Help** | | | | | | |
| Yes | 70 | 18 | 15 | 6 | 127 | 17 |
| No | 319 | 82 | 102 | 87 | 625 | 83 |
| Don't Know/Not Stated | 0 | 0 | 0 | 0 | 0 | 0 |
| **Fear of Publicity/News Coverage** | | | | | | |
| Yes | 56 | 14 | 9 | 8 | 29 | 4 |
| No | 333 | 85 | 108 | 92 | 723 | 96 |
| Don't know/Not Stated | 0 | 0 | 0 | 0 | 0 | 0 |
| **Other Reason** | | | | | | |
| Yes | 36 | 9 | 8 | 7 | 58 | 8 |
| No | 355 | 91 | 109 | 93 | 695 | 92 |
| Don't Know/Not Stated | 0 | 0 | 0 | 0 | 0 | 0 |

Figures may not add to totals due to rounding.
Source: 1999 General Social Survey, Statistics Canada

The most common locations for sexual assaults to occur were bars and restaurants and other commercial locations (23 per cent and 14 per cent, respectively), public places (21 per cent), the victim's own home (15 per cent) or the home of someone else (19 per cent).

Sexual assaults are unlikely to come to the attention of the police, and this is more often the case for unwanted sexual touching than for sexual attacks (81 per cent and 69 per cent, respectively).

## Reasons for Not Reporting to Police

Responses to questions about reasons for not reporting to police cannot be analyzed separately for victims of unwanted sexual touching and sexual attack due to small sample counts. Altogether, victims of sexual assault provided a range of reasons for not reporting incidents to police (Table 28.1). Many did not report because the incident was dealt with another way (61 per cent), they felt it wasn't important enough (50 per cent), they felt it was a personal matter (50 per cent), or they didn't want the police involved (47 per cent).[9] While 33 per cent did not report because they did not think the police could do anything, another 18 per cent felt that the police would not help them. Other reasons were fear of revenge by the offender (19 per cent), and wanting to avoid publicity over the incident (14 per cent[10]).

Reasons for not reporting to police that stand out for sexual assault victims, as compared to the other violent crimes measured by the GSS, relate to the sensitive nature of these events: higher proportions avoided calling the police because they considered it a personal matter that did not concern the police, or because they feared publicity.

# Victim Characteristics

A common pattern shown in both police and victimization survey data is that young women and girls are at the highest risk of sexual assault victimization.

## Young Women and Girls at Highest Risk

Compared to other violent crimes, females are much more likely to be victims of sexual assault than are males. Females accounted for 85 per cent of victims of sexual offences who reported to a sample of police services reporting to the Incident-based Uniform Crime Reporting Survey (UCR2) in 2002, 11 compared to 48 per cent of victims of all other violent crimes. Females also represented 82 per cent of the population 15 years and older who reported a sexual assault victimization to the 1999 GSS, compared to 43 per cent of victims of all other violent victimizations.

Victims of sexual offences also tend to be young. In 2002, over half (61 per cent) of all victims of sexual offences reported to the police were children and youth under 18 years of age. Controlling for populations served by this sample of police services, rates of sexual offences known to the police were highest among girls aged 11 to 19, with the highest rate at age 13 (781 per 100,000 population) (see Figure 28.3). Among male victims, rates were highest for boys 3 to 14 years of age.

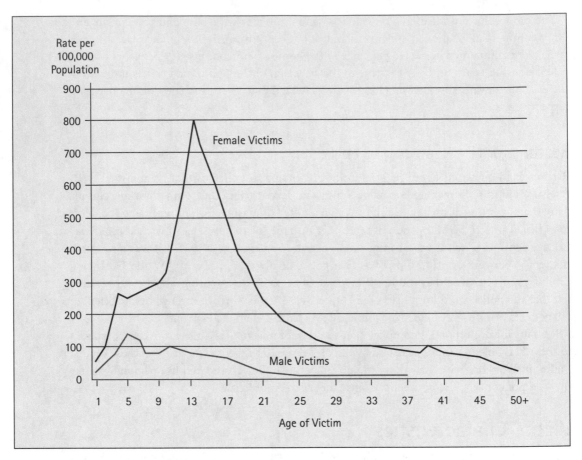

**Figure 28.3 Young Women at Highest Risk of Sexual Victimization, 2002**

Data are based in 154 police agencies (excluding OPP rural) participating in the UCR2 Survey, representing 56 per cent of the national volume of reported crime.

Source: Incident-based Uniform Crime Reporting Survey (UCR2), Canadian Centre for Justice Statistics, Statistics Canada.

While males make up a small proportion of victims of sexual offences overall (15 per cent), this proportion is higher for younger victims. In incidents involving children under 12, boys made up 29 per cent of victims compared to 12 per cent of youth aged 12–18 and 8 per cent of adults.

Among adults (aged 15 and older) interviewed for the 1999 GSS, rates of sexual assault were highest among women, those 15 to 24 years of age, those who were single, separated, or divorced, as well as students, those who participated in at least 30 evening activities outside the home per month, and those who had a household income of less than $15,000 or who lived in urban areas.

# Profile of Accused Persons

According to the UCR2, in 2002, 97 per cent of persons accused of sexual offences were male, higher than the representation of males among persons accused of all other types of violent offences (82 per cent). Overall, compared to other violent offenders, sexual offenders are somewhat older. In 2002, the mean age of persons charged by police with sexual offences was 33 years as compared to 31 for those charged with other violent offences. However, rates of sexual offending were highest among the youngest males, those aged 13 to 17, and peaked for 13- and 14-year-olds (221 and 230 per 100,000).

This peak among 13- and 14-year-olds applies to sexual assault level 1 and other sexual offences, but not to sexual assault levels 2 or 3, where there is no discernable age-related pattern among accused. Compared to their older counterparts, sexual offences involving these young teens more often involve young victims their own age, family members, or casual acquaintances, and are more likely to take place in single homes or in or around schools. They are also somewhat more likely to be dealt with informally by police.

The percentage of 12- to 15-year-old girls who reported selling drugs or engaging in property-related offences was comparable to boys (4.8 per cent and 35.9 per cent, respectively), but fewer girls reported engaging in other violent offences (10.9 per cent).[12]

## Accused Most Often Known to Victims

About half of sexual assault victims who reported to the sample of police services represented in UCR2 were assaulted by a friend or acquaintance (10 per cent and 41 per cent, respectively), 28 per cent by a family member, and 20 per cent by a stranger. Children under 12 were most often victimized by family members, especially in the case of girls (51 per cent). Parents (20 per cent) were less likely than other relatives (29 per cent) to be identified as suspects. In comparison, youth aged 12 to 17 and adults were most frequently victimized by acquaintances (47 per cent and 40 per cent, respectively).

---

**Box 28.2**  Dating Violence

Rates of dating violence reported to the police suggest that girls under the age of 16 have the highest rates of sexual violence by a dating partner, but that women aged 18 to 20 have the highest rates of physical assaults by dates. Males reported few cases of sexual violence by dating partners and lower rates of physical assault. These data include incidents involving all ages of victims, but only those who report to the police.[13]

---

## Most Offences Take Place in a Residence

The majority of sexual offences reported to police in 2002 took place in a residence (64 per cent), followed by public and open areas (26 per cent), and commercial places (11 per cent).[14]

Sexual assault level 2 was least likely to take place in a residence (52 per cent compared to 64 per cent of sexual assault level 1, 65 per cent of sexual assault level 3, and 65 per cent of other sexual offences). Sexual assault level 2 was more likely to take place in a public or open area (38 per cent), as compared to other sexual offences (27 per cent), sexual assault level 1 (25 per cent), and level 3 (23 per cent).

## Alcohol a Factor

It is not uncommon for violent crimes to be committed within the context of alcohol or drug use by offenders and sometimes by victims. Among adult victims of sexual assault responding to the 1999 GSS, 48 per cent were of the opinion that the incident was related to the perpetrator's alcohol or drug use, similar to percentages of assault and robbery victims who felt the same way (51 per cent of both). The percentage of victims who felt that the incident was related to their *own* alcohol or drug use was considerably smaller for all victims of violence (less than 10 per cent).[15]

# Methodology

## Uniform Crime Reporting Survey

The Uniform Crime Reporting (UCR) Survey was developed by Statistics Canada with the co-operation and assistance of the Canadian Association of Chiefs of Police. The survey, which became operational in 1962, collects crime and traffic statistics reported by all police agencies in Canada. UCR survey data reflect reported crime that has been substantiated through police investigation.

This is an aggregate survey that classifies incidents according to the most serious offence in the incident (generally the offence that carries the longest maximum sentence under the *Criminal Code*). As a result, less serious offences are underrepresented by the UCR survey. In the case of violent crime, a separate incident is recorded for each victim. The exception is robbery for which one incident is counted for every distinct or separate occurrence (in order to avoid inflating the number of robberies in cases with large numbers of victims, e.g., a bank robbery). In the case of non-violent crimes, one incident (categorized according to the most serious offence) is counted for every distinct occurrence.

The incident-based Uniform Crime Reporting (UCR2) survey captures detailed information on individual criminal incidents reported to police, including characteristics of victims, accused persons, and incidents. In 2001, detailed data were collected through the UCR2 survey from 154 police services in nine provinces. These data represent 59 per cent of the national volume of reported actual *Criminal Code* incidents. Other than Ontario and Quebec, the data are primarily from urban police departments. The reader is cautioned that these data are not geographically representative at the national or provincial level.

The UCR2 Trend Database contains historical data, which permits the analysis of trends in the characteristics of incidents, accused, and victims, such as weapon use and victim/

accused relationship. This database currently includes 104 police services who have reported to the UCR2 survey constantly since 1995. These police services accounted for 42 per cent of the national volume of crime in 2001.

## Homicide Survey

The Homicide Survey began collecting detailed data provided by police on homicide incidents, victims, and accused persons in 1974. Summary counts are available back to 1961. Whenever a homicide (murder, manslaughter, or infanticide) becomes known to the police, the investigating police department completes the survey questionnaire which is then forwarded to the Canadian Centre for Justice Statistics. Every effort is made to count homicides in the year in which they occurred. However, in some circumstances, homicides are counted in the year in which they were known to police, which may not be the year in which they actually occurred.

## General Social Survey on Victimization

The General Social Survey (GSS) is an annual survey that monitors changes in Canadian society and provides information on specific policy issues of current or emerging interest. Each year, the GSS has a particular focus. In 1988, 1993, and 1999, the focus of the GSS was on crime and victimization.

In 1999, approximately 26,000 Canadians aged 15 years and older residing in households were interviewed by telephone about their experiences of victimization. As with previous cycles, the response rate was quite high—81.3 per cent. Responses were weighted to represent the approximately 24.3 million non-institutionalized persons 15 years of age and older in the Canadian population. Given this sample size, an estimate of a proportion of the population, expressed as a percentage, is expected to be within approximately 0.8 per cent of the true proportion 19 times out of 20. Estimates for sub-samples of the population will have wider confidence intervals.

## Adult Criminal Court Survey

The Adult Criminal Court Survey (ACCS) provides statistical information on the processing of cases through provincial/territorial adult criminal court systems. Coverage in 2001/02 stood at 90 per cent of all adult criminal court cases. One province and two territories (Manitoba, Nunavut, and NWT) are not included in the survey at this time. British Columbia and New Brunswick began participating in 2001/02 and have been excluded from the trend analysis.

Some court locations in Quebec are not included. Information from Quebec's 140 municipal courts (which account for approximately 20 per cent of federal statute charges in that province) is not yet collected. Superior Court data from British Columbia, Alberta, New Brunswick, Prince Edward Island, and Yukon are also included.

A case is defined in the ACCS as one or more charges against an accused person or corporation that receive a final decision on the same day. Charges in each case are ranked according to the type of final decision and the charge with the most serious decision is used to represent the case.

## Youth Court Survey

The Youth Court Survey (YCS) is a census of cases heard in youth court for persons aged 12–17 at the time of the offences. Though every effort is made by respondents and the Canadian Centre for Justice Statistics to ensure complete survey coverage, slight under-coverage may occur in some jurisdictions. A case is defined by the YCS as one or more charges laid against a young person that is completed in youth court on the same day. Charges in each case are ranked according to the type of final decision and the charge with the most serious decision is used to represent the case.

## Notes

1. A subset of 154 police departments participated in the UCR2 representing 59 per cent of the national volume of crime in Canada in 2002. For the purposes of this publication, Ontario Provincial Police rural divisions have been removed from the UCR2. This is due to an absence of accurate population estimates for those areas which are needed to calculate rates. The remaining police forces used for this analysis represent 56 per cent of the national volume of reported crime in 2002.
2. This excludes a large number of recent cases in British Columbia involving missing women. These will be coded in 2002, the year in which they became known to the police as homicides.
3. A hybrid offence may be processed as a summary or indictable offence. Except where otherwise stated by law, the maximum penalty for a summary conviction is a fine not exceeding two thousand dollars or imprisonment for six months or both.
4. The section has been found to be unconstitutional by the Ontario and Quebec Courts of Appeal (R. v M(C) (1995), 98 C.C.C. (3d) 481. (Ont. C.A.) and R. v. Roy (1998), 125 C.C.C. (3d) 442 (Que. C.A.))
5. Eight per cent of incidents were reported to police, but this estimate is based on small counts and therefore has a high coefficient of variation (greater than 33.3 per cent). In 14 per cent of cases victims did not know if the incident was reported or refused to answer.
6. These questions were designed to closely resemble the *Criminal Code* definition of sexual assault.
7. Due to the relatively low counts of sexual assaults reported to each of these surveys, these estimates have large and overlapping coefficients of variation. The difference is therefore not statistically significant.
8. Coefficient of variation for this figure is between 16.6 per cent and 33.3 per cent. Use with caution.
9. Percentages exceed 100 per cent due to multiple responses.
10. Coefficient of variation for this figure is between 16.6 per cent and 33.3 per cent. Use with caution.
11. The incident-based Uniform Crime Reporting (UCR2) survey captures detailed information on individual criminal incidents reported to police, including characteristics of victims, accused persons, and incidents. In 2002, 154 police services in nine provinces participated in this survey representing 59 per cent of the national volume of reported crime. Other than Ontario and Quebec, the data are primarily from urban police departments. The reader is cautioned that these data are not nationally representative.
12. For further information on the topic of self-reported delinquency, see Fitzgerald, R. (2003). *An examination of sex differences in delinquency*. Crime and Justice Research Paper Series.
13. According to Statistics Canada's 1993 Violence Against Women Survey, 16 per cent of women 18 years of age and over (an estimated 1.7 million women) had been assaulted or sexually assaulted by a male dating partner since the age of 16. Twelve per cent of women reported being sexually assaulted and 7 per cent reported being physically assaulted (many women reported both).
14. Public places include streets, roads, and open areas such as parks. Commercial places include office buildings, stores, bars, restaurants, and other business locations.
15. The coefficient of variation for the estimates for sexual assault and robbery were between 16. 6 per cent and 33.3 per cent. Use with caution.

# References

Besserer, S. and Trainor, C. 2000. 'Criminal Victimization in Canada, 1999'. *Juristat* Catalogue 85-002-XPE. Vol. 20 No. 10. Canadian Centre for Justice Statistics. Ottawa: Minister of Industry.

Bittle, S. 2002. 'When protection is punishment: Neoliberalism and secure care approaches to youth prostitution'. *Canadian Journal of Criminology*. 44(3). 317–350.

Clark. S. and Hepworth, D. 1994. 'Effects of Reform Legislation on the Processing of Sexual Assault Cases'. In J. Roberts and R. Mohr (eds.), *Confronting Sexual Assault: A Decade of Legal and Social Change*. Toronto: University of Toronto Press, pp. 113–135.

Department of Justice. 1985. *Sexual Assault Legislation in Canada: An Evaluation*. Ottawa: Supply and Services Canada.

Fitzgerald, R. 2003. 'An examination of sex differences in delinquency'. *Crime and Justice Research Paper Series*. Catalogue 85-561-MIE2003001. Canadian Centre for Justice Statistics, Statistics Canada.

Roberts, J. and Gebotys, R. 1992. 'Reforming Rape Laws'. *Law and Human Behaviour* 16(5): 555–573.

Roberts, J. and Grossman, M. 1994. 'Changing Definitions of Sexual Assault: An Analysis of Police Statistics'. In J. Roberts and R. Mohr (eds.), *Confronting Sexual Assault: A Decade of Legal and Social Change*. Toronto: University of Toronto Press, pp. 57–83.

## Introduction

In this article, Hickey presents the different types of profiling used by forensic criminal investigations of serial killers. Based on his overview and commentary, how effective is profiling at this time? How does the process he outlines compare with the portrayal of forensic investigations in popular TV crime dramas like *Law and Order* and *CSI*?

# Profiling Serial Killers

*Eric W. Hickey*

Robert Keppel, a former detective investigating the Ted Bundy case, once remarked that apprehending serial killers is very difficult. 'Police departments generally are not equipped or trained to apprehend serial killers. They are organized to catch burglars and robbers and to intervene in family fights' (Lindsey 1984, p. 1). Several factors set the serial offender apart from typical domestic killers and other violent criminals. Serial killers can be highly mobile and traverse many law enforcement jurisdictions while still remaining in a relatively small geographic area. Offenders generally prefer strangers as victims and are usually careful to minimize the amount of evidence left at the crime scene. Consequently, months may go by before there is sufficient interagency communication to recognize a common pattern of homicides. Coordination of information can be even more difficult when offenders cross several state lines, committing murders along the way. Although there has been considerable criticism of law enforcement in tracking down serial killers, police have made concerted efforts in some cases to join forces and conduct multiagency investigations.

Public anxieties demand quick apprehension of a serial offender; however, conducting investigations requires an enormous amount of resources and agency coordination. Montgomery (1992, 1993) notes that nearly 20,000 suspect names were collected in the Green River Killer case at a cost to taxpayers of over $20 million. Police also examined data on 185,000 persons in England's Staffordshire case of serial murder (Canter 1994) and the Yorkshire Ripper case, in which 268,000 names of possible leads were collected using over 5 million man-hours of police work and $6–7 million in costs (Doney 1990). Considering the increasing costs of task force investigations, the Unabomber case, which spanned 18 years and three task forces, cost approximately $75 million including the costs of prosecution.

# Forensic Science

Physical evidence is critical to cases, and pressure is applied to find the most qualified experts who can withstand courtroom scrutiny. But forensics means much more today than simply working with physical evidence, creating even more challenges to what actually constitutes acceptable scientific evidence and who can be considered as an expert. In 1998, your present author was asked to consult as an expert witness in a federal case of stalking. Psychiatrists for both the defence and prosecution were quickly accepted by the courts as experts in their fields. Your author, although a recognized *criminologist* with considerable expertise in the area of stalking, was forced to undergo nearly two hours of examination by a most adept defence attorney. The judge finally ruled that your author qualified as an expert. This was not only an issue of having a new type of expert (in this case a criminologist) but an unlicensed expert asked to testify in a case that drew its experts primarily from licensed psychiatrists. (The offender did receive a 3 ½-year sentence.)

The term *forensics* means belonging to or used in courts of law. This has given rise to forensic medicine or the use of medical expertise in legal or criminal investigations. In turn, forensic psychology has begun to offer insights into criminal behaviour and the criminal mind. Criminology and psychology join forces to create criminal profiling, or the creation of criminal portraits that assist those in law, law enforcement, mental health, or academics to better understand crime and criminals.

Increasingly, pressure is being placed on law enforcement personnel, social scientists, and biologically oriented researchers to identify which individuals will become involved with criminal behaviour, who their victims will be, and which appropriate criminal justice measures should be used to deal with the offender. Predicting criminal behaviour accurately has never been an exact science, but more than ever a demand for accuracy exists. The movement today is toward integrating sciences and technology into an interdisciplinary approach to criminality. This approach encompasses behavioural, psychological, and biological explorations of criminal behaviour and their legal applications. This exploration must incorporate various academic and applied disciplines such as those related to the courts, corrections, law enforcement, and victimology. Disciplines such as criminology, criminal justice, psychology, psychiatry, sociology, law and jurisprudence, mathematics, statistics, geography, and behavioural medicine, to name but a few, need to be integrated into the field of forensic science. We might envision forensics as a hub of a wheel with the spokes representing the sciences. For example, geography is now becoming a tool to address issues of crime and victimization. This approach is referred to as *spatial mapping* or *environmental criminology* and is used to generate geographic profiles of offenders, victims, and crime scenes. Computers are now being used to identify crime locations in urban and suburban areas by plotting where they have occurred over time. This geo-mapping approach to crime prediction has tremendous implications for future urban development, police administration, and policy development. Spatial mapping can also be applied to understanding criminal victimization, victim profiling, and promotion of victim protection. David Canter of Liverpool, England, established a program in Investigative Psychology in which computer models are used to predict criminal offending.

Criminalists work in crime labs conducting tests and analyses in ballistics, serology, toxicology, hair-fibre evidence, DNA, latent prints, and other areas relevant to determining the nature of collected physical evidence. Physical forensics is often critical to the outcome of criminal cases. In addition, physical evidence frequently helps investigators explain the psychology of the crime and that of its perpetrator(s). Thus enlightened, criminal psychologists promote greater understanding of criminal personalities among researchers, the courts, and law enforcement agencies. Forensics is also of practical value to correctional and law enforcement administrators interested in the classification of prisoners or in the provision of training for personnel who investigate and manage offenders and offender populations.

# Profiling

The term *profiling* refers to many areas of forensics. For example, Owen (1998), noted author of *In the Mix*, developed inmate profiles by examining the lives and crimes of incarcerated women at Central California Women's Facility in Chowchilla, California. Her work has provided clarity and insight into life behind bars for female felons. Jackson (1996) explored the world of credit card fraud and the types of people who repeatedly engage in such crimes. Wallace (2001), an expert in domestic violence, profiles the types of criminals who target the elderly. Today profiling has become a tool used widely in criminal investigations. Profiling is developing as a science but continues to receive mixed reviews. Some professionals, such as Canter (2000), Godwin (1999), and Levin and Fox (1985), have been skeptical of the utility of profiling, particularly the psychologically based approach. Other researchers express varying degrees of support for the success of psychological profiling development, including Egger (1985), Geberth (1983), Holmes (1990), and Ressler and his colleagues (1988). Psychological profiling has yet to function as a 'magic wand' to solve serial killings, but it is still too early in its development to be considered a failure. Programs such as those developed around profiling often require several years of testing and refinement before we are able to evaluate them. For profiling to fulfill its potential, law enforcement personnel must be willing to collaborate with those in the academic and medical professions. For example, psychiatrists can be of particular value in profiling, provided law enforcement officials are willing to accept and use their profiles. The problem in dealing with lust killers, for example, is that as offenders they present a very complex set of behavioural and psychological characteristics. Psychologists Purcell and Arrigo (2000) illustrate the complexities of such killers by proposing an integrated model of lust killing and paraphilia. Liebert (1985), in evaluating the contributions of psychiatry to the investigation of serial murders, such as lust killings, stated:

Acceptance that the Borderline or Narcissistic Personality Disorder, with severe sociopathic and sadistic trends, can commit murder as a substitute for normal erotic pleasure or even non-violent perversion is the foundation for exploration of motivation in serial murders. With a mutually respectful desire to learn about the bizarre world of the lust murderer, the investigator and psychiatric consultant can enhance their sense of 'type' for a suspect. The investigator is less likely to make a mistake in judging the grandiosity of pathological narcissism and the manipulativeness of sociopathy with

'normalcy'. The lust murderer can present a facade of relationships and effective, perhaps even superior, performance. Not infrequently, he will be in the bright-superior
intelligence range and, therefore, potentially a skilled impostor (p. 197).

## Types of Profiling

The term *typology* has lent itself to the development of various forms of profiting that are
now used as criminal investigative techniques from white-collar crimes to serial murder. The
following forms of profiling will help to illustrate the emerging issues involved in criminal
investigations. Geographical profiling and the scientific, empirically based offender profiling
by David Canter and colleagues (2000) are both becoming leading approaches in criminal
investigations. They both can offer tremendous assistance to investigators in making profiling a more scientific and precise science. Investigative profiling today can be viewed from
several perspectives:

1. Offender Profiling—Law enforcement agencies collect data, often using case studies
   or anecdotal information, which then is transformed into general descriptions of the
   types of persons most commonly associated with a certain type of criminal activity.
   This stereotyping is common in seeking out drug couriers and terrorists. This form of
   profiling can often be invasive and legally tenuous. Civil rights advocates quickly point
   out the flaws in using physical characteristics to profile criminals. Dodd (1998) also
   found that such profiling could be very misleading. For example, one might consider
   that people involved in fraudulent insurance claims usually are in need of money. The
   opposite was reported in Dodd's study of fraudulent insurance claimants. Of the 209
   false claims, only 13 per cent were in need of the money, whereas 57 per cent earned a
   regular income. David Canter and S. Hodge along with Gabriella Salfati (1999) from
   England have made significant progress in elevating offender profiling from a street-
   level operation to a sophisticated approach to criminal investigation. Indeed, Canter (2000) takes umbrage with American profiling, stating that profiling was originally the purview of psychologists, not the FBI. He rejects the detective deductions of
   profiling as being anecdotal, 'deductive, fictional hero' approaches to solving crimes
   through 'gut-feeling' investigations (p. 26). Clinical observations alone are insufficient
   in making decisions about criminal behaviour. Indeed, criminologists, psychologists,
   and psychiatrists have been ineffectual in accurately predicting criminal behaviour.
   Our predictive capabilities are replete with *false positives,* or incorrectly predicting that
   someone will behave in a certain criminal manner. Canter (2000) believes that many
   profilers today operate under the guise of informed speculation. Like psychic detec-
   tives and astrologers, such profilers are shrouded in ambiguity and therefore can shift
   their explanations to fit the situation. In addition, Copson (1995) found that only 3 per
   cent of profilers in his study of criminal cases actually helped to identify the offender.
2. Victim Profiling—Profilers identify the personality and behavioural characteristics
   of crime victims who tend to fall prey to certain types of offenders. Information can
   be gathered through personal records; interviews with witnesses, victims, family, and

friends; crime scene examination; and autopsies. Investigators will enhance their effectiveness in murder investigations as victim–offender relationships are more closely scrutinized. Victims, even in death, are often storybooks about the offender and the circumstances of the crime.

3. Equivocal Death Profiling—Also referred to as *psychological autopsy,* investigators apply non-scientific information to explain the motivations of a person or group engaged in suicide pacts or difficult-to-explain deaths.

4. DNA Profiling—In recent years several cases of murder have been solved as a result of the advent of DNA profiling or genetic science. This includes gathering DNA from crime scenes, victims, and offenders in efforts to match up perpetrators to specific crimes. Between 1979 and 1986 a serial killer stalked, raped, and murdered at least six victims in southern California. Newly found DNA evidence from rape kits found in archived cases conclusively linked these murders. Investigators then used other profiling techniques by examining the predator's stalking and killing habits to link the killer to four more murders.

5. Crime Scene Profiling—Also referred to as *criminal investigation analysis,* this form of profiling is based upon the FBI model developed by its Behavioral Science Unit. Investigators focus on crime scene descriptions, photographs, offender behaviour before and after the criminal act(s), traffic patterns, physical evidence, and victim information and place less credence on psychological data. Psychosocial data are compared to other similar cases and investigators engage in an experiential-informational guessing technique to reconstruct the offender's personality. From the FBI's 1988 study of 36 serial sexual murderers a dichotomy of offender characteristics was developed. The 'organized' offender is methodical, premeditated, mature, resourceful, and usually involves sexual perversion in the offence. The 'disorganized' type of killer was found to act much more randomly, opportunistically—opposite characteristics of the organized offender—and often with some form of mental disorder (Ressler et al. 1988). Their dichotomous profile includes the following characteristics:

| *Organized* | *Disorganized* |
|---|---|
| Good intelligence | Average or low intelligence |
| Socially/sexually competent | Socially/sexually incompetent |
| Stable work history | Lack of stable work history |
| Controlled during crime | Anxious during crime |
| Lives with someone | Lives alone |
| Very mobile | Lives near crime scene |
| Follows investigation in media | Little interest in media |
| May leave town/change job | Little change in lifestyle |
| Uses alcohol prior to crime | Little alcohol use |
| Premeditated offence | Spontaneous offence |
| Victim a stranger | Victim or location unknown |
| Conversation with victim | Little conversation with victim |
| Demands submission | Sudden violence to victim |

| | |
|---|---|
| Uses restraints | Little use of restraints |
| Violent acts prior to death | Post-mortem sexual acts |
| Body hidden | Body left in view |
| Weapon/evidence absent | Weapon/evidence often present |
| Transports body | Body left at scene |

The problem with this dichotomous model is the lack of rigorous reliability and validity testing. Even though the model has been used extensively by investigators, it may not have the utility previously thought.

6. Psychological Profiling—Tracking the serial killer and the multitude of problems posed by such a task has led, in the past few years, to the development of psychological profiling, a tool used to prioritize a variety of homicides and other serious crimes. Psychological profiling, also known as criminal personality assessment, is applied to criminal behaviour profiling, offender profiling, victim profiling, and crime scene profiling. It is used by law enforcement agencies in the United States, Canada, and Britain. Swanson, Chamelin, and Territo (1984) define the intent and purpose of this type of profiling:

> The purpose of the psychological assessment of a crime scene is to produce a profile, that is, to identify and interpret certain items of evidence at the crime scene that would be indicative of the personality type of the individual or individuals committing the crime. The goal of the profiler is to provide enough information to investigators to enable them to limit or better direct their investigations (pp. 700–701).

Profilers match the personality characteristics of a certain type of offender with those of a suspect. Investigators use batteries of interviews and testing to establish their base of information. Experts are frequently called upon to predict future behaviour of offenders including pedophiles, child molesters, rapists, and other sexual deviants. The investigator usually has a particular offender that he or she is profiling. In efforts to improve the effectiveness and credibility of psychological, crime scene, and criminal profiling, organizations such as the *Academy of Behavioral Profiling*, founded by Brent Turvey, attract investigators and researchers interested in both the forensic and investigative criminal analysis.

7. Geographical Profiling—While investigators have been working to improve both crime scene profiling and psychological profiling, other researchers and investigators such as former detective Kim Rossmo from Canada have been actively developing a geographical approach to criminal investigations. Also referred to as spatial mapping, this technique combines geography and environmental criminology to connect crime scenes to offender habitats and hunting grounds. Such profiling is empirically based and has not placed much value on motivation or personality. It does help law enforcement personnel in deciding where to begin knocking on doors and setting up stakeouts. In the case of the 'Railroad Killer', the offender had stayed near trains and therefore was likely a drifter or transient. The geographic similarities linked him to

many killings and he was eventually identified, arrested, and sent to prison. A geographical profile includes the elements of *distance, mobility, mental maps,* and *locality demographics.* Offenders are profiled by the amount of distance covered by a serial offender. Some may travel because they have access to transportation, whereas others are limited in their access. This can create problems because some serial offenders like Ted Kaczynski, the Unabomber, used buses to transport his bombs or mailed them. *Mental maps* refer to an offender's cognitive images of his or her surroundings. As an offender becomes more comfortable with his tools and surroundings, the more likely he will be to expand those boundaries. Offender travel routes can be critical to a serial-murder investigation. Kim Rossmo (1999), one of the noted pioneers of geographic profiling, identifies four offender styles in hunting for victims:

1. Hunter—identifies a specific victim in his home area
2. Poacher—prefers to travel away from home area for hunting victims
3. Troller—an opportunistic killer, he attacks victims while carrying out his regular activities
4. Trapper—a spider-and-fly scenario in which an offender enjoys laying a trap for a victim

Rossmo (1995) conducted an impressive critical examination of serial-murder cases using data sets from the FBI and your present author. His eclectic approach to geographic profiling utilizes not only empirical data but also psychological information. A geographical profile includes a study of area maps, examination of crime scenes, interviews of witnesses and investigators, and knowledge of abduction and body dump sites where serial murder is involved. Rossmo's Criminal Geographic Targeting, a computerized program, produces a topographical map based on crime scene information. The more crime scenes, the greater the predictive ability of the program. Using the 11 crime scenes of serial killer Clifford R. Olson who raped, sodomized, and hammered boys and girls to death, Rossmo was able to pinpoint the killer's area of residence to within a four-block radius. In another case of serial rape, Rossmo used 79 crime scenes to pinpoint the actual basement of the offender's home as the location of the attacks. Scotland Yard, Dutch police, the FBI Behavioral Science Unit, and many other law enforcement agencies in need of better science to solve their cases frequently use Rossmo.

## Signatures of Violent Offenders

Cases of serial killing share commonalties and characteristics. Anger, low self-esteem, fantasy, facilitation, and objectification of victims all are common denominators in understanding the general etiological roots of serial murder. Some cases, however, have distinctive behaviours that make the crime and the offender(s) unique. These are referred to as the *signature,* or personal marking, of the offender. Signatures include verbal, sexual, and physical acts. For example, most cases of serial murder are described in terms of patterns of murder customized to fit the special needs and fantasies of each killer. The signatures are also referred to as 'calling cards' or 'trademarks' and can be used by repeat violent offenders who are not serial killers. A serial rapist may demand the victim to beg for mercy or tell him how much she is enjoying his sexual attentions to her. This pattern is not part of the modus operandi and sets the case apart from other murder cases. The 'method of operating' or (MO) is separate from motive and signature. MO includes techniques to commit the crimes that may evolve as the offender becomes more skilful and confident in his crimes. Signatures are actions of the serial offender usually unnecessary to completing the murders. There are exceptions, however, as in the case of Cary Stayner who enjoyed decapitating his female victims. Such signatures are extensions of paraphilic fantasies and can facilitate the offender in actualizing his fantasies.

Sometimes post-mortem mutilation becomes the signature of a particular killer. Others collect souvenirs such as body parts, pieces of clothing, or newspaper clippings. Harvey Glatman liked to abduct women and take photographs of them before and after the sexual assaults and murders. Dr Robert D. Keppel, an expert in serial-murder cases, explains the significance of Glatman's desire to take photographs as his personal signature for murder:

> His photos were more than souvenirs, because in Glatman's mind, they actually carried the power of his need for bondage and control. They showed the women in various poses: sitting up or lying down, hands always bound behind their backs, innocent looks on their faces, but with eyes wide with terror because they had guessed what was to come (p. 37).

Another offender liked to remove the eyeballs from his victims. One killer cannibalized the sexual organs of his young victims, whereas still another skinned his victims and made lampshades, eating utensils, and clothing. Bronswick (2001, pp. 85–89) a former psychotherapist for death row inmates, provides the following list of signature behaviours frequently found in serial-murder investigations:

- Aberrant sex
- Attacks at the face
- Body disposal
- Cannibalism
- Decapitation
- Dismemberment
- Mutilation
- Necrophilia
- Penile/object penetration
- Picquerism (sexual arousal from repeated stabbing of a victim)
- Restraints
- Souvenirs (photos, clothing, jewellery, newspaper clippings)
- Torture
- Trophies (victim body parts used for sexual arousal)
- Weapons

Signatures are helpful in profiling criminal behaviours and can link offenders to crimes. Signatures also can help determine the level of progression and sophistication of the predator.

This usually means that a first-time offender will not demonstrate the savoir-faire found amongst veteran predators. For example, a predator will sometimes change his MO in order to elude police but it is far more difficult for him to alter his signature because it is fantasy based.

## Problems in Profiling

Profiling can be very useful, but caution must be exercised to avoid constructing hasty or poorly grounded profiles that may lead investigators in wrong directions. This inevitably places a strain on resources, and, most important, additional lives may be lost. Errors in the information transmitted to NCAVC (National Center for the Analysis of Violent Crime), mistaken assessments by the evaluation team, and other potential glitches mean profiles can and do go wrong. In one case, for example, a profile on a criminal suspect told investigators the man they were looking for came from a broken home, was a high school dropout, held a marginal job, hung out in 'honky tonk' bars, and lived far from the scene of the crime. When the attacker was finally caught, it was learned the psychological assessment was 100 per cent wrong. He had not come from a broken home; he had a college degree, held an executive position with a respected financial institution, did not use alcohol, and lived near the scene of the crime. With this possibility for error, the bureau warns investigators not to become so dependent on the evaluation that they neglect other leads or become biased to the point where they blindly follow only the clues that match the scenario described in the profile's report (Goodroe 1987, p. 31). In 1996, Richard Jewell, a security guard at the Olympic Games in Atlanta, Georgia, noticed an unattended knapsack. Concerned that it might contain a bomb, he immediately reported his findings to his superiors. While Olympic visitors were being evacuated, the sack exploded, killing one woman and injuring over 100 others. Jewell quickly became a suspect because he 'fit' the profile of someone who would set a bomb and then become a hero for saving others.

He seemed to be enjoying the sudden notoriety of the event and being recognized as a public hero. Investigators also noted that he had mentioned to the media how he hoped to land a permanent job with law enforcement after the games. Jewell became a prime suspect and quickly became subject to an intensive investigation. The media harassed him for several months before investigators were forced to admit that they had the wrong man. Indeed, not until November 2000 was Eric Robert Rudolph indicted, in absentia, for several bombings of abortion clinics and three Atlanta bombings, including the explosion at the Olympic Games. Sometimes profiling does not work simply because the offenders/crimes do not fit traditional profiles. Investigators must always be prepared for exceptions. For example, no one ever considered the possibility that the DC Sniper was really a team of two offenders and they were both African American. Even more unlikely was the fact that one of the killers was only in his teen years.

Sometimes investigators ignore or fail to understand offender profiles and are quick to rush to conclusions based upon a piece of physical evidence. In the case of Cary Stayner, the Yosemite Park killer who had abducted and murdered a woman, her daughter, and her teenage friend, four suspects were arrested. The suspects had some physical evidence that linked them to the murders. The FBI was adamant that the killers were behind bars. Your present author, when interviewed by local media, explained that the probability of these murders being committed by several people was very low. Given the facts of the case at that point, the profile, given the manner in which the victims were killed, strongly suggested that this was the work of a lone predator. The suspects were also petty criminals and drug dealers, hardly the types of offenders who suddenly carry out such sadistic sexual murders. Months passed and your author continued to maintain that the real offender was still free to kill while these common criminals sat in jail. Then another brutal murder occurred involving a Yosemite Park worker, Joie Armstrong. She had been decapitated. Some investigators still maintained that the men in custody were the killers of the three park tourists. Much of that line of thinking was discarded when Cary Stayner not only confessed to the Armstrong murder, but also to the other three killings. It was the manner in which the victims were killed that linked the cases. These were sexual killings where decapitation becomes part of the sexual experience. Certainly this was not the work of petty criminals. Your author drew his conclusions based upon information about how the victims died and, using a psychological profile, determined that the killings were the work of a lone sexual predator. Stayner was sentenced to life in prison, no parole, for the Joie Armstrong case and was convicted in the three tourists' murders (author's files). The profile can be a useful tool but, like any tool, it can be misused. Profiles can complement crime scene investigations and strengthen interagency and interdisciplinary co-operation.

# References

Bronswick, A.L. 2001. *Using Sexually Related Crime Scene Characteristics to Profile Male Serial Killers: A Question of Motivation.* Unpublished dissertation, Alliant International University, Fresno, CA.

Canter, D. 1994. *Criminal Shadows.* London: Harper-Collins.

———. 2000. 'Offender Profiling and Criminal Differentiation'. *Legal and Criminological Psychology,* 5, 23–46.

Canter D.V., and Alison, L.J. (2000). *Profiling Rape and Murder* (Offender Profiling series, vol. V). Aldershot: Dartmouth.

Copson, G. 1995. Coals to Newcastle? Part 1: A Study of Offender Profiling (paper 7). London: Police Research Group Special Interest Series, Home Office.

Dodd, N.J. 1998. 'Applying Psychology to the Reduction of Insurance Claim Fraud'. *InsuranceTrends,* 18, 11–16.

Doney, R.H. 1990. 'The Aftermath of the Yorkshire Ripper: The Response of the United Kingdom Police Service'. In S.A. Egger (ed.), *Serial Murder: An Elusive Phenomenon.* New York: Praeger, pp. 95–112.

Egger, S.A. 1985. 'Serial Murder and the Law Enforcement Response'. Unpublished dissertation, College of Criminal Justice, Sam Houston State University, Huntsville, TX.

Geberth, V.J. 1983. *Practical Homicide Investigation.* New York: Elsevier.

Godwin, G.M. 1999. *Hunting Serial Predators.* New York: CRC Press.

Godwin, J. 1978. *Murder U.S.A.* New York: Random House.

Goodroe, C. 1987, July. 'Tracking the Serial Offender'. *Law and Order,* 29–33.

Holmes, R.M. 1990. *Profiling Violent Crimes.* Newbury Park, CA: Sage.

Jackson, J. 1996, Winter. 'Computer Crimes and Criminals'. *American Criminal Justice Association Journal,* 57 (1&2), 32–36.

Keppel, R.D. 1989. *Serial Murder: Future Implications for Police Investigations.* Cincinnati, OH: Anderson.

Levin, J., and Fox, J.A. 1985. *Mass Murder: The Growing Menace.* New York: Plenum Press.

Liebert, J.A. 1985, December. 'Contributions of Psychiatric Consultation in the Investigation of Serial Murder'. *International Journal of Offender Therapy and Cooperative Criminology,* 29(3), 187–200.

Lindsey, R. 1984, January 21. 'Killers Who Roam the U.S.' *New York Times,* pp. 1, 7.

Montgomery, J.E. 1992, February. Organizational Survival: Continuity or Crisis? Paper presented at the Police Studies Series, Simon Fraser University, Vancouver, British Columbia.

———. 1993. 'Organizational Survival: Continuity or Crisis?' In M. Layton (ed.), *Policing in the Global Community: The Challenge of Leadership.* Burnaby,

British Columbia: Simon Fraser University, pp. 133–142.

Owen, B. 1998. *In the Mix*. Albany: State University of New York.

Rossmo, D.K. 1995. *Geographic Profiling: Target Patterns of Serial Murderers*. Doctoral dissertation, Simon Fraser University, Burnaby, British Columbia.

———. 1999. 'Geographic Profiling'. In J. Jackson and D. Bekerian (eds.), *Offender Profiling: Theory, Practice and Research*. New York: Wiley.

Swanson, C.R., Chamelin, N.C., and Territo, L. 1984. *Criminal Investigation*. New York: Random House.

Wallace, H. 2001. *Family Violence: Legal, Medical, and Social Perspectives*. Boston: Allyn and Bacon.

# 30

## Introduction

For some time now the US has had one of the highest rates of violent crime among industrialized Western nations. And for the last two decades or so, it has taken a strong 'law and order' position on crime that advocates a harsher punitive approach to social control. One consequence has been that America currently has the highest imprisonment rate in the world. But from the mid-twentieth century on, there has also been a movement advocating 'progressive' policies toward criminals that focus on addressing the difficult socio-economic and political realities faced by lower classes and minority groups in America. In this article, Katz argues that progressives are currently having a problem effectively speaking out on criminal violence, not so much because of the popularity of conservative opinion, but because of shortcomings in their own thinking.

What are the main lines of thinking that have shaped progressive thought? What is the overall shortcoming with them? Katz argues that, despite their differences, both political approaches share a 'materialist, instrumental perspective on crime'. What exactly does he mean by this? Finally, how can conflict theory help us understand, not only the crime problem in the US, but also the current debate over it? In what ways might Katz's analysis be relevant to the debate over crime in Canada?

# Criminals' Passions and the Progressive's Dilemma

*Jack Katz*

Progressives in the United States, defined here as those who are at once critical of business elites and supportive of policies that directly benefit the lower classes, now face street crime as a daunting political problem. Conservative politicians triumph in stirring up fears of street crime; they can maintain a broadly moralistic posture even as they discard particular leaders who have become tainted by scandal. But progressives, who occasionally have their own problems with corrupt leaders, have become virtually speechless on criminal violence. Progressives risk alienating important constituencies—especially supporters of civil liberties, minority groups, and socialists—if they rail against violent predatory crime; and they appear morally weak to many voters when they drop a posture of indignation and speak in positive tones on behalf of remedial programs.

The current quandary created for progressive politicians by criminal violence is not simply the result of right-wing campaign advertising tricks, as apologists too often believe; the current difficulty is deeply rooted in the structure of progressive thought.

Since 1950, three lines of initiative, corresponding to three independent intellectual sources, have shaped progressive policies toward violent criminals. In the 1950s, theories of *depth psychology* were invoked to depict violent criminals as emotionally disturbed and to reform criminal court procedures and penal institutional policies that had been characterized as insensitive, cruel, and ineffective in reducing crime. In the 1960s, *sociological* writings that attributed criminality to a contradiction between materialist culture and inadequate economic opportunities were drawn on to develop various governmental programs in an effort called the War on Poverty. In the 1970s, progressive forces in the legal profession succeeded in implementing *norms of legality* in various American institutions, with significant if unforeseen consequences for the ability of government to implement progressive policies in criminally violent sectors of the population.

In the following pages, I will argue that the progressive's current dilemma with violent crime has been structured by (1) an emergent awareness of the repressive consequences of reforms inspired by psychological theory; (2) the inadequacies of sociological theories of crime for appreciating the passions in criminal motivations; and (3) the success of efforts to institutionalize legality, which has placed deviant sectors of the population at a historically unprecedented remove from the conventionally respectable centres of American society. The result has been a thoroughgoing failure to develop policies that can grasp the realities of criminal violence, either intellectually or practically.

## Depth Psychology and Criminal Justice

Early in twentieth century, Progressives produced a large body of social research criticizing criminal justice institutions as insensitive to the urban poor, and they mounted recurrent waves of pressure demanding institutional reforms from state legislatures. Their most celebrated permanent success in the domain of criminal justice was the creation of specialized courts and confinement facilities for juveniles. Depicting a process in which the age-indiscriminate housing of offenders led to the socialization of youths into mature criminal lifestyles, and calling for institutions responsive to the individual needs of youths, the progressives created a national climate of opinion in which resistance to the differentiation by criminal justice administration of adolescent and older offenders was regarded as barbaric and archaic. Beginning in Chicago in 1898, juvenile courts were soon established throughout the nation.[1]

Progressives originally appreciated juvenile delinquents, in a sociological perspective, as members of vulnerable social groups, namely as residents of impoverished, usually immigrant, urban neighbourhoods. By the 1950s, progressive thought about juveniles had become dominated by psychological perspectives. Settlement-house and related local-action philanthropic agencies became self-consciously 'professionalized', in part through their increasing governance by psychological social workers. When publicity about 'gang' violence in American cities created a sense of crisis in the 1950s, the psychologically trained incumbents of the old-line social agencies called for further differentiation in the treatment of juvenile delinquents, not only by age category but by type of personality disorder.[2]

During the 1960s, Progressive opinion on the juvenile court shifted in a way that came to characterize disenchantment with a series of criminal justice reforms that had been instituted to promote greater sensitivity to individual needs. If the juvenile court system had minimized earlier problems of physical abuse and moral corruption of young by older offenders, critics pointed out that the juvenile justice system had also extended the reach of state control, providing justification for state funding of an increased confinement capacity and for confinement criteria, such as being a 'person in need of supervision', that were inherently vague and administratively arbitrary. Juvenile court judges, operating in a special adjudicatory environment, sought to distinguish 'good kids' from 'hardcore offenders' within proceedings lasting a matter of minutes.[3] This prototypically modern criminal justice institution hardly seemed to exercise power in an enlightened manner.

From the 1930s to the 1960s, the insanity defence had been treated as a vehicle for bringing compassionate, progressive social science into the criminal justice process. Legal academics demonstrated the sophistication of their scholarship by bringing psychological theory into their teaching and treatises. When violent crimes drew extraordinary journalistic interest, psychological arguments were promulgated to the general public by writers intent on opposing capital punishment.[4] But discontent about discretionary power grew rapidly in the sixties, and an early target of criticism was the realm of discretion authorized by psycholegal interpretations which held that impassioned violence reflected insanity.

In the early 1960s, a criticism emerged that pointed to the ironically repressive implications of the insanity defence.[5] In some jurisdictions, the prosecution had been able to invoke the charges of insanity, over defence objections, in order to reduce its burden of proof. More generally, a defendant who had been adjudged insane and unfit to stand trial, or one who had escaped conviction on a successful insanity defence, faced a liability to confinement beyond set statutory terms and might be placed interminably under the administration of institutional psychological experts. In the 1970s, Western intellectuals found it increasingly difficult to ignore disturbing resonances from revelations of the repressive use of insanity issues in Soviet criminal processes.[6] Psychological science, previously thought to be a perspective of enlightened compassion working for the defence, now became seen as a tool of limitless state repression.

Throughout the shift among progressives away from trust in psychological expertise and toward a suspicion of repressive state power, there was little effort to appreciate the details of the lived experience of criminal violence. Progressive thought was consistently unable to grasp the non-rational, moral, and sensual logic of impassioned personal violence.

Even though offenders may not formally think out the rationale of their behaviour, their violence has a tripartite coherence.[7] First, impassioned attacks typically are righteous efforts to defend some version of the Good. A father who beats a five-week-old child to death may initially seem to have gone berserk, but the details of his mounting violence—the issuance of orders to stop crying, the shaping of violence into forms of discipline rather than into more expeditious methods of killing—commonly describe an effort not so much to kill as to restore respect according to the Biblical injunction that parents be honoured. Similarly, a spouse, in fatally attacking an adulterous mate, will not simply and temporarily go mad, but may become mad about defending the sanctity of the marital union. A fellow taking up a shotgun and levelling it at a driver who has blocked his driveway will understand himself to be standing up for the rights of property owners in general. Two fellows, enraged and in a violent struggle, will typically be refusing to accept insults that not only they, personally, but that any 'real man' should refuse to tolerate. Far from giving way to dark or evil impulses, the attackers will understand themselves as trying to be Good in some sense that they, at the moment, feel is widely embraced by the community.

Second, the violence in righteous attacks is not simply a 'release' or a resolution of frustrated emotions, but a positive, creative act. In essence, the attacker attempts to write the truth of the offence he has received in the body of the person attacked. The attack at once reconstructs and attempts to transcend the offence. This is sometimes evident in a struggle to turn the mouth into a compliant tool for delivering curses. Sometimes it is seen in the homologous relationship between the attacking acts and the background they respond to: He burned my school books in a trash can, I'll burn him in his bed; she insulted my taste in music, I'll smash her record player.

And third, the extremity of the act is felt and specifically desired by the offender, who acts out of a sense that he must take a last moral stand in defence of his respectability. Many of the paradoxes of impassioned homicide—that these serious acts occur so often during leisure times and in casual social settings, that they occur so rarely against superiors at work—make sense if we appreciate that enraged attacks, although emerging from humiliating situations, tend not to emerge when the humiliated person feels there is some other time and place where respect might be taken for granted.

Righteously impassioned violence is typically employed to coordinate an array of activities (insulting gestures and curses, pushes and shoves, attacks on inanimate objects, strategies to scar the victim's body, and so on). Such violence emerges from a logic that is profoundly moral and sensual, if not reflectively generated. These are not simply aberrations or 'mental explosions'; righteously enraged violence emerges through universal interpersonal rather than unique psychopathological dynamics. Yet these acts are also products of idiosyncratic systems of brutal meaning, emerging over an extended period of time and through multiple attacks, through an elaborated, private semiotics of violence. And there lies at least a small promise for effective intervention.

Shortly after the attack, offenders often 'wake up' to regret their new existence as criminal killers in a world that regards them not as protagonists in immortal dramas written in Biblical terms, but as mortals caught in the prosaic workings of the criminal justice system. The most recent progressive policy response to impassioned domestic violence, supported now by some suggestive experimental evidence, encourages early and sustained intervention in domestic disputes by local criminal justice agencies. Such intervention appears promising in part because arrest, confinement, court appearances, and mandated counselling may together significantly undermine the moments in which transcendent myth governs experience.[8]

What lends a perhaps surprisingly progressive character to this new impetus toward police intervention into the most intimate regions of private life is its affiliation with the feminist and anti–child abuse social movements. But the state's social welfare bureaucracies do not operate in a manner indifferent to social class. Through the administration of income and housing assistance, foster care and adoption programs, drug treatment and public medical services, the state massively and thoroughly interrogates the private lives of the poor. (The middle class knows nothing comparable. The forms used by mortgage loan officers, for example, have no place to record suspicions of spouse and child abuse.) And so, over the course of a generation, the progressive perspective has moved from a posture of compassionate, deep psychological understanding of the offender toward a moral alliance with the victim in an outraged call to expand the state's punitive and constraining powers into the private lives of the lower classes.

# Sociological Materialism and Criminals' Passions

About 50 years ago, Robert K. Merton, in his paper 'Social Structure and Anomie',[9] formalized what became the dominant sociological version of the progressive view of crime causation, at least in journalism and in the public's understanding. Once counted as the most frequently cited professional article in the history of sociology, Merton's argument had both theoretical and political appeal.

Merton developed two now-familiar themes: deviance is the result of a commercial culture that stimulates desires, within a social structure that unequally distributes the opportunities to fulfill material goals. Published when the Depression was well advanced and the Democratic party was well entrenched in national office, the theory cast a chastising eye in familiar directions, appealing to widespread sentiments that structural problems could unjustly put masses of otherwise good people to desperate choices. The argument also appealed to culture critics who disdain the false gods of mass advertising.

While positing the emergence of an intermediate state of anomie from which various lines of deviant action might emerge, Merton's theory put materialistic motives and opportunities for material gains at the driving foundation of deviance. A brief review of some central patterns in youth crime and in predatory adult crime will indicate the massive irrelevance of this materialist version of progressive thought to the lived experience of deviance.

## Delinquency

Merton's theory made its most rhetorically successful appearance in statements on youth crime, or 'delinquency'. Revised and applied specifically to juvenile delinquency by Richard Cloward and Lloyd Ohlin,[10] 'opportunity theory' became part of the intellectual foundation of the Democratic administration's War on Poverty in the 1960s.[11] Three patterns indicate the broad inadequacies of this version of progressive thought in application to youth crime.

First, despite a popular tradition of locating in the lower class a distinctive culture of toughness, a fascination with aleatory risk taking, and the death defying pursuit of illicit action, mortality statistics on males aged 15 to 19 point to a quite different contemporary social reality. In the United States, the mortality rate for white males in late adolescence is not clearly lower than the rate for blacks; in some years it is slightly higher. Teenage white males die from motor vehicle accidents at about three times the rate for their black counterparts. Teenage black males die from 'homicide and legal intervention' at almost five times the rate for their white counterparts. The white rate is not simply the product of the greater availability of cars to white adolescents; the adolescent white male rate of death from auto accidents is several times that of white female adolescents, just as the black male adolescent rate of death from 'homicide and legal intervention' is several times that of the black female adolescent rate.[12]

White male adolescent mortality seems related not simply to access to automobiles but to the way they are driven.

These mortality data indicate criminogenic forces that operate powerfully across the lines that progressive theory traditionally addresses: the fascination with tempting fate is common among young men, and is often combined with a widespread preoccupation with the cultures of alcohol and drug use. As with 'gang' violence, youths' reckless driving typically emerges spontaneously and without connection to material, instrumental objectives. In the domain of fatal criminal activity by young males, social inequality appears to structure the form more clearly than the incidence of deviance. C. Wright Mills' old argument that social pathologists are biased to focus on deviance in urban, lower-class, ethnic minority settings is still worth heeding.[13]

The irrelevance of materialist causes and intentions explains the similarly general neglect by sociologists of relatively innocent forms of youthful criminal activity. Vandalism, for example, has rarely been studied. Vandals take material destruction, not acquisition, as their objective, except when they take an item as a souvenir of an adventure. 'Joyriding' forms of auto theft are not typically instrumental efforts to remedy problems of access to transportation. Adolescents who shoplift often have the money to buy the stolen goods in their pockets, or they discard the booty soon after it has served its function as trophy. And young burglars often break and enter successfully and then wonder what they might reasonably do once inside. Some act out a version of the Goldilocks story, sitting here and there, messing up this or that room, perhaps taking a beer from the refrigerator. When caught, these amateur offenders frequently experience a metaphysical shock as they simultaneously realize, prospectively, the conventional criminal definition that their activity may be given; and retrospectively, that they had been operating in a world of myths.

None of the powerful attractions of these sneaky thrills has mattered much to social research and social theory. But precisely because these forms of deviance have cross-class appeal to amateurs, they can lead us to recognize motivational dynamics that social theory should grow to appreciate. In part, these forms of sneaky thrills are attractive as games: they have goal lines, tricky manoeuvres to fake-out the opposition, and a concern to 'get away with it' that justifies action, regardless of the value of the 'it'. In part, they are seductive plays with sexual metaphors of foreplay, penetration, and orgasmic climax. In part they are strategic interactions over social visibility in which the line between what others think and what one knows about oneself is put to the test.

And they all share as well the temptations of desecration. Vandalism pursues a pure fascination with defiling the sacred. Its outrageously senseless character, to victims, points toward its explanation. The common view misunderstands vandals as simply trying to destroy; but destruction appeals because it is a strategy to release positive powers. Across social and ethnic divisions, adolescents live in a world of material goods that, independent of their market value, serve, through orderliness and surface perfections, to provide a sense of cosmological coherence to adults.[14] Wherever things soiled and things out of place stir anxieties not rationally related to instrumental activities, there adolescents can find objects that are treated as possessing totemic power.

But it has been common to see only a negative force—'frustration' or 'deprivation'—behind vandalism, just as it is common to see only 'acting out' or 'frustration' behind a child's knocking down of a pyramid of blocks. Yet the construction has a compelling majesty for the child; as parents celebrate it with mock expressions of awe, the whole obviously attains a spiritual presence that is infinitely greater than the sum of its parts. Drawn to the visible majesty that is obviously before him, the child seeks to touch the untouchable, acting more in the spirit of exploration than of malevolence. Observers who can see only 'anger' and a 'mess' speak more about the limits of their own theories than about the lived experience of youth.

More clearly than in any other area of criminal behaviour, the traditional progressive view has dominated popular and academic understandings of street 'gang' violence. Related to the great rhetorical appeal of 'opportunity' theory and the call for expanded job opportunities to which opportunity theory predictably leads has been the extraordinarily tired intellectual texture of the field. For a while in the 1960s, books on delinquency won awards from professional research societies without working their arguments through data of any sort, quantitative or qualitative.[15]

Part of the narrowness of traditional inquiry into group delinquency has been a neglect of comparative class analysis. At least since World War II, a series of forms of collective deviance have been embraced by middle-class youth: beats, hippies, punks. What makes a comparative examination important is not simply that it makes analysis more deeply sociological; it helps isolate the essential attractions of violence to ghetto youth gangs.

Middle-class and ghetto forms of collective youth deviance have been regularly and radically different along a series of dimensions. While members of ghetto fighting groups profess a proud affiliation with a local neighbourhood and with identities as 'homeboys', middle-class youths cover up their affluent and suburban origins in tawdry dress and in trips to city locations. While middle-class youth develop 'gender blender' styles of deviance (jeans for everyone, makeup for males and females alike), ghetto gangs organize power around males and sustain emphatically dominant relations with female acquaintances and groups. Middle-class collective youth deviance movements identify with underclass and pariah groups, symbolically integrating diverse classes and ethnicities. Meanwhile ghetto gangs have a segregating thrust, dramatizing inherent, irremediable, deadly differences with just those others in society who are most like them in age, sex, geographic location, social class, and usually ethnicity. And middle-class forms of collective deviance typically take leftist overtones, often defining themselves as collective movements through historically decisive battles with police and the 'Establishment'. Ghetto gangs, on the contrary, are by and large fascistic. Even when they are being hunted by the police, they treat official authority as essentially outside their sovereign reality and employ various symbols of aristocratic, in-born rights of absolute authoritarian rule.

In crucial respects, the traditional progressive understanding of ghetto gang violence has it precisely backwards. Far from being a response to limited opportunities to enter the larger society, the gang encourages its members to look backward and downward; the gang has its attractions as a vehicle for demonstrating elite status by dominating others as aristocrats would dominate a lower caste. Thus Mexican-American *barrio* warriors do not emulate the advertised models of modern commercial affluence, they mimic the arrogant posture of premodern landed elites. And contemporary black gangs in Los Angeles continue to enact a fascination with the legacy of their southern rural heritage in which one group dominates another group on the bare basis of colour (in this case, red and blue coloured clothes).

The ghetto gang's principles of social organization and culture are those of childhood: stay close to home, relate primarily to members of the same sex, engage the myths and symbols of Knights and Lords and other fantastic pre-modern rulers. Ghetto violence is, then, not a cause of gang formation; the fabric of gang life has its own fascinations, and violence is valued, indeed treasured, as a way of transforming what might be seen as a 'punk' affiliation with childhood ways into a heroic loyalty to the neighbourhood or group.

The social divisions central to violent ghetto gangs are not between the ghetto and the affluent ethnic majority society; they are divisions within ghetto communities. The arrogant style of gang domination shows up vividly in juxtaposition to the humility of others in the gang's generational or neighbourhood background, and not at all in anticipation of a dismal occupational fate within a long biographical view or a larger socio-economic framework. What progressive commentators have not wanted to acknowledge is that America's distinctive, century-old youth gang problem is related neither to a more avidly commercial culture nor to a greater degree of rigidity in stratification in this country than in economically comparable Western societies. It is related to the distinctive external and internal migration patterns in US history that have repeatedly brought in masses of ethnic minority, peasant-origin peoples who maintain traditions of deference toward authority and vivid concerns over respectability. Along with such strange bedfellows as the Ku Klux Klan and Hell's Angels, ghetto gangs are the form that the mass appeal of the fascistic spirit, which revels in lording nativist advantages over humbled ethnic minorities, has taken in our country.

With respect to the ghetto-gang phenomenon, Progressive theorists have been caught on the horns of an inescapable dilemma. They cannot confront the sensual and moral attractions that inspire gang members and then turn to present these youths as petitioners for leftist policies. And they cannot acknowledge the central contribution of rural-urban migration patterns in establishing the framework for gang formation without turning cruelly against morally compelling masses of optimistic newcomers.

## Stickup

The contemporary social reality of robbery provides superficial support for ideas that offenders calculate crimes as instruments for obtaining material goals. Robbers, after all, typically demand money, and in interviews, robbers often say that they do it for the money. But

- Robbers are often employed when they commit their offences, and their jobs sometimes provide them with information, and with opportunities for emotional hostilities with superiors, that generate an insider's knowledge and resentments as resources for the offence. The instrumental, materialist perspective rebounds with an appreciation of the low pay and status of the jobs robbers generally hold. But the progressive's perception of white-collar crime turns the debate around once again. If good jobs don't stifle criminal motives, why assume that bad jobs breed them?

- A look at how little planning goes into the typical street robbery, and the very limited rewards and high risks of capture the offence entails, suggests that the instrumental perspective is applicable only superficially, if at all.
- If there are instrumental, materialist reasons for robbery, it is striking that poor women can virtually never grasp them. And in places where the ethnic comparison can be made clearly, as in Southern California, poor black males commit robbery four to five times more often than do poor Hispanic males. This disproportion is much greater for robbery than it is for non-property violent offences, such as assault and homicide, or for non-violent property offences, such as burglary.[16]
- The fact that robbers are typically well aware of alternative opportunities to make more money at less risk through other illegitimate activities, in non-violent property crime and in vice markets; and the fact that many burglars, cheque forgers, pimps, and drug dealers abjure robbery as a fool's game should persuade researchers to attend to the special, non-material attractions of robbery.
- If lack of legitimate opportunity motivates entry into and persistence with robbery, the Progressive is well aware that, after the many years in prison that virtually all persistent robbers will serve, legitimate job opportunities will not be any better. And yet, when the ages of robbers are noted and compared to the number of people in the population of the same ages, it appears that robbery peaks in the early twenties and declines precipitously a few years later.
- And, what is perhaps most neglected about the social reality of robbery, early experiences with robbery often show that materialist motives are clearly secondary during the formative stages of the robber's criminal career. Robbery as a 'professional' line of criminal work typically grows out of adolescent years spent cultivating an awesome presence as a badass. Teenage badasses will often go out of their way to embed robbery in a transcendent immoral project.

A repeat offender's first robberies will often victimize peers and even friends, and will not be limited to situated action, but will make robbery an ongoing feature of his identity. A fearsome fellow may, for example, ask a series of acquaintances for small 'loans' that are, it is initially promised, to be paid back at some future date. When those dates come, and when repayment dates are rescheduled again and again, the cynicism behind the debtor's excuses and promises, delivered with casually subtle intimidating undertones, will become increasingly transparent, with the result that both parties will realize retrospectively that the 'loan' was the first stage in an artfully interminable robbery.

In recent years, the instrumental, materialist perspective has reached into the patterns of robber-victim interaction to find supporting evidence. Asked to generalize about the matter, robbers will typically say that they don't want to use violence and only do when a victim's resistance makes it necessary. A great variety of studies have seemed to show support in the form of high correlations between resistance by victims and their experience of suffering injuries in robberies. The ironically inverse relationship between the means of intimidation used by a robber and the probability of injury to victims seems to provide further support. Considering nonfatal injuries, robbers who use guns are less dangerous than those who use knives, who in turn are less dangerous than those who use clubs or strong-arm force, pre-sumably because the more lethal the means of seeking compliance, the less likely one will be required to use it. Various demographic characteristics of offenders and victims—age, sex, number of co-offenders—significantly distinguish robberies from assaults and non-robbery homicides, also indicating that a different, presumably more rational, framework governs robbery than governs impassioned violence.

But a more intimate view of the meaning of robbery within its full social and processual context undermines the persuasiveness of a rational, instrumental understanding of the rob-ber's behaviour. Correlation, we must always recall, does not establish causation; but more troubling is the distinct possibility that there is a causal relation between victims' resistance and robbers' use of force that runs in a direction opposite to the one that the rationalist view would presume. Resistance by victims may be their response to a robber they perceive as bent on gratuitous violence.

Moreover, even if victims resist and trigger the offender's violence, considering the nature of the resistance victims produce, they often do not provide very compelling reasons for a violent response. What is usually coded by researchers as 'resistance' by victims is an array of behaviours, such as a slow pace in complying with the offender's demands, shouts for help, or attempts to escape, that do not threaten the offender physically and that increase the of-fender's risk of capture less than the offender's own violent response. Given the lack of plan-ning typical of the robbery, the offender would often be much more rational to abandon the current victim and move on to the next criminal opportunity he encounters.

Most importantly, offenders have so many reasons to use violence in robberies that virtu-ally all, and thus ultimately virtually none, of their brutality can be explained instrumentally. After taking all the betting money at a crap game held in a public housing project, robbers are well advised to fire a few warning shots because their victims are likely to have guns and to use them. When robbing a pimp or drug dealer whom they know, and who knows them, rob-bers are 'rational' to defend themselves from subsequent attack by killing their victims. Be-cause they often rob with others who are equally as or more fearsome than they, and because they cannot bring to legitimate forums their disputes over how to split the take, robbers send an instrumentally sensible message to their co-offenders when they viciously attack victims. And because they are frequently involved in vice activities that make them well-known carri-ers of large amounts of cash in their communities, robbers have additional reasons to display a random proclivity to 'non-rational' violence.

Given the context of the typical robber's social life, gratuitous violence carries so many instrumental benefits that it may almost always be 'rational'. Most fundamentally, the un-certainties in robbery are so numerous and so inherent in the offence that offenders can-not rationally anticipate using violence rationally. They know that they cannot know if the victim will have the means and inclination to respond irrationally to their offer to forbear violence in exchange for money. They often suspect that even if they make their use of force precisely contingent on the victim's compliance, their co-offenders, who are often under the influence of intoxicating substances and who often boast badass reputa-tions themselves, may not. At some point in their careers most offenders will realize that they do not know themselves well enough to know whether they will respond rationally to an unexpected occurrence within an offence. In the end, those who would persist in robbery know that to engage in this type of offence, they must steel themselves to it beyond rational calculation. And toward that end, gratuitous violence is an especially valuable self-portraying resource.

In referring to their offence as 'stickup', robbers summarize the attraction in the offence that makes an instrumental understanding superficial. At once phallic and fiercely wilful in its connotations, 'stickup' is attractive almost exclusively to males and to males who are inclined to treat personal relationships as well as robbery scenes as spontaneously subject to violent domination by their will. 'Stickup' promises to freeze the will of victims so that the offender can become the only being present with a purpose that must be respected. Within such an egocentric cosmological project, the robber need not have reasons for his behaviour because he need not attend to the reasons of anyone else.

## White-Collar Crime

Contemporary realities, broadcast so vividly and continuously that they can no longer be ignored, undermine social theories that would attribute deviant motives either to materialist culture or to inequalities in social structure. White-collar crime generates waves of publicity far out of proportion to the little puddles of criminal cases that are officially filed against political and business elites, and white-collar crime does not fit neatly into the critique of commercial culture. The motivational dynamics behind great political scandals, such as the abuses of power in 'Watergate' and 'Irangate', are connected less clearly to material self-seeking than to an image of national identity under attack and needing extraordinary measures of defence. When they are committed for economic gain, white-collar crimes are incompatible with notions that deviant motives are bred in disadvantaged sections of society, and they are not neatly limited to any particular national culture. International bribery scandals have demonstrated that political corruption at the highest levels effectively tempts royal families, socialist party officials, and bureaucrats throughout the Third World. And the business forms of America's white-collar crimes—from the price-fixing scandals of the 1950s, with their anti-free market design, to inside traders operating on capitalism's heart in the 1980s—show well-placed executives criminally financing conventional lifestyles, and arbitragers taking in money in amounts so fabulous that they far outpace the capacity of commercial culture to stimulate the offenders' desires. The latter talk about money not necessarily as a means to an advertised lifestyle, but in terms strikingly reminiscent of street criminals, as a way of keeping score in a game-like pursuit of high risk 'action'.

In the light of white-collar crime, the progressive view of crime causation has been pushed back from explaining the emergence and incidence of deviant motives to the politically less inspiring claim that social inequalities only shape the form or quality of deviance. But here, on the qualitative turf of common crime, the traditional view of progressives is even less convincing. In its lived details, street crime does not clearly exhibit materialistic motives but, rather, hedonistic pursuits sometimes united with gratuitous patterns of violence that border on the sadistic.

# Legality and the Marginalization of Deviance

Several indirectly connected, long-term patterns of social change that have been promoted by American progressives have had the joint, unintended consequence of increasing the social distance between the criminally violent sectors of the population and the conventionally respectable centres of society. One broadly relevant pattern of development has been the long-term expansion of higher education from the large-city-based, private universities that dominated academic research earlier in the century to rural and small-city-based state universities that became major research centres in sociology after World War II.

First-hand, qualitative, individual-case-based research on crime and deviance has typically been produced in research centres located in large cities, often through private universities that had no local public university competition and that were responsive to community concerns to address urban problems. The development of large public universities, historically justified in part as a way of opening opportunities to those not favoured by family wealth, created major research centres that were commonly located at great distances from the high-crime urban areas. Convenient access to sites for first-hand field research is not as widely distributed. Despite some crosscurrents (for example, the more recent growth of public universities in some urban centers; individually negotiated grants that enable the conduct of research away from an academic home base), the dominant trend is for academic social research on crime to be conducted at a greater social remove from the deviants studied, both in geographic terms and in terms of the methodology and types of data employed.[17]

But geographic and technological changes in the social institutional basis of academic research on deviance have played a relatively minor role in moving the lived experience of deviance to the obscured peripheries of American society. Of far greater importance has been the pursuit of legality through a variety of indirectly related social movements, movements that have promoted civil rights in racial relations and in prisons, and that have attacked political corruption and union racketeering. Without any ideological planning directing the pattern, progressive forces have been more or less consistently successful in infusing the rule of law, principally ideals of due process and equal protection, through American society; while progress in reducing substantive social inequalities has been stalled, abandoned, and reversed. One of the results of the uneven implementation of the progressive agenda has been the displacement of criminal violence to the margins of the American social structure.

One dimension of this change, the historical ironies of the Civil Rights Movement in separating an Afro-American underclass from white and black middle-class society, has now been frequently noted. By reducing racial barriers to education, employment, and housing, the Civil Rights Movement created pathways out of racially segregated southern communities, and out of northern urban ghettos, that were especially useful for upwardly mobile African-Americans.[18] As one experienced fieldworker of American ghetto life has put it, the 'old heads'—the locally respected, well-educated, professional and small-business elite of the black community—had become far more scarce in ghetto areas by the 1980s than they had been in the 1950s.[19] The American black ghetto, once a multi-class area containing the black bourgeoisie, the black working class, and the black urban poor, became increasingly dominated by a black 'underclass'. Young men who are tempted by lifestyles characterized by criminal violence have always been concentrated in ethnically segregated, poor urban neigh-bourhoods. But over the last 25 years, young African-American men attracted to a dangerous lifestyle of illicit 'action' have had decreasing personal contacts with conventionally respect-able black men, except in one area—through their frequent contacts with increasingly inte-grated police forces.

Related to the race relations side of the Civil Rights Movement, a number of ancillary movements brought legality into institutions that traditionally governed the relationship be-tween the criminal population and the centers of societal authority. In prisons, Black Mus-lims, who combined freedom of expression and freedom of religion claims with complaints about racially motivated oppression, initially spurred the judicial reform of authority rela-tions.[20] Once begun, prisoners' rights movements spread to represent white and Hispanic complainants, stimulated the formation of specialized legal action support groups, and be-came national. In the *Wolff* decision in the early 1970s, the US Supreme Court made clear that the courts would broadly place procedural requirements on prison administrators' power to discipline inmates.[21] In several states, federal courts have taken control of prisons away from incumbent officials and have appointed monitors to supervise the reconstruction of everyday authority relations.

The 'legalized repression' that now characterizes prison administration has two enduring consequences that progressives must find disturbing. One is a dramatic increase in caste-like segregation among inmate groups and between inmates and staff. Initially spurred by Black Muslims, who rode the Civil Rights Movement of the 1960s into federal courts, judicial intervention has authorized inmate associations and has undermined the ability of prison administration to select inmate leaders and shape the social structure of the inmate world,[22] with the result that US prisons today are dominated to an unprecedented extent by fascist-styled gangs organized around a bizarre array of racist mythologies, from Black Muslims to Mexican *Familias* to Aryan Brotherhoods. We should not flinch from the historical paradox that the most highly rationalized, modern form of enlightened beneficence, as represented by progressive judges battling cruelty and arbitrary power in prisons over the last 25 years, has led to the most intense expressions of peer-directed racist hatreds among contemporary in-mates, whose vengeful and creatively vicious acts of maiming and mutilation[23] are strangely reminiscent of the ancient and spectacular official brutality that the Enlightenment revolu-tions aimed to eradicate.

Second, and more subtly, the legalization of prison authority, which was finally achieved on a national scale during the 1980s, has reconstituted the control capacities of prisons, expand-ing enormously their organizational powers to incarcerate. Before the judicial revolution, correctional officers in many state systems were 'good old boys' who, through patterns of vio-lence, corruption, and limited educational achievement, maintained social ties with inmate leaders. Now, correctional officers are better educated, much more often female, preoccupied with the legalities of power (such as the proper form to 'write up' inmate infractions), and increasingly professional in their career orientations. More socially distant from inmates in gender, education, and everyday culture, correctional staffs now equip prisons with a greatly enhanced organizational sophistication. It is not a coincidence that as prisons finally became 'legalized' in their daily operations during the 1980s, the raw size of the inmate population doubled on a national scale (and in California, which has been a leader in the acceptance of legality in the prisons, the prison population quadrupled), even as crime rates ended the decade at a lower level than existed when it began. Without the professionalization and legalization of prison administration, this increase in incarcerative capacity would have been opposed by judges who, when confronted with resistant 'good old boy' administrations, have in extreme instances ordered the release of inmates subject to arbitrary, discriminatory, and 'cruel and unusual' treatment.

Legality, in the forms of judicial oversight, the reshaping of the exercise of authority to conform with published rule, and the introduction of intraorganizational procedures for questioning authority, has changed the relationship of deviant populations to the centre of American society by dismantling traditional, subterranean social bridges between the conventional center and the deviant periphery. The attack on the corruption of prison authority was paralleled by interrelated attacks on corruption in urban political machines, in police departments, and in local criminal courts. Even before Watergate, an uncoordinated but national-scale legal campaign against local political corruption had begun, as federal law enforcement institutions became gradually more professionalized and, in the non-partisan style of pre-World War I Progressives, became mobilized to 'clean' government.

Along with numerous other social trends that undermined political 'machines', anticorruption prosecutions dismantled a complex network of ties between inner-city deviants and respectable government officials.

When urban political machines mobilized the vote in ethnic neighbourhoods, neighbourhood toughs, who traditionally hung out around social and athletic, especially boxing, clubs, were appreciated as politically valuable symbols of ethnic group pride and were at times literally as well as figuratively publicly embraced by ward bosses.[24] If intervention in the criminal justice system could not always be counted on for an efficacious 'fix', many local criminals found that it made sense to keep 'connected' lawyers on 'retainer' and disposed to exercise 'influence'. A reader of the life histories of common criminals who operated in US cities from the West through the East coasts will find matter-of-fact descriptions of corrupt influences on local criminal justice institutions continuing through the 1950s,[25] descriptions that have no parallel in the ethnographies and life histories that trace criminal careers within the last 20 years.

By the time in American history that African-Americans were able to be elected municipal leaders, the traditional infrastructure through which ethnic leaders reached and were reachable by residents in ethnic neighbourhoods had been severely weakened by force of law. The dismantling of corrupt bridges to deviant inner-city populations is significant for progressive policies in at least two respects. The absence of subterranean connections in contemporary cities presents special difficulties for implementing remedial programs. A new educational, job opportunity, or drug rehabilitation program must now bootstrap its own social mechanisms for reaching its targets. On the other side, the increased social distance of predatory criminals from conventional social organization hardens the boundaries of their deviant lifestyles and makes their motivations less ambiguously anti-social.

The moral universe in which the contemporary violent criminal typically operates has been isolated gradually but firmly by the broad institutionalization of legality throughout

American society. Consider the implications of the transformation of local neighbourhood commercial culture, from the days of the urban American Jewish ghetto, as documented by Louis Wirth early in this century, to the realities of the African-American ghetto today. In Wirth's ghetto, market transactions were routinely moralized; price, quality, and service were constantly subject to bargaining; fraud was an everyday risk; any transaction could provide evidence of one's acumen or prove one a fool.[26] The implementation of mass merchandising and consumer protection legislation has eradicated the routine moral dramas of negotiating consumer transactions. The poor still pay more, but they usually pay it up front; large-scale and legally reviewable marketing has made retail negotiations too costly and bothersome for most merchandisers. Today the predatory criminal, whose objectives are superficially material but whose motives are fundamentally centred on transcending humiliation and 'taking' victims by making them fools, stands as a harsh, extreme, archaic representative of a lost moral world.

## Conclusion

The challenges that criminals' passions represent for contemporary progressive thought reflect essentially two troublesome empirical patterns. First, while legality, or procedural justice, and substantive equality, or social-class justice, have frequently been joined in progressive thought, legality has made a much steadier empirical advance in recent decades. Progressive thought has failed to adjust to this emergent disjuncture in its ideals. The increasing institutional commitment to legality in the United States has made it more difficult to reach populations of the criminally violent; in addition, legality increasingly confuses social-class interpretations of crime by enhancing public awareness of white-collar crime. While progressives may take ideological comfort from the expanded prosecutions of conservative political and business elites for corruption and fraud, they cannot in the same breath blame socio-economic conditions for deviant motives. If social-class position shapes the form more clearly than it shapes the incidence of crime, reducing crime inequalities cannot as easily be promoted by a promise of improved collective moral character.

Second, and more disturbing, as political advertising effectively parades the details of criminal victimization before the public, the lived experience of contemporary street crime is dominated by moral and sensual dynamics, not material strivings.

If the lived experience of crime poses fundamental difficulties for progressive politicians, there are equally troublesome implications for modern social theory in general. My overall argument, that criminality is best explained by moral and sensual dynamics, will seem to some anti-progressive, in part because of the nature of its approach to social explanation. Crime is neither the product of extraordinary emotional pathology ('insanity' or 'sickness') nor the instrumental execution of materialist plans. Its coherence is deep and detailed, but it is sensually embodied, not reflectively produced. But so is much of our routine, conventional, everyday behaviour. When we write, walk, or talk, we do so interactively, anticipating how our lines of action will be seen and responded to by others, but we do not live our interactive awareness rationally; we do not produce our routine action reflectively. Rather we rely on rhythms and holistic senses of the projects we are engaged in, such that our writing is better grasped as a kind of prosaic drawing; our talking, as a usually banal singing; our walking, as a dancing that typically does not parade its aesthetic dimensions even as we rely fundamentally on them. Were we able to see the moral and sensual dimensions of everyday behaviour more clearly, an analysis of the moral and sensual dynamics of crime would not stand out as damning. But we still teach a legacy of eighteenth- and nineteenth-century rationalism in our social theory classes; and our version of interactionist analysis overplays the role of reflection ('the looking-glass self') and thought, to the neglect of the embodiment of conduct (we read classic interactionist theory on 'mind, self and society', but not on 'body, self, and social interaction').

Considering the distinctive anxieties of twentieth-century life and the special horrors of its massive deaths, our clinging to centuries-old theoretical perspectives is a deep and pathetic intellectual failure. Existentialism and phenomenology, the philosophical movements that arose with the twentieth century's unprecedented, vicious chaos, remain outside the mainstream of empirical research and of American social thought. So do the central sticking points in American policy development on crime, where sensual and moral dynamics are as central as they are to crime causation.

If homicides commonly arise out of quickly developing passions, we should reduce the availability of guns so that enraged attackers might turn to less lethal instruments of violence. But guns remain symbols that are embraced with uniquely profound passions in America. The key research question about guns and American violence is not how much or whether removing guns will reduce violence, but why guns have acquired such strong moral and sensual meanings in the United States.[27]

And if robbery grows out of a fascination with dominating social interaction so that it provides signs of respect, we should acknowledge the special challenges of humiliation that are maintained within ethnically bounded, and particularly black, poverty communities. But policies of racial integration that would specifically address the unique roots of America's criminal violence evoke fears that repeatedly turn progressive political leaders to more broadly defined, and less specifically relevant, institutional solutions. Ironically working in the same direction, the recent rise of African-Americans to local political leadership positions, through electoral successes that are based on the size of segregated voting blocks, has itself contributed to the deterioration of the national commitment to integration.

And if robbery pays so poorly that a commitment to it can only be sustained when intermixed with more economically rewarding opportunities in gambling, prostitution, and illegal drug markets—vice worlds that, when combined with robbery, sustain the moral and sensual attractions to a way of life characterized by illicit action—then we should appreciate that our criminal legal framework, through making vice activities so remunerative, provides crucial support for the robber's career. But the sensualities of vice activities stir such powerfully moralized passions that we are barely able as a community to bring alternative regulatory frameworks into rational political discussion.

Dominated by a materialist, instrumental perspective on crime, progressive thought has misled us because it has directed attention away from those distinctive features of American ethnic relations and moral culture that are most closely related to the exceptionally violent dimensions of the crime problem in the United States. The progressive's failures are mirrored rather than avoided by the Right. Indeed, no voice on the contemporary political scene speaks to the distinctively national character of America's criminal violence. In a notable way, both political sides share a materialist, instrumental perspective on crime causation, the one calling for more 'opportunity', the other for higher 'costs' to offset the 'benefits' that criminals are presumed to calculate. If we would abandon the instrumental, materialist framework that supports tired remedial policies and turn research attentions to the moral and sensual dynamics that animate criminal violence, we might generate an empirically grounded progressive response to crime.

## Notes

1. Anthony M. Platt, *The Child Savers: The Invention of Delinquency* (Chicago: University of Chicago Press, 1977).
2. New York City Youth Board, *Reaching the Fighting Gang* (New York: Youth Board, 1960).
3. Robert M. Emerson, *Judging Delinquents: Context and Process in Juvenile Court* (Chicago: Aldine, 1969).
4. Psychiatrists and liberal legal academics entered public debates over crime and punishment in the 1950s and 1960s by pressing for changes in the criteria for applying the insanity defence in capital cases. Perhaps the most famous instance was the case that Truman Capote made into an immensely successful 'non-fiction novel', *In Cold Blood* (New York: Random House, 1965).
5. Joseph Goldstein and Jay Katz, 'Abolish "The Insanity Defense"—Why Not?' *Yale Law Journal* 72 (1963): 853.
6. See, for example, Zhores A. Medvedev and Roy A. Medvedev, *A Question of Madness* (New York: Norton, 1979).
7. The following paragraphs summarize Chapter 1, 'Righteous Slaughter', in Jack Katz, *Seductions of Crime* (New York: Basic Books, 1988).
8. Compare Richard A. Berk and Phyllis Newton, 'Does Arrest Really Deter Wife Battery? An Effort to Replicate the Findings of the Minneapolis Spouse Abuse Experiment', *American Sociological Review* 50 (April 1985): 253.
9. Robert K. Merton, 'Social Structure and Anomie', in his *Social Theory and Social Structure* (New York: Free Press, 1968 [1938]).
10. Richard A. Cloward and Lloyd E. Ohlin, *Delinquency and Opportunity: A Theory of Delinquent Gangs* (Glencoe, Ill.: Free Press, 1960).
11. Daniel P. Moynihan, *Maximum Feasible Misunderstanding: Community Action in the War on Poverty* (New York: Free Press, 1969).
12. Katz, *Seductions of Crime*, chapter 4, note 9.
13. C. Wright Mills, 'The Professional Ideology of Social Pathologists', *American Journal of Sociology* 49 (September 1943): 165–80. For a rare hint that the lower- or working-class youth and middle-class youth may differ not so much in their pursuit of action as in its social visibility, see Herbert J. Gans, *The Urban Villagers* (New York: Free Press, 1962), 66 (comparing the visibility of street-corner life with the cover provided by the closed doors of the fraternity).
14. Compare Mary Douglas, *Purity and Danger: An Analysis of the Concepts of Pollution and Taboo* (London: Routledge and Kegan Paul, 1976).
15. Twenty-five years later, the body of 'gang' theories that flourished in the 60s takes the appearance of an extreme phase of academic sophistry. With only rare consideration for grounding analysis in any recognizable data, theorists spun out intricate variations on such questions as the relationship between the pressures experienced by gang kids, the normative direction of their delinquent activities, and the gap between aspiration and legitimate opportunity in the larger society. For American society, the central significance of the academic debates was not in the elaborate distinctions made in book-length expositions of theory, but in the scholarly legitimizing of the simple social theory that stressed a clash between materialistic culture and inequalities in mobility opportunities, and that appeared in newspaper columns, in political speeches, and in government programs. My reference to 'opportunity theory' is to this gross progressive perspective on lower-class deviance, not to the subtleties of any particular academic text.
16. Katz, *Seductions of Crime*, 240.
17. Tempted by massive statistical data bases that are provided, ready-made, by the state, academic researchers increasingly take the bait and focus their efforts on the handful of background conditions that such data happen to cover. By itself not publishing much of the data it collects, the state, which sympathetically allows researchers access to electronic data files, effectively controls a vast portion of formally independent intellectual energies. Faced with, on the one hand, the awful but inevitable risk of coming up with nothing new in a

qualitative field study and, on the other, the certainty of 'making a contribution' by exploring a virgin portion of an electronic data set, few Ph.D. students can resist the seduction. The niggardly resource commitments of governmental units to analyze and publish the data they collect has drawn academics to become out-of-house bureaucrats, promulgating state-created versions of social reality, rather than independent investigators of social phenomena (and this applies not simply in the area of crime but also to the study of ethnic groups, social mobility, etc.).

18. William Julius Wilson, *The Declining Significance of Race*, 2nd ed. (Chicago: University of Chicago Press, 1980), 129.

19. See Elijah Anderson, *Streetwise: Race and Class in an Urban Community* (Chicago: University of Chicago Press, 1990).

20. James Jacobs, *Stateville* (Chicago: University of Chicago Press, 1977).

21. *Wolff v. McDonnell* , 418 US 539 (1974).

22. Compare John J. DiIulio, Jr. *Governing Prisons: A Comparative Study of Correctional Management* (New York: Free Press, 1987).

23. See, for example, W.G. Stone, as told to G. Hirliman, *The Hate Factory: The Story of the New Mexico Penitentiary Riot* (Agoura, Calif.: Paisano Publications, 1982).

24. See, for example, Warren Moscow, *The Last of the Big-Time Bosses: The Life and Times of Carmine De Sapio and the Rise and Fall of Tammany Hall* (New York: Stein and Day, 1971), and Steven P. Erie, *Rainbow's End: Irish-Americans and the Dilemmas of Urban Machine Politics, 1840–1985* (Berkeley and Los Angeles: University of California Press, 1988).

25. See, for example, Harry King and William Chambliss, *Box Man: A Professional Thief's Journey* (New York: Harper and Row, 1972).

26. Louis Wirth, *The Ghetto* (Chicago: University of Chicago Press, 1956).

27. The reason may have implications so sad that we would rather not appreciate them. Guns lost their popular charm and their potential to become icons in Europe when international wars brought home a level of destruction that the United States has never known. Elias remarks that the common celebratory practice of shooting off guns ended in Europe after the First World War. Norbert Elias, *The Loneliness of the Dying* (New York: Basil Blackwell, 1985). In various ways, the exceptional level of domestic criminal violence in the United States may be the trade-off for the exceptional immunity from international violence that the United States has enjoyed over the last 200 years.

# Part VIII     Issues in Moral and Legal Regulation

The topics studied within the sociology of deviance and social control are often contentious. The articles selected for this section address issues concerning areas not covered in other parts of the reader: wife abuse, corporate crime, internet deviance, and gambling. Despite their diversity, there is a common element running through them. Each of the activities occurs in an arena characterized by some degree of normative suspension that makes regulating what falls within them problematic.

Normative suspension involves removing or relaxing the applicability of some of the regular norms that prevail in a society in a specific social setting, and replacing them with ones that are often more lax, though still restrictive, and are usually formulated and enforced by participants in that setting. This can result in a zone of ambiguity and potential contest over which norms, values, ideas, and beliefs should prevail.

In Western societies, the family household is one such environment. It is a private haven set apart from a competitive public world where many of the norms pertinent to daily family life are decided and enforced by the adult participants of the family. As a result, a family may engage in customs and practices that reflect personal preferences, interpersonal agreements, or ethnic and religious traditions that vary significantly from those generally observed in public life. In effect, they constitute 'how we live together here'. There is a freedom to this institutionalized arrangement and selective suspension of public norms. But what is to be done if the principles and norms being practiced within the domestic setting are offensive to those of the wider society and have harmful consequences for some family members? For example, how do we sort out what is appropriate concerning parents using corporal punishment to discipline children within families, especially if the family arrangement is a traditional, patriarchal one where parents are often expected to be strict and exercise more severe forms of discipline as part of honourably fulfilling their duties? The issue can also arise when the norms or means of social control in the domestic setting are generally in line with those of the wider community, but are being interpreted and enacted in troubling ways.

Corporate and professional settings also generate issues in regulating sites with some institutionalized degree of normative suspension, or sites where members act as if they were exempt, or partially exempt, from certain societal norms and expectations. Consider corporate crime. Business generally claims that it is involved in an arena—the market—that works most effectively with regard to competition, innovation, and profit-making if it is free of government intervention and control. As such, it's best if business responsibly monitors itself through boards of directors, codes of ethics, associations, and ultimately, competition itself. The rise of multinational corporations and global economies has amplified this issue even more with businesses engaging in activities outside the jurisdiction of any one national society. What norms apply to doing business in a global economy, who should decide them, and who should enforce them?

There is a parallel situation encountered in understanding and responding to white-collar crime. Most professions argue with some degree of validity that only their members have the expertise and hence the authority to establish norms and guidelines for their profession and to evaluate wrongdoing. As a result, the professions establish professional associations and develop codes of ethics to guide their practitioners and to assess wrongful conduct. However, what kinds of structures are in place to present checks and balances for members engaging in, interpreting, and judging conduct primarily in terms of the profession's shared ideology and interests?

Activities that occur on the Internet occur in a different sort of arena. The Internet occupies a space, not only outside any one national society, but outside geographic territories altogether. Cyberspace is characterized by a radical openness and accessibility that is difficult to monitor and regulate. And it has given rise to a kind of anarchistic sentiment that it should be free of government surveillance and regulation or the constraints of any particular community. As with the case of Wikipedia, producing, consuming, and managing should be left to the users themselves.

Finally, governments themselves have participated in establishing arenas that can result in problematic outcomes as well as difficulties in regulating or effectively addressing those outcomes. For example, by transforming gambling into the entertainment of gaming which they themselves regulate, governments have effectively shifted the responsibility for gambling and its consequences entirely onto the individual. Gaming is portrayed as the private activity of enjoying a leisure pastime. Of course, one of the possible outcomes is problem gambling. But how can governments or communities regulate what ultimately becomes defined as being the private matter of how individuals choose to enjoy themselves, and hence, their personal responsibility?

The issues discussed in the following articles require us to contend with the kinds of ambiguities that have always been an integral part of the sociology of deviance and social control.

## Introduction

MacLeod's article, an excerpt from her report *Battered but not Beaten: Preventing Wife Battering in Canada*, makes an important contribution to a puzzling phenomenon: why do women in highly abusive relationships remain with the spouse who is physically and psychologically abusing them, rather than leaving?

MacLeod outlines, and then challenges, the two most commonly held theories concerning the origins and perpetuation of domestic violence. What exactly is the problem with both theories? How do their shortcomings interfere with assisting battered women? Can Gilligan's theory of masculine and feminine systems of valuing/morality (outlined in Chapter 15) be of use in understanding the problem and helping battered women?

# Wife Battering in Canada

*Linda MacLeod*

Battered women and batterers come from all walks of life. They may be working outside the home or in the home. They may be unemployed or have a steady job. They may be rich or poor, well-educated or illiterate, of any nationality or race, young or old, with or without children.

Despite the difficulty of understanding wife battering, two major types of explanation have been widely used to respond to battered women, their children, and the men who batter them.

## Power-Based Theories

These theories explain that violence against women is perpetuated by society's power structure which makes men dominant over women through the creation of separate and unequal roles for each gender. This dominance is reinforced through institutional rules and structures based on male supremacy.

As staff members of the Women's Research Centre in Vancouver have stated:

> Wife assault is a reality in our society because men have the socially ascribed authority to make the rules in marriage, and because violence against their wives is accepted in the eyes of society, as an appropriate instrument of control. The social and economic structure of marriage as an institution in which women are dependent on men requires this assignment of authority to men.[1]

Power-based theories of wife battering emphasizing sex-based inequality and the patriarchal structure of society have gained acceptance by policy-makers and service-providers in this field. This explanation for wife battering appears in most writings on the subject and helps guide intervention services for battered women, their partners, and their children.

Research on the power dynamics in battering families also asserts that power is more highly valued in battering families than in non-battering families. On the surface, this power may not always overtly rest with the man. However, research findings suggest that, in families where the woman is dominant in terms of decision-making or earning power, or where the woman is perceived to be superior in some other way, violence is often used by the man to shift the balance of power. Many counsellors reported that many men resort to physical violence when they feel their wives are more articulate than they are. These men frequently complain that they can't win an argument with their wives, so they 'shut them up' by the use of force.

In power-based theories, the acceptance and social reinforcement of violence in the family is a means to establish and to maintain the male in a dominant relationship over his wife.

Because male roles are socially created as dominant over female roles,

> Wife assault arises out of the socio-cultural belief that women are less important and less valuable than men and so are not entitled to equal status and respect. Thus, central to the task of dealing with the problem of wife assault is the need to recognize that wife assault is a social problem experienced by many Canadian women each year rather than an isolated interpersonal problem between two particular spouses.[2]

## Learning Theories

Learning theorists argue that witnessing or suffering violence teaches people to use violence to try to solve problems or deal with stress.[3] This argument is supported by research and by statements from service-providers which reveal that many batterers come from families where their mothers were battered and/or where they themselves were physically, sexually, or psychologically abused as children.[4] These findings are corroborated by the statistics collected for this study. Sixty-one per cent of the partners of the women who stayed in transition houses in 1985 had been abused as children. Thirty-nine per cent of the battered women reported being physically abused as children, 24 per cent reported being sexually abused, and 48 per cent reported being emotionally abused as well. Of the women who said they physically abused their own children, 69 per cent said they had themselves been physically abused during their childhood.

Learning theorists also argue that the use of violence as a discipline tool can teach violence. In this vein, researchers report a 'strong relationship between parental punishment and aggression' and suggest that

> increasing evidence indicates that a high price is paid for maintaining order in the family through violence. The norms that legitimate violence assure a family institution and a society characterized by violence for years to come.[5]

Learning theorists also frequently explain the perpetuation of violence by stating that victims, friends, and society as a whole unintentionally reinforce the violence.

> The victim after the beating, may indeed do as he insists; others may treat him with more respect and often he feels more in control. Even if he feels remorseful or guilty about her injuries he (and sometimes the victim herself) tends to blame the victim for 'causing' him to 'lose control'. He denies responsibility for the negative behaviour. Due to the tacit acceptance of family violence in society and to the lack of clear messages that his violent behaviour must stop, his violence is rarely punished.[6]

Finally, learning theorists suggest that witnessing violence vicariously can teach some men to use violence within or outside the family. This tenet has created concern about pornography as a teaching tool for violence.

These types of explanations, one based on the structure of power in our society, the other on learning theory, have clarified our understanding of wife battering, and have helped to guide intervention efforts. Yet many shelter workers and other service-providers lamented, 'These theories that seem so clear to us just don't seem to ring true for too many of the women who come to us'.

## How do Battered Women Understand the Battering?

Battered women speak of a shifting, ambiguous power. They spoke sometimes of feeling powerless against their partners. They also spoke of their power in the relationship and of the powerlessness of their partners. Many believe women are more powerful than men, as the quote below elucidates:

> I can't quite make sense of what the women here [at the shelter] are saying about the patriarchal structure of society and about power and society making men more powerful and all that. When I was growing up, my mother was for sure stronger than my Dad in every way but physically. She was smarter, could do more, and more people respected her. I think it's the same with my husband and me. There's no way he's stronger than me, except physically, and that's why he hits me, because he feels so low.

Other women elaborated this theme in terms of a mother-son model of relationships between themselves and their partners.

> My husband and all the men I've ever known are like little boys. We're really like their mothers, underneath. Everyone keeps telling me to leave him; they say he'll destroy me. But they don't know how strong I am and how weak he is underneath.

Others spoke of the power they feel in the relationship.

> Sure I feel sorry for him. He says he would have nothing without me and the kids. I know he's pretty rotten sometimes. But he really needs me. I guess that's why I keep going back. He makes me feel important.

Still others spoke of their partners as victims or losers in society.

> You can talk about men being powerful in our society if you want, but you're not talking about my husband. My husband's never had any power in his whole life. He's never had a chance. He was born poor. He was born Indian. He's never felt better than anyone. He's never felt better than me. It's because he's so low that he hits me.

Many battered women do not feel like powerless victims, and will not respond positively to services which treat them like victims instead of survivors.

These experiences remind us of the complexity of the realization of power in individual relationships. They also remind us that power in our society is not just gender-based; it is also class-, race-, and age-based.

Many battered women also understand battering as something that 'got out of hand', as an extension of a normal part of a normal relationship. Many battered women feel their relationship started out much like any other relationship and, in fact, some emphasize that they feel they had an unusually loving, intense, and dose relationship.

Intimate relationships, by definition, generate a wide range of emotions. The image of romantic love idealized in our society is characterized by highs and lows. Being 'in love' is living 'on the edge', participating in a kind of emotional aerobics. The socially accepted use of drugs, the preoccupation with 'having it all', with creative stress, the fitness craze, and even our social addiction to soap operas and violent television shows emphasize high energy and intense emotional highs and lows.

For these reasons, wife battering at the outset is often difficult to prevent, or even to identify, because some violence (rough sexual play and psychological games intended to elicit jealousy) is intertwined with our ideal of 'being in love' (isolation and possessiveness). In different socio-economic groups, this violence may be more or less psychological, or more or less physical, but the romantic desire to be alone together in a private world and the desire to have constant physical contact with your loved one are simply the 'positive' faces of the jealousy and isolation which become part of most wife-battering experiences.

Battered women often talk of the intensity of their love for the batterer. Throughout this study, many battered women made the following kinds of statements: 'I've never had better sex with anyone', 'I just can't believe he'd hit me. I know he really loves me as much as I love him', 'No one's ever loved me the way he does'. Battered women also speak of the highs and lows of the relationship:

> You know, life was a roller-coaster with Bill. In the end, of course, that became unbearable—all the tension. But in the beginning, it was just so thrilling. I never wanted to come down.

Many battered women are guilty of no greater 'weakness' than being in love with being in love. It's their attempt to stay in love, to retain an idealized vision of their partner, that often prevents many battered women from realizing they are being battered until the battering has become a part of life.

Women who are battered do not generally define themselves as battered the first time they are battered. In fact, because wife battering includes emotional, verbal, and financial battering, as well as physical and sexual battering, it may be difficult to define when the first incident actually occurred. This ambivalence is evident in the words battered women use to describe their early experiences with the batterer. It is not uncommon for battered women to say:

> I was flattered by his jealousy at first—I thought it meant he loved me. He said he would rather stay home, just with me, than go out with friends. I loved the attention and closeness at first. I thought he was the most romantic man in the world.

Even the first case of physical abuse is not always clear-cut. In many cases, the woman is 'just pushed'. While pushing can result in severe injuries, depending on the location of the push—down the stairs, over a chair, into a pot of boiling water on the stove, etc.—the push itself can be easily re-interpreted by the batterer and by the woman who is battered as something minor. The results of the push can be viewed as an accident.

> I was just baffled the first time he hit me. It wasn't really a hit, you know, not like a punch or even a slap; he just pushed me really hard. I broke an arm, but it was from falling backward over a chair, not from his push.

Another woman's statement mirrors these sentiments:

> I couldn't believe my husband had hit me. I just kept asking, is this the same man who loves me so much that he can't stand it if another man talks to me? It was really easy for me to accept his explanation that he'd had a hard day at work and a little too much to drink. I couldn't see anything else without having to ask if he really did love me, and that was just too painful. It wasn't until much later, years of violence later, that I could see that the way he loved me—his jealousy, his possessiveness—were also part of the violence.

Is this 'illogic' really so different from the logic which we call compromising, or 'forgiving and forgetting', when it does not involve identifiable violence?

While violence almost always escalates, it may not do so for months or years. The result is that women accept the violence as unpleasant but bearable, given the good things about the relationships (and most battering relationships do still provide sporadic periods of closeness during the honeymoon phases of the violence) until they are so enmeshed in the cycle of violence and so demoralized and trapped by it that they can't 'just leave'.

Many service-providers, and even women who have been battered, counsel that leaving or calling the police 'the first time it happens' is the most effective way to ensure it won't happen again. However, given that it may be hard to define 'that first incident', especially since definitions of intolerable violence are culturally relative and since most women have a lot of emotional and practical investment in their relationships, this advice frequently has an unreal, hollow ring to it.

American author Susan Schechter points to the 'normalcy' of the early reactions of most battered women, at least in terms of the current 'rules' of intimate relationships, in her comment: 'Most people feel ambivalent when ending a long-term relationship. Major change is always difficult, often slowly and haltingly undertaken.[7]

There is growing evidence that leaving provides no guarantee the battering will stop and may even escalate the violence. In the present study, 12 per cent of the women were separated or divorced. Anecdotal information suggests the majority of these women were battered by their ex-husbands, some by new partners. Michael Smith, in his telephone survey of 315 Toronto women, found that, while the rate of abuse for all women interviewed was 18.1 per cent, for women who were separated or divorced, the rate jumped to 42.6 per cent. [8]

The reactions of most battered women are often strong and logical and must be treated this way if we are to reach out to battered women and provide services for them which 'ring true', will be helpful, and will be used by a greater number of battered women. It is easy to scoff at, or be discouraged by, the astonished response of many women to the suggestion that they leave their violent husbands: 'But he's my husband, and the father of my children. I can't just abandon him'. It's easy from an outside vantage point which assumes the batterer, the battered wife, their relationship, or all three are defective, to dismiss as misguided sentiment the woman's heroic attempts to keep her marriage together, to keep her children from knowing about the violence, to insist that she loves her husband. The woman's actions and statements are easy to dismiss as long as we assume the battered woman, along with her partner and their relationship, are somehow different from us in terms of the basic personality of the man and woman and in terms of the initial quality of the relationship.

However, as this study has established repeatedly, research shows that battered women do not fit one psychological or socio-economic mould. Few common characteristics which are not the direct result of the battering have been cited. In fact, in the one study known to the author where the personality traits of battered women *before* the violence were discussed, Lenore Walker found women who are battered 'perceive themselves as more liberal than most' in their relationships with men[9]—a far cry from the stereotype of the battered woman as a traditional women totally oppressed by, and dependent on, her partner.

It is *after* prolonged battering, as a result of the battering, that battered women begin to display certain similar psychological traits. After prolonged battering, women suffer from low self-esteem and isolation. They are emotionally dependent on the batterer, are compliant, feel guilty, and blame themselves for the violence, and yet demonstrate great loyalty to the batterer. Not only do they want the relationship to continue, they state they are staying for the sake of the family. They believe the batterers' promises to change and frequently believe the violence would stop if only their partners would get the one lucky break they've always wanted.[10]

To understand the actions and perceptions of battered women, it is important to think of how we all act in relationships, what we want, and the extent to which many of us will go to preserve a relationship. As one shelter worker poignantly said:

> Relationships are hard to come by. Sure we should help women know that they have worth outside their marriages, but a marriage isn't just status and a piece of paper . . . it's warmth, belonging, and a future. Battered women don't always get these good things out of their relationships, but most of them did in the beginning, and they just keep hoping it will come back. People will go to any lengths to feel loved, and love is not just waiting around the next comer for every battered woman who leaves her batterer.

Even the majority of women who report the violence do so out of hope that she and her partner will be helped to return to their pre-violent state. Of course, she may also hope she will get attention and be listened to because she is frequently lonely and unnurtured as a result of the isolation most batterers impose on their victims. She may also hope he will be punished or 'get his just desserts'. But behind it all, she often just wants them to be happy again. The importance of these hopes should not be diminished.

Unfortunately many of the services which have been created for battered women and for their partners have been built on the assumption that the relationship is not worth saving and ignore or belittle the woman's hopes to save and rekindle it. The hope of the service-providers is most often to save or protect the woman as an individual or to help or change the batterer as an individual in some way. This well-intentioned, institutional hope often buries the woman's pleas for a different kind of help. This discrepancy between the battered woman's hopes and the hopes of the service-providers renders many of the initiatives taken inappropriate and is frustrating for the women who are battered and contributes to the burn out and despair of the people who try to help the women, their children, and their partners.

## Notes

1. Helga Jacobsen, Coordinator. *A Study of Protection for Battered Women* (Vancouver: Women's Research Centre, 1982), p. 5.
2. Marion Boyd, ed. *Handbook for Advocates and Counsellors of Battered Women* (London, Ontario: London Battered Women's Advocacy Clinic Inc., 1985), pp. 12–13.
3. Anne Ganley, 'Causes and Characteristics of Battering Men', in *Wife Assault Information Kit* (Victoria: Ministry of the Attorney General. April 1986), pp. 68–69.
4. Research supporting this hypothesis is summarized in Straus and Hotaling, *The Social Causes*, pp.14–15.
5. *Ibid.*, p. 15.
6. Ganley, 'Causes and Characteristics', p. 70.
7. Susan Schechter, *Women and Male Violence: The Visions and Struggles of the Battered Women's Movement* (Boston: South End Press, 1982), p. 20.
8. Michael D. Smith, *Woman Abuse: The Case for Surveys by Telephone.* The LaMarsh Research Programme Reports on Violence and Conflict Resolution. Report #12 (Toronto: York University, November 1985), p. 29.
9. Walker, 'The Battered Woman Syndrome Study', p. 8.
10. Albelta, Social Services and Community Health, *Breaking the Patten: How Alberta Communities Can Help Assaulted Women and Their Families* (Edmonton: November 1985), p. 17.

## Introduction

Hagan draws on a conflict theory perspective to provide a critical overview of the extent of white-collar and criminal crime as well as how they're currently processed and sanctioned. Specifically, he examines the connection between such crime and social class, the structure of modern organizations, law, regulatory agencies, and the structure of the market. He then discusses how current practices and systems are conducive to committing them, despite their significant impact in financial and human terms.

One of Hagan's main criticisms concerns how such crime is processed and sanctioned. While corporations, which have the legal status of 'fictitious persons', are subject to legal regulation, the laws that govern them are generally weak. So even when they're punished, it's not regarded as a deterrent, but a cost of doing business. What kinds of actions can be taken to address this and the other factors Hagan identifies which contribute to corporate and white-collar crime?

# Corporate and White-Collar Crime

*John Hagan*

Most of us know far more about street crime and organized crime than we do about corporate and white-collar crime. While recent cases such as the multibillion-dollar Enron bankruptcy in the United States have raised the profile of these types of crime, few Canadians are aware of the harm that is done by corporate and white-collar criminals. In fact, these crimes are much more costly in dollar terms than street crime is. The six billion dollar lost to investors in the Bre-X fraud is far greater than the money lost in all the robberies in Canadian history. Few bank robbers get away with more than a few thousand dollars, but Julius Melnitzer, an Ontario lawyer, defrauded banks and friends of $90 million to support his lavish lifestyle. Corporate and white-collar crimes also cause a large number of deaths and injuries. Laureen Snider (1988) reported that occupational deaths were the third leading cause of death in Canada and attributed at least half these deaths to unsafe and illegal working conditions.

The topic of white-collar crime raises some important issues in the field of criminology. The term itself, introduced by Edwin Sutherland (1940) more than a half century ago, is probably one of the most popularly used criminological concepts in everyday life. However, despite its popularity, there is uncertainty about the precise meaning of the term. This is less important than the fact that the concept of white-collar crime has forced a reconsideration of some very basic criminological assumptions.

No longer is it possible to take for granted the way in which crime itself is defined. No longer can the official data collected on crime by agencies of crime control be accepted uncritically. No longer can it be assumed that the poor are more criminal than the rich. The criminological enterprise has taken on new form and substance now that the topic of white-collar crime has become a central part of our thinking. This chapter will consider separately issues of class, crime, and the corporations; the social organization of work; and legal sanctions. Each is part of the topic of white-collar crime.

## The Extent of Corporate and White-Collar Crime

The business section in your daily paper normally deals with stories involving new business developments, company profits, mergers, and other related matters. However, in recent years criminal matters have become a routine part of business reporting. To give you some idea of the extent of corporate and white-collar crime, consider the following stories from the May 9, 2003 edition of the business section of the *Globe and Mail:*

- Two Ontario men were charged with theft and fraud because of activities in the mid-1990s that resulted in over $40 million in losses. Mark Eizenga and James Sylvester were accused of selling shares to support investments in Cuba and the Caribbean. Investors were allegedly misled by the pair, and most of the money has disappeared.
- Stock traders working for a unit of the Royal Bank were accused of placing stock orders late in the day in order to artificially inflate the closing price of a stock at the end of a reporting period. This would help to make the performance of a stock portfolio look more positive than it actually was.
- The Ontario Securities Commission has accused a Peterborough man of collecting at least $25 million by falsely guaranteeing individuals a high rate of return on investments.
- There is a flaw in Microsoft's Internet Passport service that could make it possible for computer hackers to gain access to the accounts of customers visiting Internet shopping sites. The system also controls access to Microsoft's Hotmail system. The security flaw placed Microsoft in possible violation of a US Federal Trade Commission order to ensure that personal consumer information was protected by the Passport system. The order resulted from previous problems with the system.
- Rupert Murdoch, owner of a global media empire that includes Fox TV, appeared before a US Congressional committee seeking approval of a takeover of DirecTV, which is the largest provider of satellite television in the United States. Critics fear that the deal would violate competition laws by allowing Murdoch's company to use its huge size to force smaller competitors out of business.
- The US government is pursuing fraud charges against HealthSouth Corporation, the largest owner of physical therapy clinics and rehabilitation clinics in the United States. Many of the company's executives have pleaded guilty to making fraudulent reports that made the company appear to be more profitable than it actually was. This inflated the stock price. Many investors who bought the stock because of its apparent profitability lost most of their money when the fraud was revealed.

- A New York stockbroker was accused of using his clients' money to pay off former employees who had threatened to reveal his illegal stock trading. He had been previously charged with 'churning' investors' accounts. 'Churning' is the practice of making unnecessary trades to generate higher commissions.
- The Dutch company Ahold NV, one of the world's largest supermarket companies, lowered its earnings estimates by $880 million after these earnings had been artificially inflated by some of its American executives in order to make the company's performance look better than it really was,
- The US Securities and Exchange Commission is looking into potential accounting fraud charges against Qwest Communications, a large phone company. The company overstated its revenues by $2.2 billion over a three-year period ending in 2001.
- Halliburton Company, once run by US Vice-President Dick Cheney, admitted paying $2.4 million in bribes to an official of the Nigerian government in order to get tax breaks for its operations in that country.

In addition to these stories involving violations and possible violations of criminal laws and securities regulations, there were also several articles dealing with ethical and regulatory issues. Among these were stories dealing with the need for better regulation of the stock market; the debate over the need to better regulate complex financial instruments known as derivatives; ethical questions about whether it was proper for Gerry Schwartz, the chief executive of the large Canadian company Onex, to appoint his wife to the board of directors of his company; the problems that were created for the Calgary-based oil company Talisman when it was accused of producing revenues that helped the Sudanese government to repress its own people in a civil war; a discussion of the reluctance of major pharmaceutical manufacturers to provide low-cost AIDS drugs for developing countries that cannot afford to pay for these treatments; and the ethics of Molson's sex-laden campaign for Bavaria beer.

## The Nature of Corporate and White-Collar Crime

Corporate and white-collar offenders have found many ways to make money. Box 32.1 shows the range of offences committed by corporations and by individuals in the course of practising legitimate occupations.

## Occupation, Organization, and Crime

White-collar crimes are often committed through, and on behalf of, corporations. The involvement of corporations in crime has been recognized at least since the early part of the twentieth century, when E.A. Ross (1907) wrote of a new type of criminal 'who picks pockets with a 'rake-off' instead of a jimmy, cheats with a company prospectus instead of a deck of cards, or scuttles his town instead of his ship'. Particular actions of corporations have been criminal offences in Canada since 1889 (Casey 1985). However, it was not until after the Great Depression that Edwin Sutherland (1940) finally attached a lasting label to these offenders

---

**Box 32.1**  Types of Corporate and Wite-Collar Crime

---

**Crimes Against the Public**
*Corporate and Business Crime*
- price-fixing (conspiring on contract bids or on prices for selling to the public)
- manipulation of stocks and securities
- commercial and political bribery and rebates
- patent and trademark infringements
- misrepresentation and false advertising
- fraudulent grading, packaging, and labelling
- tax fraud
- adulteration of food and drugs
- illegal pollution of the environment

*Crimes by Individual and Professional Practitioners*
- obtaining fees, payments, or charges through fraud and deception
- deceiving or defrauding patients, clients, customers
- immoral practices in relations with clients
- unprofessional conduct and malpractice
- falsification of statements on vital documents

**Crimes within the Organization**
*Offences Against the Organization*
- theft of funds by employees
- theft of inventory *by* employees

*Offences Against Employees*
- violation of workplace health and safety laws
- violation of labour laws
- discriminatory employment practices
- harassment

Source: Adapted from Ronald Akers. 1973. *Deviant Behavior: A Social Learning Approach.* Belmont: Wadsworth: 180–81.

---

in his influential paper 'White-Collar Crime'. Sutherland proposed in this paper that white-collar crime be defined 'as a crime committed by a person of respectability and high social status in the course of his occupation'.

Since Sutherland came up with this term, there has been confusion about the role of *occupation* and *organization* in the study of white-collar crime. A distinction is still often drawn today (see, for example, Coleman 1985: 8) between '**occupational crime**—that is, white collar crime committed by an individual or group of individuals exclusively for personal gain', and '**organizational crime**—white collar crimes committed with the support and encouragement of a formal organization and intended at least in part to advance the goals of that organization'. Organizational crime is also known as **corporate crime**.

The problem is that the occupational and organizational components of many white-collar crimes cannot be easily separated. Clinard and Yeager (1980) make this point with the example of a Firestone Tire official who aided his corporation in securing and administering illegal political contributions benefiting the corporation, but then embezzled much of the funds for himself. The illegal activities of lawyers (Reasons and Chappell 1985) are another common form of white-collar crime in which it is often difficult to separate the individual component from what is done for and through the law firm. Nonetheless, it is important to note that locating white-collar offenders in their ownership and authority positions in occupational and organizational structures is a key part of the class analysis of white-collar crime (Geis 1984; Hagan and Parker 1985; Weisburd et al. 1990). Sutherland's emphasis on 'respect' and 'status' in defining white-collar crime only begins to open up the issue of class position and the role it plays in any understanding of white-collar crime. A key element of social class is the power to commit major white-collar crimes that only ownership and authority positions in occupational and organizational structures can make possible.

However, as Sutherland recognized, the problem is not only one of our conception of white-collar offenders and their class positions, but also one of our conception of white-collar crime itself (cf. Shapiro 1990). Sometimes our confused conceptions can seem mundane, so mundane that they pass unnoticed. For example, the *New York Times* published two stories in the same edition—one that warned and possibly discouraged its readers from 'pirating' computer software (Lewis 1989), and another that informed and likely encouraged its readers to acquire newly designed devices to copy audio tapes (Fantel 1989). The contradiction probably was unnoticed, but the latter story nonetheless began with the mildly apologetic and perhaps not entirely facetious suggestion that among the higher animals and human beings, larceny seems to be an innate trait held in check by social conditioning. But inhibitions fail, and the primal impulse asserts itself when it comes to tape recording. Even decent folk, who refrain from pocketing silver spoons, think nothing of taping copyrighted music. (Fantel 1989: 27) This confusion is even more prevalent today, when a company like Sony advertises equipment that enables people to download music videos while its entertainment division fights to stop this illegal behaviour.

Sutherland (1945) insisted that insofar as there exists a 'legal description of acts as socially injurious and legal provision of a penalty for the act', such acts are, for the purposes of our research and understanding, crime (cf., Tappan 1947). This is the case even though many such acts go undetected and unprosecuted. For example, many stock and securities frauds can be prosecuted under provincial securities legislation or under the *Criminal Code of Canada*. The former are considered 'quasi-criminal' statutes. Yet the behaviours prosecuted under either body of law may be identical. It is an act of prosecutorial discretion that determines whether these behaviours are defined clearly and officially as crimes. Sutherland insisted that such acts of official discretion were not relevant to the categorization of these behaviours for the purposes of research. In either case, the behaviours were to be regarded as criminal. Such a position can make a major difference in the relationship observed between class and crime.

Consider the issue of deaths and accidents that result from events in the workplace. Occupational deaths far outnumber deaths resulting from murder. In Canada (Reasons et al. 1981), occupational deaths accounted for more than 10 times as many deaths as murder. While it cannot be assumed that all or most of such deaths result from the intentions of employers to see employees die, there nonetheless is good reason to believe that the majority of such deaths are not simply the result of employee carelessness.

One estimate (Reasons et al. 1981) holds that more than one-third of all on-the-job injuries are due to illegal working conditions, and that about another quarter are due to legal but unsafe conditions. At most, one-third of all such accidents are attributed to unsafe acts on the part of employees. There are numerous well-documented examples of employers intentionally, knowingly, or negligently creating hazards. These include failing to follow administrative orders to alter dangerous situations and covering up the creation and existence of such hazards. The penalties for these offences are very light. For example, Reasons et al. discuss the case of Quasar Petroleum of Calgary, which was fined $15,000 for violating safety regulations when three men died while cleaning out a tank containing toxic fumes. The men were not provided with protective equipment nor were they trained to recognize the need for such equipment.

The case of asbestos poisoning involving administrative decisions within the Johns-Manville Corporation is but one of the best-known examples. Swartz (1978) notes that asbestos has been recognized as a serious health hazard since the turn of the century. Nonetheless, people working with it were not informed, and the government bureaucracy and the medical community ignored the hazard. At the Johns-Manville plant in Toronto, company doctors regularly diagnosed lung diseases among the asbestos workers, but they never told the workers that their lung problems were related to asbestos. Many of the workers subsequently died of asbestos-related illnesses. The construction industry also has high rates of death and injury because of failure to implement workplace health and safety regulations. For example, in two recent Manitoba cases one company was fined $75,000 because of the death of a bridge painter who was working on a platform with no guard rails, and another was fined $27,500 for its role in the death of a young worker who was electrocuted when he was allowed to work on a high-voltage light fixture while the wires were live (McIntyre 2001). Swartz (1978) concludes that these deaths should be recognized as a form of murder, or what is sometimes called 'corporate homicide!' However, as with the Westray Mine disaster corporate executives are almost never held personally responsible for their negligence.

Corporate homicides seem likely to rival in number or even exceed those deaths resulting from homicide conceived in more traditional terms. Of immediate interest here is the meaning of corporate homicide, and crimes like it, for the relationship between class and crime.

## Social Class and Crime

To pursue this interest, a fundamental point must first be made about more conventional forms of crime and delinquency. There is increasing evidence that a relatively small number of offenders account for a rather large proportion of serious street crimes (Greenwood 1982; Wolfgang 1972). The difficulty of including such persons in conventional research designs has probably obscured the relationship that exists between class position and this type of criminality.

A parallel point may be true of many kinds of white-collar crime. For example, crimes such as corporate homicide may occur with high incidence but low prevalence among highly selected subpopulations—that is, among particular employers in particular kinds of industries. The mining and asbestos industries are examples that have already been noted. Again, it may be difficult to pinpoint such employers in conventional research designs, and this may obscure the relationship between class position and this type of criminality.

Implicit in the preceding references to street crimes and corporate homicide is the high likelihood that crime is not a unidimensional concept. That is, these are different kinds of crime that likely have different connections to the concept of class. Among adults, class probably is negatively related to making the direct physical attacks involved in street crimes of violence, and class probably is positively related to causing harms less directly through criminal acts involving the use of corporate resources. Similarly, among juveniles, it may be that some common acts of delinquency (for example, forms of theft that include the illegal copying of computer software and music and the unauthorized use of credit and bank cards) are related positively to class (Cullen et al. 1985; Hagan et al. 1985; Hagan and Kay 1990), while less frequent and more serious forms of delinquency are negatively related to class. It has sometimes appeared that measures of status are not related to crime and delinquency at all (Tittle et al. 1978). However, the study of white-collar crime and delinquency provides increasing reason to believe that measures of class are connected to crime and delinquency in interesting, albeit complicated, way.

## White-Collar Crime and the Social Organization of Work

Not all white-collar crimes are committed by white-collar persons. For example, much embezzlement is committed by relatively low-status bank tellers (Daly 1989). However, if it is true that white-collar crime is positively related to class position, it is also reasonable to ask why it should be so. The answer may lie in the power derived from ownership and authority positions in the occupational and organizational structures of modern corporations. These positions of power carry with them a freedom from control that may be criminogenic. That is, to have power is to be free from the kinds of constraints that may normally inhibit crime. As will be seen, the modern corporation facilitates this kind of freedom with the presumed goal of enhancing free enterprise and the unintended consequence of encouraging crime.

### Crime and the Corporation

It is recognized that the organizational form of the corporation is crucial to understanding most white-collar crime (Ermann and Lundman 1982; Hagan 1982; Reiss 1980). As Wheeler and Rothman (1982) succinctly note, the corporation 'is for white-collar criminals what the gun or knife is for the common criminal—a tool to obtain money from victims'. Of course, the importance of the corporation is not restricted to the world of crime. From the Industrial

Revolution on, it has become increasingly apparent that 'among the variety of interests that men have, those interests that have been successfully collected to create corporate actors are the interests that dominate the society' (Coleman, 1974). This reference to men in particular is not accidental, for corporate entities are disproportionately male in employment, ownership, and control. Our interest is in developing an understanding of the link between the power of the corporate form and the freedom that this powerful structure generates.

The corporation itself is a 'legal fiction', with, as H.L. Mencken aptly observed, 'no pants to kick or soul to damn'. That is, the law chooses to treat corporations as 'juristic persons', making them formally liable to the same laws as 'natural persons'. Some of the most obvious faults in this legal analogy become clear when the impossibility of imprisoning or executing corporations is considered. However, there are more subtle differences between corporate and individual actors with equally significant consequences.

For example, the old legal saw tells us that the corporation has no conscience or soul. Stone (1975) describes the problem well:

> When individuals are placed in an organizational structure, some of the ordinary internalized restraints seem to lose their hold. And if we decide to look beyond the individual employees and find an organizational 'mind' to work with, a 'corporate conscience' distinct from the consciences of particular individuals, it is not readily apparent where we would begin—much less what we would be talking about.

Stone goes on to suggest some interesting ways in which the corporate conscience and corporate responsibility could be increased (see also Nagorski 1989). However, the point is that these mechanisms, or others, have not been put in place. Corporate power in this sense remains unchecked, and it is in this sense criminogenic.

The problem is in part the absence of cultural beliefs to discourage corporate criminality (Geis 1962). C. Wright Mills (1956) captured part of the problem in his observation that 'it is better, so the image runs, to take one dime from each of ten million people at the point of a corporation than $ 100,000 from each of ten banks at the point of a gun'. Nonetheless, there is some evidence that cultural climates vary across time and regimes. For example, Sally Simpson (1986), who studied antitrust violations in the United States between 1927 and 1981, found that such violations were more common during Republican than Democratic administrations. However, even when condemnatory beliefs about corporate crime have been strong, there have been too few controlling mechanisms in place to impose their controlling influence effectively.

Consider, for a moment, the internal structure of a typical modern corporation, as illustrated by Woodmansee's description of the General Electric Corporation (cited in Clinard and Yeager 1980; see also Shearing et al. 1985). Note the complexity of this enterprise and its gender stratification:

> We begin by describing the way GE's employees are officially organized into separate layers of authority. The corporation is like a pyramid. The great majority of the company's workers form the base of the pyramid; they take orders coming down

from above but do not give orders to anyone else. If you were hired by GE for one of these lowest level positions, you might find yourself working on an assembly line, installing a motor in a certain type of refrigerator. You would be in a group of five to 50 workers who all take orders from one supervisor, or foreman, or manager. Your supervisor is on the second step of the pyramid; she or he, and the other supervisors who specialize in this type of refrigerator, all take orders from a General Manager.

There are about 180 of these General Managers at GE; each one heads a department with one or two thousand employees. The General Manager of your department, and the General Managers of the one or two other departments which produce GE's other types of refrigerators, are in turn supervised by the Vice President/General Manager of the Refrigerator Division. This man (there are only men at this level and above) is one of the 50 men at GE responsible for heading GE's Divisions. He, and the heads of several other Divisions which produce major appliances, look up to the next step of the pyramid and see, towering above, the Vice President/Group Executive who heads the entire Major Appliance Group. While there are over 300,000 workers at the base of the pyramid, there are only 10 men on this Group Executive level. Responsibility for overseeing all of GE's product lines is divided between the 10. At about the same level of authority in the company are the executives of GE's Corporate Staff; these men are concerned not with particular products but with general corporate matters such as accounting, planning, legal affairs, and relations with employees, with the public and with governments.

And now the four men at the top of the pyramid come into view; the three Vice Chairmen of the Board of Directors, and standing above them, GE's Chief Executive. . . . Usually, these four men confer alone, but once a month, 15 other men join them for a meeting. The 15 other members of the Board of Directors are not called up from the lower levels of the GE pyramid; they drift in sideways from the heights of neighbouring pyramids. Thirteen of them are chairmen or presidents of other corporations, the fourteenth is a former corporate chairman, and the fifteenth is a university president. (Clinard and Yeager 1980, 457–58)

Could the board of directors of the above corporation exercise the kind of control over its employees that individual actors are expected by law to exercise, for example, over their dependants? Stone (1975) points out that top officers and directors, theoretically, are liable to suit by the corporation itself (via a shareholders' action) if they allow a law violation to occur through negligence. However, the courts have not imposed a duty on directors to uncover corporate wrongdoing. This provides an incentive for senior managers and directors to remain uninformed about illegal activities.

Canadian law in this area will be tested in the case of YBM Magnex, a company that ostensibly sold a variety of products including industrial magnets and bicycles, primarily to Eastern European markets. Starting its Canadian life as a shell corporation on the Alberta Stock Exchange, YBM Magnex stock rose in value from 85 cents to $20 in less than three years. It was included as one of the stocks used in the prestigious Toronto Stock Exchange 300 index and had a total share value of about $1 billion. Several eminent Canadians served on its board of directors, including former Ontario premier David Peterson and First Marathon Securities vice-president Robert Mitchell. However, despite this face of respectability, the company had a very shady background. The company was controlled by Semion Mogilevich, one of Russia's most powerful organized criminals (Howlett 2002). YBM Magnex had been investigated in Britain for a variety of offences, including money laundering. In Canada, the RCMP had been investigating the company since it was established in 1995 (Rubin 1999). Stockholders' investments disappeared in May 1998 when the Ontario Securities Commission stopped trading in the company. Auditors had refused to accept the company's financial statements, and US law enforcement officials had raided the company's Pennsylvania headquarters investigating charges of fraud and money laundering. Directors and auditors of the company are now being sued for $635 million and charged by the Ontario Securities Commission with withholding information from the public concerning the fact that the company was under investigation for its ties to organized crime. The results of this legal action should help clarify the responsibility of directors under Canadian law, but as of June 2003 the case had not yet been resolved.

How widespread is the use of 'executive influence from afar' and 'executive distancing and disengagement' in corporate criminality? Two intriguing studies (Baumhart 1961; Brenner and Molander 1977) suggest that the problem is large. The latter of these studies reports that the percentage of executives who indicate an inability to be honest in providing information to top management has nearly doubled since the earlier research, done in the 1950s. About half of those surveyed thought that their superiors frequently did not wish to know how results were obtained as long as the desired outcome was accomplished. Furthermore, the executives surveyed 'frequently complained of superiors' pressure to support incorrect viewpoints, sign false documents, overlook superiors' wrongdoing, and do business with superiors' friends' (Brenner and Molander 1977).

The recent bankruptcy of Britain's Barings Bank provides another example of **executive disengagement**. Barings Bank, which had been controlled by the same family since 1762, was brought down by the actions of a 28-year-old trader in their Singapore office. Nicholas Leeson lost almost $1 billion of the company's money on financial derivatives, which were essentially bets on the future performance of the Tokyo stock market. When the Tokyo market fell, Barings collapsed when it could not cover the losses. The size of this gamble was in violation of British banking laws. While bank officials were quick to blame Leeson for the entire affair, it is highly unlikely that senior bank officials did not at least tacitly approve of Leeson's trading activities. Several financial experts have suggested that the profits Leeson had previously made for Barings led bank officials to allow him to risk their shareholders' money by making illegal trades (Drohan 1995).

## The Criminogenic Market Structure

Corporate crime research suggests not only a growing freedom at the top of organizations from the need to know and accept responsibility for criminal activity below, but also a growing pressure from the top down that is itself criminogenic. Farberman (1975) has referred to such pressures in the automotive industry and in other highly concentrated corporate sectors as constituting a '**criminogenic market structure**'. The crime-generating feature of these markets is their domination by a relatively small number of manufacturers who insist that their dealers sell in high volume at a small per-unit profit.

Dealerships that fail to perform risk the loss of their franchises in an industry in which the alternatives are few. A result is high pressure to maximize sales and minimize service. More specifically, Farberman suggests that dealers in the car industry may be induced by the small profit margins on new cars to compensate through fraudulent warranty work and repair rackets. The connection between these findings is that the executives of the automotive industry can distance themselves from the criminal consequences of the 'forcing model' (high volume/low per-unit profit) they impose. The result is an absence of control over repair and warranty frauds at the dealership level.

Farberman also points out that corporate concentration can be criminogenic in that it diminishes the corrective role competition can play in restraining criminal practices that increase the costs of production. Asch and Seneca (1969) conclude from their research that high concentration is in particular related to higher rates of crime in consumer-goods industries. This receives further support from Clinard and Yeager's (1980) finding that the oil, auto, and pharmaceutical industries appear to violate the law more frequently than do other industries. Particular types of crime, such as collusion and antitrust activity, may also be more common in highly concentrated industries (Coleman, 1987).

The scale of the crimes that access to corporate resources makes possible will now be considered. In an intriguing study, Wheeler and Rothman (1982) categorized white-collar offenders into three groups: those who committed offences, alone or with affiliated others, using neither an occupational nor an organizational role (individual offenders); those who committed offences alone, or with affiliated others, using an occupational role (occupational offenders); and those who committed offences in which both organization and occupation were ingredients (organizational offenders). The results of this study indicate in a variety of ways the enormous advantages accruing to those who use formal organizations in their crimes. For example, across a subset of four offences, the median 'take' for individual offenders was $5279, for occupational offenders $17,106, and for organizational offenders $117,392. In a parallel Canadian study, Hagan and Parker (1985) reported that securities violators who make use of organizational resources commit crimes that involve larger numbers of victims and are broader in their geopolitical spread. Why the organizational edge? Wheeler and Rothman (1982) answer with an example:

> Represented by its president, a corporation entered into a factoring agreement with a leading . . . commercial bank, presenting it with $1.2 million in false billings over the course of seven months; the company's statements were either inflated to reflect much more business than actually was being done, or were simply made up. Would the bank have done this for an individual? Whether we conclude that organizations are trusted more than individuals, or that they simply operate on a much larger scale, it is clear that the havoc caused when organizations are used outside the law far exceeds anything produced by unaffiliated actors.

Just as the organizational form has facilitated economic and technological development on a scale far beyond that achieved by individuals, so too has this form allowed criminal gains of a magnitude that men and women acting alone would find hard to attain.

The structure of the modern corporation allows a power imbalance to prevail in which those individuals at the top experience a relative freedom, while those at the bottom often experience pressure applied from the top that encourages various kinds of white-collar crime. The point has also been made that the corporate form itself can be used effectively to perpetrate 'bigger and better crimes' than can be achieved by individuals acting alone. Access to these corporate resources is a unique advantage of class positions involving ownership and authority in business organizations. It is in this sense that, it can be said that in the world of the modern corporation, the social organization of work itself is criminogenic.

## White-Collar Crime and Legal Sanctions

Given the distribution of freedom and pressure that has been identified within the structure of the modern corporation and the power this gives to those who run it, the question that recurs is: What does the law do to remedy the potential for abuse? This question raises issues of legal liability and the enforcement of law.

'We have arranged things', writes Christopher Stone (1975), 'so that the people who call the shots do not have to bear the full risks'. This, in a nutshell, is the consequence of the limited liabilities borne by modern corporate actors:

> Take, for example, a small corporation involved in shipping dynamite. The share-holders of such a company, who are typically also the managers, do not *want* their dynamite-laden truck to blow up. But if it does, they know that those injured cannot, except in rare cases, sue them as individuals to recover their full damages if the amount left in the corporations' bank account is inadequate to make full compensation. . . . What this means is that in deciding how much money to spend on safety devices, and whether or not to allow trucks to drive through major cities, the calculations are skewed toward higher risks than suggested by the 'rational economic corporation/free market' model that is dreamily put forth in textbooks. If no accident results, the shareholders will reap the profits of skimping on safety measures. If a truck blows up, the underlying human interests will be shielded from fully bearing the harm that they have caused. And then, there is nothing to prevent the same men from setting up a new dynamite shipping corporation the next day; all it takes is the imagination to think up a new name, and some $50 in filing fees (462–63).

It may be conceded that large corporations are not quite so free as the small corporation in the example to dissolve and reconstitute their operations. However, the separation of share-holder and management interests gives rise to a related problem of liability. Given that corporate officers gain their primary rewards through salaries, the effects of damage judgments are indirect and, judging from experience, limited.

These discussions raise the broader issue of how and why the law is used to control white-collar crime. It has already been seen that civil remedies are not very effective, We turn now to criminal sanctions. How does the state decide what kinds of upper-world indiscretions will be called criminal? The most interesting work that has been done on this issue in Canada involves the development of anticombines legislation. Given the powerful economic interests involved in forming the **monopolistic enterprises** this legislation presumably seeks to prevent, one might wonder how an **anticombines law** was ever passed in the first place. Goff and Reasons (1978) indicate that the initiative for the original legislation in 1899 'came not from the general populace but from small businessmen, who felt their firms were at the mercy of big business interests'. However, more recently Smandych (1985) has noted that a 'Royal Commission on Labour and Capital', created for the purpose of investigating industrial conditions in Canada, interviewed and recorded testimony from numerous trade-union representatives and workers. This testimony, cited in the report of the commission in 1899, specifically sought legislation against monopolistic practices, and Smandych argues that 'the possibility that worker demands for the elimination of combines went unnoticed by the government of the day is extremely doubtful'.

Smandych goes on to conclude that 'the first flourishing of Canadian anticombines legislation was the product of an essential confrontation between labour and capital, and of the state's effort to find an acceptable solution'. None of this is to say, as later noted, that this legislation was strong or effective. Quite the contrary, as Snider (1979) observes. Efforts over the years to strengthen the legislation with 'pro-consumer and pro-competition' amendments regularly 'were weakened or eliminated in the face of business opposition'. Smandych, Snider, Goff, and Reasons are all agreed that this legislation has done less than it promised to reduce monopolistic practices and to punish those who promote them. In fact, many have argued that the laws are almost totally ineffective. Prosecutions are rarely successful, and when they are, the fines are so low that they do not act as an effective deterrent to anticompetitive behaviour. Not surprisingly, business has lobbied very strongly against changes to combines legislation.

Steven Box (1981) has noted another way in which the law favours corporate offenders:

> Some people benefit more than others from these laws. . . . By the criminal law's constructing *particular* definitions of murder, rape, robbery and assault other acts, which are in many ways very similar, are excluded, and these are just the acts more likely to be committed by more powerful individuals. Thus the criminal law defines only some types of killing as murder: it excludes, for example, deaths which result from acts of negligence such as employers' failure to maintain safe working conditions in factories and mines. . . . The criminal law includes only some types of property deprivation as robbery: it excludes, for example, the separation of consumers from part of their money that follows manufacturers' malpractices or advertisers' misrepresentations. . . . The criminal law defines only some types of violence as criminal assault: it excludes those forms of assault . . . resulting from working in a polluted factory environment where the health risk was known to the employer but concealed from the employee (48–49).

But what of the white-collar offenders who are held criminally liable and processed through the criminal justice system? Are they liable to as severe sanctioning as individual actors? Notions of 'equality before the law' are perhaps nowhere more subjective in meaning than in their application to the sentencing of white-collar offenders (Hagan and Albonetti 1982). This is reflected in at least two kinds of comments made by judges about the sentences they impose for white-collar crimes. It is reflected first in the suggestion that white-collar offenders experience sanctions in a different way from other kinds of offenders, and second in the assertion that different kinds of sanctions are appropriate in white-collar cases.

The view, common among judges, that white-collar offenders experience sanctions differently is well summarized in Mann et al.'s (1980) conclusions after interviewing a sample of judges who have tried such cases: 'Most judges have a widespread belief that the suffering experienced by a white-collar person as a result of apprehension, public indictment and conviction, and the collateral disabilities incident to conviction—loss of job, professional licenses, and status in the community—completely satisfies the need to punish the individual'. This belief persists in the face of findings from a recent study by Benson (1989: 474) that 'although they commit the most serious offences, employers and managers are least likely to lose their jobs after conviction for a white-collar crime'. The argument for white-collar leniency endures in the minds of judges and others: the defendant, having suffered enough from the acts of prosecution and conviction, does not require a severe sentence. However, the sentence must still provide a deterrent. Mann et al. (1980) conclude that most judges seek a compromise in resolving this dilemma. 'The weekend sentence, the very short jail term, and the relatively frequent use of amended sentences (where a judge imposes a prison term and later reduces it) are evidence of this search for a compromise'.

It is important to acknowledge the disputed role of fines in sentencing white-collar offenders. Posner (1980) asserts that 'the white-collar criminal . . . should be punished only by monetary penalties'.His argument is that if fines are suitably large, they are an equally effective deterrent and cheaper to administer, and therefore socially preferable to imprisonment and other afflictive punishments. It has already been noted that corporate entities are liable to little else than fines. However, Mann et al. (1980) find judges to be skeptical of the effectiveness of fines. They report

a conspicuous absence of responses by judges that a fine was the appropriate sanction to be imposed on a defendant. . . . Where fines were used in conjunction with another sentence it was generally the other sentence . . . that was thought to have the intended deterrent effect. Where the fine was used alone, the idea that the commencement of the criminal process against the defendant was the punishment seemed to be more important in the judges' minds than the fine itself.

The sense that emerges is that judges are acutely aware of the issues of deterrence, disparity, and discrimination in the sentencing of white-collar offenders, and that they attempt to respond to these issues by fashioning sentences that combine sanctions in a compromise fashion. Consistent with this view, Hagan and Nagel (1982) found, in a sentencing study covering the period from 1963 to 1976 in the Southern District of New York, that judges attempted to compensate for the shorter prison terms given to white-collar offenders by adding probation or fines to their sentences. Similarly, fines were most frequently used in conjunction with prison and probation sentences. In any case, all these findings suggest that white-collar offenders are advantaged by the specific types and combination of legal sanctions that are imposed on them.

However, both in Canada and the United States, there is some evidence that the mid-1970s brought a new and somewhat harsher attitude toward white-collar crime. Katz (1980) speaks of a 'social movement against white-collar crime' that began in the United States in the late 1960s, and the evolution of public opinion documents an increasing concern with the occurrence of such crimes (Cullen et al. 1982; Schrager and Short 1978).

So, there *appears* to be a move toward tougher legal sanctions for white-collar offences. Of course, charges must be laid before sanctions can be imposed, and the power of corporations and of persons in high social-class positions makes the decision to prosecute problematic (see Benson et al. 1988). Wheeler et al. (1982) have sought to demonstrate that policies like those described above have led to the more severe sentencing of high-status white-collar offenders. Hagan and Palloni (1983) concur in reporting an increased use of imprisonment with white-collar offenders after Watergate, but they also indicate that the length of these prison sentences was unusually short. The Canadian study of the enforcement of securities laws in Ontario (Hagan and Parker 1985) reveals a similar pattern of trade-offs in the severity with which white-collar offenders are treated. Overall, treatment of white-collar offenders seems to have been lenient in the past, and despite some examples of harsher sentences, there is no unambiguous evidence that this situation has changed markedly. Even where white-collar offenders have received prison sentences, they typically obtain parole very early in their terms.

There is a possibility that the massive losses due to the failures of companies such as Enron and WorldCom will lead to harsher treatment of corporate criminals. These crimes led to a serious loss of confidence in the stock market—why would someone want to invest money in companies whose earnings reports could not be trusted? This had a major impact on the economy as investors moved their money out of the stock market. The scandals were so pervasive that it became obvious that major changes were needed in regulation and corporate governance, and governments in the United States have become more involved in regulating corporations and making their laws tougher. They have also put more resources into investigating and prosecuting corporate crime. Many senior executives have been publicly arrested and taken into custody in front of the media in so-called 'perp walks', designed to show the public that politicians have acted. Several of the lower-level executives charged in these scandals have received jail sentences, but none of the higher level officials had come to trial by the summer of 2003.

Even if sanctions are becoming tougher, governments have helped to create an environment conducive to white-collar crime through weak legislation and lax enforcement. You have already seen how Canada's ineffective competitions legislation has allowed anticompetitive business practices to flourish. An even more dramatic example is the wave of failures in the savings and loan business in the United States. A major reason for these failures was the strong belief of President Reagan and his officials that free enterprise worked best if business was left alone by government. Accordingly, they dismantled many of the agencies and regulations that controlled the industry. This move was, of course, strongly encouraged by businesspeople who ultimately benefited by the government's mistake. The result was a wave of criminal activity in the savings and loan industry. According to the government's General Accounting Office, bailing out these institutions will ultimately cost the American taxpayer between $325 and $500 billion (Pontell and Calavita 1993). Although not all the losses were due to criminal activity, crime was a major contributor to these massive financial failures. Similarly, regulatory failures were partly responsible for the billions of dollars lost to corporate crime in the late 1990s and early 2000s.

# References

Akers, R. 1973. *Deviant Behaviour: A Social Learning Approach*. Belmont: Wadsworth.

Asch, P., and Seneca, J.J. 1969. 'Is Collusion Profitable?' *Review of Economics and Statistics* 58: 1–12.

Baumhart, R. 1961. 'How Ethical Are Businessmen?' *Harvard Business Review* 39: 5–176.

Benson, M.L. 1989. 'The Influence of Class Position on the Formal and Informal Sanctioning of White-Collar Offenders'. *Sociological Quarterly* 30: 465–79.

Benson, M.L., Maakestad, M.L., Cullen, F.T., and Geis, G. (1988). 'District Attorneys and Corporate Crime: Surveying the Prosecutorial Gatekeepers'. *Criminology* 26: 505–18.

Box, S. 1981. *Deviance, Reality and Society* (2nd ed.). Toronto: Holt, Rinehart and Winston.

Brenner, S.S., and Molander, E.A. 1977. 'Is the Ethics of Business Changing?' *Harvard Business Review* 55: 57–71.

Casey, J. 1985. 'Corporate Crime and the State: Canada in the 1980s'. In Thomas Fleming (ed.), *The New Criminologies in Canada* (pp. 100–101). Toronto: Oxford University Press.

Clinard, M., and Yeager, P. 1980. *Corporate Crime*. New York: Free Press.

Coleman, J. 1974. *Power and the Structure of Society*. New York: W.W. Norton.

———. (1985). *The Criminal Elite*. New York: St. Martin's Press.

———. (1987). 'Toward an Integrated Theory of White-Collar Crime'. *American Journal of Sociology* 93: 406–39.

Cullen, F., Larson, M., and Mathers, R. 198). 'Having Money and Delinquency Involvement: The Neglect of Power in Delinquency Theory'. *Criminal Justice and Behavior* 12(2): 171–92.

Cullen, F., Link, B., and Polanzi, C. 1982. 'The Seriousness of Crime Revisited: Have Attitudes Toward White Collar Crime Changed?' *Criminology* 20: 83–102.

Daly, K. 1989. 'Gender and Varieties of White-Collar Crime.' *Criminology* 27: 769-93.

Drohan, M. 1995. 'Barings Was Warned of Risk'. *The Globe and Mail* (March 6): Al.

Ermann, M.D., and Lundman, R. 1982. *Corporate Deviance*. New York: Holt, Rinehart and Winston.

Fantel, H. 1989. 'Tape-Copying Decks Improve Their Act'. *New York Times* (July 9), p. 27.

Farberman, H. 1975. 'A Criminogenic Market Structure: The Automobile Industry'. *Sociological Quarterly* 16: 438–57.

Geis, G. 1962. 'Toward a Delineation of White-Collar Offenses'. *Sociological Inquiry* 32: 160–71.

———. 1984. 'White Collar Crime and Corporate Crime'. In Robert F. Meier (ed.), *Major Forms of Crime*. Beverly Hills: Sage.

Goff, C., and Reasons, C. 1978. *Corporate Crime in Canada*. Scarborough: Prentice Hall.

Greenwood, P. 1982. *Selective Incapacitation*. Santa Monica, CA: Rand.

Hagan, J. 1982. 'The Corporate Advantage: The Involvement of Individual and Organizational Victims in the Criminal Justice Process'. *Social Forces* 60 (4): 993–1022.

Hagan, J., and Albonetti, C. 1982. 'Race, Class and the Perception of Criminal Injustice in America'. *American Journal of Sociology* 88: 329–55.

Hagan, J., Gillis, A.R., and Simpson, J. 1985. 'The Class Structure of Gender and Delinquency: Toward a Power-Control Theory of Common Delinquent Behavior'. *American Journal of Sociology* 90: 1151–78.

Hagan, J., and Kay, F. 1990. 'Gender and Delinquency in White-Collar Families: A Power-Control Perspective'. *Crime and Delinquency* 36(3): 391–407.

Hagan, J., and Nagel, I. 1982. 'White Collar Crime, White Collar Time: The Sentencing of White Collar Criminals in the Southern District of New York', *American Criminal Law Review* 20(2): 259–301.

Hagan, J., and Palloni, A. 1983. 'The Sentencing of White Collar Offenders Before and After Watergate'. Paper presented at the American Sociological Association Meetings, Detroit.

Hagan, J., and Parker, P. 1985. 'White Collar Crime and Punishment: The Class Structure and Legal Sanctioning of Securities Violations'. *American Sociological Review* 50(3): 302–16.

Howlett, K. 2002. 'The Two Faces of YBM Magnex'.*The Globe and Mail* (December 29): Bl3.

Katz, J. 1980. 'The Movement against "White-Collar Crime"', In Egan Bittner and Sheldon Messinger (eds.), *Criminology Review Yearbook*, Vol. 2. Beverly Hills: Sage.

Lewis, P. 1989. 'Cracking Down on Computer Pirates.' *New York Times* (July 9): 10.

Mann, K., Wheeler, S., and Sarat, A. 1980. 'Sentencing the White Collar Offender'. *American Criminal Law Review* 17(4): 479.

McIntyre, M 2001. 'Deaths Cost Firms Dearly'. *Winnipeg Free Press* (March 3): A1, A4.

Mills, C.W. 1956. *The Power Elite*. New York: Oxford University Press.

Nagorski, Z. 198). 'Yes, Socrates, Ethics Can Be Taught'. *New York Times* (February 12): F2.

Pontell, H.N., and Calavita, K. 1993. 'The Savings and Loan Industry', In Michael Tonry and Albert J. Reiss (eds.), *Beyond the Law: Crime in Complex Organizations* (pp. 203–46). Chicago: University of Chicago Press.

Posner, R.A. 1980. 'Optimal Sentences for "White Collar Criminals".' *American Criminal Law Review*: 409–18.

Reasons, C., and Chappell, D. 1985, 'Crooked Lawyers: Towards a Political Economy of Deviance in the Profession'. In Thomas Fleming (ed.), *The New Criminologies in Canada.* (pp. 206–22). Toronto: Oxford University Press.

Reasons, C., Ross, L., and Paterson, C. 1981. *Assault on the Worker: Occupational Health and Safety in Canada.* Toronto: Butterworths.

Ross, E.A. 1907. *Sin and Society*. Boston: Houghton Mifflin.

Rubin, S. 1999. 'RCMP Investigated YBM in Early 1995'. *The Financial Post* (January 9).

Schrager, L., and Short, J.F. 1978. 'Toward a Sociology of Organizational Crime'. *Social Problems* 25(4): 407–19.

Shapiro, S.P. 1990. 'Collaring the Crime, Not the Criminal: Reconsidering the Concept of White-Collar Crime'. *American Sociological Review* 55: 346–65.

Shearing, C., Addario, S., and Stenning, P. 1935. 'Why Organizational Charts Cannot Be Trusted: Rehabilitating Realism in Sociology'. Paper presented at a Symposium on Qualitative Research: Ethnographic/Interactionist Perspectives. University of Waterloo (May 15–17).

Simpson, S. 1986. 'The Depression of Antitrust: Testing a Multilevel, Longitudinal Model of Profit-Squeeze'. *American Sociological Review* 51: 859–75.

Smandych, R. 1985. 'Marxism and the Creation of Law: Re-Examining the Origins of Canadian Anti-Combines Legislation, 1890-1910'. In Thomas Fleming (ed.), *The New Criminologies* (pp. 87–99). Toronto: Oxford University Press.

Snider, L. 1979. 'Revising the Combines Investigation Act: A Study in Corporate Power'. In Paul J. Brantingham and Jack M. Kress (eds.), *Structure, Law and Power: Essays in the Sociology of Law* (pp. 105–19). Beverly Hills: Sage.

——. 1988. 'Commercial Crime.' In Vincent F. Sacco (ed.), *Conformity and Control in Canadian Society* (pp. 231–83). Scarborough: Prentice Hall.

Stone, C. 1975. *Where the Law Ends: The Social Control of Corporate Behavior.* New York: Harper and Row.

Sutherland, E. 1940. 'White Collar Criminality'. *American Sociological Review* 5: 1–12.

——. 1945. 'Is 'White Collar Crime' Crime? *American Sociological Review* 10: 132–39.

Swartz, J. 1978. 'Silent Killers at Work'. In M. David Ermann and Richard Lundman (eds.), *Corporate and Governmental Deviance* (pp. 114–28). New York: Oxford University Press.

Tappan, P. 1947. 'Who Is the Criminal?' *American Sociological Review* 12: 96–102.

Tittle, C., Villemez, W.J., and Smith, D. 1978. 'The Myth of Social Class and Criminality: An Empirical Assessment of the Empirical Evidence'. *American Sociological Review* 47: 505–18.

Weisburd, D., Waring, E., and Wheeler, S. 1990. 'Class, Status and the Punishment of White-Collar Criminals'. *Law and Social Inquiry* 15(2): 223–46.

Wheeler, S., and Rothman, M. 1982. 'The Organization as Weapon in White Collar Crime'. *Michigan Law Review* 80(7): 1403–26.

Wheeler, S., Weisburd, D., and Bode, N. 1982. 'Sentencing the White Collar Offender: Rhetoric and Reality'. *American Sociological Review* 47: 641–59.

Wolfgang, M. 1972. *Delinquency in a Birth Cohort.* Chicago: University of Chicago Press.

## Introduction

Kleinknecht's study applies a symbolic interactionist approach to understanding computer hacking. Symbolic interactionism focuses on how people create and recreate society in everyday social interactions, on how those interactions are structured, and on the shared norms, values, and symbols people use to define situations. It also asks us to consider the meaning that peoples' actions have for themselves and others, and the importance of this to understanding what's going on. So what is going on with hackers?

A key concept Kleinknecht draws on is subculture. In sociology, subculture doesn't refer to a culture that is lower than another culture, but a culture shared by members of an identifiable group that is both part of the wider society, yet in important ways distinctive from it. Often the distinctive norms, values, beliefs, and ideas that members share are reflected in a jargon or 'argot' that members of the community use. In what ways is the hacker subculture a part of the wider society, and in what ways is it distinctive from it?

Ideology is another key concept relevant to his study. It can refer to a fairly explicit, coherent system of ideas, values, and beliefs that explain and justify how a society and its institutions are, or should be, organized (i.e., a political doctrine). Or it can refer to a set of deep and abiding background ideas, values and beliefs that frame reality and shape members' perceptions of the world (i.e., a world view). Kleinknecht outlines some key components of hacker ideology in the form of maxims. What are the fundamental values and ideas that underlie these maxims? How do these subcultural values, ideas, and beliefs relate to the ideology that prevails in the wider society?

# The Hacker Spirit: An Interactionist Analysis of the Hacker Ideology

*Steven Kleinknecht*

A major characteristic distinguishing a particular subculture from the broader community is its ideology or group perspective (Shibutani 1955; Fine and Kleinman 1979; Prus 1997). An ideology represents a unique way of understanding the world, which tends to justify what the subculture is all about. Within the hacker subculture, this ideology is referred to as the 'hacker ethic' or 'hacker spirit'. By engaging self-defined hackers in participant observation and in-depth interviews, the goal of this essay is to offer an ethnographic examination and analysis of the hacker ideology.

While the term 'hacker' once served as a positive label for someone who was a 'technological wizard', the term over the course of the last 50 years has come to carry a negative connotation. The public image of what *actually* constitutes a hacker has shifted, and now, hackers are more likely to be defined as 'computer criminals' or 'electronic vandals' than as being 'technological aficionados'. However, as hackers indicate, public perception is at odds with their own perspectives on what actually constitutes a hacker. Hackers are more apt to classify themselves as individuals *who passionately and creatively work towards finding a solution to any given problem*. Quite often this desire to understand is applied specifically to computers and thus, a desire to learn and improve computers is frequently at the heart of hackers' definition of what it is they do.

This article explores the hacker perspective in an in-depth fashion and offers an insider look at the hacker ideology and its applications. To evaluate and move beyond often-stereotypical outsider representations of the hacker subculture, I adopt the symbolic interactionist stance that it is essential to gain intimate familiarity with our subject matter (Blumer 1969). The data for this project are based on two years of on- and off-line fieldwork. During this time, I attended hacker meetings in the central and southwestern Ontario area and engaged in on-line participant observation with five different groups of hackers from Canada and the United States. Along with several informal conversations, 15 qualitative interviews were also conducted.

What follows is an overview of the central tenets of the hacker perspective, which updates Levy's (1984) original treatise on the hacker ethic. Analyses of how hackers draw social boundaries between different subgroups of hackers and invoke their ideology as a way of rationalizing their behaviour are also presented.

## The Hacker Spirit and the Pursuit of Knowledge

Representing the ideology of the first generation of hackers, Levy (1984: 40–5) argued that the following elements made up key components of the hacker ethic:

- Access to computers—and anything that might teach you something about the way the world works—should be unlimited and total. Always yield to the Hands-On Imperative!
- All information should be free.
- Mistrust authority—promote decentralization.
- Hackers should be judged by their hacking, not bogus criteria such as degrees, age, race, or position.
- You can create art and beauty on a computer.
- Computers can change your life for the better.

Similar to Levy's (1984) *Hacker Ethic*, seven fundamental and interrelated elements of the hacker spirit were observed in analyzing the data for this project. Each of these elements is premised on the overarching goal that one should strive to acquire an ever greater understanding of how things work. To hackers, knowledge and an unorthodox approach to learning are valued above all else. Consistent with this goal, the following principles represent the essence of the hacker perspective.

*Principle 1: Higher understanding requires an unorthodox approach.* In order to reach a level of higher understanding, hackers maintain that it is essential to take a creative approach to problem-solving. As such, it is not uncommon for hackers to define the term hacker as 'Someone who thinks outside of the box' (interview).

*Principle 2: Hacking involves hard work.* Along with taking a creative approach to problem-solving, hackers point out that to be a hacker one must realize that solving problems can be, and often is, hard work. As Raymond (2001) argues, 'Being a hacker is lots of fun, but it's a kind of fun that takes lots of effort'. Therefore, long hours of dedication to one's project(s) are essential. It was suggested that younger generations of hackers often lack this sort of concerted focus and thus, are criticized for their laziness and for misappropriating the hacker label.

*Principle 3: Hacking requires a 'learn for yourself' approach—learn by doing.* Problem-solving not only requires a great deal of ingenuity and hard work, but a hacker must also be self-motivated and seek to understand by taking a hands-on approach. Hackers suggest that you do not learn how to be a hacker, rather hacking is a way of thinking about and approaching a problem that cannot be taught; it is self-directed and something that 'comes from within'. Matthew maintains that '[To be a hacker] I had to learn how to learn . . . There is no amount of knowledge that can qualify you as a hacker, or a newbie, or what have you. It all comes down to a willingness to learn new things' (interview).

*Principle 4: Share your knowledge and information with others.* In striving for ever greater levels of understanding, hackers argue that it is imperative that people share their solutions to problems so that other hackers can devote their time to new problems and build upon one another's findings. However, hacker groups have different informal protocols that one should follow when asking for information. Knowing 'who does what' within the hacker community, developing informal networks across the community, and knowing what information the different groups covet, as well as the value (e.g., monetary, reputational, 'pure' knowledge) they place on their knowledge, for hackers, are important factors to recognize when seeking out information.

*Principle 5: You're evaluated based on what you know and your desire to learn.* Hackers indicate that physical appearance, educational degrees, and style are inconsequential in the subculture. Instead, a hacker's status and reputation are based upon his or her level of knowledge, creative self-directed problem-solving, and display of skill. Consequently, ignorance is highly disparaged. The following hacker quote is poignant in this regard: 'In grade school, I was teased for my lack of style and grace, but this is a new era, and in my world, you'll be taunted endlessly for your lack of intelligence' (interview). However, some hackers suggest that this principle does not appear to be as important to the latest generation of 'hackers'.

*Principle 6: Mistrust authority.* Hackers believe that people who hold positions of power within society value and impose conformity, which hackers see as stifling creativity. Authority figures are also seen as not always acting in society's best interests. Therefore, hackers argue that these people are to be mistrusted and their attitudes challenged. Kris's comments capture this sentiment well: 'I think the hacker mindset is to challenge everything. Always push the button that says "do not push", always try the door to see if it's locked, always challenge authority, especially when it claims to be acting in your best interests' (interview).

*Principle 7: All information should be free.* Hackers believe that information that is of any worth to society should be made available to everyone. In order to safeguard against abuses of information and to assist in the furthering of knowledge, hackers maintain that ownership of information should be opposed. As an alternative, they advocate a model based on the free-flow and sharing of knowledge. A pertinent example of information sharing is the development of open source software, to which a community of hackers contribute their programming efforts. Some hackers suggest that the *all information should be free* aspect of their ideology can be taken too far and that certain 'so-called hackers' (e.g., script kiddies, crackers) misuse the principle to justify inappropriate behaviour.

Many aspects of the hacker ethic, first described by Levy in 1984, still hold a great deal of relevance to the current generation of hackers. One significant difference, however, is the way in which the ideology is now being applied in light of 'new' hacker activities.

It is important to note how the various 'subcategories' of hackers use the ideology. For instance, hackers draw boundaries between the different subgroups within the community in terms of how they apply their ideology. When used to justify illegal behaviours within a subculture, such as copying proprietary software, the person is more appropriately identified as a 'cracker', not a hacker. So while an outsider may identify hackers in terms of their endorsement of the subculture's ideological principles, hackers further distinguish between members of their community in terms of how fully they subscribe to the hacker spirit and how the ideology is applied to rationalize their activities.

The tenets of the ideology are used to counter prevailing perspectives and rationalize certain behaviours. In this sense, we can also see how the hacker ideology becomes used as a vocabulary of motive (Mills 1940) for the different subgroups—that is, as a way of talking about hacking that justifies the behaviour. Although hackers incorporate aspects of the hacker spirit into their vocabulary, the different activities that their ideology is used to justify vary. For instance, while one group might draw upon the *all information should be free* tenet to rationalize defacing a 'corrupt' government's website, another group employs it to rationalize the communal development of open source software. For acts interpreted as deviant or criminal by outsiders, the use of the hacker ideology to rationalize these behaviours becomes a technique of neutralization—that is, as a way of neutralizing guilt and possible delinquent self-images associated with 'deviant' acts. Thus, their ideology also functions as a way of managing the stigma—a discrediting social attribute—that both outsiders and certain insiders associate with particular types of hackers and their behaviours.

## Conclusion

Hackers present a picture of their ideology, and subculture more generally, that is very much at odds with outsider characterizations. Taking a symbolic interactionist approach to the study of hackers allows us to move beyond such portrayals. While most hackers disagree with being labelled as criminals, they very much agree with the counterculture overtones of their ideology and activities. Although recognizing that outsiders see their subculture as deviant, hackers feel that their ideology and activities are normal and often admirable. Like the jazz musicians described by Becker (1963) and the mystics in Simmons's (1973) study, hackers see their perspective as being elite, as their approach represents a better way of doing things and seeing the world than other outsider belief systems. Freedom of information over ownership of information, creativity over conventionality, hard work and self-direction over indolence, intellectualism over looks and style, and unorthodoxy over conformity are highly valued, noble pursuits within the hacker subculture.

# References

Becker, H. 1963. *Outsiders*. New York: Free Press.

Blumer, H. 1969. *Symbolic Interactionism*. Berkeley, CA: University of California Press.

Fine, G.A., and Kleinman, S. 1979. 'Rethinking Subculture: An Interactionist Analysis', *American Journal of Sociology* 85, 1: 1–20.

Levy, S. 1984. *Hackers: Heroes of the Computer Revolution*. New York: Bantam Doubleday Dell.

Mills, C.W. 1940. 'Situated Actions and Vocabularies of Motive', *American Sociological Review* 5: 904–13.

Prus, R. 1997. *Subcultural Mosaics and Intersubjective Realities: An Ethnographic Research Agenda for Pragmatizing the Social Sciences*. Albany: SUNY Press.

Raymond, E.S. 2001. 'How to Become a Hacker'. Available at www.catb.org/~esr/faqs/hacker-howto.html.

Shibutani, T. 1955. 'Reference Groups as Perspectives', *American Journal of Sociology* 60: 562–9.

Simmons, J.L. 1973. 'Maintaining Deviant Beliefs', in *Deviance: The Interactionist Perspective*, pp. 308–14, E. Rubington and M.S. Weinberg, eds. New York: Macmillan Company.

## Introduction

State sponsored gambling is everywhere in Canada, the US and many other nations. But it was only a few decades ago that gambling was illegal and policed by the same governments that are now promoting and profiting from it. How did gambling become normalized? How is the social construction of gambling connected to the interests of groups and institutions that seek to influence how we think about activities like gambling?

In this article, Cosgrave focuses primarily on how the transformation occurred in Canada and raises a number of troubling questions and issues regarding the current role of the state, notably with regard to who the main consumer is and the emergence of problem gambling. What are consequences of the state's heavy involvement in promoting gambling? In the final analysis, is the common public good really being served by governments' involvement in gambling?

# Regulating Vice: The Moral Trajectory of Gambling in Canada

*James F. Cosgrave*

Watching prime time television, you see no shortage of advertisements aimed at encouraging participation in various forms of gambling: lotteries with large jackpots asking you to 'Imagine the Freedom', sports betting through the government run 'Pro-line' or 'Sports Select' systems, casino gambling with smiling, excited patrons and slogans such as 'We Deal Excitement Big Time'. There has also been a new type of gambling advertisement by the provincial governments' 'gaming' corporations—in Ontario, for example, the Ontario Lottery and Gaming Corporation (OLG) has advertisements where gambling activities are not shown, but instead, heartwarming images of all the public good that is being done with the gambling revenues are presented: scenes of recovering patients in hospitals, small children found by police officers, and the like. These newer ads take a different approach to gambling advertising: they don't promote the appeal of gambling, they rather show that gambling is good for society at large, that the money generated from the various forms of gambling is going to good causes and social programs, and that, indirectly, you are a good citizen through your gambling contributions.

How did we arrive at the point where gambling has become normalized and promoted by the state, especially given that only a few decades ago it was illegal? This article will discuss the normalization of gambling activities, with an emphasis on how the transformation of the definition and legal status of gambling sheds light on the social and historical construction of deviance. The frame of reference will be gambling in Canada, with a focus on the situation in Ontario. Of particular interest is the involvement of the state in gambling enterprises, since legal gambling is largely owned by the state rather than private gambling corporations. These enterprises (e.g., lotteries, casinos, and electronic gambling machines[1]) are part of state infrastructure and gambling activities are exploited by provincial governments for their revenue-generating capacity. An issue that has emerged with the state's involvement in gambling enterprises, and which relates directly to the social construction of deviance, is the production of 'problem' and 'pathological' gamblers. The state must find ways to manage this social problem as it poses serious issues for the legitimacy of its involvement in gambling enterprises.

In order to understand the transformation of gambling activities, this discussion will also investigate our sociological understanding of processes of 'deviantization' and stigmatization. A sociological approach to the issues will involve demonstrating the ways in which the meanings of activities change historically, and in relation to the interests of groups and institutions that seek to influence how we think about the activities. This is particularly important for understanding those activities that come to be labelled as deviant, because it shows the shifting historical understandings and relativity of the conceptions, i.e., that something is considered deviant now, but wasn't in the past, or vice versa, and that there are conflicting interpretations of, and orientations to, the activities themselves. While changing social conditions contribute to the liberalization of previously-defined deviant activities, it is important to recognize that some groups stand to benefit in various ways—economically, politically, morally, institutionally, etc.—through the changed status of the activities.

## The Transformation of Vices

There are all kinds of examples we could point to of the changing status of 'deviant' activities: not only gambling, but recreational drug use, cigarette smoking, same-sex relations, pornography, and prostitution. These activities have been considered 'vices', or have been illegal, either or wholly or partially, at some time. The term partially legal refers to a situation of legal ambiguity. Prostitution is a legal activity in Canada, but soliciting a prostitute or running a common-bawdy house is not. For some, this represents a curious form of legality, and the prostitution laws in Canada are currently being challenged. Cigarette smoking is legal, but increasingly prohibited in certain situations (e.g., indoors, in one's work place, outside buildings within a certain distance from doorways, etc.). Gambling is legal in Canada, but for the most part free-enterprise gambling (gambling run by private industry and Internet gambling) remains illegal. Broadly though, perhaps with the exception of cigarette smoking, these activities are more accepted, with citizens in Canada having a more tolerant or liberal attitude towards them.

In Canada, attitudes toward marijuana smoking are being liberalized, and it is considered acceptable activity if you have some kind of medical condition that marijuana's active medicinal ingredients can relieve. Beyond the medical use, more than half of Canadian citizens would like to see recreational marijuana use decriminalized. By contrast, cigarette smoking has been undergoing increased stigmatization for its negative health consequences. Cigarettes are bad for you, and they are bad for the people around you who inhale your 'second hand smoke'. In Canada, the Ontario provincial government is initiating lawsuits against tobacco manufacturers for the health-care costs generated by smoking-related illnesses. In the Netherlands, there is a new smoking ban aimed at tobacco: the ban will thus prohibit the tobacco that is rolled into marijuana or hash joints, but the drug smoking itself is still acceptable in Amsterdam's many cafes. By comparison, Americans have less tolerant views of recreational drug-taking than Canadians (and certainly the Dutch), with much stiffer penalties for drug possession. Marc Emery, Canada's 'Prince of Pot' and an outspoken marijuana activist, was convicted of marijuana seed sales by the US government. The Canadian government (and the RCMP) largely left him alone to conduct business, while the US was eager to have him charged. He even paid taxes in Canada on his seed sales (Mulgrew 2009).

There may be signs that official attitudes to 'soft' drug use may be changing in the US: the current administration has said that it would not prosecute users and sellers of medical marijuana, and further, the state of California is studying a marijuana tax as a way to collect much-needed revenues (McKenna 2009). As with other states in the US, California is facing serious financial problems. While many Americans would like to see marijuana laws relaxed, it is instructive to see how legal and moral positions can change if powerful actors have an interest in a changed definition of, and status for the activity.

The status of an activity as legal does not necessarily give it a *morally* clean bill of health. On the topic of cigarette smoking, there is the hypocrisy of Canadian governments toward the activity: while instituting various types of smoking ban, and demanding warning labels on packages, they nevertheless profit greatly from the taxes they receive. While the high taxes are considered a 'sin tax'—the tax on activities that are legal but which still have a connotation of vice—the governments still nevertheless benefit from them. The high taxes also create deviance by contributing to an illegal market in cigarettes, which are smuggled in and sold through some of Canada's Native reservations. The high cost of smoking offers the opportunity for money to be made in illegal markets. This pattern resembles other attempts to regulate vice. Illegal markets are created for activities and products that are prohibited, but which there is significant public demand. In the 1920s, there was the widespread production and sale of illegal alcohol by organized crime during Prohibition, and the present-day we have the phenomenon of marijuana grow operations ('grow-ops') that flourish due to the lucrative illegal markets for the drug.

On the topic of illegal markets, provincial governments in Canada, which benefit economically from legalized and liberalized gambling, actually contribute to these markets. Not only has gambling legalization in Canada contributed to a growing gambling culture (in both its legal and illegal forms), but the laws themselves have contributed to the development of the illegal markets. This is seen through the phenomenon of sports betting. While it is illegal in Canada outside of the government-run systems (such as 'Pro-line' and 'Sports-Select'), betting lines and bookie information are found in national and local newspapers. The Ontario government, through the OLG, has proposed allowing sports betting in its Ontario casinos. First of all, this change in the legal status of casino sports betting was proposed because the casinos were not making as much money as they used to, and the move was an economic strategy for the province (as the legalization of casino gambling was in the first place). But the sports betting proposal would enable Ontario to compete with both legal sports betting in other jurisdictions (like Las Vegas), and would allow the government to compete with the many Internet sports betting sites (gambling on the Internet is still illegal in Canada). The proposal would permit 'sports books' in casinos, and the opportunity to bet on single sports games. This is undoubtedly a better bet for the sports bettor. Until the proposal is implemented however, Canadian bettors who want to bet legally on sports will have to continue to patronize the Pro-line system, which is rigged to benefit the governments. How so? The system forces parlay betting, which means that you must bet on a minimum of three game outcomes or occurrences (the latter could be number of goals in an over/under bet for example), and you must get all three (or more) correct to receive any pay-out. This clearly benefits the 'house': in this case, the government gaming system. Serious sports gamblers know this is a sucker's bet and have been contributing to the illegal markets by either betting with bookies, or by utilizing the many sports betting sites on the Internet, which are set up in other jurisdictions (such as the UK, Australia, the Caribbean). While allowing sports betting into the casinos, there will no doubt be money to be made—the house always has the edge—but a consequence will be lower profits for the Pro-line system.

We thus see here a relationship between the structure of legalized gambling and the large markets for illegal gambling, and it is likely that Canadian provincial governments will find ways to 'regulate' and exploit Internet gambling, as they lose a lot of money to sites located in other jurisdictions. In the US, the fiscal problems faced by many of the states have stimulated interest in the legalization of sports betting and Internet gambling. In the US, the only legal sports betting is available through Nevada's casinos and bookies, and this represents only a small slice of the massive sports betting pie. Similarly, the legalization of Internet gambling could raise billions of dollars for cash-strapped states. If this occurs, it won't be long before other jurisdictions such as Canada follow suit.

# The Historical–Moral Career of Gambling in Canada

How have we gotten to the point where gambling appears to have been liberalized in the Canadian context? Liberalization can be understood in two senses: first, in the general sense which relates to cultural permissiveness toward an activity, whereby citizens come to accept or tolerate an activity, regarding it as socially acceptable rather than as deviant.

Secondly, we can speak of the market liberalization of an activity whereby the activity can be organized and exploited for legal economic gain, and this depends upon the permissiveness of society toward the activity.

There is no doubt that gambling has been legalized and liberalized in Canada, but this must be qualified: state gambling monopolies must be better understood as a partial or selective liberalization (Abt 1996), because a free market for gambling offerings does not exist. In Canada, the provincial governments own gambling enterprises, and privately run enterprises are not allowed to compete. If Canadians want to gamble legally, they must do so in the state-sanctioned venues. This selective liberalization thus benefits the state, primarily through the interest in revenues, but gambling has also been used to stimulate economic activity in depressed cities and towns, provide jobs, and attract tourism. The primary alibis for state-owned gambling are that the revenues can be used to fund social programs, and takes gambling enterprises out of the hands of organized crime. While this sounds good, it must be pointed out that state-owned gambling represents a serious conflict of interest, as the state, which is supposed to regulate social activities, is also the primary beneficiary of gambling revenues. In other words, it is the regulator as well as the promoter. We can compare this situation to two other vices, cigarette smoking and alcohol consumption. Both of these forms of consumption are regulated: through age of consumption laws and through state-sanctioned venues for sale of the products. A difference is this: while the sale of alcohol products in Ontario takes place through The Beer Store and the Liquor Control Board of Ontario (notice the state interest in and emphasis on 'control' here), the products are regulated, but they are not the state's products; with gambling, the individual is consuming the state's gambling products, and the state promotes its own gambling products heavily, as mentioned at the beginning of this article. Moral dissuasion is an aspect of the taxation of cigarettes and alcohol (the 'sin' of sin tax now being centred on ill health rather than vice), but this is certainly not the case with gambling and its promotion by provincial governments.

The revenue-generating imperative of legalized gambling means that the state has an economic interest in the gamblers' losses, or to shade this differently, it generates revenues from the losses of its citizens. Is this an important distinction? Since gambling enterprises are state-owned (although there is provincial variation on the relationship between state and private industry involvement) and a way of generating money for social programs, the citizen contributes to this funding through gambling. This is a form of voluntary taxation, as it depends upon individuals choosing to gamble in one form or other. However, it is also a regressive form of taxation, as lower income earners tend to spend more as a percentage of income than higher-income earners. In state-owned gambling then, the citizen becomes a consumer of state gambling products. This also suggests that gambling does not only represent another way for the state to generate tax revenues, although this deserves some discussion in itself— it represents a way of governing, or relating to, its citizens. In other words, in state-owned gambling the citizen becomes consumer of the state's gambling products, and the state has a direct interest in gambling markets and the 'entertainment' industry. As such, the state acts like any other corporation in the marketplace, marketing and promoting its products as it seeks to make money from gamblers' losses. To reiterate though, this set-up is a way in which the state conducts itself in order to govern: it needs the gambling revenues from citizens.

There is no doubt that the state could only legalize gambling in Canada if cultural attitudes would accept it, although state-run gambling in Canada is still controversial (for reasons discussed below). Think of the more liberal attitudes toward the vices mentioned earlier: the state must respond to changes in culture, for example, legalizing same-sex marriage. This does not mean though that there are not conflicts around activities, depending on individuals' and groups' social and political positions. Like the other vices, gambling liberalization has occurred with a weakening of religious influences on culture, in particular, the dominance of Protestant values in English Canada (Morton 2003). As they pertain to the gambling issue, Protestant values emphasize the rewards of hard work —in the earliest versions of the Protestant work ethic, believers were working for the glory of God (Weber 1958). Consider how gambling challenges or undermines the emphasis on work: not only is there a reliance on chance, but there is also the attempt to get 'something for nothing', rather than through hard work or God's grace (Lears 2003; Morton 2003). Now think of the gambling advertising, particularly for lotteries. Canada's Lotto 6/49 asks you to 'Imagine the Freedom'. What does this mean? The advertisements present images of consumption (cars, cottages, etc.), so one will be free to consume, without having to worry about where the money is coming from. In presenting these consumption fantasies, the advertisements also appear to undermine the work ethic itself, as in the Super 7 ads, showing the employee quitting his job, or 'Relaxo', the lottery-winning anti-super-hero, who can now afford to watch sports from his armchair, and never have to work. One of the slogans of Super 7 was: 'Earning money is great: Winning it is even better'.[2] In other words, getting money through the play of chance is better than earning it. The advertisements devalue the work ethic, and the governments themselves are happy to exploit this. Imagine the freedom from working. Are the governments that promote gambling through these slogans and representations agreeing with Karl Marx on the alienating nature of work in capitalism? Why work if you have a chance of winning? The reality of course is that the odds are stacked against you in all forms of state-owned gambling, despite those doing the 'Happy Dance' in the Lotto 6/49 commercials.

With the exception of bingo and horse racing, gambling was illegal in Canada in the twentieth century until 1969, when the federal government permitted lotteries. In 1985, the regulation of gambling was passed to the provinces, and since then, gambling has expanded rapidly. Since the early 1990s, we have seen governments expand their gambling offerings to include: sports betting, casinos, electronic gaming machines, scratch and win games in the corner store. Gambling opportunities are ubiquitous, and while Internet gambling is still illegal in Canada, this does not stop people from gambling in this way, as the popularity of Internet poker attests.

But serious social problems have emerged as a result of this gambling expansion, and the state has had to manage the very problems they've helped to create. With the expansion of gambling, governments have moved into riskier forms of gambling, such as video lottery terminals (VLTs). The riskiness refers to the ways in which this form of gambling has significantly higher rates of problem and pathological gambling associated with them. VLTs have earned the slogan the 'crack cocaine of gambling', but this has not stopped governments in some provinces from generating large revenues from them. In Nova Scotia for example, citizens groups such as GameOverVLTs have protested the government's reliance on the machines and have called for their complete elimination as the only way of solving the addiction problems they have created. There have also been a number of suicides directly related to VLT addiction (McKenna 2008). How have these governments been able to persist in justifying the existence of VLTs? They will say of course, that they need the revenues, and that people choose to gamble in this way. They will also say that it is only a certain small percentage of gamblers who develop gambling problems, while the rest of the gambling population can gamble for entertainment or leisure purposes. As such gambling problems are medicalized and individualized, in other words, the problems become problems of particular individuals who are 'pathological' or diseased individuals. While there is no doubt that excessive gambling can have very serious consequences, including suicide, the point here is that the characterization or framing of the problem locates the problem in the individual, while the spread of gambling opportunities and the state's reliance on and promotion of gambling (VLTs for example) —its gambling social policy—is depoliticized. Since state-owned gambling is controversial precisely because it does generate gambling problems, this generates legitimacy problems for the state's involvement. Do we want the state and governments involved in the creation of gambling problems, which bring with them a variety of related problems: family conflict and breakdown, bankruptcy, theft, fraud, and most disturbingly, suicide? This is a consequence of the conflict of interest mentioned earlier: governments benefit from their involvement in gambling, but they are also implicated in social harm (Law Commission of Canada 2003; McKenna 2008). Some provincial governments are facing lawsuits for this reason, as addicted gamblers are suing the respective lottery corporations for their role in the creation of addiction (Branswell 2002; Canadian Broadcasting Corporation 2008).

## The Transformation of Gambling Stigmas

If we look at the transformation of gambling away from its negative conceptions as sin or vice, we must consider the shifts in moral framework and social attitudes towards the activity. Significantly, we see a shift from a religious moral framework (sin) to a 'scientific' framework, where excessive gambling is framed as a pathology—'pathological gambling'. Along with this historical transformation, we have seen a partial shift in terminology, whereby gambling becomes re-framed as 'gaming'. How does gaming differ from gambling? Certainly gambling brings with it connotations of risk-taking, and also of shady dealings (for example, the links between illegal gambling operations and organized crime, or of gambling dens, etc.), and gambling has a long history of negative moral evaluations, although it has also been a popular, if often covert, popular cultural activity (Reith 2002; Morton 2003). By and large, these negative moral evaluations of gambling have diminished, and this must certainly be the case if states are going to promote gambling to the population. The term gaming arises in this shift, where a risk-taking activity gets re-framed as a 'game'. Certainly, we refer to poker as a game, but there is also risk involved, the risk of losing all your money. Gaming arises as a feature of the euphemizing of gambling as 'entertainment' (Kingma 1997; Cosgrave 2009), where one is not really gambling but partaking in a 'gaming' experience—a form of entertainment or leisure activity. I would suggest that the term is political, in the sense that it is a way to sanitize gambling of its riskiness, and to render it a legitimate entertainment offering. The Ontario Lottery and Gaming Corporation has a mandate to generate revenues from its various 'gaming' enterprises. So, in terms of the social construction of deviance, the shift in terminology is itself an example of how interested, and powerful, groups or organizations can influence public attitudes toward activities. The term gaming also signifies the shift in moral attitudes, since gambling now has lost much of its moral stigma, and the arguments against prohibition have lost much of their force. Indeed, not only is gambling promoted by states, but gambling is a popular topic or theme in the media, with televised poker tournaments on television, and dramas such as 'Las Vegas'. However, the morality issue around gambling has not completely disappeared, it too has been transformed.

The morality issue was touched on earlier in the discussion in terms of the promotion of gambling, where advertising messages challenge the social values related to the work ethic.

Sociologists have been discussing for some time the transformation of capitalist societies, as they move from being production to consumption-based (Baudrillard 1975, 1988; Bauman 2001; Bell 1975). The rise of the consumer society has seen with it an accompanying shift in orientations to work and leisure, where the pleasures of consumption compete with, if not overshadow, the rewards that follow from work. Further, the social emphasis on consumption contributes to the cultural liberalization of the activities mentioned earlier, as lifestyles come to be objects of marketing, and activities get understood in terms of 'consumer choice'. Significantly however, with the shift into an increasingly globalized consumer society, there is also a breakdown in opportunities for gainful employment—where long-term, stable employment is harder to come by. While we may question whether the work ethic still holds the same cultural weight as in the past, we could, in any case, suggest that, in an economic climate where many people experience job insecurity, and where many are working a lot harder for less, the gambling-friendly governments' promotion of gambling—getting 'something for nothing'—takes on added significance. If contemporary capitalist societies are no longer 'gainful employment societies' (Beck 2003, p. 6), it is unsettling that governments are exploiting gambling as people experience the precariousness of employment. It might be pointed out here that, getting something for nothing has often been a common-sense criticism of people collecting social assistance, such as welfare—why don't they get a job? With lotteries, governments themselves are participating in the promotion of the something for nothing ethic, and the denigration of work itself. If the moral framing of gambling as a sin or vice has lost its cultural power, and where governments are explicitly pro-gambling, where does morality currently lie?

Perhaps you have noticed an increase in messages in the media concerning the risks involved with gambling (for example, the 20-something male increasingly obsessed with Internet poker, and losing), or the messages advocating 'responsible gambling' with slogans such as 'know your limit, play within it'. These messages imply that gambling is not just a regular form of entertainment, but rather there can be serious negative consequences for participating. The notion of responsible gambling is interesting for a number of reasons. One understanding of gambling, and perhaps the one with the longest history, is that it is irrational, or is an encounter with chance or fate, where restraint is forgone in the fateful embrace of the uncertain outcome (Goffman 1967). This excited orientation surely sounds much different compared to the notion of the responsible gambler, who must exercise rational control or restraint over their gambling participation, thereby behaving responsibly. So what is the sociological significance of the idea of responsible gambling? Since states have entered into the gambling market to exploit the revenue potential, they have to address the legitimacy of their involvement as well as educate citizens who might choose to gamble about the dangers. In effect, since gambling involves taking risks (financial risks), the state advocates responsible gambling as a way of legitimating their involvement. Responsible gambling literature typically 'teaches' the gambler to treat gambling as a form of entertainment, and not treat gambling as a way of making money (RCGO 2002). In other words, the gambler should get used to losing their money (although all the images related to commercialized gambling emphasize winning), but should behave responsibly in the face of the losses. To be a responsible gambler then means to show restraint, and to monitor oneself for the possibility of signs of problem gambling.[3]

We can see how responsible gambling then arises as a kind of moral orientation advocated by the state's gambling agencies; since gambling is legalized and legitimized, the individual must comport themselves responsibly in the face of the numerous legal gambling opportunities available (lotteries, sports betting, casinos, Internet gambling, etc.). There is a difference however between responsible gambling and rational gambling: a professional poker player is a rational gambler who tries to minimize chance, and who seeks to win money from opponents. The responsible gambler is the gambler who loses money (certainly at some point, and often, often) but does not let the gambling (losses) get in the way of, or cause problems for, their everyday lives (family and work). There are a couple of significant issues here: one is that the state is very serious about making money from gambling, but the citizen should not orient to gambling as a way to make money. Gambling should be 'entertainment'. Casinos do not like card counters (a rational approach to playing blackjack to increase one's chances of winning), and rational gamblers know not to gamble against the house edge, as this guarantees losses over the long run—'the house always wins' as the saying goes.

Another issue is that the bulk of gambling done in Canada (and in other countries) is electronic gambling. This is chance gambling, where there is no component of skill. Governments earn much of their revenues from this type of gambling, and we have seen how the electronic machines are showing up in the horse-racing tracks; these are now referred to as 'racinos'. In one sense, these machines pose no risk to the gambler, because they are programmed to pay out (and must legally do so) a certain percentage of what goes in (let's say 90 cents is paid out for every dollar inserted). In other words, the machines are guaranteed to make money, while the gambler, who may win sporadically, will lose their money with sustained play. There is no risk here because the losses are guaranteed. Significantly however, these machines, specifically the VLTs, have the highest rates of problem and pathological gambling associated with them—they are the most addictive forms of gambling. Some governments rely heavily on this type of gambling to raise revenues, and there have been very sad cases of suicide related to gambling machine addiction (McKenna 2008).

A study of Ontario gambling revenue sources derived from problem gamblers revealed that 4.8 per cent of gamblers (a total of 3.8 moderate and 1.0 per cent severe problem gamblers as categorized by the Canadian Problem Gambling Index or CPGI) contributed 36 per cent of $4 billion generated from Ontario residents in 2003, amounting to more than $1.4 billion (Williams and Woods 2007). In Ontario, the amount spent by the provincial government on the prevention and treatment of problem gambling is about 2 per cent of total revenues from 12,000 of its more than 20,000 slot machines, which amounted to $36 million in 2004. This figure however 'represents only 2.6 per cent of the $1.41 billion dollars estimated to have been derived from problem gamblers' in the 2003/2004 time period (Williams and Wood, 2007, 383).

Despite the evidence of harm related to electronic gambling (Campbell and Smith 2007), governments nevertheless continue to generate revenues from them. We might well ask here: how does government relate to its citizens, if it is responsible for the inflicting of harm on vulnerable members of society?

As mentioned, with involvement in gambling enterprises, states are in a conflict of interest, namely that between being a regulator as well as promoter at the same time. However, we might consider some social conditions that are shaping the state's conduct in this curious direction. Many countries are legalizing gambling and allowing it to spread, indeed gambling expansion is a global phenomenon. As such, particular jurisdictions do not want to lose the potential revenues if people are going elsewhere to participate, so they legalize and expand their gambling offerings. As an example in Canada, there are large casinos built close to the border with the US: the Windsor casino across from Detroit (which has three large casinos to keep people from gambling in Canada), the Niagara Falls and Fallsview casinos across from New York state, the Thousand Islands Charity casino near Kingston, as well as casinos in British Columbia across from Washington state. There is thus heavy economic competition for gambling dollars, prompting the spread of gambling enterprises on a global scale. The Chinese island of Macau is now larger than Las Vegas as a casino gambling centre, and Aboriginally-run gambling in the US brings in more money than all the gambling in the state of Nevada. And of course, Internet gambling is increasingly popular (Internet poker for example), but is illegal in many countries, including Canada. This does not stop people from gambling in this way, however, and jurisdictions that deem Internet gambling illegal lose the revenues to other jurisdictions where it is legal. Internet gambling also poses threats to traditional forms of gambling, such as casino gambling.

The global spread of gambling enterprises places gambling squarely within the consumer society, where gambling becomes a form of legitimate, if not risky, consumption. In Canada, as discussed, the state's involvement in gambling enterprises means that it has a vested economic interest in this consumer entertainment market. However, state-owned gambling must be considered a form of political economy, i.e., a way in which the state acts politically in terms of economic considerations. Gambling then is not only consumption activity, but taxation activity, since it is a method whereby states generate revenues to allow it to fund various activities (recall the OLG ads mentioned earlier).

This represents an individualization of taxation, meaning that the ability of the state to collect revenues depends on the willingness of citizens to gamble in the legal gambling venues. As such, gambling must be promoted, and new gambling products must be introduced. Gambling has to be made appealing to the public: the advertising slogan for Casino Rama in Ontario (run by the Rama Indian Band) is 'We Deal Excitement, Big Time!'). So, like other forms of consumption, gambling has to be marketed and sold, and the images are generally ones of winning and having fun—gambling as entertainment, rather than as risk-taking. With gambling as a form of voluntary taxation, we find a particular type of tax downloading, since governments find it very difficult to introduce new or higher taxes. Corporations can get away with paying less than their fair share of taxes in a globalizing economy, so states must innovate in terms of their approaches to taxation: gambling is one of these approaches.

As mentioned, addictive gambling is strongly related to VLTs. More generally, a large percentage of gambling revenues come from a small percentage of gamblers, and government revenues rely on this problematic stream. Significantly then, not only is gambling a taxation method, but it is an activity that holds out risks for the individual, and governments seem very happy to collect the revenues. Gambling is a form of 'risky consumption' (Cosgrave 2009). The problem and pathological gamblers are very good for business, although they do represent a problem of risk management for state-owned gambling corporations.

It can be reiterated here that there is a serious conflict of interest with state-owned gambling enterprises; however, consideration of larger political and economic issues prompts us to see how, through the interests in maintaining gambling markets, states are behaving like large-scale corporations, and are quite willing to exploit their citizens for their own economic purposes.

By way of conclusion, the example of gambling makes visible the shift in the moral and legal meaning of activities in relation to changing cultural attitudes, but more importantly for an understanding of processes of deviantization, in relation to those groups and interests who stand to benefit, either from the stigmatizing or de-stigmatizing of activities.

## Notes

1. Electronic gambling machines are known as EGMs, which include slot machines and video lottery terminals, or VLTs.
2. The Super 7 lottery was replaced in September 2009 by 'Lotto Max', which costs a minimum of $5 to play, compared to $2 for the former lottery. Lotto Max promises higher jackpots in its weekly draws, starting at $10,000,000.
3. According to literature distributed by the Responsible Gambling Council (2009), here are some of the signs of problem gambling: 'Losing all track of time when you gamble'; 'Gambling with money needed for essentials like groceries or rent'; 'Often spending more money than you intended'; 'Having few interests outside of gambling'; 'Hiding your gambling from family or friends'; 'Trying to win back money that you've lost'.

## References

Abt, V. 1996. 'The Role of the State in the Expansion and Growth of Commercial Gambling in the United States', in *Gambling Cultures: Studies in History and Interpretation*, ed. Jan McMillen, London: Routledge, pp. 179–198.

Baudrillard, J. 1975. *The Mirror of Production*, St. Louis: Telos Press.

Baudrillard, J. [1970] 1988. *The Consumer Society: Myths and Structures*, London: Sage.

Bauman, Z. 2001. 'Consuming Life'. *Journal of Consumer Culture* 1(1): 9–29.

Beck, U. 2003. 'The Theory of Reflexive Mod-ernization: Problematic, Hypotheses and Research Programme', *Theory, Culture and Society* 20 (2): 1–33.

Bell, D. 1975. *The Cultural Contradictions of Capitalism*, New York: Basic Books.

Branswell, B. 2002 'Gamblers try to collect a debt to society'. *The Toronto Star*, July 13, p. J.4.

Campbell, C.S. and Smith, G.J. 2003. 'Gambling in Canada—From Vice to Disease to Responsibility: A Negotiated History'. *Canadian Bulletin of Medical History* (20)1: 121–149.

———. 2007. 'Tensions and Contentions: An Examination of Electronic Gaming Issues in Canada', *American Behavioural Scientist* (51)1: 86–101.

Canadian Broadcasting Corporation 2008 'Problem Gamblers hit Ontario casinos with $3.5 billion lawsuit', www.cbc.ca/canada/toronto/story/2008/06/11/gambling-lawsuit.html accessed August 5, 2008.

Cosgrave, J.F. 2009. 'Governing the Gambling Citizen: The State, Consumption, and Risk', in *Casino State: Legalized Gambling in Canada*, eds. James F. Cosgrave and Thomas R. Klassen, Toronto: University of Toronto Press, pp. 46–66.

Goffman, Erving. 1967. 'Where the Action Is', in *Interaction Ritual*. Garden City, NY: Anchor Books, pp. 149–270.

Kingma, S. 1997. '"Gaming is Play, It Should Remain Fun!" The Gaming Complex, Pleasure and Addiction', in *Constructing The New Consumer Society*. Eds. P. Sulkunen, J. Holmwood, H. Radner and G. Schulze: Macmillan Press.

Law Commission of Canada. 'What is a crime? Challenges and alternatives: discussion paper,' Her Majesty the Queen in Right of Canada, 2003, Cat. No. JL2-21/2003: 11–17.

Lears, J. 2003. *Something for Nothing: Luck In America*, New York: Viking.

McKenna, P. 2008. *Terminal Damage: The Politics of VLTs in Atlantic Canada*, Halifax: Fernwood Press.

McKenna, B. 2009. 'Why California is Studying Marijuana Tax', www.theglobeandmail.com/report-on-business/why-california-is-studying-marijuana-tax/article1342595/. Accessed November 1.

Morton, S. 2003. *At Odds: Gambling and Canadians, 1919–1969*, Toronto: University of Toronto Press.

Mulgrew, I. 2009. 'Prince of Pot's sentence reeks of injustice and mocks our sovereignty', http://www.vancouversun.com/health/Prince+sentence+reeks+injustice+mocks+sovereignty/2042230/story.html#. September 28.

Reith, G. 2002. *The Age of Chance: Gambling in Western Culture*. London: Routledge.

RGCO—Responsible Gambling Council (Ontario). 2002. 'It's Only a Game: The Responsible Gambling Handbook', RCGO: Toronto.

Responsible Gambling Council. 2009. 'Within Limits-Problem Gambling Prevention Week: The early warning signs of a gambling problem aren't always easy to see', Responsible Gambling Council, Toronto.

Weber, M. 1958. *The Protestant Ethic and the Spirit of Capitalism,* trans. Talcott Parsons, New York: Charles Scribner's Sons.

Williams, R.J. and Wood, R.T. 2007. 'The Proportion of Ontario Gambling Revenue Derived From Problem Gamblers', *Canadian Public Policy—Analyse De Politiques*, Vol XXXIII (3): 367–387.

# Credits

Chapter 1: George Gurley, 'Pleasures of the Fur' abridged from Vanity Fair, March 2001: 174, 176, 181–2, 184–5, 188, 193, 196.

Chapter 2: Linda Deutschmann, 'Prescientific Approaches to Deviance' abridged from *Deviance and Social Control*, 4th edn. Thomson Nelson Canada, 1998.

Chapter 3: Robert Silverman, J. Teevan, and V. Sacco, 'Lay Definitions of Crime' from *Crime in Canadian Society*, 6th edn., Harcourt Brace, 2000.

Chapter 4: Law Commission of Canada, 'What Is a Crime?' from *What is a Crime? Challenges and Alternatives*, Ottawa: Her Majesty the Queen in Right of Canada, 2003.

Chapter 5: Emile Durkheim, 'Crime and the Collective Consciousness' from *The Division of Labor in Society*, New York: The Free Press, 1984. 'The Normal and the Pathological' from *The Rules of Sociological Method*, New York: The Free Press, 1938.

Chapter 6: William O'Grady , 'Crime, Fear, and Risk' from *Crime in Canadian Context*, 2nd edn. Copyright © Oxford University Press Canada, 2011. Reprinted by permission of the publisher.

Chapter 7, page 71: 'Violent crime rises in Toronto' from *Metro* (newspaper), May 25–27, 2001.

Chapter 8: Maria Elizabeth Grabe, 'Television News Magazines and Functionalism' abridged from *Critical Studies in Mass Communication* 16, 2: July 1999.

Chapter 9: Harvey Sacks, 'On Doing "Being Ordinary"' abridged from J. M. Atkinson and J. Heritage (eds), *Structures of Social Action*, New York: Cambridge, 1984: 413–29. Reprinted with the permission of Cambridge University Press.

Chapter 10: Erving Goffman, 'Stigma and Social Identity' from *Stigma: Notes on the Management of Spoiled Identity*, Englewood Cliffs, NJ: Prentice-Hall: 1963.

Chapter 11: Michael Lynch 'Accommodation Practices: Vernacular Treatments of Madness' in *Social Problems* 31, 2: December 1983.

Chapter 12: 'Body of the Condemned' from *Discipline and Punish* by Michel Foucault. English Translation copyright © 1977 by Alan Sheridan (New York: Pantheon). Originally published in French as *Surveiller et Punir*. Copyright © 1975 by Editions Gallimard. Reprinted by permission of Georges Borchardt, Inc., for Editions Gallimard.

Chapter 13: 'Life in Prison: Interview with a Lifer' from Julian V. Roberts, *Criminal Justice in Canada: A Reader*. Toronto: Harcourt Brace Canada, 2000.

Chapter 14: Bryan Hogeveen, 'Is There Justice for Young People?' abridged from George C. Pavlich and Myra J. Hird (eds), *Questioning Sociology: A Canadian Perspective*, Don Mills, ON: Oxford University Press, 2007. Reprinted by permission of the publisher.

Chapter 15: Law Commission of Canada, 'Restorative Justice' abridged from *Transforming Relationships Through Participatory Justice*, Ottawa: Minister of Public Works and Government Services, 2003.

Chapter 16: Tamara O'Doherty, 'Off Street Commercial Sex'

Chapter 17: Chris Bruckert, 'The World of the Professional Stripper' abridged from Chris Bruckert, 'The World of the Professional Stripper,' in Merle Jacobs (ed.), *Is Anyone Listening? Women Work and Society*, Toronto: Women's Press, 2002. Reprinted by permission of Women's Press.

Chapter 18: James F. Hodgson, 'Juvenile Prostitutes' abridged from *Games Pimps Play: Pimps, Players and Wives-in-Law*, Toronto: Canadian Scholars' Press, 1997. Reprinted by permission of Canadian Scholars' Press, Inc.

Chapter 19: Sigmund Freud, 'Why is it So Difficult for People to be Happy?' abridged from *Civilization and Its Discontents*, W. W. Norton, 1961.

Chapter 20: Nancy Heitzig, 'Medical Deviance and DICA: Disorders Usually First Diagnosed in Infancy, Childhood and Adolescence' from *Deviance: Rulemakers and Rulebreakers*, Minneapolis/St Paul MN: West Publishing, 1996.

Chapter 21: D. L. Rosenhan, 'Being Sane in Insane Places,' *Science* 179, 1973.

Chapter 22: Abridged from 'Deviant Youth: The Social Construction of Youth Problems' in *Teenage Troubles: Youth and Deviance in*

*Canada,* 3rd edn. by Julian Tanner. Copyright © Oxford University Press Canada 2010. Reprinted by permission of the publisher.

Chapter 23: National Crime Prevention Centre of Public Safety Canada, 'Youth Gangs in Canada: What Do We Know?' and 'Youth Gang Involvement: What Are the Risk Factors?'

Chapter 24: Robert J. Brym, 'Hip Hop from Caps to Bling' abridged from *Sociology as a Life or Death Issue,* Pearson, Allyn and Bacon, 2008.

Chapter 25: John F. Manzo and Monetta M. Bailey, 'On the Assimilation of Racial Stereotypes among Black Canadian Young Offenders' new from *Canadian Review of Sociology and Anthropology* 42, 3, 2005.

Chapter 26: Erin Anderson, 'One on One with a Killer' from *Globe and Mail,* 25 March 1999.

Chapter 27: Barbara Boyle Torrey, 'Data Gold Mines and Minefields' from David M. Thomas and Barbara Boyle Torrey (eds), *Canada and the United States: Differences that Count,* 3rd edn. Peterborough, ON: Broadview Press, 2008.

Chapter 28: Rebecca Kong, Holly Johnson, Sara Beattie and Andrea Cardillo, 'Sexual Offences in Canada' abridged from *Juristat,* Minister of Industry: Statistics Canada – Catalogue no. 85-002, 23, 6. 2003.

Chapter 29: Eric W. Hickey, 'Profiling Serial Killers' abridged from *Serial Murderers and Their Victims,* 4th edn. Belmont, CA: Thomson Wadsworth, 2006.

Chapter 30: Jack Katz, 'Criminals' Passions and the Progressive's Dilemma' abridged from Alan Wolfe, ed., *America at Century's End,* Berkeley: University of California Press, 1991: 396–417.

Chapter 31: Linda MacLeod, 'Wife Battering in Canada' from *Battered but not Beater: Preventing Wife Battering in Canada,* Ottawa: The Canadian Advisory Council on the Status of Women, 1987.

Chapter 32: 'White-Collar Crime' abridged from Rick Linden, *Criminology: A Canadian Perspective,* 5th edn. Toronto: Thomson Nelson, 2004.

Chapter 33: Steven Kleinknecht, 'The Hacker Spirit: An Interactionist Analysis of the Hacker Ideology' from Lorne Tepperman and Harley Dickinson (eds.), *Reading Sociology: Canadian Perspectives,* Copyright © Oxford University Press Canada, 2007. Reprinted by permission of the publisher.

Chapter 34: James F. Cosgrave, 'Regulating Vice: The Moral Trajectory of Gambling in Canada'

# Index